THIRD CANADIAN EDITION

3

College Writing Skills

with Readings

JOHN LANGAN
Atlantic Community College

SHARON WINSTANLEY
Seneca College

McGraw-Hill Ryerson

Toronto Montréal Boston Burr Ridge, IL Dubuque, IA Madison, WI New York San Francisco St. Louis
Bangkok Bogotá Caracas Kuala Lumpur Lisbon London Madrid Mexico City
Milan New Delhi Santiago Seoul Singapore Sydney Taipei

McGraw-Hill
Ryerson Limited

A Subsidiary of The **McGraw·Hill** *Companies*

COLLEGE WRITING SKILLS WITH READINGS
Third Canadian Edition

ISBN: 0-07-088785-3

4 5 6 7 8 9 10 TCP 0 9 8 7 6 5 4 3

Printed and bound in Canada

Care has been taken to trace ownership of copyright material contained in this text; however, the publishers will welcome any information that enables them to rectify any reference or credit for subsequent editions.

Vice President and Editorial Director: Pat Ferrier
Sponsoring Editor: James Buchanan
Developmental Editor: Sandra de Ruiter
Marketing Manager: Sharon Loeb
Senior Supervising Editor: Margaret Henderson
Copy Editor: Ian MacKenzie
Production Coordinator: Madeleine Harrington
Composition: ArtPlus Limited
Cover Design: Liz Harasymczuk
Cover Photos: Main image: © Steve Allen/BrandX Pictures; Glass/pencils: © Steve Allen/BrandX Pictures; Pencil sharpener: © Nick Koudis/PhotoDisc
Printer: Transcontinental Printing Group

National Library of Canada Cataloguing in Publication Data

Langan, John, 1942-
        College writing skills with readings / John Langan, Sharon Winstanley.
— 3rd Canadian ed.

Includes index.
ISBN 0-07-091858-9

        1. English language—Rhetoric. 2. College readers.
I. Winstanley, Sharon II. Title.

PE1408.L27 2002   808'.0427   C2002-901574-X

rution • Description • Examples • Process • Cause and Effect • Comparison and Contrast
inition • Division and Classification • Argumentation • Narration • Description • Examples
ess • Cause and Effect • Comparison and Contrast • Definition • Division and Classification
umentation • Narration • Description • Examples • Process • Cause and Effect • Comparison and
trast • Definition • Division and Classification • Argumentation • Narration • Description

Contents

Readings Listed by Rhetorical Mode	vii
Preface	ix
Permissions	xiv

PART 1	**ESSAY WRITING**	1

1	**An Introduction to Writing**	3
	Learning Outcomes	3
	Writing Is a Skill	4
	Writing Is a Process of Discovery	4
	Benefits of Writing the Traditional Essay	5
	An Overview of the Essay	6
	Point and Support	7
	Structure of the Traditional Essay	13
	Word Processing and the Writing Process	18
	Activities	21
	Reviewing the Learning Outcomes	23

2	**The Writing Process**	24
	Learning Outcomes	24
	The Writing Process	25
	Stage 1: Prewriting	26
	Stage 2: Writing an Outline and Drafting	34
	Stage 3: Revision	41
	Activities	46
	Reviewing the Learning Outcomes	50

3	**The First and Second Steps in Essay Writing**	51
	Learning Outcomes	51
	Step 1: Begin with a Point or Thesis	52
	Step 2: Support the Thesis with Specific Evidence	57
	Practice in Advancing and Supporting a Thesis	62
	Reviewing the Learning Outcomes	71

4   The Third Step in Essay Writing   72

Learning Outcomes   72
Step 3: Organize and Connect the Specific Evidence   72
Transitions and Transitional Sentences   76
Introductions, Conclusions, and Titles   83
Practice in Organizing and Connecting Specific Evidence   90
Reviewing the Learning Outcomes   96

5   The Fourth Step in Essay Writing   97

Learning Outcomes   97
Revising Sentences   97
Editing Sentences   113
Practice in Revising Sentences   114
Reviewing the Learning Outcomes   127

6   Four Bases for Revising Essays   128

Learning Outcomes   128
Base 1: Unity   129
Base 2: Support   131
Base 3: Coherence   134
Base 4: Sentence Skills   137
Practice in Using the Four Bases   140
Reviewing the Learning Outcomes   147

PART 2   PATTERNS OF ESSAY DEVELOPMENT   149

7   Introduction to Essay Development   151
8   Narration   159
9   Description   172
10 Examples   185
11 Process   198
12 Cause and Effect   211
13 Comparison and Contrast   223
14 Definition   241
15 Division and Classification   254
16 Argumentation   267

PART 3   SPECIAL SKILLS   283

17 Taking Essay Exams   285

1. Learning Skills during the Semester   285
2. Exam Preparation and Study Skills   286
   Techniques for Writing Successful Exams   288

18   Writing a Summary   294

How to Summarize   295
Writing a Summary   298

19   Writing a Review or Evaluation Report   308

Points to Keep in Mind When Writing an Evaluation Report   315
A Model Report   315

20   Using the Library and the Internet   319

Using the Library   319
Using the Internet   326
Research Practice   332

21   Writing a Research Paper   334

PART 4   SENTENCE SKILLS: GRAMMAR, MECHANICS,
PUNCTUATION, WORD USE, AND PRACTICE   355

Grammar

22   Subjects and Verbs   357

23   Fragments   361

24   Run-Ons   373

25   Regular and Irregular Verbs   383

26   Subject–Verb Agreement   389

27   Additional Information about Verbs   394

28   Pronoun Agreement and Reference   399

29   Pronoun Types   404

30   Adjectives and Adverbs   409

31   Misplaced Modifiers   413

32   Dangling Modifiers   416

Mechanics

33   Manuscript Form   420

34   Capital Letters   422

35   Numbers and Abbreviations   428

Punctuation

36   Apostrophe   431

37   Quotation Marks   436

38   Comma   442

39   Other Punctuation Marks   450

Word Use

40 Commonly Confused Words   454

41 Effective Word Choice   462

42 ESL Pointers   466

Practice

43 Editing Tests   476

PART 5   READINGS FOR WRITING   489

44 Introduction to the Readings   491

Looking Inward

Shame *Dick Gregory*   495
Smash Thy Neighbor *John McMurtry*   501
My Body Is My Own Business *Naheed Mustafa*   508
Of Lemons and Lemonade *Sherwin Tija*   513
Wait Divisions *Tom Bodett*   519
How to Do Well on a Job Interview *Glenda Davis*   524

Observing Others

Why My Mother Can't Speak English *Garry Engkent*   530
He Was a Boxer When I Was Small *Lenore Keeshig-Tobias*   538
Five Parenting Styles *Mary Ann Lamanna and Agnes Reidmann*   544
Where the World Began *Margaret Laurence*   550
Why Are Students Turned Off? *Casey Banas*   557
Sometimes the Words Don't Come *Jeannie Marshall*   562
The Monster *Deems Taylor*   566

Considering Concepts

Here's to Your Health *Joan Dunayer*   574
Coffee *Alan Durning*   579
How to Make It in College, Now That You're Here *Brian O'Keeney* 583
In Praise of the F Word *Mary Sherry*   591
The Pain of Animals *David Suzuki*   596
A Work Community *Paul Hoffert*   603
Choose Your Battles *Andrew Clark*   607
Sex, Lies, and Conversation *Deborah Tannen*   612

Reading Comprehension Chart   620

Index   622

Correction Symbols   626

Readings Listed by Rhetorical Mode

Example

Here's to Your Health *Joan Dunayer*	574
A Work Community *Paul Hoffert*	603
Sometimes the Words Don't Come *Jeannie Marshall*	562
Sex, Lies, and Conversation *Deborah Tannen*	612
The Monster *Deems Taylor*	566

Process

How to Do Well on a Job Interview *Glenda Davis*	524
Coffee *Alan Durning*	579
How to Make It in College, Now That You're Here *Brian O'Keeney*	583

Cause and Effect

Why Are Students Turned Off? *Casey Banas*	557
Why My Mother Can't Speak English *Garry Engkent*	530
Shame *Dick Gregory*	495
Where the World Began *Margaret Laurence*	550
Sex, Lies, and Conversation *Deborah Tannen*	612

Definition

Choose Your Battles *Andrew Clark*	607
Why My Mother Can't Speak English *Garry Engkent*	530
Shame *Dick Gregory*	495
The Monster *Deems Taylor*	566

Division and Classification

Wait Divisions *Tom Bodett*   519
Five Parenting Styles *Mary Ann Lamanna and Agnes Reidmann*   544
How to Make It in College, Now That You're Here *Brian O'Keeney*   583

Description

A Work Community *Paul Hoffert*   603
Where the World Began *Margaret Laurence*   550
The Pain of Animals *David Suzuki*   596
The Monster *Deems Taylor*   566
Of Lemons and Lemonade *Sherwin Tija*   513

Narration

Why My Mother Can't Speak English *Garry Engkent*   530
Shame *Dick Gregory*   495
He Was a Boxer When I Was Small *Lenore Keeshig-Tobias*   538
Where the World Began *Margaret Laurence*   550
Sometimes the Words Don't Come *Jeannie Marshall*   562
The Pain of Animals *David Suzuki*   596

Argumentation and Persuasion

Choose Your Battles *Andrew Clark*   607
Here's to Your Health *Joan Dunayer*   574
Smash Thy Neighbor *John McMurtry*   501
My Body Is My Own Business *Naheed Mustafa*   508
In Praise of the F Word *Mary Sherry*   591
The Pain of Animals *David Suzuki*   596

Compare and Contrast

Smash Thy Neighbor *John McMurtry*   501
Sex, Lies, and Conversation *Deborah Tannen*   612
The Monster *Deems Taylor*   566
Of Lemons and Lemonade *Sherwin Tija*   513

Note: some selections are cross-referenced because they illustrate more than one rhetorical method of development.

ration · Description · Examples · Process · Cause and Effect · Comparison and Contrast
nition · Division and Classification · Argumentation · Narration · Description · Examples
ess · Cause and Effect · Comparison and Contrast · Definition · Division and Classification
mentation · Narration · Description · Examples · Process · Cause and Effect · Comparison and
trast · Definition · Division and Classification · Argumentation · Narration · Description

Preface

College Writing Skills with Readings, the third Canadian edition, will help students master the traditional five-paragraph essay and variations on—and developments from—this essay structure. It is a very practical book with a number of special features to aid instructors and their students.

- **Four principles are presented as keys to effective writing.** These four principles—unity, support, coherence, and effective sentence skills—are highlighted on the inside front cover and reinforced throughout the book. Part 1 focuses on the first three principles and to some extent on sentence skills; Part 4 serves as a concise handbook of sentence skills. Parts 2 and 3 show, respectively, how the four principles apply in the different patterns of essay development and in specialized types of writing. The ongoing success of Canadian editions of *College Writing Skills with Readings* is evidence that the four principles are easily grasped, remembered, and followed by students.
- **Writing is treated as a process.** The first chapter introduces writing as both a skill and a process of discovery. The second chapter, "The Writing Process," explains and illustrates the sequence of steps in writing an effective essay. In particular, the chapter focuses on prewriting, outlining, and revising as essential to any writing assignment. Detailed suggestions for prewriting and revising then accompany many of the writing assignments in Part 2.
- **Activities and assignments are numerous and varied.** For example, in Part 1 there are more than seventy activities to help students apply and master the four principles or bases of effective writing. There are nearly two hundred activities and tests in the entire book. A variety of writing assignments follows each of the patterns of essay development in Part 2. Some topics are highly structured, for students who are still learning the steps in the writing process; others are open-ended. Instructors thus have the option of selecting those assignments most suited to the individual needs of their students.
- **Clear thinking is stressed throughout.** The emphasis on logic and the pursuit of ideas and explanations in a sequential manner starts in the first chapter. Students are introduced to the two principles that are the bases of clear thinking and writing: *making a point and providing support to back up*

that point. The focus on these principles then continues throughout the book, helping students to learn that clear writing is inseparable from clear thinking.

■ ***The traditional essay is emphasized.*** Students are asked to write formal essays with an introduction, three supporting paragraphs, and a conclusion. Anyone who has tried to write a solidly reasoned essay knows how much work is involved. A logical essay requires a great deal of mental discipline and close attention to a set of logical rules. Writing an essay in which there is an overall thesis statement and in which each of the three supporting paragraphs begins with a topic sentence is more challenging for many students than writing a free-form or expressive essay. The demands are significant, but the rewards in both college and career are great.

■ ***Lively teaching models are provided.*** The book provides two high-interest student essays with each assignment. Students then read and evaluate these essays in terms of the four bases of unity, support, coherence, and effectiveness of sentence skills. After reading vigorous papers composed by other students as well as by the professional authors whose works are included in Part 5, and experiencing the power that good writing can have, students will be encouraged to aim for a similar honesty, realism, and detail in their own work.

■ ***The book is versatile.*** Since no two people use an English text in exactly the same way, the material has been organized in a highly accessible manner. Each section of the book deals with a distinct aspect of writing. Instructors can therefore turn quickly and easily to the skills they want to present.

■ ***Helpful learning aids accompany the book.*** *The Instructor's Manual and Test Bank* includes The Instructor's Guide along with thirty supplementary activities and tests. Also available is *Allwrite!*—a high-interest, interactive grammar tutorial program on CD-ROM. Please contact your McGraw-Hill Ryerson representative for details concerning policies, prices, and availability, as some restrictions may apply.

CHANGES IN THE THIRD CANADIAN EDITION

There are major changes and additions in this new Canadian edition of *College Writing Skills with Readings.*

■ Part 1 reflects significant revision, especially in the first two chapters, "Introduction to Writing" and "The Writing Process." More attention is devoted to each element of the paragraph and the essay to help students understand these elements in a functional sense.

■ New material on paragraph writing and structure has been added to Chapter 1 to help students review these concepts and prepare for essay writing.

■ Additional material on prewriting and outlining now strengthens emphasis on the book's approach to the writing process.

- Each chapter in Parts 1 and 2 contains Learning Outcomes and end-of-chapter Reviews of those outcomes. Students and instructors will find these useful for focusing on the essential skills and knowledge within the chapters.

- Group activities have been added, as have new assignments.

- This third Canadian edition places stronger emphasis on third-person voicing in essay writing and continues to encourage students to move beyond personal narratives toward a wider range of essay types.

- Computer and Internet use are now presumed as the norms for writing and researching activities, and both writing and research instruction reflect this view.

- Student models and practice materials have been updated, changed, and modified with a view to maintaining the text's essential values while giving it a consistently Canadian contextual quality.

- Eight new readings appear in Part 5. These selections are current, are relevant to students, and demonstrate an appropriate range of rhetorical modes to reinforce and extend the book's pedagogy.

ACKNOWLEDGMENTS

Reviewers who have provided helpful ideas and feedback include: Joan Pilz of Humber College, Elias Saari of Cambrian College, Dianna McAleer of Algonquin College, Anne Ward of Lambton College, Alisa Kay of George Brown College, Janice Burk of Sault College, Lori Dunn of Seneca College, Sandra Koncz of Cambrian College, Nancy Holmes of Okanagan University College, and Stan Bennett of University College of the Cariboo.

As always, I am grateful for the help, good humour, wise advice, and encouragement provided by my editors at McGraw-Hill Ryerson: Associate Editor Marianne Minaker, Developmental Editor Sandra de Ruiter, and Senior Supervising Editor Margaret Henderson. And I once again thank the students of Seneca College York Campus for inspiring me and for sharing their thoughts and feelings with me.

SHARON WINSTANLEY
SENECA COLLEGE

McGraw-Hill Ryerson
Online Learning Centre

McGraw-Hill Ryerson offers you an online resource that combines the best content with the flexibility and power of the Internet. Organized by chapter, the LANGAN/WINSTANLEY Online Learning Centre (OLC) offers the following features to enhance your learning and understanding of Writing Skills:

- Quizzes
- Exercises
- Current Articles
- Web Links
- Downloadable Supplements

By connecting to the "real world" through the OLC, you will enjoy a dynamic and rich source of current information that will help you get more from your course and improve your chances for success, both in the course and in the future.

For the Instructor

Downloadable Supplements

The Instructor's Manual is available, password-protected for instant access!

PageOut   **PageOut**
Create a custom course Website with PageOut, free with every McGraw-Hill Ryerson textbook.

Create your own course Web page for free, quickly and easily. Your professionally designed Web site links directly to OLC material, allows you to post a class syllabus, and much more! Visit www.pageout.net

Online Resources

McGraw-Hill Ryerson offers various online resource tools, such as Web links, to help you get the latest information to use in your class.

For the Student

Exercises and Activities

Do you understand the material? Various online exercises and activities allow you to put what you've read into practice, then grade yourself to ensure you're on the right path.

Articles

Several online articles provide further information on hot topics such as using the Internet for research purposes.

Web Links

Keep current and find out more with this feature — simply click and you're exploring issues such as plagiarism.

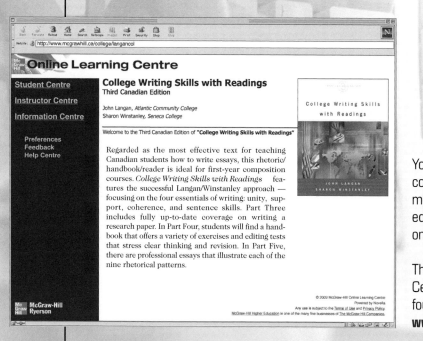

Your Internet companion to the most exciting educational tools on the Web!

The Online Learning Centre can be found at:

www.mcgrawhill.ca/college/langancol

Permissions

Banas, Casey, "Why Are Students Turned Off?" From *The Chicago Tribune*, August 5, 1979. Copyright 1979 by The Chicago Tribune. Used with permission.

Bodett, Tom, "Wait Divisions." From *Small Comforts*. Copyright 1987 by Tom Bodett. Reprinted by permission of Perseus Books Publishers, a member of Perseus Books, L.L.C.

Clark, Andrew, "Choose Your Battles." From *Saturday Night*, August 18, 2001. Reprinted by permission of *The National Post*.

Davis, Glenda, "How to Do Well on a Job Interview." Reprinted by permission of the author.

Dunayer, Joan, "Here's to Your Health." Reprinted by permission of Townsend Press.

Durning, Alan, "Coffee." From *Adbusters Quarterly*, Winter 1995: Vol 3, #3 (72-74). Alan Durning is executive director of Northwest Environmental Watch in Seattle, Washington and co-author of *Stuff: The Secret Lives of Everyday Things*. Reprinted by permission of Northwest Environmental Watch.

Engkent, Garry, "Why My Mother Can't Speak English." Reprinted by permission of the author.

Gregory, Dick, "Shame." Copyright 1964 by Dick Gregory Enterprises, Inc., from *Nigger: An Autobiography* by Dick Gregory. Used by permission of Dutton, a division of Penguin Putnam Inc.

Hoffert, Paul, "A Work Community." From *All Together Now*. Copyright 2000 by Paul Hoffert. Reprinted by permission of Stoddart Publishing Co. Limited.

Keeshig-Tobias, Lenore, "He Was a Boxer When I Was Small." Lenore Keeshig-Tobias is an award-winning author and a traditional Native storyteller from the Chippewas of Nawash First Nation. Reprinted by permission of the author.

Lamanna, Mary Ann, and Reidmann, Agnes, "Five Parenting Styles." From *Marriages and Families: Making Choices Throughout the Life Cycle*. Copyright 1981 by Wadsworth, Inc. Reprinted by permission.

Laurence, Margaret, "Where the World Began." From *Heart of a Stranger*. Used by permission of McClelland & Stewart, Inc. The Canadian Publishers.

Marshall, Jeannie, "Sometimes the Words Don't Come." Reprinted by permission of the author.

McMurtry, John, "Smash Thy Neighbor." From *Maclean's*. Reprinted by permission.

Mustafa, Naheed, "My Body Is My Own Business." From *The Globe and Mail*, June 29, 1993 (A-26). Reprinted by permission of Naheed Mustafa.

O'Keeney, Brian, "How to Make It in College, Now That You're Here." Reprinted by permission.

Sherry, Mary, "In Praise of the F Word." From "My Turn" in *Newsweek*. Reprinted by permission of the author.

Suzuki, David, "The Pain of Animals." From *Inventing the Future: Reflections on Science, Technology and Nature*. Stoddart Publishing Company, 1989. Reprinted by permission of the author.

Tannen, Deborah, "Sex, Lies, and Conversation." Copyright 1990 by Deborah Tannen, Ph.D.

Taylor, Deems, "The Monster." Copyright 1937, originally published by Curtis Brown, Ltd.

Tija, Sherwin, "Of Lemons and Lemonade." From *Adbusters Quarterly*, Winter 1995: Vol. 3, #3 (28-32). Reprinted by permission of *Adbusters Quarterly*, www.adbusters.org.

Essay Writing

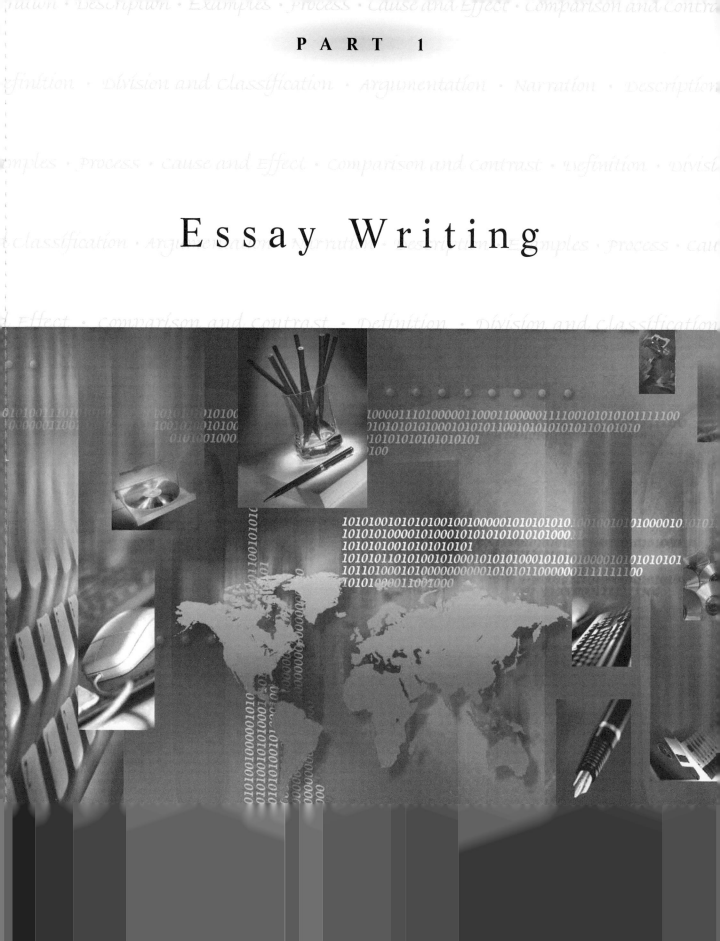

ration • Description • Examples • Process • Cause and Effect • Comparison and Contrast
finition • Division and Classification • Argumentation • Narration • Description • Examples
cess • Cause and Effect • Comparison and Contrast • Definition • Division and Classification
umentation • Narration • Description • Examples • Process • Cause and Effect • Comparison and
trast • Definition • Division and Classification • Argumentation • Narration • Description

CHAPTER 1

An Introduction to Writing

LEARNING OUTCOMES

After reading this chapter and working through its activities, you will
- **Know that writing is a skill and a process of discovering your thoughts**
- **Realize the immediate and lifelong benefits of writing the traditional essay**
- **Learn to write an effective paragraph**
- **Know the structure of the typical college essay**
- **See the value of the computer in the writing process**

The questions and experiences of Canadian college students shape this book. Those students, like you, struggled with writing paragraphs and essays. Those students asked how to make writing less confusing; they asked how to make their ideas clearer; and often they asked how writing essays would help their future careers.

Beginning with the sections that follow, you will find answers to those questions. The main concepts reinforced throughout this book are introduced in the box below.

- Writing is a skill, and confusion decreases as writers learn to follow clearly set out and workable methods and practices.
- Writing is a process of discovering, arranging, and revising thoughts, and a clear expression of ideas results from understanding and following this process.
- Writing the traditional essay, whose main point is logically supported, is the best preparation for effective, appropriate communication in most media.

College Writing Skills with Readings, third Canadian edition, offers concrete, practical help in college writing tasks. The writing process is broken down into a series of logical, easily followed steps, beginning with prewriting and concluding with revising final drafts. For the student in twenty-first-century Canada, writing and communicating information effectively are essential skills in a technology-based society.

Part 1 begins with a look at the act of writing itself, and with some basic concepts to help students approach writing with more confidence and stronger motivation.

WRITING IS A SKILL

"I can never say what I mean," "I was always bad at English," "I don't mind writing e-mails, but essays are torture," "Writing is easy for some people, but not for me."

When students say such things, they are expressing the genuine uncertainty most people feel about putting thoughts on paper. Writing exposes the writer: to himself or herself, and to others. Once thoughts and feelings are on paper for others to judge, people are vulnerable. And perhaps nowhere is anyone more vulnerable than in the classroom, where judgments have mark-values. Students may feel *they* are being judged, not the way they write.

Feeling uncertain or unvalued leads students to two mistaken conclusions: one, that they alone find writing difficult; and two, that they lack the talent to write well. These attitudes may cause them to avoid trying to improve, or even to avoid writing. Such students feel that failure is inevitable: that trying can only result in failing, so there is no reason to try. Only adopting a different attitude about writing will break them out of this cycle of self-defeat.

A realistic, positive attitude about writing begins with the idea that **writing is a skill**. All skills are acquired and mastered in stages. Like learning to cook, drive, or design websites, learning to write is a step-by-step process. Writing requires willingness, patience, and determination to learn and work through those steps.

Good writing is the result of completing tasks or meeting challenges. It is not a gift or a single flash of inspiration. The intense thinking required by clear writing is a challenge to most people. Finding words and phrases that transfer ideas to paper is demanding. Deciding what is worth keeping, out of an hour's worth of writing, is difficult. Discovering that an apparently simple topic has become complex is frustrating. **Writing well is hard work.** But learning any skill requires work—and the reward is achievement.

If you have the desire to learn, the patience to review and revise your work, and the determination to write well, this book will give you the extensive practice needed to develop and hone your writing skills.

WRITING IS A PROCESS OF DISCOVERY

Believing that writing is a natural gift leads students to another false assumption—that writing flows in a single straight line from the writer's mind to the page. Good writing is never a simple one-draft trip to a flawless final draft.

As mentioned previously, **writing is a process of discovery**—a series of stages. The process may loop and zigzag in many directions as the writer finds new ideas and connections between thoughts and associated feelings and mental images. Most writers do not know what they want to say or what their focus will be until they follow the paths of their thoughts in writing. The illustrations below demonstrate the writing process:

Seldom the case:

Starting point ————————————————————➤ Finished paper

Usually the case:

Starting point  Finished paper

Let's follow the discovery process of Tina Kallas, author of the paragraph on movie-going on page 8. Her assignment was to write about some annoyance in everyday life. With no focus in mind, she started writing about annoyances in general, to discover a topic. Traffic annoyed her, so she filled a screen with point-form ideas and details about traffic. One single detail, though, sparked a series of thoughts: the traffic she had to deal with in driving to the movies. Now Tina was thinking about traffic in the theatre-complex parking lot, and about lining up to get into a movie. She switched directions; she decided that movie-going itself was an annoyance. This apparent "detour" in Tina's writing journey was itself a rich source of ideas—the irritating aspects of movie-going.

As she pursued her new line of thought, Tina started thinking that her paper's main idea could be the irritating behaviour of other movie-goers. But describing the sound of people dropping popcorn tubs on the floor triggered memories: the smell of movie-house popcorn and the temptation of snacks at the concession stand. She changed direction a second time, finding that she had a lot to say about other movie-goers and the temptation of snacks. Now Tina was not really sure of where she was going, but she kept typing, getting down more and more details about the experience of going to the movies. She had "opened the tap" in her mind, and although she was uncertain of how to fit other movie patrons and snacks into a finished paper, she just kept writing, knowing that eventually her ideas would come together.

Writing is usually a continuing discovery; as you write, you find new avenues of thought, change direction, or even go backwards. You may work out an opening sentence and realize suddenly that this is your conclusion. Or you may find yourself caught up in explaining some detail, only to find it could be the main point of your paper. As you begin to write, be relaxed and open enough to let these things happen. You are discovering what you want to say and the shape and direction of your paper.

BENEFITS OF WRITING THE TRADITIONAL ESSAY

Now you know some reassuring facts about writing in general. But before you move on to an overview of the essay as a specific form, consider the benefits of writing the traditional essay—benefits that may surprise and motivate you.

Mastering the demands of the essay's structure and content gives you the foundation for all college writing assignments. Whether you are in the classroom, in the lab, in an online course, or on co-op, you will be assigned a variety of writing formats: reports, analyses, business or technical documents, website text, broadcast copy, and research papers. All these formats are based on the traditional essay. They contain differing numbers of body paragraphs, but the "deductive" essay structure—which leads with its main idea and follows through with clearly set out proof—is the core of almost all writing formats.

As you look ahead, and to other media, essay writing readies you for the requirements of electronic communication. During your career, you may write online as often as on paper. Stating a point and backing it up concisely are the essentials of time-efficient e-mail correspondence and website content. Screen readers impatiently scan a document's opening for its point and spend only seconds checking for evidence of support and explanation to see the pattern of point and specific support you learn from essay writing.

Disciplines you acquire in essay writing also strengthen other essential communication skills: reading and speaking. In this "age of information," you will be evaluated on how well you absorb, use, and transmit information. Learning to manage and position ideas in essays makes you a more acute reader; your judgment improves with awareness of how other writers handle ideas and proof. Structuring and creating essay-content will make you a better speaker, too. You will be prepared to develop and present ideas orally, using the elements and structure of an effective essay: an interesting opening, solid and coherent body, and reassuringly rounded conclusion.

Most important, essay writing makes you a stronger thinker. Writing a clearly reasoned traditional essay requires mental discipline and close attention to a logical progression of ideas. Each time you meet the challenge of creating an essay with a guiding thesis statement and supporting paragraphs beginning with topic sentences, your ability to express, order, and defend ideas grows stronger. To sum up, traditional essay writing trains your mind to think clearly, and that ability is of value in every phase of your life.

Now it is time for an overview of the essay and its components, beginning with four steps that will help you construct organized, coherent essays.

AN OVERVIEW OF THE ESSAY

Although the writing process may be unpredictable, there are four steps that break essay writing into clear and manageable tasks. These steps guide you to work on one thing and one goal at a time. You may go back and forth between these steps as you work; the important things are to keep writing and to refer often to the goals in each step.

Here are the four steps to help you construct an organized and coherent essay:

1 Discover and state clearly your point or thesis.

2 Provide logically ordered, detailed support for your thesis.

3 Organize and connect your supporting material.

4 Revise and edit so that your content is concise and well stated and your sentences error-free.

Part 1 of this book explains each step in detail and provides many practical materials to help you absorb and master each one. First, though, consider the two essential elements of an essay: point and support.

POINT AND SUPPORT

The traditional essay is a writing format with a purpose: It makes a point, and then defends, explains, illustrates, or proves that point.

MAKING A POINT IN SPEECH AND IN PRINT: YOUR AUDIENCES

People make points all the time in ordinary conversation, for all sorts of reasons. You might say, "C++ is really hard," "There aren't enough good videos on *MuchMusic*," or "Students should work for a while before going to college." Your listeners will not usually push you to justify your assertions. They may know you and already know your reasoning. They may agree with you and know you are just passing time with your comments, or they may not want to challenge you. As well, conversations generally move quickly from subject to subject, so people don't usually expect a long explanation.

Print is different from everyday speech. Readers of your printed words do not always know you. They cannot see or feel the context for your ideas. Your readers may not agree with you, and they are not obliged to give you a chance. You are not there with them to break into your text and clarify what you mean. (Moreover, reading even a few paragraphs requires two things of your readers—time and concentration.) Readers don't like wasting time and energy; they want to know what you are writing about and why you are writing. To communicate effectively with readers, to reward their patience, *you must make your point clearly and back it up thoroughly with specific reasons or illustrative details*.

Visualize your reading audience as reasonable people, curious about what you have to say. If you pay them the respect of thinking through your point so that you support it clearly and logically, your readers will be ready to accept what you say.

POINT AND SUPPORT IN A PARAGRAPH

You read print in blocks of sentences, or paragraphs. The look of a group of sentences placed together and surrounded by white space suggests a paragraph's purpose—it is a container for a series of thoughts tied to one idea. A paragraph is the basic unit of communication for making one point and backing up that point with logically connected details.

Paragraphs that stand alone, and body-paragraphs in an essay, support a point with details. The main difference between the two is the depth of coverage given to supporting evidence. An independent paragraph backs up its point with a variety of supporting details; a body-paragraph in an essay explores one supporting detail of the essay's thesis-point in some depth. Like Tina Kallas, author of the paragraph on movie-going below, you may begin by working on paragraphs intended as independent pieces of writing.

In a paragraph, every sentence performs a function. First is **the topic sentence**; it **states the point of the paragraph**. The point is your subject and viewpoint on that subject, as you saw in the conversational examples in the previous section. When you write your point in a topic sentence, you give a compressed version of your whole paragraph's meaning.

> **A topic sentence**
> - States the writer's intention for the paragraph that follows
> - Suggests the writer's viewpoint or judgment on the subject
> - Previews the focus and limits for supporting details
> - Guides the reader into the paragraph's content

Notice a key phrase in the topic sentence of Tina's paragraph: *drawbacks to movie-going.* This phrase expresses both the subject *(movie-going)* and the writer's attitude about that subject *(drawbacks).* Tina's intention is clear: She is writing about negative aspects of her subject, and *drawbacks* is a general enough word to suggest and cover all the supporting details in the paragraph. For this reason, topic sentences are sometimes called "umbrella sentences."

Following from the topic sentence, each sentence in a paragraph-unit performs one or more of the following supporting functions.

> **Body sentences**
> - Make the point clearer with examples
> - Prove the truth of the topic sentence's point with explanations
> - Recount one extended example or narrative to demonstrate the point
> - Clarify or expand on the point with comparisons to similar ideas or situations
> - Give logical consequences resulting from the point

The support in body-sentences is specific. As you read Tina's paragraph, you see what she means by *drawbacks;* you share her experiences looking for a parking space and walking on sticky floors. The supporting details expand the general idea in the topic sentence into specific facts. These specifics—the details, examples, and explanations—reinforce the paragraph's point and make it clearer. The **paragraph's meaning is unified because each piece of support relates back to the single point of the topic sentence**. Whether you use facts, word-pictures, quoted opinions, statistics, or personal anecdotes as supporting details, you communicate your meaning with specific ideas directly connected to your point.

Now read Tina Kallas' paragraph on why movie-going annoys her:

The Hazards of Movie-Going

Although I love movies, I've found there are drawbacks to movie-going. One problem is just the inconvenience of it all. I have to drive at least fifteen minutes to the theatre, more if traffic is bad. It can take forever to find a parking spot, and then I have to walk across a huge parking lot to the theatre. There I encounter long lines, sold-out tickets, and ever-increasing prices. And I hate sitting with my feet sticking to the floor because of other people's spilled snacks. Another problem is my lack of self-control at the theatre. I often stuff myself with unhealthy, calorie-laden snacks. My choices might include a bucket of popcorn, a box of Maple Buds, a giant pop, or all three. The worst problem is some of the other movie-goers. Kids run up and down the aisles.

Teenagers laugh and shout at the screen. People of all ages drop pop containers and popcorn tubs, cough and burp, and talk to one another. All in all, I would rather stay home and wait for the latest movie hits on cable TV in the comfort of my own living room.

Now you see what Tina's **supporting evidence** has done. The specific details catch your attention and each detail brings her point into clearer focus. By showing you the series of experiences that led to her point, she gives you a basis for understanding her views.

STRUCTURING SUPPORT IN A PARAGRAPH

During the writing process, supporting details usually come to you in random order. You then have two tasks: first, to decide which details best explain your point, and then to place those details in an order that demonstrates your point most clearly. Making an outline, such as the one you see below, is the best way to work out an effective order for your paragraph's details and explanations.

Tina Kallas' supporting evidence is clear and easy to follow because she has arranged it in a logical pattern. She offers three reasons she finds movie-going annoying; **each reason** (supporting detail) **is a subtopic**. A subtopic is a smaller division of the topic, an aspect of the proof. Tina follows each subtopic with examples or short explanations that are even more specific. The logical progression of ideas from a general point to specific pieces of proof is called **deductive structure**; by using this structure, Tina shows how she *deduced* the truth of her point.

This **movement from point to detail** (subtopic) **to explanation**, a pattern that repeats for each subtopic, is key to creating an effective paragraph.

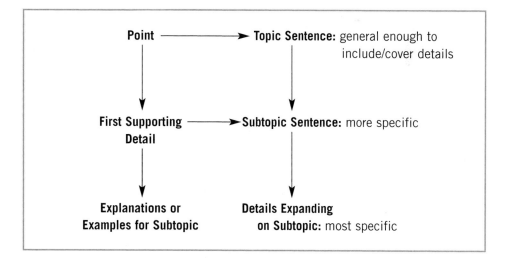

Your subject will often suggest an order for your subtopics. For example, if you are explaining why something happened to you, you may put the causes of that situation in the order in which they occurred. Or you may discover that some reasons seem more important than others do, so you may put your details in order of their importance. You will find more information on organizing supporting material on pages 72–74.

Activity

Part 1: An Individual Activity

You have learned why the paragraph on movie-going supports its point effectively. Now take the paragraph to pieces and see how its parts fit into an outline. By doing so, you will grasp the "general to specific" deductive structure more clearly. You will also practise using the paragraph outline format demonstrated in the next section.

Fill in each section of the outline below, beginning with the point stated in Tina Kallas' paragraph.

POINT   _____

_____

SUPPORT   1. _____

a. *Fifteen-minute drive to theatre* _____

b. _____

c. _____

d. _____

SUBTOPIC   2. Lack of self-control

a. *Often stuff myself with unhealthy snacks.* _____

b. *Might have popcorn, candy, pop, or all three.* _____

SUBTOPIC   3. _____

a. _____

b. _____

c. *People of all ages make noise.* _____

Part 2: A Group Activity

1. Create your group's topic by writing your version of the following phrase:

"   *(Some leisure activity)*   is   *(enjoyable, boring, healthy . . .)*   ."

2. Come up with reasons why each person might hold this view. Have someone list the reasons.
3. Decide which reasons your group finds strongest. Make a new list for those.
4. Under each reason (subtopic/supporting detail), jot down a few specific examples that make the subtopic-reason easy to understand.
5. Copy the outline format onto paper of your own. Now, make an outline as a group, consisting of your point, your supporting subtopics, and the examples or situations that illustrate your subtopics.

Compare your group's outline with those of the other groups in the class.

OUTLINING A PARAGRAPH

Students sometimes avoid making outlines or they make quick (and often odd-looking) outlines *after* writing paragraphs or essays. Outlining takes work, but it exposes repeated or similar ideas and weak connections between ideas. Outlining makes writing a good paper much easier. Rather than avoiding outlining, use it to map your thoughts and keep your intentions for your paragraph clear.

A good time to make an outline is after you have jotted down some ideas. Pause for a while so that you see your ideas with a fresh mind. Remember that outlines tend to change as you work on them, so try not to judge yourself harshly while you work.

There are many ways to start an outline, but the following method works if you allow yourself the time to go through it a step at a time.

1. Copy the outline pattern below. Write it by hand, leaving spaces to fill in, or key it in, saving it as a blank document that you can copy and paste for repeated use.

Point
Topic Sentence: _____

Support
    Subtopic 1: _____

        Suptopic Support (examples, explanations)
        a.
        b.
        c.

    Subtopic 2: _____

        Subtopic Support
        a.
        b.
        c.

    Subtopic 3: _____

        Subtopic Support
        a.
        b.
        c.

Note: This outline does not dictate a rigid pattern of three subtopics with three supporting items each. Adjust it to suit your supporting evidence—your paragraph may have two subtopics and four examples for each, or some variation on this pattern. Be sure, though, that the sections of your support are balanced; that each supporting detail and explanation unit is roughly the same length.

2. Before you begin your outline, take a clean piece of paper or open a new document onscreen. Ask yourself two questions: What is my point, and why do I believe my point is true? Write out your point in one sentence. (Be prepared to change the sentence, if you find your point changing.) Now list any words or phrases that bring to mind facts, examples, or situations that back up your point.

3. Next, look at your prewriting as well as at the page or screen document where you just noted your point and reasons for that point. See if some reasons are more important than others; if so, put your reasons (subtopics) in order of importance, or in an order that seems appropriate to you.

4. You are ready to start your outline. Don't worry if you change or eliminate examples, or think of a new way to explain a detail. If you are stalled at some point, fill in another section of the outline—you need not work from top to bottom in a straight line. The point of outlining is to see and shape your thoughts—you can always rearrange parts of your outline. A messy outline is usually a good outline.

A NOTE ABOUT PARAGRAPH LENGTH

Every day you read paragraphs in newspaper articles, on websites, and in stories or novels. Any paragraph signals to you that it covers a single idea, but some are so short that they look like "print-bytes." You know that proving your point in print requires more words than you might use in conversation, but after reading the preceding section of this book, you may wonder, How long should a paragraph be?

Paragraph length depends on three main considerations:

- The purpose of the paragraph
- The reading audience's needs
- The medium and format in which the paragraph appears

Paragraphs range from one sentence to several pages in length; the student paragraph you read contains fourteen sentences. Short paragraphs in newspapers—a disposable medium—give easy-to-manage information quickly to a wide variety of readers. Printed in narrow columns, article paragraphs are broken into short pieces so their appearance does not intimidate readers. Websites entertain and inform in a competitive electronic environment. Screens are harder to read than pages; scroll bars, back-buttons, colour, animation, and graphics tempt readers away from long periods of focus. Web-based paragraphs may appear brief to attract readers, but in fact, they use "three-dimensional support"—hypertext links to material on other parts of the same page or other sites. Stories and novels imitate life in entertaining ways, with fascinating characters and plots. Paragraphs may be only a single line of dialogue or may run to twenty sentences of intense action or vivid description—their purpose is to carry leisure-time readers along in a fictional world.

Essays, reports, text and non-fiction books, and career writing formats inform readers. These formats are generally printed so that readers can consider, judge, and sometimes act on their content. Paragraph length depends on making a point and supporting it with logical and sufficient explanation. This is the type of writing that you are practising now, and this is why "print-byte" paragraphs are rarely found in college writing. Instead of asking how long your paragraph should be, ask yourself, Does my paragraph make my point clear?

STRUCTURE OF THE TRADITIONAL ESSAY

POINT AND SUPPORT IN AN ESSAY

The best way to learn to write clearly and logically is to practise writing the traditional college essay. Typically an essay is a paper of five hundred words or more, consisting of an introductory paragraph, two to four supporting paragraphs, and a concluding paragraph. This multi-paragraph format is simply an expanded version of the paragraph structure shown in the preceding sections.

Like the paragraph, the essay supports and develops one point. The essay's main point or central idea is called a **thesis statement**, rather than a topic sentence, as it is in a paragraph. The thesis statement, following the deductive model, appears in the first paragraph; specific points that support the thesis appear in the paragraphs that make up the body of the essay. Each body paragraph develops a single supporting point, so an essay's internal paragraphs treat evidence for the essay's thesis point more fully than would be possible in a single-paragraph paper.

A MODEL ESSAY

The following model will help you clearly understand the form of an essay. Tina Kallas, the writer of the paragraph on movie-going, later decided to develop her subject more fully. Here is the essay that resulted.

The Hazards of Movie-Going

INTRODUCTORY PARAGRAPH

I am a movie fanatic. My friends count on me to know movie trivia (who was the pigtailed little girl in *E.T.: The Extra-Terrestrial?* Drew Barrymore) and to remember every big Oscar awarded since I was in grade school (best picture 1994? *Forrest Gump*). My friends, though, have stopped asking me if I want to go out to the movies. While I love movies as much as ever, the inconvenience of going out, the temptations of the theatre, and the behaviour of some patrons are reasons for me to wait and rent the video. 1

FIRST SUPPORTING PARAGRAPH

To begin with, I just don't enjoy the general hassle of the evening. Since small local movie theatres are a thing of the past, I have to drive fifteen minutes to the nearest multiplex. The parking lot is shared with several restaurants and a supermarket, so it's always jammed. I have to drive around at a snail's pace until I spot another driver backing out. Then it's time to stand in an endless line, with the constant threat that tickets for the show I want will sell out. Just as bad, the theatre will be so crowded that I won't be able to sit with my friends, or we'll have to sit in a front row gaping up at a giant screen. I have to shell out a ridiculous amount of money—up to $12—for a ticket. That entitles me to sit while my shoes seal themselves to a sticky floor coated with spilled pop, bubble gum, and crushed Rolos. 2

SECOND
SUPPORTING
PARAGRAPH

Secondly, the theatre offers tempting snacks I really don't need. Like most of us, I have to battle an expanding waistline. At home I do pretty well by simply not buying stuff that is bad for me. I can make do with snacks like celery and carrot sticks because there is no ice cream in the freezer. Going to the theatre, however, is like spending my evening in a convenience store that's been equipped with a movie screen and comfortable seats. As I try to convince myself to have just a diet Coke, the smell of fresh popcorn dripping with butter soon overcomes me. Chocolate bars the size of small automobiles seem to jump into my hands, and I risk pulling out my fillings as I chew enormous mouthfuls of Maple Buds. If I go with friends, they always seem to order nachos and miles of red licorice strings. Immediately, I feel jealous and deprived, and end up buying snacks I don't need, to console myself. By the time I leave the theatre, I feel disgusted with myself.   3

THIRD
SUPPORTING
PARAGRAPH

Many of the other patrons are even more of a problem than the concession stand. Little kids race up and down the aisles, usually in giggling packs. Teenagers try to impress their friends by talking back to the screen, whistling, and making what they consider to be hilarious noises. Adults act as if they were at home in their own living rooms. They comment loudly on the ages of the stars and reveal plot twists that are supposed to be secrets until the film's end. And people of all ages create distractions. They crinkle candy wrappers, stick gum on their seats, and drop popcorn tubs or cups of crushed ice and pop on the floor. They also cough and burp, squirm endlessly in their seats, file out for repeated trips to the washrooms or concession stands, and elbow me out of the armrest on either side of my seat.   4

CONCLUDING
PARAGRAPH

After arriving home from the movies one night, I decided that I was not going to be a movie-goer anymore. I was tired of the problems involved in getting to the theatre, resisting unhealthy snacks, and dealing with the patrons. The next day, I arranged to have premium movie channels installed as part of my cable TV service, and I also got a membership in my local video store. I may now see movies a bit later than other people, but I'll be more relaxed watching box office hits in the comfort of my own living room.   5

"The Hazards of Movie-Going" is a good example of a standard short essay, one of the most versatile of writing formats. Essays are flexible patterns for exploration—they suit personal expressions of feeling or memories as well as they do objective comparisons of technical matters or reports of events. The "voices" in which writers "speak" in essays range from the highly personal "I" of a first-person essay to the less personal third-person approach.

Tina's essay is a personal, expressive type of essay. You may begin the semester by writing about personal concerns—a personal essay lets you rely confidently on your own experience. If, like Tina, you write in the "first person" voice, as "I," when you express your views, you show readers your strong connection to your subject matter. You will discover, as you practise essay writing, that you can express personal ideas in the third-person voice as well, without using the pronoun "I." Many subjects you write about at college will lend themselves better to the third-person, "no I," approach. When you write from the non-intrusive third-person point of view, your reader focuses more on your subject, and less on your connection to it. As you progress in essay writing, you will develop a sense of which subjects benefit from which voice or approach.

Now you will see how "The Hazards of Movie-Going" makes effective use of standard college essay structure, with its one-paragraph introduction, three-paragraph body, and one-paragraph conclusion. The functions of these paragraphs as parts of essay structure are described and illustrated below.

Introductory Paragraph

In your introductory paragraph your reader sees your subject and your relationship to that subject—what your essay is about. Your first few sentences attract the reader's attention, giving context or background for the main idea you will develop. Then you advance the central idea, or thesis, that will be explored in the essay. The thesis contains your subject and viewpoint, and often includes a plan of development—a "preview" of the major points that will support the thesis. These supporting points should be listed in the order in which they will appear in the essay. In some cases, the plan of development is presented in a sentence separate from the thesis; in other cases, it is suggested in general terms.

Activity

1. In "The Hazards of Movie-Going," which sentences attract the reader's interest by offering background information?

   a. First sentence
   b. First two sentences
   c. First three sentences

2. In which sentence is the thesis of the essay presented?

   a. Third sentence
   b. Fourth sentence

3. Does the thesis contain a plan of development?

   a. Yes
   b. No

4. Write down the words in the thesis that announce the three major supporting points in the essay:

   a. _____

   b. _____

   c. _____

Body: Supporting Paragraphs

Most essays have three supporting points, developed at length over three separate paragraphs. (Some essays will have two supporting points, others four or more.) For the purposes of this book, your goal will be three supporting points (unless your instructor indicates otherwise). Each of the supporting paragraphs should begin with a *topic sentence* **that guides your choice of details and states the point to be detailed in that paragraph**. Just as the thesis provides a focus for the entire essay, the topic sentences provide a focus for each supporting paragraph. Body paragraphs expand on the pattern of the essay itself; each one examines one of the thesis statement's main points in its topic sentence, and in its "proof" or supporting details, each paragraph advances and develops its part of the entire essay.

Activity

1. What is the topic sentence for the first supporting paragraph of the essay?

   _____

   _____

2. The first topic sentence is then supported by the following details: (fill in the missing words)

   a. *Have to drive fifteen minutes* _____

   b. _____

   c. *Endless ticket line* _____

   d. _____

   e. _____

   f. *Sticky floor* _____

3. What is the topic sentence for the second supporting paragraph of the essay?

   _____

   _____

4. The second topic sentence is then supported by the following examples:

   a. *At home only snacks are celery and carrot sticks* _____

   b. *Theatre is like a convenience store with seats* _____

   c. *Friends order snacks and I feel deprived* _____

      (1) *fresh popcorn* _____

      (2) _____

      (3) _____

5. What is the topic sentence for the third supporting paragraph of the essay?

   _____

   _____

6. The third topic sentence is then supported by the following details:

a. _____

b. _____

c. *Adults talk loudly and reveal plot twists* _____

d. *People of all ages create distractions* _____

Concluding Paragraph

The concluding paragraph summarizes the essay by briefly restating the thesis and, at times, the main supporting points of the essay. In addition, the writer often presents a more general or "outward looking" concluding thought about the subject of the paper.

Activity

1. Which two sentences in the concluding paragraph restate the thesis and supporting points of the essay?

   a. First and second   b. Second and third   c. Third and fourth

2. Which two sentences contain the concluding thought of the essay?

   a. First and second   b. Second and third   c. Third and fourth

DIAGRAM OF AN ESSAY

The following diagram shows you at a glance the different parts of a standard college essay, also known as a **one-three-one essay**. This diagram will serve as a helpful guide when you are writing or evaluating essays.

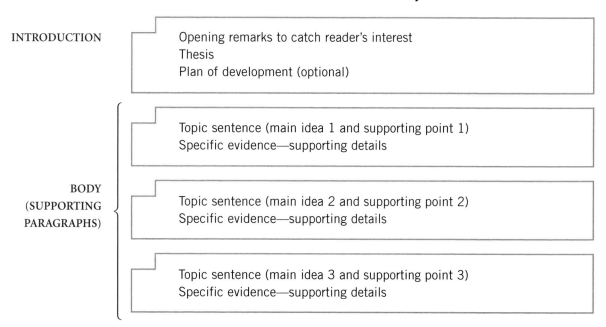

Title of the Essay

INTRODUCTION

Opening remarks to catch reader's interest
Thesis
Plan of development (optional)

BODY
(SUPPORTING
PARAGRAPHS)

Topic sentence (main idea 1 and supporting point 1)
Specific evidence—supporting details

Topic sentence (main idea 2 and supporting point 2)
Specific evidence—supporting details

Topic sentence (main idea 3 and supporting point 3)
Specific evidence—supporting details

CONCLUSION

> Summary (optional)
> General closing remarks

You now have an overview of the traditional form of the essay. In the next chapter, you will learn just how to go about writing an effective essay. First, though, consider the ways your computer can help you to write more easily and efficiently.

WORD PROCESSING AND THE WRITING PROCESS

Using a computer is an everyday activity for most people, and writing on a computer can help you at every stage of the writing process. Once you are comfortable writing onscreen, you will find prewriting, drafting, and revising easier and faster. If you are hesitant about your word-processing skills, most colleges have computer labs. Introductory courses in computer applications may be offered, or there may be free classes in word processing; take advantage of these opportunities, if necessary.

Some of the information in this section may be more meaningful and more useful *after* you have worked through Chapter 2 of the book.

General Tips on Word Processing

- Allow enough time if you are using your school's computer centre. You may have to wait for a computer or printer. In addition, you may need several sessions to complete your paper.

- Every word-processing program allows you to "save" your writing. Save your work frequently as you work on a draft. Work that is not saved is lost when the file you are working on is closed, when the computer is turned off, or if there's a power or system failure.

- If you are using your college's computers, form the habit of working only on your disk. By doing so, you avoid forgetting to copy your work to your own disk, and possibly losing it. If you are using your own computer, keep your work in two places—the hard drive or disk you are working on as well as a backup disk. At the end of each session with the computer, copy your work onto the backup disk. Then if the hard drive or working disk becomes damaged, you'll have the backup copy.

- Print out your work at least at the end of every session. Then you'll not only have your most recent draft to work on away from the computer, you'll also have a copy in case something should happen to your disks.

- Work in single-spacing so you can see as much of your writing on the screen at one time as possible. Just before you print out your work, change to double-spacing.

- Before making major changes in a paper, create a copy of your first-draft document. For example, if your file is titled "Worst Job," create a copy called "Worst Job 2." Then make all your changes in that file. If the changes don't work out, you can always go back to the original file.

Using a Computer in Each Stage of the Writing Process

Following are ways to make word processing a part of your writing. As you become familiar with working onscreen, you will find the methods that work best for you.

Prewriting: The "Discovery" Stage

Discovering and rearranging ideas are easier than ever on the computer. With freewriting, in particular, you can get ideas onto the screen almost as quickly as they occur to you. A passing thought that could prove productive is not likely to get lost. If you set aside ten minutes to freewrite on a subject, you may turn up a potential thesis, find a new direction, or discover small random details: the point is to discover your responses to a topic. Even if almost nothing seems useful that day, all you will have lost is ten minutes of your time.

After any initial freewriting, questioning, and list making on a computer, print out a hard copy. With a clean printout in front of you, you'll be able to see everything at once and revise and expand your work with hand-written comments in the margins of the paper.

You can also open several documents at once on your screen and transfer material from one to another. If you have a page or two of freewriting and a rough list of ideas for an essay outline, work with both documents at once. If you wish to add points or details from your freewriting to your list document, just highlight an item on your freewriting document, use the "copy" function, then move your cursor to the desired position on your list document and use the "paste" function to insert the highlighted words. Be sure to save your changes. This "multi-window" capability is a real benefit to writers.

If you listed items, you may be able to turn that list into an outline right on the screen. Open a new document, named "Outline," and type in the "Essay Outline" pattern on page 39 and the inside back cover of the book. Cut and paste items from your list into the outline pattern. Delete ideas you feel should not be in your paper (saving them at the end of the file in case you change your mind), and add any new ideas that occur to you. Then use the "cut" and "paste" functions to shuffle the supporting ideas until you find the best order for your paper.

Word processing also makes it easy for you to experiment with the wording of the point of your paper. You can try a number of versions in a short time. After you have decided upon the version that works best, you can easily delete the other versions—or simply move them to a temporary "leftover" section at the end of the paper.

Writing Your First Draft

Many writers create a first draft by hand and then type it into the computer for revision. As you type a handwritten draft, you may find yourself making changes and improvements. Once you have a draft on the screen, or a hard copy, you will find it much easier to revise than a handwritten one.

If you compose directly onscreen, you benefit from the computer's special features. For example, if your freewriting contains an anecdote you plan to use in your paper, simply copy the story from your freewriting document and insert it into your paper. You can refine it then or later. Or if you discover while typing that a sentence or paragraph is out of place, cut it and paste it wherever you wish. If you realize that an earlier sentence can be expanded, just move your cursor back and type in the added material.

Revising

During revision, word processing really shines. All substituting, adding, deleting, and rearranging can be done easily within an existing document. All changes instantly take their proper places within the paper, rather than being scribbled above the line or squeezed into the margin. You can concentrate on each change you want to make, rather than fight with a messy draft. You can carefully go through your paper, checking that all your supporting evidence is relevant, and adding new support where needed. Find the "undo" function to save retyping: Anything you decide to eliminate can be deleted in a keystroke, and replaced, if necessary, by another keystroke. Additions can be inserted precisely where you choose. If you change your mind, all you have to do is delete or cut and paste. Then you can sweep through the paper focusing on other changes, such as improving word choice, increasing sentence variety, eliminating wordiness, and so on.

Like many students, you may wish to print out a hard copy of your file at various points throughout the revision; number each revision, as in "Draft 2," and so on. You can then revise in longhand—adding, crossing out, and indicating changes—and later quickly make those changes in the document.

Editing and Proofreading

Editing and proofreading are also made easier by word processing. You no longer need to cross out mistakes on a page and grow frustrated as your work turns into an unreadable mess. Your screen draft stays tidy as you work. You are more likely to continue correcting errors when you work onscreen, simply because it is easier to do so and because your document looks cleaner. If you are unsure about making some change, just highlight and copy it, then move it to the bottom of your screen.

If you find editing or proofreading on the screen hard on your eyes, print out a copy. Mark any corrections on that copy, and then transfer them to the final draft.

If your word-processing package includes a spell checker, by all means use it. Spell checkers tell you when a word is not in its dictionary. You may need to check the form of spell checker in your package—use a Canadian dictionary to check your spelling. Keep in mind, however, that the spell checker cannot tell you how to spell a name correctly or when you have mistakenly used, for example, *their* instead of *there*. To a spell checker, *Thank ewe four the complement* is as correct as *Thank you for the compliment*. The "search" function can help you find words you tend to misspell, so you can locate them in a document.

Use grammar checkers with caution. These programs are still developing; they cannot magically write flawless sentences for you. Because a grammar checker recognizes certain word patterns as matching its catalogue of "correct structures," it spots some simple grammatical errors. But you must know which option to choose from the menu of corrections it offers. As well, grammar checkers ignore some errors completely or offer odd, incorrect sentence-level substitutions. Refer to Part 4 of this book any time you are unsure about a point of grammar or sentence structure.

Word-processed papers look so good that you may feel they are better than they are. Do not be fooled by your paper's appearance. Take time to carefully review your grammar, punctuation, and spelling. Do not forget to justify or leave your margins ragged, to italicize titles where necessary, to insert page numbers, and to change your essay to double-spacing before printing your final draft for marking.

Even after you hand in your paper, save the file on your disk. Your instructor may ask for revisions, and the file will save you from having to key in the paper all over again.

ACTIVITIES

Activity 1

Freewrite for fifteen minutes about your previous experiences with English classes. What problems did you have? What kinds of assignments were you given? What did you most enjoy, and what did you dislike most?

Option 1: Class Activity On the board, list four headings: Problems, Assignments, Likes, and Dislikes. List everyone's contribution under the four headings, and discuss common experiences, problems, and preferences.

Option 2: Individual Activity Based on your freewriting, create an outline for a paragraph about your experiences in English classes. For subtopics, you may concentrate only on various kinds of problems you faced, or you could contrast your "likes" with your "dislikes."

Activity 2

Following is an excerpt from one student's journal. As you read, look for a general point and supporting material that could be the basis for an interesting paper.

September 6, 2001

My first programming class was tonight. The parking lot was jammed when I got there. I thought I was going to be late for class. A guard had us park on a field next to the regular lot. When I got to the room, it had the usual painted, cinder-block construction. Every school I have ever been in since first grade seems to be made of cinder block. Everybody sat there without saying anything, waiting for the instructor to arrive. I think they were all a bit nervous like me. I hoped there wasn't going to be a tonne of work in the course. I think I was also afraid of looking foolish somehow. This goes back to grade school, when I wasn't a very good student, and teachers sometimes embarrassed me in class. I didn't like elementary school, and I hated high school. Now here I am six years later in college of all places. Who would have thought I would end up here? The instructor appeared—a woman who I think was a bit nervous herself.

I think I like her. Her name is Barbara Hanlin. She says we should call her Barbara. We got right into it, but it was interesting stuff. I like the fact that she asks questions, but then she lets you volunteer. I always hated it when teachers would call on you whether you wanted to answer or not. I also like the fact that she answers the questions and doesn't just leave you hanging. She takes the time to write important ideas on the board. I also like the way she laughs. This class may be OK.

1. If Alain, the writer of the journal entry above, was looking for ideas for an essay, he could find several in this single entry. For example, he might write about the apparently roundabout way he wound up in college. See if you can find in the entry an idea that might be the basis for an interesting paragraph, and write your point in the space below.

_____

Using the paragraph outline pattern on page 11, expand your point into an outline. Use details and examples of your own, if necessary.

2. Take fifteen minutes now to write a journal entry on this day in your life. On a separate sheet of paper, just start writing about anything that you have seen, said, heard, thought, or felt today, and let your thoughts take you where they may.

A CLOSING NOTE

Here is a suggested sequence for using this book if you are working on your own.

1 After completing this introduction, read the remaining five chapters in Part 1 and work through as many of the activities as you need to master the ideas in these chapters. By the end of Part 1, you will have covered all the basic theory needed to write effective papers.

2 Work through some of the chapters in Part 2, which describes a number of traditional patterns for organizing and developing essays. You may want to include "Examples," "Process," "Comparison and Contrast," and "Argumentation." Each chapter opens with a brief introduction to a specific pattern, followed by student essays written in that pattern. Included are a series of questions so that you can evaluate the essays in terms of the basic principles of writing explained in Part 1. Also, read the selections from Part 5 on which some essay assignments are based. Work through some writing topics presented, following the hints about prewriting and revising to help you plan and write an effective paper.

3 Turn to Part 3 as needed for help with types of writing you will do in college: exam essays, summaries, reports, and research papers. These kinds of writing are variations of the essay form you have already learned.

4 In addition, refer to Part 4 as needed to review and practise skills needed to write effective, error-free sentences.

Refer to these guides regularly; they'll help you produce clearly thought-out, well-written essays:

- On the inside front cover, a checklist of the four basic steps in effective writing
- On the inside back cover, a list of commonly used correction symbols

College Writing Skills will help you learn, practise, and apply the thinking and writing skills to communicate effectively. But the starting point must be your determination to do the work needed to become a strong writer. The ability to express yourself clearly and logically can open doors of opportunity for you, both in school and in your career. If you decide that you want such language power, this book will help you reach that goal.

REVIEWING THE LEARNING OUTCOMES FOR CHAPTER 1

To assure yourself that you have understood and met the Learning Outcomes for this chapter, answer the following questions.

- What does the concept of "writing as a learnable skill" mean to you specifically and personally?
- What benefits will you gain from essay writing during your college years? How will essay writing skills help you during your career?
- What are the components of an effective paragraph, and what is the function of each?
- Describe the structure of a college essay: What are its main parts?
- In which stages of the writing process can computers help you, and how?

Narration • Description • Examples • Process • Cause and Effect • Comparison and Contrast
Definition • Division and Classification • Argumentation • Narration • Description • Example
Process • Cause and Effect • Comparison and Contrast • Definition • Division and Classification
Argumentation • Narration • Description • Examples • Process • Cause and Effect • Comparison and
Contrast • Definition • Division and Classification • Argumentation • Narration • Description

CHAPTER 2

The Writing Process

LEARNING OUTCOMES

After reading this chapter and completing its activities and assignments, you will
- Know how to choose and narrow a topic
- Understand the concepts behind the stages of the writing process
- Be ready to use prewriting effectively to generate ideas
- Know the structure and importance of outlining

Chapter 1 introduced you to writing as a skill and a process, and then to paragraph and essay structure. Now this chapter turns to focus on the writing process itself. Prewriting, outlining, and revising are strategies that will help you create better essays every time you use them.

In this chapter, a four-step sequence for creating effective essays is set out. Internalizing this sequence will guide and direct you every time you approach a writing task. Review the four steps in the box below:

Four Steps to Effective Essay Writing
- Discover your point and write a solid thesis statement.
- Develop logical, detailed support for your thesis.
- Organize your thesis and supporting material into an outline.
- Write a first draft, then revise and edit in further drafts.

Each of these steps uses different parts of your mind, different ways of thinking. Learning how the writing process works at each step will help you to focus your mind for that step, and lessen your confusion about writing effectively. The chapters that follow cover each step in detail, allowing you to practise them and absorb the sequence thoroughly.

Before you write your first essay, and before you "test drive" the writing process, you may face a common first-semester challenge: how to choose a topic. Following is advice to help you with this preliminary issue.

CHOOSING AND MANAGING A TOPIC

Occasionally you may be assigned a specifically designed "essay-size topic or subject." When this is the case, you simply proceed to prewrite to discover your ideas—no "topic adjustment time" is needed. More often, though, you will be given a general topic area or asked to choose a topic for your paper. In either of these writing situations, the focusing and managing techniques that follow will be useful.

When you must find a focus within a wide topic-area or choose a topic of your own, follow your interests. The truest (and perhaps oldest) writing rules are, "Write about what interests you," and "Write about what you know." When you write about a subject that you connect with, your energy and interest will flow through to your words, making it easier for you to spend the time needed to produce a solid essay. When you write on a subject you already know about, your confidence allows you to relax and concentrate on shaping and expressing your ideas. Remember, experience is not your only source of "knowing" something; you "know" things from reading, thinking, talking about, or seeing things as well. If you are interested in and confident about your topic, you are ready to explore your thoughts in the prewriting phase of the writing process.

In some courses, you may be asked to write on a topic about which you have no experience or knowledge. Do whatever research is required to gain the information you need. The chapter "Using the Library and the Internet" on pages 319–333 will show you how to use these resources to look up relevant information. Without direct or indirect experience, or information gained through research, you will not be able to provide the specific evidence needed to develop the point you are trying to make. Your writing will be starved for specifics.

THE WRITING PROCESS

A blank page or screen can be an intimidating object for anyone. As you sit wondering how to develop a finished essay in a few days, you may develop a mental block instead. The blank, confused feeling is usually the result of "mental clutter," trying to think of too many things at once.

Beginning to write is difficult, but these two strategies will help you immediately:

1   Review the four steps for essay writing in the box below, and see how these steps mesh with and lead to the four clear-cut goals for an effective essay. Doing so will give you a structure and directed path to follow.

2   Focus on one thing, one writing task at a time. No one can create a solid thesis before gathering a few thoughts together and focusing on making a point about your topic; no one writes a final draft in one sitting. Begin at the beginning—this chapter will show you where and how to begin to write good essays.

Four Steps to Effective Essays	Four Goals for Essay Writing
1. Discover the main point you wish to make. Write your thesis statement.	**1. Unity:** The thesis guides and controls all supporting points and details.
2. Develop solid support for the thesis.	**2. Support:** Each supporting point is explained or illustrated by sufficient and specific details.
3. Organize and connect supporting points and details by outlining and drafting.	**3. Coherence:** Supporting points are in an order appropriate to the thesis; paragraphs, points, and details are clearly connected.
4. Write and revise to develop your thesis most clearly through points and support and to ensure that language or mechanical errors do not interfere with your message.	**4. Effective Sentence Skills:** Sentences, spelling, and punctuation are free of errors; readers will follow your essay's argument without interference.

Don't worry about trying to memorize the four steps or four goals; this book will remind you of them. As you work through this text, these steps and goals will become parts of your "writing equipment."

AN OVERVIEW OF THE WRITING PROCESS

When you start to write an essay, you begin a process that is seldom straightforward. For most writers, getting started is difficult. Accept first of all that discovering what you think will take time and energy. Your mind is not blank; it is full of ideas and connections. Writing—like drawing, speaking, or making music—is a way of finding out what your ideas are and then giving them shape. The writing process has three general stages, and each calls for a different approach. The "discovery" stage or prewriting requires different mental processes than does the "shaping" or outlining and drafting stage, or the "polishing" or revision part of the writing process.

In the following pages, you will learn how to best use your abilities during different stages of essay writing; you will explore tested strategies to help you with blocks and problems—skills you can practise in writing situations for the rest of your life.

STAGE 1: PREWRITING

Prewriting describes the first stages of writing, the creative "discovery" period. During prewriting, you want to free your mind to discover the directions in which your ideas flow most freely. This is not a time to use "ordering" or "correcting" functions in your mind—those work against the relaxed, open mental state you need for exploratory prewriting.

Writers have, by trial and error, found techniques (sometimes referred to as "brainstorming") to help open up their minds and imaginations. The following pages describe four techniques that will help you think about and develop a topic and get words on paper: (1) freewriting, (2) questioning, (3) making a list, and (4) diagramming. These prewriting techniques are an essential first stage of the writing process.

TECHNIQUE 1: FREEWRITING

Freewriting means jotting down in rough sentences or phrases everything that comes to mind about a possible topic. See if you can write non-stop for ten minutes or more. Do not worry about spelling or punctuating correctly, about erasing mistakes, about organizing material, or about finding exact words. Instead, explore an idea by putting down whatever pops into your head. If you get stuck for words, repeat yourself until more words come. There is no need to feel inhibited, since mistakes *do not count*, and you do not have to hand in your paper.

Freewriting will limber up your writing muscles and make you familiar with the act of writing. It is a way to break through mental blocks about writing. Do not worry about mistakes; **focus on discovering what you want to say** about a subject. Your initial ideas and impressions will often become clearer after you have gotten them down on paper, and they may lead to other impressions and ideas. As you get material down on the page or up on the screen, it will make what you have left to do a bit easier. Sometimes as you write down one idea, another possible focus emerges. That's fine: if your freewriting tells you that you have unexpected thoughts, go with them. Revise or review those new ideas later to take advantage of your discoveries. Through continued practice in freewriting, you will develop the habit of thinking as you write. And you will learn a technique that is a helpful way to get started on almost any paper.

Freewriting: A Student Model

As you freewrite, your mind runs along all sorts of paths branching off the general topic you are assigned. You fill up your page or screen, racing past ideas as you get them down. From this general freewriting, two possibilities usually emerge: your focus simply appears as the thing you are writing most about, or, like Tina Kallas, you consciously decide on one idea that "sparks a connection" for you. Many writers use freewriting in two stages: to generate ideas about some broad topic, and then to explore a single focus, their specific topic.

Freewriting to Generate Ideas

Tina Kallas' essay "The Hazards of Movie-Going" on pages 13–14 was in response to an assignment with the general topic of some annoyance in everyday life. Tina began by doing some general freewriting and thinking about things that annoyed her. Here is her freewriting:

> There are lots of things I get annoyed by. One of them that comes to mind is politicians, in fact I am so annoyed by them that I don't want to say anything about them the last thing I want is to write about them. Another thing that bothers me are people who keep complaining about everything. If you're having trouble, do something about it just don't keep complaining and just talking.

I am really annoyed by traffic. There are too many cars in our block and its not surprising. Everyone has a car, the parents have cars and the parents are just too indulgent and the kids have cars, and they're all coming and going all the time and often driving too fast. Speeding up and down the street. We need a speed limit sign but here I am back with politics again. I am really bothered when I have to drive to the movies all the congestion along the way plus there are just so many cars there at the mall. No space even though the parking lot is huge it just fills up with cars. Movies are a bother anyway because the people can be annoying who are sitting there in the theatre with you, talking and dropping popcorn cups and acting like they're at home when they're not.

Focused Freewriting

At this point, Tina read over her notes, and later commented, "I realized that I had several potential topics. I said to myself, 'What point can I make that I can cover in an essay? What do I have the most information about?' I decided that maybe I could narrow my topic down to the annoyances involved in going to the movies; I figured I would have more details for that topic." Tina then did a more focused freewriting to accumulate details for a paper on problems with movie-going:

I really find it annoying to go see movies anymore. Even though I love films. Traffic to Cinema Six is awful. I hate looking for a parking place, the lot isn't big enough for the theatres and other stores. You just keep driving to find a parking space and hoping someone will pull out and no one else will pull in ahead of you. Then you don't want there to be a long line and to wind up in one of the first rows with this huge screen right in front of you. Then I'm in the theatre with the smell of popcorn all around. Sitting there smelling it trying to ignore it and just wanting to pour a whole bucket of popcorn with melted butter down my throat. I can't stop thinking about the chocolate bars either. I love the stuff but I don't need it. The people who are there sometimes drive me nuts. Talking and laughing, kids running around, packs of high school kids hollering, who can listen to the movie? And I might run into my old boyfriend—the last thing I need. Also sitting thru all the previews and commercials. If I arrive late enough to miss that junk the movie may be sold out.

Tips and Comments

Tina's freewriting drafts contain errors in spelling, grammar, and punctuation. They are shown uncorrected to make three points:

- Freewriting is *for you;* you are the audience and no one is checking "over your shoulder."
- The whole point of freewriting is to go with the flow of your ideas; don't stop as you discover what's in your mind—get ideas down just as they come to you.
- Correcting problems is a mental process different from exploring; "shifting mental gears" can slow or stop the discovery stage of the writing process.

If worrying about your sentences is slowing you down, write your ideas in point form—this is *your* first step, the raw material you will return to and shape later.

Take the same approach as Tina did when freewriting: explore your topic without worrying at all about being "correct." Figuring out what you want to say and getting material down on the page to find your focus should have all of your attention at this early stage of writing.

Activity

To get a sense of freewriting, take a sheet of paper and do some general freewriting about the everyday annoyances in your life. See how much material you can accumulate in ten minutes. And remember not to worry about "mistakes"; you're just thinking on paper.

When you are finished, see if you can find an idea or two that would make a good focus for an essay.

TECHNIQUE 2: QUESTIONING

Questioning as a technique works in a way different from freewriting. If you are an "order oriented" methodical person who enjoys linear thinking, questioning may offer a comfortable framework to use. Freewriting bypasses the ordering parts of your mind; questioning requires you to confront yourself with a set of specific demands. Questioning's structured approach gives a sense of direction to prewriting. Ask yourself as many questions as you can think of about your subject; your answers will be a series of different "takes" or focuses on it. Such questions include *Why? When? Where? Who?* and *How?*

To begin, divide your page or screen into two columns: "Questions" and "Answers," as you see below. Leave enough space in the "Answers" column so that you can return to a particular response if more details come to you later. Next, ask yourself this preliminary question: "What's my subject?" Then, write your answer as a reference point for the rest of your question-and-answer series. If one question stops you, just go on to another.

Here are some questions that Tina Kallas might have asked while developing her paper:

Questioning: A Student Model

Questions	*Answers*
Why don't I like to go to the theatre?	Just too many problems involved.
When is going to the movies a problem?	Could be any time—when movie is popular the theatre is too crowded, when traffic is bad the trip is a drag.
Where are problems with movie-going?	On the highway, in the parking lot, at the concession stand, in the theatre itself.

Questions	*Answers*
Who creates the problems?	I do by wanting to eat too much. The patrons do by creating disturbances. The theatre owners do by not having enough parking space and showing too many commercials.
How can I deal with the problem?	I can stay home and watch movies on video or cable TV.

Tips and Comments

Asking questions can be an effective way of getting you to think about a topic from a number of different angles. The questions can really help you generate details about a topic.

Questioning also works as a "second stage" for your prewriting. If you have done some general freewriting, but still are not sure of a focus for your paper, then try questioning, using your freewriting as a reference.

- Questioning may reveal your focus quickly when one answer in particular is more detailed than others.
- Questioning can yield answers that may be rich sources of *connected* details—making some of your organizing and outlining a little easier.
- Questioning can show you directions for paragraphs within an essay; if you have many answers to "*Why?*" your mind may want to explore the causes of a subject.

Activity

To get a sense of the questioning process, use a sheet of paper to ask yourself a series of questions about a good or bad experience that you have had recently. See how many details you can accumulate in ten minutes. And remember not to be concerned about "mistakes," because you are just thinking on paper.

TECHNIQUE 3: LIST MAKING

List making is simply making a list of ideas and details that relate to your subject. Pile these items up, one after another, without trying to sort out major details from minor ones or trying to put the details in any special order. Your goal is just to list everything about your subject that occurs to you. You may use list making as a first or second stage of prewriting.

After Tina did her freewriting about her movie-going topic, she made up the following list of details to help her see her ideas more clearly.

List Making: A Student Model

Traffic is bad between my house and theatre
Noisy patrons

Don't want to run into Jeremy
Hard to be on a diet
Kids running in aisles
I'm crowded into seats between strangers who push me off arm rests
Not enough parking
Parking lot needs to be expanded
Too many previews
Can't pause or fast forward like you can with a VCR or DVD player
Long lines
High ticket prices
Too many temptations at snack stand
Commercials for food on the screen
I can make healthy snacks for myself at home
Tubs of popcorn with butter
Huge chocolate bars
Movie may be sold out
People who've seen movie before talk along with actors and give away plot twists
People coughing and sneezing
Icky stuff on floor
High school students yelling and showing off

Tips and Comments

One detail led to another as Tina expanded her list. Slowly more details emerged, some of which she could use in developing her paper. By the time she finished her list, she was ready to plan an outline and then to write her first draft.

List making works as a first or second stage of prewriting. As a first stage, listing is a quick, easy method you are already familiar with from making everyday "to do" lists.

- List making frees you of concerns about your sentences in prewriting; simply list your ideas as phrases.
- List making works if you like to make notes to yourself as you work; just include something like "good first idea" in parentheses after a list item.

List making is an effective "second stage" of prewriting. Like Tina, you may find it useful to make a list by referring to your page of freewriting.

- List making after freewriting can stimulate your mind so you think of more points and details.
- Listing your ideas after freewriting, questioning, or diagramming displays your thoughts in simple uncluttered form, so you can proceed to evaluate them.
- Listing is an excellent sorting method; number your points and ideas in your preferred order before outlining, or sort out points and their related supporting details from your list.
- Listing is useful for writers who like to connect ideas graphically with lines and circles.

Activity

To get a sense of list making, list a series of realistic goals, major or minor, that you would like to accomplish between today and one year from today. Your goals can involve personal, academic, and career matters.

TECHNIQUE 4: CLUSTERING

Clustering, also known as *diagramming* or *mapping*, is another strategy for generating ideas. People who enjoy thinking in a visual or graphic way can use lines, boxes, arrows, and circles to show relationships among the ideas and details that occur to them.

State your subject in a few words in the centre of a blank sheet of paper. Then, as ideas and details come to you, put them in boxes or circles around the subject. As you find connections or relationships between ideas and groups of ideas, draw lines to connect them to each other and to the subject. Put minor ideas or details in smaller boxes or circles, and use connecting lines to show how they relate.

There is no right or wrong way of clustering; it is a way to think on paper about how various ideas and details relate to one another. Below is an example of clustering that Tina might have done to develop her ideas:

Clustering: A Student Model

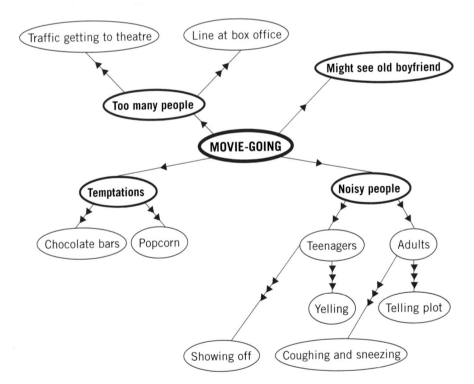

Note: This diagram shows how Tina could use clustering *after* freewriting, as a second stage of prewriting.

Her main idea groupings now show clearly as **supporting points in bold**, separate branches from the topic. The relationships of **details** to supporting points are clearly visible.

Clustering reveals the levels of structure for Tina's essay: from topic to supporting points to details for each supporting point.

Which supporting point will Tina probably not use, and why?

Where has Tina discovered a third level of details for a supporting point, and how has she indicated this level graphically?

Tips and Comments

Clustering excels as a prewriting tool for the visually minded writer, for both first and second stages of prewriting. As a primary method of generating ideas, clustering frees you from the linearity of the page or screen.

- Clustering prevents "sentence block"; you note points and details in words and phrases.
- Clustering instantly shows you connections between ideas as you use lines and arrows to link one thing with another.

Clustering's only downfall occurs when your page becomes too messy to follow. Avoid this by starting a clean second page where you distinguish visually between possible supporting points and details. Refer back to the diagram of Tina's clustering for techniques to help you clarify levels of support and connections.

As a second stage of prewriting, clustering demonstrates relationships between ideas and details. Clustering can also "preview" the content of your body paragraphs and their focus.

- Cluster diagrams clearly reveal a paragraph's focus and possible levels of details within, as Tina's "noisy people" set of clusters shows.
- Clustering as a second stage, if you show levels of links between points and details, prepares you for outlining and drafting.

Activity

Use clustering to organize the list of year-ahead goals that you created for the previous activity (page 32).

A FINAL NOTE ON THE FIRST STAGE OF THE WRITING PROCESS

Prewriting is the "no rules" first stage of the writing process. Following rules or worrying about spelling or sentence structure actually works against the "idea generating" way of using your mind. No matter which technique you prefer, there is only one guideline: go with what works for you. Any technique that gets your ideas flowing is good.

- Sometimes you may use one technique, then another, to discover your ideas and a focused topic: i.e., freewriting and listing, or clustering and questioning, or any combination that works for you.

- Occasionally you may use several techniques at once; for example, you may ask yourself questions while writing a list, or you may diagram and sort through a list as you write one.

When one technique is not working, simply stop and try another. The writing process is not a straightforward path, and each journey may begin differently.

STAGE 2: WRITING AN OUTLINE AND DRAFTING

Stage 2 of the writing process involves outlining *and* drafting. Generally you will create an outline from your prewriting, followed by a first draft: this is the sequence this book demonstrates. Outlining, and sometimes re-outlining, is needed to untangle and clarify your prewriting. True, some writers write a trial draft *before* outlining. If you have worked successfully this way, continue to do so; this is actually an extra stage of prewriting. The sorting and decision-making step of outlining is still needed. Your pre-outlining trial draft guides your outline and helps you find out where to make changes or additions.

Preparing a correctly structured detailed outline is an essential step in writing. The quality of your outline can determine the success or failure of your essay. Essays are highly organized writing patterns. They communicate effectively only when their content is logically arranged and sufficiently detailed to make a point and support it thoroughly. Therefore, an effective essay does not result from patching together random pieces of prewriting into a final draft. Essays written without good outlines are as ramshackle as buildings constructed without blueprints.

- Creating a formal outline requires three thought processes: sorting, ordering, and evaluating. You will think about the point you wish to make about your topic as you compose your thesis. You will consider and evaluate the supporting evidence (subtopics or supporting points and details) for that thesis. The quality and the arrangement of your raw material are what add up to a solid essay.
- Sorting, ordering, and evaluating are organizational skills that develop your ability to think clearly and logically. Outlining lets you work on the bare bones of your essay without the distracting clutter of phrases and sentences—you will see both your ideas and the connections between them.
- A good outline allows you to relax and write your first draft without worrying about what you will say next—you have your "blueprint" at hand.

You have seen both a paragraph outline diagram (page 11) and a diagram of an essay's general shape (pages 17–18) in Chapter 1. The full essay outline pattern simply expands the paragraph model to accommodate the thesis statement and support structure for each body paragraph in the essay. On page 39 following and on the inside back cover, you will see a complete essay outline diagram.

THE TRANSITION FROM PREWRITING TO OUTLINING

Before you become intimidated by the prospect of outlining, know that with your prewriting done, you already have most of your content. There are some informal "sorting out" techniques you can use to bridge the gap between rough notes, lists, or clusters and a finished outline. Tina Kallas, the student writing about the annoyances of movie-going, provides an example of how to make the transition from prewriting to outline.

- As Tina was working on her list of details, she suddenly realized what the plan of her essay could be. She could organize many of her details into one of three supporting groups: (1) annoyances in going out, (2) too many tempting snacks, and (3) other people. She then went back to the list, crossed out items that she now saw did not fit, and numbered the items according to the group in which they did fit:

1 Traffic is bad between my house and theatre
3 Noisy patrons
~~Don't want to run into Jeremy~~
2 Hard to be on a diet
3 Kids running in aisles
3 I'm crowded into seats between strangers who push me off arm rests
1 Not enough parking
1 Parking lot needs to be expanded
1 Too many previews
~~Can't pause or fast forward like you can with a VCR~~
1 Long lines
1 High ticket prices
2 Too many temptations at snack stand
~~Commercials for food on the screen~~
2 Can prepare healthy snacks for myself at home
2 Tubs of popcorn with butter
2 Huge chocolate bars
~~Candy has always been my downfall~~
1 Movie may be sold out
3 People who've seen movie before talk along with actors and give away plot twists
3 People coughing and sneezing
1 Icky stuff on floor
3 Teenagers yelling and showing off

- Under the list, Tina was now able to write a "trial thesis" and three supporting points or "four-point outline":

Going to the movies offers some real problems.

1. Inconvenience of going out
2. Tempting snacks
3. Other movie-goers

- Tina was now ready to work on a full outline for her essay. Once the outline was complete, she had a clear framework to follow, and writing the first draft of her essay seemed less intimidating.
- Tina used her list to find and group her supporting points, to make a transition from prewriting to outlining. You may not proceed in exactly the order or way that Tina did. You may decide on your supporting points before you try to write a trial thesis statement. Or you may find that you have lots of examples for one of your details, so that it's actually a supporting point. There are some steps you can follow, though, that will help you develop your prewriting into an outline.

1. Begin by writing a statement of your point, a "trial thesis statement." Write your focused version of your topic and your viewpoint on it. Don't worry about writing a polished thesis statement—the next chapter will give you extensive practice in creating one. You can always go back and change it later.

2. Turn your trial thesis statement into a question. Tina's trial statement was, "Going to the movies offers some real problems." Her "thesis question" might be, "Why is going to the movies such a problem?" *or* "What are the problems with going to the movies?"

3. Now, ask yourself your "thesis question" as you look over your freewriting for ideas that answer the question.

Tina could have answered a *"Why"* thesis question like this:

"Why is going to the movies such a problem?"

- Because it's inconvenient to go out
- Because theatres are full of tempting snacks
- Because of the way other movie-goers act

Asking a thesis question helps you discover the best supporting reasons for the point stated in your thesis. The best reasons are usually those for which your mind supplies lots of examples or details, or those you feel most strongly about. Don't worry if one of those reasons started out as a detail. If your thesis question changes while you are looking for answers, try that new version of the question.

4. Choose the three best answers to your thesis question.

5. Begin again with a new screen or fresh piece of paper. Write your trial thesis at the top. List your three answers below it in point form.

6. Think about an appropriate order for your answers/reasons—these are your supporting ideas or points. Is one idea or piece of evidence more important than another? Is the order in which your points occurred in time important? After deciding on an order, list the points again, leaving space after each to fill in details. Revise your trial thesis if necessary.

7. Now you have the basics of your outline; work on supplying, in point form, the examples and details that explain your reasons most clearly. Chapters 3 and 4 will give you extensive practice in discovering and selecting supporting points and adequate details.

In the box below, you will find an introduction to the four parts of a formal essay outline and instructions for filling in each part. Refer back to this box as you work through the following chapters.

- ***Thesis Statement:*** Write a "trial thesis statement." Note your overall viewpoint on your topic and your supporting points.
- ***Supporting Points:*** Number each supporting point with an upper-case Roman numeral (I, II, III); then write the point as a "trial topic sentence." Leave space after your topic sentence to list in point form your supporting details and examples.
- ***Supporting Details and Examples:*** List these in numbered point form under the topic sentence of each supporting point.
- ***Conclusion Statement:*** Write a "trial conclusion," summing up your supporting points. Try to add a final thought that follows as a result of your points, or broadens the meaning of your main point.

A blank essay outline form is shown on page 39. Tina Kallas created her own word-processed version of it, and after working out her details and a fuller thesis statement, she wrote the following formal outline. To show you how Tina Kallas progressed from her rough "four-point outline" to a nearly complete formal outline, her work is shown below. When you have completed the exercises and assignments in the chapters that follow, you will have practised the skills needed to create such outlines.

Opening Paragraph: Thesis Statement

Going to the movies is more of a hassle than a pleasure for me.
   1. *Annoyances of parking and driving*
   2. *Constant temptations to overeat*
   3. *Behaviour of other movie-goers*

Body Paragraph: Supporting Point #1

Going to the theatre is full of inconveniences.
   Supporting Details & Examples
   1. *Time wasted driving to theatre—15 minutes*
   2. *Time wasted at theatre—parking at multiplexes & malls, line-ups for tickets*
   3. *Crowds in theatres—expensive tickets for bad seating*

Body Paragraph: Supporting Point #2

Constant temptation to overeat and snack
   Supporting Details & Examples
   1. *Don't need to snack—healthy food at home*
   2. *Theatres are big convenience stores—smells of popcorn, huge chocolate bars*
   3. *Friends buy candy—I feel deprived, so I buy it too*

Body Paragraph: Supporting Point #3

Other movie-goers distract and annoy me.
   Supporting Details & Examples
   1. *Noisy little kids, high school kids—stupid behaviour*
   2. *Adults give away the plot*
   3. *Noises of paper & wrappings, people pushing past me*

Concluding Paragraph: Conclusion

There are better ways to see a movie—cable & DVDs.
   1. *No inconveniences*
   2. *No temptations*
   3. *No distractions*

Comment

After all her prewriting, and after working out her formal outline, Tina knew that she had a promising paper with a clear point and solid support. She saw that she had organized the material into a traditional essay consisting of an introduction, several supporting paragraphs, and a conclusion. Chances are that if you do enough prewriting and thinking on paper, you will eventually discover what the point and support of your essay might be. Outlining your points and support will alert you to possible weak spots, repetitions, or unrelated ideas in your support, and will allow you to relax and focus on writing a solid paper.

Activity

Create an essay outline that could serve as a guide if you were to write an essay on your year-ahead goals.

ESSAY OUTLINE DIAGRAM

Photocopy this outline pattern, or create your own on disk by setting it up and saving it as a blank document named "Essay Outline." Each time you are ready to outline, just paste your outline document onto a new document page.

Opening Paragraph: Thesis Statement
   Supporting Points
    1.
    2.
    3.

Body Paragraph: Supporting Point #1
   Supporting Details & Examples
    1.
    2.
    3.

Body Paragraph: Supporting Point #2
   Supporting Details & Examples
    1.
    2.
    3.

Body Paragraph: Supporting Point #3
   Supporting Details & Examples
    1.
    2.
    3.

Concluding Paragraph: Conclusion

DEVELOPING A FIRST DRAFT FROM AN OUTLINE

Once you have worked through your outline, writing a first draft will not be such a demanding task. Do not be "shackled" to your outline as you proceed, though.

- If additional thoughts and details come to you, put them in your draft and note them on your outline.
- If one of your points or details no longer works for you, and you feel blocked as you try to replace that material, just leave a blank space and add a comment like, "Do later" and then keep going to finish your draft.
- Don't worry about spelling, punctuation, or grammar—you will correct these things in a later draft as you revise.
- Stay fixed on the goal of stating your thesis clearly and pursuing its supporting points with plenty of specific details.

Your first draft is just that: a first try at turning your outline into sentences and paragraphs. Focus on creating the general shape of your essay, not on fine details. Revising, the next stage of the writing process, is the time for polishing your ideas, words, and sentences.

Writing a First Draft: A Student Model

Here is Tina's first draft:

> Even though I love movies, my friends have stopped asking me to go. There are just too many problems involved in going to the movies. **1**
>
> There are no small theatres anymore, I have to drive fifteen minutes to a big multiplex. Because of a supermarket and restaurants, the parking lot is filled. I have to keep driving around to find a space. Then I have to stand in a long line. Hoping that they do not run out of tickets. Finally, I have to pay too much money for a ticket. Putting out that much money, I should not have to deal with a floor that ~~is sticky~~ seems coated with rubber cement. By the end of a movie, my shoes are often sealed to a mix of spilled pop, bubble gum, and other stuff. **2**
>
> The theatre offers temptations in the form of snacks I really don't need. Like most of us I have to worry about weight gain. At home I do pretty well by simply watching what I keep in the house and not buying stuff that is bad for me. I can make do with healthy snacks because there is nothing in the house. Going to the theatre is like spending my evening in a ~~market~~ convenience store that's been equiped with a movie screen and there are seats which are comfortable. I try to convince myself to have just a diet pop, the smell of fresh popcorn soon overcomes me. My friends are as bad as I am. Choclate bars seem to jump into your hands, I am eating enormous mouthfuls of maple buds. By the time I leave the theatre I feel out of sorts with myself. **3**
>
> Some of the other movie-goers are the worst problem. There are highschoolers who try to impress their friends in one way or another. Little kids race up and down the aisles, giggling and laughing. Adults act as if they're watching the movie at home. They talk loudly about the ages of the stars and give away the **4**

plot. Other people are dropping popcorn tubs or cups of ~~pop~~ crushed ice and pop on the floor. Also coughing a lot and doing other stuff. —*be spec*

 I decided one night that I was not going to be a movie-goer anymore. I joined a local video store, and I'll watch movies comfortable in my own living room.

5

Comment

After Tina finished the first draft, she was able to put it aside until the next day. You will benefit as well if you can allow some time between finishing a draft and starting to revise.

 Review Tina's first draft as you work on the activity that follows.

Activity

1. **The Introductory Paragraph** Tina's first paragraph is very brief. She knows she can develop her opening further in a later draft. Which sentence contains her thesis statement? What is the purpose of her other sentence?

2. **The Body Paragraphs**
   a. One of Tina's paragraphs lacks a topic sentence. Knowing she can return to fix this problem later, she circles the opening of one of her paragraphs. Which paragraph's opening sentence is not a topic sentence? Why?

   b. Later in her essay, Tina can't think of details to add to clarify an example, so she writes a note to herself to "be specific." Which subtopic in which paragraph needs more attention, and why?

   c. At several points in the draft, Tina revises her phrases and images. Where does she do so, and why?

3. **The Concluding Paragraph** Tina's conclusion is very brief because she will expand it later. What could she add to make it more complete?

STAGE 3: REVISION

Revising is as essential to the writing process as prewriting, outlining, and doing the first draft. *Revising* means literally "re-seeing." It means that you rewrite a paper, building upon what has already been done, in order to make it stronger. One writer has said about revision, "It's like cleaning house—getting rid of all the junk and putting things in the right order." It is not just a "straightening up"; instead, you must be ready to roll up your sleeves and do whatever is needed to create an effective paper. Too many students think that a first draft *is* the paper. They start to become writers when they realize that revising a rough draft three or four times is often at the heart of writing.

GENERAL REVISING TIPS

- First, set your first draft aside for a while. Then come back to it with a fresh, more objective point of view.
- Second, work from typed or printed text. You'll be able to see the paper more impartially than if you were just looking at your own familiar handwriting.

- Next, read your draft aloud. Hearing how your writing sounds will help you spot problems with meaning as well as with style.
- Finally, as you do all these things, add in your thoughts and changes above the lines or in the margins of your paper. Your written comments can serve as a guide when you work on the next draft.

Revising is not a "one-shot" activity. Here its basic goals and activities are introduced; then Chapter 6 will give you instruction and practice in revision. When you revise or "re-see" your essay draft, you are not examining one aspect of your writing, but three: your content, your sentences, and finally your "mechanics" —grammar, punctuation, and spelling. Never try to revise all three levels of your writing at once. Instead, leave yourself enough time to give your ideas and language the attention they deserve.

There are three stages to the revising process:

- Revising content
- Revising sentences
- Editing

REVISING CONTENT

Recall the box on page 26 of this chapter, and note how the goals for effective essay writing guide you during revision. To revise the content of your essay, ask the following questions:

1 Is my paper **unified**?
- Do I have a thesis that is clearly stated or implied in the introductory paragraph of my essay?
- Do all of my supporting paragraphs truly support and back up my thesis?

2 Is my paper **supported**?
- Are there three separate supporting points for the thesis?
- Do I have *specific* evidence for each of the three supporting points?
- Is there *plenty* of specific evidence for each supporting point?

3 Is my paper **organized**?
- Do I have an interesting introduction, a solid conclusion, and an accurate title?
- Do I have a clear method of organizing my paper?
- Do I use transitions and other connecting words?

The next two chapters (Chapters 3 and 4) will give you practice in achieving **unity**, **support**, and **organization** in your writing.

REVISING SENTENCES

The fourth goal for essay working is effective sentence structure, and Chapter 5 in this part of the book will give you practice in revising sentences. Refer to the pages listed as you ask yourself the following questions:

1 Do I use parallelism to balance my words and ideas? (pages 98–99)

2 Do I have a consistent point of view? (pages 99–101)

3 Do I use specific words? (pages 101–104)

4 Do I use active verbs? (pages 104–105)

5 Do I use words effectively by avoiding slang, clichés, pretentious language, and wordiness? (pages 105–107)

6 Do I vary my sentences? (pages 107–112)

EDITING

After you have revised your paper for content and style, you are ready to edit for errors in grammar, punctuation, and spelling. Students often find it hard to edit a paper carefully. They have put so much work into their writing, or so little, that it is almost painful for them to look at the paper one more time. You may simply have to *will* yourself to perform this important closing step in the writing process. Remember that eliminating sentence-skills mistakes will improve an average paper and help ensure a strong mark on a good paper. Further, as you get into the habit of checking your papers, you will also get into the habit of using the sentence skills consistently. They are an integral part of clear and effective writing.

Chapter 5 in this part of the book and the handbook of skills in Part 4 (pages 355–488) will serve as guides while you are editing your paper for mistakes in **sentence skills**.

AN ILLUSTRATION OF THE REVISING AND EDITING PROCESSES

Revising with a Second Draft: A Student Model

Since Tina Kallas was using a word-processing program on a computer, she was able to print out a double-spaced version of her movie essay, leaving her plenty of room for revisions. Here is one of her revised paragraphs:

Secondly,   *tempting snacks*
The theatre offers ~~temptations in the form of snacks~~ I really don't need.
             battle an expanding waistline
Like most of us I have to ~~worry about weight gain.~~ At home I do pretty well by

simply ~~watching what I keep in the house and~~ not buying stuff that is bad for
             like celery and carrots sticks   *no ice cream*   *freezer*
me. I can make do with ~~healthy~~ snacks because there is ~~nothing~~ in the ~~house.~~
       however
Going to the theatre is like spending my evening in a convenience store that's
               comfortable   *As*
been equiped with a movie screen and ~~there are~~ seats ~~which are comfortable.~~ I
                dripping with butter
try to convince myself to have just a diet pop, the smell of fresh popcorn soon

overcomes me. ~~My friends are as bad as I am.~~ Choclate bars seem to jump
    my   *risk pulling out my fillings as I chew*   *My friends are buying*
into ~~your~~ hands. I ~~am eating~~ enormous mouthfuls of maple buds. By the time
snacks, and I feel left out.   *disgusted*
I leave the theatre I feel ~~out of sorts~~ with myself.

Comment

Tina made her changes in longhand as she worked on the second draft. As you will see when you complete the activity below, her revision serves to make the paragraph more **unified**, **supported**, and **organized**.

Activity

Fill in the missing words.

- To achieve better organization, Tina adds the transitional word *Secondly*, making clear that tempting snacks is the second of her supporting ideas.

- Tina also adds in the transition "_____" to clearly contrast the difference between being at home and being in the theatre.

- In the interest of _____, *(unity/support/organization)*, Tina crosses out the sentence _____. She realizes this sentence is not a relevant detail but really another topic idea.

- To add more _____ *(unity/support/organization)*, Tina changes *healthy snacks* to _____; she changes *nothing in the house* to _____; she adds _____ after *popcorn;* and she changes *am eating* to _____.

- In the interest of eliminating wordiness, she removes the words _____ from the third sentence.

- In the interest of parallelism, Tina changes *and there are seats which are comfortable* to _____.

- To create a consistent point of view, Tina changes *jump into your hands* to _____.

- For greater sentence variety, Tina combines two short sentences, beginning the first sentence with the subordinating word _____.

- Finally, Tina replaces the vague *out of sorts* with the more precise _____.

Editing: A Student Model

After typing into her document all the changes in her second draft, Tina printed out another clean draft of the paper. The paragraph on tempting snacks required almost no more revision, so Tina turned her attention mostly to editing changes, illustrated below with her work on the second supporting paragraph:

Secondly, the theatre offers tempting snacks I really don't need. Like most

of us, I have to battle an expanding waistline. At home I do pretty well by

simply not buying stuff that is bad for me. I can make do with snacks

like celery and carrot sticks because there is no ice cream in the freezer.

Going to the theatre, however, is like spending my evening in a convenience

store that's been ~~equiped~~ *equipped* with a movie screen and comfortable seats. As I try

to convince myself to have just a diet pop, the smell of fresh popcorn dripping

with butter soon overcomes me. ~~Choclate~~ *Chocolate* bars *the size of small automobiles* seem to jump into my hands. I

risk pulling out my fillings as I chew enormous mouthfuls of ~~maple~~ ~~buds~~. *M B* My

friends ~~are buying snacks~~ *buy nachos and licorice strings*, and I feel left out. *so I buy snacks too* By the time I leave the theatre,

I feel disgusted with myself.

Comment

Once again, Tina makes her changes in longhand right on the printed sheet of her paper. To note these changes, complete the activity below.

Activity

Fill in the missing words.

- As part of her editing, Tina checked and corrected the _____ of two words, *equipped* and *chocolate*.

- She added _____ to set off two introductory phrases (*Like most of us* in the second sentence and *By the time I leave the theatre* in the final sentence) and to set off the interrupting word *however* in the fourth sentence.

- She realized that *Maple Buds* is a brand name and added _____ to make it *Maple Buds*.

- And since revision can occur at any stage of the writing process, including editing, she made one of her details more vivid by adding the descriptive words _____ .

ACTIVITIES

You now have a good overview of the writing process, from prewriting to first draft to revising to editing. The remaining chapters in Part 1 will deepen your sense of the four goals of effective writing: unity, support, organization or coherence, and sentence skills.

To reinforce much of the information about the writing process that you have learned in this chapter, you can now work through the following activities:

1   OUTLINING SKILLS

As already mentioned (see pages 34–41), outlining is central to writing a good paper. An outline lets you see, and work on, the bare bones of a paper, without the distraction of a clutter of words and sentences. It develops your ability to think clearly and logically. Outlining provides a quick check on whether your paper will be **unified**. It also suggests right at the start whether your paper will be adequately **supported**. And it shows you how to plan a paper that is **well organized**.

The following two exercises will help you develop the outlining skills so important to planning and writing a solid essay.

Activity 1

One key to effective outlining is the ability to distinguish between **major ideas and details** that fit under those ideas. In each of the three lists below, major and supporting items are mixed together. Put the items into logical order by filling in the outline that follows each list.

1. **Thesis:** My high school had three problem areas.

   Involved with drugs

   Leaky ceilings

   Students

   Unwilling to help after class

   Formed cliques

   Teachers

   Buildings

   Ill-equipped gym

   Much too strict

   a. _____

      (1) _____

      (2) _____

   b. _____

      (1) _____

      (2) _____

   c. _____

      (1) _____

      (2) _____

2. **Thesis:** Working as a dishwasher in a restaurant was my worst job.

   Ten-hour shifts

   Heat in kitchen

   a. _____

      (1) _____

Working conditions	(2) _____
Minimum wage	b. _____
Hours changed every week	(1) _____
No bonus for overtime	(2) _____
Hours	c. _____
Pay	(1) _____
Noisy work area	(2) _____

3. **Thesis:** Joining an aerobics class has many benefits.

Make new friends	a. _____
Reduce mental stress	(1) _____
Social benefits	(2) _____
Strengthens heart	b. _____
Improves self-image	(1) _____
Mental benefits	(2) _____
Tones muscles	c. _____
Meet interesting instructors	(1) _____
Physical benefits	(2) _____

Activity 2

Read the essay on the following pages, and outline it in the spaces provided. Write out the thesis, or central point, and topic sentences, and summarize in a few words the supporting material that fits under each topic sentence. One item is summarized for you as an example.

Losing Touch

Steve, a typical Canadian, stays home on workdays. He plugs into a computer terminal in order to hook up with the office, and he sends and receives work during the day by e-mail and a fax modem. Evenings, he puts on his stereo headphones, slides a movie into his DVD player, or logs back onto the computer to spend time online. On many days, Steve doesn't talk to any other human beings, and he doesn't see any people except those on television. Steve is imaginary, but his lifestyle is very common. More and more, the inventions of modern technology seem to be cutting us off from contact with our fellow human beings.

Thesis: _____

_____

The world of business is one area in which technology is isolating us. Many people now work alone at home. With access to a large central computer, employees such as secretaries, insurance agents, and accountants do their jobs at terminals in their own homes. They no longer actually have to see the people they're dealing with. In addition, employees are often paid in an impersonal way. Workers' salaries are automatically credited to their bank accounts, eliminating the need for paycheques. Fewer people stand in line with their co-workers to receive their pay or cash their cheques. Finally, personal banking is becoming a detached process. Customers interact with machines or pay bills online rather than contacting people to deposit or withdraw money from their accounts. Even some bank loans are approved or rejected, not in an interview with a loan officer, but through a display on a bank's website.

First topic sentence: _____

_____

Support: 1. _Many people now work alone at home._ _____

2. _____

3. _____

a. _____

b. _____

Another area that technology is changing is entertainment. Music, for instance, was once a group experience. People listened to music in concert halls or at small social gatherings. For many people now, however, music is a solitary experience. Walking along the street or sitting in their living rooms, they wear headphones to build a wall of music around them. Movie entertainment is changing, too. Movies used to be social events. Now, fewer people are going out to see a movie. Many more are choosing to wait for a film to appear on cable television. Instead of being involved with the laughter, applause, or hisses of the audience, viewers watch movies in the isolation of their own living rooms.

Second topic sentence: _____

_____

Support: 1. _____

2. _____

Education is a third important area in which technology is separating us from others. From elementary schools to colleges, students spend more and more time sitting by themselves in front of computers. The computers give them feedback, while teachers spend more time tending the computers and less time interacting with their classes. A similar problem occurs in homes. As more families buy computers, increasing numbers of students practise their math and reading skills with software programs instead of with their friends, brothers and sisters, and parents. Last, alienation is occurring as a result of other high-tech inventions: CDs and DVDs. People are buying CDs and DVDs on subjects such as cooking, real estate investment, speaking, and speed-reading. They then practise their skills at home rather than taking group classes in which rich human interaction can occur.

Third topic sentence: _____

_____

Support: 1. _____

2. _____

3. _____

Technology, then, seems to be driving human beings apart. Soon, we may no longer need to communicate with other human beings in order to do our work, entertain ourselves, or pursue an education. Technology will be the co-worker and companion of the future.

2 REVISING

Activity

Following is the second supporting paragraph from an essay called "Problems of Combining School and Work." The paragraph is shown in four different stages of development: (1) the first full draft; (2) the revised second draft; (3) the edited next-to-final draft; and (4) the final draft. The four stages appear in scrambled order. Write the number 1 in the answer blank for the first full draft and number the remaining stages in sequence.

_____   I have also given up some personal pleasures in my life. On sundays for example I used to play street hockey or football, now I use the entire day to study. Good old-fashioned sleep is another lost pleasure for me now. I never get as much as I like because their just isn't time. Finally I miss having the chance to just sit in front of the TV, on weeknights. In order to watch the whole line-up of movies and sports that I used to watch regularly. These sound like small pleasures, but you realize how important they are when you have to give them up.

_____   I've had to give up pleasures in my life. I use to spend sundays playing games, now I have to study. I'm the sort of person who needs a lot of sleep, but I don't have the time for that either. Sleeping nine or ten hours a night wouldn't be unusual for me. Pyschologists say that each individual need a different amount of sleep, some people need as little as five hours, some need as much as nine or ten. So I'm not unusual in that. But Ive given up that pleasure too. And I can't watch the TV shows I use to enjoy. This is another personal pleasure Ive lost because of doing work and school. These may seem like small things, but you realize how good they are when you give them up.

_____   Besides missing the social side of college life, I've also had to give up some of my special personal pleasures. I used to spend Sunday afternoons, for example, playing street hockey or touch football depending on the season. Now I use Sunday as a catch-up day for my studies. Another pleasure I've lost is sleeping late on days off and weekends. I once loved mornings when I could check the clock, bury my head in the pillow, and drift off for another hour. These days I'm forced to crawl out of bed the minute the alarm lets out its piercing ring. Finally, I no longer have the chance to just sit watching the movies and sports shows that I enjoy. A leisurely night of playing Tomb Raider or renting a Jet Li movie is a pleasure of the past for me now.

_____   Besides missing the social side of college life, I've also had to give up some of my special personal pleasures. I used to spend sunday afternoons, for example playing street hockey or touch football, depending on the season. Now I use the day as a catch-up day for my studies. Another pleasure I've lost is sleeping late on days off and weekends. I once loved mornings when I could check the clock, then burying my head in the pillow, and you drift off to sleep for another hour. These days I'm forced to get out of bed the minute the alarm lets out it's ring. Finally I no longer have the chance to just sit watching the movies and also programs with sports that I enjoy. A leisurely night of playing Tomb Raider or renting a Jet Li movie is a pleasure of the past for me now.

Final Questions

- Which errors in some of the drafts are the most distracting to the reader?

  _____

- Which sample paragraph conveys its meaning most clearly?

  _____

  _____

  Why? _____

REVIEWING THE LEARNING OUTCOMES FOR CHAPTER 2

To assure yourself that you have met the Learning Outcomes for this chapter, answer the following questions.

- What is the key to discovering a topic or narrowing a wide general topic?
- What are the main stages of the writing process and what activities are involved in each stage?
- How do you think working on essay writing in distinct stages will improve your writing?
- What are the four prewriting techniques, and which techniques might suit which types of thinkers?
- What are the four parts of a formal outline?

The First and Second Steps in Essay Writing

LEARNING OUTCOMES

After reading this chapter and working through its activities, you will
- Discover and express your point as a solid thesis statement
- Support your point with specific evidence

Chapter 2 introduced you to the stages of the writing process. Working on any writing task stage by stage will make you a more effective writer. As you practise this approach—taking it a stage at a time and keeping your goals in front of you—two things will happen: You will begin to follow this pattern automatically whenever you have a writing assignment, and you will develop your own variations on the techniques involved.

This chapter, returning to the four steps that lead to achieving the four goals of effective essay writing, focuses on the first two steps in writing a solid essay:

1. Begin with a point expressed as **a thesis** → to guide your support, leading to **Unity**.
2. Develop your point with **specific points and details** → to explain/prove your point, leading to clear, sufficient **Support**.

The following chapters will then focus on the third and fourth steps in effective writing:

3. Organize and connect the **specific evidence** (72–96) → to create logical and complete support, leading to **Coherence**.
4. Revise and edit for **clear, error-free sentences** (97–127) → to create an essay that presents **Effective Sentence Skills**.

Working through the writing process will show you an interesting fact: most writers spend over 50 percent of their time prewriting and planning and at least 30 percent of their time revising, rewriting, and polishing. If you have spent almost all your time trying to write "one perfect first draft" in the past, consider the percentage of time writers generally spend on that draft, using the percentages above.

STEP 1: BEGIN WITH A POINT OR THESIS

Your first step in writing is to discover what overall main point you want to make about your topic or subject. Write that point in a single sentence; you want to know right from the start if you have a clear and workable thesis. You will be able to use the thesis as a guide while writing your essay. At any stage you can turn your point into a "thesis question" (page 36). You can also ask yourself if various answers to your "thesis question" really support or explain your thesis' expressed viewpoint. With the thesis as a guide, the danger of drifting away from the point of the essay is greatly reduced, and you focus on the goal of **unity** in your essay.

WRITING A GOOD THESIS

A typical college essay is between five hundred and six hundred words in length. In final word-processed form, such an essay takes up two to three pages. When you have only two or three pages to make and support a point about some subject, you can tackle only one aspect, one angle, or one "subcategory" of that subject successfully.

To write a good thesis, you must begin with a subject that is neither too broad nor too narrow. Suppose, for example, that an instructor asks you to write a paper on the Internet. A topic such as the Internet is obviously too broad to cover in a five-hundred-word essay. You would probably have to write a book to adequately support any point you might make about the general subject of the Internet. What you need to do, then, is limit your subject, as the box below demonstrates. Narrow it down until you have a thesis that you can deal with specifically in five hundred words or so. In the box that follows are

1 Several general subjects (or topics)

2 Limited versions of those general subjects

3 Thesis statements about the limited subjects

General Subject	Limited Subject	Thesis (Limited Subject + One Viewpoint on It)
The Internet	E-mail	E-mail is a great way to stay in touch with friends.
Family	Older sister	My older sister helped me overcome my shyness.
Television	Cable stations	Cable stations offer more interesting kinds of programs than network TV.

General Subject	Limited Subject	Thesis (Limited Subject + One Viewpoint on It)
College	Studying English at college	Studying English in college is very different from taking high school English.
Sports	Players' salaries	High players' salaries are bad for the game, anger the fans, and distort the values our children are developing.

Activity

Sometimes a subject must go through several stages of limiting before it is narrow enough to write about. Below are four lists reflecting several stages that writers went through in moving from a general subject to a narrow thesis statement. Number the stages in each list from 1 to 5, with 1 marking the broadest stage and 5 marking the thesis.

List 1

_____ Teachers

_____ Education

_____ Math teacher

_____ My high school math teacher was peculiar sometimes.

_____ High school math teacher

List 2

_____ Bicycles

_____ Dangers of bike riding

_____ Recreation

_____ Recreational vehicles

_____ Bike riding in the city is a dangerous activity.

List 3

_____ Retail companies

_____ Supermarket

_____ Dealing with customers

_____ Working in a supermarket

_____ I've learned how to handle unpleasant supermarket customers.

List 4

_____ Camping

_____ First camping trip

_____ Summer vacation

_____ My first camping trip was a disastrous experience.

_____ Vacations

Later in this chapter, you will get more practice in narrowing general subjects to thesis statements.

AVOIDING COMMON ERRORS IN WRITING A THESIS

Thesis statements perform two tasks:

- They state your single point clearly.
- They preview your essay's content.

As they perform these tasks, thesis statements act as guides to your readers, telling them just what to expect from the paragraphs that follow. A thesis is like the chairs in the child's story "The Three Bears": To be effective, it must be neither "too big" nor "too small," but "just right." To create the "just right" thesis that guides readers and previews your support effectively, avoid the following common errors:

- Announcements rather than thesis statements
- Thesis statements that are too broad
- Thesis statements that are too narrow
- Thesis statements containing multiple points

1 Announcements Rather than Thesis Statements

The subject of this paper will be my parents.
I want to talk about cuts to education funding in my province.
The "baby boom" generation is the concern of this essay.

In this first group, the sentences are not thesis statements but just announcements of a topic idea. Each is also guilty of "overstatement," or redundancy—any reader looking at these statements' key words assumes that paragraphs following these statements discuss "parents," "education cuts," or "the 'baby boom' generation." Readers need not be told "the subject is . . ." For instance, "The subject of this paper will be my parents" does not make a point *about* the parents but merely tells, in a rather unimaginative way, the writer's general subject. A thesis statement must advance a point about a limited subject. A thesis may be stated as a formula: "Subject + Viewpoint on Subject = Thesis."

2 Thesis Statements That Are Too Broad

My parents have been the most influential people in my life.
Cuts in education funding are a major concern of everyone in our province.
The "baby boom" generation has changed history.

In this second group, all statements are too broad to be supported adequately in a student essay. For example, "My parents have been the most influential people in my life" could not be supported with specific details in eight hundred words or less. There are many autobiographies in which entire chapters detail the influence of parents on the authors' lives.

3 Thesis Statements That Are Too Narrow

My parents had only one child.
In the last year there have been over twenty public schools closed in our city.
The members of the post–World War II "baby boom" make up the largest single age group in Canada.

In this third group, there is no room in any of the three statements for support to be given. For instance, "My parents had only one child" is too narrow to be expanded into a paper. It is a simple fact that does not require much support. Such a statement is sometimes called a *dead-end statement;* there is no place to go with it. On the other hand, "My parents helped me grow in three important ways" is a point that you could support with specific ideas in an essay.

4 Thesis Statements Containing Multiple Points

My parents helped me grow in important ways, although in other respects I was limited.

The problem of cuts to education funding must be solved, and the provincial government should start spending more on Ontario's future.

The "baby boom" generation has had many advantages, but it also faces many problems.

In this fourth group, each of the statements contains more than one idea. For instance, "My parents helped me grow in important ways, although in other respects I was limited" appears to have two separate ideas ("parents helped me grow" *and* "in other respects I was limited"). The reader is asked to focus on two quite separate points, each of which more logically belongs in an essay of its own.

Activity 1

Part A: Write *TN* in the space next to each statement that is too narrow to be developed in an essay. Write *TB* beside each statement that is too broad to be covered in an essay.

_____ 1. The way our society treats elderly people is unbelievable.

_____ 2. The first car that I owned was a Toyota.

_____ 3. Computers have changed our society.

_____ 4. People who eat a lot of red meat are almost three times more likely to get colon cancer as people who eat mostly fish and chicken.

_____ 5. Action must be taken against drugs.

Part B: Write *A* beside each sentence that is an announcement rather than a thesis statement. Write *2* beside each statement that contains more than one idea.

_____ 6. My last car was dependable, but many North American cars are poorly made.

_____ 7. The subject of this essay is computers in our public schools.

_____ 8. Soap operas show many stereotyped characters, although they also portray real problems in contemporary life.

_____ 9. I am going to write on my ideas concerning "F" grades.

_____ 10. The hardest teacher I ever had taught me a lesson I will never forget.

Activity 2

As you have read, writers may substitute an announcement of a subject for a true thesis idea. Dead-end thesis statements are too narrow to need support or development. Some thesis statements are too general, too broad to be adequately supported within the limits of a six- or seven-hundred-word essay, and others are vague or contain more than one idea. Sharpen your sense of what makes a good thesis statement by working through the following activities in pairs. Compare your results with those of classmates.

Write *A* beside the sentences that are announcements rather than thesis statements. Write *OK* beside the statement in each pair that is a clear, limited point that could be developed in an essay.

_____ 1. a. This essay will discuss the people you meet in exercise class.

_____ b. The kinds of workout clothes worn in my aerobics class identify "jocks," "strugglers," and "shopping fanatics."

_____ 2. a. I made several mistakes in the process of trying to win the respect and affection of my stepson.

_____ b. My thesis in this paper is relationships between step-parents and stepchildren.

_____ 3. a. A period of loneliness can teach you to use your creativity, sort out your values, and feel empathy for others.

_____ b. Loneliness is the subject of this paper.

Activity 3

Write *TN* beside statements that are too narrow to be developed in an essay. Write *OK* beside the statement in each pair that is a clear, limited point.

_____ 1. a. I had squash, tomatoes, and corn in my garden last summer.

_____ b. Vegetable gardening can be a frustrating hobby.

_____ 2. a. The main road into our town is lined with fast-food outlets.

_____ b. For several reasons, the number of fast-food chain outlets limited should be abolished.

_____ 3. a. There are more single-parent households in our country than ever.

_____ b. Organization is the key to being a successful single parent.

Activity 4

Write *TB* beside statements that are too broad to be developed in an essay. Write *OK* beside the statement in each pair that is a clear, limited point.

_____ 1. a. In many ways, sports are an important part of Canadian life.

_____ b. Widespread gambling in some Canadian cities has changed people's lives for the worse.

_____   2. a. Modern life makes people antisocial and unfriendly.

_____   b. Too much time at my workstation screen in my office cubicle has made me a much less social person in several ways.

_____   3. a. Toy ads on television teach children to be greedy, competitive, and snobbish.

_____   b. Advertising has bad effects on all of society.

Activity 5

For each pair, write _2_ beside the statement that contains more than one idea. Write _OK_ beside the statement in each pair that is a clear, limited point.

_____   1. a. Working with old people changed my stereotyped ideas about the elderly.

_____   b. My life has moved in new directions since the rewarding job I had working with older people last summer.

_____   2. a. The new architecture on this campus is very unpleasant, although the expansion was desperately needed.

_____   b. Our new college resource centre building is ugly, intimidating, and inefficient.

_____   3. a. Among the most entertaining ads on TV today are those on the cable shopping stations.

_____   b. Although ads on cable shopping stations are often misleading, they can still be very entertaining.

STEP 2: SUPPORT THE THESIS WITH SPECIFIC EVIDENCE

THE IMPORTANCE OF SUPPORTING POINTS

The first essential step in writing a successful essay is to formulate a clearly stated thesis. The second basic step is to support the thesis with specific reasons: your supporting points and details.

To ensure that your essay will have adequate support, you may find an informal or "four-point" outline helpful. Write down a brief version of your thesis idea, and then work out and jot down the three points that will support that thesis.

Once again, here is Tina Kallas' "four-point outline" for her essay on movie-going:

Movie-going is a problem.

1. Inconvenience of going out
2. Tempting snacks
3. Other movie-goers

A "four-point outline" looks simple, but developing one often requires careful thinking. The time spent, though, on developing a logical beginning for your outline is invaluable. Once you have planned the steps that logically support your thesis, you will be in an excellent position to go on to prepare a formal outline and write an effective essay.

Activities in this section will give you practice in the crucial skill of planning a clearly developed essay.

Activity

Complete the four-point outlines that follow by adding a third logical supporting point (*c*) that will parallel the two already provided (*a* and *b*).

1. The first day on a new job can be nerve-wracking.
   a. Meeting new people
   b. Finding your way around a new place

   c. _____

2. My stepmother has three qualities I admire.
   a. Patience
   b. Thoughtfulness

   c. _____

3. At our school, the resource centre is the worst place to study.
   a. Uncomfortable chairs and tables
   b. Little privacy

   c. _____

4. College students should live at home.
   a. Stay in touch with family
   b. Avoid distractions of residence or apartment life

   c. _____

5. _____ is the worst job I've ever had.
   a. Difficult boss
   b. Poor pay

   c. _____

THE IMPORTANCE OF *SPECIFIC* DETAILS

Just as a thesis must be developed with three (or more) supporting points, those supporting points must be developed with specific details. Specific details have two key values. First of all, details excite the reader's interest. They make writing a pleasure to read, for we all enjoy learning particulars about people, places, and things. Second, details serve to explain a writer's points. They give the evidence needed for us to see and understand general ideas.

Too often, body paragraphs in essays contain vague generalities rather than the specific supporting details that are needed to engage and convince a reader. Here is what one of the paragraphs in "The Hazards of Movie-Going" would have looked like if the writer had not detailed her supporting evidence vividly.

Some of the other patrons are even more of a problem than the theatre itself. Many people in the theatre often show themselves to be inconsiderate. They make noises and create disturbances at their seats. Included are people in every age group, from the young to the old. Some act as if they were at home in their own living rooms watching the TV set. And people are often messy, so that you're constantly aware of all the food they're eating. People are also always moving around near you, creating a disturbance and interrupting your enjoyment of the movie.

As shown in the table below, the effective paragraph from the essay provides details that clarify the point that other movie-goers are a problem. Tina *specifies* the exact age groups (little kids, high school kids, and adults) and the offences of each (giggling, talking and whistling, and loud comments). She *specifies* the various food excesses (crinkled wrappers, gum on seats, dropped popcorn, and pop containers). Finally, she *provides concrete details* that enable us to see and hear other disturbances (coughs and burps, squirming, constant trips to the bathroom, and jostling for elbow room). The ineffective paragraph asks us to guess about these details; the effective paragraph describes the details in a detailed and lively manner.

Point: "Other movie-goers are a problem."	
Vague Support	*Specific Support*
1. Many people in the theatre show themselves to be inconsiderate. They make noises and create disturbances at their seats. Included are people in every age group, from the young to the old. Some act as if they were at home in their own living rooms watching the TV set.	1. Little kids race up and down the aisles, usually in giggling packs. Teenagers try to impress their friends by talking back to the screen, whistling, and making what they consider to be hilarious noises. Adults act as if they were at home in their own living rooms and comment loudly on the ages of the stars or why movies aren't as good any more.
2. And people are often messy, so that you're constantly aware of all the food they're eating.	2. And people of all ages crinkle candy wrappers, stick gum on their seats, and drop popcorn tubs or cups of crushed ice and pop on the floor.
3. People are also always moving around near you, creating a disturbance and interrupting enjoyment of the movie.	3. They also cough and burp, squirm endlessly in their seats, file out for repeated trips to the restrooms or concession stand, and elbow you out of the armrest on either side of your seat.

The strong paragraph, then, contains sharp details to capture our interest and enable us to share the writer's experiences. Details provide pictures that make each of us feel, "I am there." The particulars also enable us to understand clearly the writer's point that patrons are a problem. Aim to make your own writing equally convincing by

- Making your details specific
- Giving examples that illustrate your details

Activity

Write *S* in front of the two selections below that provide specific evidence to support their opening points. Write *X* in front of the two selections that follow their opening points with vague, general, and wordy sentences.

1. Building a wooden deck can be an enjoyable project only if you take certain precautions.

   Get a building permit before you start. If you don't have one, you may have to tear down everything you've built when the local building inspector learns of your project. Also, purchase pressure-treated lumber for any posts that will be set into the ground. Ordinary wood, not treated with preservatives, will eventually rot from contact with soil and moisture.

2. My mother was a harsh disciplinarian.

   When I did something wrong, no matter how small, she would inflict serious punishment. She had expectations that I was to live up to, and she never changed her attitude. When I did not behave as I should, I was dealt with severely. There were no exceptions as far as my mother was concerned.

3. Some things are worse when they're "improved."

   A good cheesecake, for one thing, is perfect. It doesn't need pineapple, cherries, blueberries, or whipped cream smeared all over it. Plain old blue jeans, the ones with five pockets and copper rivets, are perfect too. Manufacturers only made them worse when they made them "low rise," took away the pockets, made them baggy-fitting, and plastered logos and designers' names all over them.

4. Pets can be more trouble than children.

   My dog, unlike my children, has never been completely housebroken. When he's excited or nervous, he still has an occasional problem. My dog, unlike my children, has never learned how to take care of himself when we're away, despite the fact that we've given him plenty of time to do so. We don't have to worry about our grown children anymore. However, we still have to hire a dog-sitter.

THE IMPORTANCE OF *ADEQUATE* DETAILS

Everyone writes from "images" they "see" in their minds. As you write, you trace some image or a pattern of ideas that you try to capture from your thoughts. Most of your effort in writing goes into trying to get these things into words as accurately as you can.

Readers cannot "see what you see" in your mind, so your words must do the work of showing your thoughts clearly. This is where providing *enough* specifics becomes important. The work of finding details and examples to explain and clarify a supporting point has a goal: to show your readers as closely as possible what you "see" that makes that point true for you.

A common and serious problem in students' writing is inadequate development. You must provide *enough* specific details to fully support the point in a body paragraph of an essay. You could not, for example, include a paragraph about a friend's unreliability and provide only a one- or two-sentence example. You would have to extend the example or add several other examples showing your friend as an unreliable person. Without such additional support, your paragraph would be underdeveloped. Readers would not *see* why your friend was unreliable.

Students may try to disguise unsupported paragraphs through repetition and generalities. Do not fall into this "wordiness trap." Be prepared to do the hard work needed to ensure that each paragraph has solid support.

Activity 1

Both of the following body paragraphs were written on the same topic, and both have clear opening points. Which one is adequately developed? Which one, on the other hand, has only several particulars and uses mostly vague, general, wordy sentences to conceal the fact that it is starved for specific details?

Turn Back Time? No Thanks

Most men wouldn't want to be teenage boys again, mainly because no one would want to worry about talking to teenage girls. If they are honest, men in their twenties still remember how nerve-wracking it was to call a girl and ask her out. Just the act of dialing a girl's phone number was enough to start a teenage boy's heart racing, make the hand holding the receiver clammy with sweat, and make his face turn bright red. Next there were the terrors about how his voice would sound if he actually got around to speaking—would he sound like some casual deep-voiced deejay or squeak like a squirrel? Then there were questions he tortured himself with: Would she be at home? If she was, would she want to talk? And if she did talk, what was there to say? Most men who admit to these worries remember a date or two that sometimes resulted from one of these calls. They still squirm as they recall staring straight ahead and silent at an empty movie screen, clutching a popcorn box, waiting for the film to start. These men are probably still wondering why those girls ever went out with them in the first place.

Terror and the Teenage Male

Most men wouldn't want to be teenagers again—first of all, because they wouldn't want to worry about talking to teenage girls. Calling up a girl to ask her out was something they completely dreaded. They felt like they didn't know what words to express or how to express them. Every time they got on the phone, they would have all kinds of nervous symptoms. They worried a great deal about how they would sound, and had a lot of doubts about the girl's reaction. And when they occasionally managed to call up a girl to go out, the evening turned out to be a disaster. Too unsure of themselves to act in a confident way, they couldn't think of anything to say and just kept quiet. Looking back on these memories, most men feel like they made fools of themselves. Agonizing over their attempts at relationships with the opposite sex made adolescence a very uncomfortable time.

The first paragraph offers a series of well-detailed examples of the author's memories of nerve-wracking experiences, as a teenager, with girls. The second paragraph, on the other hand, is underdeveloped. For instance, whereas the second paragraph makes only the general observation "Every time they got on the phone, they would have all kinds of nervous symptoms" the first paragraph states, "Just the act of dialing a girl's phone number was enough to start a teenage boy's heart racing, make the hand holding the receiver clammy with sweat . . ."

The second paragraph makes the general statement "They worried a great deal about how they would sound," whereas in the first paragraph, the author wonders if his voice will "sound like some casual deep-voiced deejay or squeak like a squirrel." And in the second paragraph, there is no specific description of an evening that turned into a disaster. In summary, the second paragraph lacks the full, detailed support needed to develop its opening point convincingly.

Note: Both paragraphs are written in the "invisible" third-person point of view. By not writing as "I," both writers try to keep the reader's focus on the topic. When readers are not distracted by an "I," or first-person presence in a paper, close attention to specific details is even more essential.

Activity 2

Take a few minutes to write a paragraph supporting the point "Managing time is a student's biggest problem." Afterward, you and your classmates, perhaps working in small groups, should read your paragraphs aloud. The best received paragraphs are almost sure to be those with plenty of specific details.

PRACTICE IN ADVANCING AND SUPPORTING A THESIS

You now know the two most important steps in competent essay writing: (1) advancing a point, or thesis, and (2) supporting that thesis. The purpose of this section is to expand and strengthen your understanding of these two basic steps. You will first work through a series of activities on *developing* a thesis:

1 Identifying the parts of an essay

2 Completing thesis statements

3 Writing a thesis statement

4 Limiting a topic and writing a thesis

You will then sharpen your understanding of how to *support* a thesis effectively by working through the following activities:

5 Providing specific evidence

6 Identifying adequate supporting evidence

7 Adding details to complete an essay

1   IDENTIFYING THE PARTS OF AN ESSAY

Activity

This activity will sharpen your sense of the parts of an essay. "Coping with Old Age" has no indentations between paragraphs. Read this essay carefully, and then double-underline the thesis and single-underline the topic sentence for each of the three supporting paragraphs and the first sentence of the conclusion. Write the numbers of those sentences in the spaces provided at the end.

Coping with Old Age

[1]I recently read about an area of Russia where many people live to be well over a hundred years old. [2]Being 115 or even 125 isn't considered unusual there, and these old people continue to do productive work right up until they die. [3]Canada, however, isn't such a healthy place for older people. [4]Since I retired from my job, I've had to cope with the physical, mental, and emotional stresses of being "old." [5]For one thing, I've had to adjust to physical changes. [6]Now that I'm over sixty, the trusty body that carried me around for years has turned traitor. [7]Aside from the deepening wrinkles on my face and neck, and the wiry grey hairs that have replaced my brown hair, I face more frightening changes. [8]I don't have the energy I used to. [9]My eyes get tired. [10]Once in a while, I miss something that's said to me. [11]My once faithful feet seem to have lost their comfortable soles, and I sometimes feel I'm walking on marbles. [12]In order to fight against this slow decay, I exercise whenever I can. [13]I walk, I stretch, and I climb stairs. [14]I battle constantly to keep as fit as possible. [15]I'm also trying to cope with mental changes. [16]My mind was once as quick and sure as a champion gymnast. [17]I never found it difficult to memorize answers in school or to remember the names of people I met. [18]Now, I occasionally have to search my mind for the name of a close neighbour or favourite television show. [19]Because my mind needs exercise, too, I challenge it as much as I can. [20]Taking a college course like this English class, for example, forces me to concentrate. [21]The mental gymnast may be a little slow and out of shape, but he can still do a back flip or turn a somersault when he has to.

[22]Finally, I must deal with the emotional impact of being old. [23]Our society typecasts old people. [24]We're supposed to be unattractive, senile, useless leftovers. [25]We're supposed to be the crazy drivers and the cranky customers. [26]At first, I was angry and frustrated that I was considered old at all. [27]And I knew that people were wrong to stereotype me. [28]Then I got depressed. [29]I even started to think that maybe I was a cast-off, one of those old animals that slow down the rest of the herd. [30]But I have now decided to rebel against these negative feelings. [31]I try to have friends of all ages and to keep up with what's going on in the world. [32]I try to remember that I'm still the same person who sat at a first-grade desk, who fell in love, who comforted a child, who got a raise at work. [33]I'm not "just" an old person. [34]Coping with the changes of old age has become my latest full-time job. [35]Even though it's a job I never applied for, and one for which I had no experience, I'm trying to do the best I can.

Thesis statement in "Coping with Old Age": _____

Topic sentence of first supporting paragraph: _____

Topic sentence of second supporting paragraph: _____

Topic sentence of third supporting paragraph: _____

First sentence of the conclusion: _____

2 COMPLETING THESIS STATEMENTS

Activity

Complete the following thesis statements by adding a third supporting point that will parallel the two already provided. Parallel structure means that items or phrases in a list follow the same grammatical pattern. You might first want to check the section on parallelism (pages 98–99) to make sure you understand parallel form.

1. Because I never took college preparatory courses in high school, I entered

   college deficient in mathematics, study skills, and _____.

2. A good salesperson needs to like people, to be aggressive, and

   _____.

3. Rather than blame myself for failing the course, I blamed the instructor, my

   advisor, and even _____.

4. Anyone who buys an old house and is planning to fix it up should be prepared

   to put in a lot of time, hard work, and _____.

5. Our old car eats gas, makes funny noises, and _____.

6. My mother, my boss, and my _____ are three people who are
   very important in my life right now.

7. Moving in together too soon was a mistake because we hadn't finished our education, we didn't know how to handle our money, and _____.

8. Some restaurant patrons seem to leave their honesty, their cleanliness, and their _____ at home.

3 WRITING A THESIS STATEMENT

Activity

This activity will give you practice in writing an effective essay thesis—one that is neither too broad nor too narrow. It will also give you practice in understanding the logical relationship between a thesis and its topic sentences.

For each item below, write an appropriate thesis statement.

1. Thesis: _____
   a. My first car was a rebellious-looking one that matched the way I felt and acted as a teenager.
   b. My next car reflected my more mature and practical adult self.
   c. My latest car seems to tell me that I'm ageing; it shows my growing concern with comfort and safety.

2. Thesis: _____
   a. Attending a college offers the chance to prepare for a career or further educational demands.
   b. If the college is nearby, there are no room-and-board costs.
   c. The course credits that are accumulated can be transferred to some universities.

3. Thesis: _____
   a. First, I tried simply avoiding the snacks aisle of the supermarket.
   b. Then I started limiting myself to only five units of any given snack.
   c. Finally, in desperation, I began keeping snack baggies in a padlocked cupboard.

4. Thesis: _____
   a. The holiday can be very frightening for little children.
   b. Drivers cannot see children without light sticks or reflecting bands on dark costumes.
   c. Skeletons, ghosts, and vampires used for decorations can still scare young children.

5. Thesis: _____
   a. First of all, I was a typical Type A personality: anxious, impatient, and hard-driving.
   b. I also had a family history of relatives with heart trouble.
   c. My unhealthy lifestyle, though, was probably the major factor.

4 LIMITING A TOPIC AND WRITING A THESIS

The following two activities will give you practice in distinguishing general from limited subjects and in writing a thesis.

Activity 1

Look carefully at the six general and six limited subjects below. Then write a thesis for four of the limited subjects.

Hint: To create a thesis, ask yourself, "What point do I want to make about _____ (my limited subject)?"

General Subject	*Limited Subject*
1. Apartment	1. Sharing an apartment with a roommate
2. Self-improvement	2. Behaviour toward others
3. Eating out	3. Fast-food restaurants
4. Automobiles	4. Bad driving habits
5. Health	5. Regular exercise
6. The Internet	6. Chatrooms

Activity 2: Group Activity

- Here is a list of six general subjects. Each group of four students will choose four of the subjects, write a limited version of each, and then produce a thesis statement for each.
- Groups will then compare their limited subjects and the thesis statements they developed.

General Subject	*Limited Subject*
1. Pets	_____
2. Television	_____
3. Work	_____
4. College	_____
5. Vacations	_____
6. Cooking	_____

5 PROVIDING SPECIFIC EVIDENCE

Activity

Provide three details that logically support each of the following points. Your details can be drawn from your own experience, or they can be invented. In each case, the details should show *specifically* what the point expresses only generally. State your details briefly in several words rather than in complete sentences.

Example   We quickly spruced up the apartment before our guest arrived.

1. *Hid toys and newspapers in spare closet*

2. *Vacuumed pet hairs off sofa*

3. *Sprayed air freshener around living room*

1. The evening was a disaster.

_____

_____

_____

2. My seven-year-old nephew has some disgusting habits.

_____

_____

_____

3. There are several reasons why I put off studying.

_____

_____

_____

4. My parents never allowed me to think for myself.

_____

_____

_____

5. There are several ways in which students can earn extra cash.

_____

_____

_____

6 IDENTIFYING ADEQUATE SUPPORTING EVIDENCE

Activity

The following body paragraphs were taken from student essays. Two of the paragraphs provide sufficient details to support their topic sentences convincingly. Write *AD* for *adequate development* beside those paragraphs. Three paragraphs use vague, wordy, general, or irrelevant sentences instead of real supporting details. Write *U* for *underdeveloped* beside those paragraphs.

_____ 1. Another consideration in adopting a dog is the cost. Initial fees for shots and a licence might add up to $50. Annual visits to the vet for heartworm pills, rabies or distemper shots, and general checkups could cost $100 or more. Then, there is the cost of food. A 10 kilogram bag of dry food (the cheapest kind) costs around $20. A large dog can eat that much in a couple of weeks.

_____ 2. People can be cruel to pets simply by being thoughtless. They don't think about a pet's needs or simply ignore those needs. It never occurs to them that their pet can be experiencing a great deal of discomfort as a result of their failure to be sensitive. The cruelty is a result of the basic lack of attention and concern— qualities that should be there, but aren't.

_____ 3. If I were in charge of the night-time programming on a TV network, I would make changes. I would completely eliminate some shows. In fact, all of the shows that proved of little interest would be cancelled. Commercials would also change, so that it would be possible to watch them without wanting to turn off the TV set. I would expand the good shows so that people would come away with an even better experience. My ideal network would be a great improvement over the average lineup we see today on any of the major networks.

_____ 4. A friend's rudeness is much more damaging that a stranger's. When a friend says sharply, "I don't have time to talk to you just now," people feel hurt instead of angry. When a friend shows up late for lunch or a shopping trip, with no good reason, it is easy to feel taken for granted. Worst, though, is when a friend pretends to be listening, but his or her wandering eyes show a lack of attention. Then anyone feels betrayed. Friends, after all, are supposed to make up for the thoughtless cruelties of strangers.

_____ 5. Giving my first shampoo and set to a real person, after weeks of practising on wigs, was a nerve-wracking experience. The customer was a woman who acted very sure about what she came for. She tried to describe what she wanted, and I tried without much success to understand what she had in mind. Every time I did something, she seemed to be indicating in one way or another that it was not what she wanted. I got more and more nervous as I worked on her hair, and the nervousness showed. The worst part of the ordeal happened at the very end, when I added the final touches. Nothing, to this woman, had turned out right.

7 ADDING DETAILS TO COMPLETE AN ESSAY

Activity

In the following essay, specific details are needed to back up the ideas in the supporting paragraphs. Using the spaces provided, add a sentence or two of clear, convincing details for each supporting idea. This activity will give you practice at supplying specific details and an initial feel for writing an essay.

INTRODUCTION

Life without Television

   When my family's only television set went to the repair shop the other day, my parents, my sister, and I thought we would have a terrible week. How could we get through the long evenings in such a quiet house? What would it be like without all the shows to keep us company? We soon realized, though, that living without television for a while was a stroke of good fortune. It became easy for each of us to enjoy some activities alone, to complete some postponed chores, and to spend rewarding time with each other and friends.

FIRST SUPPORTING
PARAGRAPH

   First of all, with no television to compete for our time, we found plenty of hours for personal interests. We all read more that week than we had read during the six months before. _____

_____

_____

_____

We each also enjoyed some hobbies we had ignored for ages. _____

_____

_____

_____

In addition, my sister and I both stopped procrastinating with our homework.

_____

_____

_____

SECOND
SUPPORTING
PARAGRAPH

Second, we did chores that had been hanging over our heads for too long. There were many jobs around the house that had needed attention for some time. _____

_____

_____

We also had a chance to do some long-postponed shopping. _____

_____

_____

_____

And each of us also did some letter writing or other paperwork that was long overdue. _____

_____

_____

THIRD
SUPPORTING
PARAGRAPH

Finally, and probably most important, we spent time with each other. Instead of being in the same room together while we stared at a screen, we actually talked for many pleasant hours. _____

_____

_____

Moreover, for the first time in years my family played some games together.

_____

_____

And because we didn't have to worry about missing this or that show, we had some family friends over on a couple of evenings and spent an enjoyable time with them. _____

CONCLUSION

Once our television set returned, we were not prepared to put it in the attic. But we had a sense of how it can take over our lives if we are not careful. We are now more selective. We turn on the set for our favourite shows, certain sports events, and the news, but we don't leave it running all night. As a result, we find we can enjoy television and still have time left over for other activities and interests.

REVIEWING THE LEARNING OUTCOMES FOR CHAPTER 3

To assure yourself that you have thoroughly grasped the content for this chapter, answer the following questions:

- Which goal for essay writing does an effectively written thesis statement help you to achieve, and how?

- What are the four most common errors encountered in writing thesis statements? Make up an example for each error; then correct each example so that you have four solid thesis statements.

- What type of brief outline helps you see if your main points truly support your thesis?

- What two characteristics must supporting details have, in order to be effective, and why?

The Third Step in Essay Writing

LEARNING OUTCOMES

After learning and practising the techniques in this chapter, you will be prepared to
- Choose and reinforce an effective pattern of organization for your supporting material
- Connect ideas and signal your intentions in body paragraphs and sentences by using transitional structures and words
- Begin and end an essay with effective introductory and concluding paragraphs

Chapter 3 demonstrated the first two steps in writing an effective essay: advancing a thesis and supporting it with specific evidence. This chapter will deal with the third step. You'll learn the chief ways to create coherence—the third goal in essay writing. You will learn and practise techniques to connect the supporting information in a paper. You'll then see how to start an essay with a suitable introductory paragraph and how to finish it with a well-rounded concluding paragraph. In short, you will learn how to create a coherent essay that flows smoothly from opening to conclusion.

STEP 3: ORGANIZE AND CONNECT THE SPECIFIC EVIDENCE

CREATE COHERENCE

Coherence, the third goal for an effective essay, is the product of conscious choices you make in the drafting and revising stages of the writing process. *Coherence* means literally "sticking together." Coherent writing shows your reader the sequence of and connections between your ideas; the reader is not puzzled by abrupt changes of subject or sentences with no apparent relationship to each other.

To create coherence, you make *conscious choices* at two stages of creating your essay. First, at the structuring stage, as you outline and draft, *organize* your entire essay according to an order appropriate to your subject and purpose. Second, as you draft and revise, *connect* paragraphs and sentences within paragraphs with appropriate methods of transition.

All elements of a **unified** essay work together to create and sustain **coherence**. Following is a boxed summary of techniques and methods that produce an essay whose ideas flow logically and naturally from its point and purpose.

---

1. **Creating Coherence at the Essay Level**
   - Write an effective thesis statement with clear, logically derived supporting points.
   - Indicate the order for the supporting points of your thesis and sustain that order through your topic sentences and body paragraphs.
2. **Creating Coherence at the Paragraph Level**
   - Write topic sentences that refer clearly to the thesis supporting point covered by that paragraph.
   - Write topic sentences that cover all details and examples found in each body paragraph.
   - Reinforce with transitional phrases or structures the order established in your thesis in each body paragraph's topic sentence.
   - Create verbal connections or transitions in each body paragraph's topic or opening sentence that connect the reader to the ending of the previous paragraph.
   - Use transitional phrases or structures in each body paragraph's closing sentence that connect that paragraph with the one that follows.
   - Use a conclusion signal and summarizing phrases to open your concluding paragraph.
3. **Creating Coherence at the Sentence Level**
   - Within each paragraph of your essay, use transitional phrases or devices to show relationships between sentences and to mark changes of direction, meaning, or emphasis.

If these three sets of tasks seem intimidating, know that by working through the activities for Chapter 3, you have already begun work on Step 1: creating coherence at your essay's structural level. You practised writing and evaluating thesis statements, supporting points, and details—demonstrating logical progress from thesis to supporting evidence is the first step to coherence.

When you connect your paragraphs to each other, and when the wording of your sentences signals their functions and connections to each other, your essay flows coherently. The sections that follow give you techniques to organize and connect your essay at both paragraph and sentence levels.

As you are generating the main points and specific details needed to support a thesis, you should be thinking about ways to **organize and connect the supporting points and details** to achieve an essay that is **unified**. All points and details in your essay must **cohere**. A well-organized essay whose ideas flow logically and relate clearly to each other meets the three goals of **unity**, **support**, and **coherence**. This section will emphasize coherence as it shows you how to organize and connect supporting details by the use of (1) common methods of organization, (2) transitions, and (3) other transitional structures.

COMMON METHODS OF ORGANIZATION

Knowing how to write an effective thesis statement gives you a good start on achieving coherence at the essay level—your thesis and supporting points guide readers' expectations about what will be found in your body paragraphs.

Now consider a first principle for achieving coherence at both the essay and paragraph levels: choosing an appropriate *order* for your supporting points and details. When you order your points in a way that follows logically from the point your thesis makes, you *organize* your support in a way that reassures your readers that your paragraphs of proof have a reasonable sequence, making your essay easier to follow.

Time order and **emphatic order** are two common methods used to organize an essay and its supporting points and details. (You will learn more specific methods of development in Part 2 of this book.)

- **Time, or chronological order**, simply means that paragraphs are ordered and details are listed as they occur in time. *First* this is done; *next* this; *then* this; *after* that, this; and so on. Here is a four-point outline of an essay in this book in which time order is used.

Note that the thesis lists its supporting points in time order, and that the topic-sentence points reinforce this order by repeating it.

Thesis: However, for success in exercise, you should follow a simple plan consisting of arranging the time, making preparations, and warming up properly.

1. To begin with, set aside a regular hour for exercise.
2. Next, prepare for your exercise session.
3. Finally, do a series of warm-up activities.

Fill in the missing word: The topic sentences in the essay use the words <u>To begin with</u>,

_____, and _____ to help show time order.

Here is one supporting paragraph from the essay:

Next, prepare for your exercise session. You do this, first, by not eating or drinking anything for an hour before the session. Why risk an upset stomach? Then, dress comfortably in something that allows you to move freely. Because you'll be in your own home, there's no need to invest in a high-fashion dance costume. A loose T-shirt and shorts are good. A bathing suit is great in summer, and in winter a set of long underwear is warm and comfortable. If your hair tends to flop in your eyes, pin it back or wear a headband or scarf. After dressing, prepare the exercise area. Turn off the phone and lock the door to prevent interruptions. Shove the coffee table out of the way so you won't bruise yourself on it. Finally, get out the simple materials you'll need to exercise on.

- To use time order effectively, list your details in time sequence in your outline and draft. Then see where "signal words" (transitions) could be used to clarify or emphasize the order or your details.

Fill in the missing words: The paragraph uses the following words to help show time order: _____*Next*_____, _____, _____, _____, and _____ .

- **Emphatic order** is sometimes described as "save the best till last." It is a way to put *emphasis* on the most interesting or important detail by placing it in the last part of a paragraph or in the final supporting paragraph of an essay. (When all the details seem equal in importance, the writer should impose a personal order that seems logical or appropriate to the details in question.) Final positions in any writing are most emphatic positions because the reader is most likely to remember the last thing read. *Finally*, *last of all*, and *most important* are typical words or phrases showing emphasis. Here is a four-point outline of an essay in this book that uses emphatic order:

Thesis: Celebrities lead very stressful lives.

    1. For one thing, celebrities don't have the privacy an ordinary person does.
    2. In addition, celebrities are under constant pressure.
    3. Most important, celebrities must deal with the stress of being in constant danger.

Fill in the missing words: The topic sentences in the essay use the words *For one thing*, _____ , and _____ to help show emphatic order and create coherence at the essay level.

Here is the third supporting paragraph from the essay:

Most important, celebrities must deal with the stress of being in constant danger. The friendly grabs, hugs, and kisses of enthusiastic fans can quickly turn into uncontrolled assaults on a celebrity's hair, clothes, and car. Photographers must bear some responsibility for the death of perhaps the major celebrity of the 1990s—Princess Diana. Whether or not their pursuit caused the crash that took her life, it's clear she was chased as aggressively as an escaping felon. And celebrity can lead to deranged and even lethal attacks. The near-fatal stabbing of the late George Harrison in his home and the murder of John Lennon came about because two unbalanced people developed obsessions with the two Beatles. Famous people must live with the fact that they are always fair game—and never out of season.

Fill in the missing words: The words _____ are used to mark the most emphatic detail in the paragraph.

Note that maintaining coherence within the paragraph, at sentence level, means careful attention to order of details and use of emphatic "signal words."

Some essays use a combination of time order and emphatic order. For example, the essay on movie-going in the first chapter includes time order: the writer first describes getting to the theatre, then the theatre itself, and finally the behaviour of patrons during the movie. At the same time, the writer uses emphatic order, ending with the most important reason for her dislike of movie-going: "Some of the other patrons are even more of a problem than the theatre itself."

Activity

A Read the essays referred to below and identify their method of organizing details—time order, emphatic order, or a combination of both.

1. "Adopting a Challenge" (pages 160–161)

_____

2. "Everyday Cruelty" (pages 186–187)

_____

B See if you can now complete the explanations that follow.

The essay titled "Adopting a Challenge" uses *(add the missing word)*

_____ order. The author begins with the challenge of learning to sit properly in the wheelchair, then moves on to learning to move in the wheelchair, and ends with several problems that occurred next, during the church service. "Everyday Cruelty" uses a combination of *(add the missing words)*

_____ order and _____ order. It moves from the beginning to the end of a particular workday. It also ends with the "worst incident of mean-spiritedness" that the writer witnessed that day.

....

TRANSITIONS AND TRANSITIONAL SENTENCES

1 TRANSITIONS

Transitions have two functions:

1. Transitions signal the direction of a writer's thought.
2. Transitions are "links," or bridges between paragraphs, sentences, and thoughts. They are like the road signs that guide travellers.

Transitions are not "ornaments," or additional words to be "plugged in" mechanically at certain points in an essay; instead, transitional words, phrases, and sentences form essential parts of an essay's coherent and logical movement from idea to idea. Writers often know the direction in which they are proceeding, but readers may not; transitions are essential for an audience's clear understanding of an essay.

Sentence-Level Transitions

To achieve coherence *within* paragraphs, at the sentence level, use transitions to guide readers through the logical pattern behind your arrangement of examples, details, and sentences. Transitions help you to "show" readers what you mean more accurately: for example, if you wish readers to contrast one detail with another, use transitions to signal your intention. Use transitions to smooth your readers' sentence-to-sentence passage through your paragraph.

In the box below are some common transitions, grouped according to the kind of signal they give to readers. Note that certain words provide more than one kind of signal.

Addition signals: one, first of all, second, the third reason, also, next, another, and, in addition, moreover, furthermore, finally, last of all

Time signals: first, then, next, after, as, before, while, meanwhile, soon, now, during, finally

Space signals: next to, across, on the opposite side, to the left, to the right, above, below, near(by)

Change-of-direction signals: but, however, yet, in contrast, although, otherwise, still, on the contrary, on the other hand

Illustration signals: for example, for instance, specifically, as an illustration, once, such as

Conclusion signals: therefore, consequently, thus, then, as a result, in summary, to conclude, last of all, finally

---

Activity

1. To sharpen your awareness of sentence-level transitions, underline the three *addition* signals in the following selection:

   Traditional college advice about making more time for difficult courses by choosing so-called easy ones does not usually work. Hallway gossip is full of such legendary courses with nearly no assignments, group tests, and dozing professors. One way to see if one of these courses exists is to ask those students in the hall just exactly which subject got them an A after 20 percent attendance. See how vague their answers will be—chances are that course has suddenly disappeared from the calendar. Also, inquire around the same hallway experts to see which professors lecture from the same notes each semester and give the same tests. Just as suddenly no one will remember the name of any professor who actually does anything that predictable. Another time-tested strategy for picking easy courses is to check the college catalogue for the telltale course titles that signal a quick trip through a painless subject— courses like "The History of Nutrition" or "Disco and Society." Now follow up by reading the course outlines for those easy-sounding subjects . . . three essays each, a report or two, and some research assignments. So much for traditional advice; just give in, register for what's required, and do the work.

2.   Underline the four *time* signals in the following selection:

After you've snagged the job of TV sports reporter, you have to begin working on the details of your image. First, invest in two or three truly loud sports jackets. Look for gigantic plaid patterns in odd colour combinations like purple and green or orange and blue. These should become familiar enough to viewers that they will associate that crazy jacket with that dynamic sportscaster. Next, try to cultivate a distinctive voice that will be just annoying enough to be memorable. A nasal whine or a gravelly growl will do it. Be sure to speak only in tough, punchy sentences that seem to be punctuated with imaginary exclamation points. Finally, you must share lots of pompous, obnoxious opinions with your viewers. Your tone of voice must convey the hidden message, "I dare anyone to disagree with me." If the home teams lose, call them bums. If players strike, talk sarcastically about the good old days. If a sports franchise leaves town, say, "Good riddance."

3.   Underline the three *space* signals in the following selection:

The vegetable bin of my refrigerator contained an assortment of weird-looking items. Next to a shrivelled, white-coated lemon was a pair of oranges covered with blue fuzz. To the right of the oranges was a bunch of carrots that had begun to sprout points, spikes, knobs, and tendrils. The carrots drooped into U-shapes as I picked them up with the tips of my fingers. Near the carrots was a net bag of onions; each onion had sent curling shoots through the net until the whole thing resembled a mass of green spaghetti. The most horrible item, though, was a head of lettuce that had turned into a pool of brown goo. It had seeped out of its bag and coated the bottom of the bin with a sticky, evil-smelling liquid.

4.   Underline the two *change-of-direction* signals in the following selection:

Taking small children on vacation, for instance, sounds like a wonderful experience for the entire family. But vacations can be scary or emotionally overwhelming times for children. When children are taken away from their usual routine and brought to an unfamiliar place, they can become very frightened. That strange bed in the motel room or the unusual noises in Grandma's spare bedroom may cause nightmares. On vacations, too, children usually clamour to do as many things in one day as they can and to stay up past their usual bedtime. And, since it is vacation time, parents may decide to give in to the children's demands. A parental attitude like this, however, can lead to problems. After a sixteen-hour day of touring the amusement park, eating in a restaurant, and seeing a movie, children can experience sensory and emotional overload. They become cranky, unhappy, or even rebellious and angry.

5. Underline the two *illustration* signals in the following selection:

Supermarkets also use psychology to encourage people to buy. For example, in most supermarkets, the milk and the bread are either at opposite ends of the store or located far away from the first aisle. Even if a shopper stops at the market only for staples like these, she must pass hundreds of items in order to reach them. The odds are that instead of leaving with just a litre of milk, the shopper leaves with additional purchases as well. Special displays, such as a pyramid of canned green beans in an aisle or a large end display of cartons of paper towels, also increase sales. Because people assume that these items are a good buy, they may pick them up. However, they may not even be on sale! Store managers know that the customer is automatically attracted to a display like this, and they will use it to move an overstocked product.

6. Underline the two *conclusion* signals in the following selection:

In summary, cleaning up a computer's hard drive is always a good idea, but saving data can be trickier than it seems. Though media storage has improved over time, there are always risks. Ten years ago, a simple keystroke or two saved a small amount of data to a big, flat, flimsy five-inch floppy diskette. This was sensible and usually motivated by fears of power outages and computers crashing and losing data. Few computer users then worried about loss of speed in data-transfers or about clogged memories—they just worried about random loss of files. Unfortunately, the big floppies were fragile and easily damaged by handling or exposure to heat or cold. Then people's increasing storage needs led to the 3.5-inch diskette, which required new disk drives on home PCs. The new, smaller hard-case disks were more durable than floppies, and like most microchip technology, they stored more data in a smaller space. Still there were drawbacks: magnets could erase their content; they were still breakable; and worst of all, data saved on them degraded over unpredictable lengths of time and became impossible to retrieve. Finally two new forms of media storage appeared: the Zip disk and the CD, which seem to be great improvements on the smaller diskettes. Harder to damage and capable of holding larger volumes of information, they are major advances. But both require different drives and neither can guarantee infinite safe preservation of data. Therefore, the wisdom of maintaining a clean hard drive is not arguable, but the question of where and how long to store data still has no absolute answer.

2 TRANSITIONAL SENTENCES

Paragraph-Level Transitions

To achieve coherence at the paragraph level of your essay, use transitional material at the "entrance" and "exit" points of each paragraph. The two functions of transitions as signals and links suggest that topic sentences should signal the order chosen for the essay and should also link that paragraph's opening with the preceding paragraph.

Following are the specific uses for transitions and transitional sentences at paragraph level, as indicated in the box on page 77:

- Topic sentence transitions: signal and reinforce time sequence, emphatic order, or other order
- Topic sentence transitions: link paragraph topic with preceding paragraph's topic
- Concluding sentence transitions: link to following paragraph's topic, or suggest conclusion

Concluding sentences in body paragraphs should contain transitional material that signals finality and generally some linking transition words to carry the reader forward to the next paragraph.

Transitional, or *linking, sentences* are used between paragraphs to help tie together the supporting paragraphs in an essay, and may be topic sentences, which begin a paragraph, or final sentences, which lead the reader on to the next paragraph. Transitional sentences enable the reader to move smoothly and clearly from the idea in one paragraph to the idea in the next paragraph. Here is the linking sentence used in the essay on movie-going on pages 13–14:

> Many of the other patrons are even more of a problem than the concession stand.

The words *concession stand* remind us of the point of the previous supporting paragraph, while *Many of the other patrons* presents the point to be developed in the second supporting paragraph.

Activity

Below is a brief sentence outline of an essay. The second and third topic sentences serve as transitional, or linking, sentences. Each reminds us of the point in the preceding paragraph and announces the point to be developed in the current paragraph. In the spaces provided, add the words needed to complete the second and third topic sentences. If possible, try to write a concluding sentence that leads into the paragraphs that follow.

THESIS The most important values I learned from my parents are the importance of family support, of hard work, and of a good education.

FIRST SUPPORTING
PARAGRAPH

> First, my parents taught me that family members should stick together, especially in times of trouble . . .

<table>
<tr><td>SECOND
SUPPORTING
PARAGRAPH</td><td>In addition to teaching me about the importance of _____

_____

my parents taught me the value of _____

_____ . . . .</td></tr>
</table>

<table>
<tr><td>THIRD
SUPPORTING
PARAGRAPH</td><td>Along with the value of _____

my parents emphasized the benefits of _____

_____ . . . .</td></tr>
</table>

3 OTHER TRANSITIONAL STRUCTURES

In addition to transitions, there are three other kinds of connecting words and phrases that help tie together the specific evidence in a paper: repeated words, pronouns, and synonyms. Each will be discussed in turn.

Repeated Words

Many of us have been taught—correctly so—not to repeat ourselves in writing. However, repeating *key* words helps tie together the flow of thought in a paper. Below, repeated words remind readers of the selection's central idea.

> One reason for studying psychology is to help you deal with children. Perhaps a young daughter refuses to go to bed when parents want her to and bursts into tears at the least mention of "lights out." A little knowledge of psychology comes in handy. Offer her a choice of staying up until 7:30 p.m. with her parents or going upstairs and playing until 8:00 p.m. Since she gets to make the choice, she does not feel so powerless and will not resist. Psychology is also useful in rewarding a child for a job well done. Instead of telling a ten-year-old son what a good boy he is when he makes his own bed, tell him how neat it looks, how pleasing it is, and how proud of him you are for doing it by himself. The psychology books all say that being a good boy is much harder to live up to than doing one job well.

Pronouns

Pronouns (*he, she, it, you, they, this, that,* and others) are another way to connect ideas. Also, using pronouns in place of other words can help you avoid needless repetition. (Note, however, that pronouns should be used with care to avoid the problems described on pages 100–101.) Here is a selection that makes good use of pronouns:

Another way for people to economize at an amusement park is to bring their own food. If they pack a nourishing, well-balanced lunch of cold chicken, carrot sticks, and fruit, they will avoid having to pay high prices for hamburgers and hot dogs. They won't eat as many calories. Also, instead of filling up on soft drinks, they should bring a Thermos of iced tea. Iced tea is more refreshing than pop, and it is a great deal cheaper. Every dollar that is not spent at a refreshment stand is one that can be spent on another ride.

Synonyms

Using synonyms (words alike in meaning) can also help move the reader clearly from one thought to the next. In addition, the use of synonyms increases variety and interest by avoiding needless repetition. To strengthen your vocabulary and widen your knowledge of synonyms, use either a thesaurus or the "thesaurus" function under "tools" on your word-processing program. Note the synonyms for *method* in the following selection:

There are several methods of fundraising that work well with small organizations. One technique is to hold an auction, with everyone either contributing an item from home or obtaining a donation from a sympathetic local merchant. Because all the merchandise, including the services of the auctioneer, has been donated, the entire proceeds can be placed in the organization's treasury. A second fundraising procedure is a car wash. Club members and their children get together on a Saturday and wash all the cars in the neighbourhood for a few dollars apiece. A final, time-tested way to raise money is to hold a bake sale, with each family contributing homemade cookies, brownies, layer cakes, or cupcakes. Sold by the piece or by the box, these baked goods will satisfyingly fill both the stomach and the pocketbook.

Activity

Read the selection below and then answer the questions about it that follow:

¹When I think about my childhood in the 1930s, life today seems like the greatest of luxuries. ²In our house, we had only a wood-burning cookstove in the kitchen to keep us warm. ³In the morning, my father would get up in the icy cold, go downstairs, and light a fire in the black iron range. ⁴When he called us, I would put off leaving my warm bed until the last possible minute and then quickly grab my school clothes. ⁵The water pitcher and washing basin in my room would be layered with ice, and my breath would come out as white puffs as I ran downstairs. ⁶My sisters and I would all dress—as quickly as possible—in the chilly but bearable air of the kitchen. ⁷Our schoolroom, once we had arrived, didn't provide much relief from the cold. ⁸Students wore woollen mitts, which left their fingers free but covered their palms and wrists. ⁹Even with these, we occasionally suffered chilblains. ¹⁰The throbbing swellings on our hands made writing a painful process. ¹¹When we returned home in the afternoon, we spent all our indoor hours in the warm kitchen. ¹²We hated to

leave it at bedtime in order to make the return trip to those cold bedrooms and frigid sheets. [13]My mother made up hot water bottles and gave us hot bricks to ⬚⬚⬚ ⬚nder the covers, but nothing could eliminate the agony of that ⬚⬚⬚⬚ating cold when we first slid under the bedclothes.

⬚⬚⬚ ⬚ny times is the key word *cold* repeated? _____

⬚ ⬚⬚⬚re the pronoun that is used for *father* (sentence 4): _____

⬚⬚⬚⬚ ⬚⬚re the words in sentence 3 that are used as a synonym for *cookstove:*

_____ ; write in the words in sentence 10 that are used as a

⬚⬚⬚ for *chilblains:* _____ ; write in the word in sentence 12

⬚⬚⬚ ⬚d as a synonym for *cold:* _____ .

CONCLUSIONS, AND TITLES

So far, this chapter has discussed ways to create coherence, organize, and connect the supporting paragraphs and sentences of an essay. A well-organized and coherent essay, however, also needs a strong introductory paragraph, an effective concluding paragraph, and a good title.

INTRODUCTORY PARAGRAPH

First paragraphs are your readers' introduction to you and your ideas. As the cliché goes, "First impressions count." So here are some guidelines for that first meeting:

- Engage your readers as quickly as possible by using a choice appropriate to your subject from the methods of introduction that follow.
- Avoid too-abrupt or bald statements of your thesis in your second sentence: readers need some context, some background information—a "cushion" between their ideas and yours.
- Try this formula: Opening material → background/context material → thesis → lead-in to first paragraph.

A good introduction welcomes readers, makes them comfortable with your subject, states your thesis, and leads on to your first body paragraph. Following is a list of the functions of the parts of a well-written introductory paragraph:

1 It attracts the readers' interest, encouraging them to continue reading the essay.

2 It supplies any background information that may be needed to understand the essay.

3 It presents a thesis statement. This clear, direct statement of the main idea of the paper usually appears near the end of the introductory paragraph.

4 It indicates a plan of development. In this "preview," the major supporting points for the thesis are listed in the order in which they will be presented. In some cases, the thesis and plan of development appear in the same sentence.

However, writers sometimes choose to omit the plan of development, relying on a general "overview" phrase that suggests the support and pattern of development for the essay.

5 It concludes with a transitional sentence leading the reader into the first body paragraph.

Common Methods of Introduction

Here are some common methods of introduction. Use any one method, or a combination of methods, as appropriate to your material, to introduce your subject in an interesting way to the reader.

1 *Begin with a somewhat general statement of your topic and narrow it down to your thesis statement.* General statements ease the reader into your thesis statement by first introducing the topic. However, avoid sweeping statements like "the world these days," or "humanity's problems": no writer could handle such huge concepts. In the example below, the writer talks generally about diets and then narrows down to comments on a specific diet.

> Bookstore shelves today are crammed with dozens of different diet books. The Canadian public seems willing to try any sort of diet, especially the ones that promise instant, miraculous results. And authors are more than willing to invent new fad diets to cash in on this craze. Unfortunately, some of these fad diets are ineffective or even unsafe. One of the worst fad diets is the "Zone Diet." It is expensive, doesn't achieve the results it claims, and is a sure route to poor nutrition.

2 *Supply background information or context.* Much of your future career writing and some assignments for your professional courses will cover subject matter unfamiliar to general readers. Therefore, this introductory approach is relevant and useful. Whenever you write about a subject that is not considered "general knowledge" or "common interest," use this method. If you must explain an accounting method, analyze some technical process, or evaluate a software's operation, always give enough background information to make your thesis and support clear and understandable to readers.

> MP3 is a three-character code seen everywhere today—even phones have MP3 players. But what is an MP3? It is simply a compressed file containing audio data: music, speech, or sound effects. Sounds are compressed from earlier, larger wav files for quick downloading. MP3 compression matches twelve bytes of a wav with only a single byte in MP3 format; it removes sounds people's ears cannot usually hear. MP3s are an important part of the downsizing of media: they offer superior audio quality, they are divisible into cuts or sections, and they are very portable—just like cell phones.

3 *Start with an idea or situation that is the opposite of the one you will develop.* This approach works because your readers will be surprised, and then intrigued, by the contrast between the opening idea and the thesis that follows it.

> When I decided to return to school at age thirty-five, I wasn't at all worried about my ability to do the work. After all, I was a grown woman who had raised a family, not a confused teenager fresh out of high school. But when I started classes, I realized that those "confused teenagers" sitting around me were in much better shape for college than I was. They still had all their classroom skills in bright, shiny condition, while mine had grown rusty from disuse. I had to learn how to locate information in a library, how to write a report, and even how to speak up in class discussions.

4 *Explain the importance of your topic to the reader.* If you can convince your readers that the subject in some way applies to them, or is something they should know more about, they will want to keep reading.

> Diseases like scarlet fever and whooping cough used to kill more young children than any other illness. Today, however, child mortality due to disease has been almost completely eliminated by medical science. Instead, car accidents are the number one killer of our children. And most of the children fatally injured in car accidents were not protected by car seats, belts, or restraints of any kind. Several steps must be taken to reduce the serious dangers car accidents pose to our children.

5 *Use an incident or brief story.* Stories are naturally interesting. They appeal to a reader's curiosity. In your introduction, an anecdote will grab the reader's attention right away. The story should be brief and should be related to your main idea. The incident in the story can be something that happened to you, something you have heard or read about. Students who must write reports for courses in Business and Human Services disciplines find anecdotal introductions useful.

> On a Friday morning in a large Canadian mall, a woman buys two sweatshirts, jeans, a doormat, baby sleepers, and a leather backpack. Her bill comes to $650.00. She pays cheerfully with a platinum credit card, smiling at the clerk who sports several piercings and a headset. Not a single customer or clerk notices her. Why should they? Well, she is sixty-seven years of age, and except for the baby pajamas, she's shopping for herself at an apparently youth-oriented store. Consumer groups used to be fairly predictable. And in stores like The Gap, Old Navy, or Roots, where this woman just shopped, demographics should be even more predictable. But in the new millennium, consumer patterns are changing rapidly, and retailers must understand and respond to new age groups, new buying habits, and new merchandise mixes.

6 *Ask one or more questions.* You may simply want the reader to think about possible answers, or you may plan to answer the questions yourself later in the paper.

> What is love? How do we know that we are really in love? When we meet that special person, how can we tell that our feelings are genuine and not merely infatuation? And, if they are genuine, will these feelings last? Love, as we all know, is difficult to define. But most people agree that true and lasting love involves far more than mere physical attraction. Love involves mutual respect, the desire to give rather than take, and the feeling of being wholly at ease.

7 *Use a quotation.* A quotation can be something you have read in a book or article. It can also be something that you have heard: a popular saying or proverb ("Never give advice to a friend"), a current or recent advertising slogan ("Reach out and touch someone"), or a favourite expression used by friends or family ("My father always says . . ."). Using a quotation in your introductory paragraph lets you add someone else's voice to your own.

> "None but a mule deserves his family," says a Moroccan proverb. Last summer, when my sister and her family came to spend their two-week vacation with us, I became convinced that the proverb was right. After only three days of my family's visit, I was thoroughly sick of my brother-in-law's corny jokes, my sister's endless complaints about her boss, and their children's constant invasions of our privacy.

Activity 1

The box below summarizes the seven kinds of introduction. Read the introductions that follow it and, in the space provided, write the letter of the kind of introduction used in each case.

A. General to narrow	E. Questions
B. Starting with an opposite	F. Quotation
C. Stating importance of topic	G. Background information
D. Incident or story	

1. The ad, in full colour on a glossy magazine page, shows a beautiful kitchen with gleaming counters. In the foreground, on one of the counters, stands a shiny new food processor. Usually, a feminine hand is touching it lovingly. Around the main picture are other, smaller shots. They show mounds of perfectly sliced onion rings, thin rounds of juicy tomatoes, heaps of matchstick-sized potatoes, and piles of golden, evenly grated cheese. The ad copy tells how wonderful, how easy, food preparation will be with a processor. Don't believe it. My processor turned out to be expensive, difficult to operate, and very limited in its use.

2. People say, "You *can* often tell a book by its cover," and when it comes to certain paperbacks, this is true. When people browse in the drugstore or supermarket and see a paperback featuring an attractive young woman in a low-cut dress fleeing from a handsome dark figure in a shadowy castle, they know exactly what they're getting. Every romance novel has the same elements: an innocent heroine, an exotic setting, and a cruel but fascinating hero.

3. Canadians in the new millennium have become incredibly lazy. Instead of cooking a simple, nourishing meal, they pop a frozen dinner into the microwave. Instead of studying daily newspapers, they scan online versions or the capsule summaries on network news. Worst of all, instead of walking even a few blocks to the local convenience store, they jump into cars. This dependence on the automobile, even for short trips, has taken away a valuable experience—walking. If people drove less and walked more, they would save money, become healthier, and discover fascinating things about their surroundings.

Activity 2

In groups or on your own, write introductory paragraphs on any three of the following topics. Follow the "introductory paragraph formula" at the beginning of this section, and use three *different* methods of introduction. Be sure your method suits your subject.

1. Computer viruses
2. Daycare problems
3. Student newspapers
4. First-semester challenges
5. Online courses
6. The best things in life . . .

CONCLUDING PARAGRAPH

A concluding paragraph is your chance to remind the reader of your thesis idea, bring the paper to a natural and graceful end, and allow readers to "return to their own thoughts."

Common Methods of Conclusion

Any one of the methods below, or a combination of methods, may be used to round off your paper.

1 *End with a summary and final thought.* When armed forces instructors train new recruits, each of their lessons follows a three-step formula:

a Tell them what you're going to tell them.

b Tell them.

c Tell them what you've told them.

An essay that ends with a summary is similar: after you have stated your thesis ("Tell them what you're going to tell them") and supported it ("Tell them"), you restate the thesis and supporting points ("Tell them what you've told them"). Don't, however, use the exact wording you used before; instead, reinforce how you arrived at your thesis. Here is a summary conclusion:

> Catalogue shopping at home, then, has several advantages. Such shopping is convenient, saves consumers money, and saves time. It is not surprising that growing numbers of devoted catalogue shoppers are welcoming those full-colour mail brochures that offer everything from turnip seeds to televisions.

Note that the summary is accompanied by a final comment that "rounds off" and broadens the scope of the paper and brings the discussion to a close. This combination of a summary and a final thought is the most common method of concluding an essay.

2 *Include a thought-provoking question or short series of questions.* A question grabs the reader's attention. It is a direct appeal to your reader to think further about what you have written. A question should follow logically from the points you have already made in the paper. A question must deal with one of these areas:

a Why the subject of your paper is important

b What might happen in the future

c What should be done about this subject

d Which choice should be made

Your conclusion may provide an answer to your question. Be sure, though, that the question is closely related to your thesis. Here is an example:

> What, then, happens now in the twenty-first century when most of the population will be over sixty years old? Retirement policies may change dramatically, with the age-sixty-five testimonial dinner and gold watch postponed for five or ten years. Even television will change as the Metamucil generation replaces the Pepsi generation. Glamorous grey-haired models might sell everything from toilet paper to televisions. New soap operas and situation comedies will reveal the secrets of the "sunset years." It will be a different world indeed when the young find themselves outnumbered.

3 *End with a prediction or recommendation.* Like questions, predictions and recommendations also involve your readers. A prediction states what may happen in the future:

> If people stopped to think before acquiring pets, there would be fewer instances of cruelty to animals. Many times, it is the people who adopt pets without considering the expense and responsibility involved who mistreat and neglect their animals. Pets are living creatures. They do not deserve to be treated as carelessly as one would treat a stuffed toy.

A recommendation suggests what should be done about a situation or problem:

> Stereotypes such as the helpless homemaker, harried female executive, and dotty grandma are insulting enough to begin with. In magazine ads or television commercials, they become even more insulting. Such hackneyed caricatures of women are not just the objects of derisive humour, these stereotypes now pitch a range of products to an unsuspecting public. Consumers should boycott companies whose advertising continues to use such stereotypes.

Activity

In the space provided, note whether each concluding paragraph ends with a summary and final thought (write *S* in the space), ends with a prediction or recommendation (write *P/R*), or ends with a question (write *Q*).

_____   1. Disappointments are unwelcome, but regular, visitors to everyone's life. We can feel depressed about them, or we can try to escape from them. The best thing, though, is to accept a disappointment and then try to use it somehow: step over the unwelcome visitor and then get on with life.

_____   2. Holidays, it is clear, are often not the fulfilling experiences they are supposed to be. They can, in fact, be very stressful. But would we rather have a holiday-free calendar?

_____   3. Some people dream of starring roles, their names in lights, and their pictures on the cover of *People* magazine. I'm not one of them, though. A famous person gives up private life, feels pressured all the time, and is never completely safe. So let someone else have that cover story. I'd rather lead an ordinary but calm life than a stress-filled one.

TITLES

A title is usually a very brief summary of what your paper is about. It is often no more than several words, and guides your audience toward the essay that will follow. You may find it easier to write the title *after* you have completed your paper.

Following is an introductory paragraph for one of the essays in this text, along with its title.

Introductory Paragraph

> Schools divide people into categories. From first grade on up, students are labelled "advanced" or "deprived" or "remedial" or "antisocial." Students pigeonhole their fellow students, too. We've all known the "brain," the "jock," the "dummy," and the "teacher's pet." In most cases, these narrow labels are misleading and inaccurate. But there is one label for a certain type of college student that says it all: "zombie."

Title: Student Zombies

Do not underline the title or put quotation marks around it. On the other hand, you should capitalize all but small connecting words in the title. Skip a space between the title and the first line of the text. (See "Manuscript Form," pages 420–421.)

Activity

Write an appropriate title for the paragraph that follows.

> When people see rock-concert audiences only on television or in newspaper photos, the audiences at these events may all seem to be excited teenagers. However, attending a few rock shows would show people that several kinds of ticket-buyers make up the crowd. At any concert, there are usually the typical fan, the out-of-place person, and the troublemaker.

Title: _____

PRACTICE IN ORGANIZING AND CONNECTING SPECIFIC EVIDENCE

You now know the third step in effective writing: organizing the specific evidence used to support the thesis of a paper. This closing section will expand and strengthen your understanding of the third step in writing. You will work through the following series of activities:

1 Organizing through time or emphatic order

2 Providing transitions

3 Identifying transitions and other connecting words

4 Completing the transitional sentences

5 Identifying introductions and conclusions

1 ORGANIZING THROUGH TIME OR EMPHATIC ORDER

Activity 1

Use **time order** to organize the scrambled lists of supporting ideas below. Write *1* beside the supporting idea that should come first in time, *2* beside the idea that logically follows, and *3* beside the idea that comes last in time.

1. **Thesis:**   When I was a child, Disney movies frightened me more than any other kind.

    _____   As a five-year-old, I was terrified by the video of *The Little Mermaid* with a nasty octopus-witch threatening poor Ariel.

_____ Although I saw *Bambi* when I was old enough to begin poking fun at "baby movies," the scene during which Bambi's mother is killed has stayed with me to this day.

_____ About a year after seeing *The Little Mermaid*, I gripped my seat in anticipation as the new versions of *Fantasia* appeared on screen.

2. **Thesis:** Applying for unemployment benefits was a confusing, frustrating experience.

_____ It was difficult to find both the office and a place to park.

_____ When I finally reached the head of the line after four hours of waiting, the clerk had problems processing my claim.

_____ There was no one to direct or help me when I entered the large office, which was packed with people.

Activity 2

Use **emphatic order**, or order of importance, to arrange the following scrambled lists of supporting ideas. For each thesis, write *1* in the blank beside the point that is perhaps less important or interesting than the other two, *2* beside the point that appears more important or interesting, and *3* beside the point that should be most emphasized.

1. **Thesis:** My after-school job has been an invaluable part of my life this year.

_____ Better yet, it has taught me how to get along with many kinds of people.

_____ Since it's in the morning, it usually keeps me from staying up too late.

_____ Without it, I would have had to drop out of school.

2. **Thesis:** We received some odd gifts for our wedding.

_____ The winner in the odd-gift category was a large wooden box with no apparent purpose or function.

_____ Someone gave us a gift certificate for a massage.

_____ Even stranger, my uncle gave me his favourite bowling ball.

2 PROVIDING TRANSITIONS

Activity

In the spaces provided, add appropriate transitions to tie together the sentences and ideas in the following essay. Draw from the words given in the boxes above the paragraphs. Use each word only once.

Annoying People

Some people keep "enemies lists" of all the people they don't especially   **1**
like. I'm ashamed to confess it, but I, too, have an enemies list—a mental one.
On this list are all the people I would gladly live without, the ones who cause
my blood pressure to rise to the boiling point. The top three places on the list
go to people with annoying nervous habits, people who talk in movie theatres,
and people who talk on car phones while driving.

For example	First of all	Another	However

_____ , there are the people with annoying nervous habits.   **2**

_____ , there are the ones who make faces. When in deep
thought, they twitch, squint, and frown, and they can be a real distraction

when I'm trying to concentrate during an exam. _____ type of
nervous character makes useless designs. These people bend paper clips into
abstract sculptures or string the clips into necklaces as they talk.

_____ , neither of these groups is as bad as the people who
make noises. These individuals, when they are feeling uncomfortable, bite
their fingernails or crack their knuckles. If they have a pencil in their hands,
they tap it rhythmically against whatever surface is handy—a desk, a book, a
head. Lacking a pencil to play with, they jingle the loose change or keys in
their pockets. These people make me wish I were hard of hearing.

On the contrary	Then	As a result	After	second

A _____ category of people I would gladly do away with is   **3**
those people who talk in movie theatres. These people are not content to sit back,

relax, and enjoy the film they have paid to see. _____ , they
feel compelled to comment loudly on everything, from the hero's hairstyle to

the appropriateness of the background music. _____ , no one

hears a word of any dialogue except theirs. _____ they have

been in the theatre for a while, their interest in the movie may fade.

_____ they will start discussing other things, and the people
around them will be treated to an instant replay of the last family scandal or
soap opera episode. These stories may be entertaining, but they don't belong in
a movie theatre.

In addition	However	Last of all

_____, there are the people who talk on the phone while **4** they're driving. One of the things that irritates me about them is they seem to be showing off. They're saying, "Look at me! I'm so important I have to make

phone calls in my *car.*" _____, such behaviour is just plain dangerous. Instead of concentrating on adjusting carefully to ever-changing traffic conditions, they're weaving all over the road or getting much too close to the car in front of them as they gossip with a friend, make doctor's appointments, or order pizza.

So long as murder remains illegal, the nervous twitchers, movie talkers, **5** and car-phone users of the world are safe from me. _____ if ever I am granted the power of life or death, these people had better think twice about annoying me. They might not have long to live.

3 IDENTIFYING TRANSITIONS AND OTHER TRANSITIONAL STRUCTURES

Activity

The following items use connecting words to help tie ideas together. The connecting words you are to identify are set off in italics. In the space, write *T* for *transition*, *RW* for *repeated word*, *S* for *synonym*, or *P* for *pronoun*.

_____   1. Maurizio wears a puffy, quilted, down-filled jacket. In this *garment*, he resembles a stack of inflated inner tubes.

_____   2. Plants like poinsettias and mistletoe are pretty. *They* are also poisonous.

_____   3. A strip of strong cloth can be used as an emergency fan-belt replacement. *In addition*, a roll of duct tape can be used to patch a leaky hose temporarily.

_____   4. I'm always losing my soft contact lenses, which resemble little circles of thick Saran Wrap. One day I dropped both of *them* into a cup of hot tea.

_____   5. The moulded plastic chairs in the classrooms are hard and uncomfortable. When I sit in one of these *chairs*, I feel as if I were sitting in a bucket.

_____   6. One way to tell if your skin is ageing is to pinch a fold of skin on the back of your hand. If *it* doesn't smooth out quickly, your skin is losing its youthful tone.

4 COMPLETING TRANSITIONAL SENTENCES

Activity

Following are brief sentence outlines from two essays. In each outline, the second and third topic sentences serve as transitional, or linking, sentences. Each reminds us of the point in the preceding paragraph and announces the point to be developed in the current paragraph. In the spaces provided, add the words needed to complete the second and third topic sentences.

THESIS 1   Cheaper cost, greater comfort, and superior electronic technology make watching football at home more enjoyable than attending a game at the stadium.

FIRST SUPPORTING PARAGRAPH

> For one thing, watching the game on TV eliminates the cost of attending the game. . . .

SECOND SUPPORTING PARAGRAPH

> In addition to saving me money, watching the game at home is more _____ than sitting in a stadium. . . .

THIRD SUPPORTING PARAGRAPH

> Even more important than _____ and _____, though, is the _____, which makes a televised game better than the "real thing.". . .

THESIS 2   In order to set up a daycare centre in your home, you must make sure your house will conform to provincial and municipal regulations, obtain the necessary legal permits, and advertise your service in the right places.

FIRST SUPPORTING PARAGRAPH

> First of all, as a potential operator of a home daycare centre, you must make sure your house will conform to provincial and municipal regulations. . . .

SECOND SUPPORTING PARAGRAPH

> After making certain that _____ _____, you must obtain _____ . . . .

THIRD SUPPORTING PARAGRAPH

> Finally, once you have the necessary _____ you can begin to _____.

5 IDENTIFYING INTRODUCTIONS AND CONCLUSIONS

Activity

In the box below are seven common kinds of introductions and three common kinds of conclusions. After reading the three pairs of introductory and concluding paragraphs that follow, use the space provided to write the number of the kind of introduction and conclusion used in each case.

Introductions	*Conclusions*
1. General to narrow	8. Summary and final thought
2. Starting with an opposite	9. Question(s)
3. Stating importance of topic	10. Prediction or recommendation
4. Incident or story	
5. Question(s)	
6. Quotation	
7. Supplying background information	

Pair 1

_____

Shortly before Easter, our local elementary school sponsored a fundraising event at which classroom pets and their babies—hamsters, guinea pigs, and baby chicks—were available for adoption. Afterward, as I was driving home, I saw a hand drop a baby hamster out of the car ahead of me. I couldn't avoid running over the tiny creature. One of the parents had taken the pet, regretted the decision, and decided to get rid of it. Such people have never stopped to consider the several real obligations involved in owning a pet.

_____

A pet cannot be thrown onto a trash heap when it is no longer wanted or tossed into a closet if it begins to bore its owner. A pet, like us, is a living thing that needs physical care, affection, and respect. Would-be owners, therefore, should think seriously about their responsibilities before they acquire a pet.

Pair 2

_____

What would life be like if we could read each other's minds? Would communications be instantaneous and perfectly clear? These questions will never be answered unless mental telepathy becomes a fact of life. Until then, we will have to make do with less perfect means of communication. Letters, e-mail, telephone calls, and face-to-face conversations do have serious drawbacks.

_____

Letters, e-mail, phone calls, or conversations cannot guarantee perfect communication. With all our sophisticated skills, we human beings often communicate less effectively than howling wolves or chattering monkeys. Even if we were able to read each other's minds, we'd probably still find some way to foul up the message.

Pair 3

_____

"Perfection in others is hard to love," some wise person said. That individual obviously knew the problems faced by siblings cursed with older brothers or sisters who are models of perfection. All our lives, my older sister, Shelley, and I have been compared. Unfortunately, in competition with my sister's virtues, my looks, talents, and accomplishments always ended up on the losing side.

_____

Although I always lost in the sibling contests of looks, talents, and accomplishments, Shelley and I have somehow managed not to turn into deadly enemies. Feeling like the ugly duckling of the family, in fact, helped me to develop a drive to succeed and a sense of humour. In our sibling rivalry, we both managed to win.

REVIEWING THE LEARNING OUTCOMES FOR CHAPTER 4

To ensure that you have met the learning outcomes for this chapter, answer the following questions:

- What are the two most common methods for organizing supporting points in an essay?
- What are the three levels at which an essay must be coherent?
- What techniques are used to achieve coherence at the paragraph level?
- What are the two functions of transitional structures?
- How many methods exist for making an essay coherent at the sentence level? Explain how three of these methods work.
- What are the seven common methods of writing introductions?
- What are three common methods of writing conclusions?

The Fourth Step in Essay Writing

LEARNING OUTCOMES

After learning the concepts and techniques for successful revision and editing in this chapter, and after working through its exercises, you will

- Be able to revise your sentences so that they flow smoothly and clearly
- Be prepared to work on competence in editing and proofreading so that your error-free sentences carry your points and details effectively

The first four chapters of this book emphasized and demonstrated three of the goals for effective essay writing: unity, support, and coherence. These are essential qualities for the content and structure of good essays. Now this chapter will introduce you to the **fourth goal for essay writing: effective sentence skills**. Effective and correctly structured sentences help guarantee your reader's ready understanding of your point and support.

- **Revise** for smooth sentence flow.
- **Edit** and **proofread** for mistakes in grammar, punctuation, and spelling.

REVISING SENTENCES

The following strategies will help you to revise your sentences effectively.

- Use parallelism.
- Use a consistent point of view.
- Use specific words.
- Use active verbs.
- Use concise words.
- Vary your sentences.

USE PARALLELISM

Words and phrases in a pair, a series, or a list should have parallel structure. By balancing the items in a pair or a series so that they have the same grammatical structure, you will make the sentence clearer and easier to read. Notice how the parallel sentences that follow read more smoothly than the non-parallel ones.

Non-parallel (Not Balanced)	*Parallel (Balanced)*
My job includes checking the inventory, initialling the orders, and to *call* the suppliers.	My job includes checking the inventory, initialling the orders, and calling the suppliers. (A balanced series of participles or -*ing* words: *checking, initialling, calling*)
The game-show contestant was told to be cheerful, charming, and *with enthusiasm.*	The game-show contestant was told to be cheerful, charming, and enthusiastic. (A balanced series of adjectives or descriptive words: *cheerful, charming, enthusiastic*)
Grandmother likes to read mystery novels, to do needlepoint, and *browsing* the Internet on her computer.	Grandmother likes to read mystery novels, to do needlepoint, and to browse the Internet on her computer. (A balanced series of infinitives or *to* verb forms: *to read, to do, to browse*)
We painted the trim in the living room; *the wallpaper was put up by a professional.*	We painted the trim in the living room; a professional put up the wallpaper. (Balanced verbs and word order: *We painted . . . ; a professional put up . . .*)

Assembling balanced sentences is not a skill to worry about when writing first drafts. But when you rewrite, you should try to put matching words and ideas into matching structures. Errors in parallel structure often show up in lists of items within sentences. You may find yourself using such lists in your thesis statements as you set out your three supporting ideas; try to make your ideas "match grammatically." Such parallelism will improve your writing style.

Activity 1

Cross out and revise the unbalanced part of each of the following sentences.

Example   Chocolate makes me gain weight, lose my appetite, and ~~breaking~~ out in hives. *break*

1. The novelty store sells hand buzzers, plastic fangs, and insects that are fake.

2. Many people share the same three great fears: being in high places, working with numbers, and speeches.

3. To decide on a career, students should think closely about their interests, hobbies, and what they are skilled at.

4. At the body shop, the car was sanded down to the bare metal, painted with primer, and red enamel was sprayed on.

5. In order to become a dancer, Tracy is taking lessons, working in amateur shows, and auditioned for professional companies.

6. Navid's last job offered security; a better chance for advancement is offered by his new job.

7. People in today's world often try to avoid silence, whether on the job, in school, or when relaxing at home.

8. If we're not careful, we'll leave the next generation polluted air, contaminated water, and forests that are dying.

Activity 2

Revise the following thesis statements so that each flows smoothly and lists its supporting points in parallel form.

1. E-mail is an asset to communication today because of its speed and convenience, online conferencing which lets people meet without travelling, and it allows for graphics and sounds to be attached.

2. Case studies in classes really bring lessons to life: students learn from real-life situations, really interesting, and make group work fun.

3. Working at each job in a kitchen brigade is a must for anyone who hopes to be a head chef responsible for daily preparation, being really good at basic sauces, and then working on menu design and budgets.

USE A CONSISTENT POINT OF VIEW

Consistent Verb Tenses

Do not shift verb tenses unnecessarily. Keep a consistent sense of time in your essay. (For information about verb tenses, refer to Chapter 28 of Part 4 of this text.) If you begin writing a paper in the present tense, do not shift suddenly to the past. If you begin in the past, do not shift without reason to the present. Notice the inconsistent verb tenses in the following example:

> Jean *punched* down the risen yeast dough in the bowl. Then she *dumps* it onto the floured worktable and *kneaded* it into a smooth, shiny ball.

The verbs must be consistently in the **present tense:**

> Jean *punches* down the risen yeast dough in the bowl. Then she *dumps* it onto the floured worktable and *kneads* it into a smooth, shiny ball.

Or the verbs must be consistently in the **past tense:**

> Jean *punched* down the risen yeast dough in the bowl. Then she *dumped* it onto the floured worktable and *kneaded* it into a smooth, shiny ball.

Activity

Make the verbs in each sentence consistent with the *first* verb used. Cross out the incorrect verb and write the correct form in the space at the left.

_____ran_____   ***Example***   Aunt Helen tried to kiss her little nephew, but he ~~runs~~ out of the room.

_____   1. An aggressive news photographer knocked a reporter to the ground as the stars arrive for the MuchMusic Video Awards.

_____   2. The winning wheelchair racer in the marathon slumped back in exhaustion and asks for some ice to soothe his blistered hands.

_____   3. On the TV commercial for mail-order kitchen knives, an actor cuts a tree branch in half and sliced an aluminum can into ribbons.

_____   4. "Martial arts movies are so incredible," said Sean, "they're more than just action, they showed real ethical values."

_____   5. The SUV swerved around the corner, went up on two wheels, and tips over on its side.

_____   6. In a zero-gravity atmosphere, water breaks up into droplets and floated around in space.

_____   7. Mike ripped open the bag of cheese puffs with his teeth, grabs handfuls of the salty orange squiggles, and stuffed them into his mouth.

_____   8. When the ice storm struck eastern Canada in 1998, several provinces are without electricity and many services for weeks.

CONSISTENT PRONOUN POINT OF VIEW

When writing a paper, you should not shift your point of view unnecessarily. Be consistent in your use of first-, second-, or third-person pronouns.

	Singular	*Plural*
First-person pronouns	I (my, mine, me)	we (our, us)
Second-person pronouns	you (your)	you (your)
Third-person pronouns	he (his, him)	they (their, them)
	she (her)	
	it (its)	

Note: Any person, place, or thing, as well as any indefinite pronoun such as *one, anyone, someone,* and so on (page 400), is a third-person word.

For instance, if you start writing in the first person, *I,* do not jump suddenly to the second person, *you.* Or if you are writing in the third person, *they,* do not shift unexpectedly to *you. Remember,* in English we do not always mean *you* literally. Look at the examples.

Inconsistent	*Consistent*
One of the fringe benefits of my job is that **you** can use a company credit card for gas. (The most common mistake people make is to let a *you* slip into their writing after they start with another pronoun.)	One of the fringe benefits of my job is that **I** can use a company credit card for gas.
Though **we** like most of **our** neighbours, there are a few **you** can't get along with. (The writer begins with the first-person pronouns *we* and *our*, but then shifts to the second-person *you*.)	Though **we** like most of **our** neighbours, there are a few **we** can't get along with.

Activity

Cross out inconsistent pronouns in the following sentences and revise with the correct form of the pronoun above each crossed-out word.

Example   When I examined the used car, ~~you~~ could see that one of the front
fenders had been replaced.

1. Many people are ignorant of side effects that diets can have on your health.

2. When I buy lipstick or nail polish, you never know how the colour will actually look.

3. It is expensive for us to take public transportation to work every day, but what choice do you have if you can't afford a car?

4. During the border crisis, each country refused to change their aggressive stance.

5. If you want to do well in this course, one should plan on attending every day.

6. One of the things I love about my new apartment is that you can own a pet.

7. Angelina refuses to eat pepperoni pizza because she says it gives you indigestion.

8. It's hard for us to keep taking student loans, but you can't afford tuition without them.

USE SPECIFIC WORDS 1

To be an effective writer, you must use specific rather than general words. Specific words create pictures in the reader's mind. They help capture interest and make your meaning clear.

Activity

Revise the following sentences, changing vague, indefinite words into sharp, specific ones.

Example   *Several of our appliances* broke down at the same time.

Our washer, refrigerator, and television broke down at the same time.

1. *Salty snacks* are my diet downfall.

_____

_____

_____

2. I swept aside the *things* on my desk in order to spread out the road map.

_____

_____

_____

3. Our neighbour's family room has *a lot of electronic equipment.*

_____

_____

_____

4. *Several sections* of the newspaper were missing.

_____

_____

_____

USE SPECIFIC WORDS 2

Again, you will practise changing vague, indefinite writing into lively, image-filled writing that captures the reader's interest and makes your meaning clear.

Compare the following sentences:

General

She walked down the street.
Animals came into the space.
The man signed the paper.

Specific

Anne wandered slowly along Rogers Lane.
Hungry lions padded silently into the sawdust-covered arena.
The biology teacher hastily scribbled his name on the course withdrawal slip.

The specific sentences create clear pictures in our minds. The details show us exactly what has happened. Here are four ways to make your sentences specific.

1 Use exact names.

He sold his *bike.*
Vince sold his *Honda.*

2 Use lively verbs.

The flag *moved* in the breeze.
The flag *fluttered* in the breeze.

3 Use descriptive words (modifiers) before nouns.

A man strained to lift the crate.
A *heavyset, perspiring* man strained to lift the *heavy wooden* crate.

4 Use words that relate to the senses—sight, hearing, taste, smell, touch.

That woman jogs three kilometres a day.
That *fragile-looking, grey-haired* woman jogs three kilometres a day. *(Sight)*

A noise told the crowd that there were two minutes left to play.
A *piercing whistle* told the *cheering* crowd that there were two minutes left to play. *(Hearing)*

When he returned, all he found in the refrigerator was bread and milk.
When he returned, all he found in the refrigerator was *stale* bread and *sour* milk. *(Taste)*

Neil stroked the kitten's fur until he felt its tiny claws on his hand.
Neil stroked the kitten's *velvety* fur until he felt its tiny, *needle-sharp* claws on his hand. *(Touch)*

Sonia placed a sachet in her bureau drawer.
Sonia placed a *lilac-scented* sachet in her bureau drawer. *(Smell)*

Activity

With the help of the methods described above, add specific details to the five sentences that follow. Note the two examples.

Example	The person got off the bus.
	The teenage boy bounded down the steps of the shiny yellow
	school bus.
Example	She worked hard all summer.
	All summer, Eva sorted peaches and blueberries in the hot, noisy
	canning factory.

1. The car would not start.

   _____

   _____

2. The test was difficult.

   _____

   _____

3. The boy was tired.

   _____

   _____

4. My room needs cleaning.

   _____

   _____

5. A vehicle blocked traffic.

   _____

   _____

USE ACTIVE VERBS

When the subject of a sentence performs the action of the verb, the verb is in the *active voice.* When the subject of a sentence receives the action of a verb, the verb is in the *passive voice.*

The passive form of a verb consists of a form of the verb to be *(am, is, are, was, were)* and the past participle of the main verb (which is usually the same as its past tense form). In general, active verbs are more effective than passive ones. Active verbs give your writing a simpler and more vigorous style.

Passive	*Active*
The computer *was turned on* by Aaron.	Aaron *turned on* the computer.
The car's air conditioner *was fixed* by the mechanic.	The mechanic *fixed* the car's air conditioner.

Activity

Revise the following sentences, changing verbs from the passive to the active voice and making any other word changes necessary.

Example   Fruits and vegetables are painted often by artists.

Artists often paint fruits and vegetables.

1. Many unhealthy foods are included in the typical Canadian diet.

   _____

2. The family picnic was invaded by hundreds of biting ants.

   _____

3. Antibiotics are used by doctors to treat many infections.

   _____

4. The fatal traffic accident was caused by a drunk driver.

   _____

USE CONCISE WORDS

Wordiness—using more words than necessary to express a meaning—is often a sign of lazy or careless writing. Your readers may resent the extra time and energy they must spend when you have not done the work needed to make your writing direct and concise.

Here are two examples of wordy sentences:

In this paper, I am planning to describe the hobby that I enjoy of collecting old comic books.
In Ben's opinion, he thinks that digital television will change and alter our lives in the future.

Omitting needless words improves these sentences:

I enjoy collecting old comic books.
Ben thinks that digital television will change our lives.

Following is a list of some wordy expressions that could be reduced to single words.

Wordy Form	Short Form
at the present time	now
in the event that	if
in the near future	soon
due to the fact that	because
for the reason that	because
is able to	can
in every instance	always
in this day and age	today
during the time that	while
a large number of	many
big in size	big
red in colour	red
five in number	five
commute back and forth	commute
postponed until later	postponed

Activity

Revise the following sentences, omitting needless words.

1. In conclusion, I would like to end my essay by summarizing each of the major points that were covered within my paper.

   _____

   _____

2. Controlling the quality and level of the television shows that children watch is a continuing challenge to parents that they must meet on a daily basis.

   _____

   _____

3. In general, I am the sort of person who tends to be shy, especially in large crowds or with strangers I don't know well.

   _____

   _____

4. Someone who is analyzing magazine advertising can find hidden messages that, once uncovered, are seen to be clever and persuasive.

   _____

   _____

AVOID PRETENTIOUS WORDS

Some people feel that they can improve their writing by using fancy and elevated words rather than more simple and natural words. Artificial and stilted language obscures meaning more often than it communicates clearly. Here are some unnatural-sounding sentences:

> It was a splendid opportunity to get some slumber.
> The officer apprehended the intoxicated operator of the vehicle.
> This establishment sells women's apparel and children's garments.

The same thoughts can be expressed more clearly and effectively by using plain, natural language, as below:

> It was a good chance to get some sleep.
> The officer arrested the car's drunken driver.
> This store sells women's and children's clothes.

Here is a list of some other inflated words and the simpler words that could replace them:

Inflated Words	Simpler Words
subsequent to	after
finalize	finish
transmit	send
facilitate	help
component	part
initiate	begin
delineate	describe
manifested	shown
to endeavour	to try

Activity

Cross out the artificial words in each sentence. Then substitute clear, simple language for the artificial words.

Example   The ~~conflagration~~ was ~~initiated~~ by an arsonist.

The fire was started by an arsonist.

1. Fernando and his brother do not interrelate in a harmonious manner.

   _____

2. The meaning of the movie's conclusion eluded my comprehension.

   _____

3. The departmental conference will commence promptly at two o'clock.

   _____

4. A man dressed in odd attire accosted me on the street.

   _____

5. When my writing implement malfunctioned, I asked the professor for another.

   _____

VARY YOUR SENTENCES

One part of effective writing is to vary the kinds of sentences you write. If every sentence follows the same pattern, writing may become monotonous to read. Although your main goal is always to write clear, straightforward sentences, you may occasionally wish to emphasize some idea within a sentence more than another idea. Following are four ways to create variety and interest in your writing style, including coordination and subordination—two important techniques for achieving different kinds of emphasis in writing.

1 Add a second complete thought (coordination).

2 Add a dependent thought (subordination).

3 Begin with a special opening word or phrase.

4 Place adjectives or verbs in a series.

Revise by Adding a Second Complete Thought

When you add a second complete thought to a simple sentence, the result is a *compound* (or double) sentence, which gives *equal weight to two closely related ideas*. The two complete statements in a compound sentence are usually connected by a comma plus a joining or coordinating word *(and, but, for, or, nor, so, yet)*. The technique of showing that ideas have equal importance is called *coordination*. Following are compound sentences where the sentence contains two ideas that the writer considers equal in importance.

> Greg worked on the engine for three hours, but the car still wouldn't start.
> Bananas were on sale this week, so I bought a bunch for the children's lunches.
> We laced up our roller skates, and then we moved cautiously onto the rink.

Activity

Combine the following pairs of simple sentences into compound sentences. Use a comma and a logical joining word *(and, but, for, so)* to connect each pair of statements.

Example   The weather was cold and windy.
Al brought a thick blanket to the football game.

The weather was cold and windy, so Al brought a thick blanket to

the football game.

1. My son can't eat peanut butter snacks or sandwiches.
   He is allergic to peanuts.

   _____

   _____

2. I tried to sleep.
   The thought of tomorrow's math exam kept me awake.

   _____

   _____

3. This coffee bar has its own bakery.
   It has take-out service as well.

   _____

   _____

4. The cardboard storage boxes were soggy.
   Rainwater had seeped into the basement during the storm.

_____

_____

Revise by Adding a Dependent Thought

When you add a dependent thought to a simple sentence, the result is a *complex* sentence. A *complex* sentence is used when you want to *emphasize one idea over another*. The dependent thought begins with one of the following subordinating words:

after	if, even if	when, whenever
although, though	in order that	where, wherever
as	since	whether
because	that, so that	which, whichever
before	unless	while
even though	until	who
how	what, whatever	whose

Look at the following complex sentence:

Although the exam room was very quiet, I still couldn't concentrate.

The idea that the writer wishes to emphasize here—*I still couldn't concentrate*—is expressed as a complete thought. The less important idea—*Although the exam room was very quiet*—is subordinated to the complete thought. The technique of *giving one idea less emphasis than another* is called subordination.

Following are other examples of complex sentences. In each case, the part starting with the dependent word is the less emphasized part of the sentence.

Even though I was tired, I stayed up to watch the horror movie.
Before I take a bath, I check for spiders in the tub.
When Ivy feels nervous, she pulls on her earlobe.

Activity

Use logical subordinating words to combine the following pairs of simple sentences into sentences that contain a dependent thought. Place a comma after a dependent statement when it starts the sentence.

Example   Rita bit into the hard taffy.
                 She broke a filling.

When Rita bit into the hard taffy, she broke a filling.
_____

1. I had forgotten to lock the front door.
   I had to drive back to the house.

   _____

   _____

2. The bear turned over the rotten log.
   Fat white grubs crawled in every direction.

   _____

   _____

3. Kevin had sent away for a set of tools.
   He changed his mind about spending the money.

   _____

   _____

4. Some people are allergic to wool.
   They buy only sweaters made from synthetic fibres.

   _____

   _____

Revise by Beginning with a Special Opening Word or Phrase

Among the special openers that can be used to start sentences are

1 Past participles of verbs, or *-ed* words

2 Present participles of verbs, or *-ing* words

3 Adverbs, or *-ly* words

4 Infinitive forms of verbs, or *to* word groups

5 Prepositional phrases

Here are examples of all five kinds of openers:

***-ed* word**	Concerned about his son's fever, Paul called a doctor.
***-ing* word**	Humming softly, the woman browsed through the rack of dresses.
***-ly* word**	Hesitantly, Winston approached the instructor's desk.
***to* word group**	To protect her hair, Eva uses the lowest setting on her blow dryer.
Prepositional phrase	During the exam, drops of water fell from the ceiling.

Activity

Combine each of the following pairs of simple sentences into one sentence by using the opener shown at the left and omitting repeated words. Use a comma to set off the opener from the rest of the sentence.

Example   *-ing* word   The pelican scooped small fish into its baggy bill. It dipped into the waves.

Dipping into the waves, the pelican scooped small fish into its baggy bill.

-LY WORD   1. Amber signed the repair contract.
She was reluctant.

_____

_____

TO WORD GROUP   2. The interns volunteered to work overtime.
They wanted to improve their chances of promotion.

_____

_____

PREPOSITIONAL   3. The accused murderer grinned at the witnesses.
PHRASE   He did this during the trial.

_____

_____

-ED WORD   4. The vet's office was noisy and confusing.
It was crowded with nervous pets.

_____

_____

-ING WORD   5. Ryan tried to find something worth watching.
He flipped from channel to channel.

_____

_____

Revise by Placing Adjectives or Verbs in a Series

Various parts of a sentence may be placed in a series. Among these parts are adjectives (descriptive words) and verbs. Here are examples of both in a series:

Adjectives

I gently applied a *sticky new* Band-Aid to the *deep, ragged* cut on my finger.

Verbs

The truck *bounced* off a guardrail, *sideswiped* a tree, and *plunged* down the embankment.

Activity

Combine the simple sentences into one sentence by using adjectives or verbs in a series and by omitting repeated words. In most cases, use a comma between the adjectives or verbs in a series.

Example   Scott spun the basketball on one finger.
He rolled it along his arms.
He dribbled it between his legs.

Scott spun the basketball on one finger, rolled it along his arms,

and dribbled it between his legs.

1. The baby toddled across the rug.
   He picked up a button.
   He put the button in his mouth.

   _____

   _____

2. Water dribbled out of the tap.
   The water was brown.
   The water was foul-tasting.
   The tap was rusty.
   The tap was metal.

   _____

   _____

3. By 6 a.m. I had read the textbook chapter.
   I had taken notes on it.
   I had studied the notes.
   I had drunk eight cups of coffee.

   _____

   _____

4. The exterminator approached the wasps' nests hanging under the eaves.
   The nests were large.
   The nests were papery.
   The eaves were old.
   The eaves were wooden.

   _____

   _____

EDITING SENTENCES

After revising sentences in a paper so that they flow smoothly and clearly, you need to edit the paper for mistakes in grammar, punctuation, mechanics, usage, and spelling. Even if a paper is otherwise well written, it will make an unfavourable impression on readers if it contains such mistakes. To edit a paper, check it against the agreed-upon rules or conventions of written English—simply called *sentence skills* in this book. Here are the most common of these conventions, followed by pages in this text where these matters are covered:

1 Write complete sentences rather than fragments. (361–372)

2 Do not write run-ons. (373–382)

3 Use verb forms correctly. (383–388)

4 Make sure that subject, verbs, and pronouns agree. (389–393)

5 Eliminate faulty modifiers. (413–419)

6 Use pronoun forms correctly. (399–403)

7 Use capital letters where needed. (422–427)

8 Use the following marks of punctuation correctly: apostrophe, quotation marks, comma, semicolon, colon, hyphen, dash, parentheses. (431–453)

9 Use correct manuscript form. (420–421)

10 Eliminate slang and clichés. (462–465)

11 Eliminate careless errors. (454–461)

These sentence skills are treated in detail in Part 4 of this book, and they can be referred to easily as needed. Both the list of sentence skills on the inside front cover of this book and the correction symbols on the inside back cover include page references so that you can turn quickly to any skill you want to check.

Proofreading and editing are necessary skills. Only by your practising them repeatedly will they become "second nature" to you.

Editing Hints

Here are hints that can help you edit the next-to-final draft of a paper for sentence-skills mistakes:

1 Have at hand two essential tools: a good dictionary and a grammar handbook (you can use the one in this book on pages 355–465). Even if you use the spell checker and grammar checker on your word-processing program, you will still need to check spellings and uses of certain phrases.

2   Use a sheet of paper to cover your essay so that you can expose only one sentence at a time. Look for errors in grammar, spelling, and typing. It may help to read each sentence out loud. If it does not read clearly and smoothly, chances are something is wrong.

3   Pay special attention to the kinds of errors you tend to make. For example, if you tend to write run-ons or fragments, be especially on the lookout for those errors.

4   Try to work on a typewritten or word-processed draft, where you'll be able to see your writing more objectively than you can on a handwritten page; use a pen with coloured ink so that your corrections will stand out.

5   Work on one problem-area at a time. Check your spelling of particular words first, and then work on your sentences.

A Note on Proofreading

Proofreading means that you check the final, edited draft of your paper closely for typos and other careless errors. A helpful strategy is to read your paper backward, from the last sentence to the first. This helps keep you from getting caught up in the flow of the paper and missing small mistakes.

A Final Note on Editing

A series of editing tests appears on pages 476–488. You will probably find it most helpful to take these tests after reviewing the sentence skills in Part 4.

PRACTICE IN REVISING SENTENCES

You now know the fourth step in effective writing: revising and editing sentences. You also know that practice in *editing* sentences is best undertaken after you have worked through the sentence skills in Part 4. This closing section, then, will focus on *revising* sentences—using a variety of methods to ensure that your sentences flow in a smooth, clear, and interesting way. You will work through the following series of Review Tests:

1   Using parallelism

2   Using a consistent point of view

3   Using specific words

4   Using active verbs

5   Using concise words

6   Varying your sentences

1 USING PARALLELISM

■ **Review Test 1**

Cross out the unbalanced part of each sentence. In the space provided, revise the unbalanced part so that it matches the other item or items in the sentence.

Example   Cigarette smoking is expensive, disgusting, and ~~a health risk.~~
                 unhealthy
                 _____

1. Marco prefers books that are short, scary, and filled with suspense.

   _____

2. A sale on electrical appliances, furniture for the home office, and stereo equipment begins this Friday.

   _____

3. To escape the stresses of everyday life, I rely upon watching television, reading books, and my kitchen.

   _____

4. The keys to improving grades are to take effective notes in class, to plan study time, and preparing carefully for exams.

   _____

5. Qualities that I look for in friends are a sense of humour, being kind, and dependability.

   _____

6. My three favourite jobs were veterinary assistant, gardener, and selling toys.

   _____

7. Housekeeping shortcuts will help you do a fast job of doing laundry, cleaning rooms, and food on the table.

   _____

8. Studying a little every day is more effective than to cram.

   _____

9. The chickens travel on a conveyor belt, where they are plucked, washed, rinsed, and bags are put on them.

   _____

10. The speaker impressed the audience because of his clear, reasonable presentation with friendliness as well.

    _____

■ **Review Test 2**

Cross out the unbalanced part of each sentence. In the space provided, revise the unbalanced part so that it matches the other item or items in the sentence.

1. Paying college tuition and not studying is as sensible as to buy tickets to a movie and not watching it.

   _____

2. The best programming on television includes news programs, shows on science, and children's series.

   _____

3. Curling overgrown vines, porch furniture that was rotted, and sagging steps were my first impressions of the neglected house.

   _____

4. The little girl came home from school with a tear-streaked face, a black eye, and her shirt was torn.

   _____

5. There are two ways to the top floor: climb the stairs or taking the elevator.

   _____

6. While waiting for the exam to start, small groups of nervous students glanced over their notes, drank coffee, and were whispering to each other.

   _____

7. In many ways, starting college at forty is harder than to start at eighteen.

   _____

8. Interesting work is as important to me as pay that is good.

   _____

9. The "street person" shuffled along the street, bent over to pick something up, and was putting it in his shopping bag.

   _____

10. A public service industry strike now would mean interruptions in food deliveries, a slowdown in the economy, and losing wages for workers.

   _____

2 USING A CONSISTENT POINT OF VIEW

■ **Review Test 1**

Change verbs where needed in the following selection so that they are consistently in the past tense. Cross out each incorrect verb and write the correct form above it, as shown in the example. You will need to make ten corrections.

My uncle's shopping trip last Thursday was discouraging to him. First of

found

all, he had to drive around for fifteen minutes until he ~~finds~~ a parking space.

There was a half-price special on paper products in the supermarket, and

every spot is taken. Then, when he finally got inside, many of the items on his

list were not where he expected. For example, the pickles he wanted are not

on the same shelf as all the other pickles. Instead, they were in a refrigerated

case next to the bacon. And the granola was not on the cereal shelves, but in

the health food section. Shopping thus proceeds slowly. About halfway through

his list, he knew there would not be time to cook dinner and decides to pick

up a barbecued chicken. The chicken, he learned, was available at the end of

the store he had already passed. So he parks his shopping cart in an aisle,

gets the chicken, and came back. After adding half a dozen more items to his

cart, he suddenly realizes it contained someone else's food. So he retraced his

steps, found his own cart, transfers the groceries, and continued to shop.

Later, when he began loading items onto the checkout counter, he notices that

the barbecued chicken was missing. He must have left it in the other cart,

certainly gone by now. Feeling totally defeated, he returned to the deli counter

and says to the clerk, "Give me another chicken. I lost the first one." My

uncle told me that when he saw the look on the clerk's face, he felt as if he'd

flunked Food Shopping.

■ Review Test 2

Cross out inconsistent pronouns in the following sentences and revise with the correct form of the pronoun above each crossed-out word.

Example   Many shoppers are staying away from the local music store because
                 they
                 ~~you~~ can now download songs from the Internet.

1. These days people never seem to get the recognition they deserve, no matter how hard you work.

2. All you could hear was the maddening rattle of the furnace fan, even though I buried my face in the pillow.

3. When we answer the telephone at work, you are supposed to say the company name.

4. Each year I pay more money for my college tuition. But, despite the cost, one must complete college in order to get a better, more meaningful job.

5. Gary bought the used car from a local dealership. The car was so clean and shiny that you could not tell that the engine needed to be replaced.

6. I would like to go to a school where one can meet many people who are different from me.

7. When I first began to work as a server, I was surprised at how rude some customers were to you.

8. When you drive on the highway, I get disgusted at the amount of trash I see.

9. Students may not leave the exam room unless you have turned in the exam.

10. Nina wanted to just browse through the store, but in every department a salesperson came up and asked to help you.

3   USING SPECIFIC WORDS

■   **Review Test 1**

Revise the following sentences, changing vague, indefinite words into sharp, specific ones.

1. When my relationship broke up, I felt *various emotions.*

   _____

   _____

   _____

2. The *food choices* in the cafeteria were unappetizing.

   _____

   _____

   _____

3. *Bugs* invaded our kitchen and pantry this summer.

   _____

   _____

   _____

4. All last week, *the weather was terrible.*

   _____

   _____

   _____

5. In the car accident, our teacher suffered *a number of injuries.*

   _____

   _____

   _____

■ Review Test 2

With the help of the methods described on pages 101–104, add specific details to the sentences that follow.

1. The salesperson was obnoxious.

   _____

   _____

   _____

2. The child started to cry.

   _____

   _____

   _____

3. The game was exciting.

   _____

   _____

   _____

4. The lounge area was busy.

   _____

   _____

   _____

5. A passenger on the bus was acting strangely.

   _____

   _____

   _____

4 USING ACTIVE VERBS

■ **Review Test**

Revise the following sentences, changing verbs from the passive to the active voice and making any other word changes necessary.

Example   Soccer is played by children all over the world.
Children all over the world play soccer.

1. The pizza restaurant was closed by the health inspector.

   _____

2. Huge stacks of donated books were sorted by the workers in the library.

   _____

3. My computer was infected by a virus.

   _____

4. Gasoline prices will not be increased by suppliers this winter.

   _____

5. High-powered lights were used by the crew during filming of the commercial.

   _____

6. An additional charge was placed on our phone bill by the telephone company.

   _____

7. The local community centre was damaged by a severe snowstorm.

   _____

8. Stress is relieved by physical activity, meditation, and relaxation.

   _____

9. Taxes will be raised by the provincial government to pay for highway improvements.

   _____

10. Studies show that violent behaviour among young children is increased by watching violent TV programs.

   _____

   _____

5 USING CONCISE WORDS

■ **Review Test 1**

Revise the following sentences, omitting needless words.

1. I finally made up my mind and decided to look for a new job.

   _____

   _____

2. Due to the fact that the printer was out of paper, Ayesha went to the store for the purpose of buying some.

   _____

   _____

3. Marika realized suddenly that her date had stood her up and was not going to show up.

   _____

   _____

4. Our teacher does not know at this point in time if she will return to our school next year.

   _____

   _____

5. The salesperson advised us not to buy the computer at this time because it was going to have a drop in price in the very near future.

   _____

   _____

■ **Review Test 2**

Revise the following sentences, omitting needless and pretentious words.

1. The policy at our company at the present time is that there are two coffee breaks, with each of them being fifteen minutes long.

   _____

   _____

2. Permit us to take this opportunity to inform you that your line of credit has been increased.

   _____

   _____

3. I have a strong preference for sugary confections over fruit, which, in my opinion, doesn't taste as good as sugary confections.

   _____

   _____

4. Denise is one of those people who rarely admit to being wrong, and it is very unusual to hear her acknowledge that she acted in an errant manner.

   _____

   _____

5. Many people are of the opinion that children should be required by law to attend school until they reach the age of sixteen years old.

   _____

   _____

6 VARYING YOUR SENTENCES

■ Review Test 1

Combine each of the following groups of simple sentences into one longer sentence. Omit repeated words. Various combinations are often possible, so try to find a combination in each group that flows most smoothly and clearly.

1. Nadine had repaired her broken watchband with a paper clip.
   The clip snapped.
   The watch slid off her wrist.

   _____

   _____

2. The physical therapist watched.
   Julie tried to stand on her weakened legs.
   They crumpled under her.

   _____

   _____

3. There were parking spaces on the street.
   Winston pulled into an expensive garage.
   He did not want to risk damage to his new car.

   _____

   _____

4. The truck was speeding.
   The truck was brown.
   The truck skidded on some ice.
   The truck almost hit a police officer.
   The police officer was startled.
   The police officer was young.

   _____

   _____

5. The rainstorm flooded our basement.
   The rainstorm was sudden.
   The rainstorm was terrible.
   It knocked shingles off the roof.
   It uprooted a young tree.

   _____

   _____

■ **Review Test 2**

Combine each of the following groups of simple sentences into two longer sentences. Omit repeated words. Various combinations are often possible, so try to find combinations in each group that flow most smoothly and clearly.

1. A sudden cold front hit the area.
   Temperatures dropped ten degrees in less than an hour.
   My teeth began to chatter.
   I was not wearing a warm jacket.

   _____

   _____

   _____

2. Darryl works as a model.
   He has to look his best.
   He gained ten pounds recently.
   He had to take off the extra weight.
   He would have lost his job.

   _____

   _____

   _____

3. The ball game was about to begin.
   A dog ran onto the field.
   The dog began nipping the infielders' ankles.
   The game had to be delayed.
   The dog was chased away.

   _____

   _____

   _____

4. The lion was hungry.
   It watched the herd of gazelle closely.
   A young or sick animal wandered away from the group.
   The lion would move in for the kill.

   _____

   _____

   _____

5. My aunt decided to find a helpful form of exercise.
She was suffering from arthritis.
She learned that swimming is very healthful.
It works every muscle group in the body without straining the muscles.

_____

_____

_____

Review Test 3

Combine the sentences in the following paragraph into four sentences. Omit repeated words. Try to find combinations in each case that flow as smoothly and clearly as possible.

Lena and Miles wanted a vacation. They wanted a vacation that was nice. They wanted one that was quiet. They wanted one that was relaxing. They rented a small lakeside cabin. Their first day there was very peaceful. The situation quickly changed. A large family moved into a nearby cabin. They played music at top volume. They raced around in a speedboat with a loud whining engine. Lena and Miles were no longer very relaxed. They packed up their things. They drove off. They returned to their quiet apartment.

_____

_____

_____

_____

_____

_____

_____

REVIEWING THE LEARNING OUTCOMES

To be certain that you have met the learning outcomes for this chapter, answer the following questions.

- What are the six strategies that will help you to write effective sentences?
- Which of these strategies is particularly helpful when you write thesis statements?
- What are two areas in which maintaining consistency is important, and why?
- Why are active verb forms preferable to passive forms?
- What is the difference between a compound sentence and a complex sentence?
- What are five types of phrases that work as sentence openings?

Four Bases for Revising Essays

After reviewing the four goals for writing effective essays and practising exercises based on these goals, you will

- Be more aware of the importance of each of these goals
- Be able to evaluate and revise your own work with techniques for achieving the four goals

Four Steps	*Four Bases*	*Four Goals Defined*
1 If you advance a single main point in your thesis and stick to that point,	your paper will have *unity*.	**Unity:** a single main idea pursued and supported by the points and details of the essay
2 If you support your thesis' point with specific evidence,	your paper will have *support*.	**Support:** for each supporting point, enough specific and definite details
3 If you organize and connect the specific evidence, at essay, paragraph, and sentence levels,	your paper will have *coherence*.	**Coherence:** paragraphs, supporting points, and details organized and connected clearly
4 If you write clear, error-free sentences,	your paper will have effective *sentence skills*.	**Effective Sentence Skills:** sentence structure, grammar, spelling, and punctuation free of errors

This chapter will discuss these four bases—unity, support, coherence, and sentence skills—and will show how the four bases can be used to evaluate and revise a paper.

BASE 1: UNITY

Activity

The following personal student essays are on the topic "Problems or Pleasures of My Teenage Years." Which one makes its point more clearly and effectively, and why?

Essay 1

Teenage Pranks

Looking back at some of the things I did as a teenager makes me break out in a sweat. The purpose of each adventure was fun, but occasionally things got out of hand. In my search for good times, I was involved in three notable pranks, ranging from fairly harmless to fairly serious. **1**

The first prank proved that good, clean fun does not have to be dull. As a high school student, I was credited with making the world's largest dessert. With several friends, I spent an entire year collecting boxes of Jell-O. Entering our school's indoor pool one night, we turned the water temperature up as high as it would go and poured in box after box of the strawberry powder. The next morning, school officials arrived to find the pool filled with fifty thousand litres of the quivering, rubbery stuff. No one was hurt by the prank, but we did suffer through three days of massive cleanup. **2**

Not all my pranks were harmless, and one involved risking my life. As soon as I got my driver's licence, I wanted to join the "Flyers' Club." Membership in this club was limited to those who could make their cars fly a distance of at least three metres. The qualifying site was an old quarry field near Orillia where friends and I had built a ramp made of dirt. I drove my battered Ford Pinto up this ramp as fast as it would go. The Pinto flew three metres, but one of the tires exploded when I landed. The car rolled on its side, and I luckily escaped with only a bruised arm. **3**

Risking my own life was bad enough, but there was another prank where other people could have been hurt, too. On this occasion, I accidentally set a valley on fire. Two of my friends and I were sitting on a hill sharing a few beers. It was a warm summer night, and there was absolutely nothing to do. The idea came like a thunderclap. We collected a supply of large plastic garbage bags, emergency highway flares, and the half tank of helium left over from a science fair experiment. Then we began to construct a fleet of UFOs. Filling the bags with helium, we tied them closed with wire and suspended several burning flares below each bag. Our UFOs leaped into the air like an army of invading Martians. Rising and darting in the blackness, they convinced even us. Our fun turned into horror, though, as we watched the balloons begin to drop onto the wooded valley of expensive homes below. Soon, a brush fire started and, quickly sobered, we hurried off to call the fire department anonymously. **4**

Every so often, I think back on the things that I did as a teenager. I chuckle   5
at the innocent pranks and feel lucky that I didn't harm myself or others with
the not-so-innocent ones. Those years were filled with wild times. Today I'm
older, wiser—and maybe just a little more boring.

Essay 2

Problems of My Adolescence

In the unreal world of television situation comedies, teenagers are care-   1
free, smart, funny, wise-cracking, secure kids. In fact, most of them are more
"together" than the adults on the shows. This, however, isn't how I recall my
teenage years at all. As a teen, I suffered. Every day, I battled the terrible
physical, family, and social troubles of adolescence.

For one thing, I had to deal with a demoralizing physical problem—acne.   2
Some days, I would wake up in the morning with a red bump the size of a tail-
light on my nose. Since I worried constantly about my appearance anyway, acne
outbreaks could turn me into a crying, screaming maniac. Plastering on a layer
of (at the time) orange-coloured Clearasil, which didn't fool anybody, I would
slink into school, hoping that the boy I had a crush on would be absent that day.
Within the last few years, however, treatments for acne have improved. Now,
skin doctors prescribe special drugs that clear up pimples almost immediately.
An acne attack could shatter whatever small amount of self-esteem I had
managed to build up.

In addition to fighting acne, I felt compelled to fight my family. As a teenager,   3
I needed to be independent. At that time, the most important thing in life was
to be close to my friends and to try out new, more adult experiences. Unfortunately,
my family seemed to get in the way. My little brother, for instance, turned into
my enemy. We are close now, though. In fact, Eddie recently painted my new
apartment for me. Eddie used to barge into my room, listen to my phone conversations, and read my secret letters. I would threaten to tie him up and leave
him in a garbage dumpster. He would scream, my mother would yell, and all
hell would break loose. My parents, too, were enemies. They wouldn't let me
stay out late, wear the clothes I wanted to wear, or hang around with the friends
I like. So I tried to get revenge on them by being miserable, sulky, and sarcastic
at home.

Worst of all, I had to face the social traumas of being a teenager. Things that   4
were supposed to be fun, like dates and dances, were actually horrible. On the few
occasions when I had a real date, I agonized over everything—my hair, my weight,
my pimples. After a date, I would come home, raid the kitchen, and drown my
insecurities in a sea of junk food. Dances were also stressful events. My friends and
I would pretend we were too cool to care or sneak a couple of beers just to get up
the nerve to walk into the school gym. Now I realize that half the kids in the gym
were just as nervous as we were and that seventeen-year-olds are not smart to drink.
They can't handle the consequences. At dances, I never relaxed. It was too
important to look exactly right, to act really cool, and to pretend I was having fun.

I'm glad I'm not a teenager anymore. I wouldn't ever want to feel so   5
unattractive, so confused, and so insecure again. I'll gladly accept the odd
line on my face in exchange for a little peace of mind.

Essay _____ makes its point more clearly and effectively because _____

_____

_____

_____

UNDERSTANDING UNITY

Essay 1 is more effective because it is unified. All the details in this essay are on target; they support and develop each of its three topic sentences ("The first prank
proved that good, clean fun does not have to be dull"; "Not all my pranks were harmless, and one involved risking my life"; and "Risking my own life was bad enough, but
there was another prank where other people could have been hurt, too").

On the other hand, essay 2 contains some details irrelevant to its topic sentences. In the first supporting paragraph (paragraph 2), the sentences "Within the
last few years, however, treatments for acne have improved. Now, skin doctors prescribe special drugs that clear up pimples almost immediately," do not support the
writer's topic statement that she had to deal with the physical problem of acne. Such
details should be left out, in the interest of unity.

Revising for Unity

Activity

Go back to essay 2 and cross out the two sentences in the second supporting paragraph (paragraph 3) and the two sentences in the third supporting paragraph
(paragraph 4) that are off target and do not help support their topic sentences.

The difference between these first two essays leads to the first base and goal of
effective writing: **unity. To achieve unity is to have all the details in your paper
related to your thesis and three supporting topic sentences.** Each time you think of
something to put into your paper, ask yourself whether it relates to your thesis and
supporting points. If it does not, leave it out. If you were writing a paper about the
problems of being unemployed and two of your sentences talked about the pleasures
of free time, you would miss the first and most essential base of good writing.

BASE 2: SUPPORT

Activity

The following essays were written in the less personal third person point of view.
Both are unified. Which one communicates more clearly and effectively, and why?

Essay 1

Dealing with Disappointment

One way to look at life is as a series of disappointments. Life can certainly **1** appear that way because disappointment crops up in the life of everyone more often, it seems, than satisfaction. How disappointments are handled can have a great bearing on how life is viewed. People can react negatively by sulking or by blaming others, or they can try to understand the reasons behind the disappointment.

Sulking is one way to deal with disappointment. This "Why does everything **2** always happen to me?" attitude is common because it is an easy attitude to adopt, but it is not very productive. Everyone has had the experience of meeting people who specialize in feeling sorry for themselves. A sulky manner will often discourage others from wanting to lend support, and it prevents the sulker from making positive moves toward self-help. It becomes easier just to sit back and sulk. Unfortunately, feeling sorry for oneself does nothing to lessen the pain of disappointment. It may, in fact, increase the pain. It certainly does not make future disappointments easier to bear.

Blaming others is another negative and nonproductive way to cope with **3** disappointment. This all-too-common response of pointing the finger at someone else doesn't help one's situation. This posture will lead only to anger, resentment, and, therefore, further unhappiness. Disappointment in another's performance does not necessarily indicate that the performer is at fault. Perhaps expectations were too high, or there could have been a misunderstanding as to what the performer actually intended to accomplish.

A positive way to handle disappointment is to try to understand the reasons **4** behind the disappointment. An analysis of the causes for disappointment can have an excellent chance of producing desirable results. Often understanding alone can help alleviate the pain of disappointment and can help prevent future disappointments. Also, it is wise to try to remember that what would be ideal is not necessarily what is reasonable to expect in any given situation. The ability to look disappointment squarely in the face and then go on from there is the first step on the road back.

Continuous handling of disappointment in a negative manner can lead to a **5** negative view of life itself. Chances for personal happiness in such a state of being are understandably slim. Learning not to expect perfection in an imperfect world and keeping in mind those times when expectations were actually surpassed are positive steps toward allowing the joys of life to prevail.

Essay 2

Reactions to Disappointment

Gertrude Stein said that people have "to learn to do everything, even to die." In **1** life, everyone may face and master many unavoidable adversities; one misery everyone experiences is disappointment. No one gets through life without experiencing many disappointments. Strangely, though, most people seem unprepared for disappointment and react to it in negative ways. They feel depressed or try to escape their troubles instead of using disappointment as an opportunity for growth.

One negative reaction to disappointment is depression. A woman trying to win a promotion, for example, works hard for over a year in her department. Halina is so sure she will get the promotion, in fact, that she has already picked out the car she will buy when her salary increase comes through. However, the boss names one of Halina's co-workers to the position. The fact that all the other department employees tell Halina that she is the one who really deserved the promotion doesn't help her deal with the crushing disappointment. Deeply depressed, Halina decides that all her goals are doomed to defeat. She loses her enthusiasm for her job and can barely force herself to show up every day. Halina tells herself that she is a failure and that doing a good job just isn't worth the work.

Another negative reaction to disappointment, and one that often follows depression, is the desire to escape. Jamal fails to get into the college his brother is attending, the college that was the focus of all his dreams, and decides to escape his disappointment. Why worry about college at all? Instead, he covers up his real feelings by giving up on his schoolwork and getting completely involved with friends, parties, and "good times." Or Carla doesn't make the college basketball team—something she wanted very badly—and so refuses to play sports at all. She decides to hang around with a new set of friends who get high every day; then she won't have to confront her disappointment and learn to live with it.

The positive way to react to disappointment is to use it as a chance for growth. This isn't easy, but it's the only useful way to deal with an inevitable part of life. Halina, the woman who wasn't promoted, could have handled her disappointment by looking at other options. If her boss doesn't recognize talent and hard work, perhaps she could transfer to another department. Or she could ask the boss how to improve her performance so that she would be a sure candidate for the next promotion. Jamal, the fellow who didn't get into the college of his choice, should look into other schools. Going to another college may encourage him to be his own person, step out of his brother's shadow, and realize that being turned down by one college isn't a final judgment on his abilities or potential. Rather than escape into drugs, Carla could improve her basketball skills for a year or pick up another sport—like swimming or tennis—that would probably turn out to be more useful to her as an adult.

Disappointments are unwelcome but regular visitors to everyone's life. People can feel depressed about them or they can try to escape from them. The best thing, though, is to accept a disappointment and then try to use it somehow: step over the unwelcome visitor on the doorstep and get on with life.

Essay _____ makes its point more clearly and effectively because _____

_____

_____

_____

UNDERSTANDING SUPPORT

Here, essay 2 is more effective; it offers specific examples of how people deal with disappointment, so we can see for ourselves people's reactions to disappointment.

Essay 1, on the other hand, gives us no specific evidence. Repeatedly, the writer *tells* us about sulking, blaming others, and trying to understand the reasons behind a disappointment: the reactions people have to a letdown. However, the writer never *shows* us any of these responses in action. Exactly what kinds of disappointments is the writer talking about? And how, for instance, does someone analyze the causes of disappointment? Would a person make up a list of causes on a piece of paper, or review the causes with a concerned friend, or speak to a professional therapist? In an essay like this one, we would want to see *examples* of how sulking and blaming others are negative responses to disappointment.

Revising for Support

Activity

On a separate sheet of paper, revise one of the three supporting paragraphs in "Dealing with Disappointment" by providing specific supporting examples.

Examining these essays leads to the second base of effective writing: **support**. After realizing the importance of **adequate and specific supporting details**, one student revised a paper on being lost in the woods, the worst experience of her childhood. In the revised paper, instead of talking about "the terror of being separated from my parents," she wrote, "tears streamed down my cheeks as I pictured the faces I would never see again," and "I clutched the locket my parents had given me as if it were a lucky charm that could help me find my way back to the campsite." All writing should include such vivid details!

BASE 3: COHERENCE

Activity

The following two essays were written on the topic "Positive or Negative Effects of Television." Both are unified, and both are supported. Which one communicates more clearly and effectively, and why?

Essay 1

Harmful Effects of Watching Television

In a recent cartoon, one character said to another, "When you think of the awesome power of television to educate, aren't you glad it doesn't?" It's true that television has the power to educate and to entertain, but unfortunately, these benefits are outweighed by the harm it does to dedicated viewers. Television is harmful because it creates passivity, discourages communication, and presents a false picture of reality.

1

Television makes viewers passive. Children who have an electronic babysitter spend most of their waking hours in a semi-conscious state. Older viewers watch tennis matches and basketball games with none of the excitement of being in the stands. Even if children are watching *Sesame Street* or TVO's children's programs, they are being educated passively. The child actors are going on nature walks, building crafts projects, playing with animals, and participating in games, but the little viewers are simply watching. Older viewers watch guests discuss issues with Mike Bullard or Jay Leno, but no one will turn to the home viewers to ask their opinions.

2

Worst of all, TV presents a false picture of reality that leaves viewers frustrated because they don't have the beauty or wealth of characters on television. Viewers absorb the idea that everyone else in North America owns a lavish condo, suburban house, sleek car, and expensive wardrobe. Although some Canadian shows use less glamorous actors, Canadian music videos show performers and extras just as unrealistically as their U.S. counterparts. The material possessions on TV shows and commercials contribute to the false image of reality. News anchors and reporters, with their perfect hair and make-up, must fit television's standard of beauty. From their modest homes or cramped apartments, many viewers tune in daily to the upper-middle-class world that TV glorifies.

3

Television discourages communication. Families watching television do very little talking except for brief exchanges during commercials. If Uncle Bernie or the next-door neighbours drop in for a visit, the most comfortable activity for everyone may be not conversation, but watching *Buffy* or *Hockey Night in Canada*. The family may not even be watching the same set; instead, in some households, all the family members head for their own rooms to watch their own sets. At dinner, plates are plopped on the coffee table in front of the set, and the meal is wolfed down during *Video Countdown* or syndicated reruns of *Frasier*. During commercials, the only communication a family has all night may consist of questions like "Do we have any popcorn?" and "Where's the television page?"

4

Television, like cigarettes or saccharine, is harmful to our health. We are becoming isolated, passive, and frustrated. And, most frightening, the average viewer spends more time watching television than ever.

5

Essay 2

The Benefits of Television

We hear a lot about the negative effects of television on the viewer. Obviously, television can be harmful if it is watched constantly to the exclusion of other activities. It would be just as harmful to listen to CDs all the time or to eat constantly. However, when television is watched in moderation, it is extremely valuable, as it provides relaxation, entertainment, and education.

1

First of all, watching TV has the value of sheer relaxation. Watching television can be soothing and restful after an eight-hour day of pressure, challenges, or concentration. After working hard all day, people look forward to a new episode of a favourite show or yet another showing of *The Godfather* or *Grease*. This period of relaxation leaves viewers refreshed and ready to take on the world again.

2

Watching TV also seems to reduce stress in some people. This benefit of television is just beginning to be recognized. One doctor, for example, advises his patients with high blood pressure to relax in the evening with a few hours of television.

In addition to being relaxing, television is entertaining. Along with the standard comedies, dramas, and game shows that provide enjoyment to viewers, television offers a variety of movies and sports events. Moreover, in most areas, viewers have cable or satellite TV programming. With this service, viewers can watch first-run movies, rock and classical music concerts, cooking shows, and specialized sports events, like international soccer and Grand Prix racing. Viewers can also buy or rent movies to show on their television sets with DVD players or VCRs. Still another growing area of TV entertainment is video games. Discs are available for everything from electronic baseball to *Myst,* allowing the owner to have a video game arcade in the living room.   3

Most important, television is educational. Preschoolers learn reading skills, numbers, and social lessons from YTV and TVO shows and *Sesame Street.* Science shows for older children run on Canadian network and cable stations; they go on location to analyze everything from life in the Arctic to rocket launches. Many adults are hooked on the History Channel. Also, television widens our knowledge by covering important events and current news. Viewers watching CNN can see and hear international news events, natural disasters, and election results as they are happening. Finally, with newer connections and services, like WebTV, television allows any member of the family to access and learn from all the information resources on the Internet.   4

Perhaps because television is such a powerful force, we like to criticize it and search for its flaws. However, the benefits of television should not be ignored. We can use television to relax, to have fun, and to make ourselves smarter. This electronic wonder, then, is a servant, not a master.   5

Essay _____ makes its point more clearly and effectively because _____

_____

_____

_____

UNDERSTANDING COHERENCE

In this case, essay 2 is more effective because the material is organized clearly and logically. Using emphatic order, the writer develops three positive uses of television, ending with the most important use: television as an educational tool. The writer includes transitional words as signposts, making movement from one idea to the next easy to follow. Major transitions include *First of all, In addition,* and *Most important;* transitions within paragraphs include such words as *Moreover, Still another, too, Also,* and *Finally.* And this writer also uses a linking sentence ("In addition to being relaxing, television is entertaining") to tie the first and second supporting paragraphs together clearly.

Although essay 1 is unified and supported, the writer does not have any clear and consistent way of organizing the material. The most important idea (signalled by the phrase *Worst of all*) is discussed in the second supporting paragraph instead of being saved for last. None of the supporting paragraphs organizes its details in a logical fashion. The first supporting paragraph discusses children, then older viewers, then younger viewers, and then jumps back to older people again. The third supporting paragraph, like the first, leaps from an opening idea (families talking only during commercials) to several intervening ideas and then back to the original idea (talking during commercials). In addition, essay 1 uses practically no transitional devices to guide the reader.

Revising for Coherence

Activity

On a separate sheet of paper, revise one of the three supporting paragraphs in "Harmful Effects of Watching Television" by providing a clear method of organizing the material and transitional words.

These two essays lead us to the third base of effective writing: **coherence. All the paragraphs supporting ideas and sentences in a paper must be organized so that they cohere, or "stick together."** As already mentioned, key techniques for tying together material in a paper include a clear method of organization (such as time order or emphatic order), transitions, and other connecting words.

BASE 4: SENTENCE SKILLS

Activity

Following are the opening paragraphs from two essays. Both are unified, supported, and organized, but which one communicates more clearly and effectively, and why?

First Part of Essay 1

"electric rock"

[1]Where would Rock & Roll be without electric guitars? [2]The answer: where Blues, Country, and folk music was in the 1940s. [3]Rock's ancestors were played on and accompanied by acoustic guitars, fragile hollow instruments. [4]Travelling Blues musicians usually played in noisy bars, so they attached microphones and amplifiers to their acoustics—what they got was mostly feedback. [5]What they really needed appeared in 1950. [6]The solid-body electric guitar. [7]Rock's tradmark instrument brought a whole new style of music, the ways for people to make new sounds, and new playing techniques.

[8]With the invention of the electric guitar by Les Paul and Leo Fender came Rock & Roll. [9]Young musicians like Chuck Berry and Elvis Presley could be heard over the crowds of teenagers they attract. [10]The new guitars were solid pieces of

lightweight plastic; performers could swing them around easily and move while they played and sang. [11]The metal strings produce louder and sharper sounds, suited to the new musics raw emotions and fast beat. [12]When Tv brought Rock to audiences in the mid-1950s the electric guitar was a required accessory for young artists—as much a part of their look as their shiny pompadour hairdos.

First Part of Essay 2

Rock Plugs In

Where would Rock & Roll be without electric guitars? The answer: where Blues, Country, and folk music were in the 1940s. Rock's ancestors were played on and accompanied by acoustic guitars, fragile hollow instruments. Travelling Blues musicians usually played in noisy bars, so they attached microphones and amplifiers to their acoustics—what they got was mostly feedback. What they really needed appeared in 1950, the solid-body electric guitar. Rock's trademark instrument brought a whole new style of music, new sounds, and new playing techniques.

With the invention of the electric guitar by Les Paul and Leo Fender came Rock & Roll. Young musicians like Chuck Berry and Elvis Presley could be heard over the crowds of teenagers they attracted. The new guitars were solid pieces of lightweight plastic; performers could swing them around easily and move while they played and sang. The metal strings produced louder and sharper sounds, suited to the new music's raw emotions and fast beat. When TV brought Rock to audiences in the mid-1950s, the electric guitar was a required accessory for young artists—as much a part of their look as their shiny pompadour hairdos.

Essay _____ makes its point more clearly and effectively because _____

_____

_____

_____

UNDERSTANDING SENTENCE SKILLS

Essay 2 is more effective because it makes good use of *sentence skills*, the fourth base of competent writing. Here are the sentence-skills mistakes in essay 1:

1 The title should not be set off in quotation marks.

2 The main words in the title should be capitalized.

3 The plural subject Blues, Country, and folk music in sentence 2 should have a plural verb: *was* should be *were.*

4 Word group 6 is a fragment; it can be corrected by attaching it to the previous sentence.

5 There is a lack of parallelism in sentence 7, the thesis statement: *the ways for people to make new sounds* should be *new sounds*.

6 The word *tradmark* in sentence 7 is misspelled; it should be *trademark*.

7 The word *attract* in sentence 9 should be *attracted* to be consistent in tense with *could be heard*, the other verb form in the sentence.

8 The word *musics* in sentence 11 should be a possessive form: an apostrophe and *s* must be added: *music's*.

9 The abbreviation *Tv* in sentence 12 must be two capitalized letters: *TV*.

10 A comma must be added in sentence 12 after the prepositional opening phrase *When TV brought Rock to audiences in the mid-1950s.*

Revising for Sentence Skills

Activity

Here are the final three paragraphs from the two essays. Edit the sentences in the first essay to make the corrections needed. Note that comparing essays 1 and 2 will help you locate the mistakes. This activity will also help you identify some of the sentence skills you may want to review in Part 4.

Last Part of Essay 1

[13]Just as the electric guitar helped create the sound and look of Rock, it also challenged musicians to create new sounds. [14]As early as the 1951 song "Rocket 88," musicians discovered that distortion wasn't necessarily a mistake. [15]Heavy Metal owe everything to this discovery. [16]British bands like the Stones first used fuzz tone when they complained about no "Satisfaction," and the wah wah pedal added something special to Psychedelic Rock, Cream, and the 70s scene. [17]Rocks sound boundaries expanded into the experimental zone.

[18]By the late 60s and early 70s artists moved beyond toying with equipment; they started to push the limits of playing techniques. [19]Eric Clapton may have been and still may be the supreme artist, but Led Zeppelin had the nerve to use a bow on their lead guitar. [20]Jimi Hendrix bent his guitar body to bend and change the notes he played, then he played with his guitar on his back finally he set it on fire. [21]But the ultimate testimony to Rock's new style and to the durability of the electric guitar is the image of the who's Pete Townshend smashing his Stratocaster against the stage. [22]He discovered that solid body guitars, just like Rock & Roll, are indestructible.

[23]So Mr. Paul's and Mr. Fender's invention, an instrument that can be moulded into any shape created a new form of music and changed the shape and style of how that music sounds. [24]No matter how many new computerized instruments are invented, the electric guitar still rules Rock.

Last Part of Essay 2

Just as the electric guitar helped create the sound and look of Rock, it also challenged musicians to create new sounds. As early as the 1951 song "Rocket 88," musicians discovered that distortion wasn't necessarily a mistake. Heavy Metal owes everything to this discovery. British bands like the Stones first used fuzz tone when they complained about no "Satisfaction," and the wah-wah pedal added something special to Psychedelic Rock, Cream, and the '70s scene. Rock's sound boundaries expanded into the experimental zone.

By the late '60s and early '70s, artists moved beyond toying with the equipment; they started to push the limits of playing techniques. Eric Clapton may have been and still may be the supreme artist, but Led Zeppelin had the nerve to use a bow on their lead guitar. Jimi Hendrix bent his guitar body to bend and change the notes he played, then he played with his guitar on his back; finally, he set it on fire. But the ultimate testimony to Rock's new style and to the durability of the electric guitar is the image of The Who's Pete Townshend smashing his Stratocaster against the stage. He discovered that solid-body guitars, just like Rock & Roll, are indestructible.

So Mr. Paul's and Mr. Fender's invention, an instrument that can be moulded into any shape, created a new form of music and changed the shape and style of how that music sounds. No matter how many new computerized instruments are invented, the electric guitar still rules Rock.

PRACTICE IN USING THE FOUR BASES

You are familiar with four standards, or bases, of effective writing: *unity*, *support*, *coherence*, and *sentence skills*. In this section you will expand and strengthen your understanding of the four bases as you evaluate and revise essays for each of them.

1   REVISING ESSAYS FOR UNITY

Activity

The following essay contains irrelevant sentences that do not relate to the thesis of the essay or support the topic sentence of the paragraph in which they appear. Cross out the irrelevant sentences and write the numbers of those sentences in the spaces provided.

Essay

Playing on the Browns

[1]For the past three summers, I have played first base on a softball team known as the Browns. [2]We play a long schedule, including playoffs, and everybody takes the games pretty seriously. [3]In that respect, we're no different from any other of the dozens of other teams in Lethbridge. [4]But in one respect, we are different. [5]In an all-male league, we have a woman on the team—me.

1

⁶Thus, I've had a chance to observe something about human nature by seeing how the men have treated me. ⁷Some have been disbelieving; some have been patronizing; and fortunately, some have simply accepted me.

⁸One new team in the league was particularly flabbergasted to see me start the game at first base. ⁹Nobody on the Comets had commented one way or the other when they saw me warming up, but playing in the actual game was another story. ¹⁰The Comet first-base coach leaned over to me with a disbelieving grin and said, "You mean, you're starting, and those three guys are on the bench?" ¹¹I nodded and he shrugged, still amazed. ¹²He probably thought I was the manager's wife. ¹³When I came up to bat, the Comet pitcher smiled and called to his outfielders to move way in on me. ¹⁴Now, I don't have a lot of power, but I'm not exactly feeble. ¹⁵I used to work out on the exercise machines at a local health club until it closed, and now I lift weights at home a couple of times a week. ¹⁶I wiped the smirks off their faces with a line drive double over the left fielder's head.

2

The number of the irrelevant sentence: _____

¹⁷The next game, we played another new team, and this time their attitude was a patronizing one. ¹⁸The Argyles had seen me take batting practice, so they didn't do anything so rash as to draw their outfield way in. ¹⁹They had respect for my ability as a player. ²⁰However, they tried to annoy me with phoney concern. ²¹For example, a red-headed Argyle got on base in the first inning and said to me, "You'd better be careful, Hon. ²²When you have your foot on the bag, somebody might step on it. ²³You can get hurt in this game." ²⁴I was mad, but I have worked out several mental techniques to control my anger because it interferes with my playing ability. ²⁵Well, this delicate little girl survived the season without injury, which is more than I can say for some of the "he-men" on the Argyles.

3

The number of the irrelevant sentence: _____

²⁶Happily, most of the teams in the league have accepted me, just as the Browns did. ²⁷The men on the Browns coached and criticized me (and occasionally cursed me) just like anyone else. ²⁸Because I'm a religious person, I don't approve of cursing, but I don't say anything about it to my teammates. ²⁹They are not amazed when I get a hit or stretch for a wide throw. ³⁰My average this year was higher than the averages of several of my teammates, yet none of them acted resentful or threatened. ³¹On several occasions I was taken out late in a game for a pinch runner, but other slow players on the team were also lifted at times for pinch runners. ³²Every woman should have a team like the Browns!

4

The number of the irrelevant sentence: _____

[33]Because I really had problems only with the new teams, I've concluded   5
that it's when people are faced with an unfamiliar situation that they react
defensively. [34]Once a rival team has gotten used to seeing me on the field,
I'm no big deal. [35]Still, I suspect that the Browns secretly feel we're a little
special. [36]After all, we won the championship with a woman on the team.

2 REVISING ESSAYS FOR SUPPORT

Activity

The essay below lacks supporting details at certain key points. Identify the spots
where details are needed.

Formula for Happiness

[1]Everyone has his or her own formula for happiness. [2]As we go through life,   1
we discover the activities that make us feel best. [3]I've already discovered three
keys for my happiness. [4]I depend on karate, music, and self-hypnosis.

[5]Karate helps me feel good physically. [6]Before taking karate lessons, I was   2
tired most of the time, my muscles felt like foam rubber, and I was twenty pounds
overweight. [7]After three months of these lessons, I saw an improvement in my
physical condition. [8]Also, my endurance has increased. [9]At the end of my workday,
I used to drag myself home to eat and watch television all night. [10]Now, I have
enough energy to play with my children, shop, or see a movie. [11]Karate has
made me feel healthy, strong, and happy.

The spot where supporting details are needed occurs after sentence _____ .

[12]Singing with a chorus has helped me achieve emotional well-being by   3
expressing my feelings. [13]In situations where other people would reveal their
feelings, I would remain quiet. [14]Since joining the chorus, however, I have an
outlet for joy, anger, or sadness. [15]When I sing, I pour my emotions into the
music and don't have to feel shy. [16]For this reason, I enjoy singing certain
kinds of music the most, since they demand real depth of feeling.

The first spot where supporting details are needed occurs after sentence _____ .

The second spot occurs after sentence _____ .

[17]Self-hypnosis gives me peace of mind. [18]This is a total relaxation technique   4
that I learned several years ago. [19]Essentially I breathe deeply and concentrate
on relaxing all my muscles. [20]I then repeat a key suggestion to myself. [21]Through
self-hypnosis, I have gained control over several bad habits that have long been
haunting me. [22]I have also learned to reduce the stress that goes along with my
secretarial job. [23]Now I can handle the boss's demands or unexpected work
without feeling tense.

The first spot where supporting details are needed occurs after sentence _____.

The second spot occurs after sentence _____.

[24]In short, my physical, emotional, and mental well-being have been greatly increased through karate, music, and self-hypnosis. [25]These activities have become important elements in my formula for happiness.

5

3   REVISING ESSAYS FOR COHERENCE

Activity

The essay that follows could be revised to improve its coherence. Answer the questions about coherence that come after the essay.

Noise Pollution

[1]Natural sounds—waves, wind, bird songs—are so soothing that companies sell CDs and tapes of them to anxious people seeking a relaxing atmosphere in their homes or cars. [2]One reason why "environmental sounds" are big business is the fact that ordinary citizens—especially city dwellers—are bombarded by noise pollution. [3]On the way to work, on the job, and on the way home, the typical urban resident must cope with a continuing barrage of unpleasant sounds.

1

[4]The noise level in an office can be unbearable. [5]From nine to five, phones and fax machines ring, modems sound, computer keyboards chatter, intercoms buzz, and copy machines thump back and forth. [6]Every time the receptionists can't find people, they resort to a nerve-shattering public address system. [7]And because the managers worry about the employees' morale, they graciously provide the endless droning of canned music. [8]This effectively eliminates any possibility of a moment of blessed silence.

2

[9]Travelling home from work provides no relief from the noisiness of the office. [10]The ordinary sounds of blaring taxi horns and rumbling buses are occasionally punctuated by the ear-piercing screech of car brakes. [11]Taking a shortcut through the park will bring the weary worker face to face with chanting religious cults, freelance musicians, screaming children, and barking dogs. [12]None of these sounds can compare with the large radios many park visitors carry. [13]Each radio blasts out something different, from heavy-metal rock to baseball, at decibel levels so strong that they make eardrums throb in pain. [14]If there are birds singing or wind in the trees, the harried commuter will never hear them.

3

[15]Even a trip to work at 6 or 7 a.m. isn't quiet. [16]No matter which route a worker takes, there is bound to be a noisy construction site somewhere along the way. [17]Hard hats will shout from third-storey windows to warn their co-workers below before heaving debris out and sending it crashing to earth. [18]Huge front-end loaders will crunch into these piles of rubble and back up, their warning signals letting out loud, jarring beeps. [19]Air hammers begin an ear-splitting chorus of rat-a-tat-tat sounds guaranteed to shatter sanity as well as concrete. [20]Before reaching the office, the worker is already completely frazzled.

4

[21]Noise pollution is as dangerous as any other kind of pollution. [22]The   5
endless pressure of noise probably triggers countless nervous breakdowns,
vicious arguments, and bouts of depression. [23]And imagine the world problems
we could solve, if only the noise stopped long enough to let us think.

1. In "Noise Pollution," what is the number of the sentence to which the
   transition word *Also* could be added in paragraph 2? _____

2. In the last sentence of paragraph 2, to what does the pronoun *This* refer?

   _____

3. What is the number of the sentence to which the transition word *But* could
   be added in paragraph 3? _____

4. What is the number of the sentence to which the transition word *Then* could
   be added in paragraph 4? _____

5. What is the number of the sentence to which the transition word *Meanwhile*
   could be added in paragraph 4? _____

6. What word is used as a synonym for *debris* in paragraph 4? _____

7. How many times is the key word *sounds* repeated in the essay? _____

8. The time order of the three supporting paragraphs is confused. Which
   supporting paragraph should come first? _____ Second? _____
   Third? _____

4 REVISING ESSAYS FOR ALL FOUR BASES: UNITY, SUPPORT, COHERENCE, AND SENTENCE SKILLS

Activity

In this activity, you will evaluate and revise two essays in terms of all four bases:
unity, support, coherence, and sentence skills. Comments follow each supporting
paragraph. Circle the letter of the *one* statement that applies in each case.

Essay 1

Chiggers

I had lived my whole life around Dauphin, Manitoba, not knowing what   1
chiggers are. I thought they were probably a type of insect Humphrey Bogart
encountered in *The African Queen*. I never had any reason to really care, until
my first winter vacation in Florida. Within twenty-four hours, I had vividly
experienced what chigger bites are, learned how to treat them, and learned
how to prevent them.

First of all, I learned that chiggers are the larvae of tiny mites found in the **2** palmetto scrub and twitch grass on the edges of Florida beaches and that their multiple bites always cause intense itching. A beautiful day in a March break seemed perfect for a walk along an empty stretch of beach. I am definitely not a city person, for I couldn't stand to be surrounded by people, parties, and hotel pools. As I walked through the beach grass, I noticed what appeared to be a dusting of reddish seeds or pollen on my slacks. Looking more closely, I realized that each speck was a tiny insect. I casually brushed off a few and gave them no further thought. I woke up the next morning feeling like an inflamed pincushion. Most of my legs were speckled with measle-like bumps that at the slightest touch burned and itched like a mosquito bite raised to the twentieth power. When antiseptics and calamine lotion failed to help, I raced to a walk-in clinic for emergency aid.

a. Paragraph 2 contains an irrelevant sentence.
b. Paragraph 2 lacks supporting details at one key spot.
c. Time order in paragraph 2 is confused.
d. Paragraph 2 contains two run-ons.

Healing the bites of chiggers, as the doctor diagnosed them to be, is not a **3** simple procedure. It seems there is really no wonder drug or commercial product to help the cure. The victim must rely on a harsh and primitive home remedy and mostly wait out the course of the painful bites. First, the doctor explained, the skin must be bathed carefully in alcohol. An antihistamine spray applied several hours later will soothe the intense itching and help prevent infection. Before using the spray, I had to saturate each bite with gasoline or nail polish to kill any remaining chiggers. A few days after the treatment, the bites finally healed. Although I was still in pain, and desperate for relief, I followed the doctor's instructions. I carefully applied gasoline to the bites and walked around for an hour smelling like a gas station.

a. Paragraph 3 contains an irrelevant sentence.
b. Paragraph 3 lacks supporting details at one key spot.
c. Time order in paragraph 3 is confused.
d. Paragraph 3 contains one fragment.

Most important of all, I learned what to do to prevent getting chigger bites **4** in future trips down south. Mainly, of course, stay out of the scrub-growth at the edge of beaches. But if the temptation is too great on an especially beautiful day, I'll be sure to wear the right type of clothing, like a long-sleeved shirt, long pants, knee socks, and closed shoes. In addition, I'll cover myself with clouds of super-strength insect repellent. I will then shower thoroughly as soon as I get home, I also will probably burn all my clothes if I notice even one suspicious red speck.

a. Paragraph 4 contains an irrelevant sentence.
b. Paragraph 4 lacks supporting details at one key spot.
c. Paragraph 4 lacks transitional words.
d. Paragraph 4 contains a run-on and a fragment.

I will never forget my lessons on the cause, cure, and prevention of chigger   **5**
bites. I'd gladly accept the challenge of rattlesnakes, wolves, and bears in the
forests of western Canada but will never again confront a siege of chiggers on
an empty Florida beach.

Essay 2

The Hazards of Being an Only Child

Many people who have grown up in multi-child families think that being an   **1**
only child is the best of all possible worlds. They point to such benefits as the
only child's annual new wardrobe and lack of competition for parental love. But
single-child status isn't as good as people say it is. Instead of having everything
they want, only children are sometimes denied certain basic human needs.

Only children lack companionship. An only child can have trouble making   **2**
friends, since he or she isn't used to being around other children. Often, the
only child comes home to an empty house; both parents are working, and
there are no brothers or sisters to play with or to talk to about the day. At
dinner, the single child can't tell jokes, giggle, or throw food while the adults
discuss boring adult subjects. An only child always has his or her own room
but never has anyone to whisper to half the night when sleep doesn't come.
Some only children thrive on this isolation and channel their energies into
creative activities like writing or drawing. Owing to this lack of companionship,
an only child sometimes lacks the social ease and self-confidence that come
from being part of a closely knit group of contemporaries.

a. Paragraph 2 contains an irrelevant sentence.
b. Paragraph 2 lacks supporting details at one key spot.
c. Paragraph 2 lacks transitional words.
d. Paragraph 2 contains one fragment and one run-on.

Second, only children lack privacy. An only child is automatically the   **3**
centre of parental concern. There's never any doubt about which child tried to
sneak in after midnight on a weekday. And who will get the lecture the next
morning. Also, whenever an only child gives in to a bad mood, runs into his or
her room, and slams the door, the door will open thirty seconds later, revealing
an anxious parent. Parents of only children sometimes don't even understand
the child's need for privacy. For example, they may not understand why a
teenager wants a lock on the door or a personal telephone. After all, the
parents think, there are only the three of us, there's no need for secrets.

a. Paragraph 3 contains an irrelevant sentence.
b. Paragraph 3 lacks supporting details at one key spot.
c. Paragraph 3 lacks transitional words.
d. Paragraph 3 contains one fragment and one run-on.

Most important, only children lack power. They get all the love; but if something goes wrong, they also get all the punishment. When a bottle of perfume is knocked to the floor or the television is left on all night, there's no little sister or brother to blame it on. Moreover, an only child has no recourse when asking for a privilege of some kind, such as permission to stay out to a late hour or to take an overnight trip with friends. There are no other siblings to point to and say, "You let them do it. Why won't you let me?" With no allies their own age, only children are always outnumbered, two to one. An only child hasn't a chance of influencing any major family decisions, either.

4

a. Paragraph 4 contains an irrelevant sentence.
b. Paragraph 4 lacks supporting details at one key spot.
c. Paragraph 4 lacks transitional words.
d. Paragraph 4 contains one fragment and one run-on.

Being an only child isn't as special as some people think. It's no fun being without friends, without privacy, and without power in one's own home. But the child who can triumph over these hardships grows up self-reliant and strong. Perhaps for this reason alone, the hazards are worth it.

5

REVIEWING THE LEARNING OUTCOMES

To be sure that you have a thorough understanding of the four goals and bases for writing effective essays, answer the following questions.

- How do you achieve unity in your essays?
- How do writers make supporting evidence effective?
- What are three items you might put on a checklist for coherence in your essays?
- How do weak sentence skills interfere with the effectiveness of an essay?

Patterns of Essay Development

tion • Description • Examples • Process • Cause and Effect • Comparison and contrast
nition • Division and Classification • Argumentation • Narration • Description • Examples
ess • Cause and Effect • Comparison and contrast • Definition • Division and Classification
mentation • Narration • Description • Examples • Process • Cause and Effect • Comparison and
trast • Definition • Division and Classification • Argumentation • Narration • Description

C H A P T E R 7

Introduction to Essay Development

LEARNING OUTCOMES

After reading this chapter, you will
- Know how this part of the text is set out
- Understand the relationship between an essay's subject and patterns of essay development
- Reinforce your understanding of pronoun viewpoint in essay writing
- Be prepared to use two methods of revision for your essays: peer review and a personal checklist

PATTERNS OF ESSAY DEVELOPMENT

Narration and description are basic to all writing. As we arrange ideas into any pattern, we create a narrative "line": a trail or thread for readers to follow. When we try to show readers how something looks, feels, or works we are describing places, emotions, business plans, or technical processes, so we use description in all writing as well.

- **Narration is the ordering and shaping voice** of writing. As a main pattern, the narrative "line," storyline, or sequence of events predominates as a way of presenting a series of ideas that explain a point.
- **Description is the camera lens** of writing. As a main pattern of development, a descriptive essay's main emphasis in explaining or clarifying its point relies on close rendering, "photographing in words" some object, feeling, and/or location.

Exposition consists of a group of patterns whose main purpose is to expose the reader to information arranged according to a method that best serves the subject matter. Expository essays literally "expose" the reader to ordered information, thereby explaining and justifying a viewpoint stated in the thesis. Patterns of exposition are different ways or modes of shaping the "proof" or supporting points in the body of the essay; one pattern, or combination of patterns, may be best suited to communicating to readers a particular type of subject.

- **Essays that mainly offer examples** clarify each supporting point with examples to illustrate specifically that point's meaning and importance.
- **Essays that demonstrate or break down a process** either instruct or show a breakdown of how some finished product or goal is achieved.
- **Essays that show or analyze causes and effects** emphasize why some point is true or has come to be.
- **Essays that compare or contrast** two subjects or two aspects of one subject can either focus on one side at a time or make a point-by-point comparison.
- **Essays that mainly define** a subject work to clarify the writer's intent and explore various meanings of a concept.
- **Essays that divide a subject and classify it** into groupings or categories offer a clear-cut method for examining potentially complex issues.

Argumentation or persuasion naturally occurs in many well-supported essays, as the thesis point is carefully explained and proved. Essays whose main goal is arguing a point use specific tactics to gain support for a potentially contentious idea or to defend a position about which there might logically be differences of opinion.

Each chapter following presents one of these methods of essay development. You will have the chance to explore how the different patterns can work to organize material for essays and other writing formats in many of your college subjects. Each pattern or method has its definite internal logic and uses, and each offers special strategies for ordering and exploring different types of subject material.

Keep two important points in mind, as you practise "pure forms" of each pattern of development:

1. **Essays rarely use only one pattern of development.**
   You will practise writing essays that follow a single predominant pattern for supporting your point. But more often than not, you will consciously or unconsciously use additional or subordinate methods to make and demonstrate your points. You will probably use at least an example or two, whether you write a process essay of instruction or trace the causes of some problem. In the "Examples" chapter, the essay "Altered States" uses Examples as a main method, but the writer also uses the *cause and effect* pattern to explain the origins of altered states of mind.

2. **Essays generally involve presenting an argument.**
   Your essay, no matter which pattern you choose for your subject, will generally offer some form of argumentation. The overall deductive essay structure of opening with a thesis, then providing support, constitutes an argument for your thesis point. The writer of "Everyday Common Scents" (pages 174-175) does not merely describe a variety of ordinary smells; her *descriptive details* make an effective argument for the importance of paying attention to everyday pleasures. Another writer contrasts his life as a college student with his working life a year before; the *contrasting support* he supplies about both is a persuasive argument for his thesis (pages 226-228). Your essays generally have the overriding purpose of persuading your reader that the argument or point you advance is valid.

Using Part 2: The Progression in Each Chapter

After each type of essay development is explained in the following chapters, student essays illustrating that type are presented, followed by questions about the papers. The questions relate to unity, support, and coherence—the principles and goals of effective writing explained earlier in this book.

You are then asked to write your own essay. In most cases, the first assignment is fairly structured and provides a good deal of guidance for the writing process. The other assignments offer a wide and interesting choice of writing topics. In each case, the last or next-to-last assignment involves writing an essay with a specific purpose and for a specific audience. And in two instances (cause-and-effect, and comparison or contrast), there are assignments requiring outside reading or research.

The chapters in this section treat writing as a process; the stages in approaching, working through, and revising a writing task appear on the pages that follow.

THE WRITING PROCESS: FIRST CONSIDERATIONS, WRITING DECISIONS, AND PEER REVIEW

Before you begin work on particular types of essays, always consider the following concerns basic to all writing tasks:

- The nature and length of the assignment
- Your understanding of your subject
- Your purpose and your reading audience
- Your viewpoint or degree of subjectivity, expressed in point of view

Understanding the Nature and Length of an Assignment

Writing tasks and assignments in Canadian colleges are highly varied. In English and Communications courses, you will sometimes write on a topic of your own choosing, or on some point you discover within a given topic. Other times, in both English and your professional subjects, highly specific assigned topics will be given to you.

Writing formats assigned may include essays, summaries, reports, letters, case studies, and analyses. Essay structures, as set out in this text, will prepare you to manage information appropriately within various types of essays as well as in formats other than the essay.

Whatever the writing task, do not begin an assignment until you know exactly *what type of paper* the instructor has in mind. Is an assignment mainly a research summary of other people's ideas? Should it be based entirely on your own ideas? Or should it consist of a comparison of your ideas with those of other authorities?

If you are uncertain about the nature of an assignment, chances are that other students feel similar confusion. Never hesitate to ask an instructor about an assignment. Most would rather clear up confusion about assignments during class time or by e-mail before a due date than spend hours reading student essays that miss the mark.

Finally, find out *how long* a paper is expected to be. Most instructors indicate the approximate length desired in assignments. Knowing the expected length of a paper will help you decide how detailed your treatment of a subject should be, and how much time to allot for its successful planning and completion.

Knowing Your Subject

Whenever possible, try to write on a subject that interests you. You will find it easier to put more time and energy into your work. More importantly, try to write on a subject that you already know something about. If you have no direct experience with the subject, you may still have some indirect experience—knowledge gained from thinking, reading, or talking about the subject as well as from prewriting.

If you are asked to write on a topic about which you have no experience or knowledge, do whatever research is needed to gain background information you may need. "Using the Library and the Internet" on pages 319–333 will show you how to find relevant information. Without direct or indirect experience, or the information you gain through research, your writing task will seem impossible and you may be unable to provide the specific evidence needed to develop your essay.

Knowing Your Purpose and Audience

The three most common purposes of writing are to inform, to persuade, and to entertain. Most of the writing this book requires of you will involve some form of persuasion. You will advance a point or thesis and then support it in a variety of ways. To some extent, you will also write papers that provide readers with information about a particular subject.

Your main audience will be your instructor, and sometimes fellow students as well. Your instructor is really a symbol of the larger audience you should see yourself as writing for—an educated, adult audience that expects you to present your ideas in a clear, direct, and organized way. If you can learn to persuade or inform such a general audience through your writing, to "speak your mind in your own voice on paper," you will have accomplished a great deal.

Occasionally you will be challenged to write some papers for a more specific audience. By so doing, you develop an ability to choose words and adopt a tone and viewpoint that is right for a given purpose and a given group of people.

Viewpoint, Subject Matter, and Degree

When you write, you can take any of three approaches, or points of view: first-person, second-person, or third-person. Each is a different "writing voice," and each creates a different response in your reader. By suggesting a certain level of involvement in your material, you set up a specific distance, or lack thereof, between you and your reader.

First-Person Approach: Variances in One Voice

In the first-person writing voice, you speak to your audience in your own voice, using pronouns like *I, me, mine, we, our,* and *us.* Speaking as *I,* you speak subjectively and individually; your audience is very aware of your presence in your writing. Using *we*, you may suggest that you include your reader or that others share your views; there is a subtle difference implied by your choice of pronoun.

The first-person approach is most common in narrative essays based on personal experience. The *I* voice in first-person writing also suits writing tasks where most of the evidence presented consists of personal observation; this is a forceful and strong voice when your main purpose is to present your personal connection to your material. The limitation of first-person viewpoint is its subjectivity; it cannot sound objective or impartial; it may be an "intrusive voice," if you wish to emphasize your information, rather than your connection to it.

We, as a point-of-view choice, may suit essays where you sense or hope for likely agreement from your reader on subjects less completely focused on your own experience. Writing as *we* allows you to "disappear" slightly as writer, to blur your presence; *we* implies, to some degree, a common viewpoint already held.

Here is a first-person supporting paragraph from an essay on balancing college and work:

> The first problem I faced when I decided to enter college in my late twenties was money. That problem had a lot of questions connected to it. How was I going to pay rent and bills, buy groceries, afford tuition fees and books, and just stay alive? My job as a data-entry clerk paid well enough to let me live pretty comfortably, but my position didn't exist as a part-time job. Because I felt I was going nowhere, and that I needed to find a career with a future, I wanted to learn new skills and to be paid for using my mind as well as my typing ability. I read about provincial student loan programs, but I hated the idea of going into debt. The only solution to my first problem was a part-time job. But I was still afraid of two years of learning without that regular weekly paycheque.

Second-Person Approach and "False Third-Person"

In the second-person approach, the writer speaks directly to the reader, using the pronoun *you*. The second-person approach is considered appropriate for giving direct instructions and explanations to the reader. That is why *you* is used throughout this book.

Use the second-person approach only when writing a process essay. Otherwise, as a general rule, never use the word *you* in essay writing.

In English, *you* is used in conversation as a "false third-person" pronoun. Students sometimes carry this habit into their writing; for example, "Internet research seems easy at first; *you* simply type in a key word." Is this writer referring to or addressing "you the reader"? Probably not. Rather than "you the reader," the student likely means "people," "students," or some specific group. If you discover a "false third-person *you*," decide whom you mean by *you*. Replace that *you* with a noun describing persons you mean. If these "false third people" occur frequently in your writing, you should review the rule about pronoun point of view on pages 100–101.

Third-Person Approach

The third-person approach is by far the most common point of view in academic, and much business, technical, and career-related writing. Writing as the third person, the writer includes no direct references to the reader *(you)* or the self *(I, me)*. Third person gets its name from the stance it suggests—that of an outsider or "third person," observing and reporting on matters of general rather than private importance. Choosing this approach, you suggest some distance from your subject; you allow readers some "space" for responses to material; you suggest that your information is derived less from direct experience than from observation, thinking, or reading.

Here is the paragraph on balancing work and college, recast in the third person. Note the third-person pronouns *their*, *them*, and *they*, and the nouns *students* and *people:* these replace the *I* of the first paragraph example. Note also your response as reader to the "newly presented" material.

> The first problem many students face when they decide to enter college as mature students is money. Money is a problem with a lot of questions connected to it. How will students without full-time incomes pay rent and bills, buy groceries, afford tuition fees and books, and just stay alive? Many students who return to their education have held jobs that paid well enough to let them live pretty comfortably, but many positions are not available as part-time jobs. People enter college because they feel their jobs are going nowhere, and they need to find a career with a future. They know they want to learn new skills and to be paid for using their minds. Provincial student loan programs are available, but the idea of going into debt may be unappealing. The only solution to such students' first problem may be a part-time job. But these students may still be afraid of two years of learning without that regular weekly paycheque.

REVISING, DEVELOPING YOUR CRITICAL SENSE, AND REVIEWING YOURSELF

Using Peer Review

In addition to having your instructor as a final audience for your writing, you will benefit in two ways from having another student in your class as an "intermediate" or "revising audience." First, you may feel less judged by one of your peers, and second, by "seeing your writing through other eyes," you develop your critical awareness as you read and respond to your peer's comments.

Step 1: Choose a peer marker. On the day a paper is due, or on a day when you are writing papers in class, your teacher may ask you to pair up with another student. That student will read your paper, and you will read his or her paper.

Step 2: Listen critically to your peer's essay. Ideally, read the other paper aloud while your peer listens. If that is too noisy or uncomfortable, read it in a whisper while your peer looks on. As you read, both you and your fellow student should look and listen for spots where the paper does not read smoothly and clearly. Check or circle the trouble spots where your reading snags. Your peer should then read your paper, marking possible trouble spots.

Step 3:   Create your marking sheet for an X-ray outline and your comments.

1   *Identification:* At the top of a separate sheet of paper, write the title and author of the paper you have read. Under it, write your own name as the reader of the paper.

2   *Outline:* "X-ray" the paper for its inner logic by making up a scratch outline. The scratch outline need be no more than twenty words or so, but it should show clearly the logical foundation on which the essay is built. It should identify and summarize the overall point of the paper and the three areas of support for the point. Your outline can look as follows:

Point: _____

Support: 1. _____

　　　　　 2. _____

　　　　　 3. _____

For example, here is a scratch outline of the essay on movie-going on pages 13–14:

Point: *Going out to the movies presents too many problems.*

Support: *1. Getting to the theatre*

　　　　　 2. Dealing with theatre itself

　　　　　 3. Putting up with other patrons

3   *Comments:* Under the outline, write the heading "Comments." Here is what you should comment on:

- First, note something you really liked about the paper. You might, for instance, mention good use of transitions or a specific detail that is especially realistic or vivid.
- Are there spots in the paper where you see problems with *unity, support,* or *organization?* If so, offer comments. For example, you might say, "More details are needed in the first supporting paragraph," or "Some of the details in the last supporting paragraph don't really back up your point."
- Finally, look at the spots where your reading of the paper snagged. Are words missing or misspelled? Is parallel structure lacking? Are there mistakes with punctuation? Is the meaning of a sentence confused? Try to figure out what the problems are and suggest ways of fixing them.

After completing your evaluation of the paper, give it to your classmate. Your teacher may provide you with the option of rewriting a paper in light of the peer feedback. Whether or not you rewrite, be sure to hand in the peer evaluation form with your paper.

Final Personal Reviewing

1 While you're in the final stages of revising an essay, use the detailed checklist on the inside front cover of this text to carefully evaluate your assignment for *unity*, *support*, and *coherence*.

2 Before you begin the final draft of your essay, check it for errors in the *sentence skills* listed on the inside front cover. Last, read the paper out loud. If any given sentence doesn't sound right—that is, if it does not read clearly and smoothly—chances are something is wrong. Revise, correct, or edit until your paper is complete.

REVIEWING THE LEARNING OUTCOMES FOR CHAPTER 7

To reassure yourself that you have met the Learning Outcomes for this chapter, answer the following questions:

- What are the main patterns for developing the content of an essay, and where will you find each in this book?

- How do the expository methods of development differ from narration and description?

- Why is argumentation or persuasion consistently part of essay writing?

- If you are assigned an essay on the subject of "Attendance and Success," which pattern of development would you choose, and why? If your essay is to show readers how to install a software package, which pattern would you choose, and why?

- Which of the three pronoun points of view is generally best suited to college writing assignments, and why?

- Where in this text will you find checklists for revising your essays?

---

tion • Description • Examples • Process • Cause and Effect • Comparison and contrast nition • Division and Classification • Argumentation • Narration • Description • Examples ess • Cause and Effect • Comparison and Contrast • Definition • Division and Classification mentation • Narration • Description • Examples • Process • Cause and Effect • Comparison and rast • Definition • Division and Classification • Argumentation • Narration • Description

Narration

LEARNING OUTCOMES

After working through the activities and writing tasks in this chapter, you will be ready to write a narrative essay that

- Narrates an experience wherein some conflict makes a definite point
- Organizes and sequences your supporting material in time order to offer an accurate and coherent narrative
- Shows careful selection of details essential to your point
- Is revised to present vivid elements that "show" readers your point and recreate events as clearly as possible
- Concludes by returning to its point in an interesting manner, rather than ending with its last event

Children beg to hear a favourite story read again and again. Over dinner, people tell each other of their day. A restless class settles down when a teacher says, "Let me tell you something strange that happened to me once." Our ancestors' myths, tales of great hunts and battles, of angry gods and foolish humans instructed as they entertained their audiences. Whatever our age, we never outgrow our hunger for stories.

Narration requires us to recount a sequence or series of events, whether we relate a single "line" of action or several intertwined ones. Narrative-based essays make a point clear by their selection of relevant details that advance the line of narration as they unfold and deepen the meaning of the piece.

Narration generally presents the details in the order in which they happened. Someone might say, "I was really embarrassed the day I took my driver's test," and then go on to develop that statement with an account of the experience. If the narrative is sharply detailed, we will be able to see and understand just why the speaker felt that way.

Narrative essays sometimes relate personal experience, but not all narrative is first-person or subjective; nor does it resemble storytelling in some of its forms. Case studies and reports require narrative skill for accurate recreation of events and their meanings. Indeed, every profession's writing tasks use narration to record and recreate events and experiences. Narrative is often simply the writer's presence as orderer and controller of ideas or events.

In this section, you will be asked to write a narrative essay that illustrates some point. To prepare for this assignment, first read the student essays that follow and work through the questions accompanying the essays. Both essays use narrative as their main method of developing their points.

STUDENT ESSAYS TO CONSIDER

Adopting a Challenge

My church recently staged a "Sensitivity Sunday" to make our congregation aware of the problems faced by people who are physically challenged. We were asked to "adopt a challenge" for several hours one Sunday morning. Some members, like me, chose to use wheelchairs; others wore sound-blocking earplugs, hobbled around on crutches, or wore blindfolds.

1

Just sitting in the wheelchair was instructive. I had never considered before how awkward it would be to use one. As soon as I sat down, my weight made the chair begin to roll. Its wheels were not locked, and I fumbled clumsily to correct that. Another awkward moment occurred when I realized I had no place to put my feet. I fumbled some more to turn the metal footrest into place. I felt psychologically awkward as well, as I took my first uneasy look at what was to be my only means of transportation for several hours. I realized that for many people, "adopting a wheelchair" is not a temporary experiment. That was a sober thought as I sank back into my seat.

2

Once I sat down, I had to learn how to cope with the wheelchair. I shifted around, trying to find a comfortable position. I thought it might be restful, even kind of nice, to be pushed around for a while. I glanced around to see who would be pushing me and then realized I would have to navigate the contraption by myself! My palms reddened and my wrist and forearm muscles started to ache as I tugged at the heavy metal wheels. I realized as I veered this way and that that steering and turning were not going to be easy tasks. Trying to make a right-angle turn from one aisle to another, I steered straight into a pew. I felt as though everyone was staring at me and commenting on my clumsiness.

3

When the service started, other problems cropped up to frustrate me further. Every time the congregation stood up, my view was blocked. I could not see the minister, the choir, or the altar. Also, as the church's aisles were narrow, I seemed to be in the way no matter where I parked myself. For instance, the ushers had to squeeze by me to pass the collection plate. This made me feel like a nuisance. Thanks to a new building program, however, our church will soon have the wide aisles and well-spaced pews that will make life easier for the physically challenged. After the service ended, when people stopped to talk to me, I had to strain my neck and look up at them. This made me feel like a little child being talked down to and added to my sense of powerlessness.

4

My wheelchair experiment was soon over. It's true that it made an impression on me. I no longer resent large tax expenditures for ramp-equipped buses, and I wouldn't dream of parking my car in a space marked "Handicapped Only." But I also realize how little I know about the daily life of a physically

5

challenged person. A few hours of voluntary "challenge" gave me only a hint of the challenges, both physical and emotional, that people with any physical limitation must overcome.

The Gift

"Only one more thing on my list," Marlena said contentedly to herself. Walking back from lunchtime errands, she paused at the holiday display in the museum's gift shop window. Atop a velvety navy blue pillow sat a lustrous silver pin. She imagined crossing that last item off her list, thinking she'd found the perfect thing for her mother. But her contentment faded as a salesperson lifted the pin away, making room for a glossy book on vintage Canadian motor boats and a toy sailboat. Sometimes moments of satisfaction and the tidiest plans just seem meant to be disturbed.

1

"My grandson would love that little boat. His father is away sailing right now, you know, off the coast of Argentina." The voice, bright as a bird's chirp, seemed to carry a melody. Its owner was an older woman who had joined Marlena at the window. Dressed head to toe in shades of green, she looked like an elf. Everything about her was bright, except for the bluish foggy layer on her eyes. Surprised to find herself so interested, Marlena listened attentively to the woman's stories of her seagoing son and of her grandson's boat collection.

2

While she listened, one thought chased round and round her mind: her boyfriend's obsession with wooden motorboats. He went to boat shows, wrote to online lists of old boat fans, and doodled endless plans for hulls and frames on his notepads. In fact, he'd priced the very book the clerk had placed in the window. But once Marlena was inside, questions nagged her. What about the Maple Leafs sweater she'd already bought and wrapped for him? If she bought the book and the sweater, her careful budget would be shot. Agonized with doubt, she entered the store and watched the older woman buy the toy boat. She envisioned her tidy mental list scarred with cross-out lines and stood arguing with herself about changing plans and spending more than she'd budgeted. Then, startled from her thoughts by a cheery "Goodbye," she nodded and smiled at the grandmother in green, and glanced back at the window display, and the book.

3

Finally, she walked purposefully to the cashier. "I'm afraid I'll have to ask you to take that book out of the window." Her brother Luciano would be the one to get the hockey sweater, she decided; in fact he would get two presents this year. She pictured her younger brother's surprise at such generosity after months of quarrels. She saw her boyfriend's face as he unwrapped the motorboat book, and smiled to herself. No longer was she bothered by visions of untidy lists and changes to her bank balance.

4

As she left the museum to return to work, Marlena spotted the green coat and hat ahead of her at the stoplights. She hoped the sailor's son would like his gift and enjoy his own voyages. Smiling again at no one in particular, she felt quite a different kind of contentment. Organization may be a gift, but sometimes an unexpected change is the best gift of all.

5

■   **Questions**

About Unity

1. Which essay lacks an opening thesis statement?

   _____

2. Which sentence in paragraph 4 of "Adopting a Challenge" should be omitted
   in the interest of paragraph unity? *(Write the opening words.)*

   _____

3. What sentence in paragraph 2 of "The Gift" should be omitted in the interest
   of paragraph unity? *(Write the opening words.)*

   _____

4. What sentence in the final paragraph of "The Gift" makes the mistake of
   introducing a new topic and so should be eliminated?

   _____

About Support

5. Label as *sight, touch, hearing,* or *smell* all the sensory details in the following
   sentences taken from the essays.
   a. "My palms reddened and my wrist and forearm muscles started to ache as I
      tugged at the heavy metal wheels."
   b. "I could not see the minister, the choir, or the altar."
   c. "Atop a velvety navy blue pillow sat a lustrous silver pin."
   d. "The voice, bright as a bird's chirp, seemed to carry a melody."

6. In a narrative, the main method of organization is time order. Which sentence
   in paragraph 3 of "The Gift" is placed out of order?

   _____

7. In "Adopting a Challenge," how many examples support the topic sentence
   of paragraph 4, "When the service started, other problems cropped up to

   frustrate me further"? _____

About Coherence

8. The first stage of the writer's experience in "Adopting a Challenge" might be called
   sitting down in the wheelchair. What are the other two stages of the experience?

   _____

   _____

9. List three time transitions used in the third paragraph of "The Gift."

_____   _____   _____

About the Introduction

10. What methods of introduction form the first paragraph of "The Gift"? Circle the appropriate letters.
    a. Broad, general statement narrowing to a thesis
    b. Idea that is the opposite of the one to be developed
    c. An incident

WRITING A NARRATIVE ESSAY

Narrative's function is to **recreate** events and emotions for readers. Making a scene "come alive," as you experienced it, requires

- A clear sense of the scenes you recount
- Knowledge of the point you wish to make about the scenes and the experience itself
- Use of vivid language to most accurately recreate your narrative

Prewriting: Stage 1
Discovering Your Story and Its Meaning

The first stage in creating an effective narrative is prewriting, letting your story or experience "replay" in your mind to discover its key events. Freewriting is a particularly helpful technique for your first stage of prewriting. (For more about freewriting, see pages 27–29.) As you consider the story or series of events you want to relate, many ideas will crowd into your head. Simply writing them down in free-form style will jog loose details you may have forgotten and help you decide what the main point of your story really is.

Lisa, the writer of "Adopting a Challenge," spent a half-hour freewriting before she wrote the first draft of her essay. Here is what she came up with:

> Our church was planning a building renovation to make the church more accessible to the physically challenged. Some people thought it was a waste of money and that challenged people could get along all right in the church the way it was. Not many people with physical challenges come to our church anyway. The minister gave a sermon on the subject. He suggested we spend one Sunday pretending to be physically challenged ourselves. We got to choose our challenge. Some people pretended to be blind or deaf or in need of crutches. I chose to use a wheelchair. I thought it might be fun to have someone push me around. A lot scarier and more disturbing than I expected. We borrowed wheelchairs and crutches from a local nursing home. I didn't like sitting down in the wheelchair. I didn't know how to work it right. It rolled when I didn't want it to. I felt clumsy trying to make it move. I even ran into a pew. I felt silly trying to be disabled and also sort of disrespectful because for most people sitting in a wheelchair isn't a choice. It also bothered me to think what it'd be like if I couldn't get up

again. It turned out that nobody was going to push me around. I though Paula would but instead she put on a blindfold and pretended to be blind. She knocked over a cup of coffee before the morning was over. She told me later that she felt really panicky when that happened. Sitting down so low in the wheelchair was weird. I couldn't see much of anything. People ignored me or talked to me like I was a little kid. I was glad when the morning was over. Making the wheels turn hurt my hands and arms.

Prewriting: Stage 2
Ordering and Outlining

1   *Ordering Your Narrative*   When you write a narrative essay, you are essentially telling a linked series of events. Most likely, you will develop that story in chronological order—in *time sequence*—from what happened first, to what happened next, and so on.

2   *Discovering Your Point*   Many narratives, especially "expository essay narratives" *recreate* an event or events to *expose* or examine the feelings and motives connected to those events. Often the writer's point emerges from freewriting about some memory or feeling, and almost always, the writer discovers some **conflict**. The conflict may be within the writer, or it may be between the writer and some force in the outside world, but conflict is the "irritant" or energy that drives the narrator to act and the narrative toward a resolution. When you discover the source of your main emotions or responses to the events in your narrative, you will have found the point you wish to illuminate for your readers.

3   *Choosing Your Key or Supporting Details*   There are two challenges in creating a successful narrative: to decide on the point of your essay and to make sure that all the material in the essay contributes to that point. You must decide which events, or aspects of the experience, contribute most directly to your main point or to the conflict of feelings you are recreating. Too many or unrelated details will "sidetrack" your reader and weaken your point. Too few details, or details not vividly described in lively words, will leave your narrative "hollow" and fail to create interest in your readers. **Accuracy in choice and type of details** is essential to good narrative writing.

4   *Deciding on a Point of View*   When you narrate in the first person, using *I* and *me*, you stress the personal nature of your narrative, and you emphasize your close connection to the experiences you recreate: *the reader's focus is on you and the events.* Writing in the third-person point of view, using *he, she, it, they,* and *them,* allows you to relate events, scenes, and emotions experienced while remaining "invisible." Case studies, law-enforcement reports, insurance, business, and medical reports all use third-person point of view for their narratives. In third-person narratives, *the reader's attention is completely on the events, conflicts, details, and characters.* Decide where you want your readers' focus to be as you decide on your point of view.

As Lisa read over her freewriting passage, she decided that the **main point** of her narrative essay was her new **realization of how difficult it would be to face a constant physical challenge**. She had felt discomfort and embarrassment as she tried to perform ordinary activities in the wheelchair. In order to support that central point, she realized, she would need to concentrate on details that demonstrated the frustrations she felt. She created a trial outline for the first draft of her essay:

Thesis Statement: A church experiment showed me the hardship of spending the morning in a wheelchair.

1. Sitting in the wheelchair
   a. Awkward because it rolled
   b. Awkward because the footrest was out of place
   c. Psychologically awkward

2. Moving the wheelchair
   a. I thought someone would push me
   b. It was hard to make the chair move and it hurt my hands
   c. Difficult to steer

3. Ways the wheelchair affected me
   a. Couldn't see
   b. I felt in the way
   c. I felt funny talking to people as they bent down over me

First Draft and Revision: Using Peer Review and Focusing on Writing Goals

Lisa based her first draft on her trial outline. Here it is:

1   The minister at our church suggested we each "adopt a challenge" for a few hours on Sunday morning. Some members, like me, chose to use wheelchairs. Others wore earplugs, used crutches, or wore blindfolds.

2   It surprised me that I felt nervous about sitting down in my wheelchair. I'm not sure why I felt scared about it. I guess I realized that most people who use wheelchairs don't do it by choice—they have to.

3   When I sat down, I thought that my friend Paula would push me around. We had talked about her doing that earlier. But she decided instead to "adopt" her own challenge, and she pretended to be blind. I saw her with a blindfold on, trying to fix herself a cup of coffee and knocking it off the table as she stirred it. So I had to figure out how to make the chair move by myself. It wasn't so easy. Pushing the wheels made my hands and arms sore. I also kept bumping into things. I felt really awkward. I even had trouble locking the wheels and finding the footrest.

4   I couldn't see well as I sat down low in my chair. When the rest of the congregation stood up, I could forget about seeing entirely. People would nod or chuckle at something that had happened up at the front of the church, and I could only

guess what was going on. Instead of sitting in the pew with everyone else, I was parked in the aisle, which was really too narrow for the chair. The new building program our church is planning will make that problem better by widening the aisles and making the pews farther apart. It's going to be expensive, but it's a worthwhile thing. Another thing I disliked was how I felt when people talked to me. They had to lean down as though I was a kid, and I had to stare up at them as though I was too. One person I talked to who seemed to understand what I was experiencing was Don Henderson, who mentioned that his brother-in-law uses a wheelchair.

1. Using Peer Review

Lisa read over her first draft and showed it to her roommate, Trish. While all peer comments may not be equally useful, an "impartial reader" can spot inconsistencies and weak points. Lisa listed the comments about how Trish thought the essay could be improved:

- The introduction should explain <u>why</u> the minister wanted us to adopt challenges.
- The second paragraph is kind of weak. Instead of saying, "I'm not sure why I felt scared," I should try to say specifically what was scary about the experience.
- The stuff about Paula doesn't really add to <u>my</u> main point. The story is about me, not Paula.
- Maybe I shouldn't talk so much about the new building plans. They're related to people with physical challenges, but putting them in doesn't really relate directly to the idea that my morning in a wheelchair was frustrating.
- Eliminate the part about Don Henderson. It doesn't contribute to my feeling frustrated.
- The essay ends too abruptly. I need to wrap it up with some sort of conclusion.

2. Focusing on Writing Goals

Lisa next approached Stage 2 of writing and revising: she refocused herself on the goals and activities needed to create an effective narrative. She had her main point, and Trish's comments nudged her toward selecting "key events" or vivid supporting details. Lisa needed to work with her outline and with the goals of using vivid language and related physical details to strengthen the effect of *what* she had felt, and *why*.

Look at Lisa's final draft of her essay on pages 160–161 of this chapter, and answer the following questions about her narrative:

- What are the conflicts Lisa feels?
- What are the origins of these conflicts?
- To which events or physical occurrences are these strong feelings connected?
- In Lisa's finished essay, which aspects of her experience are most vividly recreated? How?
- Is Lisa's narrative most effective in the first-person point of view? Why or why not?

WRITING A NARRATIVE ESSAY

■ **Writing Assignment 1**

Write an essay telling about an experience in which a certain emotion predominated. The emotion might be disappointment, embarrassment, happiness, frustration, or any of the following:

Fear	Anger	Silliness
Pride	Nostalgia	Disgust
Jealousy	Relief	Loss
Sadness	Greed	Sympathy
Terror	Nervousness	Violence
Regret	Hate	Bitterness
Shock	Surprise	Envy
Love	Shyness	Loneliness

The experience should be limited in the duration of time you cover. Note that the two essays presented in this chapter describe experiences occurring within relatively short periods. One writer described her frustration in acting as a physically challenged person at a morning church service; the second described a surprising encounter that led to a happy discovery.

Prewriting Strategies

1 Think of an experience or event in your life in which you felt a certain emotion. Then spend at least ten minutes freewriting about that experience. Do not worry at this point about such matters as spelling or grammar or putting things in the right order; instead, just try to get down as many details as you can think of that seem related to the experience.

2 This preliminary writing will help you decide whether your topic is promising enough to continue working on. If it is not, choose another emotion. If it is, do two things:

First, write out your thesis in a single sentence, underlining the emotion you will focus on. For example,

"English class always makes me incredibly nervous."

Second, think about just what makes up the conflict—the source of tension—in your narrative. What details can you add that will create enough tension to "hook" readers and keep them interested?

Third, make up a long list of all the details involved in the experience. Then arrange those details in chronological (time) order.

3 Using the list as a guide, prepare an outline showing the major stages in your narrative sequence and supporting details for each stage. Write a first draft based on your outline.

Revising Strategies

Once you have a first draft of your essay completed, review your goals as you work on a second draft:

1   *To achieve unity:* Do you state the thesis of your narrative in the introductory paragraph? If it is not stated, have you clearly implied it somewhere in the essay? Ask yourself if there are any portions of the essay that do not support the thesis and therefore should be eliminated or rewritten.

2   *To achieve support:* Do you have enough details? Careful detailing and occasional use of dialogue help make the writer's situation come alive. See if during this revision you can add more vivid, exact details that will help your readers experience the event as it actually happened.

3   *To achieve coherence:* See if you can add time signals such as *first, then, next, after, while, during,* and *finally* to help connect details as you move from the beginning, to the middle, to the end of your narrative.

   Also, be sure you have divided your narrative into separate stages (what happened first, what happened next, what finally happened). Each stage belongs in a separate paragraph. In narratives, it is sometimes difficult to write a topic sentence for each supporting paragraph. You may, therefore, want to start new paragraphs at points where natural shifts or logical breaks in the story seem to occur.

4   *To achieve correctness in sentence skills:* Refer to the checklist on the inside front cover to edit and proofread your next-to-final draft for sentence-skills mistakes, including spelling.

■ Writing Assignment 2

Think of an experience in your life that supports one of the statements below.

- "The chains of habit are too weak to be felt until they are too strong to be broken."—Samuel Johnson
- "If you don't hurry up and let life know what you want, life will damned well soon show you what you'll get."—Robertson Davies
- "Peter's Law: The unexpected always happens."—Laurence J. Peter
- "Good people are good because they've come to wisdom through failure." —William Saroyan
- "The key to everything is patience. You get the chicken by hatching the egg— not by smashing it."—Arnold Glasgow
- "A good scare is worth more to a man than good advice."—Ed Howe
- "There are some things you learn best in calm, and some in storm." —Willa Cather
- "What a tangled web we weave/When first we practise to deceive." —Walter Scott
- "Life shrinks or expands in proportion to one's courage."—Anaïs Nin
- "We lie loudest when we lie to ourselves."—Eric Hoffer

- "Criticism—a big bite out of someone's back."—Elia Kazan
- "He who opens a school door, closes a prison."—Victor Hugo
- "A little learning is a dangerous thing."—Alexander Pope
- "Nothing is so good as it seems beforehand."—George Eliot
- "Follow your heart and you perish."—Margaret Laurence

Think of an experience you have had that demonstrates the truth of one of the above statements or of another noteworthy saying—perhaps one that has guided your life. Then, using one of these statements as your thesis, write a narrative essay about that experience. Refer to the suggestions in the Prewriting Strategies and Rewriting Strategies that follow as you develop your essay.

A REVIEW OF PREWRITING AND REVISING STRATEGIES FOR YOUR NARRATIVE ESSAY

Prewriting Guidelines

The key to the success of your essay will be your choice of an incident from your life that illustrates the truth of the statement you have chosen. Here are some guidelines to consider:

- The incident should be one that includes a *conflict*, or source of tension. That conflict does not need to be dramatic or physical. Equally effective is a quieter conflict, such as between a person's conscience and desires; a decision that must be made; or a difficult situation that has no clear resolution.
- The incident should be limited in time; a brief narrative essay cannot do justice to a lengthy experience and all its details.
- The incident should evoke a definite emotional response in you, so that your essay may draw a similar response from your reader.
- The incident must *fully support* the statement you have chosen, not merely be linked by some of the same ideas.

Revising Strategies

Once you have a first draft of your essay completed, you should review it with these questions in mind:

- Have I included the essay's thesis (my chosen statement, properly cited) in my introductory paragraph, or is it clearly implied?
- Does each paragraph, and each sentence within that paragraph, help either to keep action moving or to reveal important details about the characters?
- Do transitional words and phrases, and linking sentences between paragraphs, help make the sequence of events clear?
- Should I break up the essay by using bits of interesting dialogue instead of narration?
- Are there portions of the essay that do not support my thesis, and therefore should be eliminated or rewritten?

■ **Writing Assignment 3**

In this narrative essay, you will write with a specific purpose and for a specific audience.

Imagine that you are in a town one hundred kilometres from home, that your car has broken down several kilometres from a gas station, and that you are carrying no money.

Option 1: A Personal Narrative You thought you were going to have a terrible time, but the friendly people who helped you turned your experience into a positive one. It was such a good day, in fact, that you don't want to forget what happened.

Write a narrative of the day's events in your diary, so that you can read it ten years from now and remember exactly what happened. Begin with the moment you realized your car had broken down and continue until you were safely back at home. Include a thesis at either the beginning or the end of your narration.

Option 2: An Accurate Objective Narrative Among the pleasant people who helped you was a police officer, who arranged for a tow truck and for emergency repairs to your car. However, she must file a report, which will include your record of events.

Write a third-person narrative report from the point of view of the officer. Describe the situation and all the assistance provided. Consider carefully all details needed for an accurate record of the event. Your thesis could suggest the officer's view of your accident.

Option 3: An Instructive Narrative Imagine that a friend or relative is an inexperienced and nervous driver. You wish to recreate your experience as a reassuring narrative.

Write a narrative that uses your experience as an instructive series of events to demonstrate that your reader can deal with and even learn from an accident. To discover and state your point clearly, try to visualize someone you know who is nervous about driving, and as you do so, consider the details of your narrative that would be most reassuring to him or her.

Writing Assignment 4

Writing about a Reading Selection Read the selection "He Was a Boxer When I Was Small" by Lenore Keeshig-Tobias on pages 538–541. Keeshig-Tobias' memories of her father are full of conflict and of diverse responses to her father. But the acknowledgment of their similarities pervades the essay. Write a narrative essay that recalls and explains, from your current perspective, an occasion on which you discovered you were similar to a parent or caregiver. What was the occasion? What, specifically, sparked the connection? In what respects are you like that person? What was your dominant emotion upon making this discovery? How did you respond to your realization? Why did you respond as you did? Did your own view of yourself change as a result of this knowledge? How did your view change? Did your view of your parent or caregiver change? How did it change?

REVIEWING THE LEARNING OUTCOMES FOR CHAPTER 8

When you finish any of the writing assignments in this chapter, review your paper to decide how well you have met the learning outcomes for narrative essays. How well does your paper fulfill each of these outcomes?

- Does your essay's opening paragraph state or clearly imply its point about the emotion or experience that is its subject?

- Are your details arranged in time order, with transitional words and phrases to show relationships between paragraphs and events?

- Does each detail included in your storyline add specifically to clarifying the point in your thesis?

- Are your details vivid and accurate enough to recreate your experience for readers?

- Do you conclude by returning to your point in an interesting way in your final paragraph?

Narration • Description • Examples • Process • Cause and Effect • Comparison and Contr
Definition • Division and Classification • Argumentation • Narration • Description • Exam
Process • Cause and Effect • Comparison and Contrast • Definition • Division and Classifica
Argumentation • Narration • Description • Examples • Process • Cause and Effect • Comparison
Contrast • Definition • Division and Classification • Argumentation • Narration • Description

CHAPTER 9

Description

LEARNING OUTCOMES

By working through the activities and writing tasks in this chapter, you will be prepared to write descriptive essays that

- Offer a dominant impression in the thesis that focuses the essay
- Present a rich, carefully chosen selection of sense-oriented details that reinforce aspects of the dominant impression
- Guide readers with a clear point of view and consistent method of tracking observations of your subject
- Conclude with a thought that fixes your dominant impression in the reader's mind

Descriptions are our attempts to act as "cameras with words." Camera lenses are mechanically accurate; our senses and minds record places, emotions, and people in complex ways. To make our word-pictures clear and vivid versions of our subjects, we must recall or observe them with specific details that speak to readers' senses. We must also work for accuracy in the way we "re-present" what we see in our mind's eye; descriptive essays must chart a path for readers to follow.

Descriptive papers, more than any other type of essay, need sharp, colourful detail. These essays record our responses to the world around us, responses realized through our senses. Some descriptive writing tries to evoke emotions caused by what is described; other descriptive tasks involve clear, precise recreations of something observed.

Here is a sentence in which there is almost no appeal to the senses: "In the window was a fan." In contrast, here is a description rich in sense impressions: "The blades of the rusty window fan clattered and whirled as they blew out a stream of warm, soggy air." Sense impressions in this second example include sight *(rusty window fan, whirled)*, hearing *(clattered)*, and touch *(warm, soggy air)*. The vividness and sharpness provided by the sensory details give us a clear picture of the fan and enable us to share the writer's experience.

Descriptions written for any purpose require accuracy and precision of observation and word choice; otherwise, they do not function as "word-pictures." We sometimes use descriptive skills for their own sake, but just as often we describe as part of other writing tasks. Description is basic to explaining how we see the world;

it can convey a mood or feeling; it may capture some moment that leads a reader to a decision or action; or it may record some events or technological procedures for a reader's more accurate understanding of them.

Descriptive writing skills are needed constantly in college assignments where any event, procedure, technology, human behaviour pattern, or strategy must be carefully recreated in words. Similarly, career writing tasks require the consistent precision and detail selection associated with good descriptive writing.

In this section, you will be asked to describe a person, place, or thing sharply, by using words rich in sensory details. To prepare for this assignment, first read the student essays that follow and work through the questions that accompany the essays.

STUDENT ESSAYS TO CONSIDER

Family Portrait

My mother, who is seventy years old, recently sent me a photograph of herself that I had never seen before. While cleaning out the attic of her Florida winter home, she came across a studio portrait she had taken about a year before she married my father. This picture of my mother as a twenty-year-old girl and the story behind it have fascinated me from the moment I began to consider them.
1

The young woman in the picture has a face that resembles my own in many ways. Her face is a bit more oval than mine, but the softly waving brown hair around it is identical. The small, straight nose is the same model I was born with. My mother's mouth is closed, yet there is just the slightest hint of a smile on her full lips. I know that if she had smiled, she would have shown the same wide grin and downcurving "smile lines" that appear in my own snapshots. The most haunting features in the photo, however, are my mother's eyes. They are exact duplicates of my own large, dark brown ones. Her brows are plucked into thin lines, which are like two pencil strokes added to highlight those fine, luminous eyes.
2

I've also carefully studied the clothing and jewellery in the photograph. My mother is wearing a blouse and skirt that, although the photo was taken fifty years ago, could easily be worn today. The blouse is made of heavy, eggshell-coloured satin and reflects the light in its folds and hollows. It has a turned-down cowl collar and smocking on the shoulders and below the collar. The smocking (tiny rows of gathered material) looks hand-done. The skirt, which covers my mother's calves, is straight and made of light wool or flannel. My mother is wearing silver drop earrings. They are about two inches long and roughly shield-shaped. On her left wrist is a matching bracelet. My mother can't find this bracelet now, despite the fact that we spent hours searching through the attic for it. On the third finger of her left hand is a ring with a large, square-cut stone.
3

The story behind the picture is as interesting to me as the young woman it captures. Mom, who was earning twenty-five dollars a week as a file clerk, decided to give her boyfriend (my father) a picture of herself. She spent almost two weeks' salary on the skirt and blouse, which she bought at a fancy department store downtown. She borrowed the earrings and bracelet from her older sister, my Aunt Dorothy. The ring she wore was a present from another young man she
4

was dating at the time. Mom spent another chunk of her salary to pay the portrait photographer for the hand-tinted print in old-fashioned tones of brown and tan. Just before giving the picture to my father, she scrawled at the lower left, "Sincerely, Beatrice."

When I study this picture, I react in many ways. I think about the trouble   5
that Mom went to in order to impress the young man who was to be my father. I laugh when I look at the ring that was probably worn to make my father jealous. I smile at the serious, formal inscription my mother used in this stage of the budding relationship. Sometimes, I am filled with a mixture of pleasure and sadness when I look at this frozen, long-ago moment. It is a moment of beauty, of love, and—in a way—of my own past.

Everyday Common Scents

Smells go straight to the brain, where they wake up memories and feelings.   1
A whiff of some scent wanders idly up the nostrils, then races off to work in the mind's twisty passages. The mind is a busier place than anyone knows. People usually consider only the extremes of the scent scale, a wonderful perfume or a really evil stench. But it's the ordinary smells of everyday places that bring back fragile memories of long ago and forgotten feelings about the recent past.

Offices used to have distinct smells, for instance. Workplaces today just   2
smell like whatever is whooshing through the ventilation system, but not the places where yesterday's fathers went every day. Those pale green or grey offices of the 1940s and '50s with their dark wood moldings had a whole menu of smells. There were layers of aromas that surely seeped into the people who toiled there —tired cigarette smoke, prickly twinges of hot wiring, the carbon-y traces of typewriter and elevator oil, and the odd light waft of piney aftershave. This mixture rode home on the bus every day—its name was "father," fifty years ago.

Elementary schools, on the other hand, probably still smell the way they   3
always did. The chattering hallways are full of the warm familiar smell of kids' hair and breath, soft and kind to the nose as a pet's fur. In winter, the hot breath of school furnaces ripens half-sour aromas of damp boots, sodden snowsuits, and sweet blackening bananas hiding in lockers. All seasons bring hints of that mysterious minty poisonous-looking green sweeping powder, and for some reason, canned vegetable soup. Only now classrooms may be missing one traditional ingredient in the "school aroma" recipe: the flat, nose-choking dusty smell of chalk; it's been replaced by the solvent stink of whiteboard marker.

Take a trip to the corner convenience store. Inhaling brings back dreamy   4
scents and memories—the soapy, powdery smells of baby-pink bubblegum squares, the heavy smell of chocolate, and even the strangely medicinal breath of the ice cream cooler. Adults' and children's noses alike twitch at the chemical hint of printer's ink from tied bundles of magazines and comics waiting to be shelved, but only the grown-ups remember the coarse stink of sulphur rising every May from flame-red tissue paper packs of firecrackers. Corner stores have always smelled like excitement and dreams to children, and to most adults, too, if they admit it.

So every day can be a feast for the mind and memory. The past and present   **5**
jostle for attention right under our noses. Maybe it's time to wake up and smell
the coffee, the dog, the classroom, and that fresh basket of clean laundry
waiting on the stairs.

■ **Questions**

About Unity

1. In which supporting paragraph of "Everyday Common Scents" does the topic
   sentence appear at the paragraph's end, rather than the beginning?
   a. paragraph 2
   b. paragraph 3
   c. paragraph 4

2. Which sentence in paragraph 1 of "Everyday Common Scents" should be
   eliminated in the interest of paragraph unity? *(Write the opening words.)*

   _____

3. Which of the following sentences from paragraph 3 of "Family Portrait"
   should be omitted in the interest of paragraph unity?
   a. "My mother is wearing a blouse and skirt that, although the photo was
      taken fifty years ago, could easily be worn today."
   b. "It has a turned-down cowl collar and smocking on the shoulders and
      below the collar."
   c. "My mother can't find this bracelet now, despite the fact that we spent
      hours searching through the attic for it."
   d. "On the third finger of her left hand is a ring with a large, square-cut stone."

About Support

4. How many separate items of clothing and jewellery are described in paragraph 3 of "Family Portrait"?
   a. four
   b. five
   c. six

5. Label as sight, touch, hearing, or smell all the sensory details in the following
   sentences taken from the two essays. The first one is done for you as an example.

        hearing   *touch*   *smell*
   a. "The chattering hallways are full of the warm familiar smell of kids' hair
       touch   *touch*
   and breath, soft and kind to the nose as a pet's fur."

    b. "In winter, the hot breath of school furnaces ripens half-sour aromas of damp boots, sodden snowsuits, and sweet blackening bananas hiding in lockers."

    c. "The blouse is made of heavy, eggshell-coloured satin and reflects the light in its folds and hollows."

    d. "I laugh when I look at the ring that was probably worn to make my father jealous."

6. What are three details in paragraph 3 of "Everyday Common Scents" that reinforce the idea expressed in the topic sentence that school smells do not change?

_____

_____

_____

About Coherence

7. Which of the following methods of organization does paragraph 2 of "Family Portrait" use?
   a. Time order
   b. Emphatic order

8. Which sentence in paragraph 2 of "Family Portrait" suggests the method of organization? *(Write the opening words.)*

_____

9. The last paragraph of "Everyday Common Scents" begins with a word that serves as which type of signal?
   a. time
   b. addition
   c. contrast
   d. illustration

About the Introduction

10. Which of the following best describes the introduction to "Everyday Common Scents"?
   a. It starts with an idea that is the opposite of the one then developed.
   b. It explains the importance of the topic to its readers.
   c. It begins with a general statement of the topic and narrows it down to a thesis statement.
   d. It begins with an anecdote.

WRITING A DESCRIPTION ESSAY

About Prewriting

Because the descriptive essay's main function is to provide readers with a vivid picture in words, you must choose a topic that appeals strongly to at least one of your senses. It's possible to write a descriptive essay, maybe even a good one, about a boiled potato. But it would be easier (and more fun) to describe a bowl of potato salad, with its contrasting textures of soft potato and crisp celery, its creamy dressing, and its tangy seasonings. Likewise, as you choose a topic for your essay, you should pick one that gives you plenty of sensory detail to work with.

When Luisa, the author of "Family Portrait," began considering a topic for her essay, she looked around her apartment for inspiration. First she thought about describing her own bedroom. But she had just moved into the apartment, and the room struck her as too bare and sterile. Then she looked out her window, thinking of describing the view. That seemed more promising: she noticed the sights and sounds of children playing on the sidewalks and a group of older men playing cards, as well as the smells of the exhaust of passing traffic and of neighbours' cooking. She was jotting down some details about the view when she glanced at the framed portrait of her mother sitting on her desk. "I stopped and stared at it, as I often do, wondering again about this twenty-year-old girl who became my mother," she said. "While I sat there studying it, I realized that the best topic of all was right under my nose."

As she looked at the photograph, Luisa began to freewrite. This is what she wrote:

> Mom is twenty in the picture. She's wearing a beautiful skirt and blouse and jewellery she borrowed from Dorothy. Looks a lot like me—nose, eyes, mouth. She's shorter than I am but you really can't tell in picture. Looks a lot like old photos I've seen of Grandma too—all the DaSilva women resemble each other. Earrings and bracelet are of silver and they match. Ring might be amber or topaz? We've laughed about "the other man" who gave it to her. Her brown hair is down loose on her shoulders. She's smiling a little. That doesn't really look like her—her usual smile is bigger and opens her mouth. Looking at the photo makes me a little sad even though I really like it. Makes me realize how much older she's getting and I wonder how long she'll be with us. It's funny to see a picture of your parent at a younger age than you are now—stirs up all kinds of weird feelings. Picture was taken at a studio in Hamilton to give to Dad. Signed "Sincerely, Beatrice." So serious! Hard to imagine them being so formal with each other.

Luisa looked over her notes and thought about how to organize her essay. First she thought only of describing how the photograph *looked*. With that in mind, she thought her main points might be (1) what her mother's face looked like and (2) what she was wearing. But she was stuck for a third main point.

As she looked back at the picture, two other ideas struck her. One was her own emotional reaction to the photo—how it made her feel. The other was the story of the photo—how and why it was taken. Not sure which of those two would be her third main point, she began to write. This is her first draft:

Family Portrait

I have a photograph of my mother that was taken fifty years ago, when she was only twenty. She sent it to me only recently, and I find it very interesting.

In the photo, I see a girl who looks a good deal like I do, even though it's been a long time since I was twenty. Like most of the women in her family, including me, she's got the DaSilva family nose, waving brown hair, and large brown eyes. Her mouth is closed and she is smiling slightly. That isn't my mother's usual big grin that shows her teeth and her "smile lines."

In the photo, Mom is wearing a very pretty skirt and blouse. They look like something that would be fashionable today. The blouse is made of heavy satin. The satin falls in lines and hollows that reflect the light. It has a turned-down cowl collar and smocking on the shoulders and under the collar. Her skirt is below her knees and looks like it is made of light wool. She is wearing jewellery. Her silver earrings and bracelet match. She had borrowed them from her sister. Dorothy eventually gave them both to her, but the bracelet has disappeared. On her left hand is a ring with a big yellow stone.

When I look at this photo, I feel conflicting emotions. It gives me pleasure to see Mom as a pretty young woman. It makes me sad, too, to think how quickly time passes and realize how old she is getting. It amuses me to read the inscription to my father, her boyfriend at the time. She wrote, "Sincerely, Beatrice." It's hard for me to imagine Mom and Dad ever being so formal with each other.

Mom had the photograph taken at a studio near where she worked in Hamilton. She spent nearly two weeks' salary on the outfit she wore for it. And I think she wore the ring, which another boy had given her, to make Dad jealous. She must have really wanted to impress my father to go to all that trouble and expense.

Luisa showed this first draft to her classmate Hoi Yee, who read it and returned it with these notes jotted in the margin:

Family Portrait

I have a photograph of my mother that was taken fifty years ago, when she was only twenty. She sent it to me only recently, and I find it very interesting.[1]

In the photo, I see a girl who looks a good deal like I do, even though it's been a long time since I was twenty. Like most of the women in her family, including me, she's got the DaSilva family nose,[2] waving brown hair, and large brown eyes. Her mouth is closed and she is smiling slightly. That isn't my mother's usual big grin that shows her teeth and her "smile lines."[3]

In the photo, Mom is wearing a very pretty skirt and blouse.[4] They look like something that would be fashionable today. The blouse is made of heavy satin. The satin falls in lines and hollows that reflect the light.[5] It has a turned-down cowl collar and smocking[6] on the shoulders and under the collar. Her skirt is below her knees and looks like it is made of light wool. She is wearing jewellery. Her silver earrings and bracelet match.[7] She had borrowed them from her sister. Dorothy eventually gave them both to her, but the bracelet has disappeared. On her left hand is a ring with a big yellow stone.

[1] Was this the first time you'd seen it? Where's it been? And "very interesting" doesn't really say anything. Be more specific about why it interests you.

[2] The "DaSilva family nose" isn't helpful for someone who doesn't know the DaSilva family—describe it!

[3] Nice beginning, but I still can't quite picture her. Can you add more specific detail? Does anything about her face really stand out?

[4] Colour?

[5] This is nice—I can picture the material.

[6] What is smocking?

[7] How—what are they like?

[8] *It seems to me it'd make more sense for the main points of the essay to be about your mom and the photo, instead of the third point being about you and then going back to your mom in the conclusion. How about making this—your reaction—the conclusion of the essay instead?*

[9] *This is interesting stuff—she really did go to a lot of trouble to have the photo taken. I think the story of the photograph deserves to be a main point, not just a concluding thought.*

When I look at this photo, I feel conflicting emotions.[8] It gives me pleasure to see Mom as a pretty young woman. It makes me sad, too, to think how quickly time passes and realize how old she is getting. It amuses me to read the inscription to my father, her boyfriend at the time. She wrote, "Sincerely, Beatrice." It's hard for me to imagine Mom and Dad ever being so formal with each other.

Mom had the photograph taken at a studio near where she worked in Hamilton. She spent nearly two weeks' salary on the outfit she wore for it. And I think she wore the ring, which another boy had given her, to make Dad jealous. She must have really wanted to impress my father to go to all that trouble and expense.[9]

Making use of Hoi Yee's comments and her own reactions upon rereading her essay, Luisa wrote the final draft that appears on pages 173–174.

WRITING A DESCRIPTIVE ESSAY

■ Writing Assignment 1

Write an essay about a particular place that you can observe carefully or that you already know well. You might choose one of the following, or another place that you think of.

- Pet shop
- Laundromat
- Bar or club
- Video arcade
- Library study area or a lab room
- Your bedroom or the bedroom of someone you know
- Waiting room at a train station, bus terminal, or airport
- Antique shop, a "Dollar store" or other small shop

Prewriting

1 **Dominant Impression**: Like all essays, a descriptive paper must have a thesis. Your thesis should state a dominant impression about the place you are describing. Write a short single sentence in which you name the place or object you want to describe and the dominant impression you have about that place or object. **The dominant impression is your organizing principle**—any details you include in later drafts should agree with or support this dominant impression. But for now, don't worry if your sentence doesn't seem quite right as a thesis—you can refine it later. For now, you just want to find and express a workable topic. Here are some examples of such sentences:

The study area was noisy.
The pet shop was crowded.
The bus terminal was frightening.

The bedroom was well organized.
The restaurant was noisy.
The variety store was a wild jumble.

2 **Detail Listing:** Once you have written your sentence, make a list of as many details as you can that support that general impression. For example, this is the list made by the writer of "Everyday Common Scents":

Office ventilation air	Caretakers and green sweeping powder
Old cigarette smoke	Old black bananas—smell too sweet
Overheated wiring smell	Chalk smell—sneezing?
Small machine oil—grandfather	Bubblegum—pink, powdery pieces
Hot school hallways	Freezers had a smell, odd
Wet boots—mildew smell?	Firecrackers—Mom remembers

3 **Organizing Principle:** When you describe, you act as a "camera" for your reader. Decide how you will "track" your subject, and organize your paper according to one or a combination of the following:

Physical order—Move from left to right, move from far to near, or follow some other consistent order.
Size—Begin with large features or objects and work down to smaller ones.
A special order—Use an order that is appropriate to your subject.

For example, Darren, who wrote "Everyday Common Scents," finds that his dominant impression has to do with memories and the meanings attached to scents of ordinary places. The essay is organized according to an order that makes sense with his thesis; he chooses three locations familiar to almost everyone: offices, elementary schools, and corner stores. Set up your outline according to the organizing principle most appropriate to your subject.

4 **Sensory Details:** Use as many senses as possible in describing a scene. Chiefly you will use sight, but to an extent you may be able to use touch, hearing, smell, and perhaps even taste as well. Remember that it is through the richness of your sense impressions that the reader will gain a picture of the scene.

5 Create an outline for your essay. Group your impressions into three main stages, with a balanced number of supporting details for each. Based on your outline, proceed to the first draft of your essay.

Rewriting

After you have completed the first draft of the paper, set it aside for a while—if possible, until the next day. When you review the draft, try to do so as critically as you would if it were not your own work. Ask yourself these questions:

- Does my paper have a clearly stated thesis including a dominant impression?
- Have I provided rich, specific details that appeal to a variety of senses (sight, hearing, smell, taste, touch)? Do my details all fit under "the umbrella" of my dominant impression?
- Is there any irrelevant material that should be eliminated or rewritten?
- Have I organized my essay in some consistent manner—physical order, size, time progression, or another way that is appropriate to my subject?

- Have I used transition words to help readers follow my train of thought and my organizing pattern?
- Do I have a concluding paragraph that provides a summary or final thought or both?

As you revise your essay through one or more additional drafts, continue to refer to this list until you can answer "yes" to each question. Then be sure to check the next-to-final draft of the paper for the sentence skills listed on the inside front cover.

■ Writing Assignment 2

Write an essay about a family portrait. (The picture may be of an individual or a group.)

1 Decide how you will organize your essay. Your decision will depend on what seems appropriate for the photograph. Two possibilities are these:

- As in "Family Portrait," your first supporting paragraph might describe the subjects' faces, the second, their clothing and jewellery, and the third, the story behind the picture.
- Another possible order might be, first, the people in the photograph (and how they look); second, the relationships among the people (and what they are doing in the photo); and third, the story behind the picture (time, place, occasion, other circumstances).

2 Make a trial outline for your essay, based on the organization you have chosen.

3 Using your outline as a guide, make a list of details that support each of your main points. As practice in doing this, complete this list of details based on "Family Portrait":

a. Mother's face
   Small, straight nose
   Slight smile on her full lips
   Large, dark eyes

   _____

   _____

   _____

b. Mother's clothing and jewellery
   Blouse of heavy satin
   Blouse is eggshell-coloured
   Cowl collar
   Smocking on blouse
   Light wool skirt

   _____

   _____

   _____

c.   Story behind the photo
Mother spent two weeks' salary on clothing
Borrowed jewellery from sister

_____

_____

4 Use your outline and its list of details to write your first draft.

Rewriting

Refer to the guidelines for rewriting provided on pages 180–181.

■ Writing Assignment 3

For this descriptive essay, you will write for a specific audience and with a specific purpose.

You are writing an e-mail to designers working on a new building for your college. Their firm has asked for input from students and faculty on how a college classroom *should* be designed. Choose a type of classroom or lab where you would logically spend a fair amount of class time, and describe your ideal room layout, furniture, and equipment. Give your feedback in the third-person point of view, so that emphasis is on your details.

Prewriting

1 Decide what kind of ideal classroom or lab you will describe. What subject or subjects will be taught in that room? What types of desks or equipment are needed; how should they be arranged, and why? Is some special wall colour or lighting preferable? Why is this particular room an important one to you?

2 How will you organize your description? Will you begin at the door and take the reader around the room, or will you begin with an overview and concentrate on specific articles or aspects of the room? You need not think of every single detail down to the floor tiles, but instead visualize what will make your room "ideal," and concentrate on items related to that.

3 Focus on the main ideas and objects that make up your "ideal room" and list or diagram ideas and details that support and make your concepts as clear and "visible" to your reader as possible. Do you need to give strong sense details of textures or shapes, or do you need exacting, more technical descriptions of equipment and furnishings?

4 Plan a brief opening paragraph for your e-mail that will preview for the designers the overall organization and intention for your suggested room. For instance, you might mention that lighting, windows, and tables are particularly important in drafting labs, so that you will concentrate on those elements.

5 Write an outline, showing your main points and supporting details; then write a first draft of your e-mail.

Rewriting

Once you have the first draft of your paper completed, review it with these questions in mind:

- Does my introduction indicate a clear plan of development, a suggestion of how I will show the reader my "ideal room"?
- Is my description clearly organized according to three main points?
- Have I filled each of my supporting paragraphs with vivid or precise descriptive details that help the reader clearly imagine my ideal room?
- Have I rounded off with an appropriate concluding paragraph?
- Have I proofread my e-mail, referring to the list of sentence skills on the inside front cover?

Writing Assignment 4

Write an essay describing a person. First, decide on your dominant impression of the person, and then use only those details that will add to it. Here are some examples of interesting types of people:

Campus character	Competitor	Drunk
Dentist	Dancer at a club	Employer
Bus driver	Neighbour	TV or movie personality
Close friend	Teacher	Street person
Rival	Child	Older person
Instructor	Store owner	Hero

Writing Assignment 5:
Writing about a Reading Selection

Read the selection "Of Lemons and Lemonade" on pages 513–515. Then write an essay describing a location you know well. You might consider writing about one of the following:

Your house or apartment
Cafeteria or restaurant
Office or store where you work
Your block on your street
Park or schoolyard
Waiting room
Area where you study
Inside of a bus, a subway, a train, or your own car

In your introductory paragraph, explain where the place is and your connection with it. Explain what aspects of your location are most interesting or significant to you, and why. Be sure to state in the thesis your dominant impression of the place. Use any order that you feel is appropriate (left to right, near to far, top to bottom, or other) to organize your supporting paragraphs. Use vivid images, as the author of "Of Lemons and Lemonade" does, to capture your place and its meaning to you on paper.

REVIEWING THE LEARNING OUTCOMES FOR CHAPTER 9

After completing any of writing assignments in this chapter, review your paper by asking yourself the following questions:

- Is there a clear dominant impression of my subject in the thesis?
- Have I used either vivid sense details or precise physical details to illustrate each aspect of the dominant impression?
- Does the essay sustain a clearly set out point of view and method of observing or tracking the subject I'm describing?
- Does the final paragraph contain ideas that reinforce the dominant impression in the reader's mind?

ation • Description • Examples • Process • Cause and Effect • Comparison and Contrast • tion • Division and Classification • Argumentation • Narration • Description • Examples • ss • Cause and Effect • Comparison and Contrast • Definition • Division and Classification • mentation • Narration • Description • Examples • Process • Cause and Effect • Comparison and ast • Definition • Division and Classification • Argumentation • Narration • Description

CHAPTER 10

Examples

LEARNING OUTCOMES

By working through the activities and assignments in this chapter, you will be prepared to write an expository essay that

- Contains three supporting points that are developed with relevant examples for each point
- Uses specific illustrative supporting details within those examples that relate clearly to the thesis point
- Offers enough details to make each example clear and memorable
- Ends with a conclusion that expands on the total meaning of the examples presented

In our daily conversations, we often provide examples, details, or specific instances to explain statements we make.

Examples in exposition provide readers with clearer *pictures* of what your supporting points mean to you. Each time you illustrate your ideas with sharply drawn examples, you increase the likelihood that your audience will understand what you say, helping them see for themselves the truth of your statement.

Here are several statements and supporting examples:

The first day of classes was frustrating.

My marketing class was cancelled. Then, I couldn't find the computer lab. And the lines at the bookstore were so long that I went home without buying my textbooks.

Examples are sometimes the *reasons why* we make a particular point, and they can help to prove the truth of that statement.

That washing machine is unreliable.

The water temperature can't be predicted; it stops in midcycle; and it sometimes shreds my clothing.

Examples give your readers specific *hooks that catch them;* specifics attract your readers and stay in the memory. Lively, specific examples add interest to your paper.

185

My grandfather is a thrifty person.	He washes and reuses aluminum foil. He wraps gifts in newspaper. And he's worn the same Sunday suit for twenty years.

In this section, you will be asked to provide a series of examples to support your thesis. First, read through the student essays that follow and work through the questions that accompany the essays. Both essays use examples to develop their points.

STUDENT ESSAYS TO CONSIDER

Everyday Cruelty

Last week, I found myself worrying less about problems of global politics and more about smaller evils. I came home one day with a bad taste in my mouth, the kind I get whenever I witness the little cruelties that people inflict on each other. On this particular day, I had seen too much of the cruelty of the world. **1**

I first thought about mean-spirited people as I walked from the bus stop to the office where I work. I make this walk every day, and it's my first step away from the comforts of home and into the tensions of the city. For me, a landmark on the route is a tiny patch of ground that was once strewn with rubbish and broken glass. The city is trying to make a "mini-park" out of it by planting trees and flowers. Every day this spring, I watched the skinny saplings put out tiny leaves. When I walked past, I always noted how big the tulips were getting and made bets with myself on when they would bloom. To pass time as I walk, I often make silly little bets with myself, such as predicting that the next man I see will be wearing a blue tie. But last Wednesday, as I reached the park, I felt sick. Someone had knocked the trees to the ground and trampled the budding tulips into the dirt. Someone had destroyed a bit of beauty for no reason. **2**

At lunchtime on Wednesday, I witnessed more meanness. Along with dozens of other hungry, hurried people, I was waiting in line at Harvey's. Also in line was a young mother with two tired, impatient children clinging to her legs. The mother was trying to calm the children, but it was obvious that their whining was about to give way to full-fledged tantrums. The lines barely moved, and the lunchtime tension was building. Then, one of the children began to cry and scream. As people stared angrily at the helpless mother, the little boy's blood-curdling yells resounded through the restaurant. Finally, one man turned to her and said, "Lady, you shouldn't bring your kids to a public place if you can't control them." A young woman chimed in with another piece of cruel criticism. The mother was exhausted and hungry. Someone in line could have helped her by kneeling down to interact on eye level with one of the kids. Instead, even though many of the customers in the restaurant were parents themselves, they treated her like a criminal. **3**

The worst incident of mean-spiritedness that I saw that day happened after I left work. As I walked to the bus stop, I approached an old woman huddled in a doorway. She was wrapped in a dirty blanket and clutched a plastic bag packed with her belongings. Approaching the woman from the opposite direction **4** were three teenagers who were laughing and talking in loud voices. When they saw the old woman, they began to shout crude remarks at her. They did even more cruel things to torment her. The woman stared helplessly at them, like a wounded animal surrounded by hunters. Then, having had their fun, the teenagers went on their way.

I had seen enough of the world's coldness that day and wanted to leave it behind. At home, I huddled in the warmth of my family. I wondered why we all contribute to the supply of petty cruelty. There's enough of it already.   5

Altered States

Most Canadians are not alcoholics. Most do not cruise seedy city streets looking to score crack cocaine or heroin. Relatively few try to con their doctors into prescribing unneeded mood-altering medications. And yet, many Canadians are travelling through life with their minds slightly out of kilter. In its attempt to cope with modern life, the human mind seems to have evolved some defence strategies. Confronted with inventions like the television, the shopping mall, and the Internet, the mind will slip—all by itself—into an altered state.   1

Never in the history of humanity have people been expected to sit passively for hours, staring at moving pictures emanating from an electronic box. Since too much exposure to flickering images of police officers, detectives, and talk-show hosts can be dangerous to human sanity, the mind automatically goes into a TV hypnosis state. The eyes see the sitcom or the dog food commercial, but the mind goes into a holding pattern. None of the televised images or sounds actually enters the brain. This is why, when questioned, people cannot remember commercials they have seen five seconds before or why the TV cops are chasing a certain suspect. In this hypnotic, trance-like state, the mind resembles an armoured armadillo. It rolls up in self-defence, letting the stream of televised information pass by harmlessly.   2

If a TV watcher arises from the couch and goes to a shopping mall, he or she will again cope by slipping into an altered state. In the mall, the mind is bombarded with the sights, smells, and sounds of dozens of stores, restaurants, and movie theatres competing for the mind's attention. There are hundreds of questions to be answered: Should I start with the upper or lower mall level? Which stores should I look in? Should I bother with the sweater sale at the Bay? Should I eat fried chicken or try the healthier-sounding pita wrap? Where is my car parked? To combat this mental overload, the mind goes into a state resembling the whiteout experienced by mountain climbers trapped in a blinding snowstorm. Suddenly, everything looks the same. The shopper is unsure where to go next and cannot remember what he or she came for in the first place. The mind enters this state deliberately, so that the shopper has no choice but to leave. Some kids can be in a shopping mall for hours, but they are the exceptions to the rule.   3

But no part of everyday life so quickly triggers the mind's protective shutdown mode as that favourite pastime of the new millennium: cruising the Internet. A computer user sits down with the intention of briefly checking e-mail or looking   4 up a fact for a research paper. But once tapped into the immense storehouse of information, entertainment, and seemingly intimate personal connections that the Internet offers, the user loses all sense of time and priorities. Prospects flood the mind: Should I explore real estate prices in Vancouver? Subscribe to a mailing list? Hear the life story of a lonely stranger in Kamloops? With a mind dazed with information overload, the user numbly hits one key after another, leaping from topic to topic, from distraction to distraction. Hours fly by as he or she sits hunched over the terminal, unable to account for the time that has passed.

Therefore, the next time you see TV viewers, shoppers, or Internet surfers   5
with eyes as glazed and empty as polished doorknobs, you'll know these people are in a protective altered state. Be gentle with them. They are merely trying to cope with the mind-numbing inventions of modern life.

■ Questions

About Unity

1. Which sentence in paragraph 3 of "Altered States" should be omitted in the interest of paragraph unity? *(Write the opening words.)*

   _____

2. Which supporting paragraph in one of the essays lacks a topic sentence?

   _____

3. Which sentence in paragraph 2 of "Everyday Cruelty" should be omitted in the interest of paragraph unity? *(Write the opening words.)*

   _____

About Support

4. Which sentence in paragraph 4 of "Everyday Cruelty" needs to be followed by more supporting details? *(Write the opening words.)*

   _____

5. In paragraph 3 of "Everyday Cruelty," which sentence should be followed by supporting details? *(Write the opening words.)*

   _____

6. What three pieces of evidence does the writer of "Altered States" offer to support the statement that the Internet is an "immense storehouse of information, entertainment, and seemingly intimate personal connections"?

   _____

   _____

   _____

About Coherence

7. In paragraph 3 of "Everyday Cruelty," which three time signals does the author begin sentences with? *(Write the three signals here.)*

   _____   _____   _____

8. What sentence in "Altered States" indicates that the author has used emphatic order, saving his most important point for last? *(Write the opening words.)*

   _____

About the Introduction and Conclusion

9. Of the two student essays, which indicates in its introduction the essay's plan of development? *(Write the title of the essay and the opening words of the sentence that indicates the plan.)*

   _____

10. Which of these statements best describes the concluding paragraph of "Altered States"? *(Circle one.)*
    a. It contains a prediction.
    b. It combines a summary with a recommendation of how to treat people in an altered state.
    c. It refers to the point made in the introduction about alcohol and drugs.
    d. It contains thought-provoking questions about altered states.

WRITING AN EXAMPLES ESSAY

About Prewriting

When Tony, the student author of "Altered States," was considering a topic for his example essay, he looked around his apartment at his roommates for inspiration. He first considered examples of different types of people: jocks, brains, and space-heads. Then he thought about types of rooms in shared apartments: the Slob Kingdom, the Neat Freak Room, and the Packrat's Place.

"But that evening I noticed how one roommate acted as he was cruising the Internet," Tony said. "He sat down to e-mail his brother, and three hours later he was still there, cruising from website to website. His eyes were glassy, and he seemed to be in another reality. It reminded me of how spaced out I get when I go to a mall. I began to think about how our minds have to adjust to challenges that our grandparents didn't know anything about. I added 'watching television' as the third category, and I had a pretty good idea of what my essay would be about."

Tony had his three categories, but needed to do some more work in order to generate supporting details for each. He used diagramming to help inspire his thinking. This is what his diagram looked like:

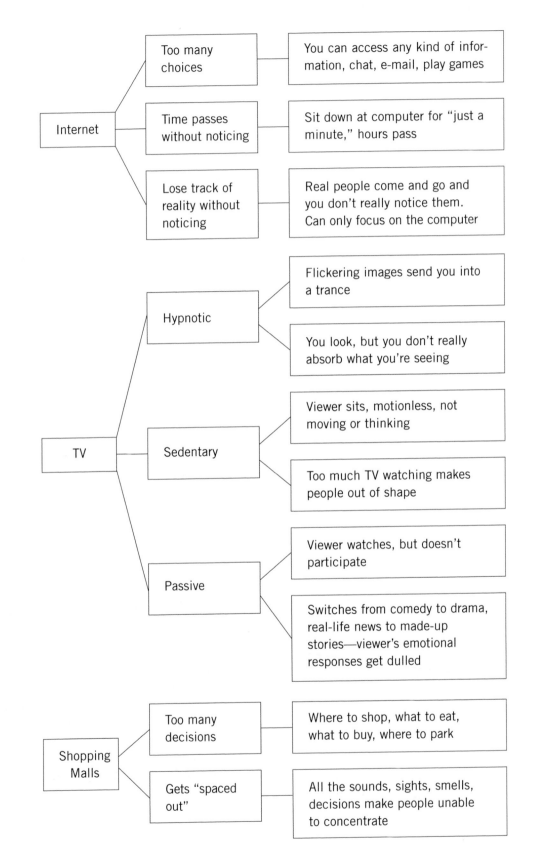

Looking at his diagram, Tony saw that he would have no trouble supporting his thesis: People's minds go into an "altered state" when they watch TV, go to shopping malls, or use the Internet. He jotted down details in diagram form and easily came up with enough ideas for his essay. He turned his diagram information into an outline and then produced his first draft.

About Revising

Tony showed his first-draft essay to a classmate for her critique. She returned his essay with the comments shown below.

Altered States

[1] *This seems to me like a separate topic—people's relationships with people they meet on the Internet.*

[2] *Your point of view isn't consistent. Sometimes you write about "a user," other times about "you," and then about "my roommate." It's confusing. Also, is the paragraph about how your roommate acts when he's on the Internet (that's what it sounds like) or what people in general are like?*

[3] *These last two sentences are good. I'd like to read more about this "altered state" you think people go into.*

[4] *The idea of the "hypnotic trance" is interesting, but you need more details to back it up.*

[5] *The point of view is a problem again. You skip from "you" to "I."*

[6] *Good image!*

[7] *I don't think this works. The essay isn't about your father. It should be about modern shoppers, not just one man.*

[8] *This final sentence seems to introduce a new topic—that we shouldn't get caught in the TV and the Internet, etc. That hasn't been your point previously in the essay.*

Modern life makes demands on the human mind that no other period in history has made. As society becomes more and more complex, the mind has developed some defence mechanisms. Confronted with inventions like the Internet, television, and the shopping mall, the mind will slip—all by itself—into an altered state.

Take the Internet, for example. A computer user sits down to check his e-mail or look up something. But once tapped into the Internet, you lose all sense of time. You can chat with strangers,[1] research any topic, play a game, or shop for any product. Some people[2] begin to think of the on-line world and on-line friends as more real than the people in their own homes. While my roommate is absorbed in the Internet, he can even have brief conversations with people who come into our room, yet not be able to remember the conversations later. He sits there in a daze from information overload. He seems numb as he hits key after key, going from website to website.[3]

Then there's TV. Our grandparents could not have imagined the idea of sitting passively for hours, staring at moving pictures emanating from a box. It's not a normal state of affairs, so the mind goes into something like a hypnotic trance.[4] You see the sitcom or the dogfood commercial, but your mind goes into a holding pattern. You don't really absorb the pictures or sounds. Five minutes after I[5] watch a show, I can't remember commercials I've seen or why the TV cops are chasing a certain suspect.

If the TV watcher arises from the couch and journeys into the real world, he often goes to the shopping mall. Here, the mind is bombarded with the sights, smells, and sounds of dozens of stores, restaurants, and movie theatres competing for its attention. Dazed shoppers begin to feel like mountain climbers trapped in a blinding snowstorm.[6] Suddenly, everything looks the same. My father is the worst of all when it comes to shopping in an altered state. He comes back from the mall looking like he'd been through a war. After about fifteen minutes of shopping, he can't concentrate enough to know what he's looking for.[7]

Internet surfers, TV viewers, and shoppers all have one thing in common. They're just trying to cope with the mind-numbing inventions of modern life. Hopefully some day we'll turn away from such inventions and return to a simpler and more healthy way of life.[8]

Tony read his classmate's comments and reviewed the essay himself. He agreed with her criticisms about point of view and the need for stronger supporting details. He also decided that the Internet was his strongest supporting point and should be saved for the last paragraph. He then wrote the final version of his essay, the version that appears on pages 187 and 188.

WRITING AN EXAMPLES ESSAY

■ Writing Assignment 1

For this assignment, you will complete an unfinished essay by adding appropriate supporting examples. Here is the incomplete essay:

Problems with My Apartment

> When I was younger, I fantasized about how wonderful life would be when I moved into my own apartment. Now I'm a bit older and wiser, and my fantasies have turned into nightmares. My apartment has given me nothing but head-aches. From the day I signed the lease, I've had to deal with an uncooperative building owner, an incompetent caretaker, and inconsiderate neighbours.

> First of all, the owner of the building has been uncooperative.

> I've had a problem, not only with the owner, but also with an incompetent caretaker.

> Perhaps the worst problem has been with the inconsiderate neighbours who live in the apartment above me.

> Sometimes, my apartment seems like a small, friendly oasis surrounded by hostile enemies. I never know what side trouble is going to come from next: the owner, the caretaker, or the neighbours. Home may be where the heart is, but my head is thinking about moving out.

Note: If you do not have experience with an apartment, write instead about problems of living in a student residence, or problems of living at home. Revise the introduction and conclusion to fit your topic. Problems in living in a college residence might include:

Restrictive residence regulations
Inconsiderate students on your floor
A difficult roommate

Problems in living at home might include:

Lack of space
Inconsiderate brothers and sisters
Conflict with your parent or parents

Prewriting Strategies

1 You have two aims: (a) to provide strong, *adequate*, specific details for the three qualities in question and (b) to provide *enough* specific details so that you solidly support each quality. Ask yourself the following questions to generate details for your paper.

  - How has the owner or your family been uncooperative?
  - In what ways have you been inconvenienced?
  - Have they been uncooperative more than once?
  - What has been your reaction?
  - What has been the owner's or the family member's reaction?
  - What kinds of things have you said to each other?

  - Who is the caretaker? Who does the cleaning at home?
  - What has he or she tried to fix in the apartment?
  - In what ways has the caretaker or cleaner been incompetent?
  - How has this person inconvenienced you?
  - Has this person's incompetence cost you time or money?
  - What is the worst example of incompetence?

  - Who are the neighbours?
  - How long have they lived nearby?
  - What kinds of problems have you had with them?
  - Have these problems happened more than once?
  - If you have spoken to the neighbours about the problems, what did they say?
  - What is the worst problem with these neighbours?

2 Use the details generated by your questioning to flesh out the three paragraphs with details and examples. Remember that you may use one extended example in each paragraph (as in the essay "Everyday Cruelty") or two or three short examples.

3 As you write your first draft, keep asking yourself these questions:

  - Do my examples truly show the family/owner as *uncooperative?*
  - Do my examples truly show the cleaner/caretaker as *incompetent?*
  - Do my examples truly show my neighbours as *inconsiderate?*

Rewriting Strategies

After you have completed the first draft of the paper, set it aside for a while if you can. When you review it, try to do so as critically as you would if it were not your own work. Ask yourself these questions:

  - Do I have a clearly stated (or implied) thesis?
  - Have I provided *relevant* specific details for the owner's uncooperativeness, the caretaker/cleaner's incompetence, and the neighbours' lack of consideration?

- Have I provided *enough* specific details to support each of the three qualities?
- Have I used transitions, including transitions between paragraphs, to help readers follow my train of thought?
- Do I have a concluding paragraph that provides a summary, or final thought, or both?

As you revise your essay through one or more additional drafts, continue to refer to this list until you can answer "yes" to each question. Then be sure to check the next-to-final draft of the paper for the sentence skills listed on the inside front cover.

■ Writing Assignment 2

Write an examples essay on the outstanding qualities (good or bad) of a person you know well. The person might be a member of your family, a friend, a roommate, a boss or supervisor, a neighbour, an instructor, or someone else.

You may approach this assignment in one of two ways. You may choose to write about three related qualities of one person. For example, "My brother is stubborn, bad-tempered, and suspicious." Or you may write about some quality that is apparent in three different aspects of a person's life and take a third-person approach. For example: "My sister's patience is apparent in her relationships with her students, her husband, and her teenage son."

Here is a list of descriptive words commonly used to describe people. Feel free to use your own words.

Honest	Persistent	Irresponsible	Spineless
Bad-tempered	Shy	Stingy	Good-humoured
Ambitious	Sloppy	Trustworthy	Co-operative
Prejudiced	Hard-working	Aggressive	Disciplined
Considerate	Supportive	Courageous	Sentimental
Argumentative	Suspicious	Compulsive	Defensive
Soft-hearted	Outgoing	Jealous	Dishonest
Energetic	Lazy	Modest	Insensitive
Patient	Independent	Sarcastic	Neat
Reliable	Stubborn	Self-centred	
Generous	Flirtatious	Cynical	

Prewriting

1 Ask yourself questions to come up with supporting details for your thesis. For instance, if you are writing about your sentimental father, you would ask yourself questions like these:

- Why do I think of Dad as being sentimental?
- When have I seen him being sentimental?
- What sort of occasions make him sentimental?
- Where are some places he's become sentimental?
- What are some memorable examples of Dad acting sentimental?

While prewriting, ask yourself *how, why, when,* and *where* the person you chose shows this outstanding quality. You will find your subject is clearly "my sentimental father," and not "I." This is exactly what you want; each time you ask yourself *why* you have an attitude toward a subject, your focus moves toward your subject and away from you.

2 Look over the material generated by your questioning and decide what your three main points will be.

3 Decide on the order of your supporting paragraphs. If one of your main points seems stronger than the others, consider making it the final point in the body of your essay.

4 Decide whether to use one extended example or two or three brief examples to support each main point.

5 Prepare an outline for your essay, drawing your main points and supporting examples from details generated by your brainstorming.

6 Write the first draft of your essay.

Rewriting

Refer to the guidelines for rewriting provided on pages 193–194.

■   **Writing Assignment 3**

Write an examples essay that develops one of the following statements or a related statement of your own. Write your essay using the third-person approach.

> If you look hard enough, you can see complete strangers being kind to one another.
> Supermarket tabloids use several techniques to lure consumers into buying them.
> Hockey is no longer Canadian nowadays.
> The best things in life are definitely not free.
> Living with a roommate can help you learn honesty, tolerance, and consideration.
> There's more joy in simple pleasures than in life's great events.
> Looking for a job is a job in itself.
> Pets in Canada are treated like surrogate children.
> Technology is no longer our servant, but our master.
> Canadian culture is American culture with different spelling.

Be sure to choose examples that actually support your thesis. They should be relevant facts, statistics, personal experiences, or incidents you have heard or read about. Focus on *why* and *how* each example clarifies your supporting points, and your focus will naturally move toward the third-person approach and away from subjective writing.

Organize each paragraph by grouping several examples that support a particular point. Or use one extended example—an incident or story that may take up a full paragraph. Save the paragraph containing the most vivid, convincing, or important examples for last. This strategy is often called "climactic order."

■   **Writing Assignment 4**

In this examples essay, you will write with a specific purpose and for a specific audience. Imagine that you have completed a year of college and have agreed to take part in your college's summer orientation program for incoming students. You will be meeting with a small group of new students to help them get ready for college life.

Prepare a brief presentation to the new students in which you make the point that they must be ready to take on more responsibility than they may have had to do in high school. Make vividly clear—using several hypothetical students as examples—just what the consequences of inappropriate behaviour can be. To organize your presentation, you might want to focus on three of the following areas: instructors, class attendance, time control, class notetaking, textbook study, establishing regular times and places for study, and getting help when needed. Each area could be developed with detailed examples in a separate supporting paragraph.

■   **Writing Assignment 5**

Writing about a Reading Selection

Read the selection titled "In Praise of the F Word" on pages 591–593. Then write an examples essay whose thesis rejects Mary Sherry's idea that failing marks in schools are vital to educational and personal development. Your thesis could be similar to this one: "Using failure as a weapon will only intimidate students, not improve their performance." In your introduction, refer to Sherry's essay and state that you disagree with her ideas. Here is a model introduction:

> In the essay "In Praise of the F Word," Mary Sherry argues that "no-fail" educational systems have led to fraudulent educations, puzzled students, and dissatisfied employers. She states that schools have become dishonest in their evaluation of students. But Sherry's views are old-fashioned and limited in their accuracy. Using failure as a weapon will only intimidate students, not improve their performance.

You might organize the essay by discussing, in separate paragraphs, any three of the following:

Failing marks, delivered to an unprepared student, can only lower self-esteem.
Failing marks may not take into account individual or cultural problems.
Failing marks may indicate inaccurate placement of a student in a course.
Failing students is a return to a "punishment-oriented" educational system.

Support each of your topic sentences with specific examples. A student writing about failing marks as a return to "punishment-oriented" education might use examples based on the following ideas to flesh out the topic sentence, "Schools have developed in a healthy direction away from offering only the 'carrot or stick' approach to marking and motivation."

1 Students are more motivated by positive goals than by negative consequences.

2 The threat of failure is a source of intimidation for uncertain or insecure students.

3 Careful attention to student performance produces more successful students than does punishment.

Your examples should be as specific and definite as you can make them in order to be convincing.

Outline your essay by listing the ideas you plan to include and the examples you will use in the order that best defends your point.

In your conclusion, you might state that schools and colleges do their best to educate in a positive and supportive way without resorting to threats and punishment.

Note: As an alternative assignment, you may wish to write an essay supporting Sherry's contention that failure in school is a valid and appropriate option for teachers and students.

REVIEWING THE LEARNING OUTCOMES FOR CHAPTER 10

Once you have finished any of the writing assignments in this chapter, review your examples essay and ask yourself the following questions:

■ Are there three definite different supporting points for my thesis?

■ Are the examples for each point clearly related to that point?

■ Do the details of each example explain the points adequately?

■ Are there enough details to make each example clear?

■ Does my conclusion expand on what my examples have shown?

Narration • Description • Examples • Process • Cause and Effect • Comparison and Contr
Definition • Division and Classification • Argumentation • Narration • Description • Examp
Process • Cause and Effect • Comparison and Contrast • Definition • Division and Classificat
Argumentation • Narration • Description • Examples • Process • Cause and Effect • Comparison
Contrast • Definition • Division and Classification • Argumentation • Narration • Description

CHAPTER 11

Process

LEARNING OUTCOMES

The goal of any process writing is for readers to be able to complete or follow the procedure set out in the paper. By working through this chapter's activities and carefully following the instructions for its writing tasks, you will be prepared to write a process paper that

- Is suitable for the knowledge level and abilities of its readers
- Opens with a clear statement of the value and purpose of the process to be followed and/or of its relative difficulty
- Tells readers exactly what they will need, in terms of time, space, and equipment, to complete the process successfully
- Offers complete, carefully sequenced steps and explanations for each stage of the process
- Uses transitions to enforce the order of the steps and connect ideas
- Mentions potential problems or setbacks that may occur, if needed
- Concludes with a reassurance of the value of the process to readers

Every day we perform many activities that are *processes*, that is, series of steps carried out in a definite order. Many of these processes are familiar and automatic: for example, opening a word-processing program on the computer or starting the car. We are thus seldom aware of the sequence of steps that makes up each activity.

Process writing involves becoming aware of the sequence of steps in a procedure and of the stages into which we group these steps. In other cases, such as when a person asks us for directions to a particular place, when we try to follow the directions for installing a new piece of software on our computers, or when we are learning a new skill in one of our college courses, we become painfully conscious of the whole series of steps involved in the process of giving information, or of learning something new.

Process essays are informative; they use *narrative* skills in creating a careful time sequence for ordering steps, they use *descriptive* skills in creating word pictures of objects, actions, and locations, and they often use *examples* to clarify instructions or the results of following those instructions.

In our jobs, we are asked to follow or to give instructions. Or we may be asked to describe technical procedures, or steps in a marketing campaign. We then become increasingly aware of the importance of understanding the goals and meaning of a process's steps and stages. We see how carefully and completely we must cover each step in a process as we focus on achieving for ourselves—or successfully leading a reader to—the results of that process.

Process writing is a type of *informative analysis.* To *analyze* something is to break it down into component parts. Whether a process paper involves *prescribing,* telling "how to" do something, or *describing,* showing how something is done, it always sets out its goals, analyzes the steps in reaching that goal, and refocuses on the value of following the process. The reader comes away with new information.

In this section, you will be asked to write a process essay—one that explains clearly how to do or make something. To prepare for this assignment, you should first read the student process papers that are presented and then respond to the questions that follow them.

STUDENT ESSAYS TO CONSIDER

Successful Exercise

Regular exercise is something like the weather—we talk about it, but we tend not to do anything about it! Exercise classes on television, exercise programs on videos and DVDs, as well as the instructions in books, magazines, and pamphlets, now make it easy to have a personal, low-cost exercise program without leaving home. However, for success in exercise, you should follow a simple plan consisting of arranging the time, making preparations, and following the sequence with care. **1**

Everyone has an excuse: a heavy schedule at work or school, being rushed in the morning and exhausted at night, too many responsibilities. However, one solution is simply to get up half an hour earlier in the morning. Look at it this way: if you're already getting up too early, what's an extra half hour? Of course, that time could be cut to fifteen minutes earlier if you could lay out your clothes, set the breakfast table, fill the coffee maker, and gather your books and materials for the next day before you go to bed. **2**

Next, prepare for your exercise session. To begin with, get yourself ready by not eating or drinking anything before exercising. Why risk an upset stomach? Then, dress comfortably in something that allows you to move freely. Since you'll be in your own home, there's no need to invest in a high-fashion dance costume. A loose T-shirt and shorts are good. A bathing suit is great in summer, and in winter a set of long underwear is warm and comfortable. If your hair tends to flop in your eyes, pin it back or wear a headband or scarf. Prepare the exercise area, too. Turn off the phone and lock the door to prevent interruptions. Shove the coffee table out of the way so you won't bruise yourself on it or other furniture. Finally, get out the simple materials you'll need to exercise on. **3**

Finally, use common sense in getting started. Common sense isn't so common, as anyone who reads the newspaper and watches the world can tell you. You do not need to do each movement the full number of times at first, but you should *try* each one. After five or six sessions, you should be able to do each one the full number of times. Try to move in a smooth, rhythmic way; doing so will help prevent injuries and pulled muscles. Pretend you're a dancer and make each **4** move graceful, even if it's just climbing up off the floor. After the last exercise, give yourself five minutes to relax and cool off—you have earned it. Finally, put those sore muscles under a hot shower and get ready for a great day.

Establishing an exercise program isn't difficult, but it can't be achieved by reading about it, talking about it, or watching models exercise on television. To begin with, you're going to have to get up off that couch and do something about it. Otherwise, as my doctor likes to say, "If you don't use it, you'll lose it."   5

How to Be a Proactive Consumer

I'm not just a consumer—I'm a victim. If I order a product, it is sure to arrive in the wrong colour, size, or quantity. If I hire people to do repairs, they never arrive on the day scheduled. If I owe a bill, the computer is bound to overcharge me. Therefore, in self-defence, I have developed the following guide to being a proactive and successful consumer.   1

The first step is getting organized. I save all sales slips and original boxes. Also, I keep a special file for warranty cards and appliance guarantees. This file does not prevent a product from falling apart the day after the guarantee runs out. One of the problems today is the shoddy manufacturing that goes into many products. However, these facts give me the ammunition I need if I must return a purchase. I know the date of the purchase, the correct price (or service charge), where the item was purchased, and an exact description of the product, including model and serial numbers. When I compose my letter asking for adjustment, I find it is not necessary to exaggerate. I just stick to the facts.   2

The next step is to send the letter to the person who will get results quickly. My experience has shown that the president of a company is the best person to contact. I call the company to find out the president's name and make sure I note the proper spelling. Then I write directly to that person, and I usually get prompt action. For example, the head of CCM arranged to replace my son's ten-speed "lemon" when it fell apart piece by piece in less than a year. Another time, the managing director of a Calgary department store finally had a twenty-dollar overcharge on my bill corrected after three months of arguing with the computer had brought no results.   3

If I get no response to a written request within ten days, I follow through with a personal telephone call. When I had a new bathtub installed a few years ago, the plumber left a gritty black substance on the bottom of the tub. No amount of scrubbing could remove it. I tried every cleanser on the supermarket shelf, but I still had a dirty tub. The plumber shrugged off my complaints and said to try Fantastik. The manufacturer never answered my letter. Finally, I made a personal phone call to the president of the firm. Within days, a well-dressed executive showed up at my door. In a business suit, white shirt, striped tie, and rubber gloves, he cleaned the tub. Before he left, he scolded in an angry voice, "You didn't have to call the president." The point is, I did have to call the president. No one else cared enough to solve the problem.   4

Therefore, my advice to consumers is to keep accurate records, and when you have to, be proactive; go right to the top. It has always worked for me.   5

■ **Questions**

About Unity

1. The (*fill in the correct answer:* first, second, third) _____
   supporting paragraph of "Successful Exercise" lacks a topic sentence. Write a
   topic sentence that expresses its main point:

   _____

   _____

2. Which of the following sentences from paragraph 4 of "Successful Exercise"
   should be omitted in the interest of paragraph unity?
   a. "Finally, use common sense in getting started."
   b. "Common sense isn't so common, as anyone who reads the newspaper and
      watches the world can tell you."
   c. "You do not need to do each movement the full number of times at first, but
      you should *try* each one."
   d. "After the last exercise, give yourself five minutes to relax and cool off—you
      have earned it."

3. Which sentence in paragraph 2 of "How to Be a Proactive Consumer" should
   be omitted in the interest of paragraph unity? (*Write the opening words.*)

   _____

About Support

4. Which sentence in paragraph 3 of "Successful Exercise" needs to be followed
   by more supporting details? (*Write the opening words.*)

   _____

5. Which supporting paragraph in "How to Be a Proactive Consumer" uses one
   extended example? Write the number of that paragraph and tell (in just a few
   words) what the example was about.

   _____

   _____

6. Which supporting paragraph in "How to Be a Proactive Consumer" depends
   on two short examples? Write the number of that paragraph and tell (in just a
   few words) what each example was about.

   _____

   _____

About Coherence

7. Read paragraph 3 of "Successful Exercise" and find the four sentences that begin with time signals. Write those four signals here.

_____   _____

_____   _____

8. In "How to Be a Proactive Consumer," which time transition word is used in the topic sentence of paragraph 2? _____ In the topic sentence of paragraph 3? _____

About the Introduction and Conclusion

9. Which best describes the introduction of "Successful Exercise"?
   a. It begins with a couple of general points about the topic and then narrows down to the thesis.
   b. It explains the importance of daily exercise to the reader.
   c. It uses a brief story about the author's experience with exercise.
   d. It asks a question about the role of exercise in life.

10. Which method of conclusion is used in both "Successful Exercise" and "How to Be a Proactive Consumer"?
   a. A summary
   b. A thought-provoking question
   c. A prediction
   d. A recommendation

WRITING A PROCESS ESSAY

A process essay requires the writer to think through the steps involved in an activity. As Fiona, the writer of "How to Be a Proactive Consumer," thought about possible topics for her essay, she asked herself, "What are some of the things I do in a methodical, step-by-step way?" A number of possibilities occurred to her: getting herself and her children ready for school in the morning, going grocery shopping (from preparing a shopping list to organizing her coupons), and the one she finally settled on: being effective at getting satisfaction as a consumer. "People tell me I'm 'so organized' when it comes to getting satisfaction on things I buy," Fiona said. "I realized that I usually get results when I ask for adjustments because I go about setting up my requests in an organized way. In order to write my essay, I just needed to put those steps into words."

Fiona began by making a list of the steps she follows when she makes a complaint. This is what she wrote:

- Save sales slips and original boxes
- Engrave items with ID number in case of burglary
- Write letter asking for adjustment

- Make photocopy of letter
- Create file of warranties and guarantees
- Send request letter directly to president
- Call company for president's name
- Follow through with telephone call if no response
- Make thank-you call after action is taken

Next, she numbered those steps in the order in which she performs them. She struck out some items she realized weren't really necessary to a successful consumer adjustment process:

1 Save sales slips and original boxes

~~Engrave items with ID number in case of burglary~~

4 Write letter asking for adjustment

~~Make photocopy of letter~~

2 Create file of warranties and guarantees

5 Send request letter directly to president

3 Call company for president's name

6 Follow through with telephone call if no response

~~Make thank-you call after action is taken~~

Next, she decided to make an outline to group her items into three stages. The stages she determined would work were (1) getting organized, (2) sending the request to the president, and (3) following up with further action.

With that preparation done, Fiona wrote her first draft:

Because I find that a consumer has to watch out for herself and be ready to speak up if a product or service isn't satisfactory, I have developed the following guide to proactive consuming. **1**

The first step is getting organized. I save all sales slips, original boxes, warranty cards, and appliance guarantees. This file does not prevent a product from falling apart the day after the guarantee runs out. One of the problems today is the shoddy workmanship that goes into many products. That way I know the date of purchase, the correct price, where the item was purchased, and an exact description of the product. **2**

The next step is to send the letter asking for adjustment to the person who will get results quickly. I call the company to find out the president's name, and then I write directly to that person. For example, the head of CCM arranged to replace my son's bike. Another time, the managing director of a Calgary department store finally had a twenty-dollar overcharge on my bill corrected. **3**

If I get no response to a written request within ten days, I follow through with a personal telephone call. When I had a new bathtub installed a few years ago, the plumber left a gritty black substance on the bottom of the tub. I tried everything to get it off. Finally, I made a personal call to the president of the firm. Within days, a well-dressed executive showed up at my door. In a business **4** suit, white shirt, striped tie, and rubber gloves, he cleaned the tub. Before he left, he said, "You didn't have to call the president."

Therefore, my advice to consumers is to keep accurate records, and when   5
you must be proactive, go right to the top. It has always worked for me.

When she was finished with her draft, Fiona set it aside for several days. When she reread it, she was able to look at it more critically. These are her comments:

> I think the first draft is okay as the "bare bones" of an essay, but it needs to be fleshed out everywhere. For instance, in paragraph 1, I need to explain *why* it's important to know the date of purchase, etc. And in paragraph 2, I need to explain more about *what happened* with the bike and the department store overcharge. In paragraph 3, especially, I need to explain *how* I tried to solve the problem with the bathtub before I called the president. I want to make it clear that I don't immediately go to the top as soon as I have a problem—I give the people at a lower level a chance to fix it first. All in all, my first draft looks to me like I just rushed to get the basic ideas down on paper. Now I need to take the time to back up my main points with better support.

With that self-critique in mind, Fiona wrote the version of "How to Be a Proactive Consumer" that appears on page 200.

WRITING A PROCESS ESSAY

■ Writing Assignment 1: Prescriptive or "How to" Process Writing

Choose a topic from the list below to use as the basis for a process essay.

> How to break a bad habit
> How to shop for a car (new or used), rent an apartment, or buy a house
> How to do a search on the Internet
> How to survive a Canadian winter
> How to find an internship (co-op position, summer job)
> How to manage your money while in college
> How to fall out of love
> How _____ became the successful person he or she is
> How to make chili, hot and sour soup, oatmeal cookies, rotis, or some other dish
> How a cell phone (or other technological or mechanical item) works

Prewriting Strategies

1 Freewrite for ten minutes on the topic you have chosen. Don't worry about spelling, grammar, organization, or anything other than getting as many steps in your process as possible down on paper. If ideas are still flowing at the end of ten minutes, keep on writing. This freewriting will give you a base of raw material that you can draw on in the next phase of your work on the essay. Judging from your freewriting, is there enough material available to you to support a process essay? If so, keep following the steps below. If not, choose another topic, and freewrite about it for ten minutes.

2 Develop a single clear sentence that will serve as your thesis. Your thesis can either (a) say it is important that your readers know about this process ("Knowing how to shop for a car can save you money, time, and future heartache") or (b) state your opinion of this process ("Falling out of love is a hard skill to learn, but a skill that that pays off in emotional health").

3 Think about or try to see your audience. What are they likely to know about your topic? Do they need some background information to follow the steps in your process? If you are explaining how to do something technical or some activity with its own vocabulary, do any of your terms or word choices need explanation?

4 Make a list of all the steps that you are describing.

5 Number your items in time order; strike out items that do not fit in the list; add others you can think of.

6 After editing the list, decide how the items can be grouped into a minimum of three steps. For example, with a topic like "How to Grow Tomatoes," you might divide the process into (a) soil preparation, (b) planting, and (c) care.

7 Use your list as a guide for your outline and the first rough draft of your paper. As you write, try to think of additional details that will develop your opening paragraph: have you mentioned any items needed or stated the value of the process? Do not expect to finish your paper in one draft. You should, in fact, be ready to write a series of lists and drafts as you work toward helping your audience successfully follow your process.

8 Look at your concluding paragraph, and consider which of the following concepts used to complete a process paper might be appropriate to your subject:

- Restating the intended results of the process
- Confirming with the reader that the process is complete and/or successful
- Reassuring the reader of the benefits offered in the opening if steps are followed correctly
- Encouraging the reader to try your process
- Emphasizing the importance of the process to the reader and/or other people
- Offering or repeating any necessary cautions, restrictions, or warnings needed at any stage of the process

Rewriting

Since the goal of all process writing is to show how to do something (or how something is done), the best way to "test" your draft is to have someone else read it.

Exchange papers with a fellow student. As it is essential that process writing describe a series of activities in a way that is easy to follow, ask yourselves these questions after reading:

1 Does the writer describe the steps in a clear, logical way?
2 Has the writer used transitions such as *first, next, also, then, after, now, during,* and *finally* to make the paper move smoothly and to guide the reader carefully from one step to another?

3 Does the paper describe the necessary steps so that a typical reader could perform the task described here, or is essential information missing?

4 Does the concluding paragraph provide (a) a summary that refocuses the reader on the intended result of the process, or (b) a final thought that encourages the reader to try the process (or any of the recommended conclusion techniques for process papers)?

5 Does the paper contain sentence-skills errors that you noticed while reading the paper aloud?

As you revise your essay through one or more additional drafts, continue to refer to this list until you can answer "yes" to each question. Then be sure to proofread the next-to-final draft of the paper for the sentence skills listed on the inside front cover.

Writing Assignment 2: Descriptive or "How It's Done" Process Writing

Everyone is an expert at something. Write a "descriptive" process essay on some skill that you can perform very well. Write from the point of view that "This is how _____ *should* be done." Remember that your skill need not be unusual. It can be anything from "creating a perfect meal" to "setting up a new stereo system" to "dealing with unpleasant customers" to "designing your first website."

1 If possible, perform the task and take notes on what you are doing as you go along. If that's not possible (as in "dealing with unpleasant customers"), think through or visualize a particular time you had to deal with such a customer and make notes about just what you did, and perhaps about points where something could or did go wrong.

2 Look over your notes and make a list of the steps you followed.

3 Considering your list, decide how you can divide the items listed into at least three stages. Some of your steps may involve telling a reader how to get ready, some may involve a change of location as part of the process, and some steps may require the reader to perform a different set of tasks: each of these could be a different stage in your process. For instance, look at the following list of items for the process of "Dealing with an Unsatisfied Customer." Then fill in the blanks on the trial outline that follows.

Dealing with an Unsatisfied Customer

This is how an unhappy customer should be dealt with, so that other customers do not become involved, and so that the customer feels that he or she has been treated fairly.

1. Introduce yourself courteously and ask for the customer's name.

2. Encourage the customer to step away from other people in the store so that he or she can explain the situation to you.

3. Use a calm and reassuring tone of voice, and suggest that you have lots of time to listen to the customer's problems.

4. Sit down with the customer, if possible, and find a notepad and pen to record the details of the situation.

5. Gently ask the customer to relate the details of the problem in the order in which the events occurred.

6. List these details and ask for clarification as you do so; never challenge the customer as he or she speaks to you.

7. If the customer is justified in any part of his or her complaint, and the product is unsatisfactory, make the adjustment calmly and quietly.

8. If the product is simply not what the customer wanted, and he or she has the receipt from its purchase, offer a refund or replacement, according to company policy.

9. If the customer has no receipt and is still displeased, state the company's policy for this situation and offer to call your supervisor or manager to provide any additional assistance.

_____   Stage 1: Introduce yourself to the customer; treat him or her calmly and courteously

Items _____ through _____

_____   Stage 2: Carefully note all details of the customer's situation

Items _____ through _____

_____   Stage 3: Provide any adjustments you can, or ask for management assistance

Items _____ through _____

4 Prepare an outline of your main points. Use it as a guide as you write the rough draft of your paper.

Rewriting

As you read through your first draft and subsequent drafts, ask yourself these questions:

- Have I introduced my essay with either a statement of the importance of the process or my opinion of the process?
- Have I included in my opening paragraph any necessary equipment or aspects of preparing to perform the process safely or well?
- Have I used any terms or described any procedures that my audience may not understand?
- Have I provided a clear step-by-step description of the process?

- Have I divided the items in the process into at least three logical stages (main points in the essay)?
- Have I carefully used transition words such as *first, next, then, during,* and *finally* to help readers to follow my train of thought?
- Have I used an appropriate concept in my concluding paragraph?

As you revise your essay through one or more additional drafts, continue to refer to this list until you can answer "yes" to each question. Then be sure to check the next-to-final draft of the paper for the sentence skills listed on the inside front cover.

■ Writing Assignment 3

In this process essay, you will write with a specific purpose for a specific audience. Imagine that your college newsaper has asked you to write an article to help prepare first-semester students for a college workload.

Write an informal but helpful essay, drawing from your own experience, in which you summarize the steps involved in meeting the challenges of a first semester and successfully managing your time in college.

Before starting this paper, you should read "Writing a Summary" on pages 294–307.

■ Writing Assignment 4

Any one of the topics below can be written as a process paper. Follow the steps suggested for Writing Assignment 1. Note that some of these topics invite humour, and some involve reversing a completed process, or "deconstructing" a finished product or process.

How to improve a college or workplace
How to "undo" that disaster (you name it), and not go there again
How to live with a two-year-old, a fifteen-year-old, or a parent
How to procrastinate with style
How I got where I am today
How to eat well on thirty dollars a week
How to organize your clothing (or your music CDs, or your books)
How to behave on a "chatgroup" (on the Internet)
How to "analyze your relationship to death"

■ Writing Assignment 5: Writing about a Reading Selection

Do *either* of the following.

Option 1: Read the selection titled "How to Do Well on a Job Interview" by Glenda Davis, on pages 524–526, noting how the author prepares you to follow her instructions and shows the value of doing so. Then write a process essay based on the topic that follows.

Your challenge with this assignment is to become "the teacher you always dreamed of." Your subject or your lesson material is something at which you are an expert: playing a certain sport, being a loyal friend, being a dynamic salesperson, winning at interactive computer games, or managing some aspect of your life especially well. Your audience is your classmates—be careful to visualize what they may need to know to benefit from your "teaching." Your essay will be a brief "training manual" for your students.

Write a *prescriptive* or "how to" process essay that both teaches your readers how to be the expert you are at your subject and shows the "connections" or relationship of your talent to other things in life—its wider implications.

Your skill may require more than three "stages," or body paragraphs, but check with your instructor to make sure the process you describe will be appropriate for a brief essay.

Start by imagining how you would teach someone else to perform this task. Then follow steps 2 through 8 in the "Prewriting Strategies" on pages 204–205.

When you are satisfied with your first draft, follow the tips for rewriting on pages 205–206, either by working with a "peer critic" or by asking the same questions of your own paper.

Option 2: Read the selection titled "How to Make It in College, Now That You're Here" on pages 583–588. Then write a process essay with the thesis, "Here are the tips that will help a student succeed in _____" (name a course in which you are now enrolled or one that you have taken in the past). To get started, think of the advice you would like to have had *before* you took that particular course: What would you have wanted to know about the professor? The assignments? The exams? Policies about attendance, lateness, and so on? Pick three tips that you believe would be most helpful to another student about to enrol in the class, and discuss each one in a separate supporting paragraph. Model your introduction after the one in "How to Make It in College" by telling your readers that, on the basis of your own experience, you are going to pass on the secrets for succeeding in this course.

Below are three sample topic sentences for "How to Succeed in Communications 101."

First topic sentence: First of all, a student who wants a good grade in Communications 101 should be prepared at every class meeting for a surprise quiz.

Second topic sentence: In addition, students should speak up during class discussion, for Professor Knox adds "participation" into final grades.

Third topic sentence: Most important, students should start early on term essays and turn them in on time.

REVIEWING THE LEARNING OUTCOMES FOR CHAPTER 11

After completing any of the writing assignments for this chapter, read through your essay and review how well you have met the learning outcomes by asking yourself these questions:

- Have I supplied enough background information to make my process understandable to readers? Are there any technical points or any special vocabulary that should be explained?

- Does my opening paragraph state why readers should follow the process, and where they might encounter any difficulties?

- Have I left out any equipment or supplies and suggested how much time may be needed for each stage?

- Are the main stages and the steps in exactly the right order to complete the process?

- Are there enough transitions to make the steps in the process clear?

- Is each step explained clearly enough; are there examples where appropriate, and are possible problems mentioned?

- Have I finished by reassuring readers that following my process is valuable?

Cause and Effect

After working through this chapter's activities and completing one or more of its writing assignments, you will write a cause-effect essay that

- Offers a thesis statement that states your viewpoint your subject and indicates whether you will examine causes or effects
- Shows as supporting points a selection of causes or effects focused on proving your thesis
- Uses true and logical causes or effects to support and clarify the thesis
- Presents its supporting points in order of importance
- Supports its causes or effects with sufficient and specific details
- Concludes with a reassurance that its thesis point is effectively supported

Why did Stacey decide to move out of her parents' house? What made you quit a well-paying job? Why are action movies so popular? **Cause and effect** essays often spring from questions like these. Humans want to know *why* things happen. We look for reasons for things; we try to connect causes to consequences. We see the results of events and actions; we crave explanations.

Situations may have many causes; we discover some easily, but others may be less obvious. Newspapers report that the low Canadian dollar is caused by various market conditions; financial analysts find causes in Asian trading activities. We realize also that a given action can have a series of effects—for good or bad. Sometimes effects may all be related; one may trigger another. At other times, effects may not really be effects at all. A TV clip states that childhood behaviour problems result from children's watching violent shows. Could there be other causes? What evidence supports these shows as the only causes? Sorting out causes and effects requires us to use logic as we try to understand things that happen in our lives.

Cause and effect essays involve *analysis*. Looking at a situation, we examine it; we break it open to discover its causes. Or we work at finding the separate effects or consequences. We must also choose accurate and logical *examples* of causes and effects. Process essays make us analyze *how* something happens; cause and effect essays make us analyze *why* it happens. You will be asked in this section to do some detective work by examining the cause of something or the effects of something. This process is not always easy; cause and effect essays need careful attention at the prewriting stage.

Cause and effect papers may treat *only* causes, or *only* effects. Or during prewriting, you may find too many of each, or only one dominant cause or effect, or weak logic in your "causal chain." Benefits of your discovery work lie in college and career writing tasks where you will explain *why* a product doesn't sell, or *why* a technical procedure gives some specific results.

Now read both essays that follow and answer the questions about them. These two essays support their thesis statements by explaining a series of causes or a series of effects.

STUDENT ESSAYS TO CONSIDER

The Joys of an Old Car

Some of my friends can't believe my car still runs. Others laugh when they see it parked outside the house and ask if it's an antique. But they aren't being fair to my fourteen-year-old Toyota Corolla. In fact, my "antique" has opened my eyes to the rewards of owning an old car.   **1**

One obvious reward is economy. Fourteen years ago, when my husband and I were newly married and nearly broke, we bought the car—a shiny, red, year-old leftover—for a mere $4200. Today it would cost five times as much. We save money on insurance, since it's no longer worthwhile for us to have collision coverage. Old age has even been kind to the Toyota's engine, which required only three major repairs in the last several years. And it still delivers twenty kilometres per litre in the city and thirty on the highway—not bad for a senior citizen.   **2**

I've heard that when a Toyota passes the fifty-thousand-kilometre mark with no major problems, it will probably go on forever. I wouldn't disagree. Our car breezed past that mark many years ago. Since then, I've been able to count on it to sputter to life and make its way down the driveway on Sudbury's coldest, snowiest mornings. When my boss at Zellers got stuck with his brand-new BMW in the worst snowstorm of the year, I sauntered into work on time. The only time it didn't start, unfortunately, was the day I had a final exam. The Toyota may have the body of an old car, but beneath its elderly hood hums the engine of a teenager.   **3**

Last of all, having the same car for many years offers the advantage of familiarity. When I open the door and slide into the driver's seat, the soft vinyl surrounds me like a well-worn glove. I know to the millimetre exactly how much room I have when I turn a corner or back into a parking space. When my gas gauge is on empty, I know that five litres are still in reserve, and I can plan accordingly. The front wheels invariably begin to shake when I go more than one hundred kilometres an hour, reminding me that I am exceeding the speed limit. With the Toyota, the only surprises I face are the ones from other drivers.   **4**

I prize my fourteen-year-old car's economy and dependability, and most of all, its familiarity. It is faded, predictable, and comfortable, like a well-worn pair of jeans. And, like a well-worn pair of jeans, it will be difficult to throw away.   **5**

Celebrity Stress

A fan who signed himself "Britney's Defender" wrote to her official site 1
with a desperate plea. "Please give me some proof," he begged, "that Britney
hasn't had plastic surgery." Luckily his question was ignored by the webmaster,
but it's typical of the fact that everyone feels entitled to know everything about
celebrities today. Stars and politicians lead stressful lives because no matter
how glamorous or powerful they are, the Internet and the media generally take
away their privacy, pressure them in public, and often endanger their safety.

For one thing, celebrities lack the privacy an ordinary person takes for 2
granted. Every personal detail and thousands of lies about them are splashed
over the front pages of the tabloids so bored shoppers waiting in line at Safeway
can read about "Celine Dion's Hidden Children" or "Beyoncé's Private Agony."
Even a celebrity's family is hauled into the spotlight. George Bush's daughters'
underage drinking or some actor's sad uncle on welfare in Saskatoon end up as
glaring headlines. Photographers hound celebrities at home, in restaurants, and
even while they're driving, hoping for Halle Berry to have another accident or
for Jim Carrey to lose his temper. When celebrities try to do the things that
normal people do, like eat out or attend a basketball game, they risk being
interrupted by thoughtless autograph seekers or harassed by aggressive fans.

In addition to losing their privacy, celebrities must cope with the constant 3
pressure to look great and act properly. Their physical appearance is always
under observation, and if they should suffer a major illness like Michael J. Fox,
the cameras will track them down, even on bad days. Famous women, especially,
suffer from nasty media comments, drawing remarks like "She's really put on
weight" or "Has she ever gotten old." Unflattering pictures of celebrities are
photographers' prizes to be sold to the highest bidder; this increases pressures
on people in public to look good at all times. Famous people are also under
pressure to act calm and collected under any circumstances. Because they
are constantly observed, they have few opportunities to blow off steam or act
a little crazy.

Most important, celebrities must deal with the stress of being in constant 4
danger. The friendly grabs, hugs, and kisses of enthusiastic fans can quickly
turn into uncontrolled assaults on a celebrity's hair, clothes, and car. Photographers
must bear some responsibility for the death of perhaps the major celebrity of
the 1990s—Princess Diana. Whether or not their pursuit caused the crash
that took her life, it's clear she was chased as aggressively as an escaping
felon. And celebrity can lead to deranged and even lethal attacks. The near-
fatal stabbing of the late George Harrison in his home and the murder of John
Lennon came about because two unbalanced people developed obsessions with
the two Beatles. Famous people must live with the fact that they are always
fair game—and never out of season.

Some people dream of starring roles, huge power, and their picture on the 5
cover of magazines. But the cost is far too high. A famous person gives up
private life, feels pressure to look and act certain ways all the time, and is
never completely safe. An ordinary mundane life is far safer and saner than a
life in the spotlight.

■ **Questions**

About Unity

1. Which supporting paragraph in "The Joys of an Old Car" lacks a topic sentence?
   a. 2
   b. 3
   c. 4

2. Which sentence in paragraph 3 of "The Joys of an Old Car" should be omitted in the interest of paragraph unity? *(Write the opening words.)*

   _____

3. Rewrite the thesis statement of "The Joys of an Old Car" to include a plan of development.

   _____

   _____

About Support

4. In paragraph 4 of "Celebrity Stress," the author supports the idea that "celebrities must deal with the stress of being in constant danger" with *(circle the letters of the two answers that apply)*
   a. statistics
   b. an explanation
   c. a quotation by an expert
   d. examples

5. After which sentence in paragraph 3 of "Celebrity Stress" are more specific details needed? *(Write the opening words.)*

   _____

6. In "The Joys of an Old Car," how many examples are given to support the topic sentence "One obvious reward is economy"?
   a. two
   b. three
   c. four
   d. five

About Coherence

7. Which topic sentence in "Celebrity Stress" functions as a linking sentence between paragraphs? *(Write the opening words.)*

   _____

8. Paragraph 3 of "Celebrity Stress" includes two main transition words or phrases. List those words or phrases.

   _____   _____

9. What are the two transition words or phrases in "The Joys of an Old Car" that signal two major points of support for the thesis?

_____   _____

About the Conclusion

10. Which of the following methods is used in the conclusion of "The Joys of an Old Car"?
    a. a summary and a final thought
    b. a thought-provoking question
    c. a recommendation

WRITING A CAUSE-EFFECT ESSAY

About Prewriting

The best essays are often those written about a topic that the author genuinely cares about. Jeannette, the author of "The Joys of an Old Car," was assigned a cause-effect essay: She explains, "My husband and I believe in enjoying what we have and living simply, rather than being 'constant consumers.' Our dinged-up old car is an example of that way of life. People keep saying, 'Surely you could buy a nicer car!' I enjoy explaining to them why we keep our old 'clunker.' I immediately thought of the car as a topic, because writing this essay was just an extension of a conversation I'd had many times."

In spite of her confidence, Jeannette wasn't sure how to divide what she had to say into three main points. She was looking for "reasons why" (causes for why) she loved her car. So, in order to get started, she made a list of all the good things about her car. Here is what she wrote:

- Starts reliably
- Has needed few major repairs
- Reminder of Alain's and my first days of marriage
- Gets good gas mileage
- Don't need to worry about scratches and scrapes
- I know exactly how much room I need to turn and park
- Saves money on insurance
- I'm very comfortable in it
- No car payment
- Cold weather doesn't seem to bother it
- Don't worry about it being stolen
- Uses regular gas
- Can haul anything in it—dog, plants—and not worry about dirt
- Know all its little ticks and shimmies and don't worry about them

When Jeannette reviewed her list, she saw that the items fell into three major categories. There were (1) the car's economy, (2) its familiarity, and (3) its dependability. These were her "causes" for loving her old car. She looked for categories for each item on her list, and crossed out those items that didn't seem to belong in any of the categories.

3 Starts reliably

1 Has needed few major repairs

~~Reminder of Alain's and my first days of marriage~~

1 Gets good gas mileage

~~Don't need to worry about scratches and scrapes~~

2 I know exactly how much room I need to turn and park

1 Saves money on insurance

2 I'm very comfortable in it

1 No car payment

3 Cold weather doesn't seem to bother it

~~Don't worry about its being stolen~~

1 Uses regular gas

~~Can haul anything in it—dog, plants, and not worry about dirt~~

2 Know all its little ticks and shimmies and don't worry about them

Now, Jeannette felt she had her three main "causes" for enjoying her car so much, and she had some "effects" of those causes on her. She produced this as a first draft:

> When people see my beat-up old car, they sometimes laugh at it. But I tell them that owning a fourteen-year-old Toyota has its good points.   **1**
>
> One obvious reward is economy. My husband and I bought the car when we were newly married. We paid $4200 for it. That seemed like a lot of money then, but today, we'd spend five times that much for a similar car. We also save money on insurance. In the fourteen years we've had it, the Toyota has needed only a few major repairs. It even gets good gas mileage.   **2**
>
> I like the familiar feel of the car. I'm so used to it that driving anything else feels very strange. When I visited my sister recently, I drove her new Plymouth to the grocery store. Everything was so unfamiliar! I couldn't even figure out how to turn on the radio. I was relieved to get back to my own car.   **3**
>
> Finally, my car is very dependable. No matter how cold and snowy it is. Sudbury gets miserable in the winter, and cars freeze up. I know the Toyota will start quickly and get me where I need to go. Unfortunately, one day it didn't and naturally that day I had a final exam. But otherwise it just keeps going and going.   **4**
>
> My Toyota reminds me of a favourite piece of clothing that you wear forever and can't bear to throw away.   **5**

About Revising

Jeannette traded first-draft copies with a classmate, Emil, and each critiqued the other's work before it was revised. Here is Jeannette's first draft with Emil's comments in the margins.

> When people see my beat-up old car, they sometimes laugh at it. But I tell them that owning a fourteen-year-old Toyota has its good points.

[1] *How? Is the insurance less expensive just because the car is old?*

[2] *Here would be a good place for a specific detail— how good is the mileage?*

[3] *This topic sentence doesn't tie in with the others—shouldn't it say "Secondly" or "Another reason I like the car..."?*

[4] *This is too much about your sister's car and not enough about yours. Tell what is so great about the familiarity of your own car.*

[5] *This is a good comparison. But draw it out more— how is your car like comfortable old clothes?*

One obvious reward is economy. My husband and I bought the car when we were newly married. We paid $4200 for it. That seemed like a lot of money then, but today, we'd spend five times that much for a similar car. We also save money on insurance.[1] In the fourteen years we've had it, the Toyota has needed only a few major repairs. It even gets good gas mileage.[2]

I like the familiar feel of the car.[3] I'm so used to it that driving anything else feels very strange. When I visited my sister recently, I drove her new Plymouth to the grocery store. Everything was so unfamiliar! I couldn't even figure out how to turn on the radio.[4] I was relieved to get back to my own car.

Finally, my car is very dependable. No matter how cold and snowy it is. Sudbury gets miserable in the winter, and cars freeze up. I know the Toyota will start quickly and get me where I need to go. Unfortunately, one day it didn't and naturally that day I had a final exam. But otherwise it just keeps going and going.

My Toyota reminds me of a favourite piece of clothing that you wear forever and can't bear to throw away.[5]

Jeannette read Emil's comments and realized two things: one, that her paragraph about familiarity needed more specific details that resulted from her point and from her own experience, and two, that actually the car's familiarity was the main reason why she loved it. She decided to "save the best for last," and place this idea as her final point.

To clear up her thinking before starting a final draft, she decided to make a more formal outline of her cause-effect essay as follows:

Situation: "I love my old Toyota because of its . . .

Cause #1: Economy
  Effects of car's age on its costs:
  • It's paid for—no payments every month
  • Insurance is cheap—no collision coverage
  • Good gas mileage, uses regular

Cause #2: Dependability
  Effects of having a dependable car:
  • Still running well
  • Starts on the coldest days

Cause #3: Familiarity
  Effects of familiarity on me as driver:
  • Know the feel of the car
  • Know how much room I need to manoeuvre
  • Know the gas tank limits
  • Know the speed tolerances of the engine

Now, Jeannette felt ready to write the final version of "The Joys of an Old Car" that appears on page 212.

WRITING A CAUSE-EFFECT ESSAY

■ **Writing Assignment 1: Deciding Between Causes and Effects and Writing the Cause or Effect Essay**

In outline form on separate paper, provide brief causes or effects for at least *four* of the six statements below. The first item is done for you as an example. Make sure that you have three *separate* and *distinct* items for each statement. Also, indicate whether you have listed three causes or three effects.

Example: Many youngsters are terrified of school.

Causes: 1. *Afraid of not being liked by other students*
2. *Afraid of failing tests*
3. *Intimidated by teachers*

1. Among winners of scholarships and holders of elected office a high percentage are products of first-generation Canadian families.

_____

_____

_____

2. Graduates of Canadian colleges and universities tend to marry later in life than they used to.

_____

_____

_____

3. Students often have trouble adjusting to college for several reasons.

_____

_____

_____

4. Wearing furs is no longer acceptable, even in a Canadian climate.

_____

_____

_____

5. Computers dominate the lives of many families.

_____

_____

_____

6. The average workweek should be no more than thirty hours long.

_____

_____

_____

When you have finished your four outlines, decide which of them would provide the best basis for a "cause" or "effect" essay you will write.

Prewriting

1 Look at the outline you produced in the previous step. You will now use it as the basis for a "cause" essay, an "effect" essay, or a cause-and-effect essay. The statement will be your thesis, and the three causes or effects will function as your main points. Make sure that each of your main points is a *separate* and *distinct* point, not a restatement of one of the other points. Make sure that *causes* really *cause* or create the situation in your statement, and don't simply "come before" that situation. Make sure that *effects* actually *result* from the situation, and don't just "occur after" that situation.

2 Decide whether you will support each of your main points with several examples or with one extended example. You may want to freewrite about each of these examples for a few minutes, or you may want to list as many details as you can think of that would go with each of the examples.

3 Write a first draft of an introduction that attracts the reader's interest, gives some background to your statement, states your thesis, and presents a plan of development.

Rewriting

After you have completed the first draft of the paper, set it aside for a while (if possible). When you reread what you have written, prepare for rewriting by asking yourself these questions:

- Does the paper have a clearly stated thesis?
- Have I backed up each main point with one extended example or several shorter examples? Do I have enough detailed support? Do I have a relatively equal amount of support for each main point?
- Have I performed a "logic check" on my causes or effects?

  1 Have I made a "time-sequence" logical error? A cause is not necessarily a cause because it happens *before* an effect: e.g., if a dog crosses the road before your car stalls, it is not the *cause* of your car trouble; a low battery or some mechanical problem may be the real reason for the stalling. Similarly, anything that simply happens *after* another event is not necessarily an effect. You must establish a clear causal connection between your ideas.

2 Have I considered "multiple causes and effects"? Choose the best causes and effects of your statement to support your point; there are often "causes behind causes," and "chains of effects." Edit or add to your details and examples to most accurately make your point. Is there irrelevant or unfocused material that should be eliminated?

- Have I used transition words to help readers follow sequence and causality in my train of thought?
- What should I provide in a concluding paragraph to wrap up my essay and either strengthen my point or give it wider meaning?

As you revise your essay through one or more additional drafts, continue to refer to this list until you can answer "yes" to each question. Then be sure to check the next-to-final draft of the paper for the sentence skills listed on the inside front cover.

Writing Assignment 2: Writing a Causes Essay

If students from another country decided to visit your college and your culture, they would encounter some surprising customs and attitudes. You would have reasons to feel both proud and perhaps embarrassed by the situations the foreign students would encounter. Write an essay explaining your feelings about specific aspects of Canadian college and culture. Give reasons for your feelings.

Prewriting Strategies

1 You will probably have an instant, gut reaction to the question "Am I more proud of or embarrassed by my everyday college and lifestyle habits?" Go with that reaction; you will find it easier to come up with supporting points for the thesis that occurred to you immediately.

2 Generate supporting details for your thesis by making a list. Call it "Reasons I'm proud of college life/my culture" or "Reasons I'm embarrassed by college life/my culture." Then list as many items as you can think of. Don't worry about whether the reasons are important, silly, significant, or trivial. Just write down as many as possible.

3 Review your list and ask yourself if some of the items could be grouped into one category. For instance, a list of reasons to be proud of Canadian college life might include items such as "we're up to date on technological career training," "students in most colleges are asked for input about their courses." These could be a category called "Advances in Canadian Colleges." That category, in turn, could serve as a main supporting point in your essay.

4 As described in 3, decide on three supporting points. Write an outline that includes those points and the examples (one extended example or several shorter ones). The point described in 3 would be outlined like this:

Point: Canadian colleges are quite advanced in courses, aims, and student concerns.

Causes: 1. Technology is used to prepare students for careers
        2. Colleges are tuned in to career growth areas, like digital animation
        3. Students are consulted about satisfaction with courses each year

5 Using your outline, write a first draft of the paper. Write an introduction that states your thesis and plan of development, and a conclusion that reminds readers of your thesis and leaves them with a final point to consider.

Rewriting

As you work through subsequent drafts, ask yourself these questions:

- Have I introduced my essay with a clearly stated thesis and plan of development? Does my opening paragraph also contain enough background information to make my point clear to the reader?
- Is each of my main points supported by solid, specific details?
- Have I used both "time and sequence" transition words such as *first, another, in addition,* and *also?* Have I used "causal" transition words such as *therefore, because of,* and *so?*
- Have I checked my writing for the sentence skills listed on the inside front cover?

Writing Assignment 3

In this essay, you will write with a specific purpose and for a specific audience. Imagine that several friends of yours complain they are having a hard time learning anything in a class taught by Professor X. You volunteer to attend the class and see for yourself. You also get information from your friends about the course requirements.

Afterwards, you write a letter to Professor X, calling attention to what you see as causes of the learning problems that students are having in the class. To organize your essay letter, you might develop each of these causes in a separate supporting paragraph. In the second part of each supporting paragraph, you might suggest changes that Professor X could make to deal with each problem.

Writing Assignment 4:
Writing about a Reading Selection

You belong to several communities or groups of people with a common interest or background (which may or may not be tied to specific physical locations). On the other hand, some groups you meet with frequently and some places where you may go every day never seem to feel like "communities."

Read the selection titled "A Work Community" by Paul Hoffert on pages 603–605. Consider the reasons Hoffert feels that his workplace has become a community, and the results or benefits he has drawn from his discovery. Write an essay that develops and defends either of the following statements with specific examples and details that make your causes or effects clear to readers.

1. There are three reasons _____ does (*or* does not) feel like a community.

2. The results of the community feeling (*or* lack of community feeling) of

   _____ are _____ , _____ , and _____ .

REVIEWING THE LEARNING OUTCOMES FOR CHAPTER 12

After completing any of the writing tasks in this chapter, review your essay to decide how well it responds to the following questions:

- Does the thesis state a clear viewpoint and indicate whether the essay deals with causes or effects?
- Is each cause or effect truly a cause or effect? Does each clearly support the point of your thesis?
- Are your causes or effects presented in an effective order with appropriate transitions to reinforce meaning and to guide the reader?
- Are the supporting points adequately explained and clarified by sufficient and specific details to make them clear?
- Does the conclusion offer reinforcement of the thesis point?

---

tion • Description • Examples • Process • Cause and Effect • Comparison and Contrast •
ition • Division and Classification • Argumentation • Narration • Description • Examples
ss • Cause and Effect • Comparison and Contrast • Definition • Division and Classification •
mentation • Narration • Description • Examples • Process • Cause and Effect • Comparison and
ast • Definition • Division and Classification • Argumentation • Narration • Description

C H A P T E R   1 3

Comparison
and Contrast

LEARNING OUTCOMES

After working through the activities and one or more of the writing tasks in this chapter, you will write a comparison or contrast essay that

- Compares or contrasts limited aspects of two subjects that have a logical reason to be considered together
- Contains in its thesis statement (1) both its subjects, (2) its intention to compare or contrast, and (3) a clear point to be made by comparing or contrasting these subjects
- Uses either the one-side-at-a-time or the point-by-point method to state and develop its comparison or contrast
- Carefully compares or contrasts each subject within one of these structures according to several appropriate bases for comparing or contrasting
- Concludes with a summing up of the results gained by comparing or contrasting the two subjects, confirming your viewpoint or judgment on these results

Comparing and contrasting are everyday thought processes. When we *compare* two things, we show how they are similar; when we *contrast* two things, we show how they are different. We may compare or contrast two brand-name products (Adidas vs. Reeboks), or two television shows, or two jobs, or two possible solutions to a problem we are having.

Comparison or contrast writing begins with this ordinary way of thinking about things, presents items with some common base for examination, and then uses *analysis* to break those ideas into sections, which may be similar or dissimilar. We use *examples* of similarities or differences to make comparisons and contrasts clear to readers.

The purpose of comparing or contrasting is to understand each of the two things more clearly and, at times, to make judgments about them. All our lives, we learn about something new by comparing or contrasting it with something we already know. Often we make decisions by comparing unknown situations ahead with familiar experiences.

Comparison essays may *inform* readers of new material by showing the similarities between familiar ideas, people, or issues, and unfamiliar or seemingly dissimilar concepts. **Essays that contrast** different ideas may sometimes *persuade* as the reader examines the differences between two points and lines up his or her sympathies with one side or the other. Both types of papers lead toward judgments or decisions.

You will be asked in this section to write a paper of comparison or contrast. Two methods of essay development are used for comparison or contrast writing. Each displays, in different ways, similarities and differences between things or ideas that reflect our natural thinking patterns.

Comparison and contrast structures are used constantly in both college and career writing requirements. You may compare one software package with another; you may contrast the accuracy of two accounting procedures; or your manager may need you to prepare a report comparing the work patterns of two employees.

To help you prepare for this assignment, first read about the two methods of development you can use in writing this type of paper. Then read the student essays that follow and work through the questions that accompany the essays.

METHODS OF DEVELOPMENT

Comparing or contrasting two ideas requires you to do three things during the prewriting stage:

1   Decide on two ideas, people, or items that have a *valid basis for comparison or contrast*. For example, you could compare or contrast *General Hospital* with *The Young and the Restless*. Your basis for comparing or contrasting would be the "common category" of soap operas: you could contrast the characters, the storylines, the themes used on the shows: all these characteristics are shared by items in the category "soap opera." *Oprah* would be much more difficult to compare or contrast with either of the two programs because it belongs to another category of show, so there would be few clear bases on which to examine the differences or similarities between a daytime talk show and a soap opera.

2   While you are in the prewriting stage with a comparison or contrast essay, develop a point of view about each "side" of your comparison or contrast; this activity will help you to form an overall thesis statement to guide your essay and your choice of supporting details for each "side." For example, if you are listing points to *compare* a year you spent in university with the year you are now spending in college, you may find that there are good points about both experiences: for instance, university courses introduced you to new ideas and ways of thinking, but your college courses add a practical or "hands-on" dimension to knowledge acquired in the classroom. Gradually, you may emerge with a thesis stating that both forms of education have value, but in differing ways.

3   Finally, when you have discovered your basis for comparison or contrast and accumulated your points on both sides, you should choose one of two methods of development. Details can be presented in a *one-side-at-a-time* format or in a *point-by-point* format. Each format is illustrated below.

One Side at a Time

The one-side-at-a-time structure may be used either for the internal structure of supporting paragraphs, or, occasionally, for an entire essay's structure. Whether you choose this method for your body paragraphs or for an essay, the one-side-at-a-time method does what its name states: it states some basis for comparison or contrast of two items, and then lists all the points for one side, followed by all the points for the other side.

Look at the following supporting paragraph from "Betting on My Future," one of the student essays that follows.

> Although I knew I could not work full-time and attend college, I did not know what life with a part-time paycheque would be like. A year ago, I ate in restaurants once or twice a week, and went to movies and hockey games: fifty dollars never seemed like much to spend for an evening out. Because I worked downtown, I enjoyed dressing well, and I never worried about putting a two-hundred-dollar jacket on my credit card; after all, I could pay off my cards every month and still save enough for a vacation every year. I was proud of myself for staying out of debt and for being able to live as well as my friends. However, I don't see those friends for a meal now, since I eat a brown-bag dinner on my break at the store where I work. I barely cover my rent, bills, and groceries, so I have to work the maximum hours and do without many things. Furthermore, since I have to watch what I spend on groceries, I don't invite people over anymore. Jeans and T-shirts are now my fashion statement; I can't afford dry cleaning these days, and my credit cards are in my safety deposit box at the bank. Because I paid my tuition fees with my savings and vacation money, and because I am still not comfortable with debt, I have avoided provincial student loans. But I no longer live the way my friends do, so maybe my pride and my lack of time have a price.

The first half of the paragraph explains fully one side of the contrast: the comfort of the student's life a year ago. The second half of the paragraph deals entirely with the other side: the financial constraints of the student's life today. When you use this method, be sure to follow the same order of points of contrast (or comparison) for each side. An outline of the paragraph shows how the points for each side are developed in a consistent sequence.

Outline (One Side at a Time)

Life with a full-time paycheque was easier than life today.

1. A year ago
   a. Restaurants, movies, hockey games
   b. Using credit cards
   c. Saving for vacations
   d. No debts

　　2. Today
　　　a. Take my lunches—have to pay rent & bills
　　　b. No credit card spending
　　　c. Savings used for tuition, no "cushion"
　　　d. Afraid of taking loan & carrying debt

Point by Point

Now look at the supporting paragraph below, which is taken from the essay "Studying: Then and Now":

> Ordinary during-the-term studying is another area where I've made changes. In high school, I let reading assignments go. I told myself that I'd have no trouble catching up on two hundred pages during a fifteen-minute ride to school. College courses have taught me to keep pace with the work. Otherwise, I feel as though I'm sinking into a quicksand of unread material. When I finally read the high school assignment, my eyes would run over the words, but my brain would be plotting how to get the car for Saturday night. Now, I use several techniques that force me to really concentrate on my reading.

The paragraph contrasts the two methods of studying point by point. The outline below illustrates the point-by-point method.

Outline (Point by Point)

Studying is something I do differently in college, compared with when I was in high school.

　　1. Keeping up with reading assignments
　　　a. High school
　　　b. College

　　2. Concentration while reading
　　　a. High school
　　　b. College

When you begin writing a comparison or contrast paper, decide whether you are going to use the one-side-at-a-time format or the point-by-point format. Use that format as you create the outline for your paper. An outline is an essential step in writing and planning a clearly organized paper.

STUDENT ESSAYS TO CONSIDER

Betting on My Future

I never thought I was a gambler, but a year ago I took a big chance: I decided to start college at the age of thirty-two. I put my money, my time, and my abilities on the line. When I look at the contrasts between my life a year ago and my life now, I feel like I'm facing uncertainties that would make any gambler nervous. The big payoff will be a career with a future, but right now, I face major changes in my income, my social life, and my self-confidence.

1

Although I knew I could not work full-time and attend college, I did not know what life with a part-time paycheque would be like. A year ago, I ate in restaurants once or twice a week, and went to movies and hockey games: fifty dollars never seemed like much to spend for an evening out. Because I worked downtown, I enjoyed dressing well, and I never worried about putting a two-hundred-dollar jacket on my credit card; after all, I could pay off my cards every month and still save enough for a vacation every year. I was proud of myself for staying out of debt and for being able to live as well as my friends. However, I don't see those friends for a meal now, since I eat a brown-bag dinner on my break at the store where I work. I barely cover my rent, bills, and groceries, so I have to work the maximum hours and do without many things. Furthermore, since I have to watch what I spend on groceries, I don't invite people over anymore. Jeans and T-shirts are now my fashion statement; I can't afford dry cleaning these days, and my credit cards are in my safety deposit box at the bank. Because I paid my tuition fees with my savings and vacation money, and because I am still not comfortable with debt, I have avoided provincial student loans. But I no longer live the way my friends do, so maybe my pride and my lack of time have a price.

2

Friends and hobbies used to fill my time. I saw my friends nearly every day after work; we went to movies and bought good seats for the major hockey games. Weekends, we partied or went skiing, and shopped for clothes and the latest in sporting equipment. Three nights a week, I worked out at a fitness club, and I was quite proud of the shape I was in. My job as a data processing clerk had a regular schedule without much pressure, and no paperwork to take home. A year ago, I never had to keep track of time; now, I juggle every minute to manage classes, assignments, job, and trying to keep it all organized. Every day as soon as my last class is over, I run for the bus to get to work by 5:00 p.m. I can't stay around to chat and make friends with other students, and, except for Sundays, I can't stay at school to work in the computer labs or the library. Spares between classes I spend trying to read my textbooks, keep up with assignments, or print out work. Evenings, I work until 9:00 p.m., and after the trip home, I try to do an hour or two of homework before I fall asleep. Sometimes, I wonder which is my biggest challenge: budgeting money or time.

3

Looking back from today, I realize my biggest problem was boredom. I liked the company I worked for; I enjoyed the people I worked with, and being downtown was always exciting. Data processing seemed like a "job," not a career. I simply moved from one project to the next, and waited for the next raise to come along. There was no push to do better and nearly no chance for promotion. No major worries meant no challenges. But now I face a series of challenges every day. The technical courses are intense, and it takes effort and concentration to do well at new subjects like digital graphics. After being out of school for fifteen years, an even bigger challenge is writing; every essay assignment feels like a battle. Because of my age and my investment in college, I pressure myself to do well. My biggest challenge may come in two years, though, from competition I will face for a new career: a lot of that competition will be younger than I am.

4

So, if I look at my life today, contrasted with one year ago, I know that I miss 5
my friends and my comfortable life. But although I may be exhausted, a little
anxious about my future, and concerned about doing well in my courses, I feel
I'm taking a "solid bet": on myself. And I never have time to be bored.

Studying: Then and Now

One June day, I staggered into a high school classroom to take my final 1
Grade 12 exam in Canadian history. I had made my usual desperate effort to
cram the night before, with the usual dismal results—I had made it only to
page seventy-five of a four-hundred-page textbook. My high school study habits,
obviously, were a mess. But, in college, I've made an attempt to reform my
notetaking, studying, and test-taking skills.

As I took notes in high school classes, I often lost interest and began doodling, 2
drawing Martians, or seeing what my signature would look like when I became
a major executive. Now, however, I try not to let my mind wander, and I pull my
thoughts back into focus when they begin to go fuzzy. In high school, my notes
often looked like something written in Arabic. In college, I've learned to use a
semi-print writing style that makes my notes understandable. When I would look
over my high school notes, I couldn't understand them. There would be a word
like *Confederation*, then a big blank, then the word *important*. Weeks later, I had
no idea what Confederation was or why it was important. I've since learned to
write down connecting ideas, even if I have to take the time to do it after class.
Taking notes is one thing I've really learned to do better since high school.

Ordinary during-the-term studying is another area where I've made changes. 3
In high school, I let reading assignments go. I told myself that I'd have no trouble
catching up on two hundred pages during a fifteen-minute bus ride to school.
College courses have taught me to keep pace with the work. Otherwise, I feel as
though I'm sinking into a quicksand of unread material. When I finally read the
high school assignment, my eyes would run over the words, but my brain would
be plotting how to get the car for Saturday night. Now I use several techniques
that force me to really concentrate on my reading.

In addition to learning how to cope with daily work, I've also learned to handle 4
study sessions for big tests. My all-night study sessions in high school were
experiments in self-torture. Around 2:00 a.m., my mind, like a soaked sponge,
simply stopped absorbing things. Now, I space out exam study sessions over
several days. That way, the night before can be devoted to an overall review
rather than raw memorizing. Most important, though, I've changed my attitude
towards tests. In high school, I thought tests were mysterious things with
completely unpredictable questions. Now, I ask instructors about the kinds of
questions that will be on the exam, and I try to "psych out" which areas or facts
instructors are likely to ask about. These practices really work, and for me they've
taken much of the fear and mystery out of tests.

Since I've reformed, notetaking and studying are not as tough as they once 5
were. And there's been one benefit that makes the work worthwhile: my college
transcripts look much different from the report cards of high school days.

■ **Questions**

About Unity

1. Which paragraph in "Betting on My Future" contains its topic sentence within the paragraph, rather than at its beginning? Write the paragraph number and the opening words of the topic sentence.

   _____

2. Which sentence in paragraph 4 of "Betting on My Future" should be omitted in the interest of paragraph unity? *(Write the opening words).*

   _____

3. In which paragraph in "Studying: Then and Now" is the topic sentence at the end rather than at the beginning, where it generally belongs in student essays? _____

About Support

4. In paragraph 3 of "Betting on My Future," what three examples does the writer give to support his claim that he must budget every minute of his time?

   _____

   _____

   _____

5. In paragraph 4 of "Betting on My Future," what sentence should be followed up by supporting details? *(Write the opening words of that sentence.)*

   _____

6. Which sentence in paragraph 3 of "Studying: Then and Now" needs to be followed by more supporting details? *(Write the opening words.)*

   _____

About Coherence

7. In paragraph 2 of "Betting on My Future," what "change of direction" signal does the author use to indicate he has finished discussing his life last year and is now going to discuss his life this year?

8. Write the words in the last section of paragraph 4 of "Betting on My Future" that indicate the writer has used emphatic order in organizing his supporting points.

About the Introduction and Conclusion

9. Which best describes the opening paragraph of "Studying: Then and Now"?
   a. Begins with a broad statement that narrows down to the thesis
   b. Explains the importance of the topic to the reader
   c. Uses an incident or brief story
   d. Asks a question

10. The conclusion of "Studying: Then and Now" falls into which category?
    a. Some observations and a prediction
    b. A summary and final thought
    c. A question or series of questions

WRITING A COMPARISON–CONTRAST ESSAY

About Prewriting

A comparison or contrast essay emphasizes how two things are alike or how they differ. Both students featured in this chapter were asked to compare or contrast some aspects of their lives as students. Max, who wrote "Betting on My Future," had started college four months earlier at the age of thirty-two.

"The evening before, a friend came into the store where I work part time," he said, "and asked why no one ever saw me any more. I tried to explain that if I wasn't in classes, or at work, or doing assignments, I was probably asleep. As I said this, I realized how different my life was now from the way it used to be less than a year ago. So the contrasts between the two parts of my life were the clearest things in my mind."

To generate ideas for his paper, Max decided to try freewriting. Feeling guilty about all the friends he hadn't seen or spoken to, he tried to write "an open letter" explaining why he never had any free time these days. Without concerning himself with organization or finding the perfect word, he wrote whatever came into his mind as he asked himself, "Why has my life changed so much? What are the differences between my life before college and my life now? If life is so demanding now, why am I doing this?" Here is what Max wrote:

> Dear friends,
>
>   I know none of you has heard from me for a while, so I thought I'd try to tell you why, and how different my life is, now that I'm back in school after nearly fifteen years. I know I never thought of myself as someone who took chances, but now I just hope the gamble is worth it. Right now, I'm betting everything on college: all my money, my time, and all my fears about what I can do. I'm so beat most of the time that I don't even pick up the phone, and I don't have the extra money to go out anyway. When Judy came into the store last night, I'd even forgotten how long it's been since we all went out to a movie, or since I worked out. And do I miss those paycheques! Right now, between tuition and textbooks, I haven't got $10 left over this week. What I make part-time barely buys me groceries after the rent and the bills. I used to be bored at

work, now I worry about failing or messing up on my courses—right now, I hardly have time to eat, let alone panic. Going back to school is a bigger change than I'd thought it would be—I feel like an outsider with a lot of the students because I'm at least 10 years older than they are, and I have to leave right after classes to get to work, so I haven't gotten to know people at college anyway. Younger students probably find me too serious, too, because I sit there in classes trying to take it all in—I can't afford not to, because I've bet my whole future on trying to train for a career.

So, I guess I'm apologizing for dropping out of the life we all used to share. I just don't feel like I have much of a choice—there's so much riding on going back to school that I don't want to take chances.

Max

As Max looked over his letter, he saw that most of what he had written fell into three categories that he could use as the three supporting points, or points for comparison, in his essay. He saw that his main feeling, or point of view, was that he felt the risk was worthwhile. Working from this view, and using these three points, he prepared this first outline for the essay:

My life this year is so different from last year, and I hope the risks pay off.

1. Used to have enough money for a social life and hobbies; now I'm scraping by.
   • Entertainment & clothes
   • Budgets & no extras
   • Debt & savings

2. Last year, I had time for people and for workouts; now I'm always rushing.
   • Movies & free time vs no free time
   • Work vs school schedules
   • Have to use every minute now

3. I was bored at work; this year everything is a challenge.
   • Nothing to try for at work
   • Courses are hard & I'm older than other students
   • It's all a competition now

Working from his outline, Max wrote the following first draft of his essay:

Judy asked me last night why no one ever sees me anymore. I told her my life feels like "risky business" right now because I've spent all my money to go back to school and everything in my life has changed this year.   1

Last year, my friends and I went to the movies nearly every week and ate in restaurants whenever we felt like it. Now, I can't even afford takeout. I had some savings put aside, but I used them for my tuition for college this year. We all used our charge cards for clothes and ski trips, now I had to put   2 my cards in the deposit box at the bank because I don't have enough income to pay the minimum on credit-card bills. Without a full-time paycheque, I'm afraid of debt, so I have to watch every penny this year. It all feels like such a gamble.

Workouts three times a week were a big part of my life last year, and so was all the time I spent with my friends. Now I barely have time to sleep. Classes, studying, and printing my assignments during spare hours, and running for the bus to work eat up every minute of my days. I fall asleep trying to do homework at night when I get home from my part-time job. Even though I miss my friends, I don't have time to meet new people at college because I'm always in such a rush, and because the other students seem so much younger and more carefree.   3

Now I am never bored, but I am not sure I enjoy the pressure of my life these days. Work used to be dull but predictable, because there were never any challenges or any chances for growth. That's why I decided to go to college—for the opportunity for a career. Every essay is a struggle for me and so are the courses like digital graphics; there are so many new things and so many things I remember that I used to find difficult, and still do. There will be so much competition for jobs when I finish, that scares me too. And most of those people applying for jobs along with me will be so much younger. At least I feel like I'm trying to make something out of my life.   4

So, if all these things sound like challenges, they are. My life has changed completely from the way it was a year ago, and I keep trying to believe the costs in money, time, and energy are worth it.   5

About Rewriting

Max put the first draft of his essay aside and took it to his English class the next day. His instructor asked Max and the other students to work in small groups, reading their drafts aloud and making revision suggestions to one another. Here are the notes Max made on his group's comments:

- I don't need to bring up Judy—I think I can explain my situation without that story.
- I'm not consistent about developing my paragraphs. I forgot to do a "one-side-at-a-time" or "point-by-point" comparison. I think I'll try a "one-side-at-a-time" technique. I'll describe in each paragraph what last year was like, then describe how different each aspect of this year is.
- I could use more support for some of my points, especially the points about where my money goes now, and about how little time I have.
- I should make my point more clearly about why this "bet" in my life is worth it—say why what I'm doing feels right to me.

After making these observations about his first draft, Max proceeded to write the version of his essay that appears on pages 226–228.

Prewriting Activity

Complete the partial outline given for the supporting paragraph that follows:

> In addition to learning how to cope with daily work, I've also learned to handle study sessions for big tests. My all-night study sessions in high school were experiments in self-torture. Around 2:00 a.m., my mind, like a soaked sponge, simply stopped absorbing things. Now, I space out exam study sessions over several days. That way, the night before can be devoted to an overall review rather than raw memorizing. Most important, though, I've changed my attitude towards tests. In high school, I thought tests were mysterious things with completely unpredictable questions. Now, I ask instructors about the kinds of questions that will be on the exam, and I try to "psych out" which areas or facts instructors are likely to ask about. These practices really work, and for me they've taken much of the fear and mystery out of tests.

In addition to learning how to cope with daily work, I've also learned to handle study sessions for big tests.

1. Planning study time

    a. _____ (all-night study sessions)

    b. College (spread out over several days)

2. _____

    a. High school (tests were mysterious)

    b. _____ (_____)

■ ## Writing Assignment 1

Write an essay of comparison or contrast on one of the topics below:

Two jobs you've held
Two bosses you've worked for
Two groups or two types of music you listen to
Two possessions you prize
Two places you've lived
Two games, sports, or leisure activities
Two magazines you read regularly
Two places you've lived
Two forms of communication: i.e., phone calls and e-mail
Two ways of spending: cash and credit cards

Prewriting Strategies

1 As you select your topic, keep in mind that you won't merely be *describing* the two things you're writing about—you will be *emphasizing* the ways they are different or alike. For instance, how does a math teacher you have in college differ from one you had in high school? How is your job as salesperson similar to a job you had as receptionist last summer?

2 Make two columns on a sheet of paper, one for each of the things you'll write about. In the left-hand column, jot down words or phrases that describe the first of the two. Write anything that comes into your head about that half of the topic. Then go back and write a corresponding word or phrase about the item in the right-hand column. For example, here is Nazima's list of characteristics about two games she plays. She began brainstorming for words and phrases to describe Scrabble:

Scrabble	*Volleyball*
Quiet	
Involves words	
Played sitting down	
Involves small group of people	
Can let mind wander when it's not your turn	
Mental concentration, not physical	
Part strategy and skill	
Some see as boring, egghead game	

Nazima then wrote a corresponding list of characteristics for volleyball, which helped her add to her first list:

Scrabble	*Volleyball*
Quiet	Noisy, talking and yelling
Involves words	Involves ball and a net
Played sitting down	Played standing up, jumping
Involves as few as 2 players	Involves 12 players
Can let mind wander when it's not your turn	Have to stay alert every minute
Mental concentration, not physical	Mental and physical concentration required
Part chance (what letters you get)	Mostly skill, strategy; little chance
Part strategy and skill	
Some see as boring, egghead game	Seen as glamorous—stars get advertising contracts
Players' size doesn't matter	Being tall helps

3 Your list of characteristics will help you decide if the two things you are writing about are more alike (in which case you'll write an essay *comparing* them) or different (in which case you'll emphasize how they *contrast*).

4 As you look over your lists, think how the characteristics you've written down (and others that occur to you) could fit into three categories that can serve as your "points of comparison or contrast," or your supporting points.

For instance, Nazima came up with three groupings of characteristics. She decided on three points or headings under which the two games could be compared or contrasted. She was almost ready to decide between a "point-by-point" and a "one-side-at-a-time" method of development.

Fill in the blanks in her outline to indicate the supporting points or points of comparison between the two games.

Thesis: Although they are two of my favourite activities, Scrabble and volleyball could hardly be more different.

Point: _____

- Scrabble requires a board and letter tiles
- Volleyball needs a ball and a net
- Scrabble can be played by two people
- Twelve people needed for a volleyball game
- Scrabble can be played anywhere there's room for two people to sit down
- Volleyball needs a large room and high ceilings or an outdoor playing area

Point: _____

- You have to concentrate mentally to play Scrabble
- You need mental and physical concentration to play volleyball
- It doesn't matter what size you are to play Scrabble
- It helps to be tall to play volleyball
- There's some chance involved in Scrabble
- Chance is not a big part of volleyball

Point: _____

- Scrabble players are seen as "eggheads" by the general public
- Star volleyball players are seen as glamorous by public
- Volleyball players get contracts to endorse athletic shoes
- Scrabble players don't endorse anything, even dictionaries
- Volleyball players are admired for the power of their spike
- Scrabble players are admired for the number of unusual two-letter words they know

5   Nazima had worked out a "point-by-point" essay as she outlined. Decide if you will design your essay with a "one-side-at-a-time" method of development or a "point-by-point" method of development. Be consistent in your use of one method or the other in your paragraphs.

6   Proceed to write the first draft of your essay.

Rewriting Strategies

As you review the first draft of your essay, ask yourself these questions:

- Have I made it clear in my opening paragraph what two things I am writing about, and whether I will compare or contrast them? Is my point of view clearly stated?
- Do my supporting points offer three areas in which I will compare or contrast my two subjects?
- Does each of my supporting paragraphs have a clear topic sentence?
- Have I consistently used either the "one-side-at-a-time" or the "point-by-point" method of development in each of my supporting paragraphs?
- Have I used transition words to help readers follow my train of thought?
- If one of my areas of comparison or contrast is stronger than the others, should I consider using emphatic order and saving that one for my final supporting paragraph?
- Have I rounded off my essay with a conclusion that suggests or confirms what my comparison or contrast has shown?

As you revise your essay through one or more additional drafts, continue to refer to this list until you can answer "yes" to each question. Then be sure to check the next-to-final draft of the paper for the sentence skills listed on the inside front cover.

■ Writing Assignment 2: Writing a Contrast Essay

Write an essay that contrasts two attitudes on a controversial subject. You may want to contrast your views with those of someone else, or contrast the way you felt about the subject in the past with the way you feel now. Essays that strongly contrast two views tend to be more dramatic and sound more forceful to readers.

This is an essay assignment where writing in the third-person point of view is recommended.

Some subjects you might consider writing about follow:

Women serving in combat positions in the Canadian Armed Forces
Legal marriage status for gay couples
Censorship of the Internet
Tax-funded shelters for street people
Cuts in education (or hospital/medical) funding
"The right to die an assisted death"
Canada's unemployment insurance system
Common-law marriage

Prewriting Strategies

1 In order to gather information for a point of view that contrasts with your own, you will need to do some research. Two approaches may help you to find useful material: going to the library to search through article indexes for recent Canadian and international news magazines (ask your instructor or library assistant if you need help), or doing an Internet search, using key words from the topics listed above to find websites on these subjects. Or interview friends and acquaintances whose attitude on the subject is different from yours.

2 To generate ideas for your paper, try the following two-part exercise:

a. Pretend a student visitor from another country who has never heard of the topic of your paper asks you to explain it. This visitor also wants to know why you hold the attitude you do about it. Using the technique of freewriting—not worrying about sentence structure, organization, spelling, repetition, etc.—write an answer for the foreign student. Include every reason you can think of for your attitude.

b. Now the student asks you to do the same thing, and you take the opposing point of view. Remember, it's up to you to make this visitor from another country understand both sides of the issue, so really try to put yourself in the other person's shoes as you represent the contrasting attitude.

3 As you look over the writing on both sides of the issue you've done for the student, note the strongest points on both sides. From them, select your three main supporting points. Are there other thoughts in your writings that can be used as supporting details for those points?

4 Write your three supporting paragraphs. Decide whether it is more effective to contrast your attitude and the opposing one, point by point within each paragraph, or to devote the first half of each paragraph to one side's attitude, and then present the other side's attitude in the last half.

5 In your concluding paragraph, summarize the contrast between your attitude and the other point of view. Consider closing with a final paragraph that makes it clear why you stand where you do.

Rewriting Strategies

Refer to the guidelines for rewriting provided on page 236.

■ ## Writing Assignment 3

In this comparison-contrast essay, you will write with a specific purpose and for a specific audience.

Option 1: Your niece or nephew is finishing high school soon and is thinking about getting a job instead of going to college or university. You would prefer to see him or her give college a try. Write him or her a letter in which you compare and contrast the advantages and disadvantages of each course of action. Use a one-side-at-a-time method in making your analysis.

Option 2: Write a letter to your boss in which you compare your abilities with those of the ideal candidate for a position to which you would like to be promoted. Use a point-by-point method in which you discuss each ideal requirement, and then describe how well you measure up to it. Use the requirements of a job you're relatively familiar with, ideally a job you would really like to apply for some day.

■ **Writing Assignment 4:**
Writing about a Reading Selection

Read the selection titled "Smash Thy Neighbor" on pages 501–505. Pay special attention to how the author compares and contrasts football and war in paragraphs 5–8 and compares football and the rest of society in paragraph 14. Notice how he makes the comparisons and contrasts in order to describe football more fully. Then write an essay in which you use a comparison to describe more fully three aspects of an activity, place, or person. You may use serious or humorous supporting details.

Following are some suggestions that you might consider for a thesis for this assignment:

Thesis: In a few significant ways,

- Going to college is like working at a career.
- The high school hallways between classes are like a three-ring circus.
- Getting divorced is like getting married.
- Caring for a pet is like caring for a child.
- Meditation is like exercise.
- Shopping for Christmas gifts is like playing professional football.
- Teachers should be like parents.
- Hate is like love.
- Raising a family is like caring for a garden.

These are only suggestions; feel free to use any other thesis that makes a comparison in order to fill out a description of an activity, person, or place. (Note that a comparison that points out similarities between things that are otherwise quite different is called an *analogy*.)

In your introduction, you should state your general thesis as well as the three points of comparison. Here, for example, is a possible introduction for an essay on meditation:

> On the surface, meditation may seem to be very different from exercise. A person who meditates is usually very still, while someone who exercises is very active. Yet the two activities are more alike than they might seem. Both require discipline, both bestow physical and mental benefits, and both can be habit-forming.

At the same time as you develop your introduction, you should prepare a general outline for your essay. The outline for the essay started by the introduction above would be as follows:

Thesis: Meditation is like exercise in three ways.

1. Both require discipline.
   a. Exercise
   b. Meditation

2. Both have physical and mental rewards.
   a. Exercise
   b. Meditation

3. Both can be habit-forming.
   a. Exercise
   b. Meditation

(Note that this outline uses the point-by-point method of development. Other topics might, of course, be more suited to the one-side-at-a-time method.)

As you work on your supporting paragraphs, *be sure to outline them first.* Such planning is very helpful in organizing and maintaining control over a comparison or contrast essay. Here, for example, is a sample trial outline for a paragraph in a point-by-point essay comparing raising children to gardening:

Topic sentence: Just as a garden benefits from both sun and rain, so do children.

1. Benefits of sun and rain to a garden
   a. Both sun and rain required for life
   b. Increase growth

2. Benefits of sunny and rainy times to children
   a. Ups and downs natural over a lifetime
   b. Personal growth

Each of your supporting paragraphs should be outlined in this way.

In your conclusion, you might round off the essay by summarizing the three areas of comparison and leaving your readers with a final thought. Do not, however, make the mistake of introducing a completely *new* idea ("Every couple should have children," for example) in your conclusion.

REVIEWING THE LEARNING OUTCOMES FOR CHAPTER 13

Once you have completed one of the writing assignments in this chapter, review your essay by responding to the following questions:

- Have you chosen two sides of one subject or two subjects that can logically be compared or contrasted? Does a worthwhile point emerge from the process of comparing or contrasting the two parts of your thesis?

- Does your thesis statement state both subjects (or both sides of your subject), whether you will compare or contrast, and the point you will make based on that action?

- Have you consistently used the method most appropriate to your subject(s)? If you have many specific details for each side, have you used the point-by-point method? If you wish to consider each side in some depth, have you used the one-side-at-a-time method?

- Within the body of your essay, whichever method you chose, are your bases for comparison or contrast and your supporting material for each base relatively equal for both sides or both subjects?

- Does the conclusion sum up the points made during the comparison or contrast process and reinforce and strengthen your main thesis point?

Definition

By working through this chapter's activities and completing at least one of its writing assignments, you will write a definition essay that

- Puts its subject in a reasonably limited category or class of similar subjects
- States in its introduction and thesis that the subject within its category is uniquely different from other similar things
- Indicates from its opening the relative degree of formality or objectivity involved in the body of the definition to follow
- Offers several supporting points to both clarify and limit the meaning of the subject—such points may be examples, anecdotes, or comparisons or contrasts
- Concludes with a summary of the meaning of the subject-term and its significance, based on what the essay has revealed

In talking with other people, we give informal definitions to explain just what we mean by a particular term. Suppose, for example, we say to a friend, "Bob is really an inconsiderate person." We might then explain what we mean by *inconsiderate* by saying, "He borrowed my accounting book 'overnight' but didn't return it for a week. And when I got it back, it was covered with coffee stains."

Definition essays continue this process of explaining and clarifying with *examples*. Words and phrases have meanings, shadings, and connotations that can and do vary from person to person. Definition writing states what a word or a phrase means and what it does not mean; definitions set boundaries around meanings.

In a written definition, we make clear in a more complete and formal way our personal understanding of a term. Such a definition typically starts with one meaning of a term. The meaning is then illustrated with a series of details.

Definition writing makes use of skills from many methods of development: *narration* creates the line and sequence for your explanation, *description* gives precision and specificity to details, *comparing or contrasting* ideas establishes what something is or is not, and *examples* demonstrate or accurately illustrate different aspects of a word or phrase's meaning.

Today, knowing what new phrases mean is a daily necessity. We hear and read new terms constantly: *spin doctor,* or *corporate stewardship,* for instance. Insurance policies and credit card agreements are filled with definitions. Accountants use terms like *statistical sampling inventory,* childcare workers speak of *attention deficits* in children, and technology creates its own vocabulary at a bewildering rate: consider *data integrity* and *ISP.*

Defining is a fundamental communications skill in most careers: engineers define *stress* differently from psychologists; police and security officers need clear understandings of *reasonable grounds* for some action they take. Instructions and reports of every kind must make many terms and phrases clear to their readers. Definitions are basic to communication.

In this section, you will be asked to write an essay in which you define and illustrate a term. To prepare for this assignment, first read the student essays that follow and work through the questions that accompany the essays.

STUDENT ESSAYS TO CONSIDER

Definition of a Baseball Fan

What is a baseball fan? The word *fan* is an abbreviation of *fanatic,* meaning "an insane or crazy person." In the case of baseball fans, the term is appropriate. They behave insanely, they are insane about trivia, and they are insanely loyal.   1

Baseball fans wear their official team T-shirts and warm-up jackets to the mall, the supermarket, the classroom, and even—if they can get away with it—to work. If the team offers a give-away item, the fans rush to the stadium to claim the hat or sports bag or water bottle that is being handed out that day. Hockey fans go similarly nuts when their favourite teams give away some attractive freebie. Baseball fans just plain behave insanely. Even the fact that fans spend the most beautiful summer months sweating at SkyDome proves it. In addition, baseball fans decorate their cars and their houses with baseball-related items of every kind. To them, Jays vanity plates are only the beginning, and team bumper stickers don't belong only on car bumpers, but also on fireplace mantels and front doors. When they go to a game, which they do as often as possible, they also decorate their bodies. True baseball fans not only put on their team jackets and grab their pennants, but also paint their heads blue to look like bluejays or wear big foam "Blue Jayheads." At the game, these fans devote enormous energy to trying to get a "wave" going.   2

Baseball fans are insanely fascinated by trivia. They talk about players as though Jose Canseco and Shawn Green were close friends. Every day, they turn to the sports page and study last night's statistics. They simply have to see who has extended his hitting streak and how many strike-outs the winning pitcher recorded. Their bookshelves are crammed with record books, magazines, team yearbooks, and baseball almanacs. They delight in remembering such significant facts as who was the last left-handed third baseman to hit into an inning-ending double play in the fifth game of the playoffs. And if you can't manage to get all that excited about such earth-shaking issues, they look at you as though *you* were the insane one.   3

Last of all, baseball fans are insanely loyal to the team of their choice, often dangerously so. Should their beloved team lose three in a row, fans may   4 begin to criticize their team. They still obsessively watch each game and spend the entire day afterwards reading and listening to the post-game commentary in newspapers, on TSN, and on sports radio. Further, this intense loyalty makes fans dangerous. To anyone who dares to say to a loyal fan that another team has better players or coaches, or God forbid, to anyone wandering near the home cheering section wearing the jacket of the opposing team, physical damage is a real possibility. And while hockey players and fans hold the record for fights, incidents of violence on the baseball field have increased in recent years and are a matter of growing concern.

From mid-October through March, baseball fans are like any other human beings. They pay their taxes, take out the garbage, and complain about the high cost of living. But when April comes, the colours and TVs go on, the record books come off the shelves, and the devotion returns. For the true baseball fan, another season of insanity has begun. 5

Student Zombies

Schools divide people up into categories. From first grade on up, students are labelled "advanced" or "deprived" or "remedial" or "antisocial." Students pigeon-hole their fellow students, too: there's the "brain," the "jock," the "dummy," and the "teacher's pet." In most cases, these narrow labels are misleading and inaccurate. But there is one label for a certain type of college student that says it all. That is, of course, "zombie." 1

Zombies are the living dead. Most people haven't known a lot of real zombies personally, but they do know how zombies act. Horror movies have provided guidance for us. The special effects in horror movies are much better these days. Over the years, movies have shown that zombies stalk around graveyards, their eyes glued open by Hollywood makeup artists, bumping like cheap toy robots into living people. Zombie students in college do just about the same thing. They stalk around campus, eyes glazed, staring off into space. When they do manage to wander into a classroom, they sit down mechanically and contemplate the ceiling. Zombie students rarely eat, dance, talk, laugh, or toss Frisbees on college lawns. Instead, they vanish when class is dismissed and return only when some mysterious zombie signal summons them back into a classroom. The signal may not occur for weeks. 2

Zombies are controlled by some mysterious force. According to legend, zombies are corpses that have been brought back to life to do the bidding of some voodoo master. Student zombies, too, seem directed by a strange power. They continue to attend school although they have no apparent desire to do so. They show no interest in college-related activities like tests, marks, papers, and projects. And yet some inner force compels them to wander through the halls of higher education. 3

An awful fate awaits all zombies unless something happens to break the spell they're under. In the movies, zombies are often shot, stabbed, drowned, or electrocuted, all to no avail. Finally the hero or heroine realizes that a counter-spell is needed. Once that spell is cast, with the appropriate props of 4 chicken feet, human hair, and bats' eyeballs, the zombie-corpse can return peacefully to its coffin. The only hope for a student zombie to change is for him or her to undergo a similarly traumatic experience. Sometimes the evil spell can be broken by a grade transcript decorated with large red "Fs." At other times, a professor will succeed through a private, intensive exorcism session. But in other cases zombies blunder around for years until they are gently persuaded by college administration to head for another institution. Then, they enrol in a new college or get a job in the family business.

Every college student knows that it's not necessary to see *Night of the Living*   5 *Dead* or *The Dead Don't Die* in order to see zombies in action—or non-action. Forget the campus film series or the late-late show. Just sit in a classroom and wait. You know who you're looking for—the students who walk in without books or papers of any kind and sit in the very last row of seats. The ones with personal stereos plugged into their ears don't count as zombies—that's a whole different category of "student." *Day of the Living Dead* is showing every day at a college near you.

■ Questions

About Unity

1. Which paragraph in "Definition of a Baseball Fan" has a topic sentence buried within the paragraph, rather than at the paragraph's beginning? *(Write the opening words.)*

2. What sentence in paragraph 2 of "Definition of a Baseball Fan" should be omitted in the interest of paragraph unity? *(Write the opening words.)*

3. Which sentence in paragraph 2 of "Student Zombies" should be omitted in the interest of paragraph unity? *(Write the opening words.)*

4. What sentence in the final paragraph of "Student Zombies" introduces a new topic and so should be eliminated? *(Write the opening words.)*

About Support

5. Which essay develops its definitions through a series of comparisons?

6. After which sentence in paragraph 4 of "Definition of a Baseball Fan" is more support needed? *(Write the opening words.)*

7. In the second paragraph of "Definition of a Baseball Fan," how many examples are given of fans' "insane" behaviour?

_____ two examples _____ four examples _____ six examples

About Coherence

8. Which paragraph in "Definition of a Baseball Fan" begins with a transitional phrase? _____

9. Which sentence in paragraph 2 of "Student Zombies" begins with a change-of-direction transitional word? *(Write the opening words.)*

About the Introduction

10. Which method of introduction is used in the opening paragraph of "Student Zombies"? *(Circle the letter of the appropriate answer.)*
    a. Anecdote
    b. Idea that is the opposite of the one to be developed
    c. Quotation
    d. Broad, general statement narrowing to a thesis
    e. Questions

WRITING A DEFINITION ESSAY

About Prewriting

In a definition essay, you provide your reader with your personal understanding of some concept. As you define what a word or phrase means to you, you illustrate its "colourings" or connotations. Although your extended definition explains your personal understanding of something, write your essay from the third-person point of view; "I"s would be intrusive and detract from your focus on your subject.

A dictionary gives you accepted meanings, synonyms, or "essential definitions" for some word or phrase. "Essential definitions" try to give the essence of a word; they put it into a broad category, then "set boundaries" around that word to separate it from other items in the same category. An example of this type is an essential definition of a couch, which puts it into the category "chair with upholstery" and then distinguishes it from other items in this category with the words "large enough for several people."

In contrast to a limited dictionary definition, your definition conveys your understanding and experience of that concept or term. As you prepare your extended definition, you may find the distinguishing or boundary-setting aspects of essential definitions useful in deciding how to limit or broaden your range of meanings.

As with other essay forms, you should think in terms of supporting your definition (which will serve as your thesis, since it contains your subject—the word or phrase, and your views of its meaning) with two or three paragraphs, each of which has its own topic sentence.

In thinking of possible topics for this essay, you should consider those you are especially qualified to discuss. A topic that you know a good deal about, or a concept that you like to think about, makes the best subject for a definition essay.

Cameron, the author of "Definition of a Baseball Fan," spent a few minutes jotting down a number of possible essay topics, keeping in mind the question, "What do I know a good deal about, or at least have an interest in exploring?" Here is a list of topic ideas. Notice how they reflect Cameron's interest in outdoor activities, sports, and history:

Definition of . . .

A person who snowboards
A soccer goalie
A person who loves forts like Fort Henry, Fort York, and so on
A war-history buff
A bodybuilder
A true Blue Jays fan
People who watch the History Channel
A hockey coach

After looking over his list, Cameron selected "A true Blue Jays fan" as the topic that interested him most. He thought it would lend itself well to a light-hearted essay that defined the sometimes loony fans of the Toronto baseball team. After giving it further thought, however, Cameron decided to broaden his topic to include all baseball fans. "I realized that, from what my cousins in Montreal said about Expos fans, as well as from what I'd seen on sports shows, trying to define the weirdness of Canadian baseball fans would make a better topic for my essay," he said.

A person who likes to think in visual terms, Cameron decided to develop ideas and details about his topic by diagramming his thoughts:

Baseball fans

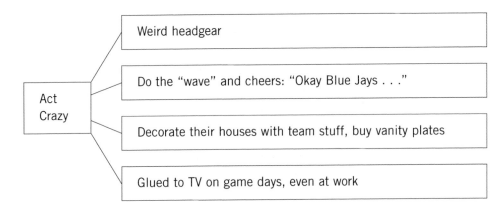

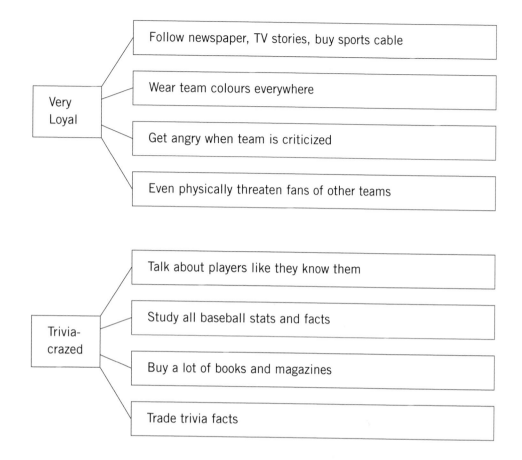

Looking over his diagramming, Cameron realized he could characterize each of his three main topics as a kind of "insanity." He decided on a thesis (he would define baseball fans as insane) that would indicate his essay's plan of development ("they act insanely, they are obsessed by trivia, and they are insanely loyal").

With that thesis and a plan of development in mind, Cameron wrote the first draft of his essay:

Baseball fans are by definition crazy. They behave insanely, they are insane about trivia, and they are insanely loyal.

If their team gives away a freebie, the fans rush to the stadium to get the hat, or whatever. Baseball fans just plain behave insanely. Hockey fans go similarly nuts when their favourite teams give away some attractive freebie. But baseball fans are even worse. Baseball fans sit sweating in order to watch their favourite game. In addition, baseball fans decorate their houses with baseball-related items of every kind. When they go to a game, which they do as often as possible, the true baseball fans make themselves look ridiculous by decorating themselves in weird, team-related ways. At the game, these fans do the "wave" more than they watch the game.

Baseball fans are insane about trivia. They talk about players as though their favourites were close friends. Every day, they turn to the sports page and study last night's statistics. Their bookshelves are crammed with record books, magazines, team yearbooks, and baseball almanacs. They remember every significant fact about the most obscure, forgotten game. They think everybody is as fascinated by all their trivial knowledge as they are.

Last of all, baseball fans are insanely loyal to the team of their choice. Baseball fans wear their team T-shirts and warm-up jackets everywhere, even to work. Of course, if they have to dress up in business clothes, they can't do that. Should their beloved team lose three in a row, their fans may begin to criticize their team. But these reactions only hide their broken hearts. They still obsessively watch each game and read all the newspaper stories about it. Their intense loyalty makes fans dangerous. To anyone who dares to say to a loyal fan that another team is better, or, God forbid, to anyone wandering near the home cheering section wearing the jacket of the opposing team, physical damage is a real possibility. Incidents of violence in the baseball stadiums have increased in recent years and are a matter of growing concern.

Baseball fans really act like they're crazy. They behave insanely, are crazy about trivia, and they're too loyal!

About Revising

The next day, Cameron showed his first draft to a study partner from his English class. She returned it with comments noted in the margins:

Baseball fans are by definition crazy. They behave insanely, they are insane about trivia, and they are insanely loyal.

If their team gives away a freebie, the fans rush to the stadium to get the hat, or whatever. Baseball fans just plain behave insanely. Hockey fans go similarly nuts when their favourite teams give away some attractive freebie. But baseball fans are even worse. Baseball fans sit sweating[1] in order to watch their favourite game. In addition, baseball fans decorate their houses with baseball-related items of every kind.[2] When they go to a game, which they do as often as possible, the true baseball fans make themselves look ridiculous by decorating themselves in weird, team-related ways.[3] At the game, these fans do the "wave" more than they watch the game.

Baseball fans are insane about trivia. They talk about players as though their favourites were close friends. Every day, they turn to the sports page and study last night's statistics. Their bookshelves are crammed with record books, magazines, team yearbooks, and baseball almanacs. They remember every significant fact about the most obscure, forgotten game. They think everybody is as fascinated by all their trivial knowledge as they are.[4]

Last of all, baseball fans are insanely loyal to the team of their choice. Baseball fans wear their team T-shirts and warm-up jackets everywhere, even to work. Of course, if they have to dress up in business clothes, they can't do that.[5] Should their beloved team lose three in a row, their fans may begin to criticize their team. But these reactions only hide their broken hearts. They still obsessively

[1] Huh? I guess this is about the weather—make it clearer.

[2] Like what? Details here.

[3] Details needed. How do they decorate themselves?

[4] I'm no baseball fan, but even I want some specific "baseball stuff" here to explain all these facts.

[5] Shouldn't this be in the first paragraph? It seems to belong to the "they act so insanely" paragraph, not the "loyalty" paragraph.

watch each game and read all the newspaper stories about it. Their intense loyalty makes fans dangerous.[6] To anyone who dares to say to a loyal fan that another team is better, or, God forbid, to anyone wandering near the home cheering section wearing the jacket of the opposing team, physical damage is a real possibility. Incidents of violence in the baseball stadiums have increased in recent years and are a matter of growing concern.

Baseball fans really act like they're crazy. They behave insanely, are crazy about trivia, and they're too loyal![7]

[6]*This doesn't support your topic statement, so take it out.*

[7]*Kind of a boring way to end it. You're just repeating your thesis.*

After reading his classmate's comments, Cameron went to work on his next draft. As he worked, he read his essay aloud several times and noticed places where his wording sounded awkward or too informal. (Example: "If their team gives away a freebie, the fans rush to the stadium to get the hat, or whatever.") A few drafts later, he produced the version of "Definition of a Baseball Fan" on pages 242–243.

WRITING A DEFINITION ESSAY

■ Writing Assignment 1

Shown below are an introduction, a thesis, and supporting points for an essay that defines the word *maturity*. Using separate paper, plan and write the supporting paragraphs and a conclusion for the essay.

The Meaning of Maturity

> Being a mature student does not mean being an old-timer. Maturity is not measured by the number of years a person has lived. Instead, the yardstick of maturity is marked by the qualities of self-denial, determination, and dependability.

> Self-denial is an important quality in the mature student . . .

> Determination is another characteristic of a mature student . . .

> Although self-denial and determination are both vital, probably the most important measure of maturity is dependability . . .

Prewriting Strategies

1 Prepare examples for each of the three qualities of maturity. For each quality, you should have one extended example that takes up an entire paragraph or two or three shorter examples that together form enough material for a paragraph.

2 To generate these details, ask yourself the following questions:

- What could I do, or have I done, that would be an example of self-denial?
- What has someone I know ever done that could be described as self-denial?
- What kind of behaviour on the part of a student could be considered self-denial?

Write down quickly whatever answers to the questions occur to you. Don't worry about writing correct sentences. Instead, concentrate on getting down as many details relating to self-denial as you can think of. Think of the opposites of the three qualities as well to help to make your illustrations of each accurate. Then repeat the questioning and writing process, substituting *determination* and *dependability* for *self-denial.*

3 Now go through the material you have compiled. If you think of other details as you read, jot them down. Next, decide just what information you will use in each supporting paragraph. List the details in the order in which you will present them.

4 Now write out the first draft of your paper.

Rewriting Strategies

After you have completed the first draft of the paper, set it aside for a while (if possible). When you reread what you have written, prepare for rewriting by asking yourself these questions:

- Have I provided enough details to support each of the three characteristics of maturity?
- Have I limited my terms for defining maturity, or are there details that should be eliminated?
- Have I used transition words to help my definition flow smoothly for readers?
- Should my concluding paragraph provide a summary or a final thought, or some wider implication of my definition?

As you revise your essay through one or more additional drafts, continue to refer to this list until you can answer "yes" to each question. Then be sure to check the next-to-final draft of the paper for the sentence skills listed on the inside front cover.

■ Writing Assignment 2

Choose one of the terms below as the subject of a definition essay. Each term refers to a certain kind of person.

Snob	Optimist	Slob
Cheapskate	Pessimist	Tease
Loser	Team player	Practical joker
Good neighbour	Scapegoat	Procrastinator
Busybody	Bully	Loner
Whiner	Spiritual person	Straight arrow
Con artist	Hypocrite	

Prewriting Strategies

1 As you devise your opening paragraph, you may want to refer to the dictionary definition of the term. Depending on your term and on your dictionary, you may find an "essential definition," or you may find a range of meanings. If you find several meanings, be sure to use only one. *Don't* begin your paper with the overused line, "According to *Oxford* . . ."

2 Remember that the thesis of a definition essay is actually some version of "What _____ means to me." The thesis presents what *you* think the term actually means.

3 As you plan your supporting paragraphs, think of the different parts or qualities of your term. Here are the three-part divisions of the student essays considered in this chapter:

   a. Maturity "is marked by the qualities of self-denial, determination, and dependability."

   b. "Stupidity exists on three levels of seriousness."

   c. (Of baseball fans) "They behave insanely, they are insane about trivia, and they are insanely loyal."

4 Support each part of your division with either a series of examples or a single extended example. Examples may also "limit" your description by saying what some quality or type of person is *not*.

5 You may find outlining to be the most helpful strategy for creating your definition essay. As a guide, put your thesis and three supporting points in the spaces below:

Thesis: _____

             _____

             _____

Support: 1. _____

           2. _____

           3. _____

Rewriting Strategies

Once you have the first draft of your essay completed, review it with these questions in mind:

- Does my thesis statement indicate how I define the term, and does it indicate my plan of development for the essay? Have I introduced my term with enough background to interest my reader?
- Does each of my supporting paragraphs have a clear topic?
- Have I supported each of my three topic sentences with one extended example or a series of examples? Does each clearly illustrate one aspect of my term?

- Have I rounded off my essay with an appropriate concluding paragraph?
- Have I proofread my essay, referring to the list of sentence skills on the inside front cover?

■ Writing Assignment 3

In this essay, you will write with a specific purpose and for a specific audience.

Option 1: You work in a doctor's office and have been asked to write a brochure that will be placed in the patients' waiting room. The brochure is intended to tell patients what a healthy lifestyle is. Write a definition of a *healthy lifestyle* for your readers, using examples wherever appropriate. Your definition might focus on both mental and physical health and might include eating, sleeping, exercise, and recreational habits.

Alternatively, you might decide to take a playful point of view and write a brochure defining an *unhealthy lifestyle*.

Option 2: The students in the first year of your college program will be hosts to some students from Quebec. The class is preparing a mini-dictionary of slang for the visitors. Your job is to write a paragraph in which you define the phrase *to gross out*.

In your introduction, consider including the non-slang definition of *gross*, which led to the slang usage. To find that definition, consult a dictionary. Your topic sentence should reflect your understanding of the slang usage of *to gross out*. Any additional paragraphs where you extend your definition can be based on illustrating an example of how the term is used, or a circumstance in which the term is appropriate.

Alternatively, you may write about any other slang term. If necessary, first get the approval of your instructor.

■ Writing Assignment 4:
Writing about a Reading Selection

Read the selection titled "Shame" on pages 495–498. Then write an essay in which you define a term, as Dick Gregory does in "Shame," through narration. You can use one of the terms listed in Writing Assignment 2 or think up one of your own. In your introduction, fill in a brief background for your readers—when and where the experience happened. Your thesis should express the idea that because of this experience, you (or the person or people you are writing about) learned the meaning of the word _____ (fill in the term you have chosen). Break the narrative at logical points to create three supporting paragraphs. You might first want to look at the examples of narrative essays given on pages 160–161.

Alternatively, you might develop your definition with three experiences that seem to embody the word you have chosen. These could be experiences of your own, ones you know about, or ones you have read about. Develop each in a separate supporting paragraph.

REVIEWING THE LEARNING OUTCOMES FOR CHAPTER 14

When you have finished one of the writing assignments in this chapter, review your essay by responding to the following questions:

- Is the subject in an appropriate and limited category of subjects?

- Does your thesis and/or introductory paragraph locate your subject within its class and set it apart from other similar subjects?

- Does the opening paragraph set the tone and degree of subjectivity or objectivity with which you defined your subject?

- Does each supporting point clearly expand on and illustrate your subject, and is the type of support chosen appropriate to your subject?

- Does the final paragraph summarize all meanings presented and suggest a significance for your particular definition?

Division and Classification

LEARNING OUTCOMES

After working on the activities and completing one of the writing tasks in this chapter, you will be prepared to write a division and classification essay that

- Divides its subject into categories according to a consistent classifying principle that logically relates to your reason for writing
- States in its thesis both the category divisions for the subject and the point of classifying the subject in this way
- Arranges its categories in an order that best supports its thesis point
- Balances the quantity of specific and adequate details for each category division or supporting points
- Presents a concluding paragraph that returns to the subject as a whole and offers final thoughts on your essay's look at its subject categories

We divide and classify every single day; we do so to make collections of items more manageable. We sort out everything from socks to documents on the computer, then place them into groups of like items, whether those "classification groups" are black ankle socks or document files. Classifying and dividing objects and ideas are attempts to organize our complex environment.

Dividing and classifying begin in infancy, as we sort and classify all the information we receive. As we move on, we constantly break down and manage large or complex subjects. Our college texts break concepts into chapters and headings, and in many subject areas, we must divide a topic into manageable or appropriate categories for writing assignments.

Sorting out your ideas for a writing task is like sorting out socks. Your first chore is to decide on a principle by which to divide your ideas: a reason to organize them into a set of classifications or categories. A principle or reason might be your purpose for those items, which dictates how you will sort and arrange or store socks.

Division and classification essays require you to choose a reason to classify your subject, or a classifying principle that suits your audience and your purpose. Writing about contemporary music for fellow students might begin with your sorting out the categories according to the tastes of your classmates; for instance, *R & B, Metal, Swing,* and so on. Writing about software for graphic design or animation for a computer animation course would require you to find categories relevant to that course's content.

Dividing and classifying ideas helps in decision making in other life and college situations. Making a decision to buy a car may involve using categories such as *financing available, gas economy,* and *repair costs,* which would be based on the general principle of *costs.*

Division and classification activities will be part of much of your college and career writing. Marketing students and professionals sort consumers into groups or categories to facilitate product development and sales decisions. Accounting students may have to sort out different procedures and programs suitable for businesses of various sizes.

In this section, you will be asked to write an essay in which you divide or classify a subject according to a single principle. To prepare for this assignment, first read the student essays that follow and then work through the questions that accompany the essays.

STUDENT ESSAYS TO CONSIDER

Mall People

Just what goes into "having fun"? For many people, "fun" involves getting out of the house, seeing other people, having something interesting to look at, and enjoying a choice of activities, all at a reasonable price. Going out to dinner or to the movies may satisfy some of those desires, but often not all. But an attractive alternative does exist in the form of the free-admission shopping mall. Teenagers, couples on dates, and the nuclear family can all be observed having a good time at the mall.   1

Teenagers are drawn to the malls to pass time with pals and be seen by other teens. The guys saunter by in sneakers, T-shirts, and baggy jeans, complete with a package of cigarettes sticking out of their pockets. The girls stumble along in high-heeled shoes and daring tank tops, with hairbrushes tucked snugly in the rear pockets of their track pants or bell-bottom jeans. Travelling in a gang that resembles a wolf pack, the teenagers make the shopping mall their hunting ground. Mall managers have obviously made a decision to attract all the teenage activity. Their raised voices, loud laughter, and occasional shouted obscenities can be heard from as far as half a mall away. They come to "pick up chicks," to "meet guys," and just to "hang out."   2

Couples find fun of another sort at shopping malls. The young lovers are easy to spot because they walk hand in hand, stopping to sneak a quick kiss after every few steps. They pause at jewellery store windows so they can gaze at diamond engagement rings and gold wedding bands. Then, they wander into furniture departments in the large mall stores. Finally, they drift away, their arms wrapped around each other's waists.   3

Mom, Dad, little Jenny, and Fred, Jr., visit the mall on Friday and Saturday evenings for inexpensive recreation. Hearing the music of the antique carousel   4 housed there, Jenny begs to ride her favourite pony with its shining golden mane. Shouting, "I'm starving!" Fred, Jr., drags the family towards the food court, where he detects the seductive odour of pizza. Mom walks through a fabric store, running her hand over the soft velvet and slippery silk materials she finds. Meanwhile, Dad has wandered into an electronics store and is admiring the sound system he'd love to buy someday. The mall provides something special for every member of the family.

Sure, some people visit the mall in a brief, businesslike way, just to pick up a specific purchase or two. But many more are shopping for inexpensive recreation. The teenagers, the dating couples, and the nuclear families all find cheap entertainment at the mall. 5

The Beer Up Here

The other night, my six-year-old son turned to me and asked for a light beer. My husband and I sat there for a moment, stunned, and then explained to him that beer was only for grown-ups. I suddenly realized how many, and how often, beer ads appear on television. To my little boy, it must seem that every Canadian drinks beer after work, or after playing ball, or at every sort of social occasion. Beer makers have pounded audiences with all kinds of campaigns to sell beer. There seems to be an ad to appeal to the self-image of every beer drinker. 1

One type of Canadian beer ad attracts people who think of themselves as grown-up kids. "Patrols" of fun-loving young men from one beer company apparently show up at people's backyard barbeques to check beverage choices, and even have recruiting sessions featuring attractive young women, who are checked for their "beer loyalty." Another ad that is a hit with the underage set as well as with adult beer drinkers shows two goofy guys ready to start a party with a broken boom box, a half-bag of cheezies, and a case of beer with a free lottery ticket attached. The ticket wins them the fantasy party of a lifetime, complete with a butler who sees them as fine young gentlemen for their choice of beer. These humorous ads suggest that beer is a necessary and socially acceptable part of a light-hearted approach to life. 2

A second kind of ad is not aimed at wannabe kids but at macho men, guys who think of themselves as "men's men," doing "guy things" together. One particular campaign features men who see themselves as victims of their nagging wives. Ads in this series show men howling with laughter about how they've fooled their wives into thinking they're home doing chores (by leaving dummy-stuffed pants lying under leaky sinks or broken furnaces) while they're really out drinking. Other beer ads show fantasy macho jobs like capping blazing oil-well fires and herding snowbound prairie cattle by helicopter. Beer is a man's drink, the ads seem to say, and women are either irrelevant or a nuisance to be gotten around. 3

European and European-sounding beers such as Amstel and Heineken like to show handsome, wealthy-looking adults enjoying their money and leisure time. A typical scene is such people enjoying an expensive hobby in a luxurious location. Beer, these ads tell us, is an essential part of "the good life." This type of ad appeals to people who want to see themselves as successful and upper class. 4

To a little boy, it may seem that beer is a necessary to every adult's life. After   5
all, we need it to make us feel young, to bond with our friends, and to celebrate
our financial success. At least, that's what advertisers tell him—and us.

■ Questions

About Unity

1. In which paragraph in "The Beer Up Here" is the topic sentence at the end
   rather than, more appropriately for student essays, at the beginning? _____

2. Which sentence in paragraph 2 of "Mall People" should be omitted in the
   interest of paragraph unity? *(Write the opening words.)*

   _____

3. What sentence in paragraph 2 of "The Beer Up Here" should be omitted in
   the interest of paragraph unity? *(Write the opening words.)*

   _____

About Support

4. After which sentence in paragraph 3 of "Mall People" are more supporting
   details needed? *(Write the opening words.)*

   _____

5. Which paragraph in "The Beer Up Here" lacks sufficient specific details?

   _____

6. Label as *sight, touch, hearing,* or *smell* all the sensory details in the following
   sentences taken from "Mall People."
   a. "Hearing the music of the antique carousel housed there, Jenny begs to ride
      her favourite pony, with its shining golden mane."
   b. "Shouting, 'I'm starving!' Fred, Jr., drags the family towards the food court,
      where he detects the seductive odour of pizza."
   c. "Mom walks through a fabric store, running her hand over the soft velvet and
      slippery silk materials she finds."

About Coherence

7. What are the time transition words used in the second supporting paragraph
   of "Mall People"?

   _____   _____   _____

8. Which topic sentence in "The Beer Up Here" functions as a linking sentence
   between paragraphs?

   _____

About the Introduction and Conclusion

9. What kind of introduction is used in "The Beer Up Here"? *(Circle the appropriate letter.)*
   a. Broad, general statement narrowing to a thesis
   b. Idea that is the opposite of the one to be developed
   c. Quotation
   d. Anecdote
   e. Questions

10. What conclusion technique is used in "Mall People"? *(Circle the appropriate letter.)*
    a. Summary
    b. Prediction or recommendation
    c. Question

Classification Prewriting Activity

This activity will sharpen your sense of the classifying process. In each of the following groups, cross out the one item that has not been classified on the same basis as the other four. Also, indicate in the space provided the single principle of classification used for the four items. Note the examples.

Examples   Shirts
          a. Flannel
          b. Cotton
          c. ~~Tuxedo~~
          d. Denim
          e. Silk

          (Unifying principle: *material*)

          Sports
          a. Swimming
          b. Sailing
          c. ~~Basketball~~
          d. Water polo
          e. Scuba diving

          (Unifying principle: *water sports*)

1. School subjects
   a. Algebra
   b. History
   c. Geometry
   d. Trigonometry
   e. Calculus

   (Unifying principle: _____)

2. Movies
   a. *The Sound of Music*
   b. *Evita*
   c. *Dracula*
   d. *Grease*
   e. *The Wizard of Oz*

   (Unifying principle: _____)

3. Clothing
   a. Sweatshirt
   b. Shorts
   c. T-shirt
   d. Evening gown
   e. Sweatpants

   (Unifying principle: _____)

4. Fasteners
   a. Staples
   b. Buttons
   c. Zippers
   d. Snaps
   e. Velcro

   (Unifying principle: _____)

5. Sources of information
   a. *Maclean's*
   b. *The Globe and Mail*
   c. *Canadian Geographic*
   d. *Chatelaine*
   e. *Saturday Night*

   (Unifying principle: _____)

6. Fibres
   a. Wool
   b. Acrylic
   c. Cotton
   d. Silk
   e. Linen

   (Unifying principle: _____)

7. Tapes
   a. Cellophane
   b. Recording
   c. Masking
   d. Duct
   e. Electrical

   (Unifying principle: _____)

8. Fairy-tale characters
   a. Witch
   b. King
   c. Fairy godmother
   d. Wicked queen
   e. Princess

   (Unifying principle: _____)

9. Emotions
   a. Depression
   b. Anger
   c. Jealousy
   d. Despair
   e. Affection

   (Unifying principle: _____)

10. Famous buildings
    a. CN Tower
    b. Expo Stadium
    c. Saddledome
    d. Molson Centre
    e. SkyDome

    (Unifying principle: _____)

WRITING A DIVISION AND CLASSIFICATION ESSAY

Prewriting Strategies

Julia liked malls and liked to look at people; she thought her observations about "people at malls" would make a good topic for a division and classification essay. But she did not immediately know how she wanted to group those people or what she wanted to say about them, so she began her prewriting by listing observations about mall shoppers. Here is what she came up with:

Julia's List Making and Outlining

Families with kids
Lots of snacking
Crowds around special displays—automobiles, kiddie rides
Older people walking mall for exercise
Groups of teenagers
Women getting made over at makeup counter
Dating couples
Blind woman with guide dog
Lots of people talking and laughing rather than shopping
Interviewers stopping shoppers to fill out questionnaires
Kids hanging out, meeting each other

As Julia reviewed her list, she concluded that the three largest groups of "mall people" were families with children, groups of teens, and dating couples. She decided to organize her essay around those three groups and created a trial outline that her essay would follow. Here is Julia's outline:

Thesis statement: Mall offers inexpensive fun for several groups.

1. Teens
   a. Roam in packs
   b. Dress alike
   c. Meet new people
2. Dating couples
   a. Act romantic
   b. Window shop for future home
   c. Have lovers' quarrels
3. Families
   a. Kids activities
   b. Cheap food
   c. Adults shop

Julia's First Draft

Julia's list making and outlining prepared her to write the first draft of her essay:

Malls aren't only places to go shopping. They also offer free, or at least cheap, fun and activities for lots of people. Teenagers, dating couples, and families all like to visit the mall.

Teenagers love to roam the mall in packs, like wolves. They often dress alike, depending on the latest fashion. They're noisy and sometimes rude, and mall security sometimes kicks them out of the building. Then they find somewhere else to go, maybe one of the warehouse-sized amusement and video-game arcades that are springing up everywhere. Those places are fun, but they tend to be more expensive than just "hanging out" at the mall. Teens are usually not as interested in shopping at the mall as they are in picking up members of the opposite sex and seeing their friends.

1

2

Dating couples also enjoy wandering around the mall. They are easy to spot   3
because they walk along holding hands and sometimes kissing. They stare at
diamond rings and wedding bands and shop for furniture together. Sometimes
they have spats, and one of them stamps off to sulk on a bench for a while.

Little kids and their parents make up a big group of mall-goers. There is   4
something for every member of the family there. There are usually some special
displays that interest the kids, and Mom and Dad can always find things they
like to window shop for. Another plus for the family is that there is inexpensive
food, like burgers and pizza, available at the mall's food court.

Revision Strategies

After completing her first draft, Julia put it aside. From previous experience, she
knew that she was a better critic of her own writing after she took a break from it.
Next morning, reading over her first draft, she noticed several places it could be
improved. Here are the observations she put in her writing journal:

- My first paragraph does present a thesis (malls offer inexpensive entertainment) and it tells how I'm going to develop that thesis (by discussing
  three groups of people). But it isn't very interesting. I think I could do a
  better job of drawing readers in by describing what is fun about malls.
- Some of the details in the essay aren't necessary; they don't support my
  main idea. For instance, the stuff about teens being kicked out of the mall
  and about dating couples having fights don't have anything to do with the
  entertainment malls provide. I'll eliminate them.
- And some of my statements that do support the main idea need more support.
  For example, when I say there are "special displays that interest the kids"
  in paragraph 4, I should give an example of such a display. I should also
  back up the idea that many teens dress alike.

With those observations in mind, Julia returned to her essay and revised it, producing the version that appears on pages 255–256.

■ Writing Assignment 1

Shown below are an introduction, a thesis, and supporting details for a classification essay on college stress. Using separate paper, plan and write the supporting
paragraphs and a conclusion for the essay.

College Stress

Jack's heart pounds as he casts panicked looks around the classroom. He
doesn't recognize the professor, he doesn't know any of the students, and he
can't even figure out what the subject is. In front of him is a test. At the last
minute his roommate awakens him. It's only another anxiety dream. The very
fact that dreams like Jack's are common suggests that college is a stressful
situation for young people. The causes of this stress can be academic,
financial, and personal.

> Academic stress is common . . .

> In addition to academic stress, the student often feels financial stress . . .

> Along with academic and financial worries, the student faces personal pressures . . .

Prewriting

1 To develop some ideas for the division and classification essay in Writing Assignment 1, freewrite for five minutes apiece on (1) *academic,* (2) *financial,* and (3) *personal problems of college students.*

2 Then add to the material you have written by asking yourself these questions:

- What are some examples of academic problems that are stressful for students?
- What are some examples of financial problems that students must contend with?
- What are some examples of personal problems that create stress in students?

Write down quickly whatever answers occur to you for the questions. As with freewriting, do not worry at this stage about writing correct sentences. Instead, concentrate on getting down as much information as you can think of that supports each of the three points.

3 Now go through all the material you have accumulated. Perhaps some of the details you have written down may help you think of even better details that would fit. If so, write down these additional details. Then make decisions about the exact information that you will use in each supporting paragraph. List the details (1, 2, 3, and so on) in the order in which you will present them.

4 Now write out the first draft of your paper.

Rewriting

After you have completed the first draft of the paper (and ideally set it aside for a while), you should prepare yourself to rewrite by asking the following questions:

- Have I included relevant examples for each of the three kinds of stress?
- Have I provided enough details to support each of the three kinds of stress?
- Have I used transition words and sentences to help readers follow my train of thought?
- Have I added a concluding paragraph that rounds out and completes the essay?
- Have I checked the paper carefully for the sentence skills listed on the inside front cover?

As you revise your essay, continue to refer to this list until you can answer "yes" to each question.

■   **Writing Assignment 2**

Choose one of the following subjects as the basis for a division and classification essay.

Music	Attitudes toward exercise
Videos	Pet owners
TV shows	Junk food
Fiction	College courses
Comic strips	Couples
Vacations	Shoppers
Answering machine messages	Bosses
Breakfast foods	Parties
Pets	Advertisements
Catalogues	Salesclerks

Prewriting

1 For a division and classification essay, outlining is essential. The success of your essay will depend on your division of your topic into three well-balanced parts. In order to create those three parts, you must use the same rule, or principle, of division for each. Most topics can be divided in several ways according to several principles. For example, the topic of "Hit Movies" could be divided in the following ways:

*Divided by the principle of
film categories:*   Action, comedy, romance

*Divided by the principle of
intended audience:*   Families, dating couples, teens

The topic of "My Favourite Books" could be divided like this:

*Divided by the principle of
book categories:*   Novels, how-to books, biographies

*Divided by the principle of
purpose they serve for me:*   Escape, self-improvement, amusement

The topic of "Places to Eat" could be divided in these ways:

Divided by the principle of cost: Cheap, moderate, expensive

*Divided by the principle of type
of food:*   North American, Italian, Chinese

If you look back at the essays that appear earlier in this chapter, you will see that the topics are divided as follows:

The topic of "Mall People" could be divided in these ways:

***Divided by the principle of
groups of shoppers:***   Teens, dating couples, families

The topic of "The Beer Up Here" could be divided in these ways:

***Divided by the principle of
beer drinkers' self-images:***   Grown-up kids, men's men,
                                 upper-class wannabes

The important point to remember is to keep your essay consistent by dividing your topic according to a single principle. It would be illogical, for example, to divide the topic of "Places to Eat" into "North American" (type of food served), "Italian" (type of food served), and "Expensive" (cost).

2 As you consider a topic for your own paper, think of principles of division you might use. Test them out by filling out this outline and answering the question.

Topic: _____

Principle of division: _____

Three-part division of topic:

a. _____

b. _____

c. _____

Have I used the same principle of division for each of the three parts? _____

When you are confident that you have chosen a topic of interest to you that you can divide into three parts according to one principle, you are ready to begin writing.

3 Before writing your first draft, you may want to freewrite on each of the three parts, make lists, or ask and answer questions to generate the supporting details you will need to develop your ideas.

Rewriting

Once you have a first draft of your essay completed, you should review it with these questions in mind:

- Have I included the essay's thesis in my introductory paragraph?
- Does my thesis state my topic and what principle of division I have chosen?
- Is each of the paragraphs in the body of my essay based on one division of my topic?
- Have I backed up statements in my essay with relevant examples or illustrations?
- Have I eliminated irrelevant material that does not support my thesis?
- Have I used transition words within the paragraphs to help readers follow my train of thought?

- Have I used linking sentences between paragraphs to help tie those paragraphs together?
- Have I included a concluding paragraph that provides the essay with a sense of completion?
- Have I reviewed my paper for sentence skills listed on the inside front cover?

As you revise your essay, continue to refer to this list until you can answer "yes" to each question.

▪ Writing Assignment 3

In this division and classification essay, you will write with a specific purpose and for a specific audience.

Unsure about your career direction, you have gone to a vocational counselling service. To help you select the type of work for which you are best suited, a counsellor has asked you to write a detailed description of your "ideal job." You will present this description to three other people who are also seeking to make a career choice.

To describe your ideal job, divide "work life" into three or more elements, such as:

> Activities done on the job
> Skills used on the job
> Physical environment
> People you work with and under
> Effects of the job on society

In your paper, explain your ideals for each element. You may have more than three supporting paragraphs, if needed. Use specific examples where possible to illustrate your points.

▪ Writing Assignment 4: Writing about a Reading Selection

Read the selection titled "Five Parenting Styles" on pages 544–547. Then write an essay in which you divide and classify a group of people. The group you classify should be *one* of the following:

- Teachers
- Friends
- Co-workers

Below are suggestions about how to write your essay.

To begin, you must think of a way—a principle of division—to divide the group you have chosen. If you were considering *co-workers*, for example, you could probably imagine several principles of division, such as these:

> Ways they treat the boss
> Efficiency at work
> Punctuality at work
> Level of neatness (desks, lockers, work turned in)

Once you have a useful principle of division, you will find that you can easily divide the people you are writing about into groups. If you decided, for instance, to use *ways they treat the boss* as your principle of division, you might write about these three groups:

1 Co-workers who "butter up" the boss
2 Co-workers who get along with the boss
3 Co-workers who dislike the boss

Here are some suggested principles of division for *teachers* and *friends*. You should feel free, of course, to come up with your own approach.

Teachers
Teaching methods
Methods of classroom control
Clothing styles
Testing methods
Level of dedication to the job

Friends
Level of loyalty
Where or how you first met them
Length of time you've been friends
Level of emotional closeness
Attitudes toward something (money, college, drugs, and so on)

To complete the essay, follow the prewriting and rewriting strategies in Writing Assignment 2 on pages 263–265.

REVIEWING THE LEARNING OUTCOMES FOR CHAPTER 15

Once you have completed one of the writing assignments, review your essay for how closely it meets this chapter's learning outcomes by responding to the questions that follow:

- Do the divisions in your essay's subject follow a consistent principle? Is this principle logically related to your purpose in writing about your subject? Does your dividing principle lead to interesting new thoughts about your subject?

- Does your thesis statement/opening paragraph mention (1) your purpose for dividing your subject as you do, (2) the point you make by doing so, and (3) your categories or classifications?

- Do your category/classification paragraphs appear in an order that best supports your thesis point?

- Is the number of supporting details for each category roughly balanced, and are all details adequately explained?

- Does your conclusion remind readers of your thesis and reinforce new ideas that emerged as a result of your division and classification?

Argumentation

After working through the activities in this chapter, and completing at least one of its writing assignments, you will write an argumentation essay that

- Opens with an appropriately introduced thesis that states a definite point to be argued
- Offers, based on some knowledge of its readers, possible counter-arguments and responses to them
- Uses a method of development best suited to the logical pattern of the argument
- Presents in its supporting points and details both solid logic and knowledge of the specifics of its subject
- Overall argues its thesis point cleanly, without slanting by emotional appeal or insulting its reader
- Concludes by reaffirming its point, as justified by the evidence presented in the essay's body

We all know someone who enjoys a good argument. Such a person likes to challenge any sweeping statement we might make. When we say something like "Ms. Lucci doesn't grade fairly," he or she comes back with, "Why do you say that? What are your reasons?"

Argumentation papers respond to our readers' natural tendency to "ask why" of any point of view or opinion we may state as part of our thesis. No two minds perceive a person or situation in exactly the same way, so readers nearly always suspend agreement with what we write until they are satisfied with our "reasons why."

The student asking why we believe Ms. Lucci marks unfairly then listens carefully as we state our case, judging if we really do have solid evidence to support our point of view. We realize that saying, "Ms. Lucci just doesn't, that's all," sounds weak and unconvincing, so we try to come up with stronger evidence to back up our statement. Such a questioner may make us feel uncomfortable, but we may also feel grateful to him or her for helping us clarify our opinions.

Arguing a point in an essay requires writers to do three things: (1) to search for logical answers to why they hold an opinion, (2) to examine and weigh the usefulness or convincing qualities of the emotions associated with their opinion, and (3) to make themselves a clear and credible source on the viewpoint they are arguing.

The ability to present sound and compelling arguments is an important skill in everyday life. You can use argumentation to make a point in a class discussion, persuade a friend to lend you money, or talk an employer into giving you a day off. Becoming skilled in clear, logical reasoning can also help you see through faulty arguments that others may make. You'll become a better critic of advertisements, newspaper articles, political speeches, and the other persuasive appeals you see and hear every day.

Argumentation writing skills hold an important place in your college and career communications needs. In a business course, you may be asked to defend a particular management style; in a technical program, you may be required to analyze and defend the use of a particular procedure. In the workplace, you may write proposals that request funding or new equipment, or you may create advertising copy to promote some product or service. The uses of good argumentation skills are endless.

In this section, you will be asked to write an essay in which you defend a position with a series of solid reasons. In a general way, you have already done this: you have made a point and supported it, with all the essays in this book. The difference is that argumentation advances a *controversial* point, one that at least some of your readers will not be inclined to accept. To prepare for this assignment, first read about five strategies you can use in advancing an argument. Then read the student essays that follow and work through the questions that accompany the essays.

STRATEGIES FOR ARGUMENTATION

Because argumentation assumes controversy, you have to work carefully to convince readers of the validity of your position. Here are five strategies you can use to help win over readers whose viewpoint may differ from yours.

1 Use Tactful, Courteous Language

In an argumentation essay, your task is to persuade readers to accept your viewpoint. It is important, therefore, not to anger them by referring to them or their opinions in rude or belittling terms. Stay away from sweeping statements like "Everybody knows that . . ." or "People with any intelligence agree that . . ." Also, *keep the focus on the issue you are discussing*, not on the people involved in the debate. Third-person viewpoint is especially useful for maintaining the readers' focus on your ideas, and for suggesting some "objective" distance between you and your subject. Don't write, "*My opponents* say that orphanages cost less than foster care." Instead, write, "*Supporters of orphanages* say they cost less than foster care." Terms like *my opponents* imply that the argument is between you and the "bad guys"—an attitude that puts more distance between you and anyone who disagrees with you. By contrast, a term such as *supporters of orphanages* suggests that those who don't agree are nevertheless reasonable people who are willing to consider differing opinions.

2 Point Out Common Ground

Another way to persuade readers to consider your opinion is to point out common ground that you share. Find points on which people on all sides of the argument can agree. You may be arguing in favour of longer access hours for the computer labs at your college. Before going into detail about your proposal, remind readers who could be opposed to increased hours that you and they share certain ideas such as enabling students with outside jobs to use the facilities and allowing more students to do better work. Readers will be more receptive to your idea once they have considered the ways in which you and they think alike.

3 Acknowledge Differing Viewpoints

It is a mistake simply to ignore points of view that conflict with yours. Acknowledging other viewpoints strengthens your position in several ways. First, it helps you spot flaws in the opposing position—as well as in your own argument. Second, and equally important, it gives the impression that you are a reasonable person, willing to see all sides of an issue. Readers are more likely to consider your point of view if you indicate a willingness to consider theirs.

At what point in your essay should you acknowledge opposing arguments? The earlier the better—ideally, in the introduction. By quickly establishing that you recognize the other side's position, you get your readers "on board" with you, ready to hear what you have to say.

One effective technique is to *cite the opposing viewpoint in your thesis statement.* Do this by dividing your thesis into two parts. In the first part, you acknowledge the other side's point of view; in the second, state your opinion, suggesting that yours is the stronger viewpoint. Below, the opposing viewpoint is underlined once; the writer's own position is underlined twice:

> <u>Although some students believe that studying another language is a waste of time,</u> <u><u>two years of second-language study should be required of all college graduates.</u></u>

For another example of a thesis that acknowledges an opposing viewpoint, look at this thesis statement, taken from the student essay entitled "Once Over Lightly: Local TV News" (pages 272–273):

> <u>While local TV newscasts can provide a valuable community resource,</u> <u><u>too often such programs provide mere entertainment at the expense of solid news.</u></u>

Another effective technique is to use one or two sentences (separate from the thesis) in the introduction to *acknowledge the alternative position.* Such sentences briefly state the "other side's" argument. To see this technique at work, look at the introduction to "Teenagers and Jobs" (pages 271–272), noting the sentence "Many people argue that working can be a valuable experience for the young."

A third technique is to *use a paragraph within the body of your essay to summarize opposing opinions in greater detail.* To do this successfully, you must spend time researching opposing arguments. A fair, even-handed summary of the other side's ideas will help convince readers that you have looked at the issue from all angles before deciding on your position. Imagine that you are writing an essay arguing that foreign ownership of Canadian businesses should be less limited. Begin by doing some library or Internet research to find information on both sides of the issue, paying attention to materials that argue for your viewpoint. You could talk to local business owners or organizations that support Canadian ownership of businesses. You would now be in a good position to write a paragraph summarizing opposing viewpoints: you might mention Canadian business owners' fears of competition from US companies, profit cuts caused by currency exchange, and so on. Once you demonstrate your understanding of opposing views, you are in a stronger position to present your own views.

4   When Appropriate, Grant the Merits of Differing Viewpoints

Sometimes an opposing argument contains a point whose validity you cannot deny. What should you do then? The strongest strategy is to admit that the point is a good one. You will lose credibility if you argue against something that clearly makes sense. Admit the merit of one aspect of the other argument while making it clear that you still believe your argument. The author of "Teenagers and Jobs" (pages 271–272) takes this approach when discussing the negative effects on students of working more than fifteen hours per week. The sentence "Many people argue that working can be a valuable experience for the young" admits that the other side has a valid point. But the author quickly follows this admission with a statement making her own viewpoint clear: "However, working more than fifteen hours a week is harmful to adolescents because it reduces their involvement with school, encourages a materialistic and expensive lifestyle, and increases the chance of having problems with drugs and alcohol."

5   Rebut Differing Viewpoints

Sometimes it may not be enough simply to acknowledge the other points of view and present your own argument. When you are dealing with an issue that your readers feel strongly about, you may need to *rebut* the opposing arguments. To *rebut* simply means to point out problems with an opposing view, to show where an opponent's argument breaks down. Imagine your essay states that your college should use money intended to build a campus fitness centre to upgrade the library instead. From reading the college paper, you know that supporters of the centre say it will help attract new students to the college. You rebut that point by citing a study conducted by college management showing that most students choose a college because of affordable tuition and because of its academic and professional programs and facilities. You also emphasize that many students, already financially strapped, would have trouble paying charges to use the centre.

A rebuttal can take two forms, similar to the two methods of development used for comparison/contrast essays: (1) you can first mention all the points raised by the other side and then present your counter-argument to each of those points; (2) you can present the first point raised by the opposition and rebut that point, then move on to the second opposing point and rebut that, and so on.

STUDENT ESSAYS TO CONSIDER

Teenagers and Jobs

"The lives of adolescents and adults are not as different as they used to be. Students juggle jobs and school and leisure time in much the same way their parents juggle careers and families; they make important choices—how often they work, what classes they take, what they spend their money on—with almost no adult input . . . if they make unwise choices, there are no safety nets." So wrote Kate Fillion of Toronto high school students ("High School Undercover," *Toronto Life*, August 1990). Many people argue that working can be a valuable experience for the young. However, working more than fifteen hours a week is harmful to adolescents because it reduces their involvement with school, encourages a materialistic and expensive lifestyle, and increases the chance of having problems with drugs and alcohol. 1

Schoolwork and the benefits of extracurricular activities tend to go by the wayside when adolescents work long hours. As more and more teens have filled the numerous part-time jobs offered by fast-food restaurants and malls, teachers have faced increasing difficulties. They must both keep the attention of tired pupils and give homework to students who simply don't have time to do it. In addition, educators have noticed less involvement in the extracurricular activities that many consider a healthy influence on young people. School bands and athletic teams are losing players to work, and sports events are poorly attended by working students. Those teenagers who try to do it all—homework, extracurricular activities, and work—may find themselves exhausted and prone to illness. A recent newspaper story, for example, described a girl who came down with mononucleosis as a result of aiming for good grades, playing on two school athletic teams, and working thirty hours a week. 2

Another drawback of too much work is that it may promote materialism and an unrealistic lifestyle. Some parents claim that working helps teach adolescents the value of a dollar. Undoubtedly that can be true. It's also true that some teens work to help out with the family budget or to save for college. However, surveys have shown that the majority of working teens use their earnings to buy luxuries—video-game systems, CD players and discs, clothing, and even cars. These young people, some of whom earn $1000 or more a month, don't worry about spending wisely—they can just about have it all. In many cases, experts point out, they are becoming accustomed to a lifestyle they won't be able to afford several years down the road, when they no longer have parents paying for car insurance, food, lodging, and so on. At that point, they'll be hard-pressed to pay for necessities as well as luxuries. 3

Finally, teenagers who work a lot are more likely than others to get involved with alcohol and drugs. Teens who put in long hours may seek a quick release from stress, just like the adults who need to drink a couple of martinis after a hard day at work. Stress is probably greater in our society today than it has been at any time in the past. Also, teens who have money are more likely to get involved with drugs. 4

Teenagers can enjoy the benefits of work while avoiding its drawbacks,   5
simply by limiting their work hours during the school year. As is often the case,
a moderate approach will be the most healthy and rewarding.

Once Over Lightly: Local TV News

Are local television newscasts a reliable source of news? Do they provide   1
in-depth coverage and analysis of important local issues? Unfortunately, all too
often they do not. While local TV newscasts can provide a valuable community
resource, too often such programs provide mere entertainment at the expense
of solid news. In their battle for high ratings, local programs emphasize news
personalities at the expense of stories. Visual appeal has a higher priority than
actual news. And stories and reports are too brief and shallow.

Local TV newscasters are as much the subject of the news as are the   2
stories they present. Nowhere is this more obvious than in weather reports.
Weatherpersons spend valuable news time joking, drawing cartoons, chatting
about weather fronts as "good guys" and "bad guys," and dispensing weather
trivia such as statistics about relative humidity and record highs and lows for
the date. Reporters, too, draw attention to themselves. Rather than just getting
the story, reporters are shown jumping into or getting out of helicopters to get
the story. When reporters interview crime victims or the residents of poor
neighbourhoods, the camera angle typically includes them and their reaction
as well as their subjects. When they report on a storm, they stand outside in
the storm, their styled hair blowing, so we can admire how they "brave the
elements." Then there are the anchorpersons, who are chosen as much for
their looks as their skills. They too dilute the news by putting their
personalities centre stage.

Often the selection of stories and the way they are presented are based on   3
visual impact rather than news value. If a story is not accompanied by an
interesting film clip, it is not likely to be shown on the local news. The result
is an over-emphasis on fires and car crashes, and little attention to such
important issues as the economy. A tractor-trailer spill on the highway slightly
injures one person and inconveniences motorists for only an hour. But because
it provides dramatic pictures—the big truck on its side, its load spilled, emergency
personnel running around, and lots of flashing lights—it is given greater emphasis
in the local newscast than a rise in local taxes, which has a far more lasting
effect on the viewer. "If it bleeds, it leads" is the unofficial motto of many
local news programs. A story that includes pictures of death and destruction,
no matter how meaningless, is preferable on the local news to a solid, important
story without flashy visuals. The mania for visuals is so strong that local news
programs will even slap irrelevant visuals on an otherwise strong story. A recent
story on falling oil prices, for example, was accompanied by footage of a working
oil well that drew attention away from the important economic information in
the report.

On the average, about half a minute is devoted to a story. Clearly, stories   4
that take less than half a minute are superficial. Even the longest stories, which
can take up several minutes, are not accompanied by meaningful analysis.

Instead, the camera jumps from one location to another, and the newscaster simplifies and trivializes the issues. For instance, one recent "in-depth" story about the homeless consisted of a glamorous reporter talking to a homeless person and asking him what should be done about the problem. The poor man was in no condition to respond intelligently. The story then cut to an interview with a city bureaucrat who mechanically rambled on about the need for more government funding. Is raising taxes the answer to every social problem? There were also shots of homeless people sleeping in doorways and on top of heating vents, and there were interviews with people in the street, all of whom said something should be done about the terrible problem of homelessness. There was, in all of this, no real exploration of the issue and no proposed solution. It was also apparent that the homeless were just the issue of the week. After the week's coverage was over, the topic was not mentioned again.

Because of the emphasis on newscasters' personalities and on the visual   5
impact of stories and the short time span for stories, local news shows provide little more than diversion. What viewers need instead is news that has real significance. Rather than being amused and entertained, we need to deal with complex issues and learn uncomfortable truths that will help us become more responsible consumers and citizens.

■ Questions

About Unity

1. Which paragraph in "Once Over Lightly" is lacking a topic sentence? _____

   Write a topic sentence for the paragraph: _____

   _____

2. What sentence in paragraph 4 of "Once Over Lightly" should be omitted in the interest of paragraph unity? *(Write the opening words.)*

   _____

3. Which sentence in paragraph 4 of "Teenagers and Jobs" should be omitted in the interest of paragraph unity? *(Write the opening words.)*

   _____

About Support

4. Which sentence in paragraph 4 of "Teenagers and Jobs" needs to be followed by more supporting details? Which sentence in paragraph 2 of "Once Over Lightly" needs to be followed by supporting details? *(Write the opening words of each sentence.)*

   _____

   _____

5. Which supporting paragraph in "Teenagers and Jobs" raises an opposing idea and then argues against that idea? _____ What transition word is used to signal the author's change of direction?" _____

6. In the second paragraph of "Once Over Lightly," the topic sentence is supported by details about three types of newscasters. What are those three types?

_____   _____   _____

About Coherence

7. Which two paragraphs of "Teenagers and Jobs" begin with an addition transition, and what are those words? _____ _____

8. Write the change-of-direction transition and the illustration transition in paragraph 3 of "Once Over Lightly."

Change-of-direction: _____   Illustration: _____

About the Introduction and Conclusion

9. Two methods of introduction are used in "Teenagers and Jobs." Circle the letters of these two methods.
    a. Broad, general statement narrowing to thesis
    b. Idea that is the opposite of the one to be developed
    c. Quotation
    d. Anecdote
    e. Questions

10. Both essays end with the same type of conclusion. What method do they use?
    a. a summary only
    b. a summary and recommendation
    c. a prediction

WRITING AN ARGUMENTATION ESSAY

Prewriting Activity: Developing "Reasons Why . . ."

In outline form on separate paper, provide brief supporting reasons for at least four of the eight statements that follow. Note the example. Make sure that you have at least three *separate* and *distinct* reasons for each statement.

Example   Recycling of newspapers, cans, and bottles should be mandatory.
    a. Towns sell recycled items rather than pay for dumping.
    b. Natural resources are protected.
    c. Respect for the environment is encouraged.

1 Couples should be required to live together for six months before marriage.
2 High schools should give birth control devices and information to students.
3 All instructors should be marked by their students.
4 Cultural diversity should be given less encouragement in Canada.
5 Gambling should not be legal in any province.
6 School does not prepare you for life.
7 All companies should be required to have daycare centres.
8 Canadian TV should not carry so much US programming.

WRITING AN ARGUMENTATION ESSAY

About Prewriting

Before choosing a topic for her essay, Anna, the writer of "Teenagers and Jobs," asked herself what controversial subject she was particularly well qualified to argue for or against. She wanted to select something she cared about, something she could "sink her teeth into." As a person who had been active in her high school community—working on the newspaper, playing basketball, and singing in a chorus—Anna first thought about "student apathy." She had never understood students ignoring opportunities available to them in school. Then she began to consider individual students she knew and their reasons for not getting more involved in school and extracurricular activities, and she changed her opinion. "I realized that 'apathy' was not really the problem," she explained. "Many of them worked so much that they literally didn't have time for school life."

After focusing her thesis on the idea of "teenagers and work," Anna made a list of what she perceived as the bad points of students working too much:

No time for sports and other activities
Students leave right after school—can't stay for clubs, practices
Don't have time to attend games, other school functions
Students sleep in class and skip homework
Stress, extra money contribute to drug and alcohol use
Teachers frustrated trying to teach tired students
Ability to buy luxuries makes teens materialistic, unrealistic about lifestyle
Some drop out of school to work full-time
Students miss the fun of being young, developing talents and social abilities
Students burned-out, even get sick

Anna reviewed her list of points, and identified three main points to develop in her essay, identifying them as 1, 2, and 3.

Realizing that some other items she had listed were related ideas that could be useful as support for her main topics, she marked those with the number of the main idea they supported in parentheses, like this: *(1).*

1 —   No time for real involvement in school and school activities
  (1)   Students leave right after school—can't stay for clubs, practices
  (1)   Don't have time to attend games, other school functions
      Students sleep in class and skip homework
2 —   Stress, extra money contribute to drug and alcohol use
  (1)   Teachers frustrated trying to teach tired students
3 —   Having extra money makes teens materialistic
  (3)   Some get so greedy for money they drop out of school to work full-time
      Students miss the fun of being young, developing talents and social abilities
      Students burn out, even get sick
  (2)   Hanging around older co-workers can contribute to drug, alcohol use
  (3)   Buying luxuries gives teens unrealistic idea of standard of living

Referring to this list, Anna wrote the following first draft of her essay:

Many people think that working is a valuable experience for young people. But when teenagers have jobs, they are too likely to neglect their schoolwork, become overly materialistic, and get into trouble with drugs and alcohol.

Schoolwork and the benefits of extracurricular activities tend to go by the wayside when adolescents work long hours. As more and more teens have taken jobs, teachers have faced increasing difficulties. They must both keep the attention of tired pupils and give homework to students who simply don't have time to do it. In addition, educators have noticed less involvement in extracurricular activities. School bands and athletic teams are losing players to work, and sports events are poorly attended by working students. Those teens who try to do it all—homework, extracurricular activities, and work—may find themselves exhausted and burned out.

Another drawback of too much work is that it may promote materialism and an unrealistic lifestyle. Most working teens use their earnings to buy luxuries. These young people don't worry about spending wisely—they can just about have it all. They are becoming accustomed to a lifestyle they won't be able to afford several years down the road, when they have to support themselves.

Finally, teenagers who work are more likely than others to get involved with alcohol and drugs. Teens who put in long hours may seek a quick release from stress, just like the adults who need to drink a couple of martinis after a hard day at work. Also, teens who have money are more likely to get involved with drugs.

In short, teens and work just don't mix.

About Revising

Anna's instructor looked over her first draft and suggested these improvements for revision:

Anna—Good beginning. Your thesis may be overstated, but each of your main topics are on the right track. Here are some points to consider:

- *Working a <u>limited</u> number of hours a week might be a good experience.*
- *Acknowledge that there can be good points to students working part-time.*
- *Good support for your first main point ("Schoolwork and the benefits of extracurricular activities tend to go by the wayside when adolescents work long hours"): the effect of too much work on scholastic achievement and extracurricular activities.*
- *<u>Less</u> effective support for points 2 and 3 ("Another drawback of too much work is that it may promote materialism and an unrealistic lifestyle" and "Finally, teenagers who work are more likely than others to get involved with alcohol and drugs").*
- *<u>How</u> do teens become too materialistic?*
- *<u>What evidence</u> is there that working teens use drugs and alcohol more than others?*
- *Can you come up with evidence beyond your own observations to support the idea that too much working is detrimental to teens?*
- *Check magazine indexes in the library and the Internet for support for your thesis.*

I look forward to seeing your final draft.

After considering her instructor's comments, Anna wrote the draft of "Teenagers and Jobs" that appears on pages 271–272.

WRITING AN ARGUMENTATION ESSAY

■ Writing Assignment 1

Shown below are three comments. Write a paper in which you argue *for* or *against* any one of the three comments (options 1–3). Support and defend your argument by drawing on your reasoning ability and general experience.

Option 1: In many ways, television has proved to be one of the worst inventions of modern times. All too often, television is harmful because of the shows it broadcasts and the way it is used in the home.

Option 2: Many of society's worst problems with drugs result from the fact that they are illegal. During Prohibition, North America discovered that making popular substances unlawful causes more problems than it solves. Like alcohol and tobacco, drugs should be legal in this country.

Option 3: Statistics show that newly licensed teenage boys cause a higher number of serious automobile accidents than any other group. It is evident that many young men are too reckless and impulsive to be good drivers. In order to protect the larger society, the age at which a boy can earn his licence should be raised to eighteen.

Prewriting

1 Take a few minutes to think about the three options. Which one in particular are you for or against—and *why?*

2 On a sheet of paper, make a brief outline of support for your position on one of the options. (Remember, you may choose to argue *against* one of the three comments, as well as for it.) Preparing the outline will give you a chance to think further about your position. And the outline will show whether you have enough support for your position. (If you find you don't, choose another position, and prepare another outline.)

3 Next, decide how you will develop each of your three supporting points. Make up brief outlines of the three supporting paragraphs. In addition to preparing brief outlines, you may also want to use other prewriting techniques. You may want to freewrite, brainstorm, and/or make up lists—all of which are described on pages 26–34.

4 Decide in which order you want to present your paragraphs. *Emphatic order* (in which you *end* with your most important reason) is often the most effective way to organize an argument. Your reader is most likely to remember your final reason.

5 As you write, think of your audience as a jury that will ultimately believe or disbelieve your argument. Have you presented a convincing case? Do you need more details? If *you* were on the jury, would you be favourably impressed with this argument?

6 Proceed to write the first draft of your essay.

Rewriting

After you have completed the first draft of the paper, set it aside for a while (if possible). When you review it, try to do so as critically as you would if it were not your own work. Ask yourself these questions:

- Have I provided persuasive details to support my argument?
- Have I acknowledged the opposing point of view, showing that I am a reasonable person willing to consider other arguments?
- Is my language tactful and courteous, or does it insult anyone who doesn't agree with me?
- Have I used transition words to help readers follow my train of thought?
- Does my final supporting paragraph include a strong argument for my position?
- What should I provide in a concluding paragraph to summarize my argument or add a final persuasive touch?

Revise your essay through added drafts, referring to this list until you can answer "yes" to each question. Then be sure to check the next-to-final draft of the paper for the sentence skills listed on the inside front cover.

Writing Assignment 2

Write a paper in which you argue *for* or *against* any one of two comments below. Support and defend your argument by drawing on your reasoning ability and general experience.

Option 1: Giving students grades does more harm than good. Schools should replace grades with written evaluations of the students' strengths and weaknesses. These would benefit both students and parents.

Option 2: Physical punishment "works" in the sense that it may stop a child from misbehaving, but adults who frequently spank and hit are also teaching children that violence is a good method of accomplishing a goal. Non-violent methods are a more effective way of training children.

Prewriting

1 As you write your opening paragraph, acknowledge the opposing point of view before stating your thesis. If you have trouble figuring out "the other side's" argument, completing this exercise will give you practice in acknowledging another way of looking at the question.

In each item, you will see a statement and then a question related to that statement. Write *two* answers to each question. First, answer "yes" to the question and briefly explain why. Then answer "no" to the question and also state why. The first item is done for you as an example:

a. Smoking has been proved to be bad for the health. Should it therefore be made illegal?

"Yes": Because smoking has been shown to have so many negative effects on the health, the sale of tobacco should be made illegal.

"No": Although smoking has been linked to various health problems, adults should have the right to make their own decisions about whether or not to smoke. Smoking should not be made illegal.

b. Animals feel pain when they are killed for food. Is eating animals therefore immoral?

"Yes": _____

_____

"No": _____

_____

c. Some high school students are sexually active. Should birth control devices and information be given out by high schools to their students?

"Yes": _____

_____

"No": _____

_____

2 Make a list of the thoughts that support your argument. Don't worry about repetition, spelling, or grammar at this point. Just write down everything that occurs to you.

Once you have written down all the thoughts that occur to you, identify your strongest points and begin your outline. Select your three main supporting points. Are there other thoughts in your list that can be used as supporting details for those points?

3 Write your three supporting paragraphs. Keep in mind that you are writing for an audience of people who, initially, will not all agree with you. It isn't enough to state your opinion. Show *why* you feel as you do, persuading your reader that your point of view is a valid one.

4 Your concluding paragraph is your final chance to persuade your readers to accept your argument. Consider ending with a prediction of what will happen if your point of view does not prevail. Will an existing situation grow worse? Will a new problem arise?

Rewriting

Follow the suggestions for rewriting provided on page 278.

■ **Writing Assignment 3**

In this argument essay, you will write with a specific purpose and for a specific audience.

Option 1: You would like to live in a big city, but your parent or spouse refuses to budge from the suburbs. Write him or her a letter in which you argue the advantages of city life. Since the success of your argument will depend to some degree on how well you overcome the other person's objections to city life, be sure to address those as well. Use specific, colourful examples wherever possible.

Option 2: Find an editorial in your local newspaper that you either strongly agree with or disagree with. Write a letter to the editor responding to that editorial, in which you state why you agree or disagree with the position taken by the paper. Provide several short paragraphs of supporting evidence for your position. Actually send your letter to the newspaper. When you turn in a copy of your letter to your instructor, also turn in the editorial to which you are responding.

■ Writing Assignment 4

Write a paper in which you use research findings to help support one of the statements in the Prewriting Activity on pages 274–275. Be sure to keep the focus on your subject by writing in the third-person point of view. Research the topic in one or both of these ways:

- Look up the topic in the subject section of your library book index or on the Internet. (Review pages 319–333 of "Using the Library and the Internet.") Think about synonyms and phrases that will be likely keywords and subject headings for some of the statements in the activity. Select the books or websites that seem likely to give you the most appropriate information about your topic. Note your sources in the ways listed in "Writing a Research Paper."

- Look up the topic in recent issues of the *Canadian Periodical Index,* or EBSCOhost, or on a search engine. (Review "Using the Library and the Internet" first.) Try some of the same keywords and headings. Select articles likely to provide information on your topic. See if you can organize your paper in the form of three reasons that support the topic. Put these reasons into an outline, use it as a guide, and note your sources as you go along. Here is an example:

Prayer should not be allowed in the public schools:

1. Children who are not religious will feel excluded.
2. Children may still pray silently whenever they please.
3. Not all schools and teachers will keep prayer nondenominational.

Note that statistical information, the results of studies, and the advice of experts may all help develop the supporting reasons for your thesis. Do not hesitate to cite such information in a limited way; it helps make your argument more objective and compelling.

■ Writing Assignment 5

Writing about a Reading Selection

Read the selection titled "In Praise of the F Word" on pages 591–593. Notice how the author acknowledges the pressures students face in schools today, and accepts the responsibility instructors face if educational standards are raised. She then uses both personal and more objective details to persuade readers of the merit of failing underprepared students.

Write an essay in which you try to persuade readers that a particular academic policy, teaching method, area of professional training, or subject is either good or bad. Clearly present your reasons in order of increasing importance. You may wish, for instance, to argue for or against one of the following:

Final examinations
Grading policies and graduation requirements
Evaluations instead of grades
"Interactive" teaching methods
Mandatory attendance

Choose a subject for which you can find three strong reasons pro or con. Each of your reasons or points will form a topic sentence for one supporting paragraph. Following, for example, is a brief outline for an essay persuading readers of the benefits of final examinations. Each of the three reasons is a topic sentence for one supporting paragraph.

Thesis: Final exams are a necessary part of students' education.

1. They motivate students to keep up with class work.
2. They allow students to demonstrate their understanding of a full semester's course material.
3. They give the student an objective view of their own achievements.

Develop your supporting paragraphs by explaining each topic sentence, using examples to illustrate your points.

REVIEWING THE LEARNING OUTCOMES FOR CHAPTER 16

When you have completed one of the argumentation essay assignments in this chapter, review how well you have met its learning outcomes by responding to the following questions:

- Does your opening paragraph provide appropriate background for your thesis? Does the thesis state the point your essay will argue clearly and straightforwardly?

- Does your essay acknowledge and counter any opposing views?

- Have you used a method of development appropriate to the type of argument, you offer: i.e., facts and statistics for a logical argument, or anecdotes or examples for an experience-based argument?

- Does each supporting point and detail clearly support your thesis viewpoint and add to the strength of your argument?

- Have you maintained both a courteous tone and an objective approach to the facts you present?

- Does your concluding statement directly reinforce your argument? Is it fully justified by the evidence you have presented in the body paragraphs of your essay?

Special Skills

Taking Essay Exams

Every semester you will write exams requiring essay answers. Your responses to essay examination questions must follow the structure and content patterns you have learned and practised in Parts 1 and 2 of this book. During an exam you may feel pressured for time or pressed to recall as much as possible, so this chapter offers ways to prepare for and write successful essay responses for college examinations.

Your main challenges with any essay exam response are these:
- Can you sort through a large body of information to focus on what the question asks?
- Can you decide what information is most relevant to answering the question?
- Can you explain why the information you present is appropriate?

Tackling these challenges successfully and responding in a clearly organized and detailed fashion is not the product of one night's frantic cramming. Therefore, this chapter's tips and techniques cover three stages of preparation: learning skills during the semester, study skills, and exam-taking tips. If you conscientiously work through these stages, you will meet the challenges each essay exam poses.

1. LEARNING SKILLS DURING THE SEMESTER

Exams are created so that instructors can measure your understanding of—and competence in explaining—key areas of subject content. How do you show that you understand enough of your course content to tackle essay responses?

- Keep up with readings and assignments right from the start of the semester. Students who do so can probably make intelligent guesses about what will be on an exam before they take it.
- Keep up with assigned readings. Doing so prepares you for classes where related subject material is being discussed and helps you to grasp relationships between concepts.
- Go to all classes and take careful notes. Good class notes add to your textbook's usefulness and help recall concepts your instructor emphasized. Be sure you will be able to understand your notes months after you make them; if necessary, spend time revising and improving your notes as soon as possible after your class.

- Participate in class discussions. By concentrating and participating in class, you will more readily absorb the material and connections between ideas and you will have less trouble recalling course content while studying.
- Form small study groups several times during each semester. Explore and review course materials and skills and compare notes. Others will catch things you might miss, even when paying attention.
- As exam time nears, find out what form each subject's exam will take. This will help you forecast which questions will be on the exam, and prepare for them.

These suggestions may seem to ask a lot of you, but you're investing time in your own success, and these techniques will save you time and misery later. Remember that you can't cram weeks of information into a single day or night of study. Why put yourself in that position?

2. EXAM PREPARATION AND STUDY SKILLS

GENERAL TIPS FOR ESSAY EXAMS

Two weeks before your exams, prepare yourself to study effectively:

- Find out from your professor the format that the exam will take: make sure you know how many questions you will be asked to answer, and how much time is allotted for the exam.
- Be sure that you have all class notes; consult classmates and your professor about anything you have missed or that seems vague to you.
- Make sure that you thoroughly know the sections of your text that illustrate the main concepts covered that semester. If the exam format is open book, be sure that you know where the main points in the text are; you lose valuable time if you have to search for relevant pages during the exam.

THREE STEPS TO PREPARE FOR ESSAY EXAMS

A week before your exam, work through three steps to focus your thinking and sharpen your response-writing skills.

Step 1: Anticipate Ten Probable Questions

Because exam time is limited, instructors can offer only certain questions, focused on the most important areas of the subject. Following are common-sense tips for determining probable questions:

- Go through class notes and mark off areas where your instructor has spent a good deal of time. The more time spent on any one area, the better the chance of an essay question on it. If the instructor spent a week talking about present-day changes in the traditional family structure, or the importance of the carbon molecule, you can reasonably expect that you will get a question on the emphasized area.

- In both class notes and textbooks, pay special attention to definitions, examples, and lists of items (enumerations). Enumerations are often the key to essay questions. For instance, if your instructor spoke at length about the causes of the Great Depression or the effects of water pollution, you should probably expect a question such as "What were the causes of the Great Depression?" or "What are the effects of water pollution?"
- If your instructor has given you study guides, look for probable essay questions there. Look for clues to essay questions on any short quizzes that have been given. Finally, carefully consider any review that the instructor provides. Write down such reviews—your instructor may be making up the exam at the time of the review and is likely to give valuable hints about it. Note also that if the instructor does not offer to provide a review, do not hesitate to *ask* for one in a friendly way. Essay questions are likely to come from areas the instructor may mention.

An Illustration of Step 1

A psychology class was given a day to prepare for an essay exam on stress—a subject covered in class that comprised a chapter in the textbook. One student, Mark, read carefully through his class notes and textbook chapter. On the basis of the headings, major enumerations, and definitions he noted, he decided that there were five likely essay questions:

1. What are the common sources of stress?
2. What are the types of conflict?
3. What are the defence mechanisms that people use to cope with stress?
4. What effects can stress have on people?
5. What are the characteristics of the well-adjusted person?

Step 2: Prepare and Memorize an Informal Outline Answer for Each Question

- Write out each question you have made up and, under it, list the main points that need to be discussed.
- Noting each main point, list important supporting information in point form as an informal outline that you can memorize.
- Pick out a *key word* in each point, and create a *catchphrase* to help you remember the key words.

Note: If you have spelling problems, make up a list of words you might have to spell in writing your answers.

An Illustration of Step 2

After identifying the likely questions on the exam, Mark made up an outline answer for each of the questions. For example, here is the outline answer that he made up for the first question:

Common sources of stress:

1. (Pressure) (internal and external)
2. (Anxiety) (sign of internal conflict)
3. (Frustration) (can't reach desired goal)
4. (Conflict) (three types of approach-avoidance)

   P A F C (People are funny creatures.)

Activity

Complete the following explanation of Mark's preparation for the essay question.

First, Mark wrote down the heading and then numbered the sources of stress under it. Also, in parentheses beside each point he added _____ _____. Then he circled the four key words, and he wrote down the first _____ of each word underneath his outline. Mark then used the first letter in each key word to make up a catchphrase that he could easily remember. Finally, he _____ himself over and over until he could recall all four of the sources of stress for which the first letters stood. He also made sure that he recalled the supporting material that went with each idea.

Step 3: Write Timed Responses to Your Questions

Practise writing under exam conditions. Doing this will show you exactly how much information you can physically place on a page in the amount of time given. If you know that an exam will have shorter essay responses worth fewer marks as well as one high-value longer question, then work out reasonable time schemes for your practice.

To help you write a better response, and to ensure that you receive *some* marks for any question, even if you do not complete your answer, always write a point-form outline first. Label it clearly as "Outline." Use your key words and catchphrases and get your main points down as quickly as possible. Allow yourself five minutes to do this for each question you try.

Give yourself revising time for each question after you have written your answers.

An Illustration of Step 3

If the exam asks you to write three essays of equal mark value in two hours (120 minutes), divide your time this way:

- Fifteen minutes' outlining time
- Thirty minutes for each essay answer, or ninety minutes
- Fifteen minutes' revising time

TECHNIQUES FOR WRITING SUCCESSFUL EXAMS

When you receive your exam, resist any temptation to begin writing answers immediately. Instead, follow the two stages of preparing to write and actually writing your response, and you will be rewarded with better marks.

STAGE 1: PREPARING YOURSELF TO WRITE

1 Read the exam instructions. Check that the format is what you were expecting.

2 Read through all the questions. Answers will come to mind immediately for some questions. In a separate exam book or piece of paper, write down key words, lists, and catchphrases now, when they're fresh in your mind. Otherwise, these ideas may be blocked or unavailable when the time comes to deal with the later questions. This strategy reduces panic and anxiety that disrupt thinking.

3 Note the *direction words* (*compare, illustrate, list,* and so on) for each question. Be sure to write the kind of answer that each question requires. If a question says "illustrate," do not "compare." The list that follows will help clarify the distinctions among various direction words.

4 Budget your time. Write in the margin the number of minutes you should spend for each essay. For example, if you have three essays worth an equal number of marks and a one-hour time limit, figure twenty minutes for each one. Make sure you are not left with only a couple of minutes to do a high mark-value essay.

5 Start with the easiest question. Getting a good answer down on paper will help build up your confidence and momentum. Number your answers plainly so your instructor knows what question you are answering first.

Direction Words Found in Essay Examination Questions

Term	*Meaning*
Compare	Show similarities between things.
Contrast	Show differences between things.
Criticize	Give the positive and negative points of a subject as well as evidence for these positions.
Define	Give the formal meaning of a term as it is used in the subject area.
Describe	Tell in detail about something; give a detailed explanation.
Diagram	Make a drawing and label it.
Discuss	Give details and, if relevant, the positive and negative points of a subject as well as evidence for your positions.
Enumerate	List points and number them 1, 2, 3, etc.
Evaluate	Give the positive and negative points of a subject as well as your judgment about which outweighs the other and why.
Illustrate	Explain by giving examples.
Interpret	Explain the meaning of something.
Justify	Give reasons for something.

Direction Words Found in Essay Examination Questions *(cont'd)*

Term	*Meaning*
List	Give a series of points and number them 1, 2, 3, etc.
Outline	Give the main points and important secondary points. Put main points at the margin and indent secondary points under the main points. Relationships may also be described with logical symbols, as follows:

I. _____

    A. _____

    B. _____

II. _____

Prove	Show to be true by giving facts or reasons.
Relate	Show connections among things.
State	Give the main points.
Summarize	Give a condensed account of the main points.
Trace	Describe the development or history of a subject.

Activity

Complete the short matching quiz below. It will help you review the meanings of some of the direction words listed on the opposite page.

1. List _____

2. Contrast _____

3. Define _____

4. Summarize _____

5. Describe _____

a. Tell in detail about something.

b. Give a series of points and number them 1, 2, 3, and so on.

c. Give a condensed account of the main points.

d. Show the difference between two things.

e. Give the normal meaning of a term.

STAGE 2: WRITING EFFECTIVE ESSAY RESPONSES

Writing a solid essay answer involves two steps: outlining and writing.

1 Outline Your Answer

Using any notes you made during step 2 of your preparation, write a point form outline for your essay answer. In a separate exam book or sheet of paper, number your main points and decide on their order, labelling your outline clearly. The five minutes spent outlining are invaluable: instructors value the clarity of an organized answer; additionally, if you do not complete your essay, you may receive marks for outline items. Follow the direction words, and check your outline to see that you have adapted your facts to the form of response required.

If there is a question on the exam similar to questions you anticipated and outlined at home, quickly write down the catchphrase that calls back the content of the outline. Below the catchphrase, write the key words represented by each letter in the catchphrase. The key words, in turn, will remind you of the concepts they represent. If you have prepared properly, this step will take only a minute or so, and you will have the guide you need to write a focused, supported, and organized answer.

An Illustration

Mark immediately wrote down his catchphrase, "People are funny creatures." He next jotted down the first letters in his catchphrase and then the key words that went with each letter. He filled in several key details and was ready to write his essay answer. Here is his brief outline:

People are funny creatures.

P   Pressure (internal and external)
A   Anxiety (internal conflict)
F   Frustration (prevented from reaching goal)
C   Conflict (approach-avoidance)

2 Write a Clear, Well-Organized Essay

If you have followed the steps to this point, you have done all the preliminary work needed to write an effective essay. Do not wreck your chances of getting a good mark by writing carelessly. Keep in mind the principles of good writing: unity, support, organization, and clear, error-free sentences.

- First, start your essay with a sentence clearly stating what your answer will be about. Then make sure that everything in your paper relates to your opening statement.
- Second, though you must obviously take time limitations into account, provide as much support as possible for each of your main points.
- Third, use transitions to guide your reader through your answer. Words such as *first, next, then, however,* and *finally* make it easy to follow your thought.
- Last, leave time to proofread your essay for sentence-skills mistakes made while concentrating on writing your answer. Look for words omitted, written incorrectly, or misspelled (if it is possible, bring a dictionary with you); for awkward phrasings or misplaced punctuation marks; and for anything that prevents the reader from understanding your thought. Cross out any mistakes and make your corrections neatly above the errors. If you want to change or add to some point, insert an asterisk at the appropriate spot, put another asterisk at the bottom of the page, and add the corrected or additional material there.

An Illustration

Read Mark's answer, reproduced below, and then do the activity that follows.

There are four common sources of stress in our lives. The first one is

pressure, which can be internal or external. Internal pressure occurs when a

person tries to live up to his or her own goals and standards. This kind of

pressure can help (when a person strives to be a better musician, for instance)

or hurt (as when someone tries to reach impossible standards of beauty).

External pressure occurs when people must compete, deal with rapid change,

or cope with outside demands. Another source of stress is anxiety. People who

are ~~anxous~~ anxious *often don't know why they feel this way. Some psychologists think*

anxiety comes from some internal conflict; for example, feeling angry and trying hard

to repress this ~~angry feeling~~ anger. A third source of stress is frustration, which

occurs when people are prevented from reaching goals or obtaining certain

needs. For example, a woman may do poorly on an important *exam because she has a*

bad cold. She feels angry and frustrated because she could not reach her goal

of an A or B grade. The most common source of stress is conflict. Conflict

results when a person is faced with two incompatible ~~goals~~ desires*. The person may*

want both goals (a demanding career and motherhood, for instance). This is

called approach/approach. Or a person may want to avoid both choices

(avoidance/avoidance). Or a person may be both attracted to and repelled by a

desire (as a woman who *wants to marry a gambler). This is approach/avoidance.*

Activity 1

Read the following comments on Mark's essay and fill in the missing word or words for each.

1. Mark begins with a sentence that clearly states what his paper _____

    _____. Always begin with such a clear statement.

2.   Notice the _____ that Mark made when writing and proof-reading his paper. He neatly crossed out incorrectly written or unwanted words, and he used insertion signs (^) to add omitted words.

3.   The four signal words that Mark used to guide his readers, and

    himself, through the main points of his answer are _____,

    _____, _____, and _____.

Activity 2

1. Make up five questions you might be expected to answer on an essay exam in a social or physical science course (sociology, psychology, biology, or other).

2. Then make up for each of the five questions an outline answer comparable to the one on anxiety.

3. Finally, write a full essay answer, in complete sentences, for one of the questions. Your outline will serve as your guide.

    Be sure to begin your essay with a statement that makes clear the direction of your answer. An example might be "The six major kinds of defence mechanisms are defined and illustrated below." If you are explaining in detail the different causes of, reasons for, or characteristics of something, you may want to develop each point in a separate paragraph. For example, if you were answering a question in sociology about the primary functions of the family unit, you could, after starting with the statement "There are three primary functions of the family unit," go on to develop and describe each function in a separate paragraph.

    You will turn in the essay answer to your English instructor, who will evaluate it using the standards for effective writing applied to your other written assignments.

Writing a Summary

In many of your courses, your instructors may ask you to write summaries. You may summarize

- An article from a magazine or a journal specific to your subject
- A TV show
- A film's storyline
- A lengthy technical procedure
- A book
- A record of stages in a business's development, or any one of a number of longer printed items

In a *summary* (or *précis* or *abstract*), you reduce material in an original work to its main points and key supporting details.

A summary is *not* an outline. A summary is written in sentence and paragraph form and does not use symbols such as *I, A, 1, 2* to indicate the relations among parts of the original material.

A summary is *not* a form of essay. A summary does not express and support *your* point of view; instead, it reproduces in the most concise form the viewpoint and main ideas of the material summarized. *You* are not present or visible in a summary; all summaries are written in the third person.

A summary is a *concentrated* form of an original text. Summaries do not quote frequently from originals, nor do they "lift" or plagiarize material from the original text. To express the condensed or concentrated main ideas in an original work, you must *paraphrase* or rework those ideas in your own words.

A summary may be a word, a phrase, several sentences, or one or more paragraphs in length. The length of the summary you prepare will depend on your instructor's expectations and the length of the original work. Most often, you will be asked to write a summary of one or more paragraphs.

Writing a summary brings together reading, study, and writing skills. To condense the original, you must preview, read, evaluate, organize, and outline the assigned material. Summarizing, then, can be a real aid to understanding; you must "get inside" the material and realize fully what is being said before you can reduce its meaning to a few words.

This chapter will demonstrate the steps involved in writing a summary. Summarizing is a skill; it does not "come naturally" to most people, but if you learn (1) to read (or watch or listen to) the original carefully, (2) to analyze and outline its main ideas, and (3) to paraphrase those main ideas in your own words, you will be prepared to face most summarizing challenges.

HOW TO SUMMARIZE

Summarizing *takes time.* Be prepared to set aside time to read shorter printed pieces several times, or to "rescan" a book you have already read, to tape and review a TV show, to watch a movie a few times, or to download and print out a website whose content you may be summarizing.

The end product may be brief, but a summary is *concentrated;* every word and phrase you write must restate essential ideas of the original. So you must know the content of the original thoroughly to restate it.

STAGE 1: PREVIEWING AND REVIEWING THE SOURCE MATERIAL

Summarizing an Article or Shorter Printed Piece

1 If you are summarizing an article or a shorter printed piece on any subject, begin by photocopying it (or downloading and printing it out, if needed) so that you can highlight important points, strike through repetitive phrases or examples, and note the main ideas right on the original.

2 Take a few minutes to preview the work. You can preview an article in a magazine or journal by taking a quick look at the following:

   a *Title.* The title often summarizes what the article is about. Think about the title and how it may condense the meaning of an article. Or a title may be eye-catching but so vague that it may not be very helpful. In *Maclean's* magazine, an article in the January 1997 issue is titled "A Plastic Revolution." The title could refer to anything from surgery to toy manufacturing.

   b *Subtitle.* A subtitle, if given, is a short summary appearing under or next to the title. In the *Maclean's* article, the subtitle is "Canadian shoppers put the 'smart card' on trial." Now you know that a new sort of bank card is the type of "plastic" the article will discuss. In short, the subtitle, the caption, or any other words in large print under or next to the title often provide a quick insight into the meaning of an article.

   c *First and last several paragraphs.* In the first paragraphs, the author may introduce the subject and state the purpose of the article. In the last several paragraphs, the writer may present conclusions or a summary. Opening and closing paragraphs are positions of *maximum attention* for readers as they seek information. Journalists and writers for special-interest journals and many website-creators know this effect and structure their content accordingly. Previews or summaries can give you a quick overview of what the entire article is about.

   d *Headings, subheadings, special typography, and graphics.* Note any headings or subheadings that appear in the article. They often provide clues to the article's main points and give an immediate sense of what each section is about. Look carefully at any pictures, charts, or diagrams that accompany the article. Page space in a magazine or journal is limited, and such visual aids are generally used to illustrate important points in the article. Note any words or phrases set off in *italic type* or **boldface print;** note also bulleted lists or boxed sections of material: such ideas have probably been emphasized because they are important points in the article. The *Maclean's* article mentioned above contains a coloured chart depicting the rise in debit card transactions since 1993, underlining the rapid shift from using cash to cards for most consumers.

3 *Read the article once through:* Read the article for a general sense of its meaning the first time through. Do not slow down or turn back and reread.

4 *Read the article a second time to note its main ideas:* Check or otherwise mark main points and key supporting details. Pay special attention to all the items noted in the preview. Also, look for definitions, examples, and enumerations (lists of items), as these often indicate key ideas. Identify important points by turning any headings into questions and reading to find the answers to the questions.

5 *Reread your checked or highlighted sections:* Go back and reread more carefully the areas you have identified as most important. Also, focus on other key points you may have missed in your first reading.

Summarizing a Book, Film, or TV Show

1 If you are assigned a longer piece of material such as a book or feature film, you must read or watch the material once before beginning the summarizing process. A single episode of a TV series or a "free-standing" one- or two-hour TV program should be taped as you are watching it, so that you can review the material to note its main ideas.

2 To begin summarizing a book, movie, or TV show, first review the aspect of that material that your course touches or focuses on. Try to readjust your own focus on the material to "see" course-related ideas, images, dialogue, or characters. Watch, read, or reread with a notepad in hand, so that you can jot down ideas as they come to you.

3 A movie or TV show is easy to watch repeatedly, and to rewind and review as needed. If you are summarizing an entire book, you may not have time to reread the entire book. To summarize a book, "narrow your focus." First, review your course material's focus: the ideas you will look for in your review of the book will be either those set out by your instructor or those related to your course material. Scan a book you have already read for the author's expressions of ideas related to your assignment.

4 If you are summarizing a book, modify the suggestions for previewing an article, and look at the following for cues to the book's main ideas:

   a *Title.* The title is often the shortest possible summary of what a book is about. Think about the title and how it may summarize the whole book.

   b *Table of contents.* The contents will tell you the number of chapters in the book and the subject of each chapter. Use the contents to get a general sense of how the book is organized. You should also note the number of pages in each chapter. If thirty pages are devoted to one episode or idea and an average of fifteen pages to other episodes or ideas, you should probably give more space to the contents of the longer chapter in your summary.

   c *Preface.* Here you will probably find out why the author wrote the book. Also, the preface may summarize the main ideas developed in the book and may describe briefly how the book is organized.

   d *First and last chapters.* In these chapters, the author may preview or review important ideas and themes developed in the book.

   e *Other items.* Note the way the author has used headings and subheadings to organize information in the book. Check the opening and closing paragraphs of each chapter to see if they contain introductions or summaries. Look quickly at charts, diagrams, and pictures in the book, since they are probably there to illustrate key points. Note any special features (index, glossary, appendixes) that may appear at the end of the book.

STAGE 2: LISTING, EDITING, AND DRAFTING YOUR SUMMARY

1 For a summary of any type of material, your first step is to list all the main ideas. Number these ideas, and leave space after each numbered item to fill in the supporting details or material for each main idea. Make your list in numbered point form, using *a, b,* and so on to list supporting details under each main idea.

2 Leave some time, if possible, before reviewing and editing your list. Check your list of ideas and support against your original material. Look for omissions, for possible repetition in either the original or in your list, as well as for duplications of ideas in examples, quotations, or explanations. A piece of supporting information may be repeated for emphasis or may be duplicated in dialogue.

3 Prepare the first draft of your summary, keeping these points in mind:

   a Identify at the start of the summary the title and author of the work. Include in parentheses the date of publication. For example, "In 'A Plastic Revolution' (*Maclean's*, January 22, 1997), Tom Fennell writes . . ."

   b Write your drafts in the third person. You are writing a reduction of the original work, with no commentary or views of your own.

   c Express the main points and key supporting details in your own words. Your task is to paraphrase the original concisely; do not imitate the style of the original.

   d Quote from the material only to illustrate key points. Also, limit your quotations. A one-paragraph summary should not contain more than one or two quoted sentences.

e Preserve the balance and proportion of the original work. If the original devoted 70 per cent of its space to one idea and only 30 per cent to another, your summary should reflect that emphasis.

f Revise the first draft, paying attention to the principles of effective writing *(unity, support, coherence, and clear, error-free sentences)* explained in Part 1.

4 Ideally, first drafts are a bit long. Better to include a few too many details than to omit necessary information. Prepare your second draft by following these tips:

a Check again for the required word count or length to aim for. Use the word count on your word-processing software to check your document, or simply count each word, including *a* and *the*.

b Review your summary to reduce *wordy phrases,* such as "because of the fact that . . ." (Why not simply "because"?), "in order to . . ." (Try simply "to.").

c Note each major idea and its support as it appears on your revised list, and note each by number on your draft. See if it can be rephrased more concisely.

d Write a final draft of your summary.

WRITING A SUMMARY

Julia Wong was asked to find and summarize an article from a general-interest Canadian magazine. As a business student, she was to find an article relating to her program. She was interested in consumer spending and retail sales, and she occasionally read *Maclean's,* so she started by checking current issues at the library and by visiting *Maclean's* website.

Her assignment asked students to choose an article of a length that could be accurately restated and summarized in one paragraph of roughly 300 words. Here is the full text of the article she decided to summarize:

A Plastic Revolution
Canadian Shoppers Put the "Smart Card" on Trial

As Drew Pullman lined up with Christmas shoppers at Mrs. B's Gift House in downtown Guelph, Ont., he had to wait as customers fumbled for cash or signed off credit-card slips. When he finally reached the till, Peter Amy, the owner of the shop, was relieved when Pullman pulled out a shiny cash card, a so-called smart card that its sponsoring banks say will revolutionize how people pay for things—from a child's weekly allowance to a new suit. With the smart card, now being tested in selected markets, consumers will use specially equipped telephones to transfer money from their bank accounts to the cash cards. When paying, consumers slide the card into small countertop terminals and the money is instantly deducted. Parents may even move funds from their own cards to their children's for use in school vending machines or to board a bus. The major banks, which are introducing the cards in Guelph and Kingston, Ont., also hope the cards will advance the use of computerized banking. In the meantime, Pullman is enjoying his cyber-cash. "I love it," he said as he used a cash card again last week at Mrs. B's. "It's so convenient."

Using computer chip technology, the new instruments resemble ordinary credit cards or the debit cards that draw money from a bank account like a cheque. But that is where the similarity ends. They are actually microcomputers with a memory that allows them to store and retrieve information on purchases and even store data such as frequent flyer miles awarded for the purchase of airline tickets. The new plastic is a key part of the banks' aggressive move into electronic commerce. The country's major financial institutions, most recently Bank of Montreal, through its mbanx program, have introduced Internet banking. Cash cards take cyber-commerce one step further by giving customers instant access to their money and allowing them to pay for products over the Internet. And if Canadians use cash cards as enthusiastically as they have used credit and debit cards, paper money will become almost obsolete, bankers contend, and banks will be a place where people go for investment advice, and not to get cash. "Canadians are taking to new technology," said Donald Gregg, general manager of Stored Value Cards for the CIBC. "Smart cards are taking off like wildfire." 2

Unlike debit cards, which were introduced in 1992 and are now widely used in Canada, cash cards do not require consumers to enter personal identification numbers. Instead, once the money is downloaded, the card becomes the equivalent of cash. To use it, the customer merely slides it into a slot in a small unit and the virtual cash moves from the card to the retailer's merchant card in a chip-to-chip transfer. 3

When placed in a tracker, a thin piece of equipment carried in a wallet and not much bigger than the card itself, the card becomes a computer. Balances can be called up and previous purchases reviewed. In future, even different currencies can be added. For security, the tracker can also lock the card so that it cannot be used without entering a specific code. A second device about the size of a hand-held calculator transfers the cash between cards. 4

The banks plan to start distributing the cards nationally in 1998. Eventually, Gregg said, medical records or a driver's licence could be carried on one card and a person's financial records, from cash in a bank account to mutual fund records, would be stored on another. They could then be downloaded to computers. "The cards will be incredibly powerful," said Gregg. "People will carry them the way they now carry laptop computers." 5

Before that, merchants in Guelph and Kingston look to the cards to simplify their operations. Among them is James Brown, owner of Brown's Fine Foods in Kingston. His company now supplies vending machines to 12 schools in the city. At the end of each school day, Brown's employees empty the machines and count hundreds of coins. As part of the smart card's introduction in Kingston, the Bank of Montreal, Toronto-Dominion Bank, and Canada Trust are encouraging students to use the new device in vending machines. If they do, Brown will be able simply to download the electronic transfers to his bank and have an immediate record of the day's receipts. Said Brown: "We hope to quit lugging cash all over town." 6

So far, the cyber-cash has met with acceptance in Guelph, where the cards are being introduced by the CIBC and the Royal Bank of Canada. But some consumers fear the banks will use the cards as an excuse to levy more service fees. 7

Said Michelle Cartier, a saleswoman at a Japan Camera store: "A lot of my friends think the banks will just use them to make more money off of them."

Bank spokesmen, however, claim cash cards could actually save money for consumers who now use debit cards. Under the current fee system, most banks charge about 40 cents every time a customer uses a debit card. But with the smart cards, clients are charged the same rate to download money onto their plastic as they are each time they withdraw cash from a bank machine. In subsequent transactions, the card is used only between retailers and their customers or in person-to-person transactions, and, unlike debit cards, the present programs involve no bank fees. **8**

The new cards could cut costs for the banks. Tom Delaney, president of the Toronto-based Tom Delaney Financial Group and a spokesman for the Consumers' Association of Canada, said that banks want to cut the number of branches they operate and electronic banking will help them to do so. "They are determined to get rid of branch banking," said Delaney. "That is their number 1 priority." And the new smart cards are their latest weapon. **9**

PREVIEWING AND REVIEWING THE ARTICLE

Julia looked at the article's title for clues to its overall meaning. "A Plastic Revolution" seemed too general to suggest much except the general thrust of the article—*revolution* meant change, and not a particular aspect of that change. She looked at the subtitle: "Canadian Shoppers Put the 'Smart Card' on Trial." Now Julia had a better sense of the piece's content: *trial* suggested testing the positive and negative possibilities of the "smart card."

She photocopied the article and checked the *Maclean's* index for more hints about the article's meaning. The index stated, "As banks test-market a new form of plastic cash, consumers fear higher service fees." Initially she thought the article was in favour of the smart cards, so she realized she needed to preview the article's important parts for evidence of opposing views of the new bank card.

Focusing on opening and closing paragraphs of the article, Julia looked for its most important ideas. Next, she noted on her photocopy what she thought were the main ideas in these paragraphs. Now she found it easier to pick out the points she would use in her summary. She made point-form notes of what she found:

Paragraph 1
- Smart card is new type of bank card
- Being tested now in some areas
- Uses special phones to move money from acct's to card
- Card goes into terminal and money is withdrawn
- Kids can have own cards with money transferred by parents
- Banks hope cards will change banking habits
- Person in example likes card—it's convenient

Last Paragraph
- Smart cards cut costs for banks
- Banks don't want so many branches
- Smart cards are "weapon" for banks to use to close branches

The article had no subheadings or boldface phrases inside it, so she looked at the chart on the page near the end of the piece to see if its information might be useful. The graph simply displayed rapid increases in the use of debit cards; it did not tell anything about "smart cards."

Julia read the article once quickly, to get a sense of its content, and to be sure there were enough interesting ideas to provide her with a good summary. She also wanted to be sure that the article could be summarized in one well-detailed paragraph. The original was just under 1000 words long, so she felt she could reduce it to roughly one-third of its original length.

Now it was time to reread the article carefully, and to highlight the main points and support in the body of the article. Julia found that highlighting helped her to distinguish the solid points of information from the repeated material in quotations. She also decided that some details included in the examples perhaps didn't belong in a summary. Since Julia had already noted the ideas she found in the first and last paragraphs, she decided to go back to the highlighted sections, and note with a check mark the points of information she had found in the body of the article. As she did so, she found some ideas she had missed in her rereading and highlighting.

LISTING THE MAIN IDEAS AND WRITING A FIRST DRAFT

Julia could now begin her list of the article's main points and supporting details. Here's what she came up with:

Paragraph 1

- Smart card is new type of bank card
- Being tested now in some areas
- Uses special phones to move money from acct's to card
- Card goes into terminal and money is withdrawn
- Kids can have own cards with money transferred by parents
- Banks hope cards will change banking habits
- Person in example likes card—it's convenient

Paragraph 2

- Smart cards use computer chip technology
- Smart cards look like credit cards or debit cards
- Debit cards take money out like a cheque
- Smart cards are microcomputers—memory stores and retrieves information
- Memories will hold flyer points
- Cards are part of banks' moving into electronic commerce
- Cash cards let customers get at money instantly & pay for things on the Net
- Canadians like credit & debit cards—money will be obsolete
- Banks will be places for investment advice, not for money transactions

Paragraph 3

- Cash cards don't need PIN numbers
- Money is downloaded & the card is the same as cash
- Card is put in a slot in a machine and cash moves to retailer's merchant card
- Money moves by chip-transfer of information

Paragraph 4

- Tracker machine (card-size) turns into computer with card in it
- Can get balances and purchase records
- Future—other currencies can be added
- Tracker can lock card so a code is needed to use it
- Other new device moves cash between cards

Paragraph 5

- Banks will give out cards in 1998
- Future—medical records & driver's licence on one card
- All financial records on another card
- Info could be downloaded onto computers
- Cards will be powerful, carried like laptops now

Paragraph 6

- Cards simplify operations for merchants
- Example—vending machines & coins vs. card-transfers
- Banks want students to use cards for school vending machines

Paragraph 7

- Example—Guelph—cards are accepted by people
- Some feel banks will charge more for services with new cards
- ?—example

Paragraph 8

- Banks say new cards will let people using debit cards save money
- Each debit transaction costs $
- Smart card lets people download a sum of money to cover several charges
- Once money is downloaded, transactions are between merchant & customer or person to person—no fees yet

Paragraph 9

- Smart cards cut costs for banks
- Banks don't want so many branches
- Smart cards are "weapon" for banks to use to close branches

After making her list, Julia felt she might have too many points for a 300-word summary. She realized also that she should probably go back and try to identify the main points and the support for those points. She decided to leave a day before doing this and attack the task of analyzing her list of information the next day, when she had a clear head.

The next day, she returned to her list, and kept the original article beside it as she worked. She did three things: She marked main ideas with an *M,* and looked for points she had listed that repeated or didn't add anything to those points. She struck out the repetitions and the points she felt weren't necessary. Finally, she marked supporting details with an *S.*

Here is her revised list:

Paragraph 1

- Smart card is new type of bank card *M*
- Being tested now in some areas *M*
- Uses special phones to move money from acct's to card *S*
- Card goes into terminal and money is withdrawn *S*
- Kids can have own cards with money transferred by parents *?*
- Banks hope cards will change banking habits *S*
- ~~Person in example likes card~~—it's convenient

Paragraph 2

- Smart cards use computer chip technology *S*
- Smart cards look like credit cards or debit cards *S*
- ~~Debit cards take money out like a cheque~~
- Smart cards are microcomputers—memory stores and retrieves information *M*
- ~~Memories will hold flyer points~~
- Cards are part of banks' moving into electronic commerce *M*
- Cash cards let customers get money instantly & pay for things on the Net *S*
- ~~Canadians like credit & debit cards~~—money will be obsolete *S*
- Banks will be places for investment advice, not for money transactions *?*

Paragraph 3

- Cash cards don't need PIN numbers *S*
- Money is downloaded & the card is the same as cash *S*
- Card goes in a slot in a machine & cash moves to retailer's merchant card *S*
- Money moves by chip-transfer of information *M*

Paragraph 4

- Tracker machine (card-size) turns into computer with card in it *M*
- Can get balances and purchase records *S*
- ~~Future—other currencies can be added~~
- Tracker can lock card so a code is needed to use it *S*
- ~~Other new device moves cash between cards~~

Paragraph 5

- Banks will give out cards in 1998 *M?*
- Future—medical records & driver's licence on one card *S*
- All financial records on another card *S*
- Info could be downloaded onto computers *S*
- Cards will be powerful, carried like laptops now *M*

Paragraph 6

- Cards simplify operations for merchants *M*
- Example—vending machines & coins vs. card-transfers *S*
- ~~Banks want students to use cards for school vending machines~~

Paragraph 7

- ~~Example—Guelph—cards are accepted by people~~
- Some feel banks will charge more for services with new cards *M*
- ~~?—example~~

Paragraph 8

- Banks say new cards will let people using debit cards save money *M*
- ~~Each debit transaction costs $~~
- Smart card lets people download money to cover several charges *S*
- Once money is downloaded, transactions are between merchant & customer or person to person—no fees yet *S*

Paragraph 9

- Smart cards cut costs for banks *M*
- Banks don't want so many branches *S*
- Smart cards are "weapon" for banks to use to close branches *S*

Now, Julia's list looked more like ideas she could turn into a summary of reasonable size. Her instructor had mentioned that naming specific individuals or their situations was not always necessary in summaries, so she felt justified in leaving most of those out. She wrote her first draft, which follows:

Note: Write summaries in the present tense. You are restating and condensing someone else's material, and such information is seen as occurring in the "written present time," or for the first time for a reader of your summary.

Tom Fennell's article "A Plastic Revolution" (*Maclean's*, January 22, 1997) covers the introduction of a new type of bank card, the "smart card," tested in the fall of 1997 in Kingston and Guelph, Ontario. This new card makes use of special phones to withdraw money from a consumer's bank account and deposit that money into a merchant's account. People like the card, and banks hope it will change banking habits. The new cards look just like credit cards or debit cards, and Canadians use debit cards more every year. Using computer chip technology, and working like microcomputers, the card transfers funds from the bank to the merchant's own banking card. The card has a memory that can store and retrieve information of all kinds. As banks move into "cyber-banking," customers can access their money instantly and make purchases on the Internet. Money may become obsolete, and banks will be used for investment consulting only, not for deposits and withdrawals. Transactions will be microchip-to-microchip actions, and the "smart card" does not need a PIN, since, once it has downloaded the money, it is the same as cash. Retailers have small units that move the cash from the customer's bank to the retailer. A "tracker," only slightly bigger than the card, gives the card memory and holds spending records, and the tracker is secure because of a personal code. Banks feel the new cards, available in 1998, will be very powerful and as common as laptops are now. They will hold all people's financial records. They simplify merchants' exchange of money in Kingston now and provide records as well. Test customers in Guelph like the card, but some feel banks will simply charge more fees for their use. Banks say the "smart card" is cheaper than the debit card, since it allows consumers to make one withdrawal for a number of purchases when they download funds. Other transactions, between individuals or between merchant and consumer, do not involve fees right now. Tom Delaney, who speaks for the Consumers' Association of Canada, says that banks are the ones who will benefit from the "smart card," though. Banks can close branches with electronic banking, and this card is their "latest weapon."

Julia was pleased with her first draft because she felt her list-making had helped her not to miss any important ideas in the article. However, she wasn't sure of how long her paragraph was. The word-count tool on her processor showed 368 words. She was 20 per cent higher than her assignment's goal, so she used three methods to revise and "tighten" her next draft. She

1 Looked for and edited wordy phrases

2 Looked for and edited repetition of ideas

3 Looked for ways of condensing related ideas into a single sentence or phrase

Here is her rough work on that first draft. Julia crossed out wordy phrases and marked them with a **W.** She then looked for repetitions and crossed those out, adding an **R** after her editing. Finally, she reminded herself to condense some ideas that could belong together by underlining them and marking them with a **C.**

Tom Fennell's article "A Plastic Revolution" (*Maclean's*, January 22, 1997) ~~covers the introduction of a new type of~~ **W** bank card, the "smart card," tested in the fall of 1997 in Kingston and Guelph, Ontario. ~~This new card~~ **R** ~~makes use of~~ **W** special phones to withdraw money from a consumer's bank account and deposit ~~that money~~ **R** into a merchant's account. People like the card and banks hope it will change banking habits. <u>The new cards look just like credit cards or debit cards, and Canadians use debit cards more every year.</u> **C** Using computer chip technology, and working like microcomputers, the card transfers funds from the bank to the merchant's own banking card. ~~The card has a memory~~ **W** that can store and retrieve information of all kinds. As banks move into "cyber-banking," customers can access their money instantly and make purchases on the Internet. ~~Money may become obsolete, and banks will be used for investment consulting only, not for deposits and withdrawals.~~ **W** Transactions will be microchip-to-microchip actions, and the "smart card" does not need a PIN, since, once it has downloaded the money, it is the same as cash. Retailers have small units that move the cash from the customer's bank to the retailer. A "tracker,"

~~only slightly bigger than the card, gives the card memory and~~ **W, R** holds spending records, and ~~the tracker is secure because of~~ **W** a personal code. Banks feel the new cards, available in 1998, will be very powerful and as common as laptops are now. ~~They will hold all people's financial records.~~ **R** <u>They simplify merchants' exchange of money in Kingston now, and provide records as well.</u> **?, C?** Test customers in Guelph like the card, but some feel banks will simply charge more fees for their use. Banks say the "smart card" is cheaper than the debit card, ~~since it allows consumers to make~~ **W** one withdrawal for a number of purchases when they download funds. Other transactions, between individuals or between merchant and consumer, do not involve fees right now. Tom Delaney, ~~who speaks for the~~ **W** Consumers' Association of Canada, says that banks ~~are the ones who~~ **W** will benefit from the "smart card," though. Banks can close branches with electronic banking, and this card is their "latest weapon."

Surprised by how much "padding" she used in writing her first draft, Julia used the cut and paste operation on her word-processing program to make a work copy of her marked-up draft. She then worked on each sentence individually, rephrasing wordy sections, taking out repetitions, and rewriting sentences where similar ideas could be joined together. After rereading the article a final time, Julia reviewed her list of main ideas and support, and wrote this final draft:

In "A Plastic Revolution" (*Maclean's*, January 22, 1997) Tom Fennell describes the "smart card," tested in the fall of 1997 in Kingston and Guelph, Ontario. Card users withdraw money by using the card and special phones to deposit funds into a merchant's account. People like the card and banks hope it will change banking habits. "Smart cards," which look like the credit or debit cards Canadians use more every year, use computer chip technology to retain memory and retrieve information; they work like microcomputers. Cards transfer funds from the bank to the merchant's own banking card. As banks move into "cyber-banking," customers can access their money instantly and make purchases on the Internet. Banks hope to become locations for investment advice, as cash becomes obsolete. "Smart card" transactions are microchip-to-microchip actions, and "smart card" users do not need a PIN, since, once the money is downloaded, it is the same as cash. Retailers have small machines that move the cash from the customer's bank to the retailer. A "tracker" device, secured by a personal code, holds the card and spending records. Banks feel the new cards, available in 1998, will be very powerful, and as common as laptops are now. Merchants like the ease of the card, and so do test customers in Guelph, but some feel banks will simply charge more fees for their use. Banks say the "smart card" is cheaper than the debit card, as customers pay for one withdrawal for a number of purchases when they download funds. Other transactions, between individuals or between merchant and consumer, do not involve fees right now. Tom Delaney, of the Consumers' Association of Canada, says that banks benefit from the "smart card," though. Banks can close branches with electronic banking, and this card is their "latest weapon."

Julia achieved three things with her final draft: She hit "the magic number" of 300 words; she eliminated her wordy phrases; and after reviewing both her first draft and her earlier revised list of main ideas and supporting details, she spotted ideas that belonged together and could be condensed or fit together into a single sentence.

Note that the process of listing an original printed source's main ideas and support in point form starts you paraphrasing or rewording an author's work. Remember not to plagiarize or use someone else's wording without quotation marks and correct citation in any summary or essay. Additional information on paraphrasing appears in the chapter on writing a research paper.

Activity 1

Write a one- or two-paragraph summary of an article from a Canadian magazine. Your summary should be roughly one-third the length of the original. Follow the sequence of steps in this chapter. The article's content should relate to your main area of study in college. For information on how to find magazine articles and journals about a specific subject, refer to this text's chapter, "Using the Library and the Internet."

Activity 2

Write an essay-length summary of either a website's or a magazine article's coverage of an issue that interests and concerns you. Subjects for your research could range from a current film that interests you to an issue affecting your life, such as tuition increases in Canadian colleges and universities. Remember that the "thesis" of your summary is the main point of the original, not your own view of the material.

Writing a Review or Evaluation Report

Each semester, you will probably be asked by at least one instructor to write a report of some type. You may be asked to review, analyze, and report on some course-related material. A review, an evaluation, or an analysis requires you to examine some piece of material, then evaluate or judge its content according to some appropriate criteria or values. Reports, evaluations, and reviews are sometimes similar in structure, length, and degree of detail required. You should, however, be aware of the differences between reports in general and evaluation reports or analytic reports.

Reports

- Have many different purposes: e.g., to inform, to explain a situation, to detail progress of a procedure or set of actions, to analyze material according to some criteria, to examine a problem and perhaps propose a solution, or to persuade
- May be of differing lengths and levels of formality
- Tend to contain appropriate quantities of objective information
- Have clearly set-out internal structures

Reviews or Evaluations

- Have two basic purposes: *to examine* some subject according to a set of points of judgment or criteria and *to deliver an evaluation* or judgment based clearly on those criteria
- Contain bases for judging their material appropriate to their subject matter and audience's needs
- Follow a specific method of development that includes *a summary, a thesis stating the criteria for evaluating the material, an evaluation based on each of those criteria, and a conclusion*

A review, evaluation, or analysis is one form of report. It follows the formula used for writing an essay. Reviews "re-see" their subject material and present it to be judged or evaluated; they are a form of critical writing. In order for readers to "re-see" the material as they read, a new element must be added to a review essay: a summary of the material reviewed. The body of the review or evaluation supports and "proves" your evaluation or judgment with specific details from the material you review.

In this chapter, you will learn how to structure and write an evaluation of any piece of material. The result of following this process is a report that breaks down a book, movie, scientific or business article, or other material into components or parts that may be judged according to appropriate "measuring criteria," and then delivers a judgment based on how well that material fulfills those requirements.

In other semesters at college, you will write either technical- or business-oriented forms of the report format, whose structures expand on and formalize the basic structure demonstrated for you in this chapter.

PART 1 OF AN EVALUATION REPORT OR REVIEW: A SUMMARY OF THE WORK

Summaries are needed in reviews and reports to supply readers with information about the material to be reviewed or reported on. Consider movie reviews: Few readers will have seen the film reviewed, so they need a summary to follow the writer's judgments in the review. A review of a technical article needs a summary so that readers know the specifics of the material and level of complexity of the original. Even a book review written for an audience familiar with the author or the book needs an opening summary to supply background information and points of focus for readers.

Writing a brief summary for a review or analytic report has one purpose: to inform readers as concisely as possible about the main ideas of the work to be reviewed.

Developing the Introductory Summary

To develop the first part of a report or review, do the following:

1 Identify the author and title of the work and include in parentheses the publisher and publication date. With magazines, give the date of publication of the issue; with films, give the director's name and year of release. Underline or italicize the titles of books, magazines or journals, and movies. Place the title of an article in double quotation marks. (See the example in the previous chapter on the summary on page 304.)

2 Write an informative summary of the material. Condense the content of the work by highlighting its main points and key supporting points. (See pages 295–307 for a complete discussion of summarizing techniques.) Use direct quotations from the work only to illustrate important ideas.

3 Do not discuss in great detail any single aspect of the work and neglect to mention other equally important points. Summarize the material so that the reader gets a general sense of *all* key aspects of the original work. Also, keep the summary objective and factual. Do not include your personal reaction to the work; your responses or evaluations will form the basis of the second part of the paper.

PART 2 OF AN EVALUATION REPORT OR REVIEW: DISCOVERING AND STATING YOUR CRITERIA

The next section of any evaluation or analytic writing is your thesis statement. In evaluating any material, you must first decide on what bases you will judge or evaluate your subject matter. These bases of judgment are your "three main ideas"; they may be any of the following:

- The points of greatest importance in a piece of material related to business or technology or humanities
- The aspects of a book or film that are most significant or most capture your interest
- Points in a general-interest piece of material that most clearly relate to the subject matter of the course for which you are assigned the report or review

You are looking for three bases of judgment, three criteria for evaluating your material in a manner relevant to your course.

As you work through the stage of developing your bases of judgment or criteria, focus on the questions below that relate to your subject area and to your assignment. You are looking for ways to "measure the value" of the material you review and report on. These questions may help you to decide on areas where you will focus your attention in your analysis or review of your material.

Questions to Help Focus an Analysis or Review

1 How is the assigned work related to ideas and concerns discussed in the course? For example, what points made in the course textbook, class discussions, or lectures are treated more fully in the work?

2 How is the work related to problems in society, to current business trends, to current technology? Does it add new information or broaden your knowledge of some aspect of its subject? How?

3 How is the work related to your understanding of life experiences, or of ideas and ways of expressing them? For instance, what emotions did it arouse in you? Did it increase your understanding of an issue or change your perspective? What techniques did the creator of the work use to stimulate your responses?

To evaluate anything, we generally ask ourselves: Is it good? Is it pleasing? Is it useful? Is it right? Does it add to what we already know? The task you face in writing an evaluation is to state *why* you answer "Yes" or "No" to any of these questions. Your answer *why* is your point of view; it is your thesis statement.

Decide on three or more points based on your self-questioning that you can apply to the work you are reviewing. List the points, leaving space beneath them on your paper or your onscreen document page where you may note in point form the aspects of the work that demonstrate how the work does (or does not) meet each of your criteria for evaluating that work.

One Student's Experience with Developing a Review or Analytic Report

Part 1: Discovering Your Message

Jeremy was assigned a book review for a course called Issues in Canadian Society. From the instructor's list of current Canadian novels, he had read Margaret Atwood's *Alias Grace*. He had enjoyed it as a mystery story but wasn't sure how the novel added to his knowledge of material in his course. Jeremy knew he needed to develop criteria or bases for judging the book related to his course content. He summarized the book in his mind: It was about a young woman who had arrived in nineteenth-century Toronto and who might or might not have murdered two people. The story covered her memories of her early life in Ireland and Toronto, of her imprisonment and her life in Kingston, and of the events that led to her apparent crime.

After looking at his class notes and at the headings on his course outline, he found areas of Canadian society covered by his course that related to large parts of *Alias Grace*. He realized he had learned a lot about life in Ontario 150 years ago while reading the story of Grace's life. Jeremy also realized that Atwood's novel had a lot of information about two sections of his course: women's place in Canadian society, and our justice and correctional systems.

He tried asking himself questions about what the book told him about these two subjects. After finding many details in *Alias Grace* that fell under these two headings, he decided he could start an outline for a review of the novel as a source of information about two concerns in Canadian society. He had his criteria for evaluating his material: He would judge the novel by how informative it was for him in two areas that were part of his course.

Here is Jeremy's first draft of an opening paragraph for his review of *Alias Grace*:

> *Alias Grace,* by Margaret Atwood (New York: Doubleday, 1996), seems like an odd place to look for information about Canadian society. It's a gripping story about a young woman who is accused of brutally murdering her employer and her supposed friend, who is her employer's housekeeper and mistress. But large parts of the story tell readers many things about life in southern Ontario in the 1800s. Grace Marks' life as an immigrant woman in early Toronto is a grim picture—young women had nearly no social or economic choices open to them. The main event in the novel, the murders of Thomas Kinnear and Nancy Montgomery, forces Grace to face the unpleasant and unfair justice and prison system of the 1800s. *Alias Grace* is interesting both as a mystery with lots of twists and as a piece of Canadian history telling readers about how the last century treated women, and how courts, lawyers, and prisons treated criminals. It's like a case study with a great plot.

Part 2: Returning to Your Purpose and Refocusing Your Message

Jeremy was satisfied that he had stated the two main areas where the novel related to his course on Canadian society, but he felt he might have too many details in his opening that belonged in his summary paragraph. He was also not sure that he had made clear that his two main points were his "measuring standards," or criteria, for judging the book as a useful research source. Because he had written the draft on his computer, he had used the spell checker, and he felt his sentence structure was fine. But he was not sure he had made clear that he was analyzing and evaluating the novel for its usefulness related to his course. He had never tried writing a review or a report before and wanted to leave his paragraph for a day, so he could "see it with fresh eyes."

The next day, Jeremy reviewed the method for writing a review and reread his paragraph, making some notes about what he really wanted to state in his opening. Here is what he came up with:

- The book was an odd choice—it was a murder mystery—but it ended up telling a lot about parts of Canadian life 150 years ago
- Don't need to put so many names and details about the plot and characters in this paragraph—I can do this in the summary—I just need a few facts from the book to make myself clear
- Two things we talked about in class, status of women & justice system, are important parts of the book
- The book was a good source of information about these things, and how they were in the 1800s—I guess I was comparing a novel with a textbook or case study as possible research source
- This novel was interesting, and I learned a lot from it because it held my interest—I didn't realize I was learning so much as I read it
- Some things have changed a lot—women's chances for different jobs, but some things haven't changed as much—deciding if someone is a criminal or mentally ill—it's still hard to decide, and hard to decide how to punish or rehabilitate someone
- Courts seem more fair these days, but prisons, like Kingston, don't seem to have improved quite so much (?)—Karla Homolka in-class case study
- I'm judging *Alias Grace* as a source of information, and it was a good one —make this clear—my "judgment points" are how good the book is as a source in the two areas: women's roles, & justice and punishment

Now he was ready to write a second draft of his opening. Jeremy knew what he wanted to say, and he knew that sometimes finding this out was not a straightforward process. He had written what he thought was a good essay opening with two main ideas, but he knew he had to *modify* this pattern to fulfill the requirements of a review or evaluation. The ideas were there, and he knew his judgment of the novel was positive; he had found good information in it. What he had to do now was return to his paragraph and subtly change its *slant* or *focus* to make it clear that he was writing an evaluation of *Alias Grace* as resource reading for issues specific to his course.

Jeremy opened a new document, and cut and pasted his first draft (page 311) onto that page. Keeping the text's "refocusing" questions (page 310) open beside his computer, he worked on the second draft that appears below:

Alias Grace, by Margaret Atwood (New York: Doubleday, 1996), is an interesting and unusual source of information about Canadian society. This gripping story tells of a young woman who is accused of two brutal murders, but how does it add to a student's knowledge of two specific aspects of Canadian life? First, *Alias Grace* shows readers many realistic and detailed pictures of life in southern Ontario in the 1800s. The book describes Grace Marks' life as an immigrant woman in early Toronto, and Atwood is grimly accurate as she shows the limited social or economic choices open to women then. As events in the novel unfold, Grace faces courts, lawyers, a madhouse, and prisons: parts of the justice system of the 1800s. A textbook or history book could give the same information, but *Alias Grace* is both a learning experience and a fascinating mystery; reading this novel makes researching the status of women, and the justice system, an intriguing pleasure, not a task.

On what basis is Jeremy evaluating *Alias Grace?*
How has Jeremy changed the *focus* of his opening paragraph?
In which sentences does he give his criteria for judging *Alias Grace?*
Which details of the novel's plot has he eliminated?
In which sentences does Jeremy give his evaluation (his thesis statement)?

PART 3 OF AN EVALUATION REPORT OR REVIEW: WRITING YOUR EVALUATION

The next section of your review or analytic report is your evaluation. You examine the work reviewed according to the criteria you choose. Each paragraph of your evaluation analyzes, or "breaks down," the work into the details that relate to your "measuring points," the ideas that fit under your headings and are relevant to the criteria you use to evaluate the material. Consider the following general guidelines for evaluating material:

- Evaluate the merit of the work: the importance of the points it makes; its accuracy, completeness, and organization; and so on.
- Evaluate how well the work measures up to the standards of other works in its category; does it offer more or less information than others? Is its information recent and timely, considering its subject-matter? Does it offer its information in a style appropriate to your needs?
- Evaluate how well the work fulfills your needs for the assignment or meets the specific expectations with which you approached it.

Although you are stating your views, opinions, and evaluations of material, you should write in the third-person viewpoint in a review. This encourages the reader to focus on the quality of your information. As well, your views and opinions will seem more objective and less personal when written in the third person. Readers welcome "the breathing space," and evaluations of business, scientific, or technical material are seldom, if ever, written in the first person.

After spending some time discovering his criteria for evaluating *Alias Grace,* Jeremy knew how he would structure his evaluation paragraphs. As well, after taking care to focus his essay on judging the novel's value as a source of information about women's lives and the justice system, he knew how to group his judgments and the details that interested him in the novel under these two headings.

Here is his rough outline for the two evaluation paragraphs that follow his summary:

Point 1:   <u>A.G. as an informative picture of women's lives in the mid-1800s</u>

- Immigrant families often fell apart or suffered major problems—affected young women
- Grace's father is irresponsible and a drunk—she has to make money somehow
- Two choices—housemaid or prostitute—she sees examples of both
- Has to learn to be a maid—rich families are demanding—not an easy job
- No office jobs or teaching—Grace is young & has no education
- Many women must have married if they were lucky, or starved—no opportunities then

Point 2:   <u>Courts, lawyers, & prisons in the 1800s—some changes</u>

- Grace's trial—unfair to her as a woman—crowds and curiosity—like some trials now
- Lawyers—biased and seem to be limited, hers was immoral—examples—people were at the mercy of how well their lawyer could impress the crowds at trials—still partly true, but law practice & education are regulated in provinces now
- Prisons—Toronto prison is primitive and unfair—Grace is put in Kingston prison—women don't have separate prison, just part of men's jail—beatings & cruel guards—is what goes on in prisons different now?

Creating a point-form outline helped Jeremy to see that he had lots of "proof" from the novel to back up each point about *Alias Grace* as an informative book. He knew that his evaluation of *Alias Grace* as a useful, well-detailed, and enjoyable source of information on two areas of Canadian society was a reasonable one.

He followed the guideline (page 313), which suggested that he decide how well a work met his needs for his assignment, and felt that the novel had exceeded his expectations in terms of its usefulness as a source of information. Jeremy then found it easy to write a conclusion, which stated his satisfaction at having learned a great deal from an unexpected source, and which recommended the book as a fascinating story as well as a source of information.

Note: Your conclusion in a review or analytic report should sum up the views your evaluation sets out. It should finalize your judgment for your readers, and it may include a recommendation of the work to others, along with reasons for that recommendation.

POINTS TO KEEP IN MIND WHEN WRITING AN EVALUATION REPORT

1 Apply the four basic standards of effective writing (unity, support, coherence, and clear, error-free sentences) when writing the report.

  a Make sure each body paragraph presents and then develops a single criterion. For example, in the model report that follows, a paragraph summarizes the book, and the two paragraphs that follow detail two points under which the student evaluated the book.

  b Support any points of evaluation with specific reasons and details drawn from the work you are reporting on. Statements such as "I agreed with many ideas in this article" or "I found the book very interesting" are meaningless without specific evidence that shows why you feel as you do. Writing such value-judgments in the first person also takes the reader's focus away from specific evidence you do provide. In the model report, the main point or topic sentence of each paragraph is developed by specific supporting evidence.

  c Proofread the paper for grammar, mechanics, punctuation, and word use.

2 Document quotations from all works by placing the page number in parentheses after the quoted material (see the model report). You may use quotations in the summary and reaction parts of the paper, but do not rely on them excessively. Use them only to emphasize key ideas.

A MODEL REPORT

Here is Jeremy's final draft of his review of *Alias Grace*:

INTRODUCTORY ⟶ PARAGRAPH CONTAINING EVALUATING CRITERIA

Alias Grace, by Margaret Atwood (New York: Doubleday, 1996), is an interesting and unusual source of information about Canadian society. This gripping story tells of a young woman who is accused of brutal murders, but how does it add to a student's knowledge of two aspects of Canadian life? First, *Alias Grace* shows readers realistic and detailed pictures of certain parts of life in southern Ontario in the 1800s. The book describes Grace Marks' life as an immigrant woman in early Toronto, and Atwood's details are grimly convincing as she shows the misery of some women's lives and the limited social or economic choices open to women then. As events in the novel unfold, Grace faces courts, lawyers, and prisons, and the cruelty and unfairness of Ontario's justice system. A textbook or history book could give the same information, but *Alias Grace* is both a learning experience and a fascinating mystery; reading this novel makes researching the status of women and the justice system in early Ontario an intriguing pleasure, not a task.

PART 1: SUMMARY ⟶
TOPIC SENTENCE
FOR SUMMARY
PARAGRAPH

Alias Grace covers the life and memories of Grace Marks, a young woman accused of murdering both her employer, Thomas Kinnear, and his mistress and housekeeper, Nancy Montgomery. Margaret Atwood begins the story in 1859, sixteen years after Grace's supposed crime. Living in Kingston and working as the housemaid for the prison governor's wife, Grace remembers her life in pieces, starting with memories sparked by newspaper clippings in the governor's wife's scrapbook. She recalls her first meeting with Dr. Jordan, the doctor studying psychiatry, whom the prison governor has allowed to study Grace. Neither Grace, nor lawyers, nor the doctor knows whether or not she is mad, nor whether or not she is guilty of murder. As her story unrolls through the letters of Dr. Jordan and through Grace's interviews with him, readers find the puzzle that is Grace's personality; she claims not to remember committing the murders. She does remember the poverty of her childhood with her parents in Ireland and the dreadful voyage to Canada. Atwood writes about every situation with careful details, even about how meals were cooked at sea where all the food was boiled together in a bag, so that "you not only got your own dinner, but a taste of what the others were eating as well." (117) Grace finds work as a maid, only to find more misery and harshness; today no one could endure the work or the hours she works. A job in Richmond Hill leads to the tangled situation of the murders, and her terror at being caught and standing trial. She finds nothing but fear and confusion in the justice system, especially as her lawyer prepares her to testify: "I was to leave out the parts I could not remember, and especially to leave out the fact that I could not remember them." (357) Finally, she experiences imprisonment in a madhouse, in the Toronto jail, and in the penitentiary in Kingston, followed by the relative comfort of her life in the governor's house, and the consolation of Dr. Jordan's company: All these scenes come alive with descriptive and historical details. Grace Marks may or may not have been a murderer, but she and the details of her world add up to a complex story of a young woman's attempts to survive and make sense of a harsh life full of contradictory experiences.

PART 2: ⟶
EVALUATION
TOPIC SENTENCE
FOR FIRST
EVALUATION
PARAGRAPH

Alias Grace gives unforgettable pictures of the hard life of a young woman in the middle of the last century. Like many Canadians' ancestors, she is an immigrant from Europe. Coming to Canada, she leaves a life of poverty in Ireland, only to find more of the same in 1840s Toronto. Her mother, who suffered with Grace's abusive father, dies on the rough voyage, leaving the family with Grace's father, who is cruel and irresponsible. Like other young women, Grace must survive alone in a new country. Her choices for work are limited: housemaid or prostitute. She has no education, as women were apparently not offered schooling at that time, and she does not even have the training needed for the demanding job of servant. She manages to support herself by learning and by enduring a number of maid's positions in homes where she is at the mercy of her employers, and her living conditions are miserable: "I was put in the attic, at the very top of the back stairs, and shared a bed with Mary Whitney . . . Our room was not large, and hot in the summer and cold in the winter, as it was next to the roof and without a fireplace or stove . . ." (148) The lack of any place, or any opportunities for young women in Grace's time is frightening for a twentieth-century reader; so is the contrast of her life and lack of choices with everything enjoyed by middle-class young women like the prison governor's wife and daughters. Marriage to a man with money was apparently the only possible way to lead a comfortable life. Even the woman who owns the rooming house where Dr. Jordan lives in Kingston lives almost in poverty, starving herself to save food for his meals. With these pictures of women of many different social levels, Margaret Atwood vividly recreates the misery and the frightening lack of choices or opportunities for women in Canada 150 years ago.

TOPIC SENTENCE FOR SECOND EVALUATION PARAGRAPH → Everyone hopes for justice from the legal system, but Grace Marks' experiences show readers both how unfair and cruel Ontario legal and correctional systems were in her time, and how some parts of the justice system have not changed. Like today, the courts always seem to have too many cases; Grace must sit in the Toronto jail for three months, where she is stared at for her fame as a female murderer. Like some of the trials on television today, Grace's trial is crowded with curious people: " . . . so many people crushed into the courthouse that the floor gave way." (359) Unlike today, witnesses seem to stand up randomly to speak for and against Grace, and she is condemned to hang. Grace's lawyer coaches her in a confusing defence that seems like something from a current TV show. He later turns against her to defend McDermott, the man who shares her murder accusation. As Dr. Jordan interviews the lawyer years later, he seems heartless and immoral, saying that Grace makes men fall in love with her to avoid punishment: "We lawyers are often cast in the role of St. George . . . Find a maiden chained to a rock and about to be devoured by a monster, rescue her, then have her yourself." (378) Grace is a victim of the unfairness of the court system and of public opinion, which both lawyers and judges seem to obey. Just as Karla Homolka was, Grace is sent to Kingston Penitentiary. But unlike today, whippings and cruelty are part of the jail experience: "Before breakfast there was a whipping, out in the courtyard; they do it before breakfast, as if those being whipped have eaten first, they are likely to spew up their food, and that makes a mess, as well as being a waste of good nourishment; and the keepers and guards say they like the exercise at that time of day, as it gives them an appetite." (238) Atwood's picture of the law and of prisons shows some similarities to today, but she also shows how some reforms have reduced the cruelty and immorality of early Canadian law.

CONCLUDING PARAGRAPH → *Alias Grace* is a remarkable piece of Canadian history and a story of the failure of society to find places or opportunities for women. Margaret Atwood has written a fascinating story of a complicated woman and a crime, but she has also written a novel that anyone curious about women's lives or about the law and prisons in the last century would find very informative and rich in interesting details. Grace Marks and her world come alive on every page as the author describes people, places, food, and clothing as they must have been 150 years ago.

Activity 1

Read a magazine or newspaper article about some subject that forms part of one of your courses. Then write an evaluation of the article. Include an introduction, a one-paragraph summary, an evaluation of one or more paragraphs, and a brief conclusion. You may, if you like, quote briefly from the article. Be sure to enclose the words that you take from the article in quotation marks and put the page number in parentheses at the end of the quoted material.

Activity 2

Read a book or watch a film or videotape suggested by your instructor. Then write a report on the piece you choose. Include an introduction, a one-paragraph summary, an evaluation of one or more paragraphs, and a brief conclusion. Also, make sure that each major paragraph in your report develops a single main point. You may quote some sentences from the book, but they should be only a small part of your report. Follow the directions in Activity 1 above when you quote material.

Activity 3

Evaluate a chapter or section of your college's student handbook. As you develop your criteria for evaluation, think about what your own needs are when you use the handbook, and consider why the section of the handbook meets your needs, or why it does not. Include an introduction identifying the section you choose, a one-paragraph summary of its content, an evaluation of one or more paragraphs, and a brief conclusion. Remember to cite your quotations correctly.

Using the Library and the Internet

This chapter provides the basic information you need to use your college library and the Internet with confidence. While using the library is the traditional way of doing such research, a college or home computer with an online service and Internet access now enables you to investigate any topic.

USING THE LIBRARY

Most students know that libraries provide study space, computer facilities, copying machines, and a reading area with recent copies of magazines and newspapers.

But the true core of a library consists of the main desk, computerized catalogues of the library's holdings, book stacks, and periodicals storage area.

For most research topics there are two steps you should take:

- Find books on your topic.
- Find articles on your topic.

LIBRARY CATALOGUE

The library catalogue will be your starting point for almost any research project. The catalogue is a list of all the holdings in the library. It is computerized and is accessed on computer terminals located throughout the library. If your college's library or learning centre is online as part of the college website, it may use a system like BIBCAT, which allows you to look up all sorts of reference materials in different media. Online library search systems allow you to search by *author, title,* or *subject,* or even by keywords, and often you will be able to access and borrow from other libraries' holdings as well.

Finding a Book: Author, Title, and Subject

There are three ways to look up a book. You can look it up according to *author, title,* or *subject.* For example, suppose you wanted to see if the library had the book called *Women in Literacy Speak,* by Betty-Ann Lloyd and two other authors. You could check for the book in any of three ways:

1 Go to the *title* section of the book file and look it up under *W.* Note that you always look up a book under the first "significant" word in the title, excluding the words *A, An,* or *The.*

2 Go to the *author* section of the book file and look it up there under *L.* An author is always listed by last name.

3 If you know the subject that the book deals with—in this case the subject is "literacy"—go to the *subject* section of the book file and look it up under *L.*

Here is the *author* entry in a computerized catalogue for Lloyd et al.'s book *Women in Literacy Speak:*

374.012x   1994   3 copies

WOM   **Lloyd, Betty-Ann.** Ennis, Frances. Atkinson, T. Canadian Congress for Learning Opportunities for Women
Women in literacy speak / — Halifax, Nova Scotia: Fernwood Press, 1994. xi. 178 p: ill. 28 con
Bibliography: p. 190–194
ISBN/ISSN 18568377

1. Literacy-Canada. 2. Adult Education-Canada.
3. Elementary Education-Canada. 4. Women's Studies-Canada/Native races. 5. Volunteer Literacy Programmes-Canada.

Status: In Library Locations: NH, King, Don Mills

Note that in addition to giving you the publisher (Fernwood Press) and year of publication (1994), the entry also gives you the *call number* (374.012x)—where to find the book in the library. If the computerized catalogue card shows that this college library is part of a network of college libraries, it lists the branches or locations where the book is available. If the book is not at your library, you can probably arrange for an interlibrary loan. The heading *Status* indicates whether the book is on the shelf at the locations where it is listed.

When you have examined all the information listed under the *author* classification of your book's catalogue entry, you may be directed to return to the main menu of the library's system. The online menu for the catalogue system will now show you codes for access to two other headings under which you can look up any given book: by *title* or by *subject.*

Using *Subject* Headings to Research a Topic

As long as you know the author or title of a publication, it is convenient to use the *author* or *title* section of the card catalogue. On the other hand, if you are researching a topic, or want to find other sources of information on your topic, or are narrowing the focus of your topic, then the *subject* section is where you should look.

The subject section performs three valuable functions:

1 It will give you a list of books, articles, and other publications on a given topic.

2 It will often provide related topics that might have information on your subject.

3 It will suggest to you more limited topics, helping you narrow your general topic.

There are three points to remember here: (1) Start researching a topic by using the *subject* section of the catalogue system. (2) Look at the titles on the catalogue entry, as well as at any cross-references listed; these sometimes suggest specific directions in which you might develop an essay. (3) Keep trying to narrow your topic.

You want to find a single limited topic, perhaps of personal interest to you, that can be adequately supported, explained, or argued in a relatively short research essay.

Activity

Use your library's catalogue to answer the following questions.

1. What is the title of one book by Austin Clarke?

   _____

2. What are two titles of books by William Gibson?

   _____

3. Who is the author of *The Northern Magus?* (Remember to look up the title under *Northern,* not *The.*)

   _____

4. Who is the author of *The English Patient?* _____

5. List two books and their authors dealing with the subject of Quebec's sovereignty:

   a. _____

   _____

   b. _____

   _____

6. Look up a book titled *Whale Music* or *Shampoo Planet* and give the following information:

   a. Author _____

   b. Publisher _____

c. Date of publication _____

d. Call number _____

e. Subject headings: _____

Electronic Books

College and public library sites increasingly provide access to e-books, whose entire content is offered online. College library websites purchase services like *books 24x7.com,* which gather and provide the full texts of books, journals, and the latest publications from sources in business and technology. You can read the entire document onscreen and print relevant sections. E-books and journals are convenient to use and are up-to-date resources in subject areas where timeliness of information is crucial.

BOOK STACKS

The book stacks are the library shelves where books are arranged according to their call numbers. The call number, as unique to your book as your Social Insurance Number is to you, appears on any catalogue file for this book, as well as on the spine and on the inside of the book itself. Your library may use electronic scanners or readers similar to those in the supermarket to locate and check out books. The call number is in the bar code on the inside cover of your book.

If your library has open stacks (which you may enter), look at the call number on your catalogue entry note, and follow these steps to find a book. If you are looking for *Women in Literacy Speak,* which has the call number 374.012x, look at the signs on the end-walls of the large bookcases that make up the stacks. Locate the number series of your book, starting with the left-hand column and working your way through your number to the final number in the right-hand column. Find the 374 classification shelves, then find 374.0 books, and 374.01 books, until you have found 374.012x, and you have your book. Don't forget to check the area around your book for other material on the same subject.

If your library has closed stacks (those you may not enter), write down the title, author, and call number on a slip of paper at the main desk (or near the card catalogue or computer terminals) and give the slip to a library assistant, who will locate the book and bring it to you.

PERIODICALS AREA

The first step in researching a topic is to check for relevant books; the second step is to locate relevant periodicals. *Periodicals* (from the word *periodic,* which means "at regular periods") are magazines, journals, and newspapers. Periodicals often contain recent information about a given subject, or very specialized information about a subject, that may not be available in a book.

To ensure that your research essay is up to date in its information, as well as timely and interesting to a professor who may have read hundreds of papers on the same subject, check specialized trade, academic, scientific, technological, or professional journals. Students in technology especially will rely on journals for the timeliness of their information. Computerized periodical indexes are updated often, even every week, and allow students in areas of rapid change and development to access information not yet printed in books. Your college or local library may have Canadian and international newspapers on computerized indexes to help with some research. Computerized systems now provide easy access to *subject* listings for periodicals.

There are several files in particular that should help you to find articles related to your topic area.

Readers' Guide to Periodical Literature

The old-fashioned way to do research is to use the familiar green volumes of the *Readers' Guide,* found in just about every library. They list articles published in more than one hundred popular (mainly US) magazines. Articles appear alphabetically under both subject and author. For example, if you wanted to learn the names of articles published on the subject of child abuse within a certain time span, you would look under the heading "Child abuse."

Here is a typical entry from the *Guide:*

```
Subject    Title of   Author
heading    article    of article   Illustrated
   ↓          ↓          ↓          ╱
 Diet                              ↙
Cancer and Diet G. Cowley. il Newsweek
   60–66    N 30 '98                 ↑
     ↑          ↖
Page numbers    Date    Name of magazine
```

Note the sequence in which information is given about the article:

1 The subject heading
2 The title of the article. In some cases, there will be bracketed words [ ] after the title that help make clear just what the article is about
3 The author (if it is a signed article). The author's first name is always abbreviated
4 Whether the article has a bibliography *(bibl)* or is illustrated with pictures *(il).* Other abbreviations sometimes used are shown in the front of the *Readers' Guide*
5 The name of the magazine. A short title like *Newsweek* is not abbreviated, but longer titles are. For example, the magazine *Popular Science* is abbreviated *Pop Sci.* Refer to the list of magazines in the front of the index to identify abbreviations
6 The volume number of the magazine (preceding the colon)
7 The page numbers on which the article appears (after the colon)
8 The date when the article appeared. Dates are abbreviated: for example, *Mr* stands for *March, Ag* for *August, O* for *October.* Other abbreviations are shown in the front of the *Guide*

The *Readers' Guide* is published in monthly supplements, with one large volume covering the entire year. The drawback of the *Readers' Guide* is that it gives you only a list of articles; you must then go to your library's periodicals area to find the magazines that contain those articles. If the magazines are available, you must read and take notes on the articles in the library, or make copies of them. More useful and convenient is the CD-ROM version of the *Readers' Guide*. Using a computer terminal that accesses the compact discs, you can quickly search for articles on a given subject. Simply type in a keyword or phrase; the computer searches for articles on your subject.

Canadian Periodical Index

This is a good place to start research on any topic of general interest in Canada. The *CPI* lists nearly four hundred popular, specialist, and academic publications; it is published monthly and bound annually. Entries are by author and subject, with cross-references to related subjects.

Here is a typical entry from the *Canadian Periodical Index:*

Subject heading   Title of article   Author of article   Name of periodical
↓   ↓   ↓   ↙

Politicians
Brains trust behind Jean Chrétien.   Peter C. Newman. *Maclean's*
    103 no 4 (Ja 22 '90): p. 29.
    ↑   ↖   ↖   ↖

Volume   Issue number   Date   Page number(s)
number   in volume

The same sequence of information appears in the *CPI* as does in the *Readers' Guide*. Computerized and CD-ROM forms of the *CPI* are available in many libraries.

Electronic Research Databases and Online Search Services

Electronic research databases and online search services are generally available through your college's library site. Much specialized or academic research information is not readily accessible online at conventional general access sites but is published electronically for specialized audiences and purchased for student use by colleges and universities.

These resources are available in three forms:

- Controlled websites to which your college has purchased access rights
- Online databases to which your college provides access
- CD-ROM databases owned by your college's library

Your college user ID and password or other student code gives you access to database publications ranging from trade and technological publications to encyclopedias and online collections like *Electric Library Canada* and *Bluebook of Canadian Business*.

Databases or online computer search services include *InfoTrac, Dialog, EBSCOhost,* and *Proquest. ERIC* (Educational Resources Information Centre), *Medline* (National Library of Medicine), and others are technical online services aimed at specialized readers and may be more difficult to understand and use. A general periodical database like *Info Trac* or *First Search* lets you access thousands of magazine articles listed and classified by subject. Often listings have summaries or abstracts, and occasionally the whole article appears. Sitting at a terminal and using *EBSCOhost,* for instance, you will be able to use keywords to quickly search many hundreds of periodicals for articles on your subject. When you find articles that are relevant for your purposes, you can either print them using a library printer (libraries may charge you about ten cents a page), or you can e-mail those articles to your home computer and print them on your own printer. Obviously, if an online resource is available, that is the way you should conduct your research.

Activity 1

At this point in the chapter, you now know the two basic steps in researching a topic in the library. What are the steps?

1. _____

2. _____

Activity 2

1. Look up a recent article on nursing home costs using your library's periodicals file or online research databases and fill in the following information:

   a. Name of the index you used _____

   b. Article title _____

   c. Author (if given) _____

   d. Name of journal, periodical, or database _____

   e. Pages _____   Date _____

2. Look up a recent article on liquid-crystal display screens, using your library's periodicals file or online research databases, and fill in the following information:

   a. Name of the index you used _____

   b. Article title _____

   c. Author (if given) _____

   d. Name of journal, periodical, or database _____

   e. Pages _____   Date _____

Your instructors may expect you to consult one or more electronic research databases to locate more specialized and professional information on a given subject.

USING THE INTERNET

The *Internet* is a giant network that connects computers at tens of thousands of educational, scientific, government, and commercial agencies around the world. The Internet is run by different utility programs called *Telnet, Gopher, e-mail, listservs,* the *World Wide Web,* and *Usenet.* These all provide information of various kinds in somewhat different formats. Within the Internet is the *World Wide Web,* a global information system whose numerous individual websites contain *links* to other sites, forming a kind of web.

To use the Internet, you need a computer with a *modem*—a device that sends or receives electronic data over a telephone line or cable. Modems are built into many computers now. Your college may provide use of online services and e-mail. To use the Internet at home, you need to subscribe to your college's service or to an ISP, an independent service provider, such as Sympatico. The service provider offers you e-mail programs that let you send and receive e-mails and use listservs, and most contain a Usenet or newsgroup utility as well. Your ISP will give you a Web browser such as *Netscape Navigator* or *Microsoft Internet Explorer;* these browsers connect you to the Web. Explore the top of your screen on your browser's page or the software pages provided by your server to locate its newsgroups and other utilities available to you.

If you have an online service as well as a printer for your computer, you can do much of your research at home. You may use search engines, read mailing lists or listservs, check newsgroups or, as you would at the library, search for books and articles on your topic. The section that follows will give information about the Net, tips to help you judge online material, and an overview of techniques for using Internet utilities.

DOMAINS, URLS, AND PROTOCOLS: DECODING YOUR SEARCH TOOLS

Just as books have call numbers, Internet sites have names and addresses that allow your computer and service provider to connect with them.

Domain Names: Each computer making up the Internet has a name; its *domain name,* made of letters or words separated by the symbol . , pronounced "dot." The domain name of Bookweb, an Internet source of information about books, is *www.bookweb.org.* The domain name describes a computer that

- Belongs to the World Wide Web—the *www*
- Is known to other computers as *bookweb*
- Is operated by a non-profit organization—*org*

URLs and Protocols: Each computer's domain must have a complete address so that your computer can locate the communication system used by that source. The address for a computer on the Internet is called a *uniform resource locator* or *URL* (pronounced "earl"), meaning a specific communication format used by Internet computers. Bookweb's URL is *http://www.bookweb.org.* With this URL, or locating address, your computer can find and connect on the Internet with Bookweb's computer. The first items in a URL make up the *protocol,* the symbol *://* and letters *http,* meaning a specific communication format. *Http* means that Bookweb uses *hypertext transfer protocol,* a Web communications format offering highlighted and underlined words that *link* to or from other Internet locations.

Other Internet communications systems are

- *Usenet* groups or *newsgroups,* accessed by and listed under "News" or "Newsgroups" in the e-mail section of your server: Their addresses begin with the letters *alt* ("alternative"), *sci* ("science"), and so on. A newsgroup's URL looks like this: *alt.rec.soccer.rules.*
- *Telnet, Gopher,* and *ftp* formats, which allow access to library computer systems *(Telnet),* search systems for Internet sites *(Gopher),* and data files on other computers *(ftp).*

Note: In an URL, the final three letters may help you to decide on the quality and type of information available at that address:

- *biz* can be used for business
- *ca* means a Canadian website
- *com* is an abbreviation for *commercial*—online retailers and businesses use it
- *edu* ends the address of educational institutions (in the United States)
- *gc.ca* refers to Canadian government agencies
- *gov* refers to US government agencies
- *name* is an extension for personal address
- *net* means Internet service provider
- *org* signifies non-profit organizations

Depending on your familiarity with using the Internet, you may mainly use the Web and its search engines, or newsgroups and mailing lists during your first year's research tasks. Each of these resources will be discussed on the pages that follow.

EVALUATING YOUR NET RESEARCH CHOICES

Two factors must be taken into account with Internet research: **time for locating information,** and **evaluation of material** found during searches. Using the Net for research is not always faster than using books or printed sources; computers load and download information at different speeds; sites with many graphics or links may be slow to load; and sometimes links between sites have expired or changed locations. Moreover, time is needed for four activities unique to Internet research:

- Choosing and refining keywords and word-strings to begin and refine searches
- Scrolling through, reading, and selecting from search-engine pages
- Pursuing links at various sites
- Bookmarking and printing screens of information

Time is also needed for you to evaluate the material you find on the Internet. On screen in front of you are thousands of sources of information, often unsorted, sometimes biased or limited, frequently commercial, and occasionally excellent. The Net's strength is its unlimited and unrestricted nature; its challenge to users is to find and evaluate the information they seek. Following are some general tips and a checklist for judging the quality and usefulness of websites and newsgroup or listserv postings:

- Consider the *credibility* of the source—is it sponsored by a retailer or the manufacturer of an item you are researching? If so, it may be biased in its favour. Is your website the creation of one individual; does it list or credit *its* sources, or offer links to sites with differing views or further information? Be cautious of trusting sites expressing strong or unbalanced views of a subject, and of sites where the creator does not offer his or her qualifications or background experience for writing about the subject, nor a bibliography or credit list of research sources.
- Consider the *three-letter sequence at the end of an URL—edu, org,* and sometimes *com* are often the most reliable sources of trustworthy and correct information. Personal webpages, no matter how impressive visually, may be seriously biased, misleading, or simply lacking in information.

Whether you are a student in a business, technical, academic, or human services program, you should use the checklist that follows to help you critically assess the content quality of any website or posting to a mailing list or newsgroup:

- **Research:** Is there a demonstration or proof of research, such as a bibliography, list of research types or methods used, or links to other reputable sites?
- **Timeliness:** Is the information current? Do dates appear as part of information offered? Does the site show how often it is updated?
- **Type of information offered:** Does the creator provide balanced examples, objective proof, statistics, or other solid material to support his or her views? Is it made clear which information is factual, and which is opinion? Would the information be credible "off-line"?
- **Credibility of source's creators:** Do you recognize the credentials or qualifications of the creators of the information? Do these persons offer background information about themselves that relates to their qualifications, research, or information? Do they acknowledge responsibility for the information provided? Do they have other sites or entries on search engines?

SEARCH ENGINES: YOUR "CYBER-LIBRARIES"

A *search engine* is a tool that combs through the vast amount of information on the Web for sites or articles that match your research needs. You activate a search engine by typing in keywords, word-strings, or a phrase that tells the engine what to look for. It then provides you with a list of "hits," or links, to websites where your keyword is found. Most search engines also provide a brief description of each site and a hypertext link to sites related to that site. Some engines rank their findings by the number of times a keyword or phrase appears on a site. Most search engines offer "Help" and "Search Tips" buttons, and many allow you to refine or streamline a search by changing or adding codes to your keywords. Take the time to read and experiment with any help or search information offered on the home page of any search engine. Well-known search engines include AltaVista, at *www.altavista.digital.com*; and Lycos, at *www.lycos.com*.

A newer type of search engine is the metasearcher, which searches a variety of engines and retrieves and sorts its findings. One of the best is Google at *www.google.com*. Google is a "smart search" engine, which not only accumulates findings but also rates them by appropriateness of content; it checks the context or words surrounding your keywords to see if they are related to the subject area you are searching for. Most search engines, including Google, search for results in different media as well—they can return findings as text files, graphic files, and sound files.

Many search engines now contain two types of searches: both give good, but different, types of information. "True" search engines like *Infoseek* or *AltaVista* search the Internet each time you type keywords into the "Search" window. But *Infoseek* and other engines will, in fact, provide both Internet "true" searches and "directory" searches. Both searches will locate websites, journal sites, and thousands of articles.

Internet-Wide Searches

The sites the Internet-wide engine locates for you are not sorted according to subcategories within a general area of information; they are sites containing your keywords, and may vary considerably in usefulness. Marina, a student in a computer technology program, finds nearly 2 million entries on *Infoseek* when she enters the keywords *liquid crystal displays*. She would have difficulty reading even the summaries of many of these entries to find useful sites. But if she has a limited topic related to her subject or has already narrowed her topic, she will have a focus to help her make a selection. In fact, since her course covers computer uses of these screens and developments in their chemical makeup, she knows she does not want commercial or entertainment media applications of the displays; she wants journal articles about recent changes to the makeup of LCDs. The screen below shows the first page of *Infoseek's* findings for the keywords *liquid crystal displays*.

Directory Searches

Directory search engines do not search the Net each time; they search their own databases based on your keywords. They present information sorted into directories or "menus" according to categories. *Yahoo,* for example, has special databases of Canadian sites as well, and these appear when you add the word *Canadian* to your keyword string. *My Virtual Reference Desk,* at *www.refdesk.com,* is another search directory; it gives you access to daily newspapers from around the world and online versions of current issues of many popular magazines. It also provides an impressive variety of reference tools as well as online links to several hundred search engines.

When Marina looks up *liquid crystal displays* using a directory engine, she is given a range of widely varied headings for sites about her subject. She finds the categories or "directory topics" *Computer>Peripherals & storage>Monitors>Monitor vendors,* and *Entertainment>Music>Computers & music>Audio on the Web>Plug-ins>Liquid Audio.* If she is working at narrowing or discovering a limited topic for a computer technology research paper, then the directory engine's breakdown of her large subject may help her to find a specific area of interest for her research. To help in the evaluation, engines often rate or rank entries with stars or graphics according to how informative they find them to be. Marina could run through and link along the sites connected to each area of information on uses of and applications for LCDs, until she discovered a specific topic in which she was interested, or which related closely to her course of study.

A Final Note about Locating Information

There are an increasing number of specialized online research resources. Check for resource sites in your area of interest by using search engines. Some of these sites are general and commercial, such as *www.elibrary.com.* Subscribers enrol monthly at a limited cost, receiving access to millions of newspaper and magazine articles as well as thousands of book chapters and television and radio transcripts. Using keyword searches, you call up lists of articles related to your subject and access full texts available for printing.

If you note the names of professional, business, or technological journals while using database indexes, you may use their names as keywords on search engines to find out if these journals have websites containing archives of articles you may download.

A note about keywords: Your skill in choosing keywords is basic to your getting useful results from any search engine. Remember when choosing, ordering, and refining your keywords that neither your computer nor the search engine knows what you mean by your keywords—they are simply codes that set off a search for identical codes in millions of documents. No one is an expert at choosing the "right" keywords; everyone proceeds by trial and error. However, there are some general guidelines to help you:

- Most search engines are *case insensitive,* meaning they don't care if you capitalize a name; however, some engines will instruct you to use capitals. It is better to capitalize as you normally would, and to read any engine's instructions about capitals; they are sometimes part of "operating codes" for information retrieval.
- Check your search engine's instructions for defining word-groups or *strings.* If you use the keywords *liquid crystal,* you want the meaning of those words to be taken as a unit; you do not want the search engine to find entries containing the word *liquid,* then all the entries containing the word *crystal.*
- Try synonyms or phrases that limit your keywords to narrow your results.
- If you are researching the Canadian aspects of some subject, limit your search by including the word *Canada* or *Canadian.*
- Try placing your keywords in order of their importance, with the most important idea first. Some engines "weight" a keyword search by the order of the words.
- Check your search engine's instructions for "codes" like + or *AND* to be inserted to link or alter the meaning of groups of keywords.

MAILING LISTS AND NEWSGROUPS AS RESEARCH RESOURCES

E-mail software allows you to access two other possible sources of information for research. Be aware that reading dozens or hundreds of postings to mailing lists or newsgroups takes time and requires you to decide how credible or useful the information in those e-mails may be. There are excellent technological and computer-application-related mailing lists and newsgroups.

- To locate and join a mailing list, use a search engine to find an Internet directory of mailing lists, check out Yahoo's listing of groups, or go to a directory called *PAML* (publicly accessible mailing lists) at *www.Neosoft.com/internet/paml/.* Once you find a mailing list on your research topic, go to the list's URL and follow its instructions for subscribing and unsubscribing later. The advantage of such lists is that you see many viewpoints on a subject and may discuss your own ideas and questions about the subject. Remember to evaluate any information appropriately.
- Newsgroups or *Usenet* groups may be accessed from the "Newsgroup" section of your e-mail server. Simply open that part of the software and set it to "receive groups." The server will load thousands of newsgroups in alphabetical order by their URLs; in other words, *alt* groups will download before *misc* groups. The number of posts currently on file from each group is listed after its name. Read through the names of the groups until you find one related to your subject; newsgroups correspond about everything from apple-growing to Buffy. Newsgroups are different from mailing lists in that you don't need to correspond with anyone; you simply use the software to download any group you choose and read its contents. Messages or posts are generally grouped by "threads," which are subject lines of groups of messages. It is important to exercise good judgment in selecting information from newsgroup postings.

USING THE NET TO FIND BOOKS ON YOUR TOPIC

One of the odd but valuable qualities of the Internet is its mixture of commercial activity and useful information. Some of the large online booksellers or book and publishing information sites will have a "search" application that will turn up a good list of available books on your topic. Here are some sites; most are American or international, but there are increasing numbers of Canadian retailers, such as Indigo, which have entered this area:

- Amazon Books at *www.amazon.ca.*
- Barnes and Noble Books at *www.barnesandnoble.com*
- Bookweb at *www.bookweb.org*
- Bookserve at *www.bookserve.com*
- Bookwire at *www.bookwire.com*
- Chapters and Indigo at *www.chapters.indigo.ca*
- UPC Link & The Independent Reader at *independentreader.com*

Many colleges have online library services available as well. Check your college's server and your college library to see what facilities and downloadable information are accessible online.

Final Thoughts

Remember that at any point you can print out information presented on the screen. You can then go to your library and know just what books you would want to borrow or visit your library online to find out in advance whether it has the books you want.

RESEARCH PRACTICE

Activity

Use your library or the Internet to research a subject that interests you. Select one of the following areas or (with your teacher's permission) one of your own choice:

Assisted suicide	Computer use and carpal tunnel
Interracial adoptions	syndrome
Ritalin and children	Noise control
Sexual harassment	Animals nearing extinction
Provincial lotteries	Animal rights movement
Greenhouse effect	Anti-gay violence
Pro-choice movement today	Drug-treatment programs for
Pro-life movement today	adolescents
Health insurance reform	Fertility drugs
Drinking-water pollution	Witchcraft today

Problems of retirement	New treatments for AIDS
Cremation	Mind–body medicine
Capital punishment	Origins of Kwanzaa
DVD technology	Hazardous substances in the home
Acid rain	Airbags
New aid for the handicapped	Gambling and youth
New remedies for allergies	Cultural diversity in Canadian cities
Censorship on the Internet	Earthquake forecasting
New prison reforms	Ethical aspects of hunting
Drug treatment programs	Ethics of cloning
Sudden infant death syndrome	Recent consumer frauds
New treatments for insomnia	Stress reduction in the workplace
Organ donation	Sex on television
Child abuse	Everyday addictions
French-language immersion in schools	Toxic waste disposal
	Self-help groups
Food poisoning (salmonella)	Telephone crimes
Alzheimer's disease	Date rape
Holistic healing	Heroes for today
Vegetarianism	Steroids
Best job prospects today	Surrogate mothers

Research the topic first through the *subject* section of a library book file or an online bookstore. Then research the topic through a library periodicals file or an online source. On a separate sheet of paper, provide the following information:

1 The topic

2 Three books that either cover the topic directly or at least in some way touch on the topic. Include these items:

Author
Title
Place of publication
Publisher
Date of publication

3 Three articles on the topic published in 1995 or later. Include these items:

Title of article
Author (if given)
Title of magazine
Date
Page(s) (if given)

4 Finally, include a paragraph describing just how you went about researching your topic. In addition, include a photocopy or printout of one of the three articles.

Writing a Research Paper

The process of writing a research paper can be divided into six steps:

1 Select a topic that you can readily research.

2 Limit your topic and make the purpose of your paper clear.

3 Gather information on your limited topic.

4 Plan your paper and take notes on your limited topic.

5 Write the paper.

6 Use an acceptable format and method of documentation.

This chapter explains and illustrates each of these steps and then provides a model research paper.

STEP 1: SELECT A TOPIC THAT YOU CAN READILY RESEARCH

Researching at a College or Local Library

First of all, go to the *Subjects* section of your library catalogue (as described on page 321) and see whether there are several books on your general topic. For example, if you initially choose the broad topic of "parenting," try to find at least three books on being a parent. Make sure that the books are actually available on the library shelves.

Next, go to the *periodicals* file and electronic research resources in your library (see pages 322–325) to see if there are a fair number of magazine, newspaper, or journal articles on your subject. John, the student writing a research paper on nanotechnology, used the "Virtual Library" section of his college's online library. He found journal indexes there, including scientific journals, containing many entries related to his subject. As he skimmed titles and summaries, he noticed that journals listed websites. He decided to print the URLs and then use his computer at home to see as many sites as possible on the general subject of nanotechnology, to try to discover an application or area of the subject he found especially interesting.

Researching on the Internet

If you have access to the Internet on a home or library computer, you can use it to determine if resources are available for your topic.

The first step is to go to the *subjects* section of either your college's or your town's or city's library website.

John went back to his college library's website; he had tried online book and CD retailers before, so he was pleased at how familiar the college library's search system was. "The site is so easy to use," he said. "The menus let me decide whether I wanted to look for books or journals or other media, and the 'Search' box let me choose between author, title, subject, and keyword. What really surprised me was that my college library has access to other libraries, and its server can even tell me how long it will take to get a book or journal from another source. It took me only a few minutes to check three libraries for books and journals, and I could access some of the journal articles onscreen on another part of the library's site."

Students may also go online to public libraries in their areas, and preview book listings under subject, author, or title. Many library systems allow people to reserve books online as well. If you find relevant books in your online search that your local library does not own, ask your research librarian if he or she can obtain them from another library through an interlibrary loan program.

"I checked out online book sites as I began my research," said Sonya Philips. "I saw that I could search for books by subject, and I knew that I was in business. All I had to do was click on a box titled 'Browse Subject.'

"Most had a category called 'Parenting and Families,' and when I clicked on that, I got sub-categories, including one for 'Teenagers.' I clicked on 'Teenagers' and that brought up a list of hundreds of books! I went through the list, and when I got to a book that sounded promising, I just clicked on that title and up came reviews of the book—and sometimes a table of contents and a summary as well! All this information helped me decide on the dozen books I eventually picked out that seemed relevant to my paper. I then went to my local library and found five of those titles on the shelves. Another title was a recent paperback, so I went to a nearby bookstore and bought it."

Next, determine if magazine or newspaper articles on your topic are available online. You can do so in one of several ways. Try a search engine or your Internet service provider; most ISPs now have a built-in "engine" that allows you to search the Internet for any topic you like. When you type in a keyword or keywords related to your topic, you'll get back a listing of sources, or "hits," on the Internet. Sonya related her experience searching the Internet in this way:

"First I typed in the word *parenting* in the keyword box," she said. "I got more than a hundred thousand hits! So I tried more specific search terms. I tried *parenting and teenagers, parenting and television, parenting and adolescents.* Those search terms worked better, and I found some useful sites—like 'The Television Project,' which is an online resource that doesn't exist anywhere else—but I was still getting lots of stuff I couldn't use, sites that were selling products, or parents' discussion groups and so on. So I asked my instructor how to look for just magazine or newspaper articles. She suggested I go directly to the sites of some popular publications. I went to three magazines' sites, and I was able to search each one for recent articles about parenting; there was plenty of material that related to my topic."

"For technology subjects, search engines are a gold mine," John said. "I got 11 million entries for sites about nanotechnology. I felt like I'd found a whole new world of people interested in this stuff. There were links pages right in the first ten sites, and lots of sites from research institutes—even things called 'fringe periodicals' and other lists of Web publications. My first move was just to start a new 'bookmarks' folder for my URLs and then to keep bookmarking sites that looked useful."

However you choose to do your research, the outcome is the same: If both books and articles are available, pursue your topic. Otherwise, you may have to choose another topic. You cannot write a paper on a topic for which research materials are not readily available.

STEP 2: LIMIT YOUR TOPIC AND MAKE THE PURPOSE OF YOUR PAPER CLEAR

A research paper should *thoroughly* develop a *limited* topic. It should be narrow and deep rather than broad and shallow. Therefore, as you read through books and articles on your general topic, look for ways to limit the topic.

For instance, as Sonya read through materials on the general topic of "parenting," she chose to limit her topic to the particular problems parents have in raising children in today's culture. Furthermore, she decided to limit it even more by focusing on what successful parents do to deal with those challenges. The broad subject "trends in retail marketing" could be reduced to television shopping networks, or online auction sites. "Symbolism in fiction" might be limited to a specific type of symbol used by one author in three works; "stress in everyday life" could be narrowed to methods of reducing stress in the workplace.

Subject headings in the book file and the magazine file will give you helpful ideas about how to limit your subject. For example, under the subject heading "parenting" in the book file were several related headings, such as "moral and ethical considerations of parenting" and "step-parenting." In addition, there was a list of seventy-eight books, with several of the titles suggesting limited directions for research: parents and discipline, parenting and adolescent girls, and parents' questions about teenagers' development. Under the subject heading "parenting" in the magazine file at the same library were subheadings and titles of many articles that suggested additional limited topics that a research paper might explore: how parents can limit the impact of TV on kids, how parents can keep the lines of communication open between parents and teenagers, and how much influence parents can have on kids. The point is that *subject headings and related headings, as well as book and article titles, may be of great help to you in narrowing your topic.* Take advantage of them.

Do not expect to limit your topic and make your purpose clear all at once. You may have to do quite a bit of reading as you work out the limited focus of your paper.

Note that many research papers have one of two general purposes. Your purpose might be to make and defend a point of some kind. (For example, your purpose in a paper might be to provide evidence that current market images of your age group in TV commercials are unrealistic.) Alternatively, depending on the course and the instructor, your purpose might simply be to present accurate, current, and focused information about a particular subject. (For instance, you might be asked to write a paper describing the most recent scientific findings about the effect of diet on heart disease.)

Note: Time factors in preparing research papers Even with the Internet to make research more comfortable, research papers take time. No one can do a respectable paper "at the last minute." You need days, or a week, for each of the early stages of discovering your topic, doing preliminary research to focus that topic, gathering information, and outlining and drafting your paper. Plan on a minimum of three weeks for initial research, narrowing your topic, accumulating your research, and making outline notes. Make a schedule for yourself, and keep adjusting it as you need to.

STEP 3: GATHER INFORMATION ON YOUR LIMITED TOPIC

After you have a good sense of your limited topic, you can begin gathering information that is relevant to it. A helpful way to proceed is to sign out the books that you need from your library. In addition, make copies of all relevant articles from magazines, newspapers, or journals. If your library has an online periodicals database, you may be able to print those articles.

In other words, take the steps needed to get all your key source materials together in one place. You can then sit and work on these materials in a quiet, unhurried way in your home or some other place of study.

STEP 4: PLAN YOUR PAPER AND TAKE NOTES ON YOUR LIMITED TOPIC

Preparing a Rough Outline

As you carefully read through the material you have gathered, think constantly about the specific content and organization of your paper. Begin making decisions about exactly what information you will present and how you will arrange it. Prepare an outline for your paper that shows both its thesis and the areas of support for the thesis. It may help to try to plan at least three areas of support.

Thesis: _____

Support: 1. _____

  2. _____

  3. _____

Here, for example, is the brief outline that Sonya Philips prepared for her paper on successful parenting:

Thesis: *There are things parents can do to overcome the negative influences hurting their families.*

Support: *1. Create quality time with families*

2. Increase families' sense of community

3. Minimize the impact of media and technology

Notetaking

With a tentative outline in mind, you can begin taking notes on information that you expect to include in your paper. Write your notes on index or file cards or on sheets of loose-leaf paper. The notes you take should be in the form of *direct quotations, summaries in your own words,* or both. (At times you may also *paraphrase*— use an equal number of your own words in place of someone else's words. Since most research involves condensing information, you will summarize much more than you will paraphrase.)

A *direct quotation* must be written *exactly* as it appears in the original work. But as long as you don't change the meaning, you may omit words from a quotation if they are not relevant to your point. Show such an omission with three spaced periods known as *ellipses* in place of the deleted words:

ORIGINAL PASSAGE   We cannot guarantee that bad things will happen, but we can argue that good things are not happening. It is the contention of this report that increasing numbers of young people are left to their own devices at a critical time in their development.

DIRECT
QUOTATION
WITH ELLIPSES   "We cannot guarantee that bad things will happen, but we can argue that good things are not happening. . . . [I]ncreasing numbers of young people are left to their own devices at a critical time in their development."

(Note that there are four dots in the above example, with the first dot indicating the period at the end of the sentence. The capital letter in brackets shows that the word was capitalized by the student, but did not begin the sentence in the original source.)

Keep in mind the following points about your research notes:

- Write on only one side of each card or sheet of paper.
- Write only one kind of information, from one source, on any one card or sheet.
- Include at the top of each card or sheet a heading that summarizes its content. This step will help you organize the different kinds of information that you gather.
- Identify the source and page number at the bottom.

Whether you quote or summarize, be sure to record the exact source and page from which you take each piece of information. In a research paper, you must document all information that is not common knowledge or a matter of historical record. For example, the birthdate of Jean Chrétien is an established fact and does not need documenting. On the other hand, the average number of hours worked annually today compared to the 1980s is a specialized fact that should be documented. As you read several sources on a subject, you will develop a sense of what authors regard as generally shared or common information about a subject and what is more specialized information that must be documented.

If you do not document specialized information or ideas that are not your own, you will be stealing (the formal term is *plagiarizing*—using someone else's work as your own work). A good deal of the material in research writing, it can usually be assumed, will need to be documented.

Online Plagiarism

Instructors are aware of the websites that sell or offer essays in every subject area. Plagiarism is theft, and a bought essay is a waste of your money and of your time; there are online tracing systems available to professors to track such submissions from students. The issue remains one of ethics; you waste an opportunity to learn when you "steal" or buy someone else's work.

An essay bought or lifted from an online site will be immediately recognizable to your instructor. Your writing style, word choices, and phrasing are as unmistakable as your fingerprints. Moreover, sections cut and pasted from a website and passed off as your own are glaringly obvious to professors as well. Papers are evaluated for the quality of the conclusions you draw from your research, not for the quantity of borrowed information piled up inside the paragraphs.

STEP 5: WRITE THE PAPER

After you have finished your reading and notetaking, you should have a fairly clear idea of the plan of your paper. Make a *final outline* and use it as a guide to write your first full draft. If your instructor requires an outline as part of your paper, you should prepare either a *topic outline,* which contains your thesis plus supporting words and phrases; or a *sentence outline,* which contains all complete sentences. In the model paper shown on pages 347–353, a topic outline appears on page 346. If you are using graphics or visual support material, specify placement of such on your outline, and supply either a printout of your material or a brief description of its content, labelling your graphics "Ill. #1," and so on. You will note that Roman numerals are used for first-level headings, capital letters for second-level headings, and numbers for third-level headings.

In an *introduction,* include a thesis statement expressing the purpose of your paper and indicate the plan of development that you will follow. The section on writing introductions for an essay (pages 83–87) is also appropriate for the introductory section of the research paper. Notice that the model research paper uses a two-paragraph introduction (page 347).

As you move from introduction to main body to conclusion, strive for unity, support, and coherence so that your paper will be clear and effective. Repeatedly ask, "Does each of my supporting paragraphs develop the thesis of my paper?" Use the checklist on the inside front cover of this book to make sure that your paper touches all four bases of effective writing.

STEP 6: USE AN ACCEPTABLE FORMAT AND METHOD OF DOCUMENTATION

Format

The model paper on pages 347–353 shows an acceptable format for a research paper. Be sure to carefully note the comments and directions that are set in small print in the margins of each page. Check with your instructor to determine whether you are to use MLA (Modern Language Association) or APA (American Psychological Association) style for your formatting, citation methods, and bibliography.

Many colleges and universities have excellent online documentation pages for both MLA and APA styles. Following are some good sites current at the time of this book's publication:

MLA Style and APA Style

- *http://www.english.uiuc.edu/cws/wworkshop/bibliostyles.htm*
- *http://www.cod.edu/library/research/Citenet.htm*

MLA Style

- *http://nutsandbolts.washcoll.edu/mla.html*
- *http://owl.english.purdue.edu/handouts/research/r_mla.html*

APA Style

- *http://webster.commnet.edu/apa/apa_index.htm*
- *http://nutsandbolts.washcoll.edu/apa.html*

Citation of Online Sources—All Styles

- *http://www.bedfordstmartins.com/online/citex.html*

Bookmark the sites you find most useful and return to them for information whenever you need to.

Documentation of Sources

You must tell the reader the sources (books, articles, and so on) of the borrowed material in your paper. Whether you quote directly or summarize ideas in your own words, you must acknowledge your sources. In the past, you may have used footnotes and a bibliography to cite your sources. Here you will learn a simplified and widely accepted documentation style used by the Modern Language Association.

Citations within a Paper: When citing a source, you must mention the author's name and the relevant page number. The author's name may be given either in the sentence you are writing or in parentheses following the sentence. Here are two examples:

In *The Way We Really Are,* author Stephanie Coontz writes, "Right up through the 1940s, ties of work, friendship, neighborhood, ethnicity, extended kin, and voluntary organizations were as important a source of identity for most Americans, and sometimes a *more* important source of obligation, than marriage and the nuclear family" (37).

"Some . . . are looking for a way to reclaim family closeness in an increasingly fast-paced society. . . . Still others worry about unsavory influences in school—drugs, alcohol, sex, violence" (Kantrowitz and Wingert 66).

There are several points to note about citations within the paper:

- When the author's name is provided within the parentheses, only the last name is given.
- There is no punctuation between the author's name and the page number.
- The parenthetical citation is placed after the borrowed material but before the period at the end of the sentence.
- If you are using more than one work by the same author, include a shortened version of the title within the parenthetical citation. For example, suppose you were using two books by Stephanie Coontz, and you included a second quotation from her book *The Way We Really Are.* Your citation within the text would be:

(Coontz, *Really Are,* 39)

Note that commas separate the author's last name and the page number from the abbreviated title.

Citations at the End of a Paper: Your paper should end with a list of "Works Cited," which includes all the sources actually used in the paper. (Don't list any other sources, no matter how many you have read.) Look at the "Works Cited" page in the model research paper (page 354) and note the following points:

- The list is organized alphabetically according to the authors' last names. Entries are not numbered.
- Entries are double-spaced, with no extra space between entries.
- After the first line of each entry, there is a half-inch indentation for each additional line in the entry.
- Use the abbreviation *qtd. in* when citing a quotation from another source. For example, a quotation from Edward Wolff on page 2 of the paper is from a book not by Wolff but by Sylvia Ann Hewlett and Cornel West. The citation is therefore handled as follows:

Economist Edward Wolff explains the loss of time:

> Over a thirty-year time span, parental time has declined 13 percent. The time parents have available for their children has been squeezed by the rapid shift of mothers into the paid labour force, by escalating divorce rates and the subsequent abandonment of children by their fathers, and by an increase in the number of hours required on the job. The average worker is now at work 163 hours a year more than in 1969, which adds up to an extra month of work annually. (qtd. in Hewlett and West 48)

Model Entries for a List of "Works Cited": Model entries of "Works Cited" are given below. Use these entries as a guide when you prepare your own list. If your paper is in the areas of science or technology, you will follow APA guidelines for your Works Cited; these are available at the APA style websites listed on page 340.

Book by One Author

Baker, Nancy. *The Night Inside.* Toronto: Penguin Books, 1993.

Note that the author's last name is written first.

Two or More Entries by the Same Author

- - -. *Blood and Chrysanthemums.* Toronto: Penguin Books, 1994.

If you cite two or more entries by the same author (in the example above, a second book by Nancy Baker is cited), do not repeat the author's name. Instead, begin with a line made up of three hyphens followed by a period. Then give the remaining information as usual. Arrange the works by the same author alphabetically by title. If your entry runs more than one line of text, tab in the second line of the listing.

Book by Two or More Authors

Burns, Edward, and David Simon. *The Corner.* New York: Broadway Books, 1997.

For a book with two or more authors, give all the authors' names but reverse only the first name. Underline or italicize book and magazine or journal titles.

Book by a Group or Committee

Department of the Secretary of State of Canada. *The Canadian Style: A Guide to Writing and Editing.* Toronto: Dundurn Press Ltd., 1991.

Magazine Article

Callwood, June. "A Date with AIDS." *Saturday Night* Mar. 1995: 52.

Write the date of the issue as follows: day, month (abbreviated in most cases to three letters), and year. The final number or numbers refer to the page or pages of the issue on which the article appears.

Article with No Author Named

"White Tigers." *Owl* Sept. 1994: 23.

Newspaper Article

Chavez, Linda. "Father Passes on Lessons of Poverty." *Philadelphia Inquirer* 25 Nov. 1998, sec. A:18.

The final letter and number refer to section A, page 18.

Editorial

"Trade Wars Laughable." Editorial. *The Winnipeg Free Press* 15 Mar. 1995, sec. A22.

List an editorial as you would any signed or unsigned article, but indicate the nature of the piece by adding *Editorial* after the article's title.

Selection in an Edited Collection

McClane, Kenneth A. "A Death in the Family." *Bearing Witness.* Ed. Henry Louis Gates, Jr. New York: Pantheon, 1991.

Revised or Later Edition

Myers, David G. *Social Psychology.* 6th ed. New York: McGraw-Hill, 1999.

Note: The abbreviations *Rev. ed., 2d ed., 3d ed.,* and so on, are placed right after the title.

Chapter or Section in a Book by One Author

Schor, Juliet B. "The Visible Lifestyle: American Symbols of Status." *The Overspent American.* New York: Basic Books, 1998. 43–64.

Pamphlet

Your Guide to Hazardous Waste in the Home. Toronto: Metro Works Planning, Control and Development Division, 1995.

Television Program

"Salmon Farming." Narr. David Suzuki. Prod. Ken Dodd. *The Nature of Things.* CBC. 21 Nov. 1993.

Film or Videotape

American History X. Dir. Tony Kaye. New Line Cinema, 1998.

Not a Love Story: A Film about Pornography. Dir. Bonnie Sherr Klein. National Film Board, 1986.

CD or Sound Recording

Jordan, Sass. *Rats.* Aquarius Records CD 108184, 1994.

Computer Software Program

SuperCalc3 Release 2.1. Computer Software. San Jose, Cal.: Computer Associates, Microproducts, 1985.

Personal Interview

Egoyan, Atom. Personal interview. 30 Mar. 1998.

Note: Online citation is developing constantly. To be certain you are accurate, check the website for the citation style you are required to use. If you quote a mailing list or newsgroup posting, check the format at the MLA or APA website to be sure of current requirements.

Online Source in a Reference Database

"Organ Transplants." *Britannica On-line.* 1 Dec. 1998
    <http://www.eb.com:180/cgi-bin/g?DocF-macro/5006/37/3.html>.

Note: The date refers to when the student researcher accessed the source.

Online Article

Woodward, Kenneth J. "Sex, Sin, and Salvation." *Newsweek On-line*
    2 Nov. 1998. 6 Nov. 1998 <http://www.newsweek.com>.

Note: The first date refers to the issue of the publication in which the article appeared; the second date refers to the day when the student researcher accessed the source.

Activity

On a separate sheet of paper, convert the information in each of the following references into the correct form for a list of "Works Cited." Use the appropriate model above as a guide.

1. A book by Paul Rutherford called *The New Icons* and published by University of Toronto Press in 2001

2. An article by Ann Shin titled "Radio Rethink" on pages 47–48 of the December 2000 issue of *Fuse* magazine

3. An article by Jane Leeman titled "Alberta Youth Leaning to Reform" on page A3 of the April 15, 2001, issue of the *Calgary Herald*

4. A book by Diane E. Papalia and Sally W. Olds titled *Human Development* and published in a seventh edition by McGraw-Hill in New York in 2001

Model Title Page

ALTHOUGH A TITLE PAGE AND OUTLINE ARE NOT STRICTLY REQUIRED, YOUR INSTRUCTOR MAY ASK YOU TO PROVIDE THEM.

[1]THE TITLE SHOULD BEGIN ABOUT ONE-THIRD OF THE WAY DOWN THE PAGE. CENTRE THE TITLE. DOUBLE-SPACE BETWEEN LINES OF THE TITLE AND YOUR NAME. ALSO CENTRE AND DOUBLE-SPACE THE INSTRUCTOR'S NAME AND THE DATE.

Successful Families:

Fighting for Their Kids[1]

by

Sonya Philips

English 101

Professor Lessig

5 May 2000

Model First Page with a Top Heading

[2]FOR A PAPER WITHOUT A TITLE PAGE OR OUTLINE, USE A TOP HEADING ON THE FIRST PAGE.

[3]DOUBLE-SPACE BETWEEN LINES. LEAVE A ONE-INCH MARGIN ON ALL SIDES.

↑ 1/2 INCH
Philips 1

↑
1 INCH

Sonya Philips

Professor Lessig

English 101

5 May 2000[2]

Successful Families: Fighting for Their Kids

It's a terrible time to be a teenager, or even a teenager's parent. That [3]message is everywhere. The TV, the magazines, and the newspapers are all full of frightening stories about teenagers and families. They say that North American families are falling apart, that kids don't care about anything, and that parents have trouble doing anything. . . .

Model Outline Page

Outline[5]

Thesis: Although these are difficult times to be raising teenagers, successful families are finding ways to cope with the challenges.

I.   Meeting the challenge of spending quality time together

    A.   Barriers to spending quality time

        1.   Increased working hours

        2.   Rising divorce rates

        3.   Women in work force

    B.   Danger of lack of quality time

    C.   Ways found to spend time together

        1.   Working less and scaling back lifestyle

        2.   Home schooling allows some families to spend more time together

II. Meeting the challenge of creating sense of community

    A.   Lack of traditional community ties

    B.   Ways found to create sense of community

        1.   Intentional communities

        2.   Religious ties

III. Meeting the challenge of limiting the negative impact of media and technology

    A.   Negative impact of media and technology

        1.   Creation of environment without protection

        2.   Flood of uncontrolled, inappropriate information

    B.   Ways of controlling media and technology

        1.   Banning TV

        2.   Using technology in beneficial ways

[4] AFTER THE TITLE PAGE, NUMBER ALL PAGES IN UPPER-RIGHT CORNER A HALF-INCH FROM THE TOP. PLACE YOUR NAME BEFORE THE PAGE NUMBER. USE SMALL ROMAN NUMERALS ON OUTLINE PAGES. USE ARABIC NUMBERS ON PAGES FOLLOWING THE OUTLINE.

[5] THE WORD OUTLINE (WITHOUT UNDERLINING OR QUOTATION MARKS) IS CENTRED ONE INCH FROM THE TOP. DOUBLE-SPACE BETWEEN LINES. LEAVE A ONE-INCH MARGIN ON ALL SIDES.

Successful Families: Fighting for Their Kids[6]

It's a terrible time to be a teenager, or even a teenager's parent. That message is everywhere. The TV, the magazines, and the newspapers are all full of frightening stories about teenagers and families. They say that North American families are falling apart, that kids don't care about anything, and that parents have trouble doing anything about it.[7] Bookstores are full of scary-sounding titles like these: *Teenage Wasteland, Cold New World, A Tribe Apart,* and *The Scapegoat Generation: America's War on Adolescents.* These books describe teenage problems that include apathy, violence, suicide, sexual abuse, depression, loss of values, poor mental health, teen crime, gang involvement, and drug and alcohol addiction.

Naturally, caring parents are worried by all this. Their worry shows in polls in which nine out of ten people said it was harder today to raise kids to be "good people" than it was twenty years ago (Donahue D1).[8] But leaving aside Canadian shows like *Ready or Not,* most popular TV shows don't give a realistic view of North American teens, so that these frightening books and statistics do not provide a complete picture of what's going on in families today. The fact is that *not* all teens and families are lost and without values. While they struggle with problems in our culture like everyone else, successful families, especially families from Canada's diverse newer cultures, are doing what they've always done: finding ways to protect and nurture their children. They are fighting the battle for their families in three ways: by fighting against the loss of quality family time, by fighting against the loss of community, and by fighting against the influence of the media and technology.[9]

It's true that these days, parents face more challenges than ever before when it comes to finding quality time to spend

[6]DOUBLE SPACE BETWEEN LINES OF THE TEXT. LEAVE A ONE-INCH MARGIN ALL THE WAY AROUND THE PAGE. YOUR NAME AND THE PAGE NUMBER APPEAR AS A HEADER HALF AN INCH FROM THE TOP OF THE PAGE.

[7]COMMON KNOWLEDGE IS NOT DOCUMENTED.

[8]THIS TYPICAL CITATION IS MADE UP OF THE AUTHOR'S LAST NAME AND THE RELEVANT PAGE NUMBER. THE "WORKS CITED" THEN PROVIDES FULL INFORMATION ABOUT THE SOURCE.

[9]THESIS, FOLLOWED BY PLAN OF DEVELOPMENT.

Philips 2

with their children. Economist Edward Wolff[10] explains the loss

of time:

> [11]Over a thirty-year time span, parental time has declined 13
> percent. The time parents have available for their children has
> been squeezed by the rapid shift of mothers into the paid
> labour force, by escalating divorce rates and the subsequent
> abandonment of children by their fathers, and by an increase
> in the number of hours required on the job. The average worker
> is now at work 163 hours a year more than in 1969, which
> adds up to an extra month of work annually. (qtd.[12] in Hewlett
> and West 48)

As a result, more children are at home alone than ever before. And this

situation does leave children vulnerable to getting in trouble. Richardson

and others report on their study of five thousand eighth graders in

California that showed children who were home alone after school were

twice as likely to experiment with drugs and alcohol than children who

had a parent (or another adult) home in the after-school hours.

But creative parents still come up with ways to be there for their

kids. For some, it's been a matter of cutting back on working hours

and living more simply. For example, in her book *The Shelter of Each*

Other, Mary Pipher[13] tells the story of a couple with three-year-old

twin boys. Edwardo worked sixty-hour weeks at a factory. Sabrina

supervised checkers at a K-Mart, cared for the boys, and tried to watch

over her mother, who had cancer. Money was tight, especially since

daycare was expensive, and the parents felt they had to keep the twins

stylishly dressed and supplied with new toys. The parents were

stressed over money problems, their lack of time together, and

especially having so little time with their boys. It bothered them that

the twins had begun to cry when their parents picked them up at

daycare, as if they'd rather stay with the daycare workers. Finally,

Sabrina and Edwardo made a difficult decision. Sabrina quit her job,

---

[10]SOURCE IS IDENTIFIED BY NAME AND AREA OF EXPERTISE.

[11]DIRECT QUOTATIONS OF FIVE TYPED LINES OR MORE ARE SINGLE-SPACED AND INDENTED TEN SPACES FROM THE LEFT MARGIN. QUOTATION MARKS ARE NOT USED.

[12]THE ABBREVIATION *QTD.* MEANS *QUOTED.* NO COMMA IS USED BETWEEN THE AUTHORS' NAMES AND THE PAGE NUMBER.

[13]WHEN CITING A WORK IN GENERAL, NOT A PART OF THE WORK, IT IS BEST TO INCLUDE THE AUTHOR'S NAME IN THE TEXT INSTEAD OF USING A PARENTHETICAL CITATION. NO PAGE NUMBER IS NEEDED AS THE CITATION REFERS TO THE FINDINGS OF THE STUDY OVERALL.

and the couple invited her mother (whose illness was in remission) to live with them. With the three adults pooling their resources, Sabrina and Edwardo found that they could manage without Sabrina's salary. The family no longer ate out, and they gave up their cable TV. Their sons loved having their grandmother in the house. Sabrina was able to begin doing relaxed, fun projects with the boys. They planted a garden and built a sandbox together. Sabrina observed, "I learned I could get off the merry-go-round" (195).[14] Other parents have "gotten off the merry-go-round"[15] by working at home, even if it means less money than they had previously. "[H]eading[16] home is a real possibility for those parents who can master the new home-office technology. . . ."[17] If enough people can manage to do this, the neighbourhoods might once again come alive for workers and their children" (Louv 285).[18]

Some parents even home-school their children as a way to be sure they have plenty of time together. Home schooling used to be thought of as a choice made only by very religious people or back-to-nature radicals. Now, teaching children at home is much less unusual. It's estimated that more than one million North American children are being home-schooled. Some universities even have admissions officers whose job it is to review applications from home-schooled kids. Parents who home-school have different reasons, but, according to a cover story in *Newsweek,* "Some . . . are looking for a way to reclaim family closeness in an increasingly fast-paced society. . . . Still others worry about unsavoury influences in school—drugs, alcohol, sex, violence" (Kantrowitz and Wingert 66). Home schooling is no guarantee that a child will resist those temptations, but some families do believe it's a great way to promote family closeness. One fifteen-year-old, home-schooled since kindergarten, explained why he liked the way he'd been raised and educated. He ended by saying, "Another

[14]ONLY THE PAGE NUMBER IS NEEDED AS THE AUTHOR HAS ALREADY BEEN NAMED IN THE TEXT.

[15]QUOTATION MARKS ACKNOWLEDGE THE PHRASE IS COPIED FROM PREVIOUS CITATION.

[16]THE CAPITAL LETTER IN BRACKETS SHOWS THE WORD WAS CAPITALIZED BY THE STUDENT, BUT DID NOT BEGIN THE SENTENCE IN THE ORIGINAL SOURCE.

[17]THE SPACED PERIODS (ELLIPSES) SHOW THAT MATERIAL FROM THE ORIGINAL SOURCE HAS BEEN OMITTED.

[18]AUTHOR AND PAGE NUMBER, WITH NO COMMA.

Philips 4

way I'm different is that I love my family. One guy asked me if I'd been brainwashed. I think it's spooky that liking my family is considered crazy" (Pipher 103).

Quitting their jobs or teaching children at home are things that many parents can't do. But other parents find a second way to nurture their children through building community ties. They help their children develop a healthy sense of belonging by creating links with positive, constructive people and activities. In the past, community wasn't so hard to find. In *The Way We Really Are,* author Stephanie Coontz writes, "Right up through the 1940s, ties of work, friendship, neighborhood, ethnicity, extended kin, and voluntary organizations were as important a source of identity for most Americans, and sometimes a *more* important source of obligation, than marriage and the nuclear family" (37). Even when today's parents were teenagers, neighbourhoods were places where kids felt a sense of belonging and responsibility. But today "parents . . .[19] mourn the disappearance of neighborhoods where a web of relatives and friends kept a close eye on everyone's kids. And they worry their own children grow up isolated, knowing more about the cast of *Friends* than the people in surrounding homes" *(USA Today).*

One way that some families are trying to build old-fashioned community is through "intentional community" or "cohousing." Begun in Denmark in 1972, the cohousing movement is modelled after the traditional village. It brings together a number of families who live in separate houses, but share some common space. For instance, families might share central meeting rooms, dining areas, gardens, daycare, workshops, or office space. They might own tools and lawn mowers together, rather than each household having its own. The point is that they treat their neighbours as extended family, not as strangers.

[19]ELLIPSES SHOW WHERE THE STUDENT HAS OMITTED MATERIAL FROM THE ORIGINAL SOURCE. THE QUOTED MATERIAL IS NOT CAPITALIZED BECAUSE THE STUDENT HAS BLENDED IT INTO A SENTENCE WITH AN INTRODUCTORY PHRASE.

Philips 5

"Creating a cohousing neighborhood can be as simple as taking down the fences between existing homes, or as complex as designing and constructing a new development from scratch," writes Wendy Priesnitz in the online magazine *Natural Life*.[20] More than five hundred such communities now exist in North America (Forsey).

Other families turn to religion as a source of community. Michael and Diane Medved, authors of *Saving Childhood,* are raising their family in a religious Jewish home. Their children attend Jewish schools, go to synagogue, and follow religious customs. They frequently visit, eat, play with, and are cared for by neighbouring Jewish families. The Medveds believe their family is stronger because of their belief "in planting roots—in your home, in your family, in your community. That involves making a commitment, making an investment both physically and emotionally, in your surroundings" (Medved and Medved 200). Other religious traditions offer a similar sense of community, purpose, and belonging for a family. Marcus and Tracy Glover are members of the Nation of Islam. They credit the Nation with making their marriage and family strong and breaking a three-generation cycle of single motherhood (Hewlett and West 201–202).[21]

A final way that families are fighting to protect their children is by controlling the impact of the media and technology. Authors Hewlett and West and Pipher use similar words to describe the effect of this impact. As they describe growing up today, Hewlett and West write about children living "without a skin" (xiii), and Pipher writes about "houses without walls" (12). The authors mean that unlike in the old days, when children were protected from the outside world while they were in the home, there is little such protection today. Even in their own living rooms, all children have to do is to turn on a TV, radio, or computer to be hit with a flood of violence, sick humour, and often

[20]CITATION FOR AN ONLINE SOURCE. NO PAGE NUMBER IS GIVEN BECAUSE THE ONLINE DOCUMENT DOES NOT PROVIDE IT.

[21]QUOTED MATERIAL EXTENDS FROM ONE PAGE TO ANOTHER, SO BOTH PAGE NUMBERS ARE GIVEN.

weird sexuality. Children are growing up watching programs like *The Jerry Springer Show,* which has featured twisted topics such as a mother stealing her twelve-year-old's boyfriend, and people who advocate associating with people only of their own race. Sadly, many parents seem to have given up even trying to protect their growing kids against garbage like this. Canadian parents are blessed with children's programming shown all over the world, but Canadian children prefer soaps, music videos, wrestling, and Home Shopping. Canadian parents are like the mother quoted in *USA Today* as saying, "How can I fight five hundred channels on TV?"

Fortunately, other parents are still insisting on control over the information and entertainment that comes into their homes. Some limit their children to public TV stations like Ontario's TVO; others subscribe to "The Television Project," an online educational organization that helps parents "understand how television affects their families and community and propose alternatives that foster positive emotional, cognitive, and spiritual development within families and communities." Others ban TV entirely from their homes. More try to find a way to use TV and other electronics as useful tools, but not allow them to dominate their homes. One American family, the Millers, who home-school their children, described to Mary Pipher their attitude towards TV. They hadn't owned a TV for years, but purchased one to watch the Olympics. The set is stored in a closet unless a program is on that the family agrees is worthwhile. Some programs the family has enjoyed together include the World Cup soccer games, the TV drama *Sarah Plain and Tall,* and an educational TV course in sign language. Pipher was impressed by the Miller children, and she thought their limited exposure to TV was one reason why. In her words:

Philips 7

Calm, happy children and relaxed, confident parents are so rare today. Probably most notable were the long attention spans of the children and their willingness to sit and listen to the grown-ups talk. The family had a manageable amount of information to deal with. They weren't stressed by more information than they could assimilate. The kids weren't overstimulated and edgy. Nor were they sexualized in the way most kids now are (107).

22THE CONCLUSION PROVIDES A SUMMARY AND RESTATES THE THESIS.

Pipher's words describe children raised by parents who won't give in to the idea that their children are lost. Such parents structure ways to be present in the home, build family ties to a community, and control the impact of the media and technology in their homes. Through their efforts, they succeed in raising nurtured, grounded, successful children. Such parents acknowledge the challenges of raising kids in today's North America, but they are up to the job.[22]

WORKS CITED SHOULD BE DOUBLE-SPACED. TITLES OF BOOKS,
MAGAZINES, AND THE LIKE SHOULD BE ITALICIZED OR UNDERLINED.

Philips 8

Works Cited

Coontz, Stephanie. *The Way We Really Are.* New York: Basic Books, 1997.

Donahue, Deirdre. "Struggling to Raise Good Kids in Toxic Times." *USA
Today* 1 Oct. 1998: D1-D2.

[24]Forsey, Helen. "Intentional Communities." *Natural Life.* 29 Mar. 2000[23]
<http://www.life.ca/nl/44/commun.html>.

Hewlett, Sylvia Ann, and Cornel West. *The War Against Parents.* Boston,
New York: Houghton Mifflin, 1998.

Kantrowitz, Barbara, and Pat Wingert. "Learning at Home: Does It Pass the
Test?" *Newsweek* 5 Oct. 1998: 64-70.

Louv, Richard. *Childhood's Future.* Boston: Houghton Mifflin, 1990.

Medved, Michael, and Diane Medved. *Saving Childhood.* New York:
HarperCollins/Zondervan, 1998.

Pipher, Mary. *The Shelter of Each Other.* New York: Grosset/Putnam, 1996.

[24]Priesnitz, Wendy. "Cohousing—A Sustainable Housing Solution."
Natural Life. 30 Mar. 2000 <http://www.life.ca/nl/62/cohousing.html>.

Richardson, J.L., et al. "Substance Abuse Among Eighth-Grade
Students Who Take Care of Themselves After School." *Pediatrics* 84
(1989): 556-66.

[24]The Television Project. Apr. 6 2000 <http://www.tvp.org>.

[23]INCLUDE THE DATE YOU ACCESSED A WEB SOURCE—IN THIS CASE, MARCH 29, 2000.

[24]SEVERAL OF THE ADJACENT SOURCES—FORSEY, PRIESNITZ, AND THE TELEVISION PROJECT—ARE ONLINE SOURCES. BY GOING ONLINE AND TYPING THE LETTERS AFTER *WWW* IN EACH CITATION, YOU CAN ACCESS ANY OF THE SOURCES. FOR EXAMPLE, YOU COULD TYPE *LIFE.CA/NL/62/ COHOUSING* TO CALL UP THE ARTICLE BY WENDY PRIESNITZ ON COHOUSING.

Sentence Skills

tion • Description • Examples • Process • Cause and Effect • Comparison and Contrast

ition • Division and Classification • Argumentation • Narration • Description • Examples

ss • Cause and Effect • Comparison and Contrast • Definition • Division and Classification

nentation • Narration • Description • Examples • Process • Cause and Effect • Comparison and

ast • Definition • Division and Classification • Argumentation • Narration • Description

C H A P T E R   2 2

Subjects and Verbs

The basic building blocks of English sentences are subjects and verbs. Understanding them is an important first step toward mastering a number of sentence skills.

Every sentence has a subject and a verb. Who or what the sentence speaks about is called the *subject;* what the sentence says about the subject is called the *verb.* In the following sentences, the subject is underlined once and the verb twice:

> The boy cried.
> That fish smells.
> Many people applied for the job.
> The show is a documentary.

A SIMPLE WAY TO FIND A SUBJECT

To find a subject, ask *whom* or *what* the sentence is about. As shown below, your answer is the subject.

> *Whom* is the first sentence about? The boy
> *What* is the second sentence about? That fish
> *Whom* is the third sentence about? Many people
> *What* is the fourth sentence about? The show

A SIMPLE WAY TO FIND A VERB

To find a verb, ask what the sentence says *about* the subject. As shown below, your answer is the verb.

> What does the first sentence *say* about the boy? He cried.
> What does the second sentence *say* about the fish? It smells.
> What does the third sentence *say* about the people? They applied.
> What does the fourth sentence *say* about the show? It is a documentary.

A second way to find the verb is to put *I, you, he, she, it,* or *they* in front of the word you think is a verb. If the result makes sense, you have a verb. For example, you could put *he* in front of *cried* in the first sentence above, with the result, *he cried,* making sense. Therefore you know that *cried* is a verb. You could use the same test with the other three verbs as well.

Finally, it helps to remember that most verbs show action. In the sentences already considered, the three action verbs are *cried, smells,* and *applied.* Certain other verbs, known as *linking verbs,* do not show action. They do, however, give information about the subject. In "The show is a documentary," the linking verb *(is)* joins the subject *(show)* with a word that identifies or describes it *(documentary).* Other common linking verbs include *am, are, was, were, feel, appear, look, become,* and *seem.*

Activity

In each of the following sentences, draw one line under the subject and two lines under the verb.

1. The ripening tomatoes glistened on the sunny windowsill.

2. Acupuncture reduces the pain of my headaches.

3. Elena nervously twisted a strand of hair around her fingers.

4. My brother made his bookshelves from bricks and planks of wood.

5. Damon's website confuses me.

6. My roommate Kerry dries her pantihose with a hairdryer.

7. The band's lead singer's earrings shone in the spotlights.

8. On St. Patrick's Day, our neighbourhood bar serves green beer.

9. My six-year-old brother lives on a diet of tuna casserole.

10. During my parents' divorce, I felt like a rag doll being torn between two people.

MORE ABOUT SUBJECTS AND VERBS

1 A sentence may have more than one verb, more than one subject, or several subjects and verbs.

The <u>engine</u> <u><u>coughed</u></u> and <u><u>sputtered</u></u>.
Broken <u>glass</u> and empty <u>cans</u> <u><u>littered</u></u> the parking lot.
<u>Joyce</u>, <u>Brenda</u>, and <u>Robert</u> <u><u>met</u></u> after class and <u><u>headed</u></u> downtown.

2 The subject of a sentence never appears within a *prepositional phrase.* A prepositional phrase is simply a group of words that begins with a preposition. Following is a list of common prepositions:

about	before	by	inside	over
above	behind	during	into	through
across	below	except	like	to
among	beneath	for	of	toward
around	beside	from	off	under
at	between	in	on(to)	with

Tip: The word *preposition* contains the word *position*. Many prepositions begin a phrase showing the position of something or someone: for example, "The printer is *beside* the computer."

Crossing out prepositional phrases will help you find the subject or subjects of a sentence.

A <u>stream</u> ~~of cold air~~ <u><u>seeps</u></u> in ~~through the space below the door.~~
<u>Specks</u> ~~of dust~~ <u><u>dance</u></u> gently ~~in a ray of sunlight.~~
The <u>people</u> ~~in the apartment above ours~~ <u><u>fight</u></u> loudly.
The murky <u>waters</u> ~~of the polluted lake~~ <u><u>spilled</u></u> ~~over the dam.~~
The amber <u>lights</u> ~~on its sides~~ <u><u>outlined</u></u> the snowplow ~~in the hazy dusk.~~

3 Many verbs consist of more than one word. Here, for example, are some of the many forms of the verb work:

Present	*Past*	
work	worked	should work
works	were working	will be working
does work	have worked	can work
is working	had worked	could be working
are working	had been working	must have worked

4 Words like *not, just, never, only,* and *always* are not part of the verb, although they may appear within the verb.

Ruby has never liked cold weather.
Our manager will not be working out with us this year.
The intersection has not always been this dangerous.

5 No verb preceded by *to* is ever the verb of a sentence.

At night, my son likes to read under the covers.
Evelyn decided to separate from her husband.

6 No *-ing* word by itself is ever the verb of a sentence. (It may be part of the verb, but it must have a helping verb in front of it.)

They going on a trip this weekend. (Not a sentence, because the verb is not complete)
They are going on a trip this weekend. (A sentence)

Activity

Draw a single line under subjects and a double line under verbs. Crossing out prepositional phrases may help you to find the subjects.

1. A great heap of dusty pots and pans covers the top of our refrigerator.

2. In June, sagging Christmas decorations were still hanging in the windows of the abandoned house.

3. The people in the all-night coffee shop seemed weary and lost.

4. Every plant in the dim room bent toward the small window.

5. A glaring headline about the conviction of a local city councillor attracted my attention.

6. Two of the biggest stores in the mall are going out of business.

7. The modem's tiny red lights suddenly started to flicker.

8. A neighbour of mine does all her work at home and e-mails it to her office.

9. The jar of peppercorns tumbled from the spice shelf and shattered on the floor.

10. The scar in the hollow of Brian's throat is the result of an emergency operation to clear his windpipe.

■ Review Test

Draw a single line under subjects and a double line under verbs. Crossing out prepositional phrases may help you to find the subjects.

1. With one graceful motion, the shortstop fielded the grounder and threw to first base.

2. Like human mothers, sheep and goat mothers develop close bonds with their babies.

3. Before class, Jorge and Aaron rushed to the coffee machine in the hall.

4. I punched and prodded my feather pillow before settling down to sleep.

5. Waiting in the long ticket line, Matt shifted his weight from one foot to the other.

6. Ancient Egyptians were branding cattle more than four thousand years ago.

7. Lilacs and honeysuckle perfume our yard on summer nights.

8. The mail carrier abruptly halted her Jeep and backed up toward the mailbox.

9. During the War of 1812, some Upper Canadian families of German background sold their land and moved to Pennsylvania, where Amish and Mennonite communities formed.

10. Frantic with anxiety, the little girl's family called a psychic to help locate the child.

Fragments

Every sentence must have a subject and a verb and must express a complete thought. A word group that lacks a subject or a verb and that does not express a complete thought is a *fragment*. Following are the most common types of fragments that people write:

1 Dependent-word fragments

2 *-ing* and *to* fragments

3 Added-detail fragments

4 Missing-subject fragments

Once you understand the specific kind or kinds of fragments that you may write, you should be able to eliminate them from your writing. The following pages explain all four fragment types.

DEPENDENT-WORD FRAGMENTS

Some word groups that begin with a dependent word are fragments. Below is a list of common dependent words. Whenever you start a sentence with one of these words, you must be careful that a fragment does not result.

after	if, even if	when, whenever
although, though	in order that	where, wherever
as	since	whether
because	that, so that	which, whichever
before	unless	while
even though	until	who
how	what, whatever	whose

In the example below, the word group beginning with the dependent word *After* is a fragment:

> After I cashed my paycheque. I treated myself to dinner.

A *dependent statement*—one starting with a dependent word like *After*—cannot stand alone. It depends on another statement to complete the thought. *After I cashed my paycheque* is a dependent statement. It leaves us hanging. We expect in the same sentence to find out *what happened after* the writer cashed the cheque. When a writer does not follow through and complete a thought, a fragment results.

To correct the fragment, simply follow through and complete the thought:

> After I cashed my paycheque, I treated myself to dinner.

Remember, then, that *dependent statements by themselves are fragments.* They must be attached to a statement that makes sense standing alone.

Here are two other examples of dependent-word fragments:

> I won't leave the house. Until I hear from you.
> Rick finally picked up the socks. That he had thrown on the floor days ago.

Until I hear from you is a fragment; it does not make sense standing by itself. We want to know in the same statement *what cannot happen* until I hear from you. The writer must complete the thought. Likewise, *That he had thrown on the floor days ago* is not in itself a complete thought. We want to know in the same statement what *that* refers to.

How to Correct a Dependent-Word Fragment

In most cases you can correct a dependent-word fragment by attaching it to the sentence that comes after it or the sentence that comes before it:

> After I cashed my paycheque, I treated myself to dinner.
> (The fragment has been attached to the sentence that comes after it.)

> I won't leave the house until I hear from you.
> (The fragment has been attached to the sentence that comes before it.)

> Rick finally picked up the socks that he had thrown on the floor days ago.
> (The fragment has been attached to the sentence that comes before it.)

Another way of correcting a dependent-word fragment is simply to eliminate the dependent word by rewriting the sentence.

> I cashed my paycheque and then treated myself to dinner.
> I will wait to hear from you.
> He had thrown them on the floor days ago.

Notes

1 Use a comma if a dependent word group comes at the *beginning* of a sentence (see above):

> After I cashed my paycheque, I treated myself to dinner.

However, do not generally use a comma if the dependent word group comes at the *end* of a sentence:

I won't leave the house until I hear from you.
Rick finally picked up the socks that he had thrown on the floor days ago.

2 Sometimes the dependent words *who, that, which,* or *where* appear not at the very start but *near* the start of a word group. A fragment often results:

I drove slowly past the old brick house. The place where I grew up.

The place where I grew up is not in itself a complete thought. We want to know in the same statement *where was the place* the writer grew up. The fragment can be corrected by attaching it to the sentence that comes before it:

I drove slowly past the old brick house, the place where I grew up.

Activity 1

Turn each of the dependent word groups into a sentence by adding a complete thought. Use a comma after the dependent word group if a dependent word starts the sentence. Note the examples.

Examples   Although I felt miserable
Although I felt miserable, I tried to smile for the photographer.

The man who found my wallet
The man who found my wallet returned it the next day.

1. If I don't get a raise soon

_____

_____

2. Because it was raining

_____

_____

3. When I heard the news of the power failure downtown

_____

_____

4. Because I couldn't find the car keys that slid under the seat

_____

_____

5. The restaurant down the street that we tried

_____

_____

Activity 2

Underline the dependent-word fragment in each selection. Then rewrite the selections, correcting each fragment by attaching it to the sentence that comes before or the sentence that comes after—whichever sounds more natural. Use a comma after the dependent word group if it starts the sentence.

1. Whenever I use a product that sprays. My cat arches her back. She thinks she is hearing a hissing enemy.

   _____

   _____

2. My father, a sales representative, was on the road all week. We had a great time playing football in the house. Until he came home for the weekend.

   _____

   _____

3. If Kim takes too long saying good-bye to her boyfriend. Her father will start flicking the porch light. Then he will come out with a flashlight.

   _____

   _____

4. Scientists are studying mummified remains. Some of which are thousands of years old. Most of the people were killed by parasites.

   _____

   _____

5. Before I turn on the microwave to cook something. I have to turn off the overhead light in the kitchen. Otherwise the circuits overload.

   _____

   _____

-*ING* AND *TO* FRAGMENTS, OR *VERBAL* FRAGMENTS

When an -*ing* word appears at or near the start of a word group, a fragment may result. Such fragments often lack a subject and part of the verb. *Doing, walking,* and other such verb forms ending in *ing* are *verbals, not complete verbs;* these words alone cannot be the "true verb" in a sentence. *To do, to receive,* and other *to* forms of verbs are *infinitive forms of verbs, not personal finite forms of verbs;* these must be "limited," or "made finite," as in *we do,* or *they received,* or used in combination with "true verbs."

Underline the word groups in the selections below that contain -*ing* words. Each is a fragment.

1. Ellen walked all over the neighbourhood yesterday. Trying to find her dog Bo. Several people claimed they had seen him only hours before.

2. We sat back to watch the movie. Not expecting anything special. To our surprise, we clapped, cheered, and cried for the next two hours.

3. I telephoned the balloon store. It being the day before our wedding anniversary. I knew my wife would be surprised to receive a dozen heart-shaped balloons.

People sometimes write *-ing* fragments because they think the subject in one sentence will work for the next word group as well. Thus, in the first selection, they think the subject *Ellen* in the opening sentence will also serve as the subject for *Trying to find her dog Bo.* But the subject must actually be *in* the sentence.

How to Correct *-ing* Fragments

1 Attach the fragment to the sentence that comes before or the sentence that comes after it, whichever makes sense. Item 1 could read, "Ellen walked all over the neighbourhood yesterday trying to find her dog Bo."

2 Add a subject and change the *-ing* verb part to the correct or "true" form of the verb. Selection 2 could read, "We didn't expect anything special."

3 Change *being* to the correct form of the verb *be (am, are, is, was, were)*. Selection 3 could read, "It was the day before our wedding anniversary."

How to Correct *to* Fragments

When *to* appears at or near the start of a word group, a fragment sometimes results:

At the Chinese restaurant, Tim used chopsticks. To impress his date. He spent one hour eating a small bowl of rice.

The second word group is a fragment and can be corrected by adding it to the preceding sentence. The *infinitive* verb form *to impress* has been made part of the "true verb" *used:*

At the Chinese restaurant, Tim used chopsticks to impress his date.

Activity 1

Underline the *-ing* fragment in each of the selections that follow. Then make it a sentence by rewriting it, using the method described in parentheses.

Example   Stepping hard on the accelerator. Stan tried to beat the truck to the intersection. He lost by a hood.
(Add the fragment to the sentence that comes after it.)

Stepping hard on the accelerator, Stan tried to beat the truck to

the intersection.

1. Flattening the young plants in the cornfield. Marble-sized hailstones fell from the sky. A year's work was lost in an hour.
(Add the fragment to the preceding sentence.)

_____

_____

2. Fire trucks raced wildly through the streets, their sirens blaring. Coming to a stop at my house. I was only burning a pile of leaves.
(Correct the fragment by adding to it a subject and by changing the verbal to a "true verb" form.)

_____

_____

3. My phone doesn't ring. Instead, a light on it blinks. The reason for this added feature being that I am partially deaf.
(Correct the fragment by changing the verbal to a "true verb" form.)

_____

_____

Activity 2

Underline the -ing or to fragment in each selection. Then rewrite each selection, correcting the fragment by using one of the three methods described above.

1. Looking with horror at the worm on the table. Shelley groaned. She knew she wouldn't like what the biology instructor said next.

_____

_____

2. I put a box of baking soda in the freezer. To try to get rid of the musty smell that greets me whenever I open it. However, my ice cubes still taste like old socks.

_____

_____

3. Staring at the clock on the far wall, perspiring like a long-distance runner, and shifting from foot to foot. I nervously began my speech. I was afraid to look at any of the people in the room.

_____

_____

4. Fantasizing wildly about the upcoming weekend's activities in a kind of hazy daydream. Winston sat quietly at his desk. He might meet the girl of his dreams at Saturday night's party.

_____

_____

5. To find the only available public transport around here. You have to walk two blocks out of your way. The endless sidewalk construction continuing throughout the season.

_____

_____

ADDED-DETAIL FRAGMENTS

Added-detail fragments lack a subject and a verb. They often begin with one of the following words:

also	especially	except	for example	like	including	such as

Underline the one added-detail fragment in each of the selections that follow:

1 Before a race, I eat starchy food. Such as bread and pasta. The carbohydrates provide quick energy.

2 Bob is taking a night course in auto mechanics. Also, one in plumbing. He wants to save money on household repairs.

3 My son keeps several pets in his room. Including hamsters, mice, and gerbils.

People often write added-detail fragments for much the same reason they write *-ing* fragments. They think the subject and verb in one sentence will serve for the next word group. But the subject and verb must be in *each* word group.

How to Correct Added-Detail Fragments

1 Attach the fragment to the complete thought that precedes it. Item 1 could read, "Before a race, I eat starchy foods such as bread and pasta."

2 Add a subject and a verb to the fragment to make it a complete sentence. Selection 2 could read, "Bob is taking a night course in auto mechanics. Also, he is taking one in plumbing."

3 Insert the fragment within the preceding sentence. Item 3 could read, "My son keeps several pets, including hamsters, mice, and gerbils, in his room."

Activity 1

Underline the fragment in each of the selections below. Then make it a sentence by rewriting it, using the method described in parentheses.

Example   My mother likes watching daytime television shows. Especially quiz shows and soap operas. She doesn't mind commercials.
(Add the fragment to the preceding sentence.)

My mother likes watching daytime television shows, especially quiz

shows and soap operas.

1. Luis works evenings in a video store. He enjoys the fringe benefits. For example, seeing the new movies first.
(Correct the fragment by adding a subject and verb to the fragment.)

_____

_____

2. Bob's fingernails are ragged from years of working as a mechanic. And his fingertips are always black. Like ink pads.
   (Add the fragment to the preceding sentence.)

   _____

   _____

3. Electronic devices keep getting smaller. Such as video cameras and cell phones. Some are so tiny they look like toys.
   (Correct the fragment by inserting it into the preceding sentence.)

   _____

   _____

Activity 2

Underline the added-detail fragment in each selection. Then rewrite to correct the fragment. Use one of the three methods described above.

1. Left-handed students face problems. For example, right-handed desks that make writing almost impossible. Spiral notebooks can also be uncomfortable to use.

   _____

   _____

2. Mrs. Daly always wears her lucky clothes to bingo. Such as a blouse printed with four-leaf clovers and dancing dollar signs. She also carries a rhinestone horseshoe.

   _____

   _____

3. Hundreds of moths were fluttering around the stadium lights. Like large flecks of snow in a blizzard. The thirty-degree weather, though, made this form of precipitation unlikely.

   _____

   _____

4. Luc buys and sells paper collectors' items. For instance, vintage comic books, trading cards, and movie posters. He sets up a display at local flea markets and fall fairs.

   _____

   _____

5. I wonder now why I had to learn certain subjects. Such as geometry. No one has ever asked me about the hypotenuse of a triangle.

   _____

   _____

MISSING-SUBJECT FRAGMENTS

In each item below, underline the word group in which the subject is missing:

1 Alicia loved getting wedding presents. But hated writing the thank-you notes.

2 Mike has orange pop and potato chips for breakfast. Then eats more junk food, like root beer, chocolate bars, and cookies, for lunch.

How to Correct Missing-Subject Fragments

1 Attach the fragment to the preceding sentence. Item 1 could read, "Alice loved getting her wedding presents but hated writing the thank-you notes."

2 Add a subject (which can often be a pronoun standing for the subject in the preceding sentence). Selection 2 could read, "Then he eats more junk food, like root beer, chocolate bars, and cookies, for lunch."

Activity

Underline the missing-subject fragment in each selection. Then rewrite that part of the selection needed to correct the fragment. Use one of the two methods of correction described above.

1. Every other day, Karen runs three kilometres. Then does fifty sit-ups. She hasn't lost weight, but she is more muscular.

_____

_____

2. I like all kinds of fresh pizza. But refuse under any conditions to eat frozen pizzas. The sauce on them is always dried out, and the crust tastes like leather.

_____

_____

3. Many people are allergic to seafood. Their mouths swell up and they choke when they eat it by mistake. And can even have trouble breathing or need to go to the emergency ward.

_____

_____

4. To distract me, the dentist tugged at the corner of my mouth. Then jabbed a needle and very speedily injected a pain killer. I hardly felt it.

_____

_____

5. Last semester, I took six courses. And worked part-time in a discount drug store, snoozing during some of the late shifts. Now that the term is all over, I don't know how I did it.

_____

_____

A Review: How to Check for Sentence Fragments

1 Read your paper aloud from the *last* sentence to the *first.* You will be better able to see and hear whether each word group you read is a complete thought.

2 Ask yourself of any word group you think is a fragment: Does this contain a subject and a verb and express a complete thought?

3 More specifically, be on the lookout for the most common fragments:

- Dependent-word fragments (starting with words like *after, because, since, when,* and *before*)
- *-ing* and *to* fragments (*-ing* or *to* at or near the start of a word group)
- Added-detail fragments (starting with words like *for example, such as, also,* and *especially*)
- Missing-subject fragments (a verb is present but not the subject)

■ **Review Test 1**

Each word group in the following student paragraph is numbered. In the space provided, write *C* if a word group is a complete sentence; write *F* if it is a fragment. You will find eight fragments in the paragraph.

1.
2.
3.
4.
5.
6.
7.
8.
9.
10.
11.
12.
13.
14.
15.
16.
17.
18.
19.
20.

¹I'm starting to think that there is no safe place left. ²To ride a bicycle. ³When I try to ride on the highway, in order to go to school. ⁴I feel like a rabbit being pursued by predators. ⁵Drivers whip past me at high speeds. ⁶And try to see how close they can get to my bike without actually killing me. ⁷When they pull onto the shoulder of the road or make a right turn. ⁸Drivers completely ignore my vehicle. ⁹On city streets, I feel more like a cockroach than a rabbit. ¹⁰Drivers in the city despise bicycles. ¹¹Regardless of an approaching bike rider. ¹²Doors of parked cars will unexpectedly open into the street. ¹³Frustrated drivers who are stuck in traffic will make nasty comments. ¹⁴Or shout out obscene propositions. ¹⁵Even pedestrians in the city show their disregard for me. ¹⁶While jaywalking across the street. ¹⁷The pedestrian will treat me, a law-abiding bicyclist, to a withering look of disdain. ¹⁸Pedestrians may even cross my path deliberately. ¹⁹As if to prove their higher position in the pecking order of the city streets. ²⁰Today, bicycling can be hazardous to the rider's health.

Now (on separate paper) correct the fragments you have found. Attach the fragments to sentences that come before or after them, or make whatever other change is needed to turn each fragment into a sentence.

■ **Review Test 2**

Underline the two fragments in each item below. Then make whatever changes are needed to turn the fragments into sentences.

Example   Sharon was going to charge her new suit. <u>But then decided to pay cash instead.</u>

She remembered her New Year's resolution. <u>To cut down on her use of credit cards.</u>

1. We both began to tire. As we passed the halfway mark in the race. But whenever I heard Reggie's footsteps behind me. I pumped my legs faster.

2. I have a few phobias. Such as fear of heights and fear of dogs. My nightmare is to be trapped in a hot-air balloon. With three German shepherds.

3. My children joke that we celebrate "Hanumas." With our Jewish neighbours. We share Hanukkah and Christmas activities. Including making potato pancakes at their house and decorating our tree.

4. Punching all the buttons on his radio in sequence. Phil kept looking for a good song. He was in the mood to cruise down the highway. And sing at the top of his voice.

5. I noticed two cartons of cigarettes. Sticking up out of my neighbour's garbage bag. I realized he had made up his mind. To give up smoking for the fifth time this year.

6. I've decided to leave home. And rent an apartment. By being away from home and on my own. I will get along better with my parents.

7. The alley behind our house was flat. Except for a wide groove in the centre. We used to sail paper boats down the groove. Whenever it rained hard enough to create a "river" there.

8. Don passed the computer school's aptitude test. Which qualifies him for nine months of training. Don kidded that anyone could be accepted. If he or she had four thousand dollars.

■ **Review Test 3**

Turn each of the following word groups into a complete sentence.

Examples   With trembling hands
With trembling hands, I headed for the front of the classroom.

As the race wore on
Some runners dropped out as the race wore on.

1. After the storm passed

   _____

2. Such as fresh fruits and vegetables

   _____

3. During the mystery movie

   _____

4. But soon grew frustrated

   _____

5. Nico, who works at his uncle's restaurant

   _____

6. To get to class on time

   _____

7. The ants swarming over the lollipop

   _____

8. Hurrying to get dressed

   _____

9. Up in the attic

   _____

10. Losing my temper

   _____

Run-Ons

A *run-on* is two complete thoughts that are run together with no adequate sign given to mark the break between them.*

Some run-ons have no punctuation at all to mark the break between the thoughts. Such run-ons are known as *fused sentences:* they are fused, or joined together, as if they were only one thought.

Fused Sentences

Mario told everyone in the room to be quiet his favourite show was on.
My blow-dryer overheated and shut off I showed up for work with clown-hair.

In other run-ons, known as *comma splices,* a comma is used to connect, or "splice" together, the two complete thoughts. However, a comma alone is *not enough* to connect two complete thoughts. Some stronger connection than a comma alone is needed.

Comma Splices

Mario told everyone in the room to be quiet, his favourite show was on.
My blow-dryer overheated and shut off, I showed up for work with clown-hair.

Comma splices are the most common kind of run-on. Students sense that some kind of connection is needed between two thoughts, and so they often put a comma at the dividing point. But the comma alone is *not sufficient.* A comma is simply a punctuation pause-mark, which cannot join ideas. A stronger, clearer mark is needed between the two complete thoughts.

---

*Note: Some instructors refer to each complete thought in a run-on as an *independent clause. A clause* is simply a group of words having a subject and a verb. A clause may be *independent* (expressing a complete thought and able to stand alone) or *dependent* (not expressing a complete thought and not able to stand alone). Using this terminology, we would say that a run-on is two independent clauses run together with no adequate sign given to mark the break between them.

A Warning—Words That Can Lead to Run-Ons: People often write run-ons when the second complete thought begins with one of the following words:

I	we	there	now
you	they	this	then
he, she, it	that	next	

Remember to be on the alert for run-ons whenever you use one of these words in writing a paper.

HOW TO CORRECT RUN-ONS

Here are three common methods of correcting a run-on:

1 Use a period and a capital letter to break the two complete thoughts into separate sentences:

Mario told everyone in the room to be quiet. His favourite show was on.
My blow-dryer overheated and shut off. I showed up for work with clown-hair.

2 Use a comma plus a joining word *(and, but, for, or, nor, so, yet)* to connect the two complete thoughts:

Mario told everyone in the room to be quiet, for his favourite show was on.
My blow-dryer overheated and shut off, and I showed up for work with clown-hair.

3 Use a semicolon to connect the two complete thoughts:

Mario told everyone in the room to be quiet; his favourite show was on.
My blow-dryer overheated and shut off; I showed up for work with clown-hair.

A semicolon, which was once called a "strong comma," is a form of "punctuation glue"; it *can* join two independent parts of a sentence without a joining word.

A fourth method of correcting a run-on is to use *subordination*. The following activities will give you practice in the first three methods. Subordination was described fully on page 109.

Method 1: Period and a Capital Letter

One way of correcting a run-on is to use a period and a capital letter between the two complete thoughts. Use this method especially if the thoughts are not closely related or if another method would make the sentence too long.

Activity

In each of the following run-ons, locate the point at which one complete thought ends and another begins. Each is a *fused sentence*—that is, each consists of two sentences fused, or joined together, with no punctuation at all between them. Reading each sentence aloud will help you "hear" where a major break or split between the thoughts occurs. At such a point, your voice will probably drop and pause.

Correct the run-on by putting a period at the end of the first thought and a capital letter at the start of the next thought.

Example   Rena's clock radio doesn't work anymore. ~~s~~he spilled a glass of pop on it.

1. The men at the door claimed to have paving material left over from another job they wanted to pave our driveway for a "bargain price."

2. Linh, a legal assistant who speaks Vietnamese, helps other people from her country write wills she assists others by going with them when they have to appear in court.

3. Vicky has her own style of dressing she wore a tuxedo with a red bow tie to her cousin's wedding.

4. In the summer, ants are attracted to water they will often enter a house through the dishwasher.

5. Humans have managed to adapt to any environment they can survive in Arctic wastes, tropical jungles, and barren deserts.

6. A five-year-old child knows over six thousand words he or she has also learned more than one thousand rules of grammar.

7. I rummaged around the crowded drawer looking for a pair of scissors then they suddenly stabbed me in the finger.

8. Squirrels like to jump from a tree onto our roof their footsteps sound like ghosts running around our attic.

Method 2: Comma and a Joining Word

Another way of correcting a run-on is to use a comma plus a joining word to connect the two complete thoughts. Joining words (also called *conjunctions*) include *and, but, for, or, nor, so,* and *yet.* Here is what the four most common joining words mean:

and   in addition

> Teresa works full-time for an accounting firm, and she takes evening classes.

(*And* means in "addition": Teresa works full-time for an accounting firm; *in addition,* she takes evening classes.)

but   however, on the other hand

> I turned to the want ads, but I knew my dream job wouldn't be listed.

(*But* means "however": I turned to the want ads; *however,* I knew my dream job wouldn't be listed.)

for   because

> Lizards become sluggish at night, for they need the sun's warmth to maintain an active body temperature.

(*For* means "because": Lizards become sluggish at night *because* they need the sun's warmth to maintain an active body temperature.)

so   as a result, therefore

> The canoe touched bottom, so Dave pushed it toward deeper water.

(*So* means "as a result": The canoe touched bottom; *as a result,* Dave pushed it toward deeper water.)

Activity 1

Insert the joining word *(and, but, for, so)* that logically connects the two thoughts in each sentence.

1. Napoleon may have been a brave general, _____ he was afraid of cats.

2. The large dog was growling at me, _____ there were white bubbles of foam around his mouth.

3. The library had just closed, _____ I couldn't get any of the reserved books.

4. He checked on the new baby every five minutes, _____ he was afraid something would happen to her.

5. Kate thought the milk was fresh, _____ it broke up into little sour flakes in her coffee.

6. Elephants have no thumbs, _____ baby elephants suck their trunks.

7. Lorne heard a noise and looked out the window, _____ the only thing there was his reflection.

8. Although I like most creatures, I am not fond of snakes, _____ I like spiders even less.

Activity 2

Add a complete and closely related thought to go with each of the following statements. Use a comma plus the italicized joining word when you write the second thought.

Example   FOR   I decided to leave school an hour early, *for I had a*

pounding headache.

BUT

1. The corner store is convenient _____

_____

FOR

2. Leo attended night class _____

_____

AND

3. Aisha studied for an hour before dinner _____

_____

SO

4. Paul can't retrieve his e-mail _____

_____

BUT

5. I needed a haircut _____

_____

Activity 3

Correct each run-on with either (1) a period and a capital letter or (2) a comma and a logical joining word. Do not use the same method of correction for every sentence.

Some of the run-ons are *fused sentences* (there is no punctuation between the two complete thoughts), and some are *comma splices* (there is only a comma between the two complete thoughts).

Example   There was a strange odour in the house,$_\wedge$ *so* Steve called the gas company immediately.

1. Luis got a can of pop from the refrigerator, then he walked outside to sit on the porch steps.

2. Cockroaches adapt to any environment they have even been found living inside nuclear reactors.

3. My dog was panting from the heat I decided to wet him down with the garden hose.

4. Our Environmental Studies class is working on a weather project with students from Russia we communicate by computer almost every day.

5. The best-selling items in the zoo gift shop are the stuffed pandas and the polar bear T-shirts the profits from these items help support the real animals in the zoo.

6. The bristles of the paintbrushes were very stiff, soaking them in turpentine made them soft again.

7. Tri Lee borrows CDs from the library to listen to on the way to work, some are music, and some are recordings of best-selling books.

8. Last week, Rita's two boys chased the babysitter out of the house, now the girl won't come back.

Method 3: Semicolon

A third method of correcting a run-on is to use a semicolon to mark the break between two thoughts. A *semicolon* (;) looks like a period above a comma and is sometimes called a *strong comma*. A semicolon signals more of a pause than a comma alone, but not quite the full pause of a period. When it is used to correct run-ons, the semicolon can be used alone or with a transitional word.

Semicolon Alone: Here are some earlier sentences that were connected with a comma plus a joining word. Now they are connected by a semicolon alone. Notice that the semicolon alone—unlike the comma alone—can be used to connect the two complete thoughts in each sentence:

> Lorne heard a noise and looked out the window; the only thing there was his reflection.

> He checked on the new baby every five minutes; he was afraid something would happen to her.

> Lizards become sluggish at night; they need the sun's warmth to maintain an active body temperature.

> The large dog was growling at me; there were white bubbles of foam around his mouth.

> We knew a power failure had occurred; all the clocks in the building were forty-seven minutes slow.

Using semicolons can add to sentence variety.

Activity

Insert a semicolon where the break occurs between the two complete thoughts in each of the following sentences.

Example   The plumber gave me an estimate of $150; I decided to repair the tap myself.

1. The children stared at the artichokes on their plates they didn't know how to eat the strange vegetable.

2. The Great Wall of China is immense it's the only architectural structure visible from the moon.

3. Elaine woke up at 3 a.m. to the smell of sizzling bacon her husband was having another insomnia attack.

4. Bissan curled up under the covers she tried to get warm by grasping her icy feet with her chilly hands.

5. Ice had formed on the inside edge of our window Joey scratched a *J* in it with his finger.

6. Charles peered into the microscope he saw only his own eyelashes.

Semicolon with a Transitional Word: A semicolon can be used with a transitional word and a comma to join two complete thoughts. Here are some examples:

Larry believes in being prepared for emergencies; therefore, he stockpiles canned goods in his basement.

I tried to cash my paycheque; however, I had forgotten to bring identification.

Athletic shoes must fit perfectly; otherwise, the wearer may injure his or her feet or ankles.

A short nap at the end of the day relaxes me; in addition, it gives me the energy to spend the evening on my homework.

Some zoo animals have not learned how to be good parents; as a result, baby animals are sometimes brought up in zoo nurseries and even in private homes.

People use seventeen muscles when they smile; on the other hand, they use forty-three muscles when they frown.

Following is a list of common transitional words (also known as *adverbial conjunctions*), with brief meanings.

Transitional Word	*Meaning*
however	but
nevertheless	however
on the other hand	however
instead	as a substitute
meanwhile	in the intervening time
otherwise	under other conditions
indeed	in fact
in addition	also, and
also	in addition
moreover	in addition
furthermore	in addition
as a result	thus, therefore
thus	as a result
consequently	as a result
therefore	as a result

Activity

For each sentence, choose a logical transitional word from the box above and write it in the space provided. Use a semicolon *before* the connector and a comma *after* it.

Example   I dread going to parties; _____ *however,* _____ my husband loves meeting new people.

1. Jasmine suffers from migraine headaches _____ her doctor has advised her to avoid caffeine and alcohol.

2. Ray's apartment is always neat and clean _____ the interior of his car looks like the aftermath of a tornado.

3. I try to attend all my math classes _____ I'll get too far behind to pass the weekly quizzes.

4. B.J. was singing Nelly Furtado tunes in the shower _____ his toast was burning in the kitchen.

5. The reporter was tough and experienced _____ even he was stunned by the tragic events.

A Note on Subordination

A fourth method of joining related thoughts is to use subordination. *Subordination* is a way of showing that one thought in a sentence is not as important as another thought. (Review the description of subordination on page 92.) Below are three earlier sentences, recast so that one idea is subordinated to (made less important than) the other idea. In each case, the subordinate (or less important) thought is underlined. Note that each subordinate clause begins with a dependent word.

Because the library had just closed, I couldn't get any of the reserved books.

When the canoe touched bottom, Dave pushed the craft toward deeper water.

I didn't make good time driving to work today because every traffic light was red.

A Review: How to Check for Run-Ons

1 To see if a sentence is a run-on, read it aloud and listen for a break marking two complete thoughts. Your voice will probably drop and pause at the break.

2 To check an entire paper, read it aloud from the *last* sentence to the *first*. Doing so will help you hear and see each complete thought.

3 Be on the lookout for words that can lead to run-on sentences:

I	he, she, it	they	this	then	now
you	we	there	that	next	

4 Correct run-ons by using one of the following methods:
- Period and a capital letter
- Comma and a joining word (*and, but, for, or, nor, so, yet*)
- Semicolon, alone or with a transitional word
- Subordination

■ Review Test 1

Correct each run-on with either (1) a period and a capital letter or (2) a comma (if needed) and the joining word *and, but, for,* or *so.* Do not use the same method of correction for every sentence.

Some of the run-ons are fused sentences (there is no punctuation between the two complete thoughts), and some are comma splices (there is only a comma between the two complete thoughts). One sentence is correct.

1. Our boss expects us to work four hours without a break, he wanders off to a vending machine at least once an hour.

2. The children in the next car were making faces at other drivers, when I made a face back the youngsters giggled and sank out of sight.

3. Joel bent over and lifted the heavy tray then he heard an ominous crack in his back.

4. The branches of the tree were bare they made a dark feathery pattern against the orange-pink sunset.

5. In the grimy bakery window, cobwebs were in every corner, and a mouse was crawling over a birthday cake.

6. Our class wanted to do something for the earthquake victims, we sent a donation to the Red Cross.

7. Aunt Jeanne wanted to live in a warmer climate for her health she moved to Vancouver.

8. The average Canadian teenager spends thirty-eight hours a week on schoolwork the average Japanese teenager spends about sixty.

■ Review Test 2

Correct each run-on by using (1) a period and a capital letter, (2) a comma and a joining word, or (3) a semicolon. Do not use one method exclusively.

1. The magazine had lain in the damp mailbox for two days its pages were blurry and swollen.

2. With a groan, Marisa pried off her high heels, then she plunged her swollen feet into a bucket of baking soda and hot water.

3. Hypnosis has nothing to do with the occult it is merely a state of deep relaxation.

4. Many young adults today live at home with their parents this allows them to save money for the future.

5. I waited for the clanking train to clear the intersection rusty boxcars just kept rolling slowly along the rails.

6. The real Laura Secord had nothing to do with chocolate, she was a brave woman who ran through the forests of southern Ontario, she relied on the help of Native Canadians to warn British troops of an American attack.

7. The words *month, silver, purple,* and *orange* have something in common, no other English words rhyme with them.

8. The broken pop machine dispensed a cup or pop, it would not provide both at the same time.

■ Review Test 3

Locate and correct the five run-ons in the passage that follows.

> My worst experience of the week was going home for lunch, rather than eating at work. My children didn't know I was coming, they had used most of the bread on hand. All I had to make a sandwich with were two thin, crumpled pieces of crust. I sat there eating my tattered sandwich and trying to relax, then the telephone rang. It was for my daughter, who was in the bathroom, she called down to me that I should get the person's name and number. As soon as I sat down again, someone knocked on the door, it was a neatly dressed couple with bright eyes who wanted to talk with me about a higher power in life. I politely got rid of them and went back to finish lunch. I thought I would relax over my coffee I had to break up a fight between my two young sons about which television channel to watch. As a last bit of frustration, my daughter came downstairs and asked me to drive her over to a friend's house before I went back to work.

■ Review Test 4

Write quickly for five minutes about what you did this past weekend. Don't worry about spelling, punctuation, finding exact words, or organizing your thoughts. Just focus on writing as many words as you can without stopping.

After you have finished, go back and correct any run-ons in your writing.

Regular and Irregular Verbs

REGULAR VERBS

A Brief Review of Regular Verbs

Every verb has four principal parts: *present, past, past participle,* and *present participle.* These parts can be used to build all the verb tenses (the times shown by a verb).

Most verbs in English are regular. The past and past participles of a regular verb are formed by adding *-d* or *-ed* to the present. The *past participle* is the form of the verb used with the helping verbs *have, has,* or *had* (or some form of *be* with passive verbs). The *present participle* is formed by adding *-ing* to the present.

Here are the principal parts of some regular verbs:

Present	*Past*	*Past Participle*	*Present Participle*
shout	shouted	shouted	shouting
prepare	prepared	prepared	preparing
surprise	surprised	surprised	surprising
tease	teased	teased	teasing
frighten	frightened	frightened	frightening

A Note about Verb Tenses and Other Languages

English verb tenses can be particularly confusing to students from other language backgrounds. Not all languages express time distinctions through their verbs in the same ways that English does. Some language groups may have only three tense-forms; others may have tenses English does not use. Because of the structural differences between Asian languages and English, ESL students from Asian cultures may find English verb tenses confusing. Asian languages do not alter verb forms to indicate changes in time referred to; instead a "time marker" word is used, and the verb's form does not change. For these students, extra patience and practice with English verb tenses are required, but with continued attention to English verb tenses, students can master their use.

Present Tense Endings: The verb ending -s or -es is needed with a regular verb in the present tense when the subject is *he, she, it,* or any *one person or thing.* Take care to make the subject *agree* with its verb.

> He read<u>s</u> every night.
> She watch<u>es</u> television every night.
> It appear<u>s</u> they have little in common.

Activity

Verbs in the sentences that follow do not agree with their subjects. Cross out each incorrect verb form and write the correct present tense of the verb in the space provided.

_____   1. My radio wake me up every morning with soft music.

_____   2. Lynn and Risa always clowns around at the start of the class.

_____   3. My wife watch our baby in the morning, and I take over afternoons.

_____   4. Many more men wants to go to nursing school next year.

_____   5. My brain work much better at night than it does in early morning.

Past Tense Endings: The verb ending -d or -ed is needed with a regular verb in the past tense.

> This morning I complet<u>ed</u> my research paper.
> The recovering hospital patient walk<u>ed</u> slowly down the corridor.
> Some students hiss<u>ed</u> when the new assignment was given out.

Activity

Some verbs in the sentences that follow need -d or -ed endings. Cross out each incorrect verb form and write the standard form in the space provided.

_____   1. One of my teeth cave in when I bit on the hard pretzel.

_____   2. The accident victim complains of dizziness right before she passed out.

_____   3. We realize a package was missing when we got back from shopping.

_____   4. I burn a hole in my shirt while I was ironing it.

_____   5. The impatient driver edges her car into the intersection while the light was still red.

IRREGULAR VERBS

Irregular verbs have irregular forms in the past tense and past participle. For example, the past tense of the irregular verb *choose* is *chose;* its past participle is *chosen.*

Almost everyone has some degree of trouble with irregular verbs. When you are unsure about the form of a verb, you can check the list of irregular verbs on the following pages. (The present participle is not shown on this list because it is formed simply by adding *-ing* to the base form of the verb.) Or you can check a dictionary, which gives the principal parts of irregular verbs.

A List of Irregular Verbs

Present	*Past*	*Past Participle*
arise	arose	arisen
awake	awoke *or* awaked	awoken *or* awaked
be (am, are, is)	was (were)	been
become	became	become
begin	began	begun
bend	bent	bent
bite	bit	bitten
blow	blew	blown
break	broke	broken
bring	brought	brought
build	built	built
burst	burst	burst
buy	bought	bought
catch	caught	caught
choose	chose	chosen
come	came	come
cost	cost	cost
cut	cut	cut
do (does)	did	done
draw	drew	drawn
drink	drank	drunk
drive	drove	driven
eat	ate	eaten
fall	fell	fallen
feed	fed	fed
feel	felt	felt
fight	fought	fought
find	found	found
fly	flew	flown
freeze	froze	frozen

Present	*Past*	*Past Participle*
get	got	got *or* gotten
give	gave	given
go (goes)	went	gone
grow	grew	grown
have (has)	had	had
hear	heard	heard
hide	hid	hidden
hold	held	held
hurt	hurt	hurt
keep	kept	kept
know	knew	known
lay	laid	laid
lead	led	led
leave	left	left
lend	lent	lent
let	let	let
lie	lay	lain
light	lit	lit
lose	lost	lost
make	made	made
meet	met	met
pay	paid	paid
ride	rode	ridden
ring	rang	rung
run	ran	run
say	said	said
see	saw	seen
sell	sold	sold
send	sent	sent
shake	shook	shaken
shrink	shrank	shrunk
shut	shut	shut
sing	sang	sung
sit	sat	sat
sleep	slept	slept
speak	spoke	spoken
spend	spent	spent
stand	stood	stood
steal	stole	stolen
stick	stuck	stuck
sting	stung	stung
swear	swore	sworn
swim	swam	swum
take	took	taken

Present	*Past*	*Past Participle*
teach	taught	taught
tear	tore	torn
tell	told	told
think	thought	thought
wake	woke *or* waked	woken *or* waked
wear	wore	worn
win	won	won
write	wrote	written

Activity

Cross out the incorrect verb form in each of the following sentences. Then write the correct form of the verb in the space provided.

flown   ***Example***   After it had ~~flew~~ into the picture window, the dazed bird huddled on the ground.

1. As graduation neared, Michelle worried about the practicality of the program she'd chose.

2. Before we could find seats, the theatre darkened and the opening credits begun to roll.

3. To be polite, I drunk the slightly sour wine that my grandfather poured from his carefully hoarded supply.

4. The inexperienced nurse shrunk from touching the patient's raw, burned skin.

5. After a day on the noisy construction site, Sam's ears rung for hours with steady hum.

6. Sheila had forget to write her student number on the test form, so the computer rejected her answer sheet.

7. If I had went to work ten minutes earlier, I would have avoided being caught in the gigantic traffic snarl.

8. Prehistoric people blowed paint over their outstretched hands to stencil their handprints on cave walls.

■ Review Test 1

Cross out the incorrect verb form in each sentence. Then write the correct form in the space provided.

1. The health inspectors walk into the kitchen as the cook was picking up a hamburger off the floor.

2. The thieves would have stole my stereo, but I had had it engraved with a special identification number.

_____   3. He had tore his girlfriend's picture into little pieces and tossed them out the window.

_____   4. Because I has asthma, I carry an inhaler to use when I lose my breath.

_____   5. Baked potatoes doesn't have as many calories as I thought.

_____   6. Yesterday I check my bank balance and saw my money was getting low.

_____   7. Many childhood diseases has almost vanished in Canada.

_____   8. Nancy sticked notes on the refrigerator with fruit-shaped magnets.

■ **Review Test 2**

Write short sentences that use the form requested for the following verbs.

Example   Past of grow   *I grew my own tomatoes last year.*_____

1. Past of *know* _____

2. Present of *take* _____

3. Past participle of *give* _____

4. Past participle of *write* _____

5. Past of *do* _____

6. Past of *talk* _____

7. Present of *begin* _____

8. Past of *go* _____

9. Past participle of *see* _____

10. Present of *drive* _____

A Note about Nonstandard Forms of Regular Verbs

Many people have grown up in communities where nonstandard forms of regular verbs are used in everyday speech. Instead of saying, for example, "That girl *looks* tired," a person using a community dialect or patois might say, "That girl *look* tired." Community dialects have richness and power but are generally not accepted in writing tasks in college and in the world of work, where regular English verb forms must be used.

tion • Description • Examples • Process • Cause and Effect • Comparison and Contrast
ition • Division and Classification • Argumentation • Narration • Description • Examples
ss • Cause and Effect • Comparison and Contrast • Definition • Division and Classification
mentation • Narration • Description • Examples • Process • Cause and Effect • Comparison and
ast • Definition • Division and Classification • Argumentation • Narration • Description

C H A P T E R   2 6

Subject–Verb Agreement

A verb must agree with its subject in number. A *singular subject* (one person or thing) takes a singular verb. A *plural subject* (more than one person or thing) takes a plural verb. Mistakes in subject–verb agreement are sometimes made in the following situations:

1 When words come between the subject and the verb
2 When a verb comes before the subject
3 With compound subjects
4 With indefinite pronouns

Each of these situations is explained on the following pages.

WORDS BETWEEN SUBJECT AND VERB

Words that come between the subject and the verb do not change subject–verb agreement. In the sentence

> The crinkly lines *around Joan's eyes* give her a friendly look.

the subject *(lines)* is plural and so the verb *(give)* is plural. The words that come between the subject and the verb are a prepositional phrase: *around Joan's eyes.* They do not affect subject–verb agreement. (A list of prepositions can be found in the box on page 358.)

To help find the subject of certain sentences, cross out prepositional phrases.

> The lumpy salt ~~in the shakers~~ needs to be changed.
> An old television ~~with a round screen~~ has sat in our basement for years.

Activity

Underline the subject and lightly cross out any words that come between the subject and the verb. Then double-underline the verb in parentheses that you believe is correct.

1. Some members of the parents' association (want, wants) to ban certain books from the school library.

2. Chung's trench coat, with its big lapels and shoulder flaps, (make, makes) him feel like a tough private eye.

3. Misconceptions about apes like the gorilla (has, have) turned a relatively peaceful animal into a terrifying monster.

4. The rising costs of necessities like food and shelter (force, forces) some people to live on the streets.

5. In my opinion, a slice of pepperoni pizza and a good video (make, makes) a great evening.

6. Members of the class (design, designs) their own websites as term work.

VERB BEFORE SUBJECT

A verb agrees with its subject even when the verb comes *before* the subject. Words that may precede the subject (when the verb comes before the subject) include *there, here,* and, in questions, *who, which, what,* and *where.*

Here are some examples of sentences in which the verb appears before the subject:

There are wild dogs in our neighbourhood.

In the distance was a billow of black smoke.

Here is the newspaper.

Where are the children's coats?

If you are unsure about the subject, ask *who* or *what* of the verb. With the first example above, you might ask, "*What* are in our neighbourhood?" The answer, *wild dogs,* is the subject.

Activity

Write the correct form of each verb in the space provided.

(IS, ARE)   1. There _____ dozens of frenzied shoppers waiting for the store to open.

(IS, ARE)   2. Here _____ the notes from yesterday's computer graphics lecture.

(DO, DOES)   3. When _____ we take our break?

(WAS, WERE)   4. There _____ scraps of yellowing paper stuck between the pages of the cookbook.

(WAS, WERE)   5. At the very bottom of the grocery list _____ an item that meant a trip all the way back to aisle one.

(IS, ARE)   6. Among the students in the class _____ those who can't keep up with the assignments.

COMPOUND SUBJECTS

A compound subject is two subjects separated by the joining word *and*. Subjects joined by *and* generally take a plural verb.

> A patchwork <u>quilt</u> and a sleeping <u>bag</u> <u><u>cover</u></u> my bed in the winter.
>
> <u>Clark</u> and <u>Lois</u> <u><u>are</u></u> a contented couple.

When subjects are joined by *either . . . or, neither . . . nor,* or *not only . . . but also,* the verb agrees with the subject closer to the verb.

> Neither the <u>negotiator</u> nor the union <u>leaders</u> <u><u>want</u></u> the strike to continue.

The nearer subject, *leaders,* is plural, so the verb is plural.

Activity

Write the correct form of the verb in the space provided.

(SIT, SITS)   1. A crusty baking pan and a greasy plate _____ on the countertop.

(COVER, COVERS)   2. Spidery cracks and a layer of dust _____ the ivory keys on the old piano.

(KNOW, KNOWS)   3. Not only the assistant manager but also the support staff _____ that the company is folding.

(WAS, WERE)   4. In eighteenth-century France, makeup and high heels _____ worn by men.

(MAKE, MAKES)   5. In my opinion, a slice of pepperoni pizza and a good video _____ a great evening.

(WANT, WANTS)   6. Neither Tasha nor the rest of the class _____ to work on that project.

(EAT, EATS)   7. Either my dog or the squirrels _____ breadcrusts I put out for the birds.

INDEFINITE PRONOUNS

The following words, known as *indefinite pronouns,* always take singular verbs:

(*-one words*)	(*-body words*)	(*-thing words*)	
one	nobody	nothing	each
anyone	anybody	anything	either
everyone	everybody	everything	neither
someone	somebody	something	

Note: *Both* always takes a plural verb.

Activity

Write the correct form of the verb in the space provided.

(SUIT, SUITS)

1. Neither of those hairstyles _____ the shape of your face.

(MENTION, MENTIONS)

2. Somebody without much sensitivity always _____ my birthmark.

(GIVE, GIVES)

3. The people at the local hardware store _____ friendly advice about home fix-it projects.

(ENTER, ENTERS)

4. Everyone _____ the college kite-flying contest in the spring.

(FALL, FALLS)

5. One of these earrings constantly _____ off my ear.

(PRINT, PRINTS)

6. Each of the students _____ in careful block letters.

(DECIDE, DECIDES)

7. Anybody in the groups we saw _____ who should belong to the committee.

◼ Review Test 1

In the space provided, write the correct form of the verb shown in the margin.

(IS, ARE)

1. As a result of a successful experiment, some users of wheelchairs _____ using trained monkeys as helpers.

(WAS, WERE)

2. Each of their children _____ given a name picked at random from a page of the Bible.

(SEEM, SEEMS)

3. Many of the headlines in the *National Enquirer* _____ hard to believe.

(IS, ARE)

4. Envelopes, file folders, and a telephone book _____ jammed into Linda's kitchen drawers.

(CONTAINS,
CONTAIN)

5. Neither of the main dishes at tonight's dinner _____ any meat.

(DAMAGE,
DAMAGES)

6. The use of metal chains and studded tires _____ highways by chipping away at the paved surface.

(MAKES, MAKE)

7. A metal grab bar bolted onto the tiles _____ it easier for elderly people to get in and out of the bathtub.

(CLEANS, CLEAN)

8. In exchange for a reduced rent, Karla and James _____ the dentist's office beneath their second-floor apartment.

Review Test 2

Cross out the incorrect verb form in each sentence. In addition, underline the subject or subjects that go with the verb. Then write the correct form of the verb in the space provided.

1. Why is Martha and her mother digging a hole in their garden so late at night?

2. Neither of my children look like me.

3. Three goats, a pot-bellied pig, and a duck was among the entrants in the pet parade.

4. Here is the low-calorie cola and the double-chocolate cake you ordered.

5. The odour of those perfumed ads interfere with my enjoyment of a magazine.

6. One of my roommates are always leaving wet towels on the bathroom floor.

7. A man or woman in his or her forties often begin to think about making a contribution to the world and not just about him- or herself.

8. Each of the child's thirty-four stuffed animals have a name and entire life history.

Review Test 3

Complete each of the following sentences using *is, are, was, were, have,* or *has*. Then underline the subject.

Example   For me, <u>popcorn</u> at the movies *is like coffee at breakfast.*

1. Under my roommate's bed _____

2. The car with the purple fenders _____

3. My boss and her secretary _____

4. Neither of the football players _____

5. Here _____

Additional Information about Verbs

The purpose of this special section is to provide additional information about verbs. Some people will find the grammar terms here a helpful reminder of what they learned earlier, in school, about verbs. For them, the terms will increase their understanding of how verbs function in English. Other people may welcome more detailed information about terms used elsewhere in the text. Remember that the most common mistakes with writing verbs have been treated earlier in this book.

VERB TENSE

Verbs tell us the time of an action. The time that a verb shows is usually called *tense*. The most common tenses are the simple present, past, and future. In addition, there are nine other tenses that enable us to express more specific ideas about time than we could with the simple tenses alone. Below and on the next page are the twelve verb tenses and examples of each tense. Read them over to increase your sense of the many different ways of expressing time in English.

The Twelve English Verb Tenses

Tenses	*Examples*
Simple Tenses	
Present	I *work*.
	Tony *works*.
Past	Ellen *worked* on her car.
Future	You *will work* on a new project next week.
Perfect Tenses	
Present perfect	We *have found* the answer to all your problems.
	The stock market *has suffered* from another major scandal in the world of business.

- The present perfect most commonly refers to an action that took place in an indefinite past, at a time that is *not* specified.

> We *have lived* in Toronto for three years.
> He *has studied* at Humber College since last September.

- With certain verbs that suggest a prolonged activity, the present perfect can indicate an action that starts in the past and continues until the present.

Past perfect	When I came home, I noticed that my brother *had eaten* all the cookies.
	By December 31, 1999, programmers *had resolved* most Y2K problems.

- The past perfect tense indicates an action that took place *before* a specified time in the past or *before* another action expressed in the simple past.

Future perfect	By the year 2010, engineers *will have developed* an efficient and economical electric car.
	I *will have done* all my homework by the time the party begins.

- The future perfect tense refers to an action taking place *before* a specified future time or another future action.

Progressive (or Continuous) Tenses

Present progressive	I *am working* on my speech for the debate.
	You *are working* too hard.
	The printer *is not working* properly.
Past progressive	He *was working* in the basement.
	The contestants *were working* on their talent routines.
Future progressive	My son *will be working* in our store this summer.

- *Progressive,* or *continuous tenses,* as the word *continuous* suggests, refer to ongoing actions in the present, past, or future.

Present perfect progressive	Sarah *has been working* late this week.
	(Sarah began *working* late earlier this week, and *continues to do so.*)
Past perfect progressive	Until yesterday, I *had been working* nights.
	(I *worked* nights for some time in the past, and *continued to do so* until yesterday. The action, while continuous, was *in the past, and is completed.*)
Future perfect progressive	My mother *will have been working* as a nurse for forty-five years by the time she retires.
	(My mother *worked* as a nurse in the past, *continues to do so, and will continue to work as a nurse* in the future, until retirement.)

Activity

On separate paper, write twelve sentences using the twelve verb tenses.

HELPING VERBS

There are three common verbs that can either stand alone or combine with (and "help") other verbs. Here are the verbs and their forms:

be (am, are, is, was, were, being, been)	do (does, did)
have (has, having, had)	

Here are examples of the verbs:

Used Alone	***Used as Helping Verbs***
I *was* angry.	I *was growing* angry.
Sheila *has* the key.	Sheila *has forgotten* the key.
He *did* well on the test.	He *did fail* the previous test.

Modal Auxiliaries

There are nine helping verbs (traditionally known as *modals,* or *modal auxiliaries*) that are always used in combination with other verbs. Here are the nine verbs and sentence examples of each:

can	I *can see* the rainbow.
could	I *could* not *find* a seat.
may	The game *may be postponed.*
might	Keesha *might resent* your advice.
shall	I *shall see* you tomorrow.
should	He *should get* his car *serviced.*
will	Terry *will want* to see you.
would	They *would* not *understand.*
must	You *must visit* us again.

Note from the examples that these verbs have only one form. They do not, for instance, add an *-s* when used with *he, she, it,* or any one person or thing.

Activity

On separate paper, write nine sentences using the nine helping verbs listed in the box above.

VERBALS

Verbals are words formed from verbs. Verbals, like verbs, often express action. They can add variety to your sentences and vigour to your writing style. (Verbals, as mentioned in Chapter 23, are not "finite," or "true verbs.") The three kinds of verbals are infinitives, participles, and gerunds.

Infinitive

An infinitive is *to* plus the base form of the verb.

I love *to dance.*
Lina hopes *to write* for a newspaper.
I asked the children *to clean* the kitchen.

Participle

A participle is *a verb form used as an adjective* (a descriptive word). The present participle ends in *-ing*. The past participle ends in *-ed* or has an irregular ending.

Peering into the cracked mirror, the *crying* woman wiped her eyes.
The *astounded* man stared at his *winning* lottery ticket.
Swinging a sharp axe, Muhammad split the *cracked* beam.

Gerund

A gerund is the *-ing* form of a verb used as a noun.

Swimming is the perfect exercise.
Eating junk food is my diet downfall.
Through *doodling,* people express their inner feelings.

Activity

On separate paper, write three sentences using infinitives, three sentences using participles, and three sentences using gerunds.

ACTIVE AND PASSIVE VERBS

When the subject of a sentence *performs the action* of a verb, the verb is in the *active voice.* When the subject of a sentence *receives the action* of a verb, the verb is in the *passive voice.*

The passive form of a verb consists of a form of the verb *be* plus the *past participle of the main verb.* Look at the active and passive forms of the verbs below and on the next page:

Active Voice	*Passive Voice*
Iva *sewed* the curtains.	The curtains *were sewn* by Iva.
(The subject, *Iva,* is the doer of the action.)	(The subject, *curtains,* does not act. Instead they receive the action of sewing.)
The tech assistant *fixed* the hard drive.	The hard drive *was fixed* by the tech assistant.
(The subject, *tech assistant,* is the doer of the action.	(The subject, the *hard drive,* does not act. Instead it receives the action of fixing.)

In general, active verbs are more effective than passive ones. Active verbs give your writing a simpler and more vigorous style. At times, however, the passive form of verbs is appropriate when the performer of the action is unknown or is less important than the receiver of the action. For example:

The tests *were graded* yesterday.
(The performer of the action is unknown.)

Alan *was hurt* by your thoughtless remark.
(The receiver of the action, Alan, is being emphasized.)

Activity

Change the following sentences from the passive to the active voice. Note that you may have to add a subject in some cases.

Examples   The dog was found by a police officer.

The police officer found the dog.

The baseball game was called off.

The official called off the baseball game.

(Here a subject had to be added.)

1. Most of our furniture was damaged by the fire.

   _____

2. Melissa's new dress was singed by a careless smoker.

   _____

3. The problem was solved by the quiet student in the back of the room.

   _____

4. The supermarket shelves were restocked after the truckers' strike.

   _____

5. The children were mesmerized by the magician's sleight of hand.

   _____

Pronoun Agreement and Reference

Pronouns are words that take the place of *nouns* (persons, places, or things). In fact, the word *pronoun* means "for a noun." Pronouns are shortcuts that keep you from unnecessarily repeating words in writing. Here are some examples of pronouns:

> Eddie left *his* camera on the bus. (*His* is a pronoun that takes the place of *Eddie's*.)
> Elena drank the coffee even though *it* was cold. (*It* replaces *coffee*.)
> As I turned the newspaper's damp pages, *they* disintegrated in my hands. (*They* is a pronoun that takes the place of *pages*.)

This section presents rules that will help you avoid two common mistakes people make with pronouns. The rules are

1 A pronoun must agree in number with the word or words it replaces.

2 A pronoun must refer clearly to the word it replaces.

PRONOUN AGREEMENT

A pronoun must agree in number with the word or words it replaces. If the word a pronoun refers to is singular, the pronoun must be singular; if that word is plural, the pronoun must be plural. (Note that the word a pronoun refers to is known as the *antecedent,* or "before-goer." The antecedent is the pronoun's point of reference in the sentence.)

Marie showed me (her) antique wedding band.

Students enrolled in the art class must provide (their) own supplies.

In the first example, the pronoun *her* refers to the singular word *Marie;* in the second example, the pronoun *their* refers to the plural word *Students.*

Activity

Write the appropriate pronoun *(their, they, them, it)* in the blank space in each of the following sentences.

Example   I opened the wet umbrella and put _____*it*_____ in the bathtub to dry.

1. Kasey and Bruce left for the movies earlier than usual, because _____ knew the theatre would be packed.

2. The clothes were still damp, but I decided to fold _____ anyway.

3. Young adults often face a difficult transition period when _____ leave home for the first time.

4. Paul's grandparents renewed _____ marriage vows at a huge fiftieth wedding anniversary celebration.

5. The car's steering wheel began to pull to one side, and then _____ started to shimmy.

Indefinite Pronouns

The following words are always singular:

(*-one words*)	(*-body words*)	
one	nobody	each
anyone	anybody	either
everyone	everybody	neither
someone	somebody	

If a pronoun in a sentence refers to one of these singular words (also known as *indefinite pronouns*), the *pronoun* should be *singular*.

Somebody left (her) backpack on the chair.

One of the servers just called and said (he) would be an hour late.

Everyone in the club must pay (his) dues next week.

Each circled *pronoun* is *singular* because it refers to an *indefinite pronoun*.

Note: There are two important points to remember about indefinite pronouns:

1 In the last example, if everyone in the club was a woman, the pronoun would be *her*. If the club had women and men, the pronoun would be *his* or *her:*

Everyone in the club must pay his or her dues next week.

Some writers follow the traditional practice of using *his* to refer to both women and men. Most writers now use *his or her* to avoid an implied sexual bias. To avoid using *his* or the somewhat awkward *his or her,* a sentence can often be rewritten in the plural:

Club members must pay their dues next week.

2 In informal spoken English, *plural* pronouns are often used with the indefinite pronouns. We would probably not say:

Everybody has *his or her* own opinion about the election.

Instead, we are likely to say:

Everybody has *their* own opinion about the election.

Here are other examples:

Everyone in the choir must buy *their* robes.
Everybody in the line has *their* ticket ready.
No one in the class remembered to bring *their* books.

In such cases, the indefinite pronouns are clearly plural in meaning. Also, the use of such plurals helps people to avoid the awkward *his or her.* In time, the plural pronoun may be accepted in formal speech or writing. **Until that happens, however, you should use the grammatically correct singular form in your writing.**

Activity

Underline the correct pronoun.

1. Neither of the potential buyers had really made up (her, their) mind.

2. Not one of the new cashiers knows what (he, they) should be doing.

3. Each of these computers has (its, their) drawbacks.

4. Anyone trying to reduce (his or her, their) salt intake should avoid canned and processed foods.

5. If anybody calls when I'm out, tell (him, them) I'll return in an hour.

PRONOUN REFERENCE

A sentence may be confusing and unclear if a pronoun appears to refer to more than one word or does not refer to any specific word. *Pronouns must have a clear point of reference, or antecedent.* Look at this sentence:

Miriam was annoyed when they failed her car for a faulty turn signal.

Who failed her car? There is no specific word that *they* refers to. Be clear:

Miriam was annoyed when the safety inspectors failed her car for a faulty turn signal.

Here are sentences with other faulty pronoun references. Read the explanations of why they are faulty and look carefully at how they are corrected.

Faulty	*Clear*
Peter told Vijay that his wife was unhappy. (Whose wife is unhappy: Peter's or Vijay's? Be clear about your *pronoun referent.*)	Peter told Vijay, "My wife is unhappy."
Mia is really a shy person, but she keeps it hidden. (There is no specific word, or *antecedent*, that *it* refers to. The adjective *shy* must be changed to a noun.)	Mia is really a shy person, but she keeps her shyness hidden.
Kizzie attributed her success to her husband's support, which was generous. (Does *which* mean that Kizzie's *action* was generous, or that her husband's *support* was generous?)	Generously, Kizzie attributed her success to her husband's support. (Or,) Kizzie attributed her success to her husband's generous support.

Activity

Rewrite each of the following sentences to make clear the vague pronoun reference. Add, change, or omit words as necessary.

Example   Susan and her mother wondered if she had been working out long enough to enter a competition.

Susan's mother wondered if Susan had been working out long enough to enter a competition.

1. Dad spent all morning birdwatching but didn't see a single one.

_____

2. At that fast-food restaurant, they give you free glasses with your soft drinks.

_____

3. Ruth told Annette that her bouts of depression were becoming serious.

_____

4. Dipping his spoon into the pot of simmering pasta sauce, Kyle felt it slip out of his hand.

_____

5. Pete visited the tutoring centre because they could help him with his economics course.

_____

■ **Review Test 1**

Underline the correct word in parentheses.

1. Each of the little girls may choose one prize for (her, their) own.

2. I asked at the body shop how quickly (they, the shop employees) could fix my car.

3. The coaches told each member of the soccer team that (his or her, their) position was the most important one in the game.

4. Marianna tried to take notes during the class, but she didn't really understand (it, the subject.)

5. When someone has a cold, (they, he or she) should take extra vitamin C and drink a lot of fluids.

■ **Review Test 2**

Cross out the pronoun error in each sentence below and write the correction in the space provided at the left. Then circle the letter that correctly describes the type of error that was made.

Example

his (or her)

Anyone without a ticket will lose ~~their~~ place in the line.
Mistake in: a. pronoun reference   ⓑ pronoun agreement

_____ 1. Could someone volunteer their services to clean up after the party?
Mistake in: a. pronoun reference   b. pronoun agreement

_____ 2. The referee watched the junior hockey game closely to make sure they didn't hurt each other during checking.
Mistake in: a. pronoun reference   b. pronoun agreement

_____ 3. If job hunters want to make a good impression at an interview, he should be sure to arrive on time.
Mistake in: a. pronoun reference   b. pronoun agreement

_____ 4. Neither of those girls appreciated their parents' sacrifices.
Mistake in: a. pronoun reference   b. pronoun agreement

_____ 5. There wasn't much to do on Friday nights after they closed the only movie theatre in the northern Manitoba town.
Mistake in: a. pronoun reference   b. pronoun agreement

Pronoun Types

This section describes some common types of pronouns: subject and object pronouns, possessive pronouns, and demonstrative pronouns.

SUBJECT AND OBJECT PRONOUNS

Pronouns change their form depending upon the place that they occupy in a sentence. In the box that follows is a list of subject and object pronouns.

Subject Pronouns	*Object Pronouns*
I	me
you	you (no change)
he	him
she	her
it	it (no change)
we	us
they	them

Subject Pronouns

Subject pronouns are subjects of verbs.

> *He* is wearing an artificial arm. (*He* is the subject of the verb *is wearing.*)
> *They* are moving into our old apartment. (*They* is the subject of the verb *are moving.*)
> *We* students should have a say in the decision. (*We* is the subject of the verb *should have.*)

Several rules for using subject pronouns—and several kinds of mistakes that people sometimes make with subject pronouns—are explained below.

Rule 1: Use a subject pronoun in spots where you have a compound (more than one) subject.

Incorrect	*Correct*
My brother and *me* are Barenaked Ladies fans.	My brother and *I* are Barenaked Ladies fans.
Him and *me* know the lyrics to all their songs.	*He* and *I* know the lyrics to all their songs.

Hint for Rule 1: If you are not sure what pronoun to use, try each pronoun by itself in the sentence. The correct pronoun will be the one that sounds right. For example, "Him knows the lyrics to all their songs" does not sound right; "He knows the lyrics to all their songs" does.

Rule 2: Use a subject pronoun after forms of the verb *be*. Forms of *be* include *am, are, is, was, were, has been, have been,* and others.

> It was *I* who left the light on.
> It may be *they* in that car.
> It is *he.*

The sentences above may sound strange and stilted to you because they are seldom used in conversation. When we speak with one another, forms such as "It was me," "It may be them," and "It is him" are widely accepted. In formal writing, however, the grammatically correct forms are still required.

Hint for Rule 2: You can avoid having to use the subject pronoun form after *be* by simply rewording a sentence. Here is how the preceding examples could be reworded:

> I was the one who left the light on.
> They may be in that car.
> He is here.

Rule 3: Use subject pronouns after *than* or *as*. The subject pronoun is used because a verb is understood after the pronoun.

> You play better than I (play). (The verb *play* is understood after *I.*)
> Jenny is as bored as I (am). (The verb *am* is understood after *I.*)
> We don't need the money as much as they (do). (The verb *do* is understood after *they.*)

Hint for Rule 3: Avoid mistakes by mentally adding the "missing" verb at the end of the sentence.

Object Pronouns

Object pronouns *(me, him, her, us, them)* are the objects of verbs or prepositions. (*Prepositions* are connecting words like *for, at, about, to, before, by, with,* and *of.* See also page 358.)

> Tamara helped *me.* (*Me* is the object of the verb *helped.*)
> We took *them* to the college. (*Them* is the object of the verb *took.*)
> Leave the children with *us.* (*Us* is the object of the preposition *with.*)
> I got in line behind *him.* (*Him* is the object of the preposition *behind.*)

People are sometimes uncertain about what pronoun to use when two objects follow the verb.

Incorrect	*Correct*
I gave a gift to Arundhati and *she.*	I gave a gift to Arundhati and *her.*
She came to the movie with Marc and *I.*	She came to the movie with Marc and *me.*

Hint: If you are not sure what pronoun to use, try each pronoun by itself in the sentence. The correct pronoun will be the one that sounds right. For example, "I gave a gift to she" does not sound right; "I gave a gift to her" does.

Activity

Underline the correct subject or object pronoun in each of the following sentences. Then show whether your answer is a subject or object pronoun by circling the *S* or *O* in the margin. The first one is done for you as an example.

S   Ⓞ   1. The sweaters Mom knitted for Victor and (I, <u>me</u>) are too small.

S   O   2. No one has a quicker temper than (she, her).

S   O   3. Your grades prove that you worked harder than (they, them).

S   O   4. (We, Us) runners train indoors when the weather turns cold.

S   O   5. (She, Her) and Betty never put the cap back on the toothpaste.

S   O   6. Chris and (he, him) are the most energetic kids in the first grade.

S   O   7. Arguing over clothes is a favourite pastime for my sister and (I, me).

S   O   8. The head of the ticket committee asked Sam and (I, me) to help with sales.

POSSESSIVE PRONOUNS

Here is a list of possessive pronouns:

my, mine	our, ours
your, yours	your, yours
his	their, theirs
her, hers	
its	

Possessive pronouns show ownership or possession.

> Peter revved up *his* motorcycle and blasted off.
> The keys are *mine*.

Note: A possessive pronoun *never* uses an apostrophe. (See also page 434.)

Incorrect	*Correct*
That coat is *hers'*.	That coat is *hers*.
The card table is *theirs'*.	The card table is *theirs*.

Activity

Cross out the incorrect pronoun form in each of the sentences below. Write the correct form in the space at the left.

Example _____hers_____ Those gloves are ~~hers'~~.

_____ 1. I discovered that my car had somehow lost its' rear licence plate.

_____ 2. Are those seats theirs'?

_____ 3. I knew the sweater was hers' when I saw the monogram.

_____ 4. The dog in that cage is our's.

_____ 5. These butter tarts are yours' if you want them.

DEMONSTRATIVE PRONOUNS

Demonstrative pronouns point to or single out a person or thing. There are four demonstrative pronouns:

this	these
that	those

> *This* is my house right in front of us.
> *Those* are your books on the shelf over there.

Generally speaking, *this* and *these* refer to things close at hand; *that* and *those* refer to things farther away. The four pronouns are commonly used in the role of demonstrative adjectives as well.

> Is anyone using *this* spoon?
> I am going to throw away *these* magazines.
> I just bought *that* white Volvo at the curb.
> Pick up *those* toys in the corner.

Note: Do not use *them, this here, that there, these here,* or *those there* to point out. Use only *this, that, these,* or *those*.

Activity

Cross out the incorrect form of the demonstrative pronoun and write the correct form in the space provided.

Example _____Those_____ ~~Them~~ tires look worn.

_____ 1. This here map is out of date.

_____ 2. Leave them keys out on the coffee table.

_____ 3. I've seen them girls somewhere before.

_____ 4. Jack entered that there dog in an obedience contest.

_____ 5. Where are them new knives?

■ Review Test

Underline the correct word in the parentheses.

1. If the contract negotiations are left up to (they, them), we'll have to accept the results.

2. (Them, Those) student crafts have won several awards.

3. Our grandmother told David and (I, me) to leave our muddy shoes outside on the porch.

4. The judge decided that the fault was (theirs', theirs) and ordered them to pay the damages.

5. The black-masked raccoon stared at Rudy and (I, me) for an instant and then ran quickly away.

6. When we saw the smashed window, Lynn and (I, me) didn't know whether to enter the house.

7. (This here, This) is my cousin Ali.

8. This coat can't be (hers, her's); it's too small.

Adjectives and Adverbs

ADJECTIVES

What Are Adjectives?

Adjectives *describe* nouns (names of persons, places, or things) or pronouns.

> Nicola is a *wise* woman. (The adjective *wise* describes the noun *woman.*)
> She is also *funny.* (The adjective *funny* describes the pronoun *she.*)
> I'll carry the *heavy* bag of groceries. (The adjective *heavy* describes the noun *bag.*)
> It is *torn.* (The adjective *torn* describes the pronoun *it.*)

Adjectives usually come before the word they describe (as in *wise* woman and *heavy* bag). But they also come after forms of the verb *be* (*is, are, was, were,* and so on). They also follow verbs such as *look, appear, seem, become, sound, taste,* and *smell.*

> That road is *slippery.* (The adjective *slippery* describes the road.)
> The printers are *noisy.* (The adjective *noisy* describes the printers.)
> Those customers were *impatient.* (The adjective *impatient* describes the customers.)
> Your room looks *neat.* (The adjective *neat* describes the room.)

Using Adjectives to Compare

For all one-syllable adjectives and some two-syllable adjectives, add -*er* when comparing two things and -*est* when comparing three or more things.

> Andrew's beard is *longer* than mine, but Lee's is the *longest.*
> Meg may be the *quieter* of the two sisters; but that's not saying much, since they're the *loudest* girls in school.

For some two-syllable adjectives and all longer adjectives, add *more* when comparing two things and *most* when comparing three or more things.

Daniel Richler is *more famous* than his brother; but their late father, Mordecai Richler, is still the *most famous* member of the family.

The red letters on the sign are *more noticeable* than the black ones, but the Day-Glo letters are the *most noticeable*.

You can usually tell when to use *more* and *most* by the sound of a word. For example, you can probably tell by its sound that "carefuller" would be too awkward to say and that *more careful* is thus correct. In addition, there are many words for which both *-er* or *-est* and *more* or *most* are equally correct. For instance, either "a more fair rule" or "a fairer rule" is correct.

To form negative comparisons, use *less* and *least*.

During my first dance class, I felt *less graceful* than an injured elephant.

When the teacher came to our house to complain to my parents, I offered her the *least comfortable* chair in the house.

Points to Remember about Comparing

Point 1: Use only one form of comparison at a time. In other words, do not use both an *-er* ending and *more* or both an *-est* ending and *most*:

Incorrect	*Correct*
My suitcase is always *more heavier* than my father's.	My suitcase is always *heavier* than my father's.
Blood and Donuts is still the *most frighteningest* movie I've ever seen.	*Blood and Donuts* is still the *most frightening* movie I've ever seen.

Point 2: Learn the irregular forms of the words shown below.

	Comparative (for comparing things)	*Superlative (for comparing three or more things)*
bad	worse	worst
good, well	better	best
little (in amount)	less	least
much, many	more	most

Do not use both *more* and an irregular comparative or *most* and an irregular superlative.

Incorrect	*Correct*
It is *more better* to give than to receive.	It is *better* to give than to receive.
Last night I got the *most worst* snack attack I ever had.	Last night I got the *worst* snack attack I ever had.

Activity

Add to each sentence the correct form of the word in the margin.

BAD

Examples   The _____*worst*_____ job I ever had was babysitting for spoiled four-year-old twins.

WONDERFUL

The __*most wonderful*__ day of my life was when my child was born.

GOOD

1. The _____ chocolate cake I ever ate had bananas in it.

YOUNG

2. Aunt Sonja is the _____ of the three sisters.

BAD

3. A rain that freezes is _____ than a snowstorm.

UNUSUAL

4. That's the _____ home I've ever seen—it's shaped like a teapot.

LITTLE

5. Being painfully shy has made Leon the _____ friendly person I know.

ADVERBS

What Are Adverbs?

Adverbs describe verbs, adjectives, or other adverbs. They usually end in *-ly.*

The father *gently* hugged the sick child. (The adverb *gently* describes the verb *hugged.*)

Newborns are *totally* innocent. (The adverb *totally* describes the adjective *innocent.*)

The lecturer spoke so *terribly* fast that I had trouble taking notes. (The adverb *terribly* describes the adverb *fast.*)

A Common Mistake with Adverbs and Adjectives

People often mistakenly use an adjective instead of an adverb after a verb.

Incorrect	*Correct*
Sam needs a haircut *bad.*	Sam needs a haircut *badly.*
I laugh too *loud* when I'm embarassed.	I laugh too *loudly* when I'm embarassed.
You might have won the race if you hadn't run so *slow* at the beginning.	You might have won the race if you hadn't run so *slowly* at the beginning.

Activity

Underline the adjective or adverb needed. (Remember that adjectives describe nouns, and adverbs describe verbs or other adverbs.)

1. As Mac danced, his earring bounced (rapid, rapidly).

2. A drop of (thick, thickly) pea soup dripped down his chin.

3. I hiccupped (continuous, continuously) for fifteen minutes.

4. The detective opened the door (careful, carefully).

5. All she heard when she answered the phone was (heavy, heavily) breathing.

Well and Good

Two words that are often confused are *well* and *good. Good* is an adjective; it describes nouns. *Well* is usually an adverb; it describes verbs.

Activity

Write *well* or *good* in each of the sentences that follow.

1. If you girls do a _____ job of cleaning the garage, I'll take you for some ice cream.

2. If I organize the office records too _____, my bosses may not need me any more.

3. When Ernie got AIDS, he discovered who his _____ friends really were.

4. Just because brothers and sisters fight when they're young doesn't mean they won't get along _____ as adults.

■ Review Test 1

Underline the correct word in the parentheses.

1. The server poured (littler, less) coffee into my cup than into yours.

2. Humid air seems to make Sid's asthma (more worse, worse).

3. The movie is so interesting that the three hours pass (quick, quickly).

4. The talented boy sang as (confident, confidently) as a seasoned performer.

5. Our band played so (good, well) that a local firm hired us for its annual dinner.

6. Tri Lee is always (truthful, truthfully), even when it might be better to tell a white lie.

7. The driver stopped the bus (sudden, suddenly) and yelled, "Everybody out!"

8. Shirt and pants in one colour make you look (more thin, thinner) than ones in contrasting colours.

■ Review Test 2

Write a sentence that uses each of the following adjectives and adverbs correctly.

1. careless
2. angrily
3. well
4. most relaxing
5. best

Misplaced Modifiers

Misplaced modifiers are words that, because of awkward placement, do not describe the words the writer intended them to describe. Misplaced modifiers often confuse the meaning of a sentence. To avoid them, place words as close as possible to what they describe.

Misplaced Words	*Correctly Placed Words*
George couldn't drive to work in his small sports car *with a broken leg.* (The sports car had a broken leg?)	With a broken leg, George couldn't drive to work in his small sports car. (The words describing George are now placed next to *George.*)
The toaster was sold to us by a charming salesperson *with a money-back guarantee.* (The salesperson had a money-back guarantee?)	The toaster with a money-back guarantee was sold to us by a charming salesperson. (The words describing the toaster are now placed next to it.)
He *nearly* brushed his teeth for twenty minutes every night. (He came close to brushing his teeth, but in fact did not brush them at all?)	He brushed his teeth for nearly twenty minutes every night. (The meaning—that he brushed his teeth for a long time—is now clear.)

Activity

Underline the misplaced word or words in each sentence. Then rewrite the sentence, placing related words together and thereby making the meaning clear.

Examples   Frozen shrimp lay in the steel pans that were thawing rapidly.

Frozen shrimp that were thawing rapidly lay in the steel pans.

The speaker discussed the problem of crowded prisons at the college.

At the college, the speaker discussed the problem of crowded prisons.

1. The patient talked about his childhood on the psychiatrist's couch.

   _____

2. The crowd watched the tennis players with swivelling heads.

   _____

3. Damian put four hamburger patties on the counter which he was cooking for dinner.

   _____

4. Steve carefully hung the new suit that he would wear to his first job interview in the bedroom closet.

   _____

5. Alexander ripped the shirt on a car door that he made in sewing class.

   _____

6. The latest Jackie Chan movie has almost opened in two hundred theatres across the country.

   _____

7. The newscaster spoke softly into a microphone wearing a bullet-proof vest.

   _____

8. The tenants left town in a dilapidated old car owing two months' rent.

   _____

■ Review Test 1

Write *MM* for *misplaced modifier* or *C* for *correct* in the space provided for each sentence.

_____   1. I nearly napped for twenty minutes during the biology lecture.

_____   2. I napped for nearly twenty minutes during the biology lecture.

_____   3. Ryan paused as the girl he had been following stopped at a shop window.

_____   4. Ryan paused as the girl stopped at a shop window he had been following.

_____   5. Marta dropped out of school after taking ten courses on Friday.

_____   6. On Friday, Marta dropped out of school after taking ten courses.

_____   7. Under his shirt, the player wore a good luck charm which resembled a tiny elephant.

_____   8. The player wore a good luck charm under his shirt which resembled a tiny elephant.

■ **Review Test 2**

Make the changes needed to correct the misplaced modifier in each sentence.

1. Margaret Atwood wrote that someone was as innocent as a bathtub full of bullets in a poem.

2. I almost filled an entire notebook with biology lab drawings.

3. The apprentice watched the master carpenter expertly fit the door with envious eyes.

4. The photographer pointed the camera at the shy deer equipped with a special night-vision scope.

5. The passengers on the bus stared at the ceiling or read newspapers with tired faces.

Dangling Modifiers

A modifier that opens a sentence must be followed immediately by the word it is meant to describe. Otherwise, the modifier is said to be dangling, and the sentence takes on an unintended meaning. For example, in the sentence

> While reading the newspaper, my dog sat with me on the front steps.

the unintended meaning is that the *dog* was reading the paper. What the writer meant, of course, was that *he* (or *she*), the writer, was reading the paper. The writer should have said,

> While reading the newspaper, *I* sat with my dog on the front steps.

The dangling modifier could also be corrected by placing the subject within the opening word group:

> While *I* was reading the newspaper, my dog sat with me on the front steps.

Here are other sentences with dangling modifiers. Read the explanations of why they are dangling and look carefully at the ways they are corrected.

Dangling	*Correct*
Shaving in front of the steamy mirror, the razor nicked Sean's chin. (*Who* was shaving in front of the mirror? The answer is not *razor,* but *Sean.* The subject *Sean* must be added.)	Shaving in front of the steamy mirror, *Sean* nicked his chin with the razor. *Or:* When *Sean* was shaving in front of the steamy mirror, he nicked his chin with the razor.
While stir-frying vegetables, hot oil splashed my arm. (*Who* is stir-frying vegetables? The answer is not *hot oil,* as it unintentionally seems to be, but *I.* The subject *I* must be added.)	While *I* was stir-frying vegetables, hot oil splashed my arm. *Or:* While stir-frying vegetables, *I* was splashed by hot oil.

Dangling	*Correct*
Taking the exam, the room was so stuffy that Keesha nearly fainted. (*Who* took the exam? The answer is not *the room,* but *Keesha.* The subject *Keesha* must be added.)	Taking the exam, *Keesha* found the room so stuffy that she almost fainted. *Or:* When *Keesha* took the exam, the room was so stuffy that she almost fainted.
To impress the interviewer, punctuality is essential. (*Who* is to impress the interviewer? The answer is not *punctuality,* but *you.* The subject *you* must be added.)	To impress the interviewer, *you* must be punctual. *Or:* For *you* to impress the interviewer, punctuality is essential.

The preceding examples make clear two ways of correcting a dangling modifier. Decide on a logical subject and do one of the following:

1 Place the subject *within* the opening word group:

When *Sean* was shaving in front of the steamy mirror, he nicked his chin.

Note: In some cases an appropriate subordinating word such as *when* must be added, and the verb may have to be changed slightly as well.

2 Place the subject right *after* the opening word group:

Shaving in front of the steamy mirror, *Sean* nicked his chin.

Activity

Ask *Who?* of the opening words in each sentence. The subject that answers the question should be nearby in the sentence. If it is not, provide the logical subject by using either method of correction described above.

Example	While pitching his tent, a snake bit Tony on the ankle.
	While Tony was pitching his tent, a snake bit him on the ankle.
Or:	*While pitching his tent, Tony was bitten on the ankle by a snake.*

1. Dancing on their hind legs, the audience cheered wildly as the elephants paraded by.

   _____

   _____

2. Last seen wearing dark glasses and a blond wig, the police spokesperson said the suspect was still being sought.

   _____

   _____

3. Pouring out the cereal, a coupon fell into my bowl of milk.

_____

_____

4. Escorted by dozens of police motorcycles, I knew the limousine carried someone important.

_____

_____

5. Tired and exasperated, the fight we had was inevitable.

_____

_____

6. Packed tightly in a tiny can, Farida had difficulty removing the anchovies.

_____

_____

7. Kicked carelessly under the bed, Lisa finally found her sneakers.

_____

_____

8. Working at the photocopy machine, the morning dragged on.

_____

_____

■ Review Test 1

Write *DM* for *dangling modifier* or *C* for *correct* in the space provided for each
sentence.

_____   1. While riding the bicycle, a vicious-looking Rottweiler snapped at Tim's ankles.

_____   2. While Tim was riding the bicycle, a vicious-looking Rottweiler snapped at
his ankles.

_____   3. Afraid to look his father in the eye, Scott kept his head bowed.

_____   4. Afraid to look his father in the eye, Scott's head remained bowed.

_____   5. Boring and silly, I turned the TV show off.

_____   6. I turned off the boring and silly TV show.

_____   7. Munching leaves from a tall tree, the giraffe fascinated the children.

_____   8. Munching leaves from a tall tree, the children were fascinated by the giraffe.

■ **Review Test 2**

Make the changes needed to correct the dangling modifier in each sentence.

1. Not having had much sleep, my concentration during class was weak.

   _____

2. Joined at the hip, a team of surgeons successfully separated the Siamese twins.

   _____

3. Wading by the lakeshore, a water snake brushed past my leg.

   _____

4. While being restrained by court officials, the judge sentenced the kidnapper.

   _____

5. In a sentimental frame of mind, Céline Dion's song brought tears to Beth's eyes.

   _____

■ **Review Test 3**

Complete the following sentences. In each case, a logical subject should follow the opening words.

Example   Looking through the door's peephole, *I couldn't see who rang the*
            doorbell.

1. Noticing the light turn yellow, _____

2. Being fragile, _____

3. While washing the car, _____

4. Although very expensive, _____

5. Driving by the cemetery, _____

Manuscript Form

When you hand in a paper for any course, it will probably be judged first by its format. It is important, then, to make the paper look attractive, neat, and easy to read. Here is a checklist you should use when preparing a paper for an instructor:

    • Is the paper full-sized, 21.5 cm × 28 cm?

    • Are there wide margins all around the paper? In particular, have you been careful not to crowd the right-hand or bottom margin?

    • If the paper is word processed, have you

    Checked whether your instructor prefers full justification or "ragged right" line format?
    Used an appropriate font, such as Times, Optima, Helvetica, or Arial?
    Chosen a readable point-size, such as 12-point?
    Double-spaced the text of each paragraph of your essay?
    Used any header information your instructor may require?

    • If the paper is handwritten, have you

    Used a blue or black pen?
    Been careful not to overlap letters or to make decorative loops on letters?
    Made all your letters distinct, with special attention to *a, e, i, o,* and *u*—five letters that people sometimes write illegibly?
    Kept all your capital letters clearly distinct from small letters?

    • Have you centred the title of your paper on the first line of page 1? Have you been careful *not* to put quotation marks around the title or to underline it? Have you capitalized all the words in the title except for short connecting words like *of, for, the, and, in,* and *to?*

    • If your paper is handwritten, have you skipped a line between the title and the first line of your paper?

    • If your paper is word processed, have you inserted two double lines of space between the title and the opening line of your paper?

- • Have you indented the first line of each paragraph about five spaces (1.25 cm) from the left-hand margin? If you are word-processing your paper, your instructor may prefer that you do not "tab" or indent a first line of a new paragraph, but leave two lines of space between each separate paragraph.

- • Have you made commas, periods, and other punctuation marks firm and clear?

- • If you have broken any words at the end of a line, have you been careful to break only between syllables?

- • Have you put your name, the date, and other information at the end of the paper, on the title page, or wherever your instructor has specified?

Also ask yourself these important questions about the title and the first sentence of your paper:

- • Is your title made up of several words that tell what the paper is about? (The title should be just several words, *not* a complete sentence.)

- • Does the first sentence of your paper stand independent of the title? (The reader should *not* have to use the words in the title to make sense of the opening sentence.)

Activity

Use the checklist to locate the seven mistakes in format in the following lines from a student paper. Explain the mistakes in the spaces provided. One mistake is described for you as an example.

	"Being alone"
	This is something that I simply cannot tolera-
	te, and I will go to great lengths to
	prevent it. For example, if I know that I need

1. Hyphenate only between syllables (*toler-ate*, not *tolera-te*).

2. _____

3. _____

4. _____

5. _____

6. _____

7. _____

Capital Letters

MAIN USES OF CAPITAL LETTERS

Capital letters are used with

1 First word in a sentence or direct quotation

2 Names of persons and the word *I*

3 Names of particular places

4 Names of days of the week, months, and holidays

5 Names of commercial products

6 Titles of books, magazines, newspapers, articles, stories, poems, films, television shows, songs, papers that you write, and the like

7 Names of companies, associations, unions, clubs, religious and political groups, and other organizations

Each use is illustrated on the pages that follow.

First Word in a Sentence or Direct Quotation

The corner grocery was robbed last night.
The alien said, "Take me to your leader."
"If you feel lonely," said Teri, "call us. We'll be over in no time."

Note: In the third example above, *If* and *We'll* are capitalized because they start new sentences. But *call* is not capitalized because it is part of the first sentence.

Names of Persons and the Word *I*

Last night, I saw a movie starring Jet Li and Chow Yun-Fat.

Names of Particular Places

Although Bill dropped out of Port Charles High School, he eventually earned his degree and got a job with Atlas Realty Company.

But: Use small letters if the specific name of a place is not given.

Although Bill dropped out of high school, he eventually earned his degree and got a job with a real estate company.

Names of Days of the Week, Months, and Holidays

On the last Friday afternoon in June, the day before Canada Day, my boss is having a barbecue for all the employees.

But: Use small letters for the seasons—summer, fall, winter, spring.

Most people feel more energetic in the spring and fall.

Names of Commercial Products

My little sister knows all the words to the jingles for Maple Leaf hot dogs, Tim Hortons doughnuts, Meow Mix cat food, and Swiss Chalet chicken.

But: Use small letters for the *type* of product (hot dogs, doughnuts, cat food, and so on).

Titles of Books, Magazines, Newspapers, Articles, Stories, Poems, Films, Television Shows, Songs, Papers That You Write, and the Like

We read the book *In the Skin of a Lion* for our cultural studies class.
In the doctor's waiting room, I watched *Canada at Noon,* read an article in *Maclean's,* and leafed through the *Winnipeg Free Press.*

Names of Companies, Associations, Unions, Clubs, Religious and Political Groups, and Other Organizations

Joe Duffy is a Roman Catholic, but his wife is Baptist.
The Hilldale Square Dancers' Club has won many competitions.
Brian, a member of the Canadian Auto Workers union and the Knights of Columbus, works for Ford Canada.

Activity

Underline the words that need capitals in the following sentences. Then write the capitalized form of each word in the space provided. The number of spaces tells you how many corrections to make in each case.

Example   In our resource management class, each student must write a report on an article in the magazine *canadian geographic.*

<u>Canadian</u>   <u>Geographic</u>

1. Leon's collection of beatles souvenirs includes a pair of tickets from their last concert at maple leaf gardens.

_____ _____ _____ _____

2. Yumi read in *Chatelaine* magazine that nelly furtado grew up in vancouver.

_____   _____   _____   _____

3. When i have a cold, I use Vicks ointment and chew listerine lozenges.

_____   _____   _____   _____

4. Since no man volunteered for the job, the boy scouts in dauphin, manitoba, have a woman pack leader.

_____   _____   _____   _____

5. A nature trail for the blind in point pelee, ontario, has signs written in braille that encourage visitors to smell and touch the plants.

_____   _____   _____

6. My father is a confirmed Edmonton oilers fan, though he lives in saskatoon.

_____   _____

7. Martha bought a pepsi to wash down her vachon flaky.

_____   _____   _____

8. Vince listened to a Barenaked ladies CD called *Stunt* while Donna read an article in *elm Street* entitled "Where's Your portfolio?"

_____   _____

OTHER USES OF CAPITAL LETTERS

Capital letters are also used with

1 Names that show family relationships
2 Titles of persons when used with their names
3 Specific school courses
4 Languages
5 Geographic locations
6 Historical periods and events
7 Races, nations, and nationalities
8 Opening and closing of a letter

Each use is illustrated on the pages that follow.

Names That Show Family Relationships

All his life, Father has been addicted to gadgets.
I browsed through Grandmother's collection of old photographs.
Aunt Florence and Uncle Bill bought a mobile home.

But: Do not capitalize words like *mother, father, grandmother, grandfather, uncle, aunt,* and so on when they are preceded by a possessive word (*my, your, his, her, our, their*).

All his life, my father has been addicted to gadgets.
I browsed through my grandmother's collection of old photographs.
My aunt and uncle bought a cabin near Tracadie.

Titles of Persons When Used with Their Names

I contributed to Premier Filmon's campaign fund.
Is Dr. Gregory on vacation?
Professor Li announced that there would be no tests in the course.

But: Use small letters when titles appear by themselves, without specific names.

I contributed to my premier's campaign fund.
Is the doctor on vacation?
The professor announced that there would be no tests in the course.

Specific School Courses

The college offers evening sections of Introductory Psychology I, Abnormal Psychology, Psychology and Statistics, and Educational Psychology.

But: Use small letters for general subject areas.

The college offers evening sections of many psychology courses.

Languages

My grandfather's Polish accent makes his English difficult to understand.

Geographic Locations

He grew up in the Maritimes but moved to the West to look for a better job.

But: Use small letters in directions.

Head west for five blocks and then turn east on Queen Street.

Historical Periods and Events

During the Middle Ages, the Black Death killed over one-quarter of Europe's population.

Races, Nations, and Nationalities

The survey asked if the head of our household was Caucasian, Asian, or Native Canadian.
Tanya has lived on armed forces bases in Germany, Italy, and Spain.
Denise's beautiful features reflect her Chinese and Filipino parentage.

Opening and Closing of a Letter

Dear Sir: Sincerely yours,
Dear Ms. Henderson: Truly yours,

Note: Capitalize only the first word in a closing.

Activity

Underline the words that need capitals in the following sentences. Then write the capitalized forms of the words in the spaces provided. The number of spaces tells you how many corrections to make in each case.

1. During world war II, some canadians were afraid that the japanese would invade British Columbia.

   _____ _____ _____ _____

2. On their job site in korea, the french, swiss, and chinese co-workers used English to communicate.

   _____ _____ _____ _____

3. When uncle harvey got the bill from his doctor, he called the Ontario Medical Association to complain.

   _____ _____

4. Dr. Freeling of the business department is offering a new course called introduction to word processing.

   _____ _____ _____

5. The new restaurant featuring vietnamese cuisine has just opened on the south side of the city.

   _____

UNNECESSARY USE OF CAPITALS

Activity

Many errors in capitalization are caused by using capitals where they are not needed. Underline the incorrectly capitalized letters in the following sentences, and write the correct forms in the spaces provided. The number of spaces tells you how many corrections to make in each sentence.

1. Kim Campbell—the first female Prime Minister—also had the shortest tenure in Office.

   _____ _____ _____

2. For her fortieth birthday, my Aunt bought herself a red Miata Convertible.

   _____ _____

3. Canadians were delighted when the Toronto Blue Jays were the first Canadian Baseball Team to win the World Series.

   _____   _____

4. In his Book titled *Offbeat Museums,* Saul Rubin tells about various Unusual Museums, such as, Believe it or not, the Barbed Wire Museum.

   _____   _____   _____   _____

5. Einstein's theory of relativity, which he developed when he was only twenty-six, led to the invention of the Electron Microscope, Television, and the Atomic bomb.

   _____   _____   _____   _____

■ Review Test 1

Add capitals where needed in the following sentences.

Example   In an injured tone, Mary demanded, "~~w~~hy wasn't ~~u~~ncle Lou invited to the party?"

(above "why" is W, above "uncle" is U)

1. To keep warm, a homeless old man sits on a steam vent near the bay store on main street.

2. Silent movie stars of the twenties, like charlie chaplin and mary pickford, earned more than a million tax-free dollars a year.

3. Unique in Canada to the carolinian zone of southwestern ontario are such plants as the green dragon Lily and sassafras trees.

4. When Jean chrétien was first in ottawa, his idols were Wilfrid laurier and Louis st. laurent.

5. In an old movie, an attractive young lady invites groucho marx to join her.

6. "why?" asks groucho. "are you coming apart?"

7. I was halfway to the wash & dry Laundromat on elm street when i realized that my box of sunlight detergent was still at home on the kitchen counter.

8. Although I know that mother loves holidays, even I was surprised when she announced a party in february to celebrate wiarton Willie and groundhog day.

■ Review Test 2

On a separate paper, write

1. Seven sentences demonstrating the seven main uses of capital letters.

2. Eight sentences demonstrating the eight other uses of capital letters.

Numbers and Abbreviations

NUMBERS

Here are three helpful rules for using numbers:

Rule 1: Spell out numbers that take no more than two words. Otherwise, use the numbers themselves.

> In Jody's kitchen is her collection of seventy-two cookbooks.
> Jody has a file of 350 recipes.

> It will take about two weeks to fix the computer database.
> Since a number of people use the database, the company will lose over 150 work days.

> Only twelve students have signed up for the field trip.
> Nearly 250 students came to the lecture.

Rule 2: Be consistent when you use a series of numbers. If some numbers in a sentence or paragraph require more than two words, then use numbers in every case throughout the selection, in the same category of items.

> After the storm, maintenance workers unclogged 46 drains, removed 123 broken tree limbs, and rescued 3 kittens that were stuck in a drain pipe.

Rule 3: Use numbers to show dates, times, addresses, percentages, and parts of a book.

> The burglary was committed on October 30, 2001, but not discovered until January 2, 2002.
> Before I went to bed, I set my alarm for 6:45 a.m.

But: Spell out numbers before *o'clock*. For example: I didn't get out of bed until seven o'clock.

The library is located at 45 West 52d Street.

When you take the skin off a piece of chicken, you remove about 40 percent of the fat.

The name of the murderer is revealed in Chapter 8 on page 236.

Activity

Cross out the mistakes in numbers and write the corrections in the spaces provided.

1. The Caribana Parade will begin at three-thirty in front of the newspaper building at one-oh-six South Forty-Second Street.

   _____   _____   _____

2. It took 4 hours to proofread all 75 pages of the manuscript.

   _____   _____

3. We expect to have fifty percent of the work completed by March tenth.

   _____   _____

ABBREVIATIONS

Using abbreviations can save you time when you take notes. In formal writing, however, you should avoid most abbreviations. Listed below are some of the few abbreviations that are considered acceptable in compositions. Note that a period is used after most abbreviations.

1 Mr., Mrs., Ms., Jr., Sr., Dr. when used with proper names:

Mrs. Levesque   Dr. DaSilva   Howard Kelley, Jr.

2 Time references:

A.M. or a.m.   P.M. or p.m.   B.C., A.D.

3 Initials in a person's name:

Pierre E. Trudeau   John F. Kennedy   Michael J. Fox

4 Organizations, technical words, and company names known primarily by their initials:

IBM   UNICEF   CBC   NHL   NDP   AIDS   CAT scan

Activity

Cross out the words that should not be abbreviated, and correct them in the spaces provided.

1. Between mid-Oct. and the beginning of Jan., I typically gain about three kgs.

   _____   _____   _____

2. I had such a bad headache this aftern. that I called my doc. for an appt.

   _____   _____   _____

3. I stopped at the p.o. at about twenty min. past ten and bought five dol. worth of stamps.

   _____   _____   _____   _____

■ Review Test

Cross out the mistakes in numbers and abbreviations, and correct them in the spaces provided.

1. Sanjay was shocked when he transferred from a small h.s. to one with over 5000 students.

   _____   _____   _____   _____

2. Grandpa lived to be ninety-nine despite smoking 2 doz. cheap cigars per mo.

   _____   _____   _____

3. Although the 2 girls are twins, they have different birthdays: one was born just before midnight on Feb. twenty-fifth, and the other a few minutes later after midnight.

   _____   _____   _____

4. In their first week of Fr. class, students learned to count from 1 to twenty-one and studied Chapter One in their textbook.

   _____   _____   _____

5. When I cleaned out the junk drawer in the kitch., I found twelve rubber bands, thirty-seven paper clips, and 3 used-up batteries.

   _____   _____

Apostrophe

The two main uses of the apostrophe are

1 To show the omission of one or more letters in a contraction

2 To show ownership or possession

Each use is explained on the pages that follow.

APOSTROPHE IN CONTRACTIONS

A *contraction* is formed when two words are combined *into one* to make one word. An apostrophe is used to show where letters are omitted in forming the contraction. Here are two contractions:

have + not = haven't (the *o* in *not* has been omitted)
I + will = I'll (the *wi* in *will* has been omitted)

Following are some other common contractions:

I + am = I'm	it + is = it's
I + have = I've	it + has = it's
I + had = I'd	is + not = isn't
who + is = who's	could + not = couldn't
do + not = don't	I + would = I'd
did + not = didn't	they + are = they're

Note: *Will* + *not* has an unusual contraction: *won't.*

Activity

Write the contractions for the words in parentheses. One is done for you.

1. (Are not) _____*Aren't*_____ the reserve books in the library kept at the circulation desk?

2. If (they are) _____ coming over, (I had) _____ better cook more pasta.

3. (I am) _____ the kind of student (who is) _____ extremely nervous before tests.

4. (We are) _____ hoping to find out (who is) _____

responsible for this error; (it is) _____ important to us to keep our customers happy.

5. I (can not) _____ remember if (there is) _____ gas in the car or not.

Note: Even though contractions are common in everyday speech and in written dialogue, it is often best to avoid them in formal writing.

APOSTROPHE TO SHOW OWNERSHIP OR POSSESSION

To show ownership or possession, we can use such words as *belongs to, possessed by, owned by,* or (most commonly) *of.*

the umbrella that *belongs to* Santo
the DVD player *owned by* the school
the gentleness *of* my father

But the apostrophe plus *s* (if the word does not end in *s*) is often the quickest and easiest way to show possession. Thus we can say

Santo's umbrella
the school's DVD player
my father's gentleness

Points to Remember

1 The *'s* goes with the owner or possessor (in examples given, *Santo, the school, my father*). What follows is the person or thing possessed (in the examples given, *the umbrella, the DVD player, gentleness*).

2 When showing possession, the apostrophe should always come before the *s*.

Santo's   not   *Santos'*

Yes   No

Activity 1

Rewrite the *italicized* part of each of the sentences below, using the *'s* to show possession. Remember that the *'s* goes with the owner or possessor.

Example   *The wing of the bluejay* was broken.

        The bluejay's wing was broken.

1. *The annoying voice of the comedian* irritated me, so I changed the TV channel.

   _____

2. *The performance of the goalie* is inconsistent.

   _____

3. *The thin hand belonging to the old lady* felt as dry as parchment.

   _____

4. *In the window of the jewellery store* is a sign reading "Ears Pierced While You Wait."

   _____

5. A fly flew into *the mouth of the TV weather person.*

   _____

6. *The new denim shirt belonging to Josh* was as scratchy as sandpaper.

   _____

7. *The hair belonging to Rachel* is usually not green—she coloured it for Halloween.

   _____

8. *The bowl of cereal belonging to Ahmed* refused to snap, crackle, or pop.

   _____

Activity 2

Add *'s* to each of the following words to make them the possessors or owners of something. Then write sentences using the words. The first one is done for you.

1. rock star *rock star's* _____

   The rock star's limousine pulled up to the curb. _____

2. Javier _____

   _____

3. pilot _____

   _____

4. neighbour _____

   _____

Apostrophe versus Possessive Pronouns

Do not use an apostrophe with possessive pronouns. They already show ownership. Possessive pronouns include *his, hers, its, yours, ours,* and *theirs.*

Incorrect	*Correct*
The sun warped his' vinyl albums.	The sun warped his vinyl albums.
The restored Meteor is theirs'.	The restored Meteor is theirs.
The decision is yours'.	The decision is yours.
The plaid suitcase is ours'.	The plaid suitcase is ours.
The lion charged its' prey.	The lion charged its prey.

Apostrophe versus Simple Plurals

When you want to make a word plural, just add an *s* at the end of the word. Do *not* add an apostrophe. For example, the plural of the word *movie* is *movies,* not *movie's* or *movies'.* Look at this sentence:

Tim coveted his roommate's collection of cassette tapes and compact discs.

The words *tapes* and *discs* are simple plurals, meaning more than one tape, more than one disc. The plural is shown by adding *s* only. On the other hand, the *'s* after *roommate* shows possession—that the roommate owns the tapes and discs.

Activity

Insert an apostrophe where needed to show possession in the following sentences. Write *plural* above words where the *s* ending simply means more than one thing.

	plural	*plural*

Example   Arlene's tinted contact lenses protect her eyes from glare.

1. Harry grasped his wifes arm as she stood up on in-line skates for the first time.

2. Vivians decision to study computer science is based on predictions of good opportunities for women in that field.

3. The fires extreme heat had melted the telephones in the office and welded the metal chairs into a twisted heap.

4. At the doctors request, Troy pulled up his shirt and revealed the zipper-like scars from his operation.

5. Of all the peoples names in all the worlds countries, the most common is Mohammed.

6. At the end of the day, Cams shirt and pants smelled like gasoline, and his fingernails were rimmed with grease.

7. The childrens shouts of delight grew louder as the clown added eggs, lightbulbs, and a bowling ball to items he was juggling.

8. Tinas camping handbook suggests that we bring water purification tablets and nylon ropes.

Apostrophe with Words Ending in -*s*

Plurals that end in -*s* show possession simply by adding the apostrophe, rather than an apostrophe plus *s*.

> the Thompsons' porch
> the players' victory
> her parents' motor home
> the Barenaked Ladies' last album
> the soldiers' hats

Activity

Add an apostrophe where needed.

1. Several campers tents collapsed during the storm.

2. The Murrays phone bills are often over $100 a month.

3. Users of wheelchairs cannot get up the steep steps at the entrances to many buildings.

4. The twins habit of dressing alike was started by their parents when the twins were children.

5. At the crowded intersection, several young men rushed out to wash the cars windshields.

■ Review Test

In each sentence, underline the two words that need apostrophes. Then write the words correctly in the spaces provided.

_____ 1. The sagging sofas stuffing was coming out in places, and one of the chairs legs was broken.

_____ 2. A shaky rope ladder led from the barns wooden floor to the haylofts dusty shadows.

_____ 3. The paperback books glaring purple and orange cover was designed to attract a hurrying customers eye.

_____ 4. Alicias essay was due in a matter of hours, but she suffered a writers block that emptied her brain.

_____ 5. While she waited in her bosss office, Marlas nervous fingers shredded a Styrofoam coffee cup into a pile of jagged white flakes.

_____ 6. Ivan couldnt remember whether he had left his wallet in his cars glove compartment or at home.

_____ 7. Members of the parents association constructed a maze made of old tires for the childrens playground.

_____ 8. The cats great green eyes grew even wider as the curious dogs sniffing nose came too close to her.

Quotation Marks

The two main uses of quotation marks are

1 To set off the exact words of a speaker or writer
2 To set off the titles of short works

Each use is explained on the pages that follow.

QUOTATION MARKS TO SET OFF THE WORDS OF A SPEAKER OR WRITER

Use quotation marks to show the exact words of a speaker or writer.

"I feel as though I've been here before," Angie murmured to her husband.
(Quotation marks set off the exact words that Angie spoke to her husband.)

Margaret Atwood wrote, "Fear has a smell . . ."
(Quotation marks set off the exact words that Margaret Atwood wrote.)

"Did you know," said the nutrition expert, "that it's healthier to be a few kilos overweight?"
(Two pairs of quotation marks are used to enclose the nutrition expert's exact words.)

The biology professor said, "Ants are a lot like human beings. They farm their own food and raise smaller insects as livestock. And, like humans, ants send armies to war."
(Note that the end quotation marks do not come until the end of the biology professor's speech. Place quotation marks before the first quoted word and after the last quoted word. As long as no interruption occurs in the speech, do not use quotation marks for each new sentence.)

Punctuation Hint: In the four examples on the preceding page, notice that a comma sets off the quoted part from the rest of the sentence. Also, observe that commas and periods at the end of a quotation always go *inside* quotation marks.

Complete the following statements that explain how capital letters, commas, and periods are used in quotations. Refer to the four examples as guides.

1. Every quotation begins with a _____ letter.

2. When a quotation is split (as in the sentence about the nutrition expert), the second part does not begin with a capital letter unless it is a _____ sentence.

3. _____ are used to separate the quoted part of a sentence from the rest of the sentence.

4. Commas and periods that come at the end of a quotation go _____ the quotation marks.

Activity 1

Place quotation marks around the exact words of a speaker or writer in the sentences that follow.

1. Several people have been credited with saying, The more I see of people, the more I like dogs.

2. Beata asked, Do you give a discount to senior citizens?

3. This hamburger is raw! cried Leo.

4. The bumper sticker on the rear of the battered old car read, Don't laugh—it's paid for.

5. I know why Robin Hood robbed only the rich, said the comedian. The poor don't have any money.

6. These CDs, proclaimed the television announcer, are not sold in any store.

7. When chefs go to great lengths, the woman at the weight-loss centre said, I go to great widths.

8. On a tombstone in a Saskatchewan cemetery are the words, Here lies an atheist, all dressed up and no place to go.

Activity 2

1. Write a sentence in which you quote a favourite expression of someone you know. In the same sentence, identify the person's relationship to you.

Example   My grandfather loves to say, "It can't be as bad as all that."

_____

_____

_____

2. Write a quotation that contains the words *Paulo asked Teresa.* Write a second quotation that includes the words *Teresa replied.*

_____

_____

_____

_____

_____

_____

_____

_____

3. Quote an interesting sentence or two from a book or magazine. In the same sentence, identify the title and author of the work.

Example   In The Dilbert Desk Calendar by Scott Adams, cartoon character

Dilbert says, "I can please only one person per day. Today isn't your

day, and tomorrow isn't looking good either."

_____

_____

_____

_____

_____

_____

_____

_____

Indirect Quotations

An indirect quotation is a rewording of someone else's comments rather than a word-for-word direct quotation. The word *that* often signals an indirect quotation.

Direct Quotation	*Indirect Quotation*
The nurse said, "Some babies cannot tolerate cows' milk." (The nurse's exact spoken words are given, so quotation marks are used.)	The nurse said that some babies cannot tolerate cows' milk. (We learn the nurse's words indirectly, so no quotation marks are used.)
Vicky's note to Dan read, "I'll be home by 7:30." (The exact words that Vicky wrote in the note are given, so quotation marks are used.)	Vicky left a note for Dan that said she would be home by 7:30. (We learn Vicky's words indirectly, so no quotation marks are used.)

Activity

Rewrite the following sentences, changing words as necessary to convert the sentences into direct quotations. The first one has been done for you as an example.

1. Ted asked Maria if she wanted to see his spider collection.

   Ted asked Maria, "Do you want to see my spider collection?"

2. Sonya said that her uncle looks just like a large basset hound.

   _____

   _____

3. Angelo said that he wanted a box of the extra-crispy chicken.

   _____

   _____

4. My boss told me that I could make mistakes as long as I didn't repeat them.

   _____

   _____

5. The instructor announced that Thursday's test had been cancelled.

   _____

   _____

QUOTATION MARKS TO SET OFF TITLES OF SHORT WORKS

Titles of short works are usually set off by quotation marks, while titles of long works are underlined or italicized. Use quotation marks to set off titles of such short works as articles in books, newspapers, or magazines; chapters in a book; short stories; poems; and songs. But you should underline or italicize titles of books, newspapers, magazines, plays, movies, record albums, and television shows. Following are some examples.

Quotation Marks	*Underlined or Italicized*
the essay "Bicycles"	in the book <u>Urban Scrawl</u>
the article "New Social Union Deal"	in the newspaper <u>The National Post</u>
the article "Living with Inflation"	in the magazine <u>Maclean's</u>
the chapter "Chinese Religion"	in the book <u>Paths of Faith</u>
the story "The Sin Eater"	in the book <u>Bluebeard's Egg</u>
the poem "When I Have Fears"	in the book <u>Complete Poems of John Keats</u>
the song "Apparitions"	in the album <u>The Dave Matthews Band</u>
the episode "Old Memories"	in the television show <u>Cold Squad</u>
	in the movie <u>Exotica</u>

Note: In printed works, including papers that are prepared on a word processor, italic type—slanted type that looks *like this*—is used instead of underlining.

Activity

Use quotation marks or underlines as needed.

1. In her short story A Sea Worry, Maxine Hong Kingston describes a group of teenage surfers and a mother who tries to understand them.

2. I bought the National Enquirer to read an article entitled Painful Beauty Secrets of the Stars.

3. We studied the chapter The Motive for Metaphor in Northrop Frye's book The Educated Imagination.

4. Jamila used an article titled A Certain Hunger by Maggie Helwig from This Magazine in her research paper about eating disorders.

5. The movie Casablanca, which starred Humphrey Bogart, was originally cast with Ronald Reagan in the leading role.

6. My favourite old TV show on Nick at Nite is Thriller, a horror series hosted by Boris Karloff, the man who starred in the 1931 movie Frankenstein.

7. When the Spice Girls' movie Spice World was first shown, fans screamed so much that no one could hear the songs or the dialogue.

8. On my father's wall is a framed front page of The Vancouver Sun of February 25, 1940—the day he was born.

OTHER USES OF QUOTATION MARKS

Quotation marks are also used as follows:

1 To set off special words or phrases from the rest of a sentence:

In elementary school, we were taught a little jingle about the "*i* before *e*" spelling rule.
What is the difference between "it's" and "its"?
(In this book, *italics* are often used instead of quotation marks to set off words.)

2 To mark off a quotation within a quotation:

The physics professor said, "For class on Friday, do the problems at the end of the chapter titled 'Work and Energy.'"

Brendan remarked, "Did you know that Humphrey Bogart never actually said, 'Play it again, Sam' in the movie *Casablanca?*"

Note: A quotation within a quotation is indicated by *single* quotation marks, as shown above.

Review Test 1

Insert quotation marks where needed in the sentences that follow.

1. The psychology class read a short story called Silent Snow, Secret Snow, about a young boy who creates his own fantasy world.

2. While filming the movie *Vertigo,* actress Kim Novak was agonizing over how to play a particular scene until director Alfred Hitchcock reminded her, Kim, it's only a movie!

3. I'm against elementary school students using calculators, said Fred. I spent three years learning long division, and so should they.

4. Composer George Gershwin wrote many hundreds of hit songs, including classics like Summertime and Somebody Loves Me.

5. When I gagged while taking a foul-tasting medicine, my wife said, Put an ice cube on your tongue first, and then you won't taste it.

6. Gene reported to his business class on an article in *Canadian Business* magazine entitled Cashing In on the Energy Boom.

7. When a guest at the wedding was asked what he was giving the couple, he replied, About six months.

8. Pierre Elliott Trudeau, an occasionally controversial prime minister, once said, Power only tires those who don't exercise it.

Review Test 2

Go through the comics section of a newspaper to find a comic strip that amuses you. Be sure to choose a strip where two or more characters are speaking to each other. Write a full description that will enable people who have not read the comic strip to visualize it clearly and appreciate its humour. Describe the setting and action in each panel, and enclose the words of the speakers in quotation marks.

Narration • Description • Examples • Process • Cause and Effect • Comparison and Cont
Definition • Division and Classification • Argumentation • Narration • Description • Exan
Process • Cause and Effect • Comparison and Contrast • Definition • Division and Classific
Argumentation • Narration • Description • Examples • Process • Cause and Effect • Compariso
Contrast • Definition • Division and Classification • Argumentation • Narration • Descriptio

CHAPTER 38

Comma

SIX MAIN USES OF THE COMMA

Commas are used mainly as follows:

1 To separate items in a series

2 To set off introductory material

3 On both sides of words that interrupt the flow of thought in a sentence

4 Between two complete thoughts connected by *and, but, for, or, nor, so, yet*

5 To set off a direct quotation from the rest of a sentence

6 For certain everyday material

You may find it helpful to remember that the comma often marks a slight pause or break in a sentence. Read aloud the sentence examples given for each rule, and listen for the minor pauses or breaks that are signalled by commas.

1 Comma between Items in a Series

Use commas to separate items in a series.

> The street vendor sold watches, necklaces, and earrings.
> The pitcher adjusted his cap, pawed the ground, and peered over his shoulder.
> The exercise instructor told us to inhale, exhale, and relax.
> Joe peered into the hot, still-smoking engine.

Notes

1 The final comma in a series is optional, but it is often used. *Be consistent* in your use of commas when you list items.

2 A comma is used between two descriptive words in a series only if *and* inserted between the words sounds natural. You could say

> Joe peered into the hot *and* still-smoking engine.

But notice in the following sentence that the descriptive words do not sound natural when *and* is inserted between them. In such cases, no comma is used.

> Theo wore a pale green tuxedo. (A pale *and* green tuxedo does not sound right, so no comma is used.)

Activity

Place commas between items in a series.

1. The old kitchen cabinets were littered with dead insects crumbs and dust balls.

2. Rudy stretched out on the swaying hammock popped open a frosty can of pop and balanced it carefully on his stomach.

3. The children splashed through the warm deep swirling rainwater that flooded the street.

4. The police officer's warm brown eyes relaxed manner and pleasant smile made him easy to talk to.

5. The musty shadowy cellar with the crumbling cement floor was our favourite playground.

2 Comma after Introductory Material

Use a comma to set off introductory material.

> Just in time, Kami slid a plastic tray under the overwatered philodendron.
> Muttering under his breath, Matthias reviewed the terms he had memorized.
> In a wolf pack, the dominant male holds his tail higher than the other pack members.
> Although he had been first in the checkout line, Devon let an elderly woman go ahead of him.
> After the fire, we slogged through the ashes of the burned-out house.

Note: If the introductory material is brief, the comma is sometimes omitted. In the activities here, you should include the comma.

Activity

Place commas after introductory material.

1. As Chen struggled with the stuck window gusts of cold rain blew in his face.

2. His heart pounding wildly Jesse opened the letter that would tell him whether or not he had been accepted at college.

3. Along the once-pretty Don River people had dumped old tires and loads of household trash.

4. When the band hadn't taken the stage forty-five minutes after the concert was supposed to begin the audience members started shouting and stamping their feet.

5. Setting down a smudged glass of murky water the server tossed Dennis a greasy menu and asked if he'd care to order.

3 Comma around Words Interrupting the Flow of Thought

Use a comma on both sides of words or phrases that interrupt the flow of thought in a sentence.

> The vinyl car seat, sticky from the heat, clung to my skin.
> Marty's personal computer, which his wife got him as a birthday gift, occupies all of his spare time.
> The hallway, dingy and dark, was illuminated by a bare bulb hanging from a wire.

Usually you can "hear" words that interrupt the flow of thought in a sentence by reading it aloud. In cases where you are not sure if certain words are interrupters, remove them from the sentence. If it still makes sense without the words, you know that the words are interrupters and that the information they give is nonessential. *Such nonessential or extra information is set off with commas.*

In the sentence

> Joanna Dodd, who goes to aerobics class with me, was in a serious car accident.

the words *who goes to aerobics class with me* are extra information not needed to identify the subject of the sentence, *Joanna Dodd*. Commas go around such nonessential information. On the other hand, in the sentence

> The woman who goes to aerobics class with me was in a serious accident.

the words *who goes to aerobics class with me* supply essential information—information needed for us to identify the woman being spoken of. If the words were removed from the sentence, we would no longer know exactly who was in the accident: "The woman was in a serious accident." Here is another example:

> *Watership Down,* a novel by Richard Adams, is the most thrilling adventure story I've ever read.

Here the words *a novel by Richard Adams* could be left out, and we would still know the basic meaning of the sentence. Commas are placed around such nonessential material. But in the sentence

> Richard Adams' novel *Watership Down* is the most thrilling adventure story I've ever read.

the title of the novel is essential. Without it the sentence would read, "Richard Adams' novel is the most thrilling adventure story I've ever read." We would not know which of Richard Adams' novels was so thrilling. Commas are not used around the title because it provides essential information.

Activity

Use commas to set off interrupting words. The first has been done for you.

1. A slight breeze, hot and damp, ruffled the bedroom curtains.

2. The defrosting chickens loosely wrapped in plastic left a pool on the counter.

3. Lenny's wallet which he kept in his front pants pocket was linked to his belt with a metal chain.

4. Mr. LaCroix who is an avid Canadiens fan remembers the grand days of Jacques Plante and Bernie Geoffrion.

5. The fleet of tall ships a majestic sight made its way into Halifax Harbour.

4 Comma between Complete Thoughts

Use a comma between two complete thoughts connected by *and, but, for, or, nor, so, yet.*

Sam closed all the windows, but the predicted thunderstorm never arrived.
I like wearing comfortable clothing, so I buy oversized shirts and sweaters.
Peggy doesn't envy the skinny models in magazines, for she is happy with her own healthy-looking body.

Notes

1 The comma is optional when the complete thoughts are short.

The ferris wheel started and Wilson closed his eyes.
Irene left the lecture hall for her head was pounding.
I made a wrong turn so I doubled back.

2 Be careful not to use a comma to separate two verbs that belong to one subject. The comma is used only in sentences made up of two complete thoughts (two subjects and two verbs). In the sentence

The doctor stared over his bifocals and lectured me about smoking.

there is only one subject (*doctor*) and a double verb (*stared* and *lectured*). No comma is needed. Likewise, the sentence

Aaron switched the lamp on and off and then tapped it with his fingers.

has only one subject (*Aaron*) and a double verb (*switched* and *tapped*); therefore, no comma is needed.

Activity

Place a comma before a joining word that connects two complete thoughts (two subjects and two verbs). Remember, do *not* place a comma within a sentence that has only one subject and a double verb. (Some items may be correct as given.)

1. My favourite soap was interrupted for a news bulletin about an ice storm and I poked my head out of the kitchen to listen to the announcement.

2. The puppy was beaten by its former owner and cringes at the sound of a loud voice.

3. The eccentric woman brought all her own clips and rollers to the hairdressers for she was afraid to use the ones there.

4. The tuna sandwich in my lunch is crushed and the cream-filled cupcake is plastered to the bottom of the bag.

5. The property owner promised repeatedly to come and fix the leaking shower but three months later he hasn't done a thing.

6. Bonita was tired of summer reruns so she visited the town library to pick up some interesting books.

7. You can spend hours driving all over town to look for a particular type of camera or you can telephone a few stores to find it quickly.

8. Many people strolled among the exhibits at the comic book collectors' convention and stopped to look at a rare first edition of *Superman*.

5 Comma with Direct Quotations

Use a comma to set off a direct quotation from the rest of a sentence.

> The carnival barker cried, "Step right up and win a prize!"
> "Now is the time to yield to temptation," my horoscope read.
> "I'm sorry," said the restaurant host. "You'll have to wait."
> "For my first writing assignment," said Scott, "I have to turn in a five-hundred-word description of a stone."

Note: Commas and periods at the end of a quotation go inside quotation marks. See also page 437.

Activity

Use commas to set off direct quotations from the rest of the sentence.

1. The coach announced "In order to measure your lung capacity, you're going to attempt to blow up a plastic bag with one breath."

2. "A grapefruit" said the comedian "is a lemon that had a chance and took advantage of it."

3. My father asked "Did you know that the family moving next door has thirteen children?"

4. "Speak louder" a man in the back row said to the guest speaker. "I paid five dollars to hear you talk, not whisper."

5. The zookeeper explained to the visitors "We can't tell the sex of a giant tortoise for almost ten years after its birth."

6 Comma with Everyday Material

Use a comma with certain everyday material.

Persons Spoken to

If you're the last to leave, Paul, please switch off the lights.
Omar, I think we're on the wrong road.
Did you see the playoff game, Lisa?

Dates

June 30, 2003, is the day I make the last payment on my car.

Addresses

I buy discount children's clothing from Bouncy Baby Wear, Box 900, Vancouver, British Columbia V6H 4Z1.

Note: No comma is used before a postal code.

Openings and Closings of Letters

Dear Santa,   Sincerely yours,
Dear Roberto,   Truly yours,

Note: In formal letters, a colon is used after the opening: Dear Sir: *or* Dear Madam: *or* Dear Allan: *or* Dear Ms. Mohr:.

Numbers

The insurance agent sold me a $50,000 term life insurance policy.

Activity

Place commas where needed.

1. Would you mind Manuel if we borrowed your picnic cooler this weekend?

2. The rotis made at Island Foods 468 Queen Street West are the best in town.

3. On December 29 1989 Vaclav Havel the dissident Czech playwright became president of Czechoslovakia.

4. The mileage chart shows Elaine that we'll have to drive 1231 kilometres to get to Red Deer Alberta.

5. The coupon refund address is 2120 Maritime Highway Halifax Nova Scotia B3J 1V2.

■ **Review Test 1**

Insert commas where needed. In the space provided below each sentence, summarize briefly the rule that explains the comma or commas used.

1. "Kleenex tissues" said the history professor "were first used as gas mask filters in World War I."

   _____

2. Dee ordered a sundae with three scoops of rocky road ice cream miniature marshmallows and raspberry sauce.

   _____

3. While waiting to enter the movie theatre we studied the faces of the people just leaving to see if they had liked the show.

   _____

4. I had left my wallet on the store counter but the clerk called me at home to say that it was safe.

   _____

5. The demonstrators protesting nuclear arms carried signs reading "Humans have never invented a weapon that they haven't used."

   _____

6. Large flowering bushes which now sell for very high prices are being stolen from provincial parks.

   _____

7. At the age of 21 Tiger Woods won the 1997 Masters Tournament with the highest margin of victory in the golfing tournament's history.

   _____

8. The talk show guest a former child star said that one director threatened to shoot her dog if she didn't cry on cue.

   _____

■ **Review Test 2**

Insert commas where needed. Mark the one sentence that is correct with a *C*.

1. Before leaving for the gym Nikki added extra socks and a tube of shampoo to the gear in her duffel bag.

2. My father said "Golf isn't for me. I can't afford to buy lots of expensive sticks so that I can lose lots of expensive white balls."

3. Oscar took a time-exposure photo of the busy highway so the cars' tail lights appeared in the developed print as winding red ribbons.

4. The graduating students sweltering in their hot gowns fanned their faces with commencement programs.

5. After her tragic death in Paris France as many as 2.5 billion people worldwide watched the televised funeral of Princess Diana on September 6 1997.

6. In November 1998 thousands of people died in Honduras from the mud slides flooding and high winds caused by Hurricane Mitch.

7. "When I was little" said Ernie "my brother told me it was illegal to kill praying mantises. I still don't know if that's true or not."

8. On July 1 1867 Upper and Lower Canada united with two other colonies to form the Dominion of Canada.

■ Review Test 3

In the following passage, there are ten missing commas. Add the commas where needed. The types of mistakes to look for are shown in the box below.

---

two commas missing between items in a series
one comma missing after introductory material
four commas missing around interrupting words
two commas missing between complete thoughts
one comma missing with a direct quotation

When I was about ten years old I developed several schemes to avoid eating liver, a food I despise. My first scheme involved my little brother. Timmy too young to realize what a horrible food liver is always ate every bit of his portion. On liver nights, I used to sit next to Tim and slide my slab of meat onto his plate when my parents weren't paying attention. This strategy worked until older and wiser Tim decided to reject his liver along with the rest of us. Another liver-disposal method I used was hiding the meat right on the plate. I'd cut the liver into tiny squares half the size of postage stamps and then I would carefully hide the pieces. I'd put them inside the skin of my baked potato beneath some mashed peas, or under a crumpled paper napkin. This strategy worked perfectly only if my mother didn't look too closely as she scraped the dishes. Once she said to me "Do you know you left a lot of liver on your plate?" My best liver trick was to hide the disgusting stuff on a three-inch-wide wooden ledge that ran under our dining-room table. I'd put little pieces of liver on the ledge when Mom wasn't looking; I would sneak the dried-up scraps into the garbage early the next day. Our dog would sometimes smell the liver try to get at it, and bang his head noisily against the bottom of the table. These strategies seemed like a lot of work but I never hesitated to take whatever steps I could. Anything was better than eating a piece of meat that tasted like old socks soaked in mud.

■ Review Test 4

On separate paper, write six sentences, one illustrating each of the six main comma rules.

Narration · Description · Examples · Process · Cause and Effect · Comparison and Cont
Definition · Division and Classification · Argumentation · Narration · Description · Exan
Process · Cause and Effect · Comparison and contrast · Definition · Division and Classific
Argumentation · Narration · Description · Examples · Process · Cause and Effect · Compariso
contrast · Definition · Division and Classification · Argumentation · Narration · Descriptic

CHAPTER 39

Other Punctuation Marks

COLON (:)

Use the colon at the end of a complete statement to introduce a list or an explanation.

1 A list:

The store will close at noon on the following dates: October 5, December 24, and December 31.

2 An explanation:

Here's a temporary solution to a dripping faucet: Tie a string to it, and let the drops slide down the string to the sink.

Activity

Place colons where needed in the sentences below.

1. Bring these items to registration a ballpoint pen, your student ID card, and a cheque made out to the college.

2. The road was closed owing to an emergency an enormous tree had fallen and blocked both lanes.

SEMICOLON (;)

The main use of the semicolon is to mark a break between two complete thoughts, as explained on pages 378–379. Another use is to mark off items in a series when the items themselves contain commas. Here are some examples:

Maya's children are named Melantha, which means "black flower"; Yonina, which means "dove"; and Cynthia, which means "moon goddess."
My parents' favourite albums are *Rubber Soul,* by the Beatles; *Songs in the Key of Life,* by Stevie Wonder; and *Bridge over Troubled Water,* by Simon and Garfunkel.

Activity

Place semicolons where needed in the sentences below.

1. Strange things happen at very low temperatures a rose will shatter like glass.

2. My sister had a profitable summer: by mowing lawns, she earned $125 by washing cars, $85 and by walking the neighbour's dogs, $110.

3. The children who starred in the play were Kari Rosoff, nine years old Flora Junco, twelve years old and Ezra Johnson, three years old.

DASH (—)

A dash signals a pause longer than a comma but not as long as a period. Use a dash to set off words for dramatic effect:

I was so exhausted that I fell asleep within seconds—standing up.
He had many good qualities—sincerity, honesty, and thoughtfulness—yet he had few friends.

Notes

1 A dash is formed on a keyboard by striking the hyphen twice (- -). In handwriting, a dash is as long as two letters would be.

2 Be careful not to overuse dashes.

3 Colons used to begin lists of items are generally more acceptable in formal writing than dashes.

Activity

Place dashes where needed in the following sentences.

1. The victim's leg broken in three places lay twisted at an odd angle on the pavement.

2. The wallet was found in a garbage can minus the cash.

3. After nine days of hiking in the wilderness, sleeping under the stars, and communing with nature, I could think of only one thing a hot shower.

PARENTHESES ( )

Parentheses are used to set off extra or incidental information from the rest of a sentence:

In 1913, the tax on an annual income of $4000 (a comfortable wage at that time) was one penny.
Arthur C. Clarke, author of science fiction books (including *2001: A Space Odyssey*), was inspired as a young man by the magazine *Astounding Stories*.

Note: Do not use parentheses too often in your writing.

Activity

Add parentheses where needed.

1. Though the first *Star Trek* series originally ran for only three seasons 1965–1968, it can still be seen on many stations around the world.

2. Whenever Jack has too much to drink even one drink is sometimes too much, he gets loud and abusive.

3. When I opened the textbook, I discovered that many pages mostly ones in the first chapter were completely blank.

HYPHEN (-)

1 Use a hyphen with two or more words that act as a single unit describing a noun.

The light-footed burglar silently slipped open the sliding-glass door.
While being interviewed on the late-night talk show, the quarterback announced his intention to retire.
With a needle, Enio punctured the fluid-filled blister on his toe.

2 Use a hyphen to divide a word at the end of a line of writing or typing. When you need to divide a word at the end of a line, divide it between syllables. Use your dictionary to be sure of correct syllable divisions.

Selena's first year at college was a time filled with numerous new pres-sures and responsibilities.

Notes

1 Do not divide words of one syllable.

2 Do not divide a word if you can avoid dividing it.

3 Word processing has eliminated the need to divide words at the end of lines. Unless they contain hyphenation dictionaries, software programs will not split your final word on a line; the word will be fitted into the line you are typing or moved to the beginning of the next line.

Activity

Place hyphens where needed.

1. The blood red moon hanging low on the horizon made a picture perfect atmosphere for Halloween night.

2. My father, who grew up in a poverty stricken household, remembers putting cardboard in his shoes when the soles wore out.

3. The well written article in *Saturday Night* magazine described the nerve wracking experiences of a journalist who infiltrated the Mob.

■ **Review Test**

At the appropriate spot, place the punctuation mark shown in the margin.

— 1. A bad case of flu, a burglary, the death of an uncle it was not what you would call a pleasant week.

( ) 2. My grandfather who will be ninety in May says that hard work and a glass of wine every day are the secrets of a long life.

- 3. The passengers in the glass bottomed boat stared at the colourful fish in the water below.

( ) 4. Ellen's birthday December 27 falls so close to Christmas that she gets only one set of presents.

; 5. The dog-show winners included Freckles, a springer spaniel King Leo, a German shepherd and Big Guy, a miniature schnauzer.

- 6. Cold hearted stepmothers are a fixture in many famous fairy tales.

; 7. Some people need absolute quiet in order to study they can't concentrate with the soft sounds of a radio, air conditioner, or television in the background.

: 8. A critic reviewing a bad play wrote, "I saw the play under the worst possible circumstances the curtain was up."

Narration • Description • Examples • Process • Cause and Effect • Comparison and Cont
Definition • Division and Classification • Argumentation • Narration • Description • Exam
Process • Cause and Effect • Comparison and Contrast • Definition • Division and Classifica
Argumentation • Narration • Description • Examples • Process • Cause and Effect • Compariso
Contrast • Definition • Division and Classification • Argumentation • Narration • Descriptio

CHAPTER 40

Commonly Confused Words

HOMONYMS

The commonly confused words (also known as *homonyms*) on the following pages have the same sounds but different meanings and spellings. Complete the activity for each set of words, and check off and study the words that give you trouble.

all ready   completely prepared
already   by then; not earlier than

> It was *already* four o'clock by the time I thought about lunch.
> My report was *all ready*, but the class was cancelled.

Fill in the blanks: Tyrone was _____ to sign up for the course when

he discovered that it had _____ closed.

brake   stop
break   come apart

> The mechanic advised me to add *brake* fluid to my car.
> During a commercial *break,* Marie lay on the floor and did fifty sit-ups.

Fill in the blanks: Avril, a poor driver, _____ at the last minute and

usually _____ the speed limit as well.

course   part of a meal; a school subject; direction
coarse   rough

> At the movies, I tried to decide on a *course* of action that would put an end to the *coarse* language of the man behind me.

Fill in the blanks: Over the _____ of time, jagged, _____
rocks will be polished to smoothness by the pounding waves.

hear perceive with the ear
here in this place

I can *hear* the performers so well from *here* that I don't want to change my seat.

Fill in the blanks: The chairperson explained that the meeting was held

_____ in the auditorium to enable everyone to _____ the debate.

hole an empty spot
whole entire

A *hole* in the crumbling brick mortar made a convenient home for the small bird and its *whole* family.

Fill in the blanks: The _____ in Jason's arguments wouldn't exist if

he put his _____ concentration into his thinking.

its belonging to it
it's the shortened form for *it is* or *it has*

The tall giraffe lowered *its* head (the head belonging to the giraffe) to the level of the car window and peered in at us.
It's (it is) too late to sign up for the theatre trip to Toronto.

Fill in the blanks: I decided not to take the course because _____

too easy; _____ content offers no challenge whatever.

knew past form of *know*
new not old

No one *knew* our *new* phone number, but the obscene calls continued.

Fill in the blanks: Even people who _____ Andrew well didn't

recognize him with his _____ beard.

know to understand
no a negative

By the time students complete that course, they *know* two computer languages and have *no* trouble writing their own programs.

Fill in the blanks: Dogs and cats usually _____ by the tone of the

speaker's voice when they are being told "_____."

passed went by; succeeded in; handed to
past a time before the present; by, as in "I drove past the house"

As Yvonne *passed* exit six on the highway, she knew she had gone *past* the correct turn-off.

Fill in the blanks: Lewis asked for a meeting with his boss to learn why he had been _____ over for promotion twice in the _____ year.

peace   calm
piece   a part

The best *piece* of advice she ever received was to maintain her own inner *peace.*

Fill in the blanks: Upon hearing that _____ of music, my angry mood was gradually replaced by one of _____.

plain   simple
plane   aircraft

The *plain* box contained a very expensive model *plane* kit.

Fill in the blanks: After unsuccessfully trying to overcome her fear, Alexandra finally admitted the _____ truth: she was terrified of flying in _____.

principal   main; a person in charge of a school
principle   a law or standard

If the *principal* ingredient in this stew is octopus, I'll abandon my *principle* of trying everything at least once.

Fill in the blanks: Our _____ insists that all students adhere to the school's _____ regarding dress, tardiness, and smoking.

right   correct; opposite of *left*
write   what you do in English

Without the *right* amount of advance planning, it is difficult to *write* a good research paper.

Fill in the blanks: Connie wanted to send for the CDs offered on TV, but she could not _____ fast enough to get all the _____ information down before the commercial ended.

than (thăn)   used in comparisons
then (thĕn)   at that time

I made more money *then,* but I've never been happier *than* I am now.

Fill in the blanks: When I was in high school, I wanted a racy two-seater convertible more _____ anything else; but _____ my friends pointed out that only one person would be able to ride with me.

their   belonging to them
there   at that place; a neutral word used with verbs like *is, are, was, were, have,*
and *had*
they're   the shortened form of *they are*

> The tenants *there* are complaining because *they're* being cheated by *their* building owner.

Fill in the blanks: The tomatoes I planted _____ in the back of the

garden are finally ripening, but _____ bright red colour will attract

hungry raccoons, and I fear _____ going to be eaten.

threw   past form of *throw*
through   from one side to the other; finished

> As the inexperienced pizza maker *threw* the pie into the air, he punched a hole *through* its thin crust.

Fill in the blanks: As the prime minister moved slowly _____ the

cheering crowd, the RCMP officer suddenly _____ himself at a man
waving a small metal object.

to   a verb part, as in *to smile;* toward, as in "I'm going *to* heaven"
too   overly, as in "The pizza was *too* hot"; also, as in "The coffee was hot, *too.*"
two   the number *2*

> I ran *to* the car *to* roll up the windows. (The first *to* means "toward"; the
> second *to* is a verb part that goes with *roll.*)
> That amusement park is *too* far away; I hear that it's expensive, *too.* (The first
> *too* means "overly"; the second *too* means "also.")
> The *two* players (2 players) jumped up to tap the basketball away.

Fill in the blanks: The _____ of them have been dating for a year, but

lately they seem _____ be arguing _____ often to pretend
nothing is wrong.

wear   to have on
where   in what place

> *Where* I will *wear* a purple feather boa is not the point; I just want to buy it.

Fill in the blanks: _____ were we going the night I refused to

_____ a tie?

weather   atmospheric conditions
whether   if it happens that; in case; if

> Although meteorologists are *weather* specialists, even they can't predict
> *whether* a hurricane will change course.

Fill in the blanks: The gloomy _____ report in the paper this morning

ended all discussion of _____ to pack a picnic lunch for later.

whose   belonging to whom
who's   the shortened form for *who is* and *who has*

    "*Who's* the patient *whose* filling fell out?" the dentist's assistant asked.

Fill in the blanks: _____ the salesperson _____ customers
are always complaining about his high-pressure tactics?

your   belonging to you
you're   the shortened form of *you are*

    You're making a fool of yourself; *your* Elvis imitation isn't funny.

Fill in the blanks: If _____ having trouble filling out _____
tax return, why don't you call Revenue Canada's local line?

OTHER WORDS FREQUENTLY CONFUSED

Here is a list of other words that people frequently confuse. Complete the activities for each set of words, and check off and study the words that give you trouble.

a   Both *a* and *an* are used before other words to mean "one."
an   Generally you should use *an* before words starting with a vowel *(a, e, i, o, u):*

    an orange   an umbrella   an indication   an ape   an effort

Generally you should use *a* before words starting with a consonant (all other letters):

    a genius   a movie   a speech   a study   a typewriter

Fill in the blanks: The morning after the party, I had _____ pounding

headache and _____ upset stomach.

accept (ăk sĕpt′)   receive; agree to
except (ĕk sĕpt′)   exclude; but

    It was easy to *accept* the book's plot, *except* for one unlikely coincidence at the very end.

Fill in the blanks: Sanka would have _____ the position,

_____ that it would add twenty minutes to his daily commute.

advice (ăd vīs′)   a noun meaning "an opinion"
advise (ăd vīz′)   a verb meaning "to counsel, to give advice"

    I have learned not to take my sister's *advice* on straightening out my life.
    A counsellor can *advise* you about the courses you'll need next year.

Fill in the blanks: Ayesha seems so troubled about losing her job that I

_____ her to seek the _____ of a professional counsellor.

affect (uh fĕkt′)   a verb meaning "to influence"
effect (ĭ fĕkt′)   a verb meaning "to bring about something"; a noun
                          meaning "result"

> The bad weather will definitely *affect* the outcome of the election.
> If we can *effect* a change in George's attitude, he may do better in his courses.
> One *effect* of the strike will be dwindling supplies in the supermarkets.

Fill in the blanks: Scientists have studied the _____ of large
quantities of saccharine on lab animals but have yet to learn how similar

amounts _____ human beings.

among   implies three or more
between implies only two

> After the team of surgeons consulted *among* themselves, they decided that the
> bullet was lodged *between* two of the patient's ribs.

Fill in the blanks: _____ halves, one enthusiastic fan stood up

_____ his equally fanatic friends and took off his coat and shirt.

beside   along the side of
besides in addition to

> *Besides* doing daily inventories, I have to stand *beside* the cashier whenever
> the store gets crowded.

Fill in the blanks: _____ those books on the table, I plan to use these

magazines stacked _____ me while doing my research paper.

fewer used with things that can be counted
less   refers to amount, value, or degree

> I've taken *fewer* classes this semester, so I hope to have *less* trouble finding
> time to study.

Fill in the blanks: This beer advertises that it has _____ calories and

is _____ filling.

former refers to the first of two items named
latter refers to the second of two items named

> Sue yelled at her sons, Greg and John, when she got home; the *former* had left
> the refrigerator open and the *latter* had left wet towels all over the bathroom.

Fill in the blanks: Marco collects coupons and parking tickets: the

_____ save him money, and the _____ are going

to cost him a great deal of money some day.

learn   to gain knowledge
teach   to give knowledge

I can't *learn* a new skill unless someone with lots of patience *teaches* me.

Fill in the blanks: Because she is quick to _____ new things, Mandy

has offered to _____ me how to play the latest video games.

loose (lōōs)   not fastened; not tight-fitting
lose (lōōz)   misplace; fail to win

In this strong wind, the house may *lose* some of its *loose* roof shingles.

Fill in the blanks: A _____ wire in the television set was causing us

to _____ the picture.

quiet (kwi′ĭt)   peaceful
quite (kwīt)   entirely; really; rather

Avivah seems *quiet* and demure, but she has *quite* a temper at times.

Fill in the blanks: Most people think the library is _____ a good

place to study, but I find the extreme _____ distracting.

Activity

These sentences check your understanding of *its, it's; there, their, they're; to, too, two;* and *your, you're.* Underline the two incorrect spellings in each sentence. Then spell the words correctly in the spaces provided.

_____   1. "Its not a very good idea," yelled Alexandra's boss, "to tell you're customer that the striped dress she plans to buy makes her look like a pregnant tiger."

_____   2. You're long skirt got stuck in the car door, and now its sweeping the highway.

_____   3. When your young, their is a tendency to confuse a crush with true love.

_____   4. After too hours of writing, Lin was to tired to write any longer.

_____   5. It is unusual for a restaurant to lose it's licence, but this one had more mice in its' kitchen than cooks.

_____   6. The vampires bought a knife sharpener in order too sharpen there teeth.

_____   7. Your sometimes surprised by who you're friends turn out to be in difficult times.

_____   8. When the children get to quiet, Clare knows their getting into trouble.

■ **Review Test 1**

Underline the correct word in the parentheses. Rather than guessing, look back at the explanations of the words when necessary.

1. I (know, no) that several of the tenants have decided (to, too, two) take (their, there, they're) case to court.

2. (Whose, Who's) the author of that book about the (affects, effects) of eating (to, too, two) much protein?

3. In our supermarket is a counter (where, wear) (your, you're) welcome to sit down and have free coffee and doughnuts.

4. (Its, It's) possible to (loose, lose) friends by constantly giving out unwanted (advice, advise).

5. For a long time, I couldn't (accept, except) the fact that my husband wanted a divorce; (then, than) I decided to stop being angry and get on with my life.

6. I spent the (hole, whole) day browsing (threw, through) the chapters in my business textbook, but I didn't really study them.

7. The newly appointed (principal, principle) is (quite, quiet) familiar with the problems (hear, here) at our school.

8. I found that our cat had (all ready, already) had her kittens (among, between) the weeds (beside, besides) the porch.

■ **Review Test 2**

On separate paper, write short sentences using the ten words shown below.

1. accept
2. its
3. you're
4. too
5. then

6. principal
7. their
8. passed
9. fewer
10. who's

Narration · Description · Examples · Process · Cause and Effect · Comparison and Cont
Definition · Division and Classification · Argumentation · Narration · Description · Exam
Process · Cause and Effect · Comparison and Contrast · Definition · Division and Classific
Argumentation · Narration · Description · Examples · Process · Cause and Effect · Compariso
Contrast · Definition · Division and Classification · Argumentation · Narration · Descripti

CHAPTER 41

Effective Word Choice

Choose your words carefully when you write. Always take the time to think about your word choices rather than simply using the first word that comes to mind. You need to develop the habit of selecting words that are appropriate and exact for your purposes. One way you can show your sensitivity to language is by avoiding slang and clichés.

SLANG

We often use slang expressions when we talk because they are so vivid and colourful. However, slang is usually out of place in formal writing. Here are some examples of slang expressions:

> Someone *ripped off* Ken's new Nike running shoes from his locker.
> After the game, we *pigged out* at the restaurant.
> I finally told my parents to *get off my case*.
> The movie really *grossed me out*.

Slang expressions have a number of drawbacks. They go out of date quickly, they become tiresome if used excessively in writing, and they may communicate clearly to some readers but not to others. Also, the use of slang can be an evasion of the specific details that are often needed to make one's meaning clear in writing. For example, in "The movie really grossed me out," the writer has not provided the specific details about the movie necessary for us to clearly understand the statement. Was it the acting, the special effects, or the violent scenes in the movie that the writer found so disgusting? In general, then, you should avoid the use of slang in your writing. If you are in doubt about whether an expression is slang, it may help to check a recently published dictionary.

Activity

Rewrite the following sentences, replacing the italicized slang words with more formal ones.

Example   When we told the neighbours to *can the noise,* they *freaked out.*

When we told the neighbours to be quiet, they were upset.

1. I didn't realize how *messed up* Joey was until he stole some money from his parents and *split* for a month.

2. After a hard day, I like to *veg out* in front of the *idiot box.*

3. Kwame was *so wiped out* after his workout at the gym that he couldn't *get it together* to defrost a frozen dinner.

4. When Alex tried to put *the move on* Elaine at the school party, she told him to *shove off.*

CLICHÉS

A *cliché* is an expression that has been worn out through constant use. Some typical clichés are

short but sweet	last but not least
drop in the bucket	work like a dog
had a hard time of it	all work and no play
word to the wise	it goes without saying
it dawned on me	at a loss for words
sigh of relief	taking a big chance
too little, too late	took a turn for the worse
singing the blues	easier said than done
in the nick of time	on top of the world
too close for comfort	time and time again
saw the light	make ends meet

Clichés are common in speech but make your writing seem tired and stale. Also, they are often an evasion of the specific details that you must work to provide in your writing. Avoid clichés and try to express your meaning in fresh, original ways.

Activity 1

Underline the cliché in each of the following sentences. Then substitute specific, fresh words for the trite expression.

Example   My boyfriend has stuck with me <u>through thick and thin</u>, <u>through good times and bad times.</u>

My boyfriend has stuck with me through difficult times and all sorts

of problems.

1. As the only girl in an otherwise all-boy family, I got away with murder.

   _____

2. When I realized I'd lost my textbook, I knew I was up the creek without a paddle.

   _____

3. My suggestion is just a shot in the dark, but it's better than nothing.

   _____

4. Nadine got more than she bargained for when she offered to help Larry with his math homework.

   _____

5. Jacques is pushing his luck by driving a car with bald tires.

   _____

6. On a hot, sticky, midsummer day, iced tea or any frosty drink really hits the spot.

   _____

7. Melissa thanks her lucky stars that she was born with brains, beauty, and humility.

   _____

8. Even when we are up to our eyeballs in work, our boss wonders if we have enough to do.

   _____

Activity 2

Write a short paragraph describing the kind of day you had. Try to put as many clichés as possible into your writing. For example, "I got up at the crack of dawn, ready to take on the world. I grabbed a bite to eat. . . ." By making yourself aware of clichés in this way, you will lessen the chance that they will appear in your writing.

■ Review Test

Certain words are italicized in the following sentences. In the space provided, identify the words as slang *(S)* or a cliché *(C)*. Then replace the words with more effective word choices.

_____ 1. Losing weight is *easier said than done* for someone with a sweet tooth.

_____

_____ 2. Mike wore *truly phat* pants and jacket, he was *so there.*

_____

_____ 3. Brendan is so stubborn that talking to him is like *talking to a brick wall.*

_____

_____ 4. Michelle spent the summer *watching the tube* and *catching rays.*

_____

_____ 5. The fans, *all fired up* after the game, *peeled out* of the parking lot and honked their horns.

_____

_____ 6. The stew I made *contained everything but the kitchen sink.*

_____

_____ 7. That dude isn't really a criminal; he's just gotten a *bum rap.*

_____

_____ 8. I failed the test, and to *add insult to injury,* I got a low grade on my paper.

_____

ESL Pointers

This section covers rules that most native speakers of English take for granted. Nonetheless, the following is useful information for speakers of English as a second language (ESL).

ARTICLES WITH COUNT AND NON-COUNT NOUNS

Articles are noun markers: they signal that a noun will follow. The indefinite articles are *a* and *an*. (Use *a* before a word that begins with a consonant sound: **a c**ar, **a p**iano, **a u**niform—the *u* in *uniform* sounds like the consonant *y* plus *u*. Use *an* before a word beginning with a vowel sound: **an e**gg, **an o**ffice, **an h**onour—the *h* in *honour* is silent.) The definite article is *the*. An article may immediately precede a noun: **a** smile, **the** reason. As an alternative, it may be separated from the noun by modifiers: **a** slight smile, **the** very best reason.

To know whether to use an article with a noun and which article to use, you must recognize count and non-count nouns. (A noun is a word used to name something—a person, place, thing, or idea.)

Note: There are various other noun markers, including quantity words *(some, several, a lot of)*, numerals *(one, ten, 120)*, demonstrative adjectives *(this, these)*, possessive adjectives *(my, your, our)*, and possessive nouns *(Jaime's, the school's)*.

Count nouns name people, places, things, or ideas that can be counted and made into plurals, such as *teacher, washroom,* and *joke (one teacher, two washrooms, three jokes)*.

Non-count nouns refer to things or ideas that cannot be counted, such as *flour, history,* and *truth*. The box below lists and illustrates common types of non-count nouns.

The quantity of a non-count noun can be expressed with a word or words called a **qualifier,** such as *some, some of, a lot of,* and *a unit of*. (In the following two examples, the qualifiers are shown in *italic* type, and the non-count nouns are shown in **boldface** type.)

Please have *some* **patience.**
We need to buy *two bags of* **flour** today.

Some words can be either count or non-count nouns, depending on whether they refer to one or more individual items or to something in general.

Certain **cheeses** give some people headaches.

This sentence refers to individual cheeses; *cheese* in this case is a count noun.

Cheese is made in almost every country where milk is produced.

This sentence refers to cheese in general; in this case, *cheese* is a non-count noun.

Common Non-Count Nouns

Abstractions and emotions: anger, bravery, health, pride, truth

Activities: baseball, jogging, reading, teaching, travel

Foods: bread, broccoli, chocolate, cheese, flour

Gases and vapours: air, helium, oxygen, steam

Languages and areas of study: Korean, Spanish, algebra, history, physics

Liquids: blood, gasoline, lemonade, tea, water

Materials that come in bulk form: aluminum, cloth, dust, sand, soap

Natural occurrences: magnetism, moonlight, rain, snow, thunder

Other things that cannot be counted: clothing, furniture, homework, machinery, money, news, transportation, vocabulary, work

---

Using *a* or *an* with Non-specific Singular Count Nouns

Use *a* or *an* with singular nouns that are non-specific. A noun is non-specific when the reader doesn't know its specific identity.

A left-hander faces special challenges with right-handed tools.

The sentence refers to any left-hander, not a specific one.

Today, our cat proudly brought **a** baby bird into the house.

The reader isn't familiar with the bird. This is the first time it is mentioned.

Using *the* with Specific Nouns

In general, use *the* with all specific nouns—specific singular, plural, and non-count nouns.

A noun is specific in the following cases:

- When it has already been mentioned once

  Today, our cat proudly brought a baby bird into the house. Luckily, **the** bird was still alive.

  The is used with the second mention of *bird.*

- When it is identified by a word or phrase in the sentence

  The pockets in the boy's pants are often filled with sand and dirt.

  Pockets is identified by the words *in the boy's pants.*

- When its identity is suggested by the general context

  At Willy's Diner last night, **the** service was terrible and **the** food was worse.

  The reader can conclude that the service and food being discussed were at Willy's Diner.

- When it is unique

  There will be an eclipse of **the** moon tonight.

  Earth has only one moon.

- When it is preceded by a superlative adjective *(best, biggest, wisest)*

  The best way to store broccoli is to refrigerate it in an open plastic bag.

Omitting Articles

Omit articles with non-specific plurals and non-count nouns. Plurals and non-count nouns are non-specific when they refer to something in general.

Pockets didn't exist until the end of the 1700s.
Service is as important as **food** to a restaurant's success.
Iris serves her children homemade **lemonade.**

Using *the* with Proper Nouns

Proper nouns name particular people, places, things, or ideas and are always capitalized. Most proper nouns do not require articles; those that do, however, require *the.* Following are general guidelines about when and when not to use *the.*

Do not use *the* for most singular proper nouns, including names of the following:

- *People and animals* (Jean Chrétien, Fido)
- *Continents, provinces or states, cities, streets, and parks* (North America, Canada, Alberta, Lethbridge, Portage Street, Banff National Park)
- *Most countries* (France, Mexico, Russia)
- *Individual bodies of water, islands, and mountains* (Lake Erie, Prince Edward Island, Mount Everest)

Use *the* for the following types of proper nouns:

- *Plural proper nouns* (the Turners, the United States, the Great Lakes, the Rocky Mountains)
- *Names of large geographic areas, deserts, oceans, seas, and rivers* (the South, the Gobi Desert, the Atlantic Ocean, the Black Sea, the Mississippi River)
- *Names with the format* the _____ of _____ (the People's Republic of China, the University of Manitoba)

Activity

Underline the correct form of the noun in parentheses.

1. (A library, Library) is a valuable addition to a town.

2. This morning, the mail carrier brought me (a letter, the letter) from my cousin.

3. As I read (a letter, the letter), I began to laugh at what my cousin wrote.

4. We are going to visit our friends in (the British Columbia, British Columbia) next week.

5. Children should treat their parents with (the respect, respect).

6. A famous park in Toronto is (High Park, the High Park).

7. My son would like to eat (the spaghetti, spaghetti) at every meal.

8. It is dangerous to stare directly at (the sun, sun).

SUBJECTS AND VERBS

Avoiding Repeated Subjects

In English, a particular subject can be used only once in a clause. Don't repeat a subject in the same clause by following a noun with a pronoun.

> Incorrect: The *manager he* asked Dmitri to lock up tonight.
> Correct: The **manager** asked Dmitri to lock up tonight.
> Correct: **He** asked Dmitri to lock up tonight.

Even when the subject and verb are separated by a long word group, the subject cannot be repeated in the same clause.

> Incorrect: The *girl* who danced with you *she is* my cousin.
> Correct: The **girl** who danced with you **is** my cousin.

Including Pronoun Subjects and Linking Verbs

Some languages may omit a pronoun as a subject, but in English, every clause other than a command must have a subject. (In a command, the subject *you* is understood: [**You**] Hand in your papers now.)

> Incorrect: The Yellowhead Highway is in central Alberta. Runs across the province.
> Correct: The Yellowhead Highway is in central Alberta. **It** runs across the province.

Every English clause must also have a verb, even when the meaning of the clause is clear without the verb.

> Incorrect: Angelita's piano teacher very patient.
> Correct: Angelita's piano teacher **is** very patient.

Including *there* and *here* at the Beginning of Clauses

Some English sentences begin with *there* or *here* plus a linking verb (usually a form of *to be: is, are,* and so on). In such sentences, the verb comes before the subject.

There are masks in every culture on Earth.

The subject is the plural noun *masks,* so the plural verb *are* is used.

Here is your driver's licence.

The subject is the singular noun *licence,* so the singular verb *is* is used.

In sentences like the above, remember not to omit *there* or *here.*

Incorrect: *Are* several chickens in the Bensons' yard.
Correct: **There are** several chickens in the Bensons' yard.

Not Using the Progressive (or Continuous) Tense of Certain Verbs

The progressive (or continuous) tenses are made up of forms of *be* plus the *-ing* form of the main verb. They express actions or conditions still in progress at a particular time.

George **will be taking** classes this summer.

However, verbs for mental states, the senses, possession, and inclusion are normally not used in the progressive tense.

Incorrect: All during the movie they *were hearing* whispers behind them.
Correct: All during the movie they **heard** whispers behind them.
Incorrect: That box *is containing* a surprise for Paulo.
Correct: That box **contains** a surprise for Paulo.

Common verbs not generally used in the progressive tense are listed in the box below.

Common Verbs Not Generally Used in the Progressive Tense

Thoughts, attitudes and desires: agree, believe, imagine, know, like, love, prefer, think, understand, want, wish

Sense perceptions: hear, see, smell, taste

Appearances: appear, seem, look

Possession: belong, have, own, possess

Inclusion: contain, include

Using Only Transitive Verbs for the Passive Voice

Only *transitive* verbs—verbs that need direct objects to complete their meaning—can have a passive form (one in which the subject receives the action instead of performing it). Intransitive verbs cannot be used in the passive voice.

Incorrect: If you don't fix those brakes, an accident *may be happened.*

Happen is an intransitive verb—no object is needed to complete its meaning.

Correct: If you don't fix those brakes, an accident **may happen.**

If you aren't sure whether a verb is transitive or intransitive, check your dictionary. Transitive verbs are indicated with an abbreviation such as *tr. v.* or *v. t.* Intransitive verbs are indicated with an abbreviation such as *intr. v.* or *v. i.*

Using Gerunds and Infinitives after Verbs (Idiomatic Verb Structures)

A gerund is the *-ing* form of a verb that is used as a noun: "For Walter, **eating** is a day-long activity." An infinitive is *to* plus the basic form of the verb (the form in which the verb is listed in the dictionary): **to eat.** The infinitive can function as an adverb, an adjective, or a noun. Some verbs can be followed by only a gerund or only an infinitive; other verbs can be followed by either. Examples are given in the following lists. There are many others; watch for them in your reading.

Verb + gerund   *(admit + stealing)*
Verb + preposition + gerund   *(apologize + for + yelling)*

Some verbs can be followed by a gerund but not by an infinitive. In many cases, there is a preposition (such as *for, in,* or *of*) between the verb and the gerund. Following are some verbs and verb/preposition combinations that can be followed by gerunds but not by infinitives:

admit	deny	look forward to
apologize for	discuss	postpone
appreciate	dislike	practise
approve of	enjoy	suspect of
avoid	feel like	talk about
be used to	finish	thank for
believe in	insist on	think about

Incorrect: He must *avoid to jog* until his knee heals.
Correct: He must **avoid jogging** until his knee heals.
Incorrect: The instructor *apologized for to be* late to class.
Correct: The instructor **apologized for being** late to class.

Verb + infinitive   *(agree + to leave)*

Following are common verbs that can be followed by an infinitive but not by a gerund:

agree	decide	plan
arrange	have	refuse
claim	manage	wait

Incorrect: The children *want going* to the beach.
Correct: The children **want to go** to the beach.

Verb + noun or pronoun + infinitive   *(cause + them + to flee)*

Below are common verbs that are first followed by a noun or pronoun and then by an infinitive (not a gerund):

cause	force	remind
command	persuade	warn

Incorrect: The coach *persuaded Carmelo studying* harder.
Correct: The coach **persuaded Carmelo to study** harder.

Following are common verbs that can be followed either by an infinitive alone or by a noun or pronoun and an infinitive:

ask	need	want
expect	promise	would like

Dena asked to have a day off next week.
Her boss asked her to work on Saturday.

Verb + gerund or infinitive   *(begin + packing or begin + to pack)*

Following are verbs that can be followed by either a gerund or an infinitive:

begin	hate	prefer
continue	love	start

The meaning of each of the above verbs remains the same or almost the same whether a gerund or an infinitive is used.

Faith hates **being** late.
Faith hates **to be** late.

With the verbs below, the gerunds and the infinitives have very different meanings.

forget	remember	stop

Esta **stopped to call** home.
(She interrupted something to call home.)

Esta **stopped calling** home.
(She discontinued calling home.)

Activity

Underline the correct form in parentheses.

1. The doctor (asked me, she asked me) if I smoked.

2. The coffee is very fresh. (Is, It is) strong and delicious.

3. (Are mice, There are mice) living in our kitchen.

4. The box (is containing, contains) a beautiful necklace.

5. Unless you take your foot off the brake, the car will not (be gone, go).

6. Most basketball players (very tall, are very tall).

7. Many people (enjoy to spend, enjoy spending) a day in the city.

8. The teacher (plans taking, plans to take) us on a field trip tomorrow.

ADJECTIVES

Following the Order of Adjectives in English

Adjectives modify nouns and pronouns. In English, an adjective usually comes directly before the word it describes or after a linking verb (a form of *be* or a "sense" verb such as *look, seem* and *taste*), in which case it modifies the subject. In each of the following two sentences, the adjective is **boldfaced** and the noun it describes is *italicized*.

That is a **false** *story.*
The *story* is **false.**

When more than one adjective modifies the same noun, the adjectives are usually stated in a certain order, though there are often exceptions. Following is the typical order of English adjectives:

Typical Order of Adjectives in a Series

1 **An article or other noun marker:** a, an, the, Lee's, this, three, your

2 **Opinion adjective:** dull, handsome, unfair, useful

3 **Size:** big, huge, little, tiny

4 **Shape:** long, short, round, square

5 **Age:** ancient, medieval, old, new, young

6 **Colour:** blue, green, scarlet, white

7 **Nationality:** Italian, Korean, Mexican, Vietnamese

8 **Religion:** Buddhist, Catholic, Jewish, Muslim

9 **Material:** cardboard, gold, marble, silk

10 **Noun used as an adjective:** house (as in *house call*), tea (as in *tea bag*), wall (as in *wall hanging*)

Here are some examples of the above order:

a long cotton scarf
the beautiful little silver cup
your new lavender evening gown
Anna's sweet Italian grandmother

In general, use no more than *two or three* adjectives after the article or other noun marker. Numerous adjectives in a series can be awkward: **the beautiful big new blue cotton** sweater.

Using the Present and Past Participles as Adjectives

The present participle ends in *-ing*. Past participles of regular verbs end in *-ed* or *-d*; a list of the past participles of many common irregular verbs appears on pages 385–387. Both types of participles may be used as adjectives. A participle used as an adjective may precede the word it describes: It was an **exciting** *ballgame*. It may also follow a linking verb and describe the subject of the sentence: The *ballgame* was **exciting.**

While both present and past participles of a particular verb may be used as adjectives, their meanings differ. Use the present participle to describe whoever or whatever causes a feeling: an **embarrassing** *incident* (the incident is what causes the embarrassment). Use the past participle to describe whoever or whatever experiences the feeling: the **embarrassed** *parents* (the parents are the ones who are embarrassed).

> The long day of holiday shopping was **tiring.**
> The shoppers were **tired.**

Following are pairs of present and past participles with similar distinctions:

annoying / annoyed	exhausting / exhausted
boring / bored	fascinating / fascinated
confusing / confused	frightening / frightened
depressing / depressed	surprising / surprised
exciting / excited	interesting / interested

Activity

Underline the correct form in parentheses.

1. The Johnsons live in a (stone big, big stone) house.

2. Mr. Kim runs a (popular Korean, Korean popular) restaurant.

3. For her party, the little girl asked if her mother would buy her a (beautiful long velvet, beautiful velvet long) dress.

4. When their son didn't come home by bedtime, Mr. and Mrs. Singh became (worried, worrying).

5. In the centre of the city is a church with (three enormous, colourful, stained-glass; three stained-glass, colourful, enormous) windows.

Prepositions Used for Time and Place

The use of prepositions in English is often idiomatic, and exceptions to general rules are not rare. Therefore, correct preposition use must be learned gradually through experience. Following is a chart showing how three of the most common prepositions are used in some customary references to time and place:

> ### The Use of On, In, and At to Refer to Time and Place
>
> *Time*
>
> > **On** *a specific day:* on Monday, on January 1, on your anniversary
> > **In** *a part of a day:* in the morning, in the daytime (but at night)
> > **In** *a month or a year:* in December, in 1867
> > **In** *a period of time:* in an hour, in a few days, in a while
> > **At** *a specific time:* at 10:00 a.m., at midnight, at sunset, at dinnertime
>
> *Place*
>
> > **On** *a surface:* on the desk, on the counter, on a ceiling
> > **In** *a place that is enclosed:* in my room, in the office, in the box
> > **At** *a specific location:* at the mall, at his house, at the ballpark

Activity

Underline the correct preposition in parentheses.

1. Can you babysit my children (on, at) Thursday?

2. Please come to my office (on, at) 3:00 p.m.

3. You will find some computer disks (in, on) the desk drawer.

4. Miguel will begin his new job (in, at) two weeks.

5. A fight broke out between two groups of friends (on, at) the park.

■ Review Test

Underline the correct form in parentheses.

1. During the storm, I was startled by the loud (thunder, thunders).

2. (Is, Here is) your new textbook.

3. The ending of the movie was very (surprised, surprising).

4. Many animals that sleep all day are active (at, in) night.

5. (The people, People) in the photograph are my mother's relatives.

6. The city streets were full of (big yellow, yellow big) taxis.

7. My friend and I (are usually agreeing, usually agree) with each other.

8. In the West, New Year's Day is celebrated (in, on) January 1.

Editing Tests

The twelve editing tests in this chapter will give you practice in revising for sentence-skills mistakes. Remember that if you don't edit carefully, you run the risk of sabotaging much of the work you have put into a paper. If readers see too many surface flaws, they may assume you don't place much value on what you have to say, and they may not give your ideas a fair hearing. Revising to eliminate sentence-skills errors is a basic part of clear, effective writing.

In half of the tests, the spots where errors occur have been underlined; your job is to identify and correct each error. In the rest of the tests, you must locate as well as identify and correct the errors.

Editing Hints

Here are hints that can help you edit the next-to-final draft of a paper for sentence skills mistakes:

1 Have at hand two essential tools: a good dictionary and a handbook (you can use Part 4 of this book).

2 Use a sheet of paper to cover your essay so that you will expose only one sentence at a time. Look for errors in grammar, spelling, and typing. It may help to read each sentence out loud. If it does not read clearly and smoothly, chances are something is wrong.

3 Pay special attention to the kinds of errors you tend to make. For example, if you tend to write run-ons or fragments, be especially on the lookout for those errors.

4 Proofreading symbols that may be of particular help are the following:

___ ℓ	omit	draw two ~~two~~ conclusions
i ∧	insert missing letter or word	achᵢeve ∧
cap, lc	Add a capital (or a lowercase) letter	My english ₵lass

Editing Test 1

In the spaces at the bottom, write the numbers of the ten word groups that contain fragments or run-ons. Then, in the spaces between the lines, edit by making the necessary corrections.

[1]I remember my childhood as being generally happy and can recall experiencing some of the most carefree times of my life. [2]But I can also remember, even more vividly, other moments. [3]When I was deeply frightened. [4]As a child, I was truly terrified of the dark and of getting lost. [5]These fears were very real, they caused me some extremely uncomfortable moments.

[6]Maybe it was the strange way things looked and sounded in my familiar room at night. [7]That scared me so much. [8]The streetlight outside or passing car lights would create shadows in my room. [9]As a result, clothes hung over a chair taking on the shape of an unknown beast. [10]Out of the corner of my eye, I saw curtains move when there was no breeze. [11]A faint creak in the floor would sound a hundred times louder than in daylight, my imagination would take over. [12]Creating burglars and monsters on the prowl. [13]Because darkness always made me feel so helpless. [14]I would lie there motionless so that the "enemy" would not discover me.

[15]Another of my childhood fears was that I would get lost. [16]Especially on the way home from school. [17]After school, all the buses lined up along the curb I was terrified that I'd get on the wrong one. [18]Scanning the bus windows for the faces of my friends. [19]I'd also look to make sure that the bus driver was the same one I had in the morning.

1. _____   3. _____   5. _____   7. _____   9. _____

2. _____   4. _____   6. _____   8. _____   10. _____

■ **Editing Test 2**

Identify the five sentence fragments and five run-on sentences in the student paper that follows. From the box below, choose the letters that describe the five mistakes and write those letters in the spaces provided. Then correct each mistake.

a. fragment	b. run-on

A Unique Object

[1]A unique object in my family's living room is an ashtray. [2]Which I made in second grade. [3]I can still remember the pride I felt. [4]When I presented it to my mother. [5]To my second-grade eyes, it was a thing of beauty. [6]Now, I'm amazed that my parents didn't hide it away at the back of a shelf it is a remarkably ugly object. [7]The ashtray is made out of brown clay. [8]I had tried to mould it into a perfect circle, unfortunately my class was only forty-five minutes long. [9]The best I could do was to shape it into a lopsided oval. [10]Its most distinctive feature, though, was the grooves sculpted into its rim. [11]I had theorized that each groove could hold a cigarette or cigar, I made at least fifty of them. [12]I somehow failed to consider that the only person who smoked in my family was my father. [13]Who smoked about five cigars a year. [14]Further, although our living room is decorated in sedate tans and blue, my ashtray is bright purple. [15]My favourite colour at the time. [16]Just for variety, it also has stripes around its rim they are coloured neon green. [17]For all its shortcomings, my parents have proudly displayed my little masterpiece on their coffee table for the past ten years. [18]If I ever wonder if my parents love me. [19]I look at that ugly ashtray, the answer is plain to see.

1. _____   3. _____   5. _____   7. _____   9. _____

2. _____   4. _____   6. _____   8. _____   10. _____

Editing Test 3

Identify the ten sentence-skills mistakes at the underlined spots in the student paper that follows. From the box below, choose the letter that describes each mistake and write that letter in the space provided. (The same kind of mistake may appear more than once.) Then, in the spaces between the lines, edit and correct each mistake.

a. fragment	d. dangling modifier
b. run-on	e. missing comma
c. inconsistent verb tense	f. spelling mistake

I had a strange experience last <u>winter, I</u> was shopping for Christmas
1
presents when I came to a small clothing shop. I was going to pass it by.

<u>Until I saw a beautiful purple robe on a mannequin in the window.</u> <u>Stopping to</u>
2   **3**
<u>look at it</u>, the mannequin seemed to wink at me. I was really <u>startled, I</u> looked
4
around to see if anyone else was watching. Shaking my <u>head</u> I stepped closer
5
to the window. Then I really began to question my <u>sanity, it</u> looked as if the
6
mannequin moved <u>it's</u> legs. My face must have shown alarm because the
7
mannequin then <u>smiles</u>. <u>And even waved her arm.</u> I sighed with <u>relief, it</u> was a
8   **9**   **10**
human model after all.

1. _____   3. _____   5. _____   7. _____   9. _____

2. _____   4. _____   6. _____   8. _____   10. _____

■ Editing Test 4

Identify the ten sentence-skills mistakes at the underlined spots in the student paper that follows. From the box below, choose the letter that describes each mistake and write that letter in the space provided. (The same kind of mistake may appear more than once.) Then, in the spaces between the lines, edit and correct each mistake.

a. run-on	d. missing quotation marks
b. mistake in subject–verb agreement	e. wordiness
	f. slang
c. faulty parallelism	g. missing comma

<u>It is this writer's opinion that</u> smokers should quit smoking for the sake of
1
those who are around them. Perhaps the most helpless creatures that suffer

from being near a smoker <u>is</u> unborn <u>babies, one</u> study suggests that the risk of
2   **3**
having an undersized baby is doubled if pregnant women are exposed to

cigarette smoke for about two hours a day. Pregnant women both should refrain

from smoking and <u>to avoid</u> smoke-filled rooms. Spouses of smokers are also
4
<u>in big trouble.</u> They are more likely than spouses of non-smokers to die of heart
5
disease and <u>the development of</u> fatal cancers. Office workers are a final group
6
that can be harmed by a smoke-filled environment. The Minister of Health and

Welfare has <u>said "Workers</u> who smoke are a health risk to their <u>co-workers.</u>
7   **8**
<u>While it is undoubtedly true that</u> one can argue that smokers have the right to
9
hurt <u>themselves they</u> do not have the right to hurt others. Smokers should
10
abandon their deadly habits for the health of others at home and at work.

1. _____   3. _____   5. _____   7. _____   9. _____

2. _____   4. _____   6. _____   8. _____   10. _____

■ **Editing Test 5**

Identify the ten sentence-skills mistakes at the underlined spots in the student paper that follows. From the box below, choose the letter that describes each mistake and write that letter in the space provided. (The same kind of mistake may appear more than once.) Then, in the spaces between the lines, edit and correct each mistake.

a. fragment	e. dangling modifier
b. run-on	f. missing comma
c. mistake in subject–verb agreement	g. wordiness
d. misplaced modifier	h. slang

North America will never be a drug-free <u>society but</u> we could eliminate many of
                                            1
our drug-related problems by legalizing drugs. Drugs would be sold by companies

and not criminals <u>if they were legal</u>. The drug trade would then take place like any
                    2
other <u>business freeing</u> the police and courts to devote their time to other problems.
        3
Lawful drugs would be sold at a fair <u>price, no</u> one would need to steal in order to
                                        4
buy them. <u>By legalizing drugs</u>, organized crime would lose one of its major sources
            5
of revenue. <u>It goes without saying that</u> we would, instead, create important tax
              6
revenues for the government. Finally, if drugs <u>was</u> sold through legal outlets, we
                                                 7
could reduce the drug problem among our young people. It would be illegal to sell

drugs to people under a certain age. <u>Just as is the case now with alcohol.</u> And
                                        8
because the profits on drugs would no longer <u>be out of sight</u>, there would be little
                                                9
incentive for drug pushers to sell to young people. Decriminalizing drugs, in short,

could be a solution. <u>To many of the problems that result from the illegal drug trade.</u>
                                                  10

1. _____   3. _____   5. _____   7. _____   9. _____

2. _____   4. _____   6. _____   8. _____   10. _____

▓ Editing Test 6

Identify the ten sentence-skills mistakes at the underlined spots in the student paper that follows. From the box below, choose the letter that describes each mistake and write that letter in the space provided. (The same kind of mistake may appear more than once.) Then, in the spaces between the lines, edit and correct each mistake.

a. fragment	e. mistake with quotation marks
b. run-on	f. mistake in pronoun point of
c. mistake in subject–verb	view
agreement	g. spelling error
d. mistake in verb tense	h. missing comma

One reason that I enjoy the commute to school is that the drive gives me

<u>uninterupted</u> time to myself. The classes and socializing at college <u>is</u> great,
     1   **2**

and so is the time I spend with my family, but sometimes all this togetherness

keeps <u>you</u> from being able to think. In fact, I look forward to the time I have
     3

<u>alone</u>, it gives me a chance to plan what I'll accomplish in the day ahead. For
  4

example, one Tuesday afternoon my Marketing professor <u>announces</u> that a
                                                 5

rough outline for our semester report was due that Friday. <u>Fortunatly</u>, I had
                                                            6

already done some <u>reading and I</u> had checked my proposed topic with her the
                        7

week before. <u>Therefore, on the way home in the car that evening.</u> I planned the
                                      8

entire history report in my mind. Then all I had to do when I got home was quickly

jot it down before I forgot it. <u>When I handed the professor the outline at 8:30</u>
                                                             9

<u>Wednesday morning.</u> She asked me <u>"if I had stayed up all night working on it."</u>
                                                         10

She was amazed when I told her that I owed it all to commuting.

1. _____ 3. _____ 5. _____ 7. _____ 9. _____

2. _____ 4. _____ 6. _____ 8. _____ 10. _____

■ Editing Test 7

Identify the ten sentence-skills mistakes at the underlined spots in the student paper that follows. From the box below, choose the letter that describes each mistake and write that letter in the space provided. (The same kind of mistake may appear more than once.) Then, in the spaces between the lines, edit and correct each mistake.

a. fragment	f. dangling modifier
b. run-on	g. homonym mistake
c. mistake in subject–verb agreement	h. missing apostrophe
d. missing comma	i. cliché
e. missing capital letter	j. spelling mistake

Cars can destroy your ego. First of <u>all the</u> kind of car you drive can make
1
you feel like a second-class citizen. <u>If you can't afford a new, expensive car,</u>
2
<u>and are forced to drive an old clunker.</u> You'll be the object of pitying stares and

nasty sneers. Drivers of newer-model cars just <u>doesn't</u> appreciate it when a
3
<u>'78 buick</u> with terminal body rust lurches into the next parking space.
4
You may even find that drivers go out of <u>there</u> way not to park near you.
5
Breakdowns, too, can damage your self-respect. You may be an assistant bank

manager or a job <u>foreman, you'll</u> still feel <u>like two cents</u> when <u>you'r</u> sitting on
6   **7**   **8**
the side of the road. As the other cars whiz past, you'll stare helplessly at your

<u>cars</u> open hood or steaming radiator. In cases like this, you may even be turned
9
into that lowest of creatures, the pedestrian. <u>Shuffling humbly along the</u>
10
<u>highway to the nearest pay phone,</u> your car has delivered another staggering

blow to your self-esteem.

1. _____   3. _____   5. _____   7. _____   9. _____

2. _____   4. _____   6. _____   8. _____   10. _____

■ **Editing Test 8**

See if you can locate the ten sentence-skills mistakes in the following passage. The mistakes are listed in the box below. As you locate each mistake, write the number of the word group in the space provided. Then, in the space between the lines, edit and correct each mistake.

one fragment _____	one mistake in pronoun point of
one run-on _____	view _____
one mistake in verb tense_____	one missing comma after
one non-parallel structure_____	introductory material _____
one dangling modifier_____	two missing quotation marks
one missing apostrophe_____	_____ _____

¹The greatest of my everyday fears is technology. ²Beginning when I couldn't master bike riding and extending to the present day. ³Fear kept me from learning to operate a jigsaw, start an outboard motor, or even using a simple tape recorder. ⁴I almost didn't learn to drive a car. ⁵At age sixteen, Dad lifted the hood of our Chevy and said, All right, you're going to start learning to drive. ⁶Now, this is the distributor . . . When my eyes glazed over he shouted, "Well, I'm not going to bother if youre not interested!" ⁷Fortunately, the friend who later taught me to drive skipped what goes on under the hood. ⁸My most recent frustration is the 35 mm camera, I would love to take professional-quality pictures. ⁹But all the numbers and dials and meters confuse me. ¹⁰As a result, my unused camera is hidden away on a shelf in my closet. ¹¹Just last week, my sister gives me a beautiful digital watch for my birthday. ¹²I may have to put it on the shelf with the camera—the alarm keeps going off, and you can't figure out how to stop it.

■ Editing Test 9

See if you can locate the ten sentence-skills mistakes in the following passage. The mistakes are listed in the box below. As you locate each mistake, write the number of the word group in the space provided. Then, in the space between the lines, edit and correct each mistake.

---

one fragment _____	one mistake in subject–verb
one run-on _____	agreement _____
one missing comma around an	two missing quotation marks
interrupter _____	_____ _____
two apostrophe mistakes	one misplaced modifier _____
_____ _____	one non-parallel structure _____

---

¹I was six years old when, one day, my dog was struck by a car while getting ready for school. ²My mother and I heard the terrifying sound of squealing brake's. ³In a low voice, she said, Oh, my God—Dusty. ⁴I remember trailing her out the door and seeing a car filled with teenagers and a spreading pool of bright blood on our cobblestoned street. ⁵To me, it seemed only a matter of seconds until a car pulled up. ⁶The driver glanced at the crumpled dog under the car. ⁷And said something about "putting Dusty down." ⁸My mother shouted, "No!" ⁹She crawled halfway under the car and took the dog, like a sack of flour, out from under the wheels. ¹⁰Her clothes were splashed with blood, she cradled the limp dog in her arms and ordered the officers to drive her to the vets office. ¹¹It was only then that she remembered me, I think. ¹²She patted my head, was telling me to walk up to school, and reassured me that Dusty would be all right. ¹³The rest of the story including Dusty's slow recovery and few more years of life, are fuzzy and vague now. ¹⁴But the sights and sounds of those few moments are as vivid to me now as they were twenty-five years ago.

■ Editing Test 10

See if you can locate the ten sentence-skills mistakes in the following passage. The mistakes are listed in the box below. As you locate each mistake, write the number of the word group in the space provided. Then, in the space between the lines, edit and correct each mistake.

---

two fragments _____ _____   one non-parallel structure _____

one run-on _____   two apostrophe mistakes _____

one mistake in subject–verb   _____

    agreement _____   three missing commas _____

    _____ _____

---

¹Most products have little or nothing to do with sex a person would never know that by looking at ads'. ²A television ad for a headache remedy, for example shows the product being useful because it ends a womans throbbing head pain just in time for sex. ³Now she will not say "Not tonight, Honey." ⁴Another ad features a detergent that helps a single woman meet a man in a laundry room. ⁵When it comes to products that do relate to sex appeal advertisers often present more obvious sexuality. ⁶A recent magazine ad for women's clothing, for instance, make no reference to the quality of or how comfortable are the company's clothes. ⁷Instead, the ad features a picture of a woman wearing a low-cut sleeveless T-shirt and a very short skirt. ⁸Her eyes are partially covered by semi-wild hair. ⁹And stare seductively at the reader. ¹⁰A recent television ad for perfume goes even further. ¹¹In this ad, a boy not older than twelve reaches out to a beautiful woman. ¹²Sexily dressed in a dark room filled with sensuous music. ¹³With such ads, it is no wonder that young people seem preoccupied with sex.

■ Editing Test 11

See if you can locate the ten sentence-skills mistakes in the following passage. The mistakes are listed in the box below. As you locate each mistake, write the number of the word group in the space provided. Then, in the space between the lines, edit and correct each mistake.

---

one fragment _____   two missing apostrophes _____

one run-on _____   _____

one mistake in subject–verb   one non-parallel structure _____

   agreement _____   one dangling modifier _____

two missing commas after   one mistake in pronoun point of

   introductory material   view _____

_____ _____

---

¹Being a server is an often under-rated job. ²A server needs the tact of a diplomat, she must be as organized as a business executive, and the ability of an acrobat. ³Working as the link between customers and kitchen, the most demanding diners must be satisfied and the often-temperamental kitchen help must be kept tamed. ⁴Both groups tend to blame the server whenever anything goes wrong. ⁵Somehow, she is held responsible by the customer for any delay (even if it's the kitchens fault), for an overcooked steak, or for an unavailable dessert. ⁶While the kitchen automatically blames her for the diners who change their orders or return those burned steaks. ⁷In addition she must simultaneously keep straight who ordered what at each table, who is yelling for the bill, and whether the new arrivals want cocktails or not. ⁸She must be sure empty tables are cleared, everyone has refills of coffee, and no one is scowling because a request for more rolls are going unheard. ⁹Finally the server must travel a hazardous route between the busy kitchen and the crowded dining room, she has to dodge a diners leg in the aisle or a swinging kitchen door. ¹⁰And you must do this while balancing a tray heaped with steaming platters. ¹¹The hardest task of the server, though, is trying to maintain a decent imitation of a smile on her face—most of the time.

■ Editing Test 12

See if you can locate the ten sentence-skills mistakes in the following passage. The mistakes are listed in the box below. As you locate each mistake, write the number of the word group in the space provided. Then, in the space between the lines, edit and correct each mistake.

---

two fragments _____ _____   two missing capital letters _____

one run-on _____   _____

two irregular verbs _____ _____ one mistake in pronoun point of

one misplaced modifier _____   view _____

                                     one subject pronoun mistake _____

---

[1]The thirtieth anniversary party of my uncle and aunt was the worst family gathering I've ever attended. [2]On a hot saturday morning in july, Mom and I drove out into the country to Uncle Ted's house. [3]It had already rained heavily, and the only place left to park was in a muddy field. [4]Then, you would not believe the crowd. [5]There must have been two hundred people in Uncle Ted's small yard, including his five daughters with their husbands and children, all the other relatives, all the neighbours, and the entire congregation of their church. [6]Since the ground was soaked and light rain was falling. [7]Mom and me went under the big rented canopy with everybody else. [8]We couldn't move between the tables, and the humidity fogged my glasses. [9]After wiping my glasses, I seen that there was a lot of food. [10]It was mainly cold chicken and potato and macaroni salads, I ate a lot just because there was nothing else to do. [11]We were surprised that Uncle Ted and his wife were doing all the work themselves. [12]They ran back and forth with trays of food and gathered trash into plastic bags staggering with exhaustion. [13]It didn't seem like much of a way to celebrate. [14]Mom was upset that she didn't get to speak with them. [15]When we left, I was hot, sticky, and sick to my stomach from overeating. [16]But quickly pushed our car out of the mud and got us on the road. [17]I have never been happier to leave a party.

Readings for Writing

Introduction to the Readings

The reading selections in Part 5 will help you find topics for writing. Each selection deals in some way with interesting, often thought-provoking concerns or experiences of contemporary life. One selection, for example, describes new kinds of stress that students face in college, and another reminds us of neighbourhoods where we grew up. The varied subjects should inspire lively class discussions as well as serious individual thought. The selections should also provide a continuing source of high-interest material for a wide range of writing assignments.

The selections serve another purpose as well. They will help develop reading skills with direct benefits to you as a writer. Through close reading, you will learn how to recognize the thesis in a selection and to identify and evaluate the supporting material that develops the thesis. In your own writing, you will aim to achieve the same essential structure: an overall thesis with detailed and valid support for that thesis. Close reading will also help you to thoroughly explore a selection and its possibilities. The more you understand about what is said in a piece, the more ideas and feelings you may have about writing on an assigned topic or a related topic of your own. A third benefit of close reading is becoming more aware of authors' stylistic devices—for example, their introductions and conclusions, their ways of presenting and developing a point, their use of transitions, and their choice of language to achieve a particular tone. Recognizing these devices in other people's writing will help you enlarge your own range of ideas and writing techniques.

THE FORMAT OF EACH SELECTION

Each selection begins with a short overview that gives helpful background information and stimulates interest in the piece. The selection is followed by two sets of questions.

- First, there are reading comprehension questions to help you measure your understanding of the material. These questions involve several important reading skills: understanding vocabulary in context, recognizing a subject or topic, determining the thesis or main idea, identifying key supporting points, and making inferences. Answering the questions will enable you and your instructor to check your basic understanding of a selection quickly. More significantly, as you move from one selection to the next, you will sharpen your reading skills as well as strengthen your thinking skills—two key factors in making you a better writer.

- Following the comprehension questions are at least seven discussion questions. In addition to dealing with issues of content, these questions focus on matters of structure, style, and tone.

Finally, several writing assignments accompany each selection. The assignments range from personal narratives to expository and persuasive essays about issues in the world at large. Many assignments provide detailed guidelines on how to proceed, including suggestions for prewriting and appropriate methods of development. When writing your essay responses to the readings, you will have opportunities to apply all the methods of development presented in Part 3 of this book.

HOW TO READ WELL: FOUR GENERAL STEPS

Skillful reading is an important part of becoming a skillful writer. Following is a series of four steps that will make you a better reader—of the selections here and in your reading at large.

1 Concentrate as You Read

To improve your concentration, follow these tips:

- First, read in a place where you can be quiet and alone. Don't choose a spot where there is a TV or stereo on or where friends or family are talking nearby.
- Next, sit in an upright position when you read. If your body is in a completely relaxed position, sprawled across a bed or nestled in an easy chair, your mind is also going to be completely relaxed. The light muscular tension that comes from sitting in an upright chair promotes concentration and keeps your mind ready to work.
- Third, consider using your index finger (or a pen) as a pacer while you read. Lightly underline each line of print with your index finger as you read down a page. Hold your hand slightly above the page and move your finger at a speed that is a little too fast for comfort. This pacing with your index finger, like sitting upright on a chair, creates a slight physical tension that will keep your body and mind focused and alert.

2 Skim Material before You Read It

In skimming, you spend about two minutes rapidly surveying a selection, looking for important points and skipping secondary material. Follow this sequence when skimming:

- Begin by reading the overview that precedes the selection.
- Then study the title of the selection for a few moments. A good title is the shortest possible summary of a selection; it often tells you in several words—

or even a single word—just what a selection is about. For example, the title "Shame" suggests that you're going to read about a deeply embarrassing condition or incident in a person's life.

- Next, form a basic question (or questions) out of the title. For instance, for the selection titled "Shame," you might ask, "What exactly is the shame?" "What caused the shame?" "What is the result of the shame?" Forming questions out of a title is often a key to locating a writer's thesis, your next concern in skimming.

- Read the first and last couple of paragraphs in the selection. Very often a writer's thesis, *if* it is directly stated, will appear in one of these places and will relate to the title.

- Finally, look quickly at the rest of the selection for other clues to important points. Are there any subheadings you can relate in some way to the title? Are there any words the author has decided to emphasize by setting them off in *italic* or **boldface** type? Are there any major lists of items signalled by words such as *first, second, also,* and *another?*

3 Read the Selection Straight Through with a Pen in Hand

Read the selection without slowing down or turning back; just aim to understand as much as you can the first time through. Place a check or star beside answers to basic questions you formed from the title and beside other ideas that seem important. Number as *1, 2, 3* . . . lists of important points. Circle words you don't understand. Put question marks in the margin next to passages that are unclear and that you will want to reread.

4 Work with the Material

Go back and reread passages that were not clear the first time through. Look up words that block your understanding of ideas and write their meanings in the margin. Also, reread carefully the areas you identified as most important; doing so will enlarge your understanding of the material. Now that you have a sense of the whole, prepare a short written outline of the selection by answering the following questions:

- What is the thesis?
- What key points support the thesis?
- What seem to be other important ideas in the selection?

By working with the material in this way, you will significantly increase your understanding of a selection. Effective reading, just like effective writing, does not happen all at once. Rather, it must be worked on. Often you begin with a general impression of what something means, and then, by working at it, you move to a deeper level of understanding of the material.

HOW TO ANSWER THE COMPREHENSION QUESTIONS: SPECIFIC HINTS

Several important reading skills are involved in the reading comprehension questions that follow each selection. The skills are

- Understanding vocabulary in context
- Summarizing the selection in a title
- Determining the main idea
- Recognizing key supporting details
- Making inferences

The following hints will help you apply each of these reading skills:

- *Vocabulary in context* To decide on the meaning of an unfamiliar word, consider its context. Ask yourself, Are there any clues in the sentence that suggest what this word means?
- *Subject or title* Remember that the title should accurately describe the entire selection. It should be neither too broad nor too narrow for the material in the selection. It should answer the question "What is this about?" as specifically as possible. Note that you may at times find it easier to answer the title question *after* the main-idea question.
- *Main idea* Choose the statement that you think best expresses the main idea— also known as the *main point* or *thesis*—of the entire selection. Remember that the title will often help you focus on the main idea. Then ask yourself the question, Does most of the material in the selection support this statement? If you can answer yes to this question, you have found the thesis.
- *Key details* If you were asked to give a two-minute summary of a selection, the key details are the ones you would include in that summary. To determine the key details, ask yourself the question, What are the major supporting points for the thesis?
- *Inferences* Answer these questions by drawing upon the evidence presented in the selection and your own common sense. Ask yourself, What reasonable judgments can I make on the basis of the information in the selection?

On pages 620–621 is a chart on which you can keep track of your performance as you answer the questions for each selection. The chart will help you identify reading skills you may need to strengthen.

Looking Inward

Dick Gregory

In this selection, Dick Gregory—the comedian and social critic—narrates two painful experiences from his boyhood. Although the incidents show graphically what it can be like to grow up black and poor, the essay also deals with universal emotions: shame, embarrassment, and the burning desire to hold onto one's self-respect.

I never learned hate at home, or shame. I had to go to school for that. I was about 1 seven years old when I got my first big lesson. I was in love with a little girl named Helene Tucker, a light-complected little girl with pigtails and nice manners. She was always clean and she was smart in school. I think I went to school then mostly to look at her. I brushed my hair and even got me a little old handkerchief. It was a lady's handkerchief, but I didn't want Helene to see me wipe my nose on my hand. The pipes were frozen again, there was no water in the house, but I washed my socks and shirt every night. I'd get a pot, and go over to Mister Ben's grocery store, and stick my pot down into his soda machine. Scoop out some chopped ice. By evening the ice melted to water for washing. I got sick a lot that winter because the fire would go out at night before the clothes were dry. In the morning I'd put them on, wet or dry, because they were the only clothes I had.

Everybody's got a Helene Tucker, a symbol of everything you want. I loved her 2 for her goodness, her cleanness, her popularity. She'd walk down my street and my brothers and sisters would yell, "Here comes Helene," and I'd rub my tennis sneakers on the back of my pants and wish my hair wasn't so nappy and the white folks' shirt fit me better. I'd run out on the street. If I knew my place and didn't come too close, she'd wink at me and say hello. That was a good feeling. Sometimes I'd follow her all the way home, and shovel the snow off her walk and try to make friends with her Momma and her aunts. I'd drop money on her stoop late at night on my way back from shining shoes in the taverns. And she had a Daddy, and he had a good job. He was a paper hanger.

I guess I would have gotten over Helene by summertime, but something happened in that classroom that made her face hang in front of me for the next twenty-two years. When I played the drums in high school it was for Helene and when I broke track records in college it was for Helene and when I started standing behind microphones and heard applause I wished Helene could hear it, too. It wasn't until I was twenty-nine years old and married and making money that I finally got her out of my system. Helene was sitting in that classroom when I learned to be ashamed of myself. **3**

It was on a Thursday. I was sitting in the back of the room, in a seat with a chalk circle drawn around it. The idiot's seat, the troublemaker's seat. **4**

The teacher thought I was stupid. Couldn't spell, couldn't read, couldn't do arithmetic. Just stupid. Teachers were never interested in finding out that you couldn't concentrate because you were so hungry, because you hadn't had any breakfast. All you could think about was noontime, would it ever come? Maybe you could sneak into the cloakroom and steal a bite of some kid's lunch out of a coat pocket. A bite of something. Paste. You can't really make a meal of paste, or put it on bread for a sandwich, but sometimes I'd scoop a few spoonfuls out of the big paste jar in the back of the room. Pregnant people get strange tastes. I was pregnant with poverty. Pregnant with dirt and pregnant with smells that made people turn away, pregnant with cold and pregnant with shoes that were never bought for me, pregnant with five other people in my bed and no Daddy in the next room, and pregnant with hunger. Paste doesn't taste too bad when you're hungry. **5**

The teacher thought I was a troublemaker. All she saw from the front of the room was a little black boy who squirmed in his idiot's seat and made noises and poked the kids around him. I guess she couldn't see a kid who made noises because he wanted someone to know he was there. **6**

It was on a Thursday, the day before the Negro payday. The eagle always flew on Friday. The teacher was asking each student how much his father would give to the Community Chest. On Friday night, each kid would get the money from his father, and on Monday he would bring it to the school. I decided I was going to buy a Daddy right then. I had money in my pocket from shining shoes and selling papers, and whatever Helene Tucker pledged for her Daddy I was going to top it. And I'd hand the money right in. I wasn't going to wait until Monday to buy me a Daddy. **7**

I was shaking, scared to death. The teacher opened her book and started calling out names alphabetically. **8**

"Helene Tucker?" **9**

"My Daddy said he'd give two dollars and fifty cents." **10**

"That's very nice, Helene. Very, very nice indeed." **11**

That made me feel pretty good. It wouldn't take too much to top that. I had almost three dollars in dimes and quarters in my pocket. I stuck my hand in my pocket and held onto the money, waiting for her to call my name. But the teacher closed her book after she called everybody else in the class. **12**

I stood up and raised my hand. **13**

"What is it now?" **14**

"You forgot me?" **15**

She turned toward the blackboard. "I don't have time to be playing with **16** you, Richard."

"My Daddy said he'd . . ."   **17**

"Sit down, Richard, you're disturbing the class."   **18**

"My Daddy said he'd give . . . fifteen dollars."   **19**

She turned around and looked mad. "We are collecting this money for you and **20** your kind, Richard Gregory. If your Daddy can give fifteen dollars you have no business being on relief."

"I got it right now, I got it right now, my Daddy gave it to me to turn in today, **21** my Daddy said . . ."

"And furthermore," she said, looking right at me, her nostrils getting big and **22** her lips getting thin and her eyes opening wide, "we know you don't have a Daddy."

Helene Tucker turned around, her eyes full of tears. She felt sorry for me. Then **23** I couldn't see her too well because I was crying, too.

"Sit down, Richard."   **24**

And I always thought the teacher kind of liked me. She always picked me to **25** wash the blackboard on Friday, after school. That was a big thrill, it made me feel important. If I didn't wash it, come Monday the school might not function right.

"Where are you going, Richard!"   **26**

I walked out of school that day, and for a long time I didn't go back very often. **27** There was shame there.

Now there was shame everywhere. It seemed like the whole world had been **28** inside that classroom, everyone had heard what the teacher had said, everyone had turned around and felt sorry for me. There was shame in going to the Worthy Boys Annual Christmas Dinner for you and your kind, because everybody knew what a worthy boy was. Why couldn't they just call it the Boys Annual Dinner, why'd they have to give it a name? There was shame in wearing the brown and orange and white plaid mackinaw the welfare gave to three thousand boys. Why'd it have to be the same for everybody so when you walked down the street the people could see you were on relief? It was a nice warm mackinaw and it had a hood, and my Momma beat me and called me a little rat when she found out I stuffed it in the bottom of a pail full of garbage way over on Cottage Street. There was shame in running over to Mister Ben's at the end of the day and asking for his rotten peaches, there was shame in asking Mrs. Simmons for a spoonful of sugar, there was shame in running out to meet the relief truck. I hated that truck, full of food for you and your kind. I ran into the house and hid when it came. And then I started to sneak through alleys, to take the long way home so the people going into White's Eat Shop wouldn't see me. Yeah, the whole world heard the teacher that day, we all know you don't have a Daddy.

It lasted for a while, this kind of numbness. I spent a lot of time feeling sorry **29** for myself. And then one day I met this wino in a restaurant. I'd been out hustling all day, shining shoes, selling newspapers, and I had googobs of money in my pocket. Bought me a bowl of chili for fifteen cents, and a cheeseburger for fifteen cents, and a Pepsi for five cents, and a piece of chocolate cake for ten cents. That was a good meal. I was eating when this old wino came in. I love winos because they never hurt anyone but themselves.

The old wino sat down at the counter and ordered twenty-six cents worth of **30** food. He ate it like he really enjoyed it. When the owner, Mister Williams, asked him to pay the check, the old wino didn't lie or go through his pocket like he suddenly found a hole.

He just said: "Don't have no money." **31**

The owner yelled: "Why in hell you come in here and eat my food if you don't **32** have no money? That food cost me money."

Mister Williams jumped over the counter and knocked the wino off his stool **33** and beat him over the head with a pop bottle. Then he stepped back and watched the wino bleed. Then he kicked him. And he kicked him again.

I looked at the wino with blood all over his face and I went over. "Leave him **34** alone, Mister Williams. I'll pay the twenty-six cents."

The wino got up, slowly, pulling himself up to the stool, then up to the counter, **35** holding on for a minute until his legs stopped shaking so bad. He looked at me with pure hate. "Keep your twenty-six cents. You don't have to pay, not now. I just finished paying for it."

He started to walk out, and as he passed me, he reached down and touched my **36** shoulder. "Thanks, sonny, but it's too late now. Why didn't you pay it before?"

I was pretty sick about that. I waited too long to help another man. **37**

■ Reading Comprehension Questions

1. The word *pregnant* in "pregnant with poverty" (paragraph 5) means
   a. full of
   b. empty of
   c. sick
   d. satisfied

2. The word *hustling* in "I'd been out hustling all day" (paragraph 29) means
   a. learning
   b. stealing
   c. making friends
   d. working hard

3. Which of the following would be a good alternative title for this selection?
   a. Helene Tucker
   b. The Pain of Being Poor
   c. Losing a Father
   d. Mr. Williams and the Wino

4. Which sentence best expresses the main idea of the selection?
   a. Richard felt that being poor was humiliating.
   b. Richard liked Helene Tucker very much.
   c. Richard had to work hard as a child.
   d. The wino refused Richard's money.

5. The teacher disliked Richard because he
   a. was dirty
   b. liked Helene

    c. was a troublemaker
    d. ate paste

6. *True or false?* Helene Tucker felt sorry for Richard when the teacher embarrassed him.

7. Richard's problems in school were due to his being
    a. hungry
    b. distracted by Helene
    c. lonely
    d. unable to read

8. The author implies that Richard
    a. was not intelligent
    b. was proud
    c. had many friends
    d. and Helene became friends

9. The author implies that
    a. Mr. Williams felt sorry for the wino
    b. Richard's teacher was insensitive
    c. Richard liked people to feel sorry for him
    d. Richard's father was dead

10. The author implies that
    a. the mackinaws were poorly made
    b. Helene was a sensitive girl
    c. Helene disliked Richard
    d. the wino was ashamed of his poverty

Discussion Questions

About Content

1. How might Dick Gregory's teacher have handled the Community Chest incident without making him feel ashamed?

2. What are some of the lessons Gregory learns from the incident involving the wino at the restaurant?

3. Where in "Shame" do we find evidence that Dick Gregory finally does escape from poverty?

About Structure

4. Since Dick Gregory is actually writing about an embarrassing incident in school, why does he devote his first three paragraphs to his feelings about Helene Tucker?

5. What is the connection between the incident involving the wino at the restaurant and the rest of the essay?

About Style and Tone

6. In the paragraph beginning, "Now there was shame everywhere," Gregory uses a device called *repetition* when he begins several sentences with the words "There was shame . . ." What is the effect of this repetition?

7. Why does Gregory use dialogue when he narrates the incidents in the classroom and in the restaurant?

■   ## Writing Assignments

Assignment 1

Dick Gregory tells us in "Shame" that he was ashamed of his poverty and of being on welfare—to the point that he threw away the warm-hooded mackinaw he had been given simply because it was obvious proof that he and his family were on welfare. Do you think Gregory was justified in feeling so ashamed of his situation? Are other people who are on welfare justified if they feel ashamed? Choose either of the following thesis statements and develop it in an essay of several paragraphs:

> People on welfare are justified in feeling ashamed.
> People on welfare should not feel ashamed.

Then develop your thesis by thinking of several reasons to support the statement you have chosen.

You might think along the following lines:

Availability of jobs
Education or lack of education
Number of young children at home requiring care
Illness, physical disability
Psychological factors—depression, work habits, expectations, mental illness
Society's attitude toward people on welfare

Assignment 2

At some time in your life, you probably had an experience like Dick Gregory's in "Shame"—something that happened in a classroom, with a group of friends or peers, or a family situation that proved to be both embarrassing and educational. At the time, the experience hurt you very much, but you learned from it. Write a narrative essay in which you retell this experience. Try to include vivid details and plenty of conversation so that the incident will come to life.

Assignment 3

Write an essay about three basic things that people must have in order to feel self-respect. In your thesis statement, name these three necessities and state that a person must possess them in order to feel self-respect. On the following page are some ideas to consider:

A certain number of material possessions
A job
A loving family or a special person
A clear conscience
A feeling of belonging
Freedom from addictions

In your supporting paragraphs, discuss the factors you have chosen, showing specifically why each is so important. In order to avoid falling into the trap of writing generalities, you may want to give examples of people who lack these necessities and show how such people lose self-respect. Your examples may be drawn from personal experience, or they may be hypothetical examples.

SMASH THY NEIGHBOR

John McMurtry

We think of football as one of those great North American sports, like hockey or basketball. Children play football from grade school through university. Hours of network TV are devoted to football coverage of Grey Cup games and *Monday Night Football*. In this selection, however, a former Canadian football player says that football games are cruel contests that injure players and bring out the worst in fans.

A few months ago my neck got a hard crick in it. I couldn't turn my head; to look left or right I had to turn my whole body. But I'd had cricks in my neck since I started playing grade-school football and hockey, so I just ignored it. Then I began to notice that when I reached for any sort of large book (which I do pretty often as a philosophy teacher at the University of Guelph), I had trouble lifting it with one hand. I was losing the strength in my left arm, and I had such a steady pain in my back that I often had to stretch out on the floor to relieve the pressure.   1

Several weeks after my problems with book-lifting, I mentioned to my brother, an orthopedic surgeon, that I'd lost the power in my arm since my neck began to hurt. Twenty-four hours later I was in a Toronto hospital, not sure whether I might end up with a wasted upper limb. Apparently the steady pounding I had received playing college and professional football in the late fifties and early sixties had driven my head into my backbone so that the disks had crumpled together at the neck—"acute herniation"—and had cut the nerves to my left arm like a pinched telephone wire (without nerve stimulation, of course, the muscles atrophy, leaving the arm crippled). So I spent my Christmas holidays in the hospital in heavy traction, and much of the next three months with my neck in a brace. Today most of the pain has gone, and I've recovered most of the strength in my arm. But from time to time I still have to don the brace, and surgery remains a possibility.   2

Not much of this will surprise anyone who knows football. It is a sport in which **3** body wreckage is one of the leading conventions. A few days after I went into the hospital for that crick in my neck, another brother, an outstanding football player in college, was undergoing spinal surgery in the same hospital two floors above me. In his case it was a lower, more massive herniation, which every now and again buckled him so that he was unable to lift himself off his back for days. By the time he entered the hospital for surgery he had already spent several months in bed. The operation was successful, but, as in all such cases, it will take him a year to recover fully.

These aren't isolated experiences. Just about anybody who has ever played foot- **4** ball for any length of time, in high school, college, or one of the professional leagues, has suffered for it later.

Indeed, it is arguable that body shattering is the very *point* of football, as killing **5** and maiming are of war. (In the United States, for example, the game results in fifteen to twenty deaths a year and about fifty thousand major operations on knees alone.) To grasp some of the more conspicuous similarities between football and war, it is instructive to listen to the imperatives most frequently issued to the players by their coaches, teammates, and fans. "Hurt 'em!" "Level 'em!" "Kill 'em!" "Take 'em apart!" Or watch for the plays that are most enthusiastically applauded by the fans, where someone is "smeared," "knocked silly," "creamed," "nailed," "broken in two," or even "crucified." (One of my coaches when I played corner linebacker with the Calgary Stampeders in 1961 elaborated, often very inventively, on this language of destruction: admonishing us to "unjoin" the opponent, "make 'im remember you," and "stomp 'im like a bug.") Just as in hockey, where a fight will bring fans to their feet more often than a skillful play, so in football the mouth waters most of all for the really crippling block or tackle. For the kill. Thus the good teams are "hungry," the best players are "mean," and "casualties" are as much a part of the game as they are of a war.

The family resemblance between football and war is, indeed, striking. Their **6** languages are similar: "field general," "long bomb," "blitz," "take a shot," "front line," "pursuit," "good hit," "the draft," and so on. Their principles and practices are alike: mass hysteria, the art of intimidation, absolute command and total obedience, territorial aggression, censorship, inflated insignia and propaganda, blackboard maneuvers and strategies, drills, uniforms, formations, marching bands, and training camps. And the virtues they celebrate are almost identical: hyperaggressiveness, coolness under fire, and suicidal bravery.

One difference between war and football, though, is that there is little or no **7** protest against football. Perhaps the most extraordinary thing about the game is that the systematic infliction of injuries excites in people not concern, as would be the case if they were sustained at, say, a rock festival, but a collective rejoicing and euphoria. Players and fans alike revel in the spectacle of a combatant felled into semiconsciousness, "blindsided," "clotheslined," or "decapitated." I can remember, in fact, being chided by a coach in pro ball for not "getting my hat" injuriously into a player who was lying helpless on the ground.

After every game, of course, the papers are full of reports on the day's injuries, **8** a sort of post-battle "body count," and the respective teams go to work with doctors and trainers, tape, whirlpool baths, cortisone, and morphine to patch and deaden the wounds before the next game. Then the whole drama is reenacted—

athletes held together by adhesive, braces, and drugs—and the days following it are filled with even more feverish activity to put on the show yet again at the end of the week. (I remember being so taped up in college that I earned the nickname "Mummy.") The team that survives this merry-go-round spectacle of skilled masochism with the fewest incapacitating injuries usually wins. It is a sort of victory by ordeal: "We hurt them more than they hurt us."

My own initiation into this brutal circus was typical. I loved the game from the **9** moment I could run with a ball. Played shoeless on a green, open field with no one keeping score and in a spirit of reckless abandon and laughter, it's a very different sport. Almost no one gets hurt, and it's rugged, open, and exciting (it still is for me). But, like everything else, it starts to be regulated and institutionalized by adult authorities. And the fun is over.

So it was as I began the long march through organized football. Now there were **10** a coach and elders to make it clear by their behavior that beating other people was the only thing to celebrate and that trying to shake someone up every play was the only thing to be really proud of. Now there were severe rule enforcers, audiences, formally recorded victors and losers, and heavy equipment to permit crippling bodily moves and collisions (according to one survey, more than 80 percent of all football injuries occur to fully equipped players). And now there was the official "given" that the only way to keep playing was to wear suffocating armor, to play to defeat, to follow orders silently, and to renounce spontaneity in favor of joyless drill. The game has been, in short, ruined. But because I loved to play, and play skillfully, I stayed. And progressively and inexorably, as I moved through high school, college, and pro leagues, my body was dismantled. Piece by piece.

I started off with torn ligaments in my knee at thirteen. Then, as the organization **11** and the competition increased, the injuries came faster and harder. Broken nose (three times), broken jaw (fractured in the first half and dismissed as a "bad wisdom tooth," so I played with it for the rest of the game), ripped knee ligaments again. Torn ligaments in one ankle and a fracture in the other (which I remember feeling relieved about because it meant I could honorably stop drill-blocking a 270-pound defensive end). Repeated rib fractures and cartilage tears (usually carried, again, through the remainder of the game). More dislocations of the left shoulder than I can remember (the last one I played with because, as the Calgary Stampeders' doctor said, it "couldn't be damaged any more"). Occasional broken or dislocated fingers and toes. Chronically hurt lower back (I still can't lift with it or change a tire without worrying about folding). Separated right shoulder (as with many other injuries, like badly bruised hips and legs, needled with morphine for the games). And so on. The last pro game I played—against the Winnipeg Blue Bombers in the Western finals in 1961—I had a recently dislocated left shoulder, a more recently wrenched right shoulder, and a chronic pain center in one leg. I was so tied up with soreness that I couldn't drive to the airport. But it never occurred to me that I should miss a play as a corner linebacker.

By the end of my football career, I had learned that physical injury—giving it **12** and taking it—is the real currency of the sport. And that in the final analysis, the "winner" is the man who can hit to kill even if only half his limbs are working. In brief, a warrior game with a warrior ethos into which (like almost everyone I played with) my original boyish enthusiasm had been relentlessly conditioned.

In thinking back on how all this happened, though, I can pick out no villains. **13**
As with the social system as a whole, the game has a life of its own. Everyone grows
up inside it, accepts it, and fulfills its dictates as obediently as Helots. Far from questioning the principles of the activity, most men simply concentrate on executing
these principles more aggressively than anybody else. The result is a group of people who, as the leagues become of a higher and higher class, are progressively insensitive to the possibility that things could be otherwise. Thus, in football, anyone
who might question the wisdom or enjoyment of putting on heavy equipment on
a hot day and running full speed at someone else with the intention of knocking
him senseless would be regarded as not really a devoted athlete and probably
"chicken." The choice is made straightforward. Either you, too, do your very utmost
to smash efficiently and be smashed, or you admit incompetence or cowardice and
quit. Since neither of these admissions is very pleasant, people generally keep any
doubts they have to themselves, and carry on.

Of course, it would be a mistake to suppose that there is more blind acceptance **14**
of brutal practices in organized football than elsewhere. On the contrary, a recent
Harvard study argues that football's characteristics of "impersonal acceptance of
inflicted injury," an overriding "organization goal," the "ability to turn oneself on
and off," and being, above all, "out to win" are prized by ambitious executives in
many large corporations. Clearly, football is no sicker than the rest of our society.
Even its organized destruction of physical well-being is not anomalous. A very large
part of our wealth, work, and time is, after all, spent in systematically destroying
and harming human life; manufacturing, selling, and using weapons that tear
opponents to pieces; making ever bigger and faster predator-named cars with
which to kill and injure one another by the million every year; and devoting our
very lives to outgunning one another for power in an ever-more-destructive rat
race. Yet all these practices are accepted without question by most people, even zeal-
ously defended and honored. Competitive, organized injuring is integral to our way
of life, and football is one of the more intelligible mirrors of the whole process: a
sort of colorful morality play showing us how exciting and rewarding it is to Smash
Thy Neighbor.

Now, it is fashionable to rationalize our collaboration in all this by arguing that, **15**
well, men *like* to fight and injure their fellows, and such games as football should
be encouraged to discharge this original-sin urge into less harmful channels than,
say, war. Public-show football, this line goes, plays the same sort of cathartic role
as Aristotle said stage tragedy does: without real blood (or not much), it releases
players and audience from unhealthy feelings stored up inside them.

As an ex-player in this seasonal coast-to-coast drama, I see little to recommend **16**
such a view. What organized football did to me was make me *suppress* my natural
urges and reexpress them in alienating, vicious form. Spontaneous desires for free
bodily exuberance and fraternization with competitors were shamed and forced
under ("If it ain't hurtin', it ain't helpin'"), and in their place were demanded
armored, mechanical moves, and cool hatred of all opposition. Endless authori-
tarian drill and dressing-room harangues (ever wonder why competing teams can't
prepare for a game in the same dressing room?) were the kinds of mechanisms
employed to reconstruct joyful energies into mean and alien shapes. I am quite cer-

tain that everyone else around me was being similarly forced into this heavily equipped military precision and angry antagonism, because there was always a mutinous attitude about full-dress practices, and everybody (the pros included) had to concentrate incredibly hard for days to whip himself into just one hour's hostility a week against another club. The players never speak of these things, of course, because everyone is anxious to appear tough.

The claim that men like seriously to battle one another to some sort of finish **17** is a myth. It endures only because it wears one of the oldest and most propagandized of masks—the romantic combatant. I sometimes wonder whether the violence all around us doesn't depend for its survival on the existence and preservation of this tough-guy disguise.

As for the effect of organized football on the spectator, the fans are not so much **18** released from supposed feelings of violent aggression by watching their athletic heroes perform it as they are encouraged in the view that people-smashing is an admirable mode of self-expression. The most savage attackers, after all, are, by general agreement, the most efficient and worthy players of all (the biggest applause I ever received as a football player occurred when I ran over people or slammed them so hard that they couldn't get up). . . . Watching well-advertised strong men knock other people around, make them hurt, is in the end like other tastes. It does not weaken with feeding and variation in form. It grows.

I got out of football in 1962. In a preseason intersquad game, I ripped the car- **19** tilage in my ribs on the hardest block I'd ever thrown. I had trouble breathing, and I had to shuffle-walk with my torso on a tilt. The doctor in the local hospital said three weeks rest; the coach said scrimmage in two days. Three days later I was back home reading philosophy.

■ Reading Comprehension Questions

1. The word *atrophy* in "without nerve stimulation, of course, the muscles atrophy, leaving the arm crippled" (paragraph 2) means
    a. get stronger
    b. flex
    c. weaken
    d. are unaffected

2. The word *imperatives* in "It is instructive to listen to the imperatives most frequently issued to the players. . . . 'Hurt 'em!' 'Level 'em!' 'Kill 'em!'" (paragraph 5) means
    a. insults
    b. commands
    c. compliments
    d. questions

3. Which of the following would be a good alternative title for this selection?
    a. The Violence of Football
    b. Football in North America
    c. A Man Who Played Football
    d. Football and Corporate Competition

4. Which sentence best expresses the main idea of the selection?
   a. Playing football has caused the author much physical pain.
   b. Most football coaches try to make the game less violent.
   c. Football's popularity is a reflection of some negative aspects of society.
   d. Violence is a central part of organized football both for the teams and for the fans.

5. The author says that organized football is like
   a. all other sports
   b. philosophy
   c. war
   d. football played without coaches and rules

6. For the author, football was ruined by
   a. people who play without equipment
   b. the regulation of adult authorities
   c. people who dislike its violence
   d. ambitious executives

7. According to the author, watching football makes people
   a. believe that "smashing thy neighbor" is good
   b. realize that football is too violent
   c. feel a great release from their own violent feelings
   d. escape from the anxieties of their jobs

8. The author implies that
   a. society is much less brutally competitive than football
   b. football players never have doubts about the brutality of the game
   c. the brutal values of football exist in other parts of society
   d. many people question the violence in football

9. The author implies that fans
   a. get rid of unhealthy feelings when watching football
   b. encourage the violence in football
   c. are unaware of the violence in football
   d. discourage the really savage attacks in football

10. In the last paragraph of the selection, the author implies that
    a. his injuries were mild
    b. the doctor exaggerated the extent of his injuries
    c. the coach thought that his injuries were mild
    d. the coach cared more about winning than about his players' injuries

■ Discussion Questions

About Content

1. According to McMurtry, what qualities of our society are reflected in football?

2. The author makes an analogy between war and football. In what ways are the two activities alike?

3. Do you agree with McMurtry that the violence of football encourages people's taste for "people-smashing [as] an admirable mode of self-expression" (paragraph 18)?

About Structure

4. What method of introduction does the author use?
   a. Anecdote
   b. An opposite
   c. Quotation

5. What method of development is used in paragraphs 5 and 6?
   a. Reasons
   b. Comparison
   c. Examples

About Style and Tone

6. Why does the author call his essay "Smash Thy Neighbor"? To answer, think about how the title may be a play on the words in a familiar biblical command.

7. McMurtry uses terms such as *body wreckage, body shattering*, and *skilled masochism* to describe organized football. What effect does he hope this language will have on the reader? Find three other phrases the author uses to describe football (beginning with paragraph 9).

■ Writing Assignments

Assignment 1

Imagine that you are a professional football coach (or, if you prefer, the head coach of your school's football team). You have just read "Smash Thy Neighbor" in a national magazine, and you feel angered and hurt by McMurtry's opinion of football. How would you answer his accusations about the sport? Write a letter to the editor of the magazine in which you give three reasons John McMurtry is wrong about football and its effects on people. You might want to get started with this thesis statement:

I feel John McMurtry is wrong about football for several reasons.

Then continue your letter, describing each reason in detail. Write a separate paragraph for each detail.

Alternatively, imagine that, as a coach, you agree with McMurtry, and write a letter in which you detail three reasons for agreeing.

Assignment 2

Write a narrative essay about a bad experience you had with sports. Among the topics you might write about are

> An injury
> Not being chosen for a team
> Missing an important point or goal
> Being pressured by a parent or coach
> Being the clumsiest person in gym class
> Being embarrassed while trying to learn a sport

You could begin the essay with a sentence or two about your experience with sports in general—whether sports have been an area of pain or pleasure for you. Your thesis should name the particular experience you will write about and tell your readers that this experience was bad (or embarrassing, or humiliating, or disillusioning, or any other word that seems appropriate).

Then organize your supporting paragraphs by dividing your experience into two or three time phases. You may want to first review the chapter on the narrative essay (pages 159–171).

Assignment 3

Write an essay about a sport you feel is a good one. In each of your supporting paragraphs, give one reason this sport is good for either players or spectators.

MY BODY IS MY OWN BUSINESS

Naheed Mustafa

On many streets in Canada today, women and girls from African and Near or Far Eastern nations wear the traditional long robes of Muslim female dress and the *hijab*, or head covering, as well. Those accustomed to feminist thought of the last thirty years see such dress as symbolic of male oppression in Islamic cultures, but Naheed Mustafa presents an opposing argument. Mustafa, educated at the University of Toronto and Ryerson University, is a journalist in her native Pakistan, who *chooses* to wear the *hijab* for reasons that are at odds with stereotypes of Muslim belief and behaviour.

I often wonder whether people see me as a radical, fundamentalist Muslim terrorist packing an AK-47 assault rifle inside my jean jacket. Or maybe they see me as the poster girl for oppressed womanhood everywhere. I'm not sure which it is. 1

I get the whole gamut of strange looks, stares and covert glances. You see, I wear the *hijab*, a scarf that covers my head, neck and throat. I do this because I am a Muslim woman who believes her body is her own private concern. 2

Young Muslim women are reclaiming the *hijab*, reinterpreting it in light of its **3** original purpose—to give back to women ultimate control of their own bodies.

The Koran teaches us that men and women are equal, that individuals should **4** not be judged according to gender, beauty, wealth or privilege. The only thing that makes one person better than another is her or his character.

Nonetheless, people have a difficult time relating to me. After all, I'm young, **5** Canadian born and raised, university-educated—why would I do this to myself, they ask.

Strangers speak to me in loud, slow English and often appear to be playing cha- **6** rades. They politely inquire how I like living in Canada and whether or not the cold bothers me. If I'm in the right mood, it can be very amusing.

But why would I, a woman with all the advantages of a North American **7** upbringing, suddenly, at 21, want to cover myself so that with the *hijab* and the other clothes I choose to wear, only my face and hands show?

Because it gives me freedom. **8**

Women are taught from early childhood that their worth is proportional to their **9** attractiveness. We feel compelled to pursue abstract notions of beauty, half realizing that such a pursuit is futile.

When women reject this form of oppression, they face ridicule and con- **10** tempt. Whether it's women who refuse to wear makeup or to shave their legs or to expose their bodies, society, both men and women, have trouble dealing with them.

In the Western world, the *hijab* has come to symbolize either forced silence **11** or radical, unconscionable militancy. Actually, it's neither. It is simply a woman's assertion that judgment of her physical person is to play no role whatsoever in social interaction.

Wearing the *hijab* has given me freedom from constant attention to my phys- **12** ical self. Because my appearance is not subjected to public scrutiny, my beauty, or perhaps lack of it, has been removed from the realm of what can legitimately be discussed.

No one knows whether my hair looks as if I just stepped out of a salon, whether **13** or not I can pinch an inch, or even if I have unsightly stretch marks. And because no one knows, no one cares.

Feeling that one has to meet the impossible male standards of beauty is tiring **14** and often humiliating. I should know, I spent my entire teenage years trying to do it. I was a borderline bulimic and spent a lot of money I didn't have on potions and lotions in hopes of becoming the next Cindy Crawford.

The definition of beauty is ever-changing; waifish is good, waifish is bad, ath- **15** letic is good—sorry, athletic is bad. Narrow hips? Great. Narrow hips? Too bad.

Women are not going to achieve equality with the right to bare breasts in pub- **16** lic, as some people would like to have you believe. That would only make us party to our own objectification. True equality will be had only when women don't need to display themselves to get attention and won't need to defend their decision to keep their bodies to themselves.

■ **Reading Comprehension Questions**

1. The word *unconscionable* in "radical, unconscionable militancy"
   (paragraph 11) means
   a. unbelievable
   b. unsuitable
   c. unmanageable
   d. unthinkable

2. The word *waifish* in "waifish is good, waifish is bad, athletic is good"
   (paragraph 15) means
   a. womanly, robust in appearance
   b. curvaceous, shapely
   c. sickly
   d. skinny, neglected-looking

3. Which of the following would be a good alternative title for this selection?
   a. The Mysterious Eastern Woman
   b. Eastern Privacy and Western Prejudice
   c. Habits and Headgear
   d. My Culture and My Choice of Clothing

4. Which sentence best expresses the main idea of the selection?
   a. Muslim women have the right to dress as they wish.
   b. Women should wear clothing that disguises their bodies to avoid
      harassment.
   c. Women will be truly free when their appearance is no longer of primary
      importance.
   d. Every woman has the right to privacy of her person.

5. People don't know what to make of Naheed Mustafa because
   a. she chooses to dress in an outlandish Eastern way
   b. the *hijab* symbolizes stereotypes of women as victims or Islamic terrorists
   c. her clothing disguises her true identity
   d. she is hiding her identity as an educated Canadian under an ethnic costume

6. *True or false?* Only men have trouble dealing with women who no longer pursue media-dictated ideals of grooming and beauty.

7. The Koran's teaching about the sexes states
   a. that women unintentionally represent temptation to men
   b. that men and women are judged by their actions
   c. that no one should be judged by external factors
   d. that both sexes have the right to privacy

8. The author implies that
   a. people see her as a militant feminist
   b. people find stereotyping easier than looking beyond appearances

      c. people don't want to know her

      d. her Canadian upbringing and education are disadvantages

9. The author implies that

      a. women can achieve a degree of personal freedom by clothing choices

      b. Western women are slow to catch up with Muslim wisdom about dress

      c. women will never understand what beauty is all about

      d. women everywhere are totally obsessed by impossible ideas of beauty

10. Wearing the *hijab* has given the author

      a. a decent anti-fashion statement appropriate to her religion

      b. a sense of being able to be whoever she truly is by her own standards

      c. a place to hide from men's expectations of her

      d. an exotic refuge from the everyday world of Canadian society

◼ Discussion Questions

About Content

1. How does the author feel that people on the street see her? Why does the author feel that way?

2. What are the practical advantages of wearing the *hijab?* What are the ideological reasons for Mustafa's adoption of the garments?

3. What does the author suggest is the basic problem with beauty?

About Structure

4. The clearest statement of the author's thesis is in the last third of the essay. Find the statement and write it down.

5. What is the "change of direction" word in paragraph 11?

About Style and Tone

6. What is the effect on your perception of Naheed Mustafa when you read such statements as "I was a borderline bulimic" who "spent a lot of money I didn't have . . . in hopes of becoming the next Cindy Crawford," and "waifish is good, waifish is bad . . ."?

7. We describe subjects by saying what they are not, as well as by saying what they are. In what terms does the author set up her reasons for believing the *hijab* is an ideal form of clothing for her?

8. The author begins her essay with an exaggerated description of one stereotyped image and confesses her defeat at trying to become another stereotyped ideal. Do the essay's examples give you a clear picture of the "real" person?

■ Writing Assignments

Assignment 1

Naheed Mustafa writes about a personal decision to wear certain clothing, which defines her in one way to observers but means something very different to her as wearer. Our clothing choices *do*, in some ways, define us and communicate information about us to others. The message sent out may not always be the one we intend to communicate. Think about the clothes and accessories you wear to class every day. What is the result of your choice(s) on those who observe you? What do certain garments and jewellery "say" about you, to yourself, and to others? Do these messages occasionally conflict?

Write an article for your college newspaper to defend some choice of personal attire or decoration that may be misinterpreted by others. You could discuss something ordinary like a baseball cap, a pierced nostril, a garment belonging to your ethnic background, or even a certain type of makeup.

In your argument, use the cause and effect method of organizing your points of defence. Notice how Mustafa has repeatedly used the word *because* and various transition words like *actually* before setting out her points of explanation. Set out your own details about your clothing or accessories in this pattern of causes, effects, and explanations.

Assignment 2

The image of beauty in any society is constantly changing and subject to the whims of advertising. Should any of us, men or women, model ourselves on TV and magazine concepts of what is attractive? Nearly our entire consumer economy is based on selling various products to us that will make us more like someone else's ideal of what is a beautiful, strong, healthy, or even "good" person.

Write an essay in which you choose one of the following sentences as the basis for your thesis statement, and argue for its validity from your own experience and knowledge.

> We are losing our ability to decide what we should look like because of ads that promote famished supermodels and Schwarzenegger/Stallone look-alikes. We choose ideals of male and female beauty *knowingly and willingly* because they appeal to our desire to be the best we can be. Fitness and beauty aren't sins.

Assignment 3

What stereotypes, based on aspects of appearance or behaviour, do we carry around with us of various national and cultural groups? Are there any points of truth in these stereotypes? Do such preconceived notions blind us to the characters of people inside the clothing or behind the counter at the store? Think about one such stereotype based on appearance or on behaviour patterns.

Discuss in an examples essay your own reaction to this stereotype. Has your reaction changed as a result of knowing individuals who broke down this stereotype, or is your attitude unchanged?

OF LEMONS AND LEMONADE

Sherwin Tija

Like many people today, Sherwin Tija grew up in the suburbs, in the "familiar gridiron of Scarborough, Ontario." Vividly contrasting the reality of childhood surroundings with the "dreamscape" of a holiday in Algonquin Park, the writer wonders what changes a knowledge of natural beauty might have made to character and thinking. Tija, still a university student, describes with equal intensity the alien familiarity of a home neighbourhood and the unfamiliar, exquisite sheen of lake water at night.

When I came across the word "cornflowers" in Margaret Laurence's The Diviners, *I didn't know what it meant. I couldn't tell you whether cornflowers were proud and glowing or taciturn and sweet; I just didn't know. The same thing occurred when I stumbled over "couchgrass" and "peonies." I had heard of them before, the names were familiar, yet, I couldn't put the names to a face, to a fragrance, or a touch.*   1

I can however, tell you about concrete, steel, tar and glass, and go on endlessly   2
about the myriad uses of bricks. Of these, their structures and lines remain rigid in my visual vocabulary; of these I can envision with clarity. Though disgracefully ignorant about the natural world, this is my world, this world of malls and lawns and faceless houses, generic streets and measured sidewalks and parks where one can see the other side by standing at one end. And while sometimes one grows strangely nostalgic for a world one's never really seen, except through a movie lens or the inscribed word, for what experience would I leave my familiar gridiron of Scarborough, Ontario? Would I leave it for a world of limitless lands, unscarred sunsets and fields? In a second. What kind of fields? I don't care; fields of wheat, grain, weeping willow leaves—fields of anything but shorn green grass and playgrounds. But I've never been to those places, so let me tell you about what I can see.

I can tell you about skinning bare knees on the coarse schoolyard lot, and get-   3
ting up bleeding and crying with pebbles still embedded like shrapnel around one's wicked-looking wound. I can tell you about the tremendous impetus the fixed playground was for our imaginations. When every recess game had to be new, the jungle gym becomes an island, a base, a prison, a fortress. The angular teeter-totters become skyward-gazing missile silos; the swings jet planes, or catapults; the sand pit the Middle East, the baseball cage an enemy wall to be climbed—everything was something. The playground was a proving ground.

When I do come across flora in the books though, I can't just dismiss it. To keep   4
the illusion of the story intact I have to pull them in somehow; they must still exist somewhere. In such cases, I contrive a scattershot barrage of green, like in a Seurat painting, and let that pass. Or maybe I see pretty pink and red and yellow flowers and dot them among the green, but all to the purpose of setting the atmosphere that I want to feel as I'm sinking into the narrative. A flower's a flower, I tell myself, so it doesn't feel as if I'm missing much.

Suburban nights are quiet, if you're in among the houses deep. I can tell you **5** about the reflected glow of lamplight in rain-wet streets, dark like soil, but solid like glass, and how each car that passes glares with eyes of opulence and self-proclaimed righteousness. I can tell you about the perversion of grass that we cultivate; not long and billowy, but short and flat and uniform. Conform, they seem to say, even as I mow them angrily down and fret at the uselessness of the task. But we all do this because there is a law against not doing it, passed by those who can afford to pay others to do it for them. And so we conform, and grow affectionate for our lawns rather than standing up for what we believe. I can tell you about dull, repetitive genetic housing, as if they're all spawned from the same master plan—a monotonous mother brick. There's the fear of getting lost in one's own neighborhood, or even on one's own street if we're just not good with numbers. When all the streets for blocks all look the same at night, and when all the people stay safe with the face of the same expression, and we allow ourselves to grow detached, and we look warily at our neighbors for lack of knowing—this would make me leave. This is the essence of freshly mowed grass.

Once I went up north to Algonquin Park, and though I didn't know the name of **6** *anything, I picked up a water flower, fragrant and wet, and I knew that was what I would see first the next time I thought about canoeing on a lake. It was a water lily, I later learned, and I smiled because it should have been obvious.*

Let me tell you about the beauty of hydrofields, the great open spaces of our **7** land, with their gigantic metal men, striding into the distance, clutching their living lines. Sometimes these lines hum and join the crickets in a chorus in the blazing summer's heat. Sometimes they are downed in storms and children are electrocuted, and these children's dogs, and then scavengers which come to feed . . . in the late summer, when the grass is yellow in the sunset, I like to pretend that it's Africa, on the Serengeti Plain. The animals are there, if only in my mind. Though sometimes the hazing of the heat causes them to appear in earnest and I wonder if it's sunstroke or an altered state of consciousness. Most often there are lone figures like me with their dogs before them, and once when I was very young, a couple making love. I remember the shadow on her upturned face as a very intense blue.

Sometimes I wish I had that natural vocabulary, and that I had grown up close to **8** *water, and that some old woman had taken me by the hand, and showed me the woods and pointed with gnarled stick at nature's ornaments, revealing their nature and their name.*

Let me tell you about the curious relationship between a sidewalk's crack and **9** your mother's back.

Sometimes I wish I could take my experiences in the wilderness for granted, like **10** *those who have had cabins up north all their lives. For while I would lose the aching awe of the wild world that I carry today, a childhood growing up among such wonders might have shaped me into a different person; possibly one more comfortable in situations requiring relinquishing thought and reason in favor of intuition and instinct. I don't know, maybe I would be less constrained, repressed. It is this possibility I regret, even if I had no choice at the time.*

Let me tell you about the brilliance of the clouds at night over the car dealer- **11**
ships on the next street. Let me tell you about the ubiquitous red stop signs, complementing green grass and vivid against a blue sky. Let me tell you about the stream
of cars that flows continuously, under formidable bridges that span neighborhood
to neighborhood, district to district. Let me tell you about the crescents and the
lanes, the circles and circuits, groves and gates, courts and squares, all connected like
a madman's maze, in some secular sequence. And even in the rurality of Suburbia,
the churches are not the tallest structures as they once used to be. Today it's the
apartment buildings. Are we losing or finding ourselves? Or do we have to do both?

The next time I think about entering the gates of heaven, what I'll remember is **12**
coasting in a canoe across glassy water at night, shining a flashlight through the
rising mists off the lake; the paddles not making a sound.

Let me tell you about the all-night donut shops, immaculate, unchanging and **13**
overcharging; the perpetual light even at night; the charisma and cheap intensity
of malls; the lack of open-ended gathering places; the solace of libraries; the ele-
phantine dumpsters; daily road kill to greet school kids walking home; the reined
imagination in knowing what's over the next horizon—more of the same; and
parking lot wastelands and furtive gropings.

Sometimes I am glad of the mystery of nature. That I cannot name with a glance **14**
every plant or leaf that comes into view, is important. That I can look at a land-
scape and wonder at its being, instead of understanding it by clarifying it, defining
it, is a freedom. Despite this, when I first swam in an Algonquin lake at sunset, when
the colors imbued the waters, my first thought was that of swimming in a postcard.

Let me tell you a tale of lemons and lemonade. A boy and a girl are selling lemon- **15**
ade by the side of the road. From a card table with a plastic tablecloth hangs a sign
alerting passersby that a cup of their brew costs only 50 cents. I buy a cup and when I
ask them if it's made out of real lemons, they tell me no, it's from a can of concentrate,
the same can wherein they have deposited my two quarters with a self-satisfied clink.

"But why didn't you use real lemons?" I say, finishing my cup. **16**

"Because this is all we had," the girl said. **17**

The cups are styrofoam, and I drop mine into their plastic garbage bag. **18**

■ Reading Comprehension Questions

1. The word *impetus* in "the tremendous impetus [of] the fixed playground"
   (paragraph 3) means
   a. toy
   b. arena
   c. drive
   d. space

2. The word *ubiquitous* in "the ubiquitous red stop signs, complementing green
   grass" (paragraph 11) means
   a. hideous
   b. bright-coloured

   c. found everywhere
   d. beautiful

3. Which phrase of the following might be a good alternative title for this essay?
   a. Of Loneliness and Landscapes
   b. Neighbourhood Nostalgia
   c. Paradise Lost
   d. Playgrounds and Plastic Cups

4. Which sentence best expresses the main idea of the selection?
   a. The suburbs are a hideous place in which to grow up.
   b. Knowing both nature and urban life helps people to know themselves.
   c. The suburbs have their own beauty and mystery.
   d. Nature is beautiful, but beyond our knowledge.

5. The writer remembers the school playground
   a. as harsh and dangerous
   b. as causing the children's aggressive and warlike behaviour
   c. as barren and empty
   d. as an inspiration to flights of fancy

6. *True or false?* The author finds nature more "real" than a suburban neighbourhood.

7. The author's main problem with the streets in his area is
   a. that the neighbours drive expensive cars and employ lawn-care services
   b. having to trim the lawn to legal standards
   c. a fear of getting lost near home
   d. the sense of imposed order and distance from neighbours

8. The writer implies that
   a. a person with a suburban upbringing will never understand nature
   b. environments may, but need not, limit our imaginations
   c. children will never experience the truth of natural things
   d. the beauty of nature can be understood only by relating it to pictures

9. The writer implies that
   a. there is a reality beyond one's ability to define it
   b. the suburbanite cannot really understand his or her "world"
   c. suburban childhood was dreary and boring
   d. suburban childhood leaves people alienated and alone

10. *True or false?* The author implies that the children selling concentrated lemonade are pathetic because they haven't experienced the "real thing."

▪ Discussion Questions

About Content

1. Sherwin Tija tells readers about knowing certain flowers and plants only by name. What were his only sources of information about these aspects of nature? What features of daily surroundings does the writer know instead?

2. Which elements of the suburban landscape are appealing, and which are described as unattractive?

3. What do you think are the writer's feelings toward the children who are selling lemonade at the end of the essay? Which experiences described in "Of Lemons and Lemonade" would lead to these feelings?

About Structure

4. Why does the author alternate between paragraphs in italics and paragraphs in normal print? Do the two types of paragraphs change in length as the essay progresses? Why do they change?

5. What is the connection between the final episode, the "tale" with dialogue about two children selling lemonade, and the rest of the essay?

About Style and Tone

6. Why do you think the writer "personifies," or gives human qualities to, various things in paragraphs 5 and 7?

7. Tija consciously repeats certain words and phrases like "I can tell you," "Let me tell you," and "sometimes." What is the effect of this repetition?

■ Writing Assignments

Assignment 1

All of us have memories of the areas where we grew up. Many people in Canadian cities spent their childhoods in suburbs similar to Scarborough and experienced natural settings only occasionally. But not all of our reactions to either our childhood environments or nature are similar to Sherwin Tija's.

Write a letter to a friend in which you describe the streets, neighbourhood, or area where you grew up. Try to capture clearly the sights, sounds, and sense details of the place, and to recreate in words the emotions those details awakened in you. Limit the dimensions of the area you describe as much as possible so that your description is intense and clearly focused. Choose a path or route you will follow as you describe your chosen place, and try to take your reader with you.

Remember that a letter follows the same structural patterns as an essay, with an introductory paragraph like a thesis statement to give your reader a clear idea of both your dominant impression and the three strongest memories of places or objects that support that impression. Be sure your conclusion follows naturally from your supporting details, and end with a final thought to sum up your feelings and reconnect with the reader of your letter.

Assignment 2

Sherwin Tija effectively contrasts personal reflections awakened by nature with those caused by everyday surroundings. Choose an environment you do *not* particularly enjoy but must frequent for some purpose (perhaps a workplace or a relative's home), and a place where you are very happy. Try to ensure that the two locations are of relatively equal time- or detail-value so that your contrast is not lopsided. Contrast the two environments in terms of what pleases or displeases you about them. Use order of importance to lead up to your strongest point of contrast, and use point-by-point format for your essay, as Tija has, to bring out specific elements of contrast. Your conclusion may point to a "moral" about why your feelings may be divided, or it may point to the absolute superiority of one place over the other.

Assignment 3

You are an environmental columnist for your local community newspaper. Two possible assignments are offered to you: one a puff-piece selling your community's building restoration and quality of life to build investor interest in your community, the other a slam at recent and older social, lighting, and drainage problems that have been causing trouble for residents and visitors. While trying to decide which job to take, you make a list of words under the simple headings of "good" and "bad" and try to group your words under some headings.

Since you're trying to find out which assignment would make the more forceful article, you are looking for the position where your strongest feelings lie. You tend to write a better argument for your own side.

Here is your rough, unfinished list of "goods" and "bads," and the tentative headings:

Good	*Bad*
1 Streets	**1** Streets
• New fronts/stores, restaurants • Clean, crisp architectural details	• Dirty/ominous alleyways/threats • Forbidding, frightening unlit areas • Rickety doorways & shattered glass
2 People	**2** People
• Entrepreneurs/exciting retail • Young families/fresh money	• Panhandlers/pathetic, annoying • Teen gangs, loitering/lingering
3 Enviro/Atmosphere	**3** Enviro/Atmosphere
• Revived, reawakened • Air quality/? • Trees/natural, verdant, leafy	• Streetcars/clean, but racket of grinding • Sewers/stench, fetid

Make your own list of words based on three distinct aspects of your community. Write either the positive or the negative article about the part of the town or city where you live. Structure your argument to be convincing, and begin with a solid thesis statement containing your major ideas, with your strongest point in the final position.

WAIT DIVISIONS

Tom Bodett

How long and how often did you wait for something today? Chances are, if you are like most of us, you wait for so many things that you lose count. Tom Bodett attacks the subject head-on; he examines waiting and finds that not all waits are the same. Next time you are in line or on hold, decide what category of wait you're enduring.

I read somewhere that we spend a full third of our lives waiting. I've also read that   **1**
we spend a third of our lives sleeping, a third working, and a third at our leisure. Now either somebody's lying, or we're spending all our leisure time waiting to go to work or sleep. That can't be true or league softball and Winnebagos never would have caught on.

So where are we doing all of this waiting, and what does it mean to an impa-   **2**
tient society like ours? Could this unseen waiting be the source of all our problems? A shrinking economy? The staggering deficit? Declining mental health and moral apathy? Probably not, but let's take a look at some of the more classic "waits" anyway.

The very purest form of waiting is what we'll call the *Watched-Pot Wait.* This   **3**
type of wait is without a doubt the most annoying of all. Take filling up the kitchen sink. There is absolutely nothing you can do while this is going on but keep both eyes glued to the sink until it's full. If you try to cram in some extracurricular activity, you're asking for it. So you stand there, your hands on the faucets, and wait. A temporary suspension of duties. During these waits it's common for your eyes to lapse out of focus. The brain disengages from the body and wanders around the imagination in search of distraction. It finds more and springs back into action only when the water runs over the edge of the counter and onto your socks.

The phrase "a watched pot never boils" comes of this experience. Pots don't care   **4**
whether they are watched or not; the problem is that nobody has ever seen a pot actually come to a boil. While people are waiting, their brains turn off.

Other forms of the Watched-Pot Wait would include waiting for your dryer to   **5**
quit at the laundromat, waiting for your toast to pop out of the toaster, or waiting for a decent idea to come to mind at a typewriter. What they all have in common is that they render the waiter helpless and mindless.

A cousin to the Watched-Pot Wait is the *Forced Wait.* Not for the weak of will,   **6**
this one requires a bit of discipline. The classic Forced Wait is starting your car in the winter and letting it slowly idle up to temperature before engaging the clutch. This is every bit as uninteresting as watching a pot, but with one big difference. You have a choice. There is nothing keeping you from racing to work behind a stone-cold engine save[1] the thought of the early demise of several thousand dollars' worth of equipment you haven't paid for yet. Thoughts like that will help you get through a Forced Wait.

[1]*save:* except

Properly preparing packaged soup mixes also requires a Forced Wait. **7**
Directions are very specific on these mixes. "Bring three cups of water to boil, add
mix, simmer three minutes, remove from heat, let stand five minutes." I have my
doubts that anyone has actually done this. I'm fairly spineless when it comes to
instant soups and usually just boil the bejeezus out of them until the noodles sink.
Some things just aren't worth a Forced Wait.

All in all, Forced Waiting requires a lot of a thing called patience, which is a **8**
virtue. Once we get into virtues I'm out of my element and can't expound on the
virtues of virtue, or even lie about them. So let's move on to some of the more far-
reaching varieties of waiting.

The *Payday Wait* is certainly a leader in the long-term anticipation field. The **9**
problem with waits that last more than a few minutes is that you have to actually
do other things in the meantime. Like go to work. By far the most aggravating feature of the Payday Wait is that even though you must keep functioning in the interludes,[2] there is less and less you are able to do as the big day draws near. For some
of us the last few days are best spent alone in a dark room for fear we'll accidentally do something that costs money. With the Payday Wait comes a certain amount
of hope that we'll make it, and faith that everything will be right once we do.

With the introduction of faith and hope, I've ushered in the most potent wait class **10**
of all, the *Lucky-Break Wait*, or the *Wait for One's Ship to Come In.* This type of wait is
unusual in that it is for the most part voluntary. Unlike the Forced Wait, which is also
voluntary, waiting for your lucky break does not necessarily mean that it will happen.

Turning one's life into a waiting game of these proportions requires gobs of the **11**
aforementioned faith and hope, and is strictly for the optimists among us. For these
people life is the thing that happens to them while they're waiting for something
to happen to them. On the surface it seems as ridiculous as following the directions
on soup mixes, but the Lucky-Break Wait performs an outstanding service to those
who take it upon themselves to do it. As long as one doesn't come to rely on it,
wishing for a few good things to happen never hurt anybody.

In the end it is obvious that we certainly do spend a good deal of our time waiting. **12**
The person who said we do it a third of the time may have been going easy on us.
It makes a guy wonder how anything at all gets done around here. But things do
get done, people grow old, and time boils on whether you watch it or not.

The next time you're standing at the sink waiting for it to fill while cooking **13**
soup mix that you'll have to eat until payday or until a large bag of cash falls out of
the sky, don't despair. You're probably just as busy as the next guy.

■   **Reading Comprehension Questions**

1. The word *apathy* in "Declining mental health and moral apathy?"
   (paragraph 2) means
   a. energy
   b. misery
   c. indifference
   d. curiosity

---

[2]*interludes:* times in between

2. The word *demise* in "the thought of the early demise of several thousand dollars' worth of equipment" (paragraph 6) means
   a. death
   b. loss
   c. start
   d. failure

3. Which of the following would be a good alternative title for this selection?
   a. Waiting Wastes Time
   b. Waiting Keeps Us Busy
   c. Waiting Can Be Worthwhile
   d. Wait for Success

4. Which sentence best expresses the main idea of the selection?
   a. I read somewhere that we spend a full third of our lives waiting.
   b. While people are waiting, their brains turn off.
   c. In the end it is obvious that we certainly do spend a good deal of our time waiting.
   d. Turning one's life into a waiting game of these proportions requires gobs of the aforementioned faith and hope, and is strictly for the optimists among us.

5. How many "classic waits" does Bodett write about? For how many does he give several examples?

6. *True or false?* The worst thing about waiting is the time involved.

7. Bodett believes the main difference between the "Watched-Pot Wait" and the "Forced Wait" is
   a. the time involved
   b. that it's easier to endure a Forced Wait
   c. almost none
   d. the choice involved

8. *True or false?* Bodett usually makes "Forced Wait" decisions based on logic.

9. The author implies that
   a. anticipating lucky breaks is a humane deed
   b. consistently relying on changes of fortune may lead to ignoring life-events
   c. waiting for lucky breaks is foolish
   d. relying on luck leads to pessimism

10. The author implies that
    a. waiting itself is an action and a choice
    b. people have no choice but to wait sometimes
    c. waiting is a major cause of inefficiency
    d. waiting wastes most of our lives

■ **Discussion Questions**

About Content

1. For how many forms of the "classic wait" does Bodett provide examples? How many examples are offered for each, and how effective are they? Why are they effective?

2. What are the physical and mental responses to the "Watched-Pot Wait"?

3. What, according to the author, are the challenges associated with the "Payday Wait"?

About Structure

4. Bodett's essay does not follow the strict one-three-one model of the five-paragraph essay usually written by students. Instead, its form is a looser one that includes an introduction, several topics for development, and a conclusion. How many topics does the author present? Indicate in the following outline the topics and how the paragraphs of Bodett's essay are broken up.

   Introduction: Paragraph(s):_____

   Topic # 1: _____ Paragraph(s):_____

   Topic # 2: _____ Paragraph(s):_____

   Topic # 3: _____ Paragraph(s):_____

   Topic # 4: _____ Paragraph(s):_____

   Conclusion: Paragraph(s):_____

5. What transitional phrase links the first sentence of paragraph 6 to the preceding three paragraphs?

6. What order does Bodett use for organizing the waits?
   a. from the most harmful to the least harmful
   b. from the shortest waits to the longest
   c. from the most difficult wait to the easiest one
   d. no particular order

7. Which method best describes the introduction to "Wait Divisions"?
   a. Quotation
   b. Idea that is the opposite of the one to be developed
   c. Anecdote
   d. Broad, general statement narrowing to thesis

About Style and Tone

8. In paragraph 2, Bodett introduces several possible effects of waiting, then dismisses them with a "probably not." Is it a sign of careless writing that the author mentions irrelevant topics only to dismiss them? Could he intend a particular tone or effect? If so, how would you describe his tone? How would such a tone suit the essay's topic and why?

9. A sentence fragment lurks in paragraph 9. What is it? Why would a professional writer like Bodett choose to break the rules in the case of this fragment? What is the effect of such a stylistic choice in terms of the general style of the essay and of the topic of the paragraph?

■ Writing Assignments

Assignment 1

Tom Bodett chose the all-too-common human experience of waiting to divide up and classify. Choose another ordinary situation or activity with which you have some experience and divide it into three classifications or categories, according to one principle. You might choose studying, for example. Classify it by styles of studying; then divide it into such groupings as "frantic, last-minute studying," "casual, unfocused studying," and so on. Be sure to write an introductory paragraph that sets out the background, range, and tone for your treatment of your subject and suggests your intention to divide and classify it.

Assignment 2

In the twenty-first century, technology moves life along more quickly than ever, but we still end up waiting for things. We communicate electronically, but we wait for slow servers to respond; we use cell phones and speed dialing, but we wait for people to answer . . . or wait for them to pick up our messages.

   Write an essay about some aspect of life or activity that technology has not changed or improved. Defend your views with specific examples and details that illustrate and clarify the point of your thesis.

Assignment 3

The "Lucky-Break Wait" is apparently a universal phenomenon; we all hope for some lucky break or lottery win, no matter how steep the odds against us. Write an essay that defines your ultimate "lucky break," and why it would mean so much to you. Refer to the tips in the chapter on "definition" essays (pages 241–253) for help.

HOW TO DO WELL ON A JOB INTERVIEW

Glenda Davis

Job interviews and how to handle them are major matters of interest to college students and the general public alike. Applying for positions is often a trying experience, no matter how well prepared the applicant may be. Glenda Davis, the author of this selection, offers practical tips and techniques, as well as some reassurances to readers.

Ask a random selection of people for a listing of their least favorite activities, and right up there with "getting my teeth drilled" is likely to be "going to a job interview." The job interview is often regarded as a confusing, humiliating, and nerve-racking experience. First of all, you have to wait for your appointment in an outer room, often trapped there with other people applying for the same job. You sit nervously, trying not to think about the fact that only one of you may be hired. Then you are called into the interviewer's office. Faced with a complete stranger, you have to try to act both cool and friendly as you are asked all sorts of questions. Some questions are personal: "What is your greatest weakness?" Others are confusing: "Why should we hire you?" The interview probably takes about twenty minutes but seems like two hours. Finally, you go home and wait for days and even weeks. If you get the job, great. But if you don't, you're rarely given any reason why. 1

The job-interview "game" may not be much fun, but it is a game you *can* win if you play it right. The name of the game is standing out of the crowd—in a positive way. If you go to the interview in a Bozo the Clown suit, you'll stand out of the crowd, all right, but not in a way that is likely to get you hired. 2

Here are guidelines to help you play the interview game to win: 3

Present yourself as a winner. Instantly, the way you dress, speak, and move gives the interviewer more information about you than you would think possible. You doubt that this is true? Consider this: a professional job recruiter, meeting a series of job applicants, was asked to signal the moment he decided *not* to hire each applicant. The thumbs-down decision was often made *in less than forty-five seconds—even before the applicant thought the interview had begun.* 4

How can you keep from becoming a victim of an instant "no" decision? 5

- *Dress appropriately.* This means business clothing: usually a suit and tie or a conservative dress or skirt suit. Don't wear casual student clothing. On the other hand, don't overdress: you're going to a job interview, not a party. If you're not sure what's considered appropriate business attire, do some spying before the interview. Walk past your prospective place of employment at lunch or quitting time and check out how the employees are dressed. Your goal is to look as though you would fit in with that group of people.
- *Pay attention to your grooming.* Untidy hair, body odor, dandruff, unshined shoes, a hanging hem, stains on your tie, excessive makeup or cologne, a sloppy

job of shaving—if the interviewer notices any of these, your prospect of being hired takes a probably fatal hit.

- *Look alert, poised, and friendly.* When that interviewer looks into the waiting room and calls your name, he or she is getting a first impression of your behavior. If you're slouched in your chair, dozing or lost in the pages of a magazine; if you look up with an annoyed "Huh?"; if you get up slowly and wander over with your hands in your pockets, he or she will not be favorably impressed. What *will* earn you points is rising promptly and walking briskly toward the interviewer. Smiling and looking directly at that person, extend your hand to shake his or hers, saying, "I'm Lesley Brown. Thank you for seeing me today."
- *Expect to make a little small talk.* This is not a waste of time; it is the interviewer's way of checking your ability to be politely sociable, and it is your opportunity to cement the good impression you've already made. The key is to follow the interviewer's lead. If he or she wants to chat about the weather for a few minutes, do so. But don't drag it out; as soon as you get a signal that it's time to talk about the job, be ready to get down to business.

Be ready for the interviewer's questions. The same questions come up again **6** and again in many job interviews. *You should plan ahead for all these questions!* Think carefully about each question, outline your answer, and memorize each outline. Then practice reciting the answers to yourself. Only in this way are you going to be prepared. Here are common questions, what they really mean, and how to answer them:

- *"Tell me about yourself."* This question is raised to see how organized you are. The *wrong* way to answer it is to launch into a wandering, disjointed response or—worse yet—to demand defensively, "What do you want to know?" or "What do you mean?" When this question comes up, you should be prepared to give a brief summary of your life and work experience—where you grew up, where your family lives now, where you went to school, what jobs you've had, and how you happen to be here now looking for the challenge of a new job.
- *"What are your strengths and weaknesses?"* In talking about your strong points, mention traits that will serve you well in this particular job. If you are well-organized, a creative problem-solver, a good team member, or a quick learner, be ready to describe specific ways those strengths have served you in the past. Don't make this mistake of saying, "I don't have any real weaknesses." You'll come across as more believable if you admit a flaw—but make it one that an employer might actually like. For instance, admit that you are a workaholic or a perfectionist.
- *"Why should we hire you?"* Remember that it is up to *you* to convince the interviewer that you're the man or woman for this job. If you just sit there and hope that the interviewer will magically discern your good qualities, you are likely to be disappointed. Don't be afraid to sell yourself. Tell the recruiter that from your research you have learned that the interviewer's company is one you would like to work for, and that you believe the company's needs and your skills are a great match.
- *"Why did you leave your last job?"* This may seem like a great opportunity to cry on the interviewer's shoulder about what a jerk your last boss was or how

unappreciated you were. It is not. The experts agree: never badmouth *anyone* when you are asked this question. Say that you left in order to seek greater responsibilities or challenges. Be positive, not negative. No matter how justified you may feel about hating your last job or boss, if you give voice to those feelings in an interview, you're going to make the interviewer suspect that you're a whiner and hard to work with.

• *"Do you have any questions?"* This is the time to stress one last time how interested you are in this particular job. Ask a question or two about specific aspects of the job, pointing out again how well your talents and the company's needs are matched. Even if you're dying to know how much the job pays and how much vacation you get, don't ask. There will be time enough to cover those questions after you've been offered the job. Today, your task is to demonstrate what a good employee you will be.

Send a thank-you note. Once you've gotten past the interview, there is one more   7
chance for you to make a fine impression. As soon as you can—certainly no more than one or two days after the interview—write a note of thanks to your interviewer. In it, briefly remind him or her when you came in and what you applied for. As well as thanking the interviewer for seeing you, reaffirm your interest in the job and mention again why you think you are the best candidate for it. Make the note courteous, businesslike, and brief—just a paragraph or two. It the interviewer is wavering between several equally qualified candidates, such a note could tip the scales in your favor.

No amount of preparation is going to make interviewing for a job your favorite   8
activity. But if you go in well prepared and with a positive attitude, your potential employer can't help thinking highly of you. And the day will come when you are the one who wins the job.

◼ Reading Comprehension Questions

1. The word *attire* in "If you're not sure what's considered appropriate business attire" (paragraph 5) means
   a. behaviour
   b. clothing
   c. grooming
   d. ethics

2. The word *discern* in "If you just sit there and hope that the interviewer will magically discern your good qualities" (paragraph 6) means
   a. appreciate
   b. enjoy
   c. decide on
   d. notice

3. Which of the following would be a good alternative title for this selection?
   a. Entering the Interview Market
   b. Handling Interview Questions
   c. Mastering the Art of Job Interviews
   d. Enjoying the Interview Game

4. Which sentence best expresses the main idea of this selection?
   a. The job-interview "game" may not be much fun, but it is a game you can win if you play it right.
   b. The job interview is often regarded as a confusing, humiliating, and nerve-racking experience.
   c. No amount of preparation is going to make interviewing for a job your favourite activity.
   d. Don't be afraid to sell yourself.

5. During a job interview, you may find it hard to act composed and warm because
   a. you are worried about the other applicants
   b. you are asked challenging questions
   c. you don't have enough time to talk
   d. you want the position so badly

6. *True or false?* Grooming details are not that crucial; your attitude is what counts with interviewers.

7. Davis stresses the value of self-presentation because
   a. interviewers meet so many applicants
   b. interviewers care only about how applicants dress
   c. first impressions are often decisive
   d. the job market today is based on superficial values

8. *True or false?* Davis suggests that presenting yourself as a winner means not admitting to weaknesses.

9. The author implies that
   a. interviewers will figure out how you'll fit into a position
   b. you should lie about your interest in the interviewer's company
   c. you should truly feel as if you are the best candidate
   d. research is a necessary adjunct to selling yourself

10. The author implies that
    a. preparation and the right attitude bring several rewards
    b. doing well in interviews puts people on the road to job success
    c. learning to tailor the truth is the way to succeed
    d. eventually you'll begin to enjoy interviews

Discussion Questions

About Content

1. What are the three sets of reasons that Davis gives to support the statement that job interviews are "confusing, humiliating, and nerve-racking"?

2. What are the supporting details for the list item "dress appropriately" in paragraph 5?

3. What is the author's *reason* for advising job applicants to send a thank-you letter?

About Structure

4. In paragraph 6, which statement would best serve as a topic sentence for the list item about strengths and weaknesses? Give reasons for your choice.
   a. A quality such as perfectionism or workaholism can be seen as both a strength and a weakness.
   b. As you talk about your strengths and weaknesses, tailor what you say to the job you're applying for.
   c. Claiming to be "a creative problem-solver" is a good idea as you apply for almost any position.
   d. The interviewer is not likely to be impressed if you claim to have no major weaknesses.

5. What is the main method of organization in paragraph 1? How is this method indicated?

6. What "change of direction" transitional signal phrase begins a sentence in the first list item in paragraph 5?

About Style and Tone

7. Davis uses bullets and headings to divide her paragraphs into sections. How is the first section of bulleted items introduced? How is the second introduced?
   Are there ordering methods or sequences to the bulleted items in each of the two sections? If so, what are they?

8. The author is writing a helpful article that gives friendly advice. Who is her main audience? How would you describe the tone of the article and its appropriateness to this audience? What level of vocabulary and what phrases does Davis use that support your opinion of her tone?

■ Writing Assignments

Assignment 1

Davis tells us how to succeed at a job interview. However, there are other situations where people could benefit from some guidelines—for instance, making a presentation in class, going out on a first date, borrowing something, or handling some problem at work. Choose one of these situations, or some other potentially annoying, difficult, or humorous situation, and write your own guide to managing it successfully. Give three general tips or rules, one for each body paragraph, and develop each paragraph with more specific aspects or "refinements" of each tip, as Davis has done. Conclude with a statement or prediction of the value of following your guidelines.

Assignment 2

What kind of position do you seek after you graduate from your program? Do some research about the specific types of jobs that will be available to you; do this by speaking to some of your instructors and by reading newspaper classified sections and online resources such as job-search sites and company sites. What are the requirements for the positions that interest you?

Now put yourself in the position of the interviewer wishing to hire someone for the job you find most appealing. Write an essay, using third-person point of view, that describes the ideal applicant for this position. Begin by giving some background on the company (feel free to invent a name for it), its aims, and why it is offering the position. Your body paragraphs could cover such things as the educational background desired, the experience needed, any special skills, and personal characteristics.

Assignment 3

What has happened to you at job interviews? Were some of them disasters and others simply forgettable? What did you learn from these experiences? Write an essay that compares or contrasts two different job interviews you have survived. Areas for comparison or contrast could include the interviewers, the physical environments, your feelings during the interviews, your degree of preparation, and the importance of the interview to you.

Observing Others

Garry Engkent

Adjustment to Canadian culture and to the English language is difficult and long for anyone new to this country. Becoming comfortable and productive within any culture is in many ways tied to the ability to use its dominant language. English is a difficult and complex tongue, incredibly rich in vocabulary and shades of meaning, but also incredibly confusing in its usage, grammar, and spelling, even to native English speakers. Engkent's mother suffered with a dilemma common among first-generation immigrants to Canada: the fear of losing one's original identity and past history along with one's original language. The author, who still speaks Cantonese, successfully accustomed himself to Canada to the extent of becoming a writer and a teacher of English language and literature at universities and colleges. Nonetheless, he felt his mother's frustration and misery most acutely while experiencing the annoyance and frustration of one aware of the demands, rules, and expectations of his new country.

1   My mother is seventy years old. Widowed for five years now, she lives alone in her own house except for the occasions when I come home to tidy her household affairs. She has been in *gum san*, the golden mountain, for the past thirty years. She clings to the old-country ways so much so that today she astonishes me with this announcement:

2   "I want to get my citizenship," she says as she slaps down the *Dai Pao*, "before they come and take away my house."

3   "Nobody's going to do that. This is Canada."

4   "So everyone says," she retorts, "but did you read what the *Dai Pao* said? Ah, you can't read Chinese. The government is cutting back on old-age pensions. Anybody who hasn't got citizenship will lose everything. Or worse."

5   "The *Dai Pao* can't even typeset accurately," I tell her. Sometimes I worry about the information Mother receives from the biweekly community newspaper. "Don't worry—the Ministry of Immigration won't send you back to China."

"Little you know," she snaps back. "I am old, helpless, and without citizenship. **6**
Reasons enough. Now, get me citizenship. Hurry!"

"Mother, getting citizenship papers is not like going to the bank to cash in your **7**
pension cheque. First, you have to—"

"Excuses, my son, excuses. When your father was alive—" **8**

"Oh, Mother, not again! You throw that at me every—" **9**

"—made excuses, too." Her jaw tightens. "If you can't do this little thing for **10**
your own mother, well, I will just have to go and beg your cousin to . . ."

Every time I try to explain about the ways of the *fan gwei*, she thinks I do not **11**
want to help her.

"I'll do it, I'll do it, okay? Just give me some time." **12**

"That's easy for you," Mother snorts. "You're not seventy years old. You're not **13**
going to lose your pension. You're not going to lose your house. Now, how much
lai-shi will this take?"

After all these years in *gum san* she cannot understand that you don't give **14**
government officials *lai-shi*, the traditional Chinese money gift to persons who do
things for you.

"That won't be necessary," I tell her. "And you needn't go to my cousin." **15**

Mother picks up the *Dai Pao* again and says, "Why should I beg at the door of **16**
a village cousin when I have a son who is a university graduate?"

I wish my father were alive. Then he would be doing this. But he is not here, **17**
and as a dutiful son, I am responsible for the welfare of my widowed mother. So I
take her to Citizenship Court.

There are several people from the Chinese community waiting there. Mother **18**
knows a few of the Chinese women and she chats with them. My cousin is there, too.

"I thought your mother already got her citizenship," he says to me. "Didn't **19**
your father—"

"No, he didn't." **20**

He shakes his head sadly. "Still, better now than never. That's why I'm getting **21**
these people through."

"So they've been reading the *Dai Pao*." **22**

He gives me a quizzical look, so I explain to him, and he laughs. **23**

"You are the new generation," he says. "You didn't live long enough in *hon san*, **24**
the sweet land, to understand the fears of the old. You can't expect the elderly to
renounce all attachments to China for the ways of the *fan gwei*. How old is she, seventy now? Much harder."

"She woke me up this morning at six, and Citizenship Court doesn't open **25**
until ten."

The doors of the court finally open, and Mother motions me to hurry. We wait **26**
in line for a while.

The clerk distributes applications and tells me the requirements. Mother wants **27**
to know what the clerk is saying, so half the time I translate for her.

The clerk suggests that we see one of the liaison officers. **28**

"Your mother has been living in Canada for the past thirty years and she still **29**
can't speak English?"

"It happens," I tell the liaison officer.   **30**

"I find it hard to believe that—not one word?"   **31**

"Well, she understands some restaurant English," I tell her. "You know, French   **32**
fries, pork chops, soup, and so on. And she can say a few words."

"But will she be able to understand the judge's questions? The interview with   **33**
the judge, as you know, is an important part of the citizenship procedure. Can she
read the booklet? What does she know about Canada?"

"So you don't think my mother has a chance?"   **34**

"The requirements are that the candidate must be able to speak either French   **35**
or English, the two official languages of Canada. The candidate must be able to pass
an oral interview with the citizenship judge, and then he or she must be able to
recite the oath of allegiance—"

"My mother needs to speak English," I conclude for her.   **36**

"Look, I don't mean to be rude, but why didn't your mother learn English   **37**
when she first came over?"

I have not been translating this conversation, and Mother, annoyed and agi-   **38**
tated, asks me what is going on. I tell her there is a slight problem.

"What problem?" Mother opens her purse, and I see her taking a small red   **39**
envelope—*lai-shi*—I quickly cover her hand.

"What's going on?" the liaison officer demands.   **40**

"Nothing," I say hurriedly. "Just a cultural misunderstanding, I assure you."   **41**

My mother rattles off some indignant words, and I snap back in Chinese, "Put   **42**
that away! The woman won't understand, and we'll be in a lot of trouble."

The officer looks confused, and I realize that an explanation is needed.   **43**

"My mother was about to give you a money gift as a token of appreciation for   **44**
what you are doing for us. I was afraid you might misconstrue it as a bribe. We have
no intention of doing that."

"I'm relieved to hear it."   **45**

We conclude the interview, and I take Mother home. Still clutching the appli-   **46**
cation, Mother scowls at me.

"I didn't get my citizenship papers. Now I will lose my old-age pension. The   **47**
government will ship me back to China. My old bones will lie there while your
father's will be here. What will happen to me?"

How can I teach her to speak the language when she is too old to learn, too old   **48**
to want to learn? She resists anything that is *fan gwei*. She does everything the
Chinese way. Mother spends much time staring blankly at the four walls of her
house. She does not cry. She sighs and shakes her head. Sometimes she goes about
the house touching her favourite things.

"This is all your dead father's fault," she says quietly. She turns to the photo-   **49**
graph of my father on the mantel. Daily, she burns incense, pours fresh cups of
fragrant tea, and spreads dishes of his favourite fruits in front of the framed picture as is the custom. In memory of his passing, she treks two miles to the cemetery to place flowers by his headstone, to burn ceremonial paper money, and to
talk to him. Regularly, rain or shine, or even snow, she does these things. Such
love, such devotion, now such vehemence. Mother curses my father, her husband,
in his grave.

When my mother and I emigrated from China, she was forty years old, and I, **50** five. My father was already a well-established restaurant owner. He put me in school and Mother in the restaurant kitchen, washing dishes and cooking strange foods like hot dogs, hamburgers, and French fries. She worked seven days a week from six in the morning until eleven at night. This lasted for twenty-five years, almost to the day of my father's death.

The years were hard on her. The black-and-white photographs show a robust **51** woman; now I see a withered, frail, white-haired old woman, angry, frustrated with the years, and scared of losing what little material wealth she has to show for the toil in *gum san.*

"I begged him," Mother says. "But he would either ignore my pleas or say, 'What **52** do you need to know English for? You're better off here in the kitchen. Here you can talk to the others in our own tongue. English is far too complicated for you. How old are you now? Too old to learn a new language. Let the young speak *fan gwei.* All you need is to understand the orders from the waitresses. Anyway, if you need to know something, the men will translate for you. I am here; I can do your talking for you.'"

As a conscientious boss of the young male immigrants, my father would force **53** them out of the kitchen and into the dining room. "The kitchen is no place for you to learn English. All you do is speak Chinese in here. To survive in *gum san,* you have to speak English, and the only way you can do that is to wait on tables and force yourselves to speak English with the customers. How can you get your families over here if you can't talk to the immigration officers in English?"

A few of the husbands who had the good fortune to bring their wives over to **54** Canada hired a retired school teacher to teach a bit of English to their wives. Father discouraged Mother from going to those once-a-week sessions.

"That old woman will get rich doing nothing. What have these women learned? **55** *Fan gwei* ways—make-up, lipstick, smelly perfumes, fancy clothes. Once she gets through with them, they won't be Chinese women any more—and they certainly won't be white either."

Some of the husbands heeded the words of the boss, for he was older than they, **56** and he had been in the *fan gwei's* land longer. These wives stayed home and tended the children, or they worked in the restaurant kitchen, washing dishes and cooking *fan gwei* foods, and talking in Chinese about the land and the life they had been forced to leave behind.

"He was afraid that I would leave him. I depended on him for everything. I could **57** not go anywhere by myself. He drove me to work and he drove me home. He only taught me how to print my name so that I could sign anything he wanted me to, bank cheques, legal documents . . ."

Perhaps I am not Chinese enough any more to understand why my mother **58** would want to take in the sorrow, the pain, and the anguish, and then to recount them every so often.

Once, I was presumptuous enough to ask her why she would want to **59** remember in such detail. She said that the memories didn't hurt any more. I did not tell her that her reminiscences cut me to the quick. Her only solace now is to be listened to.

When my father died five years ago, she cried and cried. "Don't leave me in this **60** world. Let me die with you."

Grief-stricken, she would not eat for days. She was so weak from hunger **61** that I feared she wouldn't be able to attend the funeral. At his graveside, she chanted over and over a dirge, commending his spirit to the next world and begging the goddess of mercy to be kind to him. By custom, she set his picture on the mantel and burned incense in front of it daily. And we would go to the cemetery often. There she would arrange fresh flowers and talk to him in the gentlest way.

Often she would warn me: "The world of the golden mountain is so strong, *fan* **62** *gwei* improprieties, and customs. They will have you abandon your own aged mother to some old-age home to rot away and die unmourned. If you are here long enough, they will turn your head until you don't know who you are—Chinese."

My mother would convert the months and the days into the Chinese lunar cal- **63** endar. She would tell me about the seasons and the harvests and festivals in China. We did not celebrate any *fan gwei* holidays.

My mother sits here at the table, fingering the booklet from the Citizenship **64** Court. For thirty-some years, my mother did not learn the English language, not because she was not smart enough, not because she was too old to learn, and not because my father forbade her, but because she feared that learning English would change her Chinese soul. She only learned enough English to survive in the restaurant kitchen.

Now, Mother wants *gum san* citizenship. **65**

"Is there no hope that I will be given it?" she asks. **66**

"There's always a chance," I tell her. "I'll hand in the application." **67**

"I should have given that person the *lai-shi*," Mother says obstinately. **68**

"Maybe I should teach you some English," I retort. "You have about six months **69** before the oral interview."

"I am seventy years old," she says. "*Lai-shi* is definitely much easier." **70**

My brief glimpse into Mother's heart is over, and it has taken so long to come **71** about. I do not know whether I understand my aged mother any better now. Despite my mother's constant instruction, there is too much *fan gwei* in me.

The booklet from the Citizenship Court lies, unmoved, on the table, gathering **72** dust for weeks. She has not mentioned citizenship again with the urgency of that particular time. Once in a while, she would say, "They have forgotten me. I told you they don't want old Chinese women as citizens."

Finally, her interview date is set. I try to teach her some ready-made phrases, **73** but she forgets them.

"You should not sigh so much. It is bad for your health," Mother observes. **74**

On the day of her examination, I accompany her into the judge's chamber. **75** I am more nervous than my mother.

Staring at the judge, my mother remarks, "*Noi yren.*" The judge shows interest **76** in what my mother says, and I translate it: "She says you're a woman."

The judge smiles, "Yes. Is that strange?" **77**

"If she is going to examine me," Mother tells me, "I might as well start packing for **78** China. Sell my house. Dig up your father's bones, and I'll take them back with me."

Without knowing what my mother said, the judge reassures her. "This is just a **79**
formality. Really. We know that you obviously want to be part of our Canadian
society. Why else would you go through all this trouble? We want to welcome you
as a new citizen, no matter what race, nationality, religion, or age. And we want you
to be proud—as a new Canadian."

Six weeks have passed since the interview with the judge. Mother receives a **80**
registered letter telling her to come in three weeks' time to take part in the oath of
allegiance ceremony.

With patient help from the same judge, my mother recites the oath and **81**
becomes a Canadian citizen after thirty years in *gum san*.

"How does it feel to be a Canadian?" I ask. **82**

"In China, this is the eighth month, the season of harvest." Then she adds, "The **83**
Dai Pao says that the old-age pension cheques will be increased by nine dollars
next month."

As we walk home on this bright autumn morning, my mother clutches her **84**
piece of paper. Citizenship. She says she will go up to the cemetery and talk to my
father this afternoon. She has something to tell him.

■ Reading Comprehension Questions

1. The word *quizzical* in "He gives me a quizzical look, so I explain to him, and
   he laughs" (paragraph 23) means
   a. ridiculous
   b. questioning
   c. angry
   d. confused

2. The word *dirge* in "At his graveside, she chanted over and over a dirge"
   (paragraph 61) means
   a. prayer
   b. name
   c. sad song
   d. request

3. Which of the following would be a good alternative title for this selection?
   a. Mother and the Judge
   b. A Woman's Struggle
   c. The Red Envelope
   d. A Long Life and a New Language

4. Which sentence best expresses the main idea of the selection?
   a. Immigrants find it easier to stick to the patterns and languages of their
      native countries.
   b. Engkent's mother can't speak English because of her late husband's attitude
      toward his fellow immigrants' learning the language.
   c. Engkent's mother learned only a few words of English to avoid losing
      her pension.
   d. Engkent's mother's greatest problem in learning English was her fear of
      losing her Chinese identity.

5. The author's explanations of Canadian ways are taken by his mother as
    a. excuses for his own unwillingness to do as she wishes
    b. evidence that he doesn't want to help her
    c. evidence of his feeling of superiority as a university graduate
    d. ignorance of the information printed in the *Dai Pao*

6. *True or false?* Engkent's mother's greatest fear at her first citizenship interview is that she will be sent back to China.

7. The author's father did not teach his wife English because
    a. he wished her to remain dependent on him so that she would not leave him
    b. he felt she was not intelligent enough to learn such a complex language
    c. he wanted her to maintain her Chinese heritage
    d. he did not want her to become more successful than he was

8. The author's cousin, whom he meets at the Citizenship Court,
    a. is kinder to the author's mother than is the author
    b. has more importance in the Chinese community than the author does
    c. offers an insight into the dilemma faced by the author's mother
    d. feels superior because of living longer in China than the author

9. The author implies that
    a. his mother's feelings for her husband are based mainly on Chinese traditions
    b. his mother's feelings for her husband remain intense and strongly mixed
    c. his mother remembers only the best about her deceased husband
    d. his mother despises the memory of his late father

10. The author implies that
    a. his mother is intimidated by the citizenship hearing
    b. his mother is unaware of the importance of becoming a Canadian citizen
    c. his mother has already decided her own fate
    d. his mother has a down-to-earth view of citizenship, but also realizes its import

■ Discussion Questions

About Content

1. Why does Engkent's mother so suddenly decide she must become a Canadian citizen? What are the problems with her ideas about obtaining citizenship?

2. What three qualifications are required to obtain Canadian citizenship, according to the liaison officer at the Citizenship Court? How many of these are actually relevant or necessary when Engkent's mother finally sees the citizenship judge? Why does the judge alter the requirements?

3. What is the difference between the author's mother's feelings about recalling the details of her life with her husband and the author's own feelings about hearing her recollections? Why are their feelings different?

About Structure

4. In which paragraphs in the essay do you find three of the main *causes* for Engkent's mother's inability to speak English after thirty years in Canada? What is the final *effect* that comes out at the end of the essay?

5. Where in the essay do you find the author's thesis statement, the answer to the question posed by the title? What relationship exists between the facts of the thesis and the concluding statements of the essay?

6. Why has the author chosen to use so many brief paragraphs, rather than longer sections of indirect reporting of the actions and ideas of the essay? What effect do all these short sections have on your sense of his feelings about his subject?

About Style and Tone

7. There are many Chinese phrases in this essay. Are their meanings clearly explained? List three such phrases and their meanings. How does their inclusion affect your sense of the people and situations involved?

8. "Why My Mother Can't Speak English" is written mainly in the present tense and is mainly told through dialogue. How do these two stylistic choices by the author make the narrative more or less lively? How do they bring you closer to the characters and their problems?

■ Writing Assignments

Assignment 1

Many of us have relatives who have emigrated to Canada from another country. For each person, there are different adjustments to be made, different cultural problems to be faced. But some dilemmas, some problems, have common elements for all who arrive in a new country.

Write an essay that is a descriptive character sketch about either you or a relative facing some learning experience in a new country or location. Ideally, your essay should tell a story involving adjustment to, and/or resistance to, new circumstances in a new environment. What were the *causes* of the problems experienced? What were the *effects* of the effort to try to resolve the problems? How did you or your relative change as a result of the challenge? Try to isolate and clearly define the nature and personal ramifications of the problem. When you are making your essay outline, list what you see as the major causes of this problem and the results of trying to overcome aspects of this difficulty.

Assignment 2

Canada is a nation that has called itself a "mosaic," where those from other countries are encouraged, and often funded, to maintain their native languages and cultures. Communities across the country celebrate various multicultural holidays and festivals. Many cities have TV, radio, and printed material available in a number of languages. Does this recognition of diversity always result in a country with a distinct and unique personality or unified identity? Are we enriched by having many sides to our national character, or are we merely confused? Do newcomers maintain isolated groupings within our country, or do we have a genuinely exciting and diverse character as a country?

State and defend one side or another of this issue with clear examples drawn either from your personal experience or from outside reading.

Assignment 3

At some time in our lives, most of us have struggled with someone else's stubbornness, as Engkent did with his mother's. We are frustrated by such a struggle, but we learn from it. Write a narrative essay about your own experience. As you explain what you felt and learned, use vivid details and dialogue to bring your essay to life.

HE WAS A BOXER WHEN I WAS SMALL

Lenore Keeshig-Tobias

Lenore Keeshig-Tobias is an Ojibway writer and filmmaker. In the essay that follows, she remembers her childhood and her father. She remembers not merely a one-time boxer, but a father, who emerges as a complex, troubled, and even spiritual man, perhaps as mythic in stature as the Ojibway trickster, Nanabush. The author's memories unfold a series of vivid scenes of two characters tied by blood and by fighting spirit. As Keeshig-Tobias remembers, she discovers two fighters—her father and his eldest daughter.

His thundering rages are most vivid, his tears subtle. Watching and feeling for them, but unable to bridge the gap, I learned to love, hate him all in the same breath. No one ever knew this. They saw a kid in love with her father.   1

He was a boxer when I was small. People say he was good and would have made it had he started younger, but he had a wife and growing family to provide for. Amateur boxing paid nothing, but he loved it. I think he must have been about twenty-two then. He claims that we were too young to have seen him fight, but I remember.   2

I remember the lights, the ring, my mother shouting "Kill him, Don, kill him!" and my sister eating popcorn. I remember how he'd shadow box at home, punching, dancing lightly, swinging left—left—right, and missing because there was nothing there except air.   3

His prowess in the ring must have cowed my mother during his drunken rages. Or maybe it was his thundering voice, or the way the furniture went flying. Yet, with all his storming and her crying, I couldn't help but think that there was something more,   4 something he couldn't articulate. When his ferocity gave way to tears of exasperation, I would cry with him, my dad, the boxer, the young man out to beat the world.

"It's not his fault," I would argue, "It's not all his fault, it's Mom's fault too," I would tell Gramma, even if I didn't know whose fault it was. She would disdainfully look off into the tree whenever I answered with this. Mom had Gramma to stick up for her. Dad had no one, only me.   5

There were, of course, times when things were fine. Dad would have a good job, Mom would be fresh with child, and my sisters and brothers carefree. We would spread a blanket in the front yard, or gather around the kitchen table. Dad would tell stories of Nanabush, stories of long ago when only the Indians and animals lived here. Good ole Nanabush danced before our eyes. We saw his courage, his generosity and love for the animals and our people. We also saw his anger, miserly ways, and blundering practical jokes, but we loved him and would laugh until we cried.   6

At other times we would play, all of us, seven, eight, nine of us rolling and tumbling while Mom sat back beaming like a big fat sun. We'd pretend box, then race, roll, and tumble again. How I wished those times would go on and on. He would stand shoulders up to the sky, as we climbed. He could carry all of us on his back.   7

One summer my sides ached with laughter. Then one day, I moved to the edge of the blanket and sat back to watch my sisters and brothers giggle and climb. Dad leaned forward, then down on hands and knees, all those laughing children on his back. That was when I noticed grey hairs hiding in his side-burns. I went to my room, dug out his boxing pictures, and cried.   8

I was about ten at the time, my dad about twenty-nine, and my mother twenty-eight. After that summer I never again played like that with the others. I felt too old, and instead I stood back and watched. I watched my sisters and brothers grow up. I watched him grow older, fighting all the way.   9

When he went to school, he tells us, he spoke only Ojibway and a bit of French. His grandmother was French. The only English he knew was yes and no. Indian kids, in those days, were not allowed to speak anything but English in school. So besides being punished for speaking Ojibway, he was also punished for giving the wrong answer which was either yes or no.   10

He says he eventually learned to read, write, and do arithmetic, and he laughs when he tells us how he would get on the teacher's good side and then steal test answers for the rest of the class. She never had to keep any of them in after class, but then she never realized how they had cheated and helped each other. She never realized what a bunch of stupid kids she graduated.   11

My Dad never graduated. He learned enough to be able to go out and get a job.   12

Once, Dad was working in Toronto as an industrial painter (Indian men are noted for their surefootedness in high places). Mom, the kids, and I sat around the supper table. We didn't expect him home until the weekend, but there he was, standing in the doorway with his suitcase. Later that evening, I heard him confiding to Mom his reason for coming home.   13

He had beat up a fellow worker, a wisecracking whiteman, who had been bugging him for weeks. The ambulance was being called for when he left. My dad was afraid, afraid because he was Indian and because he had once been a boxer.   14

In between the various jobs on the reserve or high-painting and ironwork off **15** in some big city, there were bouts of drinking and bouts of fanatical Christianity with thunderous preaching. We cowered every weekend waiting for him to erupt.

"Damn you, goddamn you," I would curse under my breath. "Why do you **16** make our lives so miserable?"

We grew up as Christians, something I shall never forgive those Catholic mis- **17** sionaries for, although for a time it was the most settling thing in our lives. Dad made sure, in spite of everything else, his kids went to church. If he couldn't be a good father to us, then God would. But God wasn't an Indian, or a boxer, and my Dad was. His visits to the parish priest taught him fear of the Lord. But we went faithfully to church because of fear of our Dad, and fear for our furniture.

We should all be good at sports because Indians are known for that. Look at **18** Jim Thorpe, Tom Longboat, George Armstrong. We should all get a good education and not be stupid like him. We should all go to church every Sunday and not drink like him . . . he'd preach.

I got fed up with things, eventually. I was no good at sports. School was bor- **19** ing. I stopped going to church and even dared to argue with my Dad. Finally, Mom and Dad had the priest come talk to me, to get me to go back to church and school.

The old man would listen when I told him that I would like to pray under the **20** trees. He laughed. We argued. He laughed again, shook his head, and said something about excommunication. I told him off, that I would rather go to hell and burn with the rest of my heathen savage ancestors because there would be too few Indians in heaven and I'd probably get lonely. The old missionary wobbled into the house, quite shaken, and told my dad that I was "lost." Dad came out, white-faced, and beat me. He told me to leave, that he had other kids to worry about.

I settled into my own life, fighting bouts of my own, but continued hearing of **21** his through letters and phone calls.

Was there no end? Mom and the kids kept looking to me for answers, as if I **22** were the referee. I'd listen, but offer no solution. I was beginning to see what was driving him. I was beginning to understand that he was fighting the world, and there was no way I'd turn on him behind his back.

Afraid at first, I began to meet him blow for blow. People would say that I was **23** like my dad. I thought I was like myself. I never did learn to box. He always laughed at the way I clenched my fists. I never was really interested in boxing. Being the eldest daughter of a boxer was enough, quite enough. But I can, however, thunder as loud as he can.

He's mellowed somewhat. And there have been times in quiet talk when he has **24** acknowledged his weaknesses, his aspirations and exasperations for all of us in our effort to grow up and become educated. I guess these talks are what comes with being the oldest of ten.

Thundering rages, subtle tears . . . I have seen him cry with frustration, cry out **25** in anger, and in pride, pride in his beautiful young looking wife and her accomplishments, his kids and grandchildren. Yet, the tears that touch me the most are those that roll down his cheeks when he talks of Nanabush.

Good ole Nanabush, the paradox, the son of a mortal woman and the thun- **26** dering West Wind, a boy raised by his grandmother, the best loved of all Ojibway spirits. It was through his transgressions as well as his virtue that Nanabush taught his people. And they never negated or attempted to cover up his imperfections. Dad cries when he talks of Nanabush.

I dreamed of Dad. This was after he had argued and I told him why I would never **27** go to church and how I could not understand why he still went. After all, the church, like the government, had set out to break the Indian, to make him feel less than what he was. I did not hold back that time and told him everything I had ever felt or thought about concerning our people. He couldn't answer and politely admitted, "You've got me. But I can't argue with you now, I'll answer you when I'm not drinking."

This was the first time I had won an argument against him, and it didn't dawn **28** on me until days later. We had talked, sipping our beer and not shouting. Arguments in our house were usually won by whomever could shout the loudest.

In my dreams I was fighting. Someone or something evil, disguised, was pushing **29** me the wrong way, trying to make me do something I did not want to do. Thinking to expose this by disrobing it, I reached out and tugged. It turned to fend me off and guard its robe fiercely. We struggled until I stood alone with a bundle of clothes and flesh in my arms, and dread realization that I had killed another human being. Overwhelmed with guilt, I started to cry. Who would believe this act was unintentional? Then I saw him off in the distance, standing alone, his boxer's dressing-gown over his shoulders.

I could tell him. I could tell him everything. But would he listen? Understand? **30** Lowering my burden, covering and folding it carefully I cowered toward him. His head was down, his shoulders slouched. He didn't see me until I spoke.

"Dad," I sobbed, "I killed someone who was pushing me the wrong way. I didn't **31** mean to do it, Dad, help me."

He put his arms around me, tightly. **32**

"I'll beat the world," he said and punched at the air. **33**

■ **Reading Comprehension Questions**

1. The word *prowess* in "His prowess in the ring" (paragraph 4) means
   a. size
   b. skill
   c. endurance
   d. power

2. The word *excommunication* in "shook his head, and said something about excommunication" (paragraph 20) means
   a. explanation
   b. exhaustion
   c. expulsion
   d. exhilaration

3. Which of the following would be a good alternative title for this selection?
   a. My Father, My Enemy
   b. Violent Memories
   c. An Aboriginal Legend
   d. Two Fighters

4. Which sentence best expresses the main idea of the selection?
    a. Lenore felt that her childhood was damaged by her father's rage.
    b. Keeshig-Tobias' father wanted the children to be athletes and Christians.
    c. Time showed the author the similarities between her and her father.
    d. Don felt like a failure as a boxer, and this feeling affected his family.

5. Keeshig-Tobias' father frightened her mother because
    a. he was a violent and brutal boxer
    b. he shouted loudly and threw furniture
    c. he burst out weeping during his rages
    d. she knew she was to blame

6. The author's father was punished in school
    a. because he spoke Ojibway, and knew only two English words
    b. as a result of his cheating and theft
    c. because he started fights with other students
    d. because he never learned the basic subject matter

7. *True or false?* After leaving home, Keeshig-Tobias no longer had a role to play in her family's disagreements.

8. The author implies that
    a. her mother was as much to blame as her father for their arguments
    b. only the times "when things were fine" helped her to endure her father
    c. her father's frustration touched a similar chord in her
    d. her mother detested her father's boxing days

9. The author implies that
    a. Native myths like ones about Nanabush were at odds with Christian teaching
    b. stories of Nanabush were simply parts of good childhood memories
    c. like those of Nanabush, her father's flaws outweighed his virtues
    d. both Nanabush and her father were loved for their errors as well as for their strengths

10. Keeshig-Tobias' dream suggests that
    a. she still thought of her father as the "something evil" in her life
    b. she and her father share guilt and other aspects of each other's character
    c. she sees her father as a lonely failure
    d. she hated herself for winning the argument with him

■ Discussion Questions

About Content

1. Why does Keeshig-Tobias defend her father and claim, during family arguments, "It's not his fault" (paragraph 5)?

2. What pieces of her father's past does the author learn, and how do his experiences contribute to what he has become?

3. Where in Keeshig-Tobias' essay do we see the author finally defeat her father? How does each person react to her victory?

About Structure

4. What phrases in paragraphs 2, 9, and 21 indicate that Keeshig-Tobias' essay is divided into three sections? How would you describe these three sections of her narrative?

5. The author includes two anecdotes about the Ojibway character Nanabush: one in paragraph 6 and another in paragraph 26. What aspects of Nanabush relate to aspects of the character of the author's father?

About Style and Tone

6. What phrase in the opening sentence of "He Was a Boxer When I Was Small" does the author repeat late in the essay? How does this repetition create coherence or continuity in the essay? What further ideas do you connect with this phrase in its second use?

7. Keeshig-Tobias includes snippets of dialogue in paragraphs 3 and 5, as well as in closing paragraphs 27, 31, and 33. What do these pieces of reported conversation say about the characters and their situations in the two sections of the essay?

■ Writing Assignments

Assignment 1

Most people have experienced conflicting emotions about someone, and most know, or have known, someone whose behaviour was often contradictory or paradoxical. Our reactions to such a person might ultimately be positive or negative, but our feelings, in the end, are the sum of dealing with and learning from both "sides" of this individual.

Write an essay that contrasts two aspects of a parent or of some influential person in your life. Your thesis will state your ultimate feelings about this person, as does Keeshig-Tobias' opening, and should offer supporting points related to the contradictions in his or her behaviour.

Assignment 2

As a Canadian member of the Ojibway tribe, Keeshig-Tobias finds her memories coloured by achievements, limitations, and themes related to Native Canadian culture. Each of us has experiences that are at once common to all humanity and shaped by the culture(s) of which we are a part. As Canadians, we form part of a diverse country with many common aims and feelings whose origins may lie in widely differing experiences.

Using the format of a letter, write a narrative in which you explain to a friend who is *not* of the same cultural background three or more aspects of you that are clearly shaped by habits, beliefs, and cultural patterns of your own background. As Keeshig-Tobias does, try to include vivid pictures of events, characters, and scenarios that you recall. Each experience, conversation, or recollection should clearly lead to, or be a result of, the aspect of your current self you wish to explain.

Assignment 3

Does some activity help to define you? Perhaps a hobby, an interest, or a sport? Boxing is clearly linked to Lenore Keeshig-Tobias' perceptions of her father. What might your chosen activity or interest say about you? How does it tie in to your strengths, needs, and enjoyment of your chosen activity or interest? Why is it so much a part of you as a unique individual?

Write an article for a magazine dedicated to your area of interest or activity. This article is a "Portrait of a _____." Base your article on the "definition" method of development in Chapter 14 of Part 2 of this text. In your thesis statement in the opening paragraph, define your own view of someone who pursues your interest or activity, then explain three or more aspects of your definition and how your abilities and inclinations lead you to fit into these categories. Your conclusion may suggest possible futures for someone with your interests, based on aptitudes involved in mastering and participating in your area of interest.

FIVE PARENTING STYLES

Mary Ann Lamanna and Agnes Reidmann

Parenting has been called "the biggest on-the-job training program ever." Parents have to raise children without much guidance or advance instruction, and sometimes this situation results in a "parenting style" that causes problems. In the following textbook selection, the authors discuss five parenting styles. See if you can identify your parents—or yourself—in one of the classifications.

Considering the lack of consensus about how to raise children today, it may seem   1
difficult to single out styles of parenting. From one point of view there are as many parenting styles as there are parents. . . . Yet certain elements in relating to children can be broadly classified. One helpful grouping is provided in E. E. LeMasters' listing of five parenting styles: the martyr, the pal, the police officer, the teacher-counselor, and the athletic coach. . . . We will discuss each of these.

The Parent as Martyr. Martyring parents believe "I would do anything for my   2
child." . . . Some common examples of martyring are parents who habitually wait on their children or pick up after them; parents who nag children rather than letting them remember things for themselves; parents who buy virtually anything the child asks for; and parents who always do what the children want to do.

This parenting style presents some problems. First, the goals the martyring parent **3**
sets are impossible to carry out, and so the parent must always feel guilty. Also, . . .
martyring tends to be reciprocated by manipulating. In addition, it is useful to ask
if persons who consistently deny their own needs can enjoy the role of parenting and
if closeness between parent and child is possible under these conditions.

The Parent as Pal. Some modern parents, mainly those of older children and **4**
adolescents, feel that they should be pals to their children. They adopt a **laissez-
faire** policy, *letting their children set their own goals, rules, and limits*, with little or
no guidance from parents. . . . According to LeMasters, "pal" parents apparently
believe that they can avoid the conflict caused by the generation gap in this way.

Pal parenting is unrealistic. For one thing, parents in our society *are* responsi- **5**
ble for guiding their children's development. Children deserve to benefit from the
greater knowledge and experience of their parents, and at all ages they need some
rules and limits, although these change as children grow older. Much research
points to the conclusion that laissez-faire parenting is related to juvenile delinquency, heavy drug use, and runaway behavior in children. . . .

LeMasters points out that there are also relationship risks in the pal-parent **6**
model. If things don't go well, parents may want to retreat to a more formal, author-
itarian style of parenting. But once they've established a buddy relationship, it is
difficult to regain authority. . . .

The Parent as Police Officer. The police officer (or drill sergeant) model is just **7**
the opposite of the pal. These parents make sure the child obeys all the rules at
all times, and they punish their children for even minor offenses. Being a police
officer doesn't work very well today, however, and **autocratic discipline**, *which
places the entire power of determining rules and limits in the parents' hands*—like
laissez-faire parenting—has been associated with juvenile delinquency, drug use,
and runaway teenagers. . . .

There are several reasons for this. First, Americans have tended to resist any- **8**
thing that smacks of tyranny ever since the days of the Boston Tea Party. Hence,
children are socialized to demand a share of independence at an early age.

A second reason why policing children doesn't work well today is that rapid **9**
social change gives the old and the young different values and points of view and even
different knowledge. In our complex culture, youth learn attitudes from specialized
professionals, such as teachers and school counselors, who often "widen the intellectual gap between parent and child." . . . For example, many young people today may
advocate Judy Blume's novel for teens, *Forever* (1975), which is explicit about and
accepting of premarital sex. Many parents, however, disapprove of the book.

A third reason why the police officer role doesn't work is that children, who find **10**
support from their adolescent peers, will eventually confront and challenge their
parents. LeMasters points out that the adolescent peer group is "a formidable opponent" to any cop who insists on strict allegiance to autocratic authority. . . .

A fourth reason is that autocratic policing just isn't very effective in molding **11**
children's values. One study of 451 college freshmen and sophomores at a large
western university found that adolescents were far more likely to be influenced by
their parents' referent or expert power . . . than by coercive or legitimate power. The

key was respect and a close relationship; habitual punishment or the "policing" of adolescents were far less effective modes of socialization. . . .

The Parent as Teacher-Counselor. The parent as teacher-counselor acts in **12** accord with the **developmental model of child rearing,** *in which the child is viewed as an extremely plastic organism with virtually unlimited potential for growth and development.* The limits to this rich potential are seen as encompassed in the limits of the parent to tap and encourage it. . . . This model conceptualizes the parent(s) as almost omnipotent in guiding children's development. . . . If they do the right things at the right time, their children will more than likely be happy, intelligent, and successful.

Particularly during the 1960s and 1970s, authorities have stressed the ability of **13** parents to influence their children's intellectual growth. Psychologist J. McVicker Hunt, for example, stated that he believes "you could raise a middle-class child's I.Q. by twenty points with what we know about child-rearing." . . .

The teacher-counselor approach has many fine features, and children do benefit **14** from environmental stimulation. Yet this parenting style also poses problems. First, it puts the needs of the child above the parents' needs. It may be unrealistic for most parents to always be there, ready to stimulate the child's intellect or to act as a sounding board. Also, parents who respond as if each of their child's discoveries is wonderful may give the child the mistaken impression that he or she is the center of everyone's universe. . . .

A second difficulty is that this approach expects parents to be experts—an **15** expectation that can easily produce guilt. Parents can never learn all that psychologists, sociologists, and specialized educators know. Yet if anything goes wrong, teacher-counselor parents are likely to feel they have only themselves to blame. . . .

Finally, contemporary research suggests more and more that this view greatly **16** exaggerates the power of the parent and the passivity of children. Children also have inherited intellectual capacities and needs. Recent observers point instead to an **interactive perspective**, *which regards the influence between parent and child as mutual and reciprocal,* not just a "one-way street." . . .

The "athletic coach" model proceeds from this perspective. **17**

The Parent as Athletic Coach. Athletic-coach parenting incorporates aspects **18** of the developmental point of view. The coach (parent) is expected to have sufficient ability and knowledge of the game (life) and to be prepared and confident to lead players (children) to do their best and, it is hoped, to succeed.

This parenting style recognizes that parents, like coaches, have their own per- **19** sonalities and needs. They establish team rules, or *house rules* (and this can be done somewhat democratically with help from the players), and teach these rules to their children. They enforce the appropriate penalties when rules are broken, but policing is not their primary concern. Children, like team members, must be willing to accept discipline and, at least sometimes, to subordinate their own interests to the needs of the family team.

Coaching parents encourage their children to practice and to work hard to **20** develop their own talents. But they realize that they cannot play the game for their players. LeMasters says:

The coach's position here is quite analogous to that of parents; once the game has begun it is up to the players to win or lose it. . . . [He] faces the same prospect as parents of sitting on the sidelines and watching players make mistakes that may prove disastrous.

LeMasters also points out that coaches can put uncooperative players off the **21** team or even quit, but no such option is available to parents.

■ **Reading Comprehension Questions**

1. The word *plastic* in "an extremely plastic organism" (paragraph 12) means
   a. sickly
   b. stiff
   c. transparent
   d. pliable

2. The word *autocratic* in "autocratic discipline, which places the entire power . . . in the parents' hands" (paragraph 7) means
   a. unfocused
   b. independent
   c. dictatorial
   d. generous

3. Which of the following would be a good alternative title for this selection?
   a. Mistakes Parents Make
   b. How to Be a Good Parent
   c. Kinds of Parents
   d. Parents as Coaches

4. Which sentence best expresses the main idea of the selection?
   a. There are as many parenting styles as there are parents.
   b. Styles of parenting can be broadly classified into five groups.
   c. The "police officer" parenting approach can lead to delinquency.
   d. The influence between parent and child must be mutual.

5. Martyr parents
   a. act as buddies to their children
   b. buy anything the child asks for
   c. insist on strict obedience
   d. establish house rules

6. *True or false?* The athletic-coach approach regards the parent–child relationship as a one-way street.

7. Teacher-counsellor parents
   a. often blame themselves if something goes wrong
   b. use autocratic discipline
   c. adopt a laissez-faire policy
   d. let their children set their own limits

8. The authors imply that
   a. the teacher-counsellor style of parenting is most effective
   b. the athletic-coach style of parenting is most effective
   c. "pal" parents have solved the problem of the generation gap
   d. parents should set all the rules for the household

9. *True or false?* Sometimes children learn different values at school from those held by their parents.

10. We might conclude from this selection that
    a. parenting is a complex and difficult role
    b. the best parents are unsophisticated ones
    c. different parenting styles are appropriate at different stages of growth
    d. the authors favour the parent as teacher-counsellor

Discussion Questions

About Content

1. What reasons do the authors give for saying that parents cannot be pals to their children? Do you agree?

2. Which parenting style do you think the authors prefer? How can you tell?

3. Why is it difficult for parents to act as teacher-counsellors? Give examples from your own experience.

About Structure

4. What method of development is used in the section "The Parent as Police Officer"?
   a. Reasons
   b. Contrast
   c. Narrative

5. Analyze the third paragraph of "The Parent as Teacher-Counselor." Where is the topic sentence? What kind of support is given for this topic sentence?

6. What are three transition words used in paragraph 3?

7. Find at least four terms that are defined in the selection.

About Style and Tone

8. Below are aids to understanding often used in textbooks. Which three appear in this selection?
   a. Preview and summary
   b. Charts
   c. Headings and subheadings

  d. Definitions and examples
  e. Boldface and italic type
  f. Graphs

■ Writing Assignments

Assignment 1

Write a description of "three childing styles." In other words, write an essay similar to "Five Parenting Styles" in which you discuss three different behaviour patterns of being a child in a family. Choose from the following behaviour patterns or others that may occur to you.

The child as

Prima donna or spoiled brat
Miniature adult
Helpless baby
"Daddy's girl" or "Mama's boy"
Tough kid
Rebel
Show-off
Carbon copy of parent
Little angel

In separate supporting paragraphs, describe in detail how each of your three types behaves.

Assignment 2

Write an essay that uses the following thesis statement:

My parents were (tried to be) _____.

Fill in the blank with one of the five parenting styles described in the article (or with another one that you think up). Then present three different incidents that show your parents acting according to that style. (You may, of course, choose to write about only one parent.)

Assignment 3

Write an essay in which you argue that "a _____ (name a particular parenting style described in the selection) is the ideal parent." Develop the essay by giving three reasons such parents are best.

  Feel free to use any of the styles the authors describe; you could, for example, come up with a convincing argument that "police officer" parents are best, based on your own experience or reasoning.

WHERE THE WORLD BEGAN

Margaret Laurence

Small towns, big cities, suburbs: we all begin somewhere. This "somewhere" is where our perceptions of ourselves, of others, of good and bad begin. All the perceptions of our lives are coloured by the tints of where we start out. Worlds begin small and grow with us, but we carry the images and the colours of the world in which we begin.

A strange place it was, that place where the world began. A place of incredible happenings, splendours and revelations, despairs like multitudinous pits of isolated hells. A place of shadow-spookiness, inhabited by the unknowable dead. A place of jubilation and of mourning, horrible and beautiful. 1

It was, in fact, a small prairie town. 2

Because that settlement and that land were my first and for many years my only real knowledge of this planet, in some profound way they remain my world, my way of viewing. My eyes were formed there. Towns like ours, set in a sea of land, have been described thousands of times as dull, bleak, flat, uninteresting. I have had it said to me that the railway trip across Canada is spectacular, except for the prairies, when it would be desirable to go to sleep for several days, until the ordeal is over. I am always unable to argue this point effectively. All I can say is—well, you really have to live there to know that country. The town of my childhood could be called bizarre, agonizingly repressive or cruel at times, and the land in which it grew could be called harsh in the violence of its seasonal changes. But never merely flat or uninteresting. Never dull. 3

In winter, we used to hitch rides on the back of the milk sleigh, our moccasins squeaking and slithering on the hard rutted snow of the roads, our hands in ice-bubbled mitts hanging onto the box edge of the sleigh for dear life, while Bert grinned at us through his great frosted moustache and shouted the horse into speed, daring us to stay put. Those mornings, rising, there would be the perpetual fascination of the frost feathers on windows, the ferns and flowers and eerie faces traced there during the night by unseen artists of the wind. Evenings, coming back from skating, the sky would be black but not dark, for you could see a cold glitter of stars from one side of the earth's rim to the other. And then the sometime astonishment when you saw the Northern Lights flaring across the sky, like the scrawled signature of God. After a blizzard, when the snowploughs hadn't yet got through, school would be closed for the day, the assumption being that the town's young could not possibly flounder through five feet of snow in the pursuit of education. We would then gaily don snowshoes and flounder for miles out into the white dazzling deserts, in pursuit of a different kind of knowing. If you came back too close to night, through the woods at the foot of the town hill, the thin black branches of poplar and chokecherry now meringued with frost, sometimes you heard coyotes. Or maybe the banshee wolf-voices were really only inside your head. 4

Summers were scorching, and when no rain came and the wheat became **5** bleached and dried before it headed, the faces of farmers and townsfolk would not smile much, and you took for granted, because it never seemed to have been any different, the frequent knocking at the back door and the young men standing there, mumbling or thrusting defiantly their requests for a drink of water and a sandwich if you could spare it. They were riding the freights, and you never knew where they had come from, or where they might end up, if anywhere. The Drought and Depression were like evil deities which had been there always. You understood and did not understand.

Yet the outside world had its continuing marvels. The polar bluffs and the small **6** river were filled and surrounded with a zillion different grasses, stones, and weed flowers. The meadowlarks sang undaunted from the twanging telephone wires along the gravel highway. Once we found an old flat-bottomed scow, and launched her, poling along the shallow brown waters, mending her with wodges of hastily chewed Spearmint, grounding her among the tangles of yellow marsh marigolds that grew succulently along the banks of the shrunken river, while the sun made our skins smell dusty-warm.

My best friend lived in an apartment above some stores on Main Street (its real **7** name was Mountain Avenue, goodness knows why), an elegant apartment with royal-blue velvet curtains. The back roof, scarcely sloping at all, was corrugated tin, of a furnace-like warmth on a July afternoon, and we would sit there drinking lemonade and looking across the back lane at the Fire Hall. Sometimes our vigil would be rewarded. Oh joy! Somebody's house burning down! We had an almost-perfect callousness in some ways. Then the wooden tower's bronze bell would clonk and toll like a thousand speeded funerals in a time of plague, and in a few minutes the team of giant black horses would cannon forth, pulling the fire wagon like some scarlet chariot of the Goths, while the firemen clung with one hand, adjusting their helmets as they went.

The oddities of the place were endless. An elderly lady used to serve, as her **8** afternoon tea offering to other ladies, soda biscuits spread with peanut butter and topped with a whole marshmallow. Some considered this slightly eccentric, when compared with chopped egg sandwiches, and admittedly talked about her behind her back, but no one ever refused these delicacies or indicated to her that they thought she had slipped a cog. Another lady dyed her hair a bright and cheery orange, by strangers often mistaken at twenty paces for a feather hat. My own beloved stepmother wore a silver fox neckpiece, a whole pelt, *with the embalmed (?) head still on.* My Ontario Irish grandfather said, "sparrow grass," a more interesting term than asparagus. The town dump was known as "the nuisance grounds," a phrase fraught with weird connotations, as thought the effluvia of our lives was beneath contempt but at the same time was subtly threatening to the determined and sometimes hysterical propriety of our ways.

Some oddities were, as idiom had it, "funny ha ha"; others were "funny peculiar." **9** Some were not so very funny at all. An old man lived, deranged, in a shack in the valley. Perhaps he wasn't even all that old, but to us he seemed a wild Methuselah figure, shambling among the underbrush and the tall couchgrass, muttering indecipherable curses or blessings, a prophet who had forgotten his prophesies. Everyone in town knew him, but no one knew him. He lived among us as though only occasionally and momentarily visible. The kids called him Andy Gump, and feared him. Some sought to prove their bravery by tormenting him. They were the mediaeval bear baiters, and he the lumbering bewildered bear, halfblind, only rarely turning to snarl. Everything is to be found in a town like mine. Belsen, writ small but with the same ink.

All of us cast stones in one shape or another. In grade school, among the vul-   10
nerable and violet girls we were, the feared and despised were those few older girls from what was charmingly termed "the wrong side of the tracks." Tough in talk and tougher in muscle, they were said to be whores already. And may have been, that being about the only profession readily available to them.

The dead lived in that place, too. Not only the grandparents who had, in local   11
parlance, "passed on" and who gloomed, bearded or bonneted, from the sepia photographs in old albums, but also the uncles, forever eighteen or nineteen, whose names were carved on the granite family stones in the cemetery, but whose bones lay in France. My own young mother lay in that graveyard, beside other dead of our kin, and when I was ten, my father, too, only forty, left the living town for the dead dwelling on the hill.

When I was eighteen, I couldn't wait to get out of that town, away from the   12
prairies. I did not know then that I would carry the land and town all my life within my skull, that they would form the mainspring and source of the writing I was to do, wherever and however far away I might live.

This was my territory in the time of my youth, and in a sense my life since then   13
has been an attempt to look at it, to comes to terms with it. Stultifying to the mind it certainly could be, and sometimes was, but not to the imagination. It was many things, but it was never dull.

The same, I now see, could be said for Canada in general. Why on earth did   14
generations of Canadians pretend to believe this country dull? We knew perfectly well it wasn't. Yet for so long we did not proclaim what we knew. If our upsurge of so-called nationalism seems odd or irrelevant to outsiders, and even to some of our own people *(what's all the fuss about)*, they might try to understand that for many years we valued ourselves insufficiently, living as we did under the huge shadows of those two dominating figures, Uncle Sam and Britannia. We have only just begun to value ourselves, our land, our abilities. We have only just begun to recognize our legends and to give shape to our myths.

There are, God knows, enough aspects to deplore about this country. When I see   15
the killing of our lakes and rivers with industrial wastes, I feel rage and despair. When I see our industries and natural resources increasingly taken over by America, I feel an overwhelming discouragement, especially as I cannot simply say "damn Yankees." It should never be forgotten that it is we ourselves who have sold such a large amount of our birthright for a mess of plastic Progress. When I saw the War Measures Act being invoked in 1970, I lost forever the vestigial remains of the naive wish-belief that repression could not happen here, or would not. And yet, of course, I had known all along in the deepest and often hidden caves of the heart that anything can happen

anywhere, for the seeds of both man's freedom and his captivity are found everywhere, even in the microcosm of a prairie town. But in raging against our injustices, our stupidities, I do so as *family*, as I did, and still do in writing about those aspects of my town which I hated and which are always in some ways aspects of myself.

The land still draws me more than other lands. I have lived in Africa and in **16** England, but as splendid as both can be, they do not have the power to move me in the same way as, for example, that part of southern Ontario where I spent four months last summer in a cedar cabin beside a river. "Scratch a Canadian, and you find a phony pioneer," I used to say to myself in warning. But all the same it is true, I think, that we are not yet totally alienated from physical earth, and let us only pray we do not become so. I once thought that my lifelong fear and mistrust of cities made me a kind of old-fashioned freak; now I see it differently.

The cabin has a long window across its front western wall, and sitting at the **17** oak table there in the mornings, I used to look out at the river and at the tall trees beyond, green-gold in the early light. The river was bronze; the sun caught it strangely, reflecting upon its surface the near-shore sand ripples underneath. Suddenly, the crescenting of a fish, gone before the eye could clearly give image to it. The old man next door said these leaping fish were carp. Himself, he preferred muskie, for he was a real fisherman and the muskie gave him a fight. The wind most often blew from the south, and the river flowed toward the south, so when the water was wind-riffled, and the current was strong, the river seemed to be flowing both ways. I liked this, and interpreted it as an omen, a natural symbol.

A few years ago, when I was back in Winnipeg, I gave a talk at my old college. **18** It was open to the public, and afterward a very old man came up to me and asked me if my maiden name had been Wemyss. I said yes, thinking he might have known my father or my grandfather. But no. "When I was a young lad," he said, "I once worked for your great-grandfather, Robert Wemyss, when he had the sheep ranch at Raeburn." I think that was a moment when I realized all over again something of great importance to me. My long-ago families came from Scotland and Ireland, but in a sense that no longer mattered so much. My true roots were here.

I am not very patriotic, in the usual meaning of that word. I cannot say "My **19** country right or wrong" in any political, social or literary context. But one thing is inalterable, for better or worse, for life.

This is where my world began. A world which includes the ancestors—both my **20** own and other people's ancestors who become mine. A world which formed me, and continues to do so, even while I fought it in some of its aspects, and continue to do so. A world which gave me my own lifework to do, because it was here that I learned the sight of my own particular eyes.

■ ## Reading Comprehension Questions

1. The word *repressive* in "The town of my childhood could be called bizarre, agonizingly repressive or cruel at times" (paragraph 3) means
   a. mean
   b. overbearing
   c. boring
   d. odd

2. The word *sepia* in "who gloomed, bearded or bonneted, from the sepia photographs in old albums" (paragraph 11) means
   a. faded
   b. dark
   c. brownish
   d. blurry

3. Which of the following would be a good alternative title for this selection?
   a. The Sad Place Where I Started
   b. Prairie Memories
   c. The Beauty of Childhood
   d. My Origins and My Life

4. Which sentence best expresses the main idea of the selection?
   a. Canada leaves an indelible mark on those who are born here.
   b. Childhood experiences stick with us for life.
   c. Small towns are more complex than they seem.
   d. Where we begin shapes our views of what follows.

5. The author's memories of her childhood
   a. are all positive and coloured by the sweetness of nostalgia
   b. vary in mood, according to season, place, and person recalled
   c. are all tied to outdoors experiences
   d. had mainly to do with how hard life was in the Depression

6. *True or false?* The prairie town was, without exception, tolerant of its "odd" folks.

7. Canadians were not loudly patriotic, according to Laurence, because
   a. they did not feel as powerful or important as the United States or England
   b. they thought Canada really was dull
   c. they didn't know their own country well enough to be patriotic
   d. Canada's culture did not stimulate the imagination

8. The author implies that
   a. people in her town simply accepted odd behaviour in its inhabitants
   b. under their surface tolerance, people were just as judgmental as people anywhere
   c. the small size of the town encouraged cruelty and prejudice
   d. only good manners and propriety kept people from being intolerant

9. The author implies that
   a. she can forget Canada's mistakes and shortcomings because of its natural beauty
   b. Canadians' attachment to their country is based on deluding themselves
   c. her attachment to her country is tempered by her understanding of, and resistance to, its weakness
   d. the world she began in is now a thing of the past

10. *True or false?* We can infer that Laurence has found a settled and comfortable relationship with her beginnings and her country.

■ Discussion Questions

About Content

1. Why would Laurence never describe life in her town as "dull"? What specific examples and descriptive passages clarify her use of the words *bizarre, harsh, repressive,* and *cruel?*

2. Canadian winters are known for their severity and frequently depicted as miserable. What does Laurence remember about prairie winters? How do her memories of summer compare to those of winter?

3. What specific aspects of Canada does Laurence find similar or comparable to what she experienced in her home town? Do you agree or disagree with her views of Canada and Canadians?

About Structure

4. Where in the selection do you find the first statement of the author's thesis? What is the thesis?

5. Where do you find echoes or reiterations of Laurence's thesis in the essay? What goal of all good writing is achieved by the repetition and reappearance of the thesis?

6. How many different organizing principles do you find in the selection, and what are they?

7. What method of introduction does the author use in her opening paragraphs?
   a. Anecdote
   b. Beginning with an opposite
   c. General to specific

About Style and Tone

8. In this text's chapter on descriptive writing, the importance of using lively and specific words is emphasized. Laurence's descriptive passages in this selection contain some remarkable examples of words appealing to our senses, words that capture a sight or sensation; for example, mitts are "ice-bubbled" (paragraph 4). Find three other examples of such words or phrases appealing to at least two of our senses.

9. Laurence uses the literary technique of alliteration, of placing words that begin with the same letter together for effect. She describes "the perpetual fascination of the frost feathers on windows" in winter (paragraph 4). Find three other examples of alliteration in the selection, and describe the effect on you as a reader of such word use for the items so described.

10. Laurence also makes use of figures of speech, in this case similes, to try to capture a larger meaning for some concept. Find, in paragraphs 4 and 5, two similes, and discuss their meanings related to the selection and the possible relationship between the similes in terms of the passages mentioned.

■ Writing Assignments

Assignment 1

Where did *your* world begin? What influences, visions, and memories do you carry from the place where you started out?

Using as your thesis your answers to the questions *what* do you carry with you, and *why*, write an essay relating how your place of origin shaped your views of your current life. Did the climate, the people, the buildings or physical features of the place form you in special ways? The body of your essay, which should make use of the descriptive process method of development (pages 172–184), will answer specifically *how* some aspects of "where you began" shape your perceptions of your life now.

Assignment 2

Imagine you must make a presentation to students visiting your college from another country. Your section of your college's orientation for these students involves offering your own definition of "what makes a Canadian distinctively Canadian." You have been asked to speak from your own experience and viewpoint, and to offer genuine, non-media-generated perceptions to which these students can relate.

Write an essay that is the script for such a presentation. Make use of the definition method of development for your main points and examples, which should be drawn from your own experiences and observations. Refer to the chapter on definition, pages 241–253.

Assignment 3

Margaret Laurence describes characters from her prairie town who were distinctive, if not outright peculiar. Every town and every neighbourhood contains such people, and children are particularly quick to observe, if not to judge, such characters. Making use of the techniques and methods of description, write an essay describing one such character (who may have been "funny ha ha," *or* "funny peculiar") you recall from the area where you grew up. Part of your essay may include your own and others' responses to this person's character and actions, and your thesis should give your view of the possible significance of the character to you as you consider him or her relative to your life today.

WHY ARE STUDENTS TURNED OFF?

Casey Banas

A teacher pretends to be a student and sits in on several classes. What does she find in the typical class? Boredom. Routine. Apathy. Manipulation. Discouragement. If this depressing list sounds familiar, you will be interested in the following analysis of why classes often seem to be more about killing time than about learning.

1   Ellen Glanz lied to her teacher about why she hadn't done her homework; but, of course, many students have lied to their teachers. The difference is that Ellen Glanz was a twenty-eight-year-old high school social studies teacher who was a student for six months to improve her teaching by gaining a fresh perspective of her school.

2   She found many classes boring, students doing as little as necessary to pass tests and get good grades, students using ruses to avoid assignments, and students manipulating teachers to do the work for them. She concluded that many students are turned off because they have little power and responsibility for their own education.

3   Ellen Glanz found herself doing the same things as the students. There was the day when Ellen wanted to join her husband in helping friends celebrate the purchase of a house, but she had homework for a math class. For the first time, she knew how teenagers feel when they think something is more important than homework.

4   She found a way out and confided: "I considered my options: Confess openly to the teacher, copy someone else's sheet, or make up an excuse." Glanz chose the third—the one most widely used—and told the teacher that the pages needed to complete the assignment had been ripped from the book. The teacher accepted the story, never checking the book. In class, nobody else did the homework; and student after student mumbled responses when called on.

5   "Finally," Glanz said, "the teacher, thinking that the assignment must have been difficult, went over each question at the board while students copied the problems at their seats. The teacher had 'covered' the material and the students had listened to the explanation. But had anything been learned? I don't think so."

6   Glanz found this kind of thing common. "In many cases," she said, "people simply didn't do the work assignment, but copied from someone else or manipulated the teacher into doing the work for them."

7   "The system encourages incredible passivity," Glanz said. "In most classes one sits and listens. A teacher, whose role is activity, simply cannot understand the passivity of the student's role," she said. "When I taught," Glanz recalled, "my mind was going constantly—figuring out how best to present an idea, thinking about whom to call on, whom to draw out, whom to shut up; how to get students involved, how to make my point clearer, how to respond; when to be funny, when serious. As a student, I experienced little of this. Everything was done to me."

Class methods promote the feeling that students have little control over or **8**
responsibility for their own education because the agenda is the teacher's, Glanz
said. The teacher is convinced the subject matter is worth knowing, but the student
may not agree. Many students, Glanz said, are not convinced they need to know
what teachers teach; but they believe good grades are needed to get into college.

Students, obsessed with getting good grades to help qualify for the college of **9**
their choice, believe the primary responsibility for their achievement rests with the
teacher, Glanz said. "It was his responsibility to teach well rather than their responsibility to learn carefully."

Teachers were regarded by students, Glanz said, not as "people," but as "role- **10**
players" who dispensed information needed to pass a test. "I often heard students
describing teachers as drips, bores, and numerous varieties of idiots," she said. "Yet
I knew that many of the same people had traveled the world over, conducted fascinating experiments or learned three languages, or were accomplished musicians,
artists, or athletes."

But the sad reality, Glanz said, is the failure of teachers to recognize their **11**
tremendous communications gap with students. Some students, she explained,
believe that effort has little value. After seeing political corruption they conclude
that honesty takes a back seat to getting ahead any way one can, she said. "I sometimes estimated that half to two-thirds of a class cheated on a given test," Glanz said.
"Worse, I've encountered students who feel no remorse about cheating but are
annoyed that a teacher has confronted them on their actions."

Glanz has since returned to teaching at Lincoln-Sudbury. Before her stint as a **12**
student, she would worry that perhaps she was demanding too much. "Now I know
I should have demanded more," she said. Before, she was quick to accept the excuses
of students who came to class unprepared. Now she says, "You are responsible for
learning it." But a crackdown is only a small part of the solution.

The larger issue, Glanz said, is that educators must recognize that teachers and **13**
students, though physically in the same school, are in separate worlds and have an
ongoing power struggle. "A first step toward ending this battle is to convince students that what we attempt to teach them is genuinely worth knowing," Glanz said.
"We must be sure, ourselves, that what we are teaching is worth knowing." No
longer, she emphasized, do students assume that "teacher knows best."

■ Reading Comprehension Questions

1. The word *ruses* in "students using ruses to avoid assignments" (paragraph 2)
   means
   a. questions
   b. sicknesses
   c. parents
   d. tricks

2. The word *agenda* in "the agenda is the teacher's" (paragraph 8) means
   a. program
   b. boredom

    c. happiness

    d. book

3. Which of the following would be a good alternative title for this selection?

    a. How to Get Good Grades

    b. Why Students Dislike School

    c. Cheating in Our School System

    d. Students Who Manipulate Teachers

4. Which sentence best expresses the main idea of the selection?

    a. Ellen Glanz is a burned-out teacher.

    b. Ellen Glanz lied to her math teacher.

    c. Students need good grades to get into college.

    d. Teachers and students feel differently about schooling.

5. How much of a class, according to the author's estimate, would often cheat on a test?

    a. One-quarter or less

    b. One-half

    c. One-half to two-thirds

    d. Almost everyone

6. *True or false?* As a result of her experience, Glanz now accepts more of her students' excuses.

7. Glanz found that the school system encourages an incredible amount of

    a. enthusiasm

    b. passivity

    c. violence

    d. creativity

8. The author implies that

    a. few students cheat on tests

    b. most students enjoy schoolwork

    c. classroom teaching methods should be changed

    d. Glanz had a lazy math teacher

9. The author implies that

    a. Glanz should not have become a student again

    b. Glanz is a better teacher than she was before

    c. Glanz later told her math teacher that she lied

    d. social studies is an unimportant subject

10. The author implies that

    a. most students who cheat on tests are caught by their teachers

    b. most teachers demand too little of their students

    c. students who get good grades in high school also do so in college

    d. students never question what teachers say

◾ Discussion Questions

About Content

1. What were Ellen Glanz's main discoveries when she first re-entered high school classes as a student? What did she conclude as a result of these observations?

2. Why, in paragraph 5, did the teacher believe that an assignment must have been too challenging?

3. Why, according to Glanz, is it so difficult for teachers to understand students' passivity? Why, in turn, do students tend to be passive?

4. What could cause a student caught cheating to respond with anger?

About Structure

5. Which method of introduction does Banas use in her essay?
   a. Broad to narrow
   b. Anecdote
   c. Background context
   d. Questions
   Why do you think she chose this approach?

6. List the time transitions that Banas uses in paragraph 12. How do they help the author make her point?

About Style and Tone

7. Throughout "Why Are Students Turned Off?" Banas shifts between summarizing Ellen Glanz's words and quoting Glanz directly. Find an instance in the essay in which both direct and indirect quotations are used in the same paragraph. What does the author gain or lose from using this technique? (Refer to pages 436–439 for definitions and examples of direct and indirect quotations.)

8. Parallel structures are often used to emphasize similar information. They can create a smooth, readable style. For example, note the series of participles or -*ing* verb forms in the following sentence from paragraph 2: "students *doing* as little as necessary to pass tests and get good grades, students *using* ruses to avoid assignments, and students *manipulating* teachers to do the work for them." Find two other uses of parallelism, one in paragraph 4 and one in paragraph 7.

◾ Writing Assignments

Assignment 1

Play the role of student observer in one of your college classes. Then write an essay with *either* of the following theses:

- In _____ class, students are turned off because . . .
- In _____ class, students are active and interested because . . .

In each supporting paragraph, state and detail one reason why the atmosphere in that particular class is either boring or interesting. You might want to consider areas such as these:

> **Instructor:** presentation, tone of voice, level of interest and enthusiasm, teaching aids used, ability to handle questions, sense of humour
> **Students:** level of enthusiasm, participation in class, attitude (as shown by body language and other actions)
> **Other factors:** conditions of classroom, length of class period, noise level in classroom

Assignment 2

Glanz says that students like to describe their teachers as "drips, bores, and numerous varieties of idiots." Write a description of one of your instructors, past or present, who either *does* or *does not* fit that description. *Show* in your essay that your instructor was weak, boring, and idiotic—or just the opposite (dynamic, creative, and bright). In either case, your focus should be on providing specific details that *enable your readers to see for themselves* that your thesis is valid.

Assignment 3

How does the classroom situation Ellen Glanz describes compare with a classroom situation with which you are familiar—either one from your earlier educational experience or one from the college you presently attend? Select one class you were or are a part of, and write an essay in which you compare or contrast your class with those Ellen Glanz describes. Here are some areas for comparison or contrast you might wish to include in your essay:

> How interesting the class was/is
> How many of the students did/do their assignments
> What the teaching methods were/are
> How much was/is actually learned
> How active the instructor was/is
> How passive or engaged the students were/are
> What the students thought/think of the instructor

Choose any three of these areas for comparison or contrast, or any three other areas that come to mind. Then decide which method of development you will use: *one side at a time* or *point by point*. (See pages 223–240.)

SOMETIMES THE WORDS DON'T COME

Jeannie Marshall

Most people take being able to read for granted. In fact, you are probably doing so right now. But over 20 per cent of adult Canadians have difficulty reading. As Jeannie Marshall explains in the article below, there are many reasons for adult literacy problems and many people struggling with major, often undiagnosed learning challenges. What help do our educational systems and social programs offer?

1   The first time I see Richard Cook, it's almost 9 a.m. and he's at the cash register in the cafeteria of the Bickford Centre, a Toronto school, making change for a customer. He's wearing a sweater, jeans and a baseball-style cap. Richard hands over the change with one hand, shakes my hand with the other and closes the cash drawer with a hip check.

2   He takes me by the elbow and steers me out the door and toward his basic literacy class, run by the Toronto District Board of Education, bounding ahead gallantly to open any doors in my way. Richards is 47 and, as he likes to explain to people up front, he can't read and write very well.

3   Richard wants to get me into the classroom so he can show me some photographs of his custom-made bicycle. He's happy to talk about his difficulties with literacy, too, but he thinks the bike is a lot more interesting. He made it himself using the frame of an old rowing machine, some old pipes and the wheels from old bicycles. It has mirrors, mud flaps, a stick shift, a radio/tape deck and eight speakers. It's painted with a sparkling, multi-coloured lacquer.

4   "I went to Canadian Tire and Wal-Mart looking for the right paint. One day I was at a flea market and I saw this nail polish. I got one bottle and then got the address of the company so I could buy 600 more bottles. They gave me a deal," says Richard. "You should see it when the sun hits. It just shines."

5   People in his neighbourhood and at the Bickford Centre know Richard as the guy who built "that" bike. Brian Nicholson, who oversees the literacy programs, says he saw Richard's bicycle locked up outside on his first day on the job and he knew this was going to be a fun place to work.

6   People who have made it into adulthood without reading often develop some interesting skills to compensate. And the enormous effort and discipline it takes to learn to read as an adult means they are a tenacious group. Since the Province of Ontario provides money for these adult literacy programs, each student is supposed to have a career objective. But it's not always easy for them to articulate their goals. Some students, such as the one who wanted to be a porn star but thought he would learn to read in the meantime, proved to the administrators that careers and literacy are not always directly related.

7   Richard wants to learn to read and write well enough to be able to get and keep a job so that he can build more interesting bicycles and maybe even sell them. The bike is at the centre of his world and seems to be what motivates him to work so hard in class. "I'm always thinking about it, how I can make it look better or be more

comfortable," he says. He has worked at various jobs in warehouses and breweries, but usually he has to complete work that is written out on a work-order sheet. He needs to be able to do this without asking someone else to read it to him.

Right now he and his wife of 22 years live on social assistance. He says they don't drink or smoke and they have few expenses. He attends classes five days a week from 9 a.m. until 3 p.m. He's up every morning at 5 and then rides his bicycle (in winter he uses an old ten-speed bike) to the centre, where he volunteers in the cafeteria from 6 a.m. until classes begin. He also works during coffee breaks and lunch hour. He does it because he likes to be busy, he likes the socializing. His math skills are improving through his use of the cash register and he can have breakfast and lunch for free.   **8**

"When I was about nine I fell off the top bunk and hit my head and I didn't know anybody for six months. And everything that I knew up until then was just gone," says Richard, making a whistling sound and pointing over his shoulder with his thumb to indicate the sudden flight of his childhood memories.   **9**

He carried on through the public school system without getting the special attention he needed when he was younger to help him.   **10**

Richard's classmates are older adults like himself who for various reasons did not learn to read. Tom is a retired former employee of the city's Parks and Recreation Department who wants to be able to read the newspaper; Stanley has a vision problem and needs to use a magnifying glass to help him see the letters, and Peter has a learning disability that makes reading a chore. There are 21 students in this class and each one has a different reason for not being able to read.   **11**

On this particular day, as they work on an exercise for which they have to fill in missing letters to complete various words, Richard admonishes Stanley for peeking at his neighbour's work. Stanley just laughs at his joke because any cheating he might do would be fairly conspicuous with his magnifying glass. Each time Richard gets stuck on a word, he goes to the front of the room and works his pencil up to a lethal point in the manual sharpener. The breaks seem to refresh his memory and after each trip he comes up with the letters he needs. "My problem is when I want to spell a word sometimes it doesn't sound the way it's supposed to. Sometimes the words don't come," says Richard.   **12**

Their instructor, Gordon Bynoe, explains that these people are here for many reasons, ranging from inadequate education in another country to not paying attention in class and being pushed through the system. "But they are not stupid," says Bynoe. "You can give them a piece of machinery to take apart or something to fix, and they have no problem. I have seen Richard drawing detailed pictures of that bicycle of his from memory. They can't read and write but that's not because of their intelligence."   **13**

Nicholson says they remind him of people of his grandfather's generation who were often skilled craftsmen but didn't have much formal education.   **14**

"It's something you think wouldn't happen any more but it does," says Nicholson. "We've got people here with high school diplomas." Statistics Canada's most recent report on literacy shows 22% of adult Canadians have difficulty reading.   **15**

Some of the Bickford Centre students are able to go on and take courses for high school credit and even attend community college.   **16**

Richard says he wants to get to the point where he can find streets in a new **17** neighbourhood without having to sound out each letter carefully as he tries to read the unfamiliar names. He practices at home with books, car magazines and, of course, motorcycle and bike magazines.

"If I want to read something, I want to be able to pick it up and read it and I **18** don't want to worry about anybody else telling me what the words say. It feels great when I can," says Richard. "I'm already pretty good at math. It's because of money." He nods toward the cafeteria to indicate that this practical experience has helped. "When it comes to counting money, nobody can beat me."

■ **Reading Comprehension Questions**

1. The word *tenacious* in "means they are a tenacious group" (paragraph 6) means
   a. eager
   b. determined
   c. backward
   d. busy

2. The word *admonishes* in "Richard admonishes Stanley for peeking at his neighbour's work" (paragraph 12) means
   a. insults
   b. attacks
   c. scolds
   d. rejects

3. Which of the following would be a good alternative title for this selection?
   a. The Literacy Problem
   b. Special Needs, Special People
   c. School for Survivors
   d. The Practical Power of Knowledge

4. Which sentence best expresss the main idea of the selection?
   a. "If I want to read something, I want to be able to pick it up and read it and I don't want to worry about anybody else telling me what the words say."
   b. People who have made it into adulthood without reading often develop some interesting skills to compensate.
   c. Statistics Canada's most recent report on literacy shows 22% of adult Canadians have difficulty reading.
   d. There are 21 students in this class and each one has a different reason for not being able to read.

5. Richard Cook's devotion and attention to his bicycle are proofs of
   a. his obsession with mechanical devices
   b. his slower development levels
   c. his level of skill, good memory, and attention span
   d. his technical abilities

6. *True or false?* People who lack literacy skills as adults are usually content to be dependent on others.

7. Brian Nicholson and Gordon Bynoe explain that
   a. skilled tradespeople are no longer valued
   b. educational achievements are not necessarily related to literacy
   c. school systems have tried to adapt to such students
   d. attention-deficit problems are usually the cause of literacy problems

8. The author implies that
   a. adults with literacy problems are often unmotivated
   b. adults with literacy problems are looking for easy solutions
   c. adults with literacy problems have physical disabilities
   d. adults with literacy problems have often managed quite well

9. *True or false?* Richard Cook's literacy challenges may never be completely conquerable.

10. The author implies that
    a. independence may be the biggest reward of literacy
    b. the main reward of learning basic reading skills is a better job
    c. every student in adult programs goes on to postsecondary education
    d. Ontario school systems are mainly to blame for adult literacy problems

■ **Discussion Questions**

About Content

1. What are the most interesting aspects of Richard Cook's bicycle? Why are they important?

2. What are Richard Cook's main reasons for attending literacy classes?

3. What evidence is given of Cook's attention to the task at hand and of his single-minded pursuit of his goal?

About Structure

4. What method does the author use for the introduction?
   a. Situation opposite to the one to be developed
   b. Explaining the importance of the situation
   c. An anecdote
   d. A general statement narrowing to the thesis

5. Where in Marshall's article could you find a sentence or group of sentences that expresses the thesis of the piece? Why do you think that the thesis may not appear near the beginning, as it would in many traditional essays?

About Style and Tone

6. To what extent is the selection an "opinion piece" on a subject of general concern, and to what extent is it a portrait of an interesting individual? Why does the author include direct dialogue, and where in the article does she do so? What is the effect of hearing from the various speakers?

7. As a journalist, the author is trained to supply vivid details and specific facts. In which paragraph do you find the most striking facts and details, and how do these add to your sense of the selection's meaning?

■ **Writing Assignments**

Assignment 1

Do you know someone who, like Richard Cook, is a surprising and unexpected mix of qualities and abilities? Do you know someone who defies people's preconceived notions of what he or she is likely to be?

Write an essay about such a person that you know or have met. Your thesis can suggest something about what makes this person so intriguing, and your body paragraphs can explain with examples what the surprising aspects of your subject are.

Assignment 2

Why is reading so important, or is it? Does it give people power over their lives? Using examples and details from your own life, argue for or against the importance of being able to read in today's society.

Assignment 3

Richard Cook's bicycle is not only his most prized possession; it is what has motivated him to tackle his learning challenges. Do you have some object, interest, or hobby that is very important to you? Using the cause/effect method of development (pages 211–222), write an essay that examines the reasons (causes) your interest is so valuable to you *or* the effects that having this interest has had on you.

THE MONSTER

Deems Taylor

You're about to be introduced to someone you won't like at all. By standards too numerous to count, this individual deserves dislike, disrespect, and dishonour. And yet you will be invited to admire him and overlook his many faults. Can you? Should you? This essay by Deems Taylor, a noted American composer of operas, may challenge your perceptions in suggesting that extraordinary people can't be measured by ordinary yardsticks.

He was an undersized little man, with a head too big for his body—a sickly little   **1** man. His nerves were bad. He had skin trouble. It was agony for him to wear anything next to his skin coarser than silk. And he had delusions of grandeur.

He was a monster of conceit. Never for one minute did he look at the world or at people, except in relation to himself. He was not only the most important person in the world, to himself; in his own eyes he was the only person who existed, He believed himself to be one of the greatest dramatists in the world, one of the greatest thinkers, and one of the greatest composers. To hear him talk, he was Shakespeare, and Beethoven, and Plato, rolled into one. And you would have had no difficulty in hearing him talk. He was one of the most exhausting conversationalists that ever lived. An evening with him was an evening spent in listening to a monologue. Sometimes he was brilliant; sometimes he was maddeningly tiresome. But whether he was being brilliant or dull, he had one sole topic of conversion: himself—what *he* thought and what *he* did.   **2**

He had a mania for being in the right. The slightest hint of disagreement, from anyone, on the most trivial point, was enough to set him off on a harangue that might last for hours, in which he proved himself right in so many ways, and with such exhausting volubility,[1] that in the end his hearer, stunned and deafened, would agree with him, for the sake of peace.   **3**

It never occurred to him that he and his doings were not of the most intense and fascinating interest to anyone with whom he came in contact. He had theories about almost any subject under the sun, including vegetarianism, the drama, politics, and music; and in support of these theories he wrote pamphlets, letters, books . . . thousands upon thousands of words, hundreds and hundreds of pages. He not only wrote these things, and published them—usually at somebody's else's expense—but he would sit and read them aloud, for hours, to his friends and his family.   **4**

He wrote operas; and no sooner did he have the synopsis of a story, but he would invite—or rather summon—a crowd of his friends to his house and read it to them: not for criticism; for applause. When the complete poem was written, the friends had to come again, and hear *that* read aloud. Then he would publish the poem, sometimes years before the music that went with it was written. He played the piano like a composer, in the worst sense of what that implies, and he would sit down at the piano before parties that included some of the finest pianists of his time, and play for them, by the hour, his own music, needless to say. He had a composer's voice. And he would invite eminent vocalists to his house and sing them his operas, taking all the parts.   **5**

He had the emotional stability of a six-year-old child. When he felt out of sorts, he would rave and stamp, or sink into suicidal gloom and talk darkly of going to the East to end his days as a Buddhist monk. Ten minutes later, when something pleased him, he would rush out of doors and run around the garden, or jump up and down on the sofa, or stand on his head. He could be grief-stricken over the death of a pet dog, and he could be callous and heartless, to a degree that would have made a Roman emperor shudder.   **6**

He was almost innocent of any sense of responsibility. Not only did he seem incapable of supporting himself, but it never occurred to him that he was under any obligation to do so. He was convinced that the world owed him a living. In support   **7**

[1] *volubility:* excessive talking

of this belief, he borrowed money from everybody who was good for a loan—men, women, friends, or strangers. He wrote begging letters by the score, sometimes groveling without shame, in others loftily offering his intended benefactor the privilege of contributing to his support, and being mortally offended if the recipient declined the honor. I have found no record of his ever paying or repaying money to anyone who did not have a legal claim upon it.

8   What money he could lay his hands on he spent like an Indian rajah.[2] The mere prospect of a performance of one of his operas was enough to set him to running up bills amounting to ten times the amount of his prospective royalties. On an income that would reduce a more scrupulous man to doing his own laundry, he would keep two servants. Without enough money in his pocket to pay his rent, he would have the walls and ceiling of his study lined with pink silk. No one will ever know—certainly he never knew—how much money he owed. We do know his greatest benefactor gave him $6,000 to pay the most pressing of his debts in one city, and a year later had to give him $16,000 to enable him to live in another city without being thrown into jail for debt.

9   He was equally unscrupulous in others ways. An endless procession of women marched through his life. His first wife spent twenty years enduring and forgiving his infidelities. His second wife had been the wife of his most devoted friend and admirer, from whom he stole her. And even while he was trying to persuade her to leave her first husband he was writing to a friend to inquire whether he could suggest some wealthy woman—*any* wealthy woman—whom he could marry for her money.

10   He was completely selfish in his other personal relationships. His liking for his friends was measured solely by the completeness of their devotion to him, or by their usefulness to him, whether financial or artistic. The minute they failed him— even by so much as refusing a dinner invitation—or began to lessen in usefulness, he cast them off without a second thought. At the end of his life he had exactly one friend left whom he had known even in middle age.

11   He had a genius for making enemies. He would insult a man who disagreed with him about the weather. He would pull endless wires in order to meet some man who admired his work and was able and anxious to be of use to him—and would proceed to make a mortal enemy of him with some idiotic and wholly uncalled-for exhibition of arrogance and bad manners. A character in one of his operas was a caricature of one of the most powerful music critics of his day. Not content with burlesquing[3] him, he invited the critic to his house and read him the libretto[4] aloud in front of his friends.

12   The name of this monster was Richard Wagner. Everything that I have said about him you can find on record—in newspapers, in police reports, in the testimony of people who knew him, in his own letters, between the lines of his autobiography. And the curious thing about this record is that it doesn't matter in the least.

[2]*rajah:* prince in India

[3]*burlesquing:* mocking

[4]*libretto:* opera text

Because this undersized, sickly, disagreeable, fascinating little man was right all   13
the time. The joke was on us. He *was* one of the world's great dramatists; he *was* a
great thinker; he *was* one of the most stupendous musical geniuses that, up to now,
the world has ever seen. The world did owe him a living. People couldn't know
those things at the time, I suppose; and yet to us, who know his music, it does seem
as though they should have known. What if he did talk about himself all the time?
If he had talked about himself for twenty-four hours every day for the span of his
life he would not have uttered half the number of words that other men have spoken and written about him since his death.

When you consider what he wrote—thirteen operas and music dramas, eleven   14
of them still holding the stage, eight of them unquestionably worth ranking among
the world's great musico-dramatic masterpieces—when you listen to what he
wrote, the debts and heartaches that people had to endure from him don't seem
much of a price. Eduard Hanslick, the critic whom he caricatured in *Die
Meistersinger* and who hated him ever after, now lives only because he was caricatured in *Die Meistersinger*. The women whose hearts he broke are long since dead;
and the man who could never love anyone but himself has made deathless atone-
ment, I think, with *Tristan und Isolde*. Think of the luxury with which for a time,
at least, fate rewarded Napoleon, the man who ruined France and looted Europe;
and then perhaps you will agree that a few thousand dollars' worth of debts were
not too heavy a price to pay for the *Ring* trilogy.

What if he was faithless to his friends and to his wives? He had one mistress to   15
whom he was faithful to the day of his death: Music. Not for a single moment did
he ever compromise with what he believed, with what he dreamed. There is not a
line of his music that could have been conceived by a little mind. Even when he is
dull, or downright bad, he is dull in the grand manner. There is greatness about his
worst mistakes. Listening to his music, one does not forgive him for what he may
or may not have been. It is not a matter of forgiveness. It is a matter of being dumb
with wonder that his poor brain and body didn't burst under the torment of the
demon of creative energy that lived inside him, struggling, clawing, scratching to
be released; tearing, shrieking at him to write the music that was in him. The mir-
acle is that what he did in the little space of seventy years could have been done at
all, even by a great genius. Is it any wonder that he had no time to be a man?

▦ Reading Comprehension Questions

1. The word *harangue* in "The slightest hint of disagreement, from anyone, on
   the most trivial point, was enough to set him off on a harangue that might last
   for hours" (paragraph 3) means
   a. sarcastic joke
   b. offended silence
   c. arrogant speech
   d. state of depression

2. The word *caricature* in "A character in one of his operas was a caricature of one of the most powerful music critics of his day" (paragraph 11) means
   a. mistake
   b. friend
   c. flattering description
   d. exaggerated, mocking portrayal

3. Which of the following would be a good alternative title for this selection?
   a. Wagner: His Personal Life
   b. Operas and Their Composers
   c. A Selfish Man Who Gave Much
   d. Wagner: A Musical Genius

4. Which sentence best expresses the main idea of this selection?
   a. Wagner's personal failings are less important than the great works he produced.
   b. Although Wagner was famous during his lifetime, very few of his operas are still performed.
   c. Wagner was an unfaithful lover as well as a spendthrift who borrowed money he never intended to repay.
   d. Wagner's operas are still considered among the best ever composed.

5. While trying to persuade his best friend's wife to leave her husband, Wagner was
   a. writing *Tristan und Isolde*
   b. still married to his first wife
   c. searching for a rich woman to marry
   d. borrowing money from her husband

6. *True or false?* Wagner was once thrown into jail for debt.

7. In paragraph 14, the author implies that
   a. the *Ring* trilogy is one of Wagner's less successful works
   b. Hanslick came to enjoy the character based on him in *Die Meistersinger*
   c. *Tristan und Isolde* is a magnificent love story
   d. Wagner had stopped writing music years before his death

8. The author implies that Wagner
   a. was often able to get the money he desired from others
   b. neglected the dogs that belonged to him
   c. despised vegetarians
   d. was self-conscious about his odd appearance

9. The author implies that
   a. no one recognized Wagner's talent during his own lifetime
   b. Wagner was embarrassed to ask others for money
   c. Wagner thrived on attention
   d. Wagner may have suffered from a brain disorder

10. The author implies that Wagner
    a. respected those people who would argue energetically with him
    b. was chronically depressed, unable to feel pleasure
    c. was genuinely brilliant about nonmusical subjects as well as musical ones
    d. profoundly regretted, at the end of his life, his loss of friends

■ Discussion Questions

About Content

1. What aspects of Wagner's physical appearance does Taylor note in paragraph 1? What aspects of Wagner's personality and character does the author present in the second and third paragraphs? What is the effect on you as a reader of these two sets of details being presented so close together?

2. In what ways, according to Taylor, was Wagner like a six-year-old child? In what ways was the composer like an Indian rajah?

3. What evidence does the author present for Wagner's selfishness? What proofs are offered for his "ability to make enemies"?

4. Why does Taylor say, "The joke was on us"?

About Structure

5. The author avoids revealing the name of his subject until paragraph 12. Why do you think he made this choice? Why does Taylor wait until the twelfth paragraph to balance the negative information about Wagner's behaviour with positive comments about his musical works?

6. Why, given the content and point of Taylor's essay, do you think there is an almost complete absence of transitional words or structures other than repetition? At the beginning of which paragraph do you find the only transitional "signal word" and why?

About Style and Tone

7. Why do you think the author chose to title his essay "The Monster"?

8. What wording in paragraph 2 is echoed in paragraph 13? How has it been changed when used the second time? What is the effect of this change?

9. Taylor uses unexpected wording in some of his descriptions. What is surprising about the wording in the following excerpts, and how is the meaning affected by that wording?

   "He was almost innocent of any sense of responsibility." (Paragraph 7)
   "He had a genius for making enemies." (Paragraph 11)
   "There is a greatness about his worst mistakes." (Paragraph 15)

■   **Writing Assignments**

Assignment 1

People often inspire confused or ambiguous feelings in us. Write an essay about a person in your life toward whom you have such mixed feelings. Perhaps you enjoy someone's company but do not fully trust him or her. Or you may admire someone's values or ethics, but find him or her narrow-minded. In your thesis, state both sides of your feelings, as in the following sample thesis statement:

> While Marina is often caring and generous, she can also be too critical.

Then, in your body paragraphs, fully describe one side of your subject's personality before you begin describing the other. Throughout your essay, illustrate both sides of your point with specific revealing comments and incidents.

Assignment 2

Everyone seems to know a "monster," someone who has managed to alienate nearly everyone in his or her life. Using the classification and division method for arranging your evidence, write an essay in the third-person point of view about such a person. Divide your essay's body into three sections. Those sections could be about *individuals* this person has alienated, such as any of these:

A former best friend
A former partner or spouse
A parent or parents
A co-worker

Alternatively, divide your essay's body into *categories* of people the person has alienated, such as any of the following:

Family members
Neighbours
Co-workers
Classmates

Describe in what ways your subject has made enemies of these people (or at least lost their goodwill or friendship). Your thesis statement for this assignment might be like this one:

> By being extremely self-centred and unkind, _____ has managed to alienate several people in his life.

Assignment 3

Wagner was a person who had no qualms about taking advantage of the people in his life—by insisting that they listen to him, endlessly borrowing money he never repaid, or having careless affairs. Although few people are as manipulative as

Wagner, most of us know what it's like to have someone take advantage of us for selfish reasons. Write an essay about how it feels to be taken advantage of. Select several specific instances in your life when you felt someone else was "using" you. In your essay, devote each supporting paragraph to one such anecdote or situation, describing what happened and how you responded. Below is the start of an outline of such a paper.

Thesis: When I was younger, I was taken advantage of by several important people in my life.

Topic Sentences
a. My sister often borrowed my things and then carelessly damaged or lost them.
b. A good friend of mine in high school used our friendship to spend time with my brother, on whom she had a crush.
c. My boss at work took advantage of the fact that I needed the job by forcing me to do a lot of his tasks.

Considering Concepts

HERE'S TO YOUR HEALTH

Joan Dunayer

Dunayer contrasts the glamorous "myth" about alcohol, as presented in advertising and popular culture, with the reality—which is often far less appealing. After reading her essay, you will be more aware of how we are encouraged to think of alcohol as being tied to happiness and success. You may also become a more critical observer of images presented by advertisers.

As the only freshman on his high school's varsity wrestling team, Tod was anxious to fit in with his older teammates. One night after a match, he was offered a tequila bottle on the ride home. Tod felt he had to accept, or he would seem like a sissy. He took a swallow, and every time the bottle was passed back to him, he took another swallow. After seven swallows, he passed out. His terrified teammates carried him into his home, and his mother then rushed him to the hospital. After his stomach was pumped, Tod learned that his blood alcohol level had been so high that he was lucky not to be in a coma or dead. 1

Although alcohol sometimes causes rapid poisoning, frequently leads to long-term addiction, and always threatens self-control, our society encourages drinking. Many parents, by their example, give children the impression that alcohol is an essential ingredient of social gatherings. Peer pressure turns bachelor parties, fraternity initiations, and spring-semester beach vacations into competitions in "getting trashed." In soap operas, glamorous characters pour Scotch whiskey from crystal decanters as readily as most people turn on the faucet for tap water. In films and rock videos, trend-setters party in nightclubs and bars. And who can recall a televised baseball or basketball game without a beer commercial? By the age of 21, the average American has seen drinking on TV about 75,000 times. Alcohol ads appear with pounding frequency—in magazines, on billboards, in college newspapers—contributing to a harmful myth about drinking. 2

Part of the myth is that liquor signals professional success. In a slick men's mag-   3
azine, one full-page ad for Scotch whiskey shows two men seated in an elegant
restaurant. Both are in their thirties, perfectly groomed, and wearing expensive-
looking gray suits. The windows are draped with velvet, the table with spotless
white linen. Each place-setting consists of a long-stemmed water goblet, silver uten-
sils, and thick silver plates. On each plate is a half-empty cocktail glass. The two men
are grinning and shaking hands, as if they've just concluded a business deal. The
caption reads, "The taste of success."

Contrary to what the liquor company would have us believe, drinking is more   4
closely related to lack of success than to achievement. Among students, the heavi-
est drinkers have the lowest grades. In the work force, alcoholics are frequently late
or absent, tend to perform poorly, and often get fired. Although alcohol abuse
occurs in all economic classes, it remains most severe among the poor.

Another part of the alcohol myth is that drinking makes you more attractive to   5
the opposite sex. "Hot, hot, hot," one commercial's soundtrack begins, as the camera scans a crowd of college-age beachgoers. Next it follows the curve of a woman's
leg up to her bare hip and lingers there. She is young, beautiful, wearing a bikini.
A young guy, carrying an ice chest, positions himself near to where she sits. He is
tan, muscular. She doesn't show much interest—until he opens the chest and takes
out a beer. Now she smiles over at him. He raises his eyebrows and, invitingly, holds
up another can. She joins him. This beer, the song concludes, "attracts like no other."

Beer doesn't make anyone sexier. Like all alcohol, it lowers the levels of male   6
hormones in men and of female hormones in women—even when taken in small
amounts. In substantial amounts, alcohol can cause infertility in women and impo-
tence in men. Some alcoholic men even develop enlarged breasts, from their
increased female hormones.

The alcohol myth also creates the illusion that beer and athletics are a perfect   7
combination. One billboard features three high-action images: a baseball player
running at top speed, a surfer riding a wave, and a basketball player leaping to make
a dunk shot. A particular light beer, the billboard promises, "won't slow you down."

"Slow you down" is exactly what alcohol does. Drinking plays a role in over six mil-   8
lion injuries each year—not counting automobile accidents. Even in small amounts,
alcohol dulls the brain, reducing muscle coordination and slowing reaction time. It also
interferes with the ability to focus the eyes and adjust to a sudden change in bright-
ness—such as the flash of a car's headlights. Drinking and driving, responsible for over
half of all automobile deaths, is the leading cause of death among teenagers. Continued
alcohol abuse can physically alter the brain, permanently impairing learning and
memory. Long-term drinking is related to malnutrition, weakening of the bones,
and ulcers. It increases the risk of liver failure, heart disease, and stomach cancer.

Finally, according to the myth fostered by the media in our culture, alcohol   9
generates a warm glow of happiness that unifies the family. In one popular film,
the only food visible at a wedding reception is an untouched wedding cake, but
beer, whiskey, and vodka flow freely. Most of the guests are drunk. After shouting
into the microphone to get everyone's attention, the band leader asks the bride and
groom to come forward. They are presented with two wine-filled silver drinking
cups branching out from a single stem. "If you can drink your cups without spilling

any wine," the band leader tells them, "you will have good luck for the rest of your lives." The couple drain their cups without taking a breath, and the crowd cheers.

A marriage, however, is unlikely to be "lucky" if alcohol plays a major role in it.   10
Nearly two-thirds of domestic violence involves drinking. Alcohol abuse by parents is strongly tied to child neglect and juvenile delinquency. Drinking during pregnancy can lead to miscarriage and is a major cause of such birth defects as deformed limbs and mental retardation. Those who depend on alcohol are far from happy: over a fourth of the patients in state and county mental institutions have alcohol problems; more than half of all violent crimes are alcohol-related; the rate of suicide among alcoholics is fifteen times higher than among the general population.

Alcohol, some would have us believe, is part of being successful, sexy, healthy,   11
and happy. But those who have suffered from it—directly or indirectly—know otherwise. For alcohol's victims, "Here's to your health" rings with a terrible irony when it is accompanied by the clink of liquor glasses.

■ Reading Comprehension Questions

1. The word *caption* in "The caption reads 'the taste of success'" (paragraph 3) means
   a. menu
   b. man
   c. words accompanying the picture
   d. contract that seals the business deal

2. The word *impairing* in "Continued alcohol abuse can physically alter the brain, permanently impairing learning and memory" (paragraph 8) means
   a. postponing
   b. doubling
   c. damaging
   d. teaching

3. Which one of the following would be a good alternative title for this selection?
   a. The Taste of Success
   b. Alcohol and Your Social Life
   c. Too Much Tequila
   d. Alcohol: Image and Reality

4. Which sentence best expresses the main idea of the selection?
   a. Sports and alcohol don't mix.
   b. The media and our culture promote false images about success and happiness.
   c. The media and our culture promote false beliefs about alcohol.
   d. Liquor companies should not be allowed to use misleading ads about alcohol.

5. According to the selection, drinking can
   a. actually unify a family
   b. lower hormone levels
   c. temporarily improve performance in sports
   d. increase the likelihood of pregnancy

6. *True or false?* Alcohol abuse is most severe among the middle class.

7. *True or false?* The leading cause of death among teenagers is drinking and driving.

8. From the first paragraph of the essay, we can conclude that
    a. even one encounter with alcohol can actually lead to death
    b. tequila is the worst type of alcohol to drink
    c. wrestlers tend to drink more than other athletes
    d. by the time students reach high school, peer pressure doesn't influence them

9. *True or false?* The author implies that one or two drinks a day are probably harmless.

10. The author implies that heavy drinking can lead to
    a. poor grades
    b. getting fired
    c. heart disease
    d. all of the above

Discussion Questions

About Content

1. According to Dunayer, how many parts are there to the myth about alcohol? Which part do you consider the most dangerous?

2. Drawing on your own experience, provide examples of ways in which our culture encourages drinking.

About Structure

3. What method does Dunayer use to begin her essay?
    a. Broad to narrow
    b. Idea that is contrary to what will be developed
    c. Incident

4. The body of Dunayer's essay is made up of four pairs of paragraphs (paragraphs 3 and 4; 5 and 6; 7 and 8; 9 and 10) that serve to introduce and develop each of her four main supporting points. What is the pattern by which she divides each point into two paragraphs?

5. Dunayer introduces the first part of the myth about alcohol with the words "Part of the myth is …" (See the first sentence of paragraph 3.) Then she goes on to use an addition transition to introduce each of the three other parts of the myth—in the first sentences of paragraphs 5, 7, and 9. What are those addition transitions?

6. What method does Dunayer use to conclude her essay?
    a. Prediction or recommendation
    b. Summary and a final thought
    c. Thought-provoking question

About Style and Tone

7. Why is the title of the essay appropriate?

■ Writing Assignments

Assignment 1

Describe and analyze several recent advertisements for wine, beer, or liquor on television or radio, in newspapers or magazines, or on billboards. Argue whether the ads are socially and humanly responsible or irresponsible in the way that they portray drinking. Your thesis might be something like one of the following examples:

> In three recent ads, ad agencies and liquor companies have acted irresponsibly in their portrayal of alcohol.
> In three recent ads, ad agencies and liquor companies have acted with a measure of responsibility in their portrayal of alcohol.

Alternatively, write about what you consider responsible or irresponsible advertising for some other product or service: cigarettes, weight loss, and cosmetics are possibilities to consider.

Assignment 2

Imagine you have a friend, relative, or classmate who drinks a lot, and write a letter warning him or her about the dangers of alcohol. If appropriate, use information from Dunayer's essay. Remember that since your purpose is to get someone you care about to control or break a dangerous habit, you should make your writing very personal. Don't bother explaining how alcoholism affects people in general. Instead, focus directly on what you see it doing to your reader.

Divide your argument into at least three supporting paragraphs. You might, for instance, talk about how your reader is jeopardizing his or her relationship with three of the following: family, friends, boss and co-workers, teachers and classmates.

Assignment 3

Dunayer describes how alcohol advertisements promote false beliefs, such as the idea that alcohol will make you successful. Imagine that you work for a public service ad agency given the job of presenting the negative side of alcohol. What images would you choose to include in your ads?

Write a report to your boss in which you propose in detail three anti-alcohol ads. Choose from among the following:

> An ad counteracting the idea that alcohol leads to success
> An ad counteracting the idea that alcohol is sexy
> An ad counteracting the idea that alcohol goes well with athletics
> An ad counteracting the idea that alcohol makes for happy families

COFFEE

Alan Durning

Is there a mug of coffee in your hand as you read this page? Have you ever stopped to think about what went into that mug before it reached your hands? You may have gone as far as to grind the beans, measure the coffee, pour the water into the tank of the coffee maker, place a filter in the machine's basket, and then turn on the power, but where did the ingredients themselves come from? How did they reach you? In his essay, Alan Durning "deconstructs" a simple cup of coffee into its basic elements and traces them back to their origins. In this "reverse process essay," we see the complex nature of an everyday substance.

Beans

I brewed a cup of coffee. It took 100 beans—about one fortieth of the beans that 1
grew on the coffee tree that year. The tree was on a small mountain farm in the region of Colombia called Antioquia. The region was cleared of its native forests in the first coffee boom three generations ago. These "cloud forests" are among the world's most endangered ecosystems.

The beans ripened in the shade of taller trees. Growing them did not require 2
plowing the soil, but it did take several doses of insecticides, which were synthesized in factories in the Rhine River Valley of Europe. Some of the chemicals entered the respiratory systems of farm workers. Others washed downstream and were absorbed by plants and animals.

The beans were picked by hand. In a diesel powered crusher they were removed 3
from the fruit that encased them. They were dried under the sun and shipped to New Orleans in a 132 pound bag. The freighter was fueled by Venezuelan oil and made in Japan. The shipyard built the freighter out of Korean steel. The Korean steel mill used iron mined on tribal lands in Papua New Guinea.

At New Orleans the beans were roasted for 13 minutes at temperatures above 4
400 degrees F. The roaster burned natural gas pumped from the ground in Oklahoma. The beans were packaged in four-layer bags constructed of polyethylene, nylon, aluminum foil and polyester. They were trucked to a Seattle warehouse and later to a retail store.

Bag

I carried the beans out of the grocery in a brown paper bag made at an 5
unbleached kraft paper mill in Oregon. I transported them home in an automobile that burned one sixth of a gallon of gasoline during the five mile round-trip to the market.

Grinder

In the kitchen, I measured the beans in a disposable plastic scoop molded in New   **6**
Jersey and spooned them into the grinder. The grinder was assembled in China
from imported steel, aluminum, copper, and plastic parts. It was powered by electricity generated at the Ross Dam on the Skagit River.

I dumped the coffee into a gold-plated mesh filter made in Switzerland of   **7**
Russian ore. I put the filter into a plastic-and-steel drip coffee maker.

I poured eight ounces of tap water into the appliance. The water came by pipe   **8**
from the Cedar River on the west slope of the Cascade Mountains. An element
heated the water to more than 200 degrees F. The hot water seeped through the
ground coffee and dissolved some of its oils and solids. The brew trickled into a
glass carafe.

Paper Cup

The coffee mugs were all dirty so I poured the coffee into a paper cup. The cup was   **9**
made from bleached wood pulp in Arkansas. A fraction of the chlorine in the bleach
was discharged from the pulp mill into the Arkansas River. In the river, the chlorine ended up as TCDD, which is often simply called dioxin. It is the most car-
cinogenic substance known.

Cream

I stirred in one ounce of cream. The cream came from a grain-fed dairy cow in the   **10**
lowlands north of Seattle. The cow liked to graze on a stream bank and walk in the
stream. This muddied the water and made life difficult for native trout.

The cow's manure was rich in nitrogen and phosphorus. The soils of the pas-   **11**
ture where the cow grazed were unable to absorb these quickly enough, so they
washed into the stream when it rained. The infusion of nutrients fertilized algae,
which absorbed a larger share of the oxygen dissolved in the water. The shortage of
oxygen made life more difficult for native trout.

Sugar

I measured out two tablespoons of sugar. It came from the canefields south of Lake   **12**
Okeechobee in Florida. These plantations have deprived the Everglades of water,
endangering waterfowl and reptile populations.

■ Reading Comprehension Questions

1. The word *synthesized* in "several doses of insecticides, which were synthesized
   in factories in the Rhine River Valley of Europe" (paragraph 2) means
   a. processed
   b. manufactured
   c. combined
   d. packaged

2. The word *infusion* in "The infusion of nutrients fertilized algae, which absorbed a larger share of the oxygen dissolved in the water" (paragraph 11) means
   a. pollution
   b. instilling
   c. formula
   d. combination

3. Which one of the following would make a good alternative title for this selection?
   a. Eco-Disaster in the a.m.
   b. Juan Valdez or the *Exxon Valdez?*
   c. The Whole World in Your Pot
   d. Your Daily Cup of Toxins

4. Which statement best expresses the main idea of the selection?
   a. No single item in our world is detachable from other aspects of existence.
   b. The production of coffee entails many polluting and harmful processes.
   c. Everything is more complex than it first seems.
   d. All foods are ecologically disastrous to manufacture.

5. According to the selection,
   a. destruction of Colombian rainforests is the most disastrous effect of coffee-growing and production
   b. coffee production is a completely automated process
   c. producing coffee is a combination of agriculture, human labour, and technical expertise
   d. world resources are being depleted to produce coffee

6. *True or false?* All the paper products mentioned by the author create toxic substances in their manufacture.

7. *True or false?* The normal habits of a dairy cow affect the balance of the ecology.

8. From the first three paragraphs of the article, we can conclude that the author
   a. feels nothing but environmentally based guilt about making his cup of coffee
   b. worries too much about problems caused by coffee production
   c. feels sorry for the farm labourers involved in coffee growing
   d. understands both the industrial problems and the global trade inter-connections in coffee production

9. *True or false?* All instances of water pollution in the essay arise from industrial waste.

10. We might infer that the author
    a. believes we often don't know when we are harming the environment
    b. believes we don't care about pollution or Third World industrial oppression
    c. is careful to use only "ecologically safe," "nonexploitive" products
    d. puts all the blame for ecological imbalances on human beings

■ **Discussion Questions**

About Content

1. In the opening paragraphs of his essay, the author points out two major industrially caused ecological problems. What are they? Which would seem the more harmful to you, and why?

2. How many countries does it take to produce Alan Durning's cup of coffee? How many American states are needed to assist in the process? What do these numbers tell you about products we use every day?

About Structure

3. This essay "deconstructs" a cup of coffee. If this is a "process essay in reverse," which method of introduction has the author used "in reverse"?
   a. Stating the importance of the topic
   b. Starting with an opposite
   c. Going from broad to narrow

4. Durning divides his essay into sections with sparse headings. Does each section cover only the subject named by its title? If not, which sections cover more than one subject? Why do they cover more than one subject?

5. This is a rare example of a process essay almost devoid of simple or obvious transitions. If there are no ordinary "connecting word" transitions, what rhetorical device has the author used in their place? What method of ordering ideas common to all process writing has the author used? How does this method help you to follow the sequence of ideas?

About Style and Tone

6. Durning's style in "Coffee" is as plain and severe as his title. How many sentences are simple statements starting with *I?* What is the effect of this style on you as a reader? Is the information conveyed by the essay as uncomplicated as the style?

7. Writers with strong biases or social concerns are often accused of being unfair or overbearing because of the vehement tone of their work. Alan Durning is a prominent environmentalist. Does his tone "suffocate" or badger the reader? Are there "objective" concepts in the essay? Is the article calm enough to allow readers room to consider their own point of view? If so, how is this goal achieved?

■ **Writing Assignments**

Assignment 1

Coffee is an ordinary product with a fascinating story behind it. How much does any of us know about everyday foods and beverages? Choose one fairly simple item, preferably one whose package does not have thousands of untraceable chemicals, and do some research into the origins of its ingredients. Phone the manufacturer, visit some websites, or consult your library to find out where its ingredients originate.

Write a descriptive or explanatory process essay about the history and the geographical origins of the raw materials in your chosen product. Place the ingredients in three groups for ease of paragraphing. You should organize your essay as Durning has done, starting "from the end" and taking your product apart piece by piece. You may choose to start with either the largest or the smallest of its ingredients, depending on the order you feel your reader will find most interesting.

Assignment 2

If our world is shrinking and we are all interdependent, why do we still drink coffee and drive cars powered by fossil fuels? Many manufacturers and retailers would like the public to believe that they are doing their best to preserve the world's ecological balance. Are their claims sincere or just more sophisticated marketing tactics? Will concern for the world's biological condition ever change business? Will damage to the world's ecosystems force business to change its methods?

Write an essay in which you either defend the efforts of one "world-conscious" company or argue that such efforts are merely a way of "jumping on the bandwagon." Justify your argument logically, and make use of some objective information from your own knowledge or from outside reading.

Assignment 3

You have chosen to write an article for the "World Watch" column in your college newspaper. Your article describes three specific ways in which college students could be active in improving their college and local environment. Your column may extend each example to a relevant global concern.

HOW TO MAKE IT IN COLLEGE, NOW THAT YOU'RE HERE

Brian O'Keeney

The author of this selection presents a compact guide to being a successful student. He will show you how to pass tests, how to avoid becoming a student zombie, how to find time to fit in everything you want to do, and how to deal with personal problems while keeping up with your studies. These and other helpful tips have been culled from the author's own experience and his candid interviews with fellow students.

Today is your first day on campus. You were a high school senior three months ago.   **1**
Or maybe you've been at home with your children for the last ten years. Or maybe you work full time and you're coming to school to start the process that leads to a better

job. Whatever your background is, you're probably not too concerned today with staying in college. After all, you just got over the hurdle (and the paperwork) of applying to this place and organizing your life so that you could attend. And today, you're confused and tired. Everything is a hassle, from finding the classrooms to standing in line at the bookstore. But read my advice anyway. And if you don't read it today, clip and save this article. You might want to look at it a little further down the road.

By the way, if this isn't your very first day, don't skip this article. Maybe you   2
haven't been doing as well in your studies as you'd hoped. Or perhaps you've had problems juggling your work schedule, your class schedule, and your social life. If so, read on. You're about to get the inside story on making it in college. On the basis of my own experience as a final-year student, and of dozens of interviews with successful students, I've worked out a no-fail system for coping with college. These are the inside tips every student needs to do well in school. I've put myself in your place, and I'm going to answer the questions that will cross (or have already crossed) your mind during your stay here.

What's the Secret of Getting Good Grades?

It all comes down to getting those grades, doesn't it? After all, you came here for   3
some reason, and you're going to need passing grades to get the credits or degree you want. Many of us never did much studying in high school; most of the learning we did took place in the classroom. College, however, is a lot different. You're really on your own when it comes to passing courses. In fact, sometimes you'll feel as if nobody cares if you make it or not. Therefore, you've got to figure out a study system that gets results. Sooner or later, you'll be alone with those books. After that, you'll be sitting in a classroom with an exam sheet on your desk. Whether you stare at that exam with a queasy stomach or whip through it fairly confidently depends on your study techniques. Most of the successful students I talked to agreed that the following eight study tips deliver solid results.

1   **Set Up a Study Place.**   Those students you see "studying" in the cafeteria or   4
game room aren't learning much. You just can't learn when you're distracted by people and noise. Even the library can be a bad place to study if you constantly find yourself watching the clouds outside or the students walking through the stacks. It takes guts to sit, alone, in a quiet place in order to study. But you have to do it. Find a room at home or a spot in the library that's relatively quiet—and boring. When you sit there, you won't have much to do except study.

2   **Get into a Study Frame of Mind.**   When you sit down, do it with the atti-   5
tude that you're going to get this studying done. You're not going to doodle in your notebook or make a list for the supermarket. Decide that you're going to study and learn *now*, so that you can move on to more interesting things as soon as possible.

3   **Give Yourself Rewards.**   If you sweat out a block of study time, and do a   6
good job on it, treat yourself. You deserve it. You can "psych" yourself up for studying by promising to reward yourself afterwards. A present for yourself can be anything from a favorite TV show to a relaxing bath to a dish of double chocolate ice cream.

4   Skim the Textbook First. Lots of students sit down with an assignment   **7**
like "read chapter five, pages 125–150" and do just that. They turn to page 125 and
start to read. After a while, they find that they have no idea what they just read. For
the last ten minutes, they've been thinking about their five-year-old or what they're
going to eat for dinner. Eventually, they plod through all the pages but don't
remember much afterwards.

In order to prevent this problem, skim the textbook chapter first. This means: **8**
look at the title, the subtitles, the headings, the pictures, the first and last paragraphs.
Try to find out what the person who wrote the book had in mind when he or she
organized the chapter. What was important enough to set off as a title or in bold
type? After skimming, you should be able to explain to yourself what the main points
of the chapter are. Unless you're the kind of person who would step into an empty
elevator shaft without looking first, you'll soon discover the value of skimming.

5   Take Notes on What You're Studying. This sounds like a hassle, but it   **9**
works. Go back over the material after you've read it, and jot down key words and
phrases in the margins. When you review the chapter for a test, you'll have handy
little things like "definition of rationalization" or "example of assimilation" in the
margins. If the material is especially tough, organize a separate sheet of notes. Write
down definitions, examples, lists, and main ideas. The idea is to have a single sheet
that boils the entire chapter down to a digestible lump.

6   Review after You've Read and Taken Notes. Some people swear that talk-   **10**
ing to yourself works. Tell yourself about the most important points in the chapter. Once you've said them out loud, they seem to stick better in your mind. If you
can't talk to yourself about the material after reading it, that's a sure sign you don't
really know it.

7   Give Up. This may sound contradictory, but give up when you've had   **11**
enough. You should try to make it through at least an hour, though. Ten minutes
here and there are useless. When your head starts to pound and your eyes develop
spidery red lines, quit. You won't do much learning when you're exhausted.

8   Take a College Skills Course If You Need It. Don't hesitate or feel embar-   **12**
rassed about enrolling in a study skills course. Many students say they wouldn't
have made it without one.

How Can I Keep Up with All My Responsibilities without Going Crazy?

You've got a class schedule. You're supposed to study. You've got a family. You've got   **13**
a husband, wife, boyfriend, girlfriend, child. You've got a job. How are you possibly going to cover all the bases in your life and maintain your sanity? This is one of
the toughest problems students face. Even if they start the semester with the best
of intentions, they eventually find themselves tearing their hair out trying to do
everything they're supposed to do. Believe it or not, though, it is possible to meet
all your responsibilities. And you don't have to turn into a hermit or give up your
loved ones to do it.

The secret here is to organize your time. But don't just sit around half the   **14**
semester planning to get everything together soon. Before you know it, you'll be
confronted with midterms, papers, family, and work all at once. Don't let yourself
reach that breaking point. Instead, try these three tactics.

    1   Monthly Calendar.   Get one of those calendars with big blocks around the   **15**
dates. Give yourself an overview of the whole term by marking down the due dates
for papers and projects. Circle test and exam days. This way those days don't sneak
up on you unexpectedly.

    2   Study Schedule.   Sit down during the first few days of this semester and   **16**
make up a sheet listing the days and hours of the week. Fill in your work and class
hours first. Then try to block out some study hours. It's better to study a little every
day than to create a huge once-or-twice-a-week marathon session. Schedule study
hours for your hardest classes for the times when you feel most energetic. For
example, I battled my tax law textbook in the mornings; when I looked at it after
7:00 P.M., I may as well have been reading Chinese. The usual proportion, by the
way, is one hour of study time for every class hour.

    In case you're one of those people who get carried away, remember to leave   **17**
blocks of free time, too. You won't be any good to yourself or anyone else if you
don't relax and pack in the studying once in a while.

    3   A "To Do" List.   This is the secret that single-handedly got me through col-   **18**
lege. Once a week (or every day if you want to), write a list of what you have to do.
Write down everything from "write English paper" to "buy cold cuts for lunches."
The best thing about a "to do" list is that it seems to tame all those stray "I have to"
thoughts that nag at your mind. Just making the list seems to make the tasks
"doable." After you finish something on the list, cross it off. Don't be compulsive
about finishing everything; you're not Superman or Wonder Woman. Get the
important things done first. The secondary things you don't finish can simply be
moved to your next "to do" list.

What Can I Do If Personal Problems Get in the Way of My Studies?

One student, Roger, told me this story: **19**

> *Everything was going OK for me until the middle of the spring semester. I went
> through a terrible time when I broke up with my girlfriend and started seeing her
> best friend. I was trying to deal with my ex-girlfriend's hurt and anger, my new
> girlfriend's guilt, and my own worries and anxieties at the same time. In addition
> to this, my mother was sick and on a medication that made her really irritable. I
> hated to go home because the atmosphere was so uncomfortable. Soon, I started
> missing classes because I couldn't deal with the academic pressures as well as my
> own personal problems. It seemed easier to hang around my girlfriend's apartment
> than to face all my problems at home and at school.*

Another student, Marian, told me: **20**

I'd been married for eight years and the relationship wasn't going too well. I saw the handwriting on the wall, and I decided to prepare for the future. I enrolled in college, because I knew I'd need a decent job to support myself. Well, my husband had a fit because I was going to school. We were arguing a lot anyway, and he made it almost impossible for me to study at home. I think he was angry and almost jealous because I was drawing away from him. It got so bad that I thought about quitting college for a while. I wasn't getting any support at home and it was just too hard to go on.

Personal troubles like these are overwhelming when you're going through   **21** them. School seems like the least important thing in your life. The two students above are perfect examples of this. But if you think about it, quitting or failing school would be the worst thing for these two students. Roger's problems, at least with his girlfriends, would simmer down eventually, and then he'd regret having left school. Marian had to finish college if she wanted to be able to live independently. Sometimes, you've just got to hang tough.

But what do you do while you're trying to live through a lousy time? First of   **22** all, do something difficult. Ask yourself, honestly, if you're exaggerating small problems as an excuse to avoid classes and studying. It takes strength to admit this, but there's no sense in kidding yourself. If your problems are serious, and real, try to make some human contacts at school. Lots of students hide inside a miserable shell made of their own troubles and feel isolated and lonely. Believe me, there are plenty of students with problems. Not everyone is getting A's and having a fabulous social and home life at the same time. As you go through the term, you'll pick up some vibrations about the students in your classes. Perhaps someone strikes you as a compatible person. Why not speak to that person after class? Share a cup of coffee in the cafeteria or walk to the parking lot together. You're not looking for a best friend or the love of your life. You just want to build a little network of support for yourself. Sharing your difficulties, questions, and complaints with a friendly person on campus can make a world of difference in how you feel.

Finally, if your problems are overwhelming, get some professional help. Why   **23** do you think colleges spend countless dollars on counseling departments and campus psychiatric services? More than ever, students all over the country are taking advantage of the help offered by support groups and therapy sessions. There's no shame attached to asking for help, either; in fact, almost 40 percent of college students (according to one survey) will use counseling services during their time in school. Just walk into a student center or counseling office and ask for an appointment. You wouldn't think twice about asking a dentist to help you get rid of your toothache. Counselors are paid—and want—to help you with your problems.

Why Do Some People Make It and Some Drop Out?

Anyone who spends at least one semester in college notices that some students give   **24** up on their classes. The person who sits behind you in accounting, for example, begins to miss a lot of class meetings and eventually vanishes. Or another student comes to class without the assignment, doodles in his notebook during the lecture, and leaves during the break. What's the difference between students like this and the ones who succeed in school? My survey may be nonscientific, but everyone I asked said the same thing: attitude. A positive attitude is the key to everything else—good study habits, smart time scheduling, and coping with personal difficulties.

What does "a positive attitude" mean? Well, for one thing, it means avoiding the   **25** zombie syndrome. It means not only showing up for your classes, but also doing something while you're there. Really listen. Take notes. Ask a question if you want to. Don't just walk into a class, put your mind in neutral, and drift away to never-never land.

Having a positive attitude goes deeper than this, though. It means being mature   **26** about college as an institution. Too many students approach college classes like six-year-olds who expect first grade to be as much fun as *Sesame Street*. First grade, as we all know, isn't as much fun as *Sesame Street*. And college classes can sometimes be downright dull and boring. If you let a boring class discourage you so much that you want to leave school, you'll lose in the long run. Look at your priorities. You want a degree, or a certificate, or a career. If you have to, you can make it through a less-than-interesting class in order to achieve what you want. Get whatever you can out of every class. But if you simply can't stand a certain class, be determined to fulfill its requirements and be done with it once and for all.

After the initial high of starting school, you have to settle in for the long haul.   **27** If you follow the advice here, you'll be prepared to face the academic crunch. You'll also live through the semester without giving up your family, your job, or *Monday Night Football*. Finally, going to college can be an exciting time. You do learn. And when you learn things, the world becomes a more interesting place.

■ **Reading Comprehension Questions**

1. The word *queasy* in "with a queasy stomach" (paragraph 3) means
   a. intelligent
   b. healthy
   c. full
   d. nervous

2. The word *tactics* in "try these three tactics" (paragraph 14) means
   a. proofs
   b. problems
   c. methods
   d. questions

3. Which of the following would be a good alternative title for this selection?
   a. Your First Day on Campus
   b. Coping with College
   c. How to Budget Your Time
   d. The Benefits of College Skills Courses

4. Which sentence expresses the main idea of the selection?
   a. In high school, most of us did little homework.
   b. You should give yourself rewards for studying well.

   c. Sometimes personal problems interfere with studying.
   d. You can succeed in college by following certain guidelines.

5. According to the author, "making it" in college means
    a. studying whenever you have any free time
    b. getting a degree by barely passing your courses
    c. quitting school until you solve your personal problems
    d. getting good grades without making your life miserable

6. If your personal problems seem overwhelming, you should
    a. drop out for a while
    b. try to ignore them
    c. tell another student
    d. seek professional help

7. Which of the following is *not* described by the author as a means of time control?
    a. Monthly calendar
    b. To-do list
    c. Study schedule
    d. Flexible job hours

8. We might infer that the author
    a. is a writer for the school newspaper
    b. is president of his or her class
    c. has taken a study skills course
    d. was not a successful student in his or her first year of college

9. From the selection we can conclude that
    a. college textbooks are very expensive
    b. it is a good practice to write notes in your textbook
    c. taking notes on your reading takes too much time
    d. a student should never mark up an expensive textbook

10. The author implies that
    a. fewer people than before are attending college
    b. most students think that college is easy
    c. most students dislike college
    d. coping with college is difficult

■ Discussion Questions

About Content

1. What pitfalls does O'Keeney think are waiting for students just starting college? Are there other pitfalls not mentioned in the article?

2. What is the secret that the author says got him through college? What do you think is the most helpful or important suggestion the author makes in the selection?

3. Do you agree with the author that Roger and Marian should stay in school? Are there any situations where it would be better for students to quit school or leave temporarily?

About Structure

4. What is the thesis of the selection? In which paragraph is it stated?

5. Why does the article begin with the first day on campus?

6. What method of introduction does the author use in the section on personal problems (starting on page 586)? What is the value of using this method?

About Style and Tone

7. This essay is obviously written for college students. Can you guess where an essay like this one would appear? (**Hint:** Reread the first paragraph.)

■ Writing Assignments

Assignment 1

Write a process essay similar to the one you've just read that explains how to succeed in some other field—for example, a job, a sport, marriage, child rearing. First, brainstorm the three or four problem areas a newcomer to this experience might encounter. Then, under each area you have listed, jot down some helpful hints and techniques for overcoming these problems. For example, a process paper on "How to Succeed as a Server" might describe the following problem areas in this kind of job:

> Developing a good memory
> Learning to do tasks quickly
> Coping with troublesome customers

Each supporting paragraph in this paper would discuss specific techniques for dealing with these problems. Be sure that the advice you give is detailed and specific enough to really help a person in such a situation.

You may find it helpful to look over the process essays on pages 198–210.

Assignment 2

Write a letter to Roger or Marian, giving advice on how to deal with the personal problem mentioned in the article. You could recommend any or all of the following:

> Face the problem realistically. (By doing what?)
> Make other contacts at school. (How? Where?)
> See a counsellor. (Where? What should this person be told?)
> Realize that the problem is not so serious. (Why not?)
> Ignore the problem. (How? By doing what instead?)

In your introductory paragraph, explain why you are writing the letter. Include a thesis statement that says what plan of action you are recommending. Then, in the rest of the paper, explain the plan of action (or plans of action) in detail.

Assignment 3

Write an essay contrasting college *as you thought it would be* with college *as it is*. You can organize the essay by focusing on three specific things that are different from what you expected. Or you can cover three areas of difference. For instance, you may decide to contrast your expectations of (1) a college residence room, (2) your roommate, and (3) dining hall food, with reality. Or you could contrast your expectations of (1) fellow students, (2) college professors, and (3) college courses, with reality.

Refer to the section on comparison and contrast essays in this book (pages 223–240) to review point-by-point and one-side-at-a-time methods of development. Be sure to make an outline of your essay before you begin to write.

IN PRAISE OF THE F WORD

Mary Sherry

What does it take to get by in high school? Too little, according to the author, a teacher in an "educational-repair shop." In this article, which originally appeared in *Newsweek*, Mary Sherry describes the ways she sees students being cheated by their schools and proposes a remedy you may find surprising.

Tens of thousands of 18-year-olds will graduate this year and be handed meaningless diplomas. These diplomas won't look any different from those awarded their luckier classmates. Their validity will be questioned only when their employers discover that these graduates are semiliterate.   1

Eventually a fortunate few will find their way into educational-repair shops— adult-literacy programs, such as the one where I teach basic grammar and writing. There, high school graduates and high school dropouts pursuing graduate-equivalency certificates will learn the skills they should have learned in school. They will also discover they have been cheated by our educational system.   2

As I teach, I learn a lot about our schools. Early in each session I ask my students to write about an unpleasant experience they had in school. No writers' block here! "I wish someone would have had made me stop doing drugs and made me study." "I liked to party and no one seemed to care." "I was a good kid and didn't cause any trouble, so they just passed me along even though I didn't read well and couldn't write." And so on.   3

I am your basic do-gooder, and prior to teaching this class I blamed the poor   **4**
academic skills our kids have today on drugs, divorce and other impediments to
concentration necessary for doing well in school. But, as I rediscover each time I
walk into the classroom, before a teacher can expect students to concentrate, he has
to get their attention, no matter what distractions may be at hand. There are many
ways to do this, and they have much to do with teaching style. However, if style
alone won't do it, there is another way to show who holds the winning hand in the
classroom. That is to reveal the trump card of failure.

I will never forget a teacher who played that card to get the attention of one of   **5**
my children. Our youngest, a world-class charmer, did little to develop his intellectual talents but always got by. Until Mrs. Stifter.

Our son was a high school senior when he had her for English. "He sits in the   **6**
back of the room talking to his friends," she told me. "Why don't you move him to
the front row?" I urged, believing the embarrassment would get him to settle down.
Mrs. Stifter looked at me steely-eyed over her glasses. "I don't move seniors," she
said. "I flunk them." I was flustered. Our son's academic life flashed before my eyes.
No teacher had ever threatened him with that before. I regained my composure and
managed to say that I thought she was right. By the time I got home I was feeling
pretty good about this. It was a radical approach for these times, but, well, why not?
"She's going to flunk you," I told my son. I did not discuss it any further. Suddenly
English became a priority in his life. He finished out the semester with an A.

I know one example doesn't make a case, but at night I see a parade of students   **7**
who are angry and resentful for having been passed along until they could no
longer even pretend to keep up. Of average intelligence or better, they eventually
quit school, concluding they were too dumb to finish. "I should have been held
back," is a comment I hear frequently. Even sadder are those students who are high
school graduates who say to me after a few weeks of class, "I don't know how I ever
got a high school diploma."

Passing students who have not mastered the work cheats them and the employers   **8**
who expect graduates to have basic skills. We excuse this dishonest behavior by saying
kids can't learn if they come from terrible environments. No one seems to stop to think
that—no matter what environments they come from—most kids don't put school first
on their list unless they perceive something is at stake. They'd rather be sailing.

Many students I see at night could give expert testimony on unemployment,   **9**
chemical dependency, abusive relationships. In spite of these difficulties, they have
decided to make education a priority. They are motivated by the desire for a better
job or the need to hang on to the one they've got. They have a healthy fear of failure.

People of all ages can rise above their problems, but they need to have a reason
to do so. Young people generally don't have the maturity to value education in the
same way my adult students value it. But fear of failure, whether economic or academic, can motivate both.

Flunking as a regular policy has just as much merit today as it did two genera-   **10**
tions ago. We must review the threat of flunking and see it as it really is—a positive
teaching tool. It is an expression of confidence by both teachers and parents that the
students have the ability to learn the material presented to them. However, making
it work again would take a dedicated, caring conspiracy between teachers and

parents. It would mean facing the tough reality that passing kids who haven't learned the material—while it might save them grief for the short term—dooms them to long-term illiteracy. It would mean that teachers would have to follow through on their threats, and parents would have to stand behind them, knowing their children's best interests are indeed at stake. This means no more doing Scott's assignments for him because he might fail. No more passing Jodi because she's such a nice kid.

This is a policy that worked in the past and can work today. A wise teacher, with **11** the support of his parents, gave our son the opportunity to succeed—or fail. It's time we return this choice to all students.

■ Reading Comprehension Questions

1. The word *validity* in "[the diplomas'] validity will be questioned only when their employers discover that these graduates are semiliterate" (paragraph 1) means
   a. soundness
   b. dates
   c. age
   d. supply

2. The word *impediments* in "I blamed the poor academic skills our kids have today on drugs, divorce and other impediments to concentration" (paragraph 4) means
   a. questions
   b. paths
   c. skills
   d. obstacles

3. Which one of the following would be a good alternative title for this selection?
   a. Learning to Concentrate in School
   b. Teaching English Skills
   c. A Useful Tool for Motivating Students
   d. Adult Literacy Programs

4. Which sentence best expresses the main idea of the selection?
   a. Many adults cannot read or write well.
   b. English skills can be learned through adult literacy programs.
   c. Schools should include flunking students as part of their regular policy.
   d. Before students will concentrate, the teacher must get their attention.

5. Sherry's night students are
   a. usually unemployed
   b. poor students
   c. motivated to learn
   d. doing drugs

6. According to the author, many students who get "passed along"
   a. are lucky
   b. never find a job
   c. don't get into trouble
   d. eventually feel angry and resentful

7. Sherry feels that to succeed, flunking students as a regular policy requires
   a. adult-literacy programs
   b. graduate-equivalency certificates
   c. the total co-operation of teachers and parents
   d. a strong teaching style

8. The author implies that the present educational system is
   a. the best in the world
   b. doing the best that it can
   c. very short of teachers
   d. not demanding enough of students

9. *True or false?* Sherry implies that high school students often don't realize the value of academic skills.

10. From the selection, we may conclude that the author based her opinion on
    a. statistics
    b. educational research
    c. her personal and professional experiences
    d. expert professional testimony

■ Discussion Questions

About Content

1. Sherry writes that "before a teacher can expect students to concentrate, he has to get their attention, no matter what distractions may be at hand." What distractions does she mention in the article? Can you think of any others?

2. Do you feel your high school made an honest effort to give you the skills you need—and to make you aware of the importance of those skills? If not, what should your school have done that it did not do?

About Structure

3. The main method of development of this selection is
   a. narration
   b. description
   c. argumentation and persuasion

4. In which paragraph does the author first state her main idea? What are the other paragraphs in which she states her main idea?

5. What contrast transitions are used in the first sentences of paragraphs 7 and 10? What ideas are being contrasted in those sentences?

About Style and Tone

6. Why do you think Sherry titles her essay "In Praise of the F Word"? Why doesn't she simply use the word *fail?*

7. What stylistic method does Sherry use in paragraph 11 to add rhythm and force to her points about flunking as a regular policy?

Writing Assignments

Assignment 1

Write an essay that has as its thesis one of the following points:

- In my opinion, students have no one to blame but themselves if they leave school without having learned basic skills.
- When students graduate or quit school lacking basic skills, they are the victims of an inadequate educational system.
- Flunking students has more disadvantages than advantages.

Support your thesis with several points, each developed in its own paragraph.

Assignment 2

Sherry proposes using "flunking as a regular policy" as a way to encourage students to work harder. What else might school systems do to help students? Write an essay in which you suggest a few policies for our public schools and give the reasons you think those changes will be beneficial. Here are some policies to consider:

More writing in all classes
Shorter summer vacations
Less emphasis on memorization and more on thinking skills
A language requirement
A daily quiet reading session in elementary grades

Assignment 3

Here are two letters sent to *Newsweek* by teachers in response to Sherry's article:

Letter 1

Mary Sherry's essay advocating the use of flunking as a teaching tool was well intentioned but naive. In the first place, my local school district—and I doubt it's unique—discourages the practice by compiling teachers' failure rates for comparison (would you want to rank first?). More important though, F's don't even register on many kids' Richter scales. When your spirit has been numbed—as some of my students' spirits have—by physical, sexual, and psychological abuse, it's hard to notice an F. Walk a mile in one of my kids' shoes. Real fear has little to do with school.

Kay Keglovits
Arlington, Texas

Letter 2

Sherry is right: flunking poor students makes sense. But, as she notes, "making it work again would take a dedicated, caring conspiracy between teachers and parents." I once failed a high school junior for the year. I received a furious call from the student's mother. I was called to a meeting with the school superintendent, the principal, the mother, and the student. There it was decided that I would tutor the student for four months so that the F could be replaced with a passing grade. This was a total sham; the student did nothing during this remedial work, but she was given a passing grade. No wonder education is in the condition that we find it today.

Arthur J. Hochhalter
Minot, North Dakota

These letters suggest that schools that want to try using flunking as a regular policy will have to plan their policy carefully. Write an essay in which you discuss ways to make the failing of poor students as a regular policy work. Your thesis statement can be something like this: "In order for a policy of flunking to work, certain policies and attitudes would need to be changed in many schools." As support in your essay, use the ideas in these letters, Sherry's ideas, and any other ideas you have heard or thought of. Describe your supporting ideas in detail and explain why each is necessary or useful.

THE PAIN OF ANIMALS

David Suzuki

David Suzuki is a noted geneticist, and he is well known to most Canadians from his television series, *Suzuki on Science* and *The Nature of Things*. In the essay that follows, he offers some insights into the development of his own attitudes toward animal life. In "The Pain of Animals," Suzuki reveals his views of the universality of pain and of human and animal rights within "the great chain of being." How is our view of ourselves as "supreme among beasts" now being affected by the suffering and death we inflict upon animals?

Medical technology has taken us beyond the normal barriers of life and death and   1
thereby created unprecedented choices in *human* lives. Until recently, we have taken for granted our right to use other species in any way we see fit. Food, clothing, muscle power have been a few of the benefits we've derived from this exploitation. This tradition has continued into scientific research where animals are studied and "sacrificed" for human benefit. Now serious questions are being asked about our right to do this.

Modern biological research is based on a shared evolutionary history of organisms that enables us to extrapolate from one organism to another. Thus, most fundamental concepts in heredity were first shown in fruit flies, molecular genetics began using bacteria and viruses and much of physiology and psychology has been based on studies in mice and rats. But today, as extinction rates have multiplied as a result of human activity, we have begun to ask what right we have to use all other animate forms simply to increase human knowledge or for profit or entertainment. Underlying the "animal rights" movement is the troubling question of where we fit in the rest of the natural world.   2

When I was young, one of my prized possessions was a BB gun. Dad taught me how to use it safely and I spent many hours wandering through the woods in search of prey. It's not easy to get close enough to a wild animal to kill it with a BB gun, but I did hit a few pigeons and starlings. I ate everything I shot. Then as a teenager, I graduated to a .22 rifle and with it, I killed rabbits and even shot a pheasant once.   3

One year I saw an ad for a metal slingshot in a comic book. I ordered it, and when it arrived, I practised for weeks shooting marbles at a target. I got to be a pretty good shot and decided to go after something live. Off I went to the woods and soon spotted a squirrel minding its own business doing whatever squirrels do. I gave chase and began peppering marbles at it until finally it jumped onto a tree, ran to the top and found itself trapped. I kept blasting away and grazed it a couple of times so it was only a matter of time before I would knock it down. Suddenly, the squirrel began to cry—a piercing shriek of terror and anguish. That animal's wail shook me to the core and I was overwhelmed with horror and shame at what I was doing—for no other reason than conceit with my prowess with a slingshot, I was going to *kill* another being. I threw away the slingshot and my guns and have never hunted again.   4

All my life, I have been an avid fisherman. Fish have always been the main source of meat protein in my family, and I have never considered fishing a sport. But there is no denying that it is exciting to reel in a struggling fish. We call it "playing" the fish, as if the wild animal's desperate struggle for survival is some kind of game.   5

I did "pleasure-fish" once while filming for a television report on the science of fly fishing. We fished a famous trout stream in the Catskill Mountains of New York state where all fish had to be caught and released. The fish I caught had mouths gouged and pocked by previous encounters with hooks. I found no pleasure in it because to me fish are to be caught for consumption. Today, I continue to fish for food, but I do so with a profound awareness that I am a predator of animals possessing well-developed nervous systems that detect pain. Fishing and hunting have forced me to confront the way we exploit other animals.   6

I studied the genetics of fruit flies for twenty-five years and during that time probably raised and killed tens of millions of them without a thought. In the early seventies, my lab discovered a series of mutations affecting behaviour of flies, and this find led us into an investigation of nerves and muscles. I applied for and received research funds to study behaviour in flies on the basis of the *similarity* of their neuromuscular systems to ours. In fact, psychologists and neurobiologists analyse behaviour, physiology and neuroanatomy of guinea pigs, rats, mice and   7 other animals as *models* for human behaviour. So our nervous systems must closely resemble those of other mammals.

These personal anecdotes raise uncomfortable questions. What gives us the right to exploit other living organisms as we see fit? How do we know that these other creatures don't feel pain or anguish just as we do? Perhaps there's no problem with fruit flies, but where do we draw the line? I used to rationalize angling because fish are cold blooded, as if warm-bloodedness indicates some kind of demarcation of brain development or greater sensitivity to pain. But anyone who has watched a fish's frantic fight to escape knows that it exhibits all the manifestations of pain and fear.   **8**

I've been thinking about these questions again after spending a weekend in the Queen Charlotte Islands watching grey whales close up. The majesty and freedom of these magnificent mammals contrasted strikingly with the appearance of whales imprisoned in aquariums. Currently, the Vancouver Public Aquarium is building a bigger pool for some of its whales. In a radio interview, an aquarium representative was asked whether even the biggest pool can be adequate for animals that normally have the entire ocean to rove. Part of her answer was that if we watched porpoises in the pool, we'd see that "they are quite happy."   **9**

That woman was projecting human perceptions and emotions on the porpoises. Our ability to empathize with other people and living things is one of our endearing qualities. Just watch someone with a beloved pet, an avid gardener with plants or, for that matter, even an owner of a new car and you will see how readily we can personalize and identify with another living organism or an object. But are we justified in our inferences about captive animals in their cages?   **10**

Most wild animals have evolved with a built-in need to move freely over vast distances, fly in the air or swim through the ocean. Can a wild animal imprisoned in a small cage or pool, removed from its habitat and forced to conform to the impositions of our demands, ever be considered "happy"?   **11**

Animal rights activists are questioning our right to exploit animals, especially in scientific research. Scientists are understandably defensive, especially after labs have been broken into, experiments ruined and animals "liberated." But just as I have had to question my hunting and fishing, scientists cannot avoid confronting the issues raised, especially in relation to our closest relatives, the primates.   **12**

People love to watch monkeys in a circus or zoo and a great deal of the amusement comes from the recognition of ourselves in them. But our relationship with them is closer than just superficial similarities. When doctors at Loma Linda hospital in California implanted the heart of a baboon into the chest of Baby Fae, they were exploiting our close *biological* relationship.   **13**

Any reports on experimentation with familiar mammals like cats and dogs are sure to raise alarm among the lay public. But the use of primates is most controversial. In September 1987, at the Wildlife Film Festival in Bath, England, I watched a film shot on December 7, 1986, by a group of animal liberationists who had broken into SEMA, a biomedical research facility in Maryland. It was such a horrifying document that many in the audience rushed out after a few minutes. There were many scenes that I could not watch. As the intruders entered the facility, the cam-   **14** era followed to peer past cage doors, opened to reveal the animals inside. I am not ashamed to admit that I wept as baby monkeys deprived of any contact with other animals seized the fingers of their liberators and clung to them as our babies would to us. Older animals cowered in their tiny prisons, shaking from fear at the sudden appearance of people.

The famous chimpanzee expert, Jane Goodall, also screened the same film and   **15** as a result asked for permission to visit the SEMA facility. This is what she saw (*American Scientist*, November-December 1987):

> *Room after room was lined with small, bare cages, stacked one above the other, in which monkeys circled round and round and chimpanzees sat huddled, far gone in depression and despair.*
>
> *Young chimpanzees, three or four years old, were crammed, two together into tiny cages measuring 57 cm by 57 cm and only 61 cm high. They could hardly turn around.*
>
> *Not yet part of any experiment, they had been confined in these cages for more than three months.*
>
> *The chimps had each other for comfort, but they would not remain together for long. Once they are infected, probably with hepatitis, they will be separated and placed in another cage. And there they will remain, living in conditions of severe sensory deprivation, for the next several years. During that time they will become insane.*

Goodall's horror sprang from an intimate knowledge of chimpanzees in their   **16** native habitat. There, she has learned, chimps are nothing like the captive animals that we know. In the wild, they are highly social, requiring constant interaction and physical contact. They travel long distances, and they rest in soft beds they make in the trees. Laboratory cages do not provide the conditions needed to fulfill the needs of these social, emotional and highly intelligent animals.

Ian Redmond (*BBC Wildlife*, April 1988) gives us a way to understand the hor-   **17** ror of what lab conditions do to chimps:

> *Imagine locking a two- or three-year-old child in a metal box the size of an iso-lette—solid walls, floor and ceiling, and a glass door that clamps shut, blotting out most external sounds—and then leaving him or her for months, the only con-tact, apart from feeding, being when the door swings open and masked figures reach in and take samples of blood or tissue before shoving him back and clamp-ing the door shut again. Over the past 10 years, 94 young chimps at SEMA have endured this procedure.*

Chimpanzees, along with the gorilla, are our closest relatives, sharing ninety-   **18** nine per cent of our genes. And it's that biological proximity that makes them so useful for research—we can try out experiments, study infections and test vaccines on them as models for people. And although there are only about 40,000 chimps left in the wild, compared to millions a few decades ago, the scientific demand for more has increased with the discovery of AIDS.

No chimpanzee has ever contracted AIDS, but the virus grows in them, so scien-   **19** tists argue that chimps will be invaluable for testing vaccines. On February 19, 1988, the National Institute of Health in the U.S. co-sponsored a meeting to discuss the use of chimpanzees in research. Dr. Maurice Hilleman, Director of the Merck Institute for Therapeutic Research, reported:

> *We need more chimps. . . . The chimpanzee is certainly a threatened species and there have been bans on importing the animal into the United States and into other countries, even though . . . the chimpanzee is considered to be an agricultural pest in many parts of the world where it exists. And secondly, it's being destroyed by virtue of environmental encroachment—that is, destroying the natural habitat. So these chimpanzees are being eliminated by virtue of their being an agricultural pest and by the fact that their habitat is being destroyed. So why not rescue them? The number of chimpanzees for AIDS research in the United States [is] somewhere in the hundreds and certainly, we need thousands.*

20 Our capacity to rationalize our behaviour and needs is remarkable. Chimpanzees have occupied their niche over tens of millennia of biological evolution. We are newcomers who have encroached on *their* territory, yet by defining them as *pests* we render them expendable. As Redmond says, "The fact that the chimpanzee is our nearest zoological relative makes it perhaps the unluckiest animal on earth, because what the kinship has come to mean is that we feel free to do most of the things to a chimp that we mercifully refrain from doing to each other."

21 And so the impending epidemic of AIDS confronts us not only with our inhumanity to each other but to other species.

■ Reading Comprehension Questions

1. The word *extrapolate* in "Modern biological research is based on a shared evolutionary history . . . that enables us to extrapolate from one organism to another" (paragraph 2) means
   a. stretch
   b. move
   c. estimate
   d. evolve

2. The word *expendable* in "We are newcomers who have encroached on *their* territory, yet by defining them as *pests* we render them expendable" (paragraph 20) means
   a. disposable
   b. useless
   c. pathetic
   d. hostile

3. Which one of the following would be a good alternative title for this selection?
   a. The Inhumane Society

  b. Global Cruelty
  c. Our Innate Right to Inflict Misery
  d. Science, Recreation, and Sadism

4. Which sentence best expresses the main idea of the selection?
   a. Because all animate life exists on a continuum, we have no right to kill any creature.
   b. Because of the threats of disease and our nutritional needs, we must sacrifice some animals.
   c. All creatures have similar nervous systems; therefore, any damage to an animal causes the same pain we would feel.
   d. Alternative testing procedures and alterations in our attitudes toward animal intelligence and emotion must come about.

5. According to the selection
   a. the author is a vegetarian who finds all killing of animals hateful
   b. fish are a necessary source of protein, but fishing makes him uncomfortable
   c. insects are unsuitable as scientific research subjects
   d. our emotions and reactions are mirrored in most animals

6. *True or false?* Caged primates show behaviour patterns similar to those they demonstrate in their native habitat.

7. The AIDS researcher Dr. Hilleman states that chimpanzees
   a. harm farming land and will be destroyed anyway in some areas
   b. should not be imported into the United States
   c. should be rescued from their shrinking environments and used for experiments
   d. are an endangered species and the United States has a duty to save them

8. The author implies that
   a. he was always idealistic
   b. despite his work and recreational practices, his attitudes toward animals are changing
   c. he was not a "typical boy"
   d. he finds hunting, fishing, and all forms of animal captivity and testing repulsive

9. After reading the essay, we can conclude that the author regards humans as
   a. selfish enough to justify our needs and to ignore our place in the ecosystem
   b. unwilling to face the tragic proportions of the AIDS epidemic
   c. aware of threats to other life-forms, but unwilling to do anything about them
   d. ready to make any sacrifice to prolong human life

10. *True or false?* The author implies that the human capacity for self-delusion or "double think" is generally supported by the scientific community.

■ Discussion Questions

About Content

1. What benefits have we derived from the use of animals in the past? What new "benefit" have we acquired from such use? In which areas of present-day life are animals now most useful, according to the second paragraph? With which of these uses does the author take issue? Which does he not dispute?

2. Does anything distinguish the responses of mammals from those of cold-blooded animals? Are the reactions we see in animals always understandable, based on human experience?

3. What examples does Suzuki use to point out the irony of our relationship with chimpanzees? Why are the examples ironic?

About Structure

4. What method of introduction does the author use?
   a. Anecdote
   b. Broad to narrow
   c. Explaining the importance of the subject
   d. Starting with an opposite

   Does the second paragraph imitate or reverse the technique used in the first?

5. How many personal anecdotes does Suzuki use to clarify his ideas in the first half of the essay? How are they ordered? Which phrases in these paragraphs indicate the ordering method used? What is the significance of the order used to the subject discussed?

6. Several paragraphs contain objective examples, based on impartial scientific data or statistics. Are these more or less convincing than the author's personal experiences?

About Style and Tone

7. How many of the essay's paragraphs take the first-person approach to point of view? How many use a third-person approach, with an inclusive, impersonal "we"? How do the subjects of these two groups of paragraphs relate to the two types of point of view? What is the effect on you as a reader of this mixture of two viewpoints? Is it more or less convincing as a form of argument than one consistent point of view?

8. The second half of the essay includes three citations from other sources. Are these sources unbiased? How strongly does each speaker make his or her case? Does each quotation add equally to Suzuki's argument?

■ **Writing Assignments**

Assignment 1

David Suzuki quotes Ian Redmond's statement in this essay: "The fact that the chimpanzee is our nearest zoological relative makes it perhaps the unluckiest animal on earth, because . . . we feel free to do most of the things to a chimp that we mercifully refrain from doing to each other" (paragraph 20). We may well be most inhumane to those who cannot fight back against our treatment of them. We may well be ignoring, as Durning also claims in his article "Coffee," the global nature and interconnection of many of our actions. Using the model of Suzuki's essay argument, write a persuasive essay of your own about your feelings and thoughts on some aspect of animal treatment. Consider circuses and zoos, trapping, hunting, food production, fashion, or cosmetic and scientific testing. Choose your subject based on two criteria: personal experience or knowledge and the strength of your opinion or conviction.

Assignment 2

Are the porpoises in the Vancouver Public Aquarium really "quite happy"? How do you think zoo inmates feel? What might a cow feel during the truck ride to a packing plant? Try an exercise in writing from a different point of view. Become another species for a while, perhaps a salmon unknowingly swimming upstream toward fishing nets. Write an essay that describes what another creature might feel from its perspective, in its native environment, as it progresses through "a day in the life." You may not wish to reveal your adopted identity until the end of your essay. Whether or not you write a horror story is up to you.

Assignment 3

Transplanted baboon hearts, animal bone marrow transplants for AIDS patients . . . Big Macs and leather backpacks: Can we justify any of these uses of animals?

Write an essay that contrasts three "acceptable" uses of animals with three unnecessary/unjustifiable examples of such use. A statement of your point of view of what is "acceptable and necessary" in the use of animals should appear in your thesis statement.

A WORK COMMUNITY

Paul Hoffert

You spend a fair amount of your time at college; do you get a sense of "belonging," a level of comfort, from your time there? Colleges and workplaces can provide a sense of community, as York University professor and futurist Paul Hoffert argues. But what makes one campus or one office a community and another just a "place to go"? Read Hoffert's selection, and then look around your college and make your own decision.

I've had first-hand experiences that have influenced my views on local communities. Since 1986, I have maintained an office on the Keele Street campus of York University in Toronto. York University was founded in the 1950s at a suburban location, which was meant to take the load off the downtown University of Toronto. By the 1980s, it was still in the middle of nowhere with respect to Toronto cultural activities, although the student body had grown to more than 40,000, the population of a decent-sized town.

Good restaurants, good shopping, art galleries, movie theatres, and the like were not within walking distance, and hardly any were within driving distance. There was lots of green space between buildings, but there was no "main street" where students and faculty could sustain a physical community. In the evening, the campus emptied and felt more like an archeological restoration than a living community. It was clear that a large localized population did not, on its own, constitute much of a community.

By the early 1990s, however, the university's president, Harry Arthurs, spurred the construction of a campus mall that connected several of the central buildings. It provided the "main street" place of congregation that had eluded the campus previously. Now there was hustle and bustle, benches where students and faculty could sit and chat, protection from the elements in winter, and an array of shops and activities that drew the local community together.

Stalls selling trinkets, cheap clothing, music CDs, watches, and posters gave the area a bazaar-like atmosphere, with hawkers collaring passers-by to sell them their wares and political agendas. Now there were diverse restaurants serving Japanese, Korean, Middle Eastern, and Chinese foods plus a fast-food strip with the more mundane burgers, pizzas, fried chicken, and tacos, as well as coffee, muffins, and doughnut shops.

There were clothing stores, a hair salon, a pharmacy, a doctor, a dentist, an optometrist, banks, a travel agency, a post office, a computer store, a copy/instant print, odds and ends, and the campus bookstore. There was also a pool hall, complete with video and pinball games, that stayed open until midnight. The pool-hall trade encouraged a few restaurants to stay open late as well, prolonging activity into the night and providing a sense of security for those of us who worked late or lived in student residences.

Gradually, my experience at the York University campus changed. I opened an account at the local credit union and began to get my hair cut and my teeth cleaned at the mall instead of downtown. I began to work late on campus, doing some reading while dining at the local eateries, watching a few innings of baseball while having a burger at the pub, and shooting a game of pool when my body tightened up from too many hours in front of my computer screen.

I got to know the guy who ran the computer store. He would order software, put it aside for me, and leave me a message when it came in, and I would pick it up when I passed the store. The woman proprietor of the Japanese restaurant, appreciative that I was a regular customer, routinely put an extra free item on my tray. When my first book came out, I gave her a copy as a Christmas gift. I began getting my medical prescriptions filled at the drugstore, got to know the pharmacist, and asked if she could find a cheaper supplier for my arthritis pills. A few days later she told me that her chain did not carry alternatives, but that she had asked a friend at a health-food outlet to pick up a cheaper variety and send them over. She provided these to me at her cost, as a courtesy.

Staff in the stores that I frequent know me by name, and I've become **8** acquainted with faculty members who lunch and dine at the same spots that I haunt. Many faces have become familiar. I have come to know who many faculty members are, even without exchanging words with them, because one or another of my colleagues knows them, points them out and offers me tidbits of professional information or gossip. In short, my workplace community of interest has become a local neighbourhood for me, and its members have become an extended family.

■ Reading Comprehension Questions

1. The word *sustain* in "where students and faculty could sustain a physical community" (paragraph 2) means
   a. harass
   b. manage
   c. create
   d. support

2. The word *mundane* in "the more mundane burgers, pizzas, fried chicken, and tacos" (paragraph 4) means
   a. delicious
   b. ordinary
   c. exotic
   d. nutritious

3. Which of the following would be a good alternative title for this selection?
   a. University Life
   b. Faces and Places
   c. My Weekday World
   d. Community Communication

4. Which sentence best expresses the main idea of the selection?
   a. Gradually, my experience at the York University campus changed.
   b. It was clear that a large localized population did not, on its own, constitute much of a community.
   c. In short, my workplace community of interest has become a local neighbourhood for me, and its members have become an extended family.
   d. I've had first-hand experiences that have influenced my views on local communities.

5. Why, according to the author, did York University establish itself away from Toronto's core?
   a. Downtown university campuses were overcrowded.
   b. Attracting students from suburban and outlying areas became important in the 1980s.
   c. York needed to establish its own identity as a new university.
   d. York wanted to create a new cultural community.

6. *True or false?* One of the main reasons York's campus was not a place for people to gather was its lack of central focus.

7. The main virtue of the campus mall's pool hall, according to Hoffert, was
   a. that students were attracted to its video and pinball games
   b. that its late hours attracted activity, making people on campus feel safe
   c. that it tempted him to work late
   d. that it offered him the chance for some recreation

8. The author implies that
   a. the campus mall's services were mainly low-end
   b. the mall had a chaotic, disorganized feel to it
   c. the mall was like any suburban shopping mall
   d. the mall was a lively and functional place from the start

9. *True or false?* The mall tempted Hoffert to neglect his work.

10. The author implies that
    a. the people he sees every day are as important as the services he uses
    b. the campus mall has replaced the community near his home
    c. he has become dependent on the campus mall and its conveniences
    d. he is surprised that the mall has succeeded

Discussion Questions

About Content

1. What were the main things lacking on the new campus, according to Hoffert, and what was the result of these deficiencies?

2. What were the initial benefits provided by construction of the campus mall?

3. Why might there be such a diverse character to the mall's vendors and services?

About Structure

4. Where does Hoffert place his thesis statement and why has he chosen that location for it?

5. What transition word opens the paragraph in which the author begins to incorporate his own relationship with the place he describes?

6. How many specific examples does the author supply in the two paragraphs that describe the campus mall? How many details are furnished about two of these examples?

About Style and Tone

7. How would you describe the language the author uses for this selection? Supply some examples of vocabulary that support your judgment. Based on your opinion, who would be likely audiences for such a piece?

8. In which paragraphs does Hoffert use first-person viewpoint, and in which does he use third-person viewpoint? Why, in terms of the selection's content, may he have chosen these points of view for these paragraphs?

■ Writing Assignments

Assignment 1

We all live in a variety of communities: the community around where we live, cultural communities, our college's community, and others as well. Write an essay that describes one of the communities to which you belong. What elements of your life and which people connected to you make up that community? How did you come to be part of it? Why is that community important to you? Remember to use, as Hoffert has, lots of specific details in your description.

Assignment 2

In paragraph 7, Hoffert notes his growing connections with people who work at the campus mall. Write a character sketch of someone you deal with almost every day who adds something interesting or unique to your life. As mentioned in the chapter on writing descriptive essays (pages 172–184), your thesis should contain a "dominant impression" of this person, a "hook" for readers to attach themselves to; then your body paragraphs will explain why this person is important to you.

Assignment 3

What would be your ideal campus and why? In a persuasive essay, describe the college or university campus of your dreams. Do you dream of tall trees, stone buildings, and interesting coffee houses, or something more technologically oriented, with state-of-the-art equipment? Are daycare, restaurants, gyms, and shopping essentials? What would be so beneficial about the college community you create on paper?

CHOOSE YOUR BATTLES

Andrew Clark

Recent world events brought our Armed Forces to Canadians' attention. But in general, compared to other nations such as the United States, how military-minded are we? Our international reputation is as peacekeepers, but as Andrew Clark's article argues, Canadians have a remarkable history as warriors as well. Do we choose to forget this aspect of our national character?

Tomorrow, Canadians will pause to reflect on the events of August 19, 1942. Fifty-   1
nine years ago, on a beach on the coast of France, 3,367 Canadian men were killed,

wounded, or captured, all in the space of eight hours at a battle called Dieppe. Whether remembered as a pointless slaughter or as a necessary step towards success two years later on D-Day, Dieppe is the best known engagement in our country's military history; it's been the subject of countless school lessons, numerous documentaries, and a controversial miniseries. Of a force that set off from England 4,963 strong, only 2,210 came back. All for a raid that was intended to cause temporary havoc on German defences, not to take land.

It was, in other words, one of Canada's greatest military defeats. As such, it is a strange touchstone for our military, an organization with a distinguished record. What is it about Canadians that moves us to commemorate defeat while ignoring our country's triumphs? Is there something ennobling about a losing effort? It is not as though there is a dearth of decisive actions to remember. Since the spring, the anniversaries of three of Canada's finest military victories have passed with little or no attention. On May 23, 1944, the Canadian Army broke the Hitler Line, a seemingly impenetrable system of bunkers, minefields, trenches, and German infantry that had been blocking the Allied advance on Rome. In July, 1943, in Sicily, the Hastings and Prince Edward Regiment scaled a sheer 1,000-foot cliff to capture an ancient castle held by the German Army near the small town of Assoro. During the First World War, in August, 1917, the Canadian Army captured Hill 70, a key strategic victory to follow up the success at Vimy Ridge.

The fact that we mythologize disasters while neglecting victories is a telling statement on our national character. The notion that war is embodied by the willingness to die reflects a passive, civilian perception of combat. For the vast majority of Canadians, it is easy to imagine a soldier perishing as he steps off a landing craft into a hail of bullets. It is more difficult to contemplate a soldier orchestrating a 350-gun artillery barrage that moves from target to target at a rate of 100 yards every six minutes. That requires the kind of skill that is difficult for today's Canadians to commemorate—perhaps because it runs contrary to our idealized notion that the army fighting overseas was made up of civilians in uniform, not soldiers.

Yet, a casual perusal of military records proves that those who returned were capable, professional warriors. After hostilities ended in 1945, the Canadian Army asked its officers to relate, among other things, fighting techniques, by completing battle-experience questionnaires. In report after report, Canadian citizen-soldiers coolly described the best ways to create enfilading machine-gun fire, time mortar barrages, and clear out enemy dugouts: in other words, the best way to kill as many of the enemy as possible. There is a chatty matter-of-fact tone to some, as if gardening tips are being traded. "A Tommy gun by the turret and a few grenades can be quite handy when crossing slit trenches," wrote one tank captain.

No battle better illustrates this skill and tenacity than the breaking of the Gothic Line. Between August 30 and September 1, 1944, Canadians tore through German defences in Northern Italy. After an initial breach of the German fortification, the Canadian commanders decided to break military protocol. Normally, Allied armies advanced slowly; infantry gains would be held until artillery support could be moved up, which could take up to seventy-two hours. At the Gothic Line, however, the Canadians decided not to wait. They raced through. It was a daring risk that resulted in the Germans fleeing with the Canadians in hot pursuit. On September 4, a platoon from the Hastings and Prince Edward Regiment, which was chasing the Germans, found itself partially surrounded near the small village of Santa Maria di Scacciano. During a lull in the fighting, a German officer yelled out, "Surrender you English gentlemen. You are surrounded and will only die." "We ain't English," called back Canadian private "Slim" Sanford. "We ain't gentlemen—and be goddamned if we'll surrender." According to historian Bill McAndrew, who for the last fifteen years has returned to Italy to retrace the battle, "The Gothic Line was arguably the finest single action of the Canadian corps during the entire Second World War."

When these soldiers returned home they collided with a country that was incapable of comprehending their time overseas. One of the distinct characteristics of the Canadian Army has always been that the fighting is done abroad. As such, there are two societies—the military one that does the fighting and the civilian one that stays home, and there is very little connection between the two. Even in the Second World War, in which over a million Canadians participated in uniform, the details about what the soldiers were actually doing abroad tend to get ignored when we memorialize battles.   6

The combination of tactics and courage displayed at the Gothic Line is what made the Canadian Army a finely tuned machine by the end of the Second World War. On Remembrance Day, a nation of civilians remembers a generation of soldiers. It is important that when we commemorate those who perished, we also honour the military gains that were made. To commemorate sacrifice without acknowledging achievement does a disservice to history. The truth is that the men who fought not only risked their lives, they took lives—it's a difficult truth for us to contemplate, and perhaps that's why we neglect it. Taking lives is another form of sacrifice, one that none of us will ever come close to understanding. The only thing we can say with certainty is that we are still enjoying the fruits of their terrible labour. So be grateful that men were willing to fight and die in countries they had never seen, for generations they would never know. Be glad you never had to do the same. But more than that, be grateful that they won.   7

■ **Reading Comprehension Questions**

1. The word *dearth* in "It is not as though there is a dearth of decisive actions to remember" (paragraph 2) means
   a. abundance
   b. scarcity
   c. collection
   d. history

2. The word *turret* in "A Tommy gun by the turret and a few grenades can be quite handy when crossing slit trenches" (paragraph 4) means
   a. tower
   b. edge
   c. machine
   d. belt

3. Which of the following would be a good alternative title for this selection?
   a. Canadian Bravery
   b. Forgotten Failures of World War II
   c. Soldiers, Civilians, and Memories
   d. What We Choose to Remember

4. Which sentence best expresses the main idea of the selection?
   a. It is important that when we commemorate those who perished, we also honour the military gains that were made.
   b. One of the distinct characteristics of the Canadian Army has always been that the fighting is done overseas.
   c. The fact that we mythologize disasters while neglecting victories is a telling statement about our national character.
   d. Taking lives is another form of sacrifice, one that none of us will ever come close to understanding.

5. Canadian soldiers, according to records, were
   a. raw untrained recruits
   b. well-trained and knowledgeable fighters
   c. ordinary men in uniforms, equipped for battle
   d. often foolhardy

6. *True or false?* The risk undertaken by Canadian forces at the Gothic Line gave the advantage to German troops.

7. The author implies that
   a. Canadians diminish their own capacity for martial action
   b. Canadians ignore what doesn't happen at home
   c. Canadians citizens rejected homecoming soldiers
   d. Canadians still have incomplete war records

8. *True or false?* Because Canada regards itself as peace-loving, acknowledging that part of our heritage is based on battle success is problematic.

9. The author implies that
   a. military arts are neglected in Canadian society
   b. fighting and killing are hard to understand, so we don't try
   c. killing is an inevitable part of military success
   d. fighting in wars is often a thankless matter, whose benefits go unnoticed

■ Discussion Questions

About Content

1. What is ironic about the fact that Canadian education and media devote so much attention to the Battle of Dieppe?

2. Why does Clark suggest that most Canadians more easily visualize the suffering of the Dieppe landing than they do heroic actions?

3. Describe the events at the Gothic Line and how these demonstrate the "skill and tenacity" (paragraph 5) of Canadian soldiers.

About Structure

4. What "change of direction" transitional word opens paragraph 4? What ideas in paragraph 3 are contradicted by evidence in paragraph 4?

5. Nearly all the body paragraphs of Clark's essay open with their topic sentences. One paragraph does not; which one? Where is the topic sentence in this paragraph and why might it be where it is?

About Style and Tone

6. In paragraph 4, Clark describes the tone of Canadian soldiers' reports as "chatty" and "matter-of-fact." What simile or comparison does the author use to underline his sense of the reports' tone? What effect does this comparison have on you as a reader, in terms of the subject the soldiers are writing about?

7. The author bases much of his argument on two sets of opposed ideas:
   • mythologizing defeats vs. neglecting victories
   • "civilians in uniform" vs. professional soldiers

   Which paragraphs treat the first set of ideas? Which paragraphs treat the second set? How has the author shaped his essay to reflect these two concepts? Where are the two pairs of opposed ideas brought together? Which sentence sums up a kind of resolution of the two sets of oppositions?

■ Writing Assignments

Assignment 1

There are many prevalent myths about Canadians: we're always polite; we fight viciously during hockey games; and we eat more doughnuts than any other nation.

Explore one "Canadian myth" in an essay. Look at the truths behind that myth as well as the fallacies by using specific examples and situations that explain and demonstrate the truth or falsehood of particular elements of the myth you choose.

Assignment 2

Define and analyze the Canadian temperament as you know it. What have you experienced that shows you our strengths, and what weak spots can you identify? What do the strengths and weaknesses add up to as an identity?

Remember, your essay will be fairly brief, so it is important to use very specific situations and experiences to illustrate and prove your points.

Assignment 3

In this new century, the concept of Remembrance Day is nearly 100 years old and few people are even well informed about World War II, much less World War I. To those from other cultural backgrounds, these wars may be of less significance. However, recent events may have returned war to the forefront of everyone's mind.

Should we remember wars at all? Do we owe a debt to those who fought and died, or does commemorating war perpetuate the idea and give it value?

Write an essay defending your view on this point.

SEX, LIES, AND CONVERSATION

Deborah Tannen

Most divorced women cite poor communication as a major contributor to their divorces. Few men even mention it as a factor. How is it that men and women perceive their communication so differently? According to the linguist Deborah Tannen, the discrepancy takes root in childhood and reflects the different roles played by verbal communication in men's and women's lives. This selection, adapted from Tannen's book *You Just Don't Understand: Women and Men in Conversation,* helps us understand the opposite gender and its very different conversational culture.

I was addressing a small gathering in a suburban Virginia living room—a women's 1 group that had invited men to join them. Throughout the evening, one man had been particularly talkative, frequently offering ideas and anecdotes, while his wife sat silently beside him on the couch. Toward the end of the evening, I commented that women frequently complain that their husbands don't talk to them. This man quickly concurred. He gestured toward his wife and said, "She's the talker in our family." The room burst into laughter; the man looked puzzled and hurt. "It's true," he explained. "When I come home from work I have nothing to say. If she didn't keep the conversation going, we'd spend the whole evening in silence."

This episode crystallizes the irony that although American men tend to talk 2 more than women in public situations, they often talk less at home. And this pattern is wreaking havoc with marriage.

The pattern was observed by political scientist Andrew Hacker in the late '70s. **3** Sociologist Catherine Kohler Riessman reports in her new book *Divorce Talk* that most of the women she interviewed—but only a few of the men—gave lack of communication as the reason for their divorces. Given the current divorce rate of nearly 50 percent, that amounts to millions of cases in the United States every year—a virtual epidemic of failed conversation.

In my own research, complaints from women about their husbands most often **4** focused not on tangible inequities such as having given up the chance for a career to accompany a husband to his, or doing far more than their share of daily life-support work like cleaning, cooking, social arrangements, and errands. Instead, they focused on communication: "He doesn't listen to me," "He doesn't talk to me." I found, as Hacker observed years before, that most wives want their husbands to be, first and foremost, conversational partners, but few husbands share this expectation of their wives.

In short, the image that best represents the current crisis is the stereotypical **5** cartoon scene of a man sitting at the breakfast table with a newspaper held up in front of his face, while a woman glares at the back of it, wanting to talk.

Linguistic Battle of the Sexes

How can women and men have such different impressions of communication in **6** marriage? Why the widespread imbalance in their interests and expectations?

In the April [1990] issue of *American Psychologist*, Stanford University's Eleanor **7** Maccoby reports the results of her own and others' research showing that children's development is most influenced by the social structure of peer interactions. Boys and girls tend to play with children of their own gender, and their sex-separate groups have different organizational structures and interactive norms.

I believe these systematic differences in childhood socialization make talk between **8** women and men like cross-cultural communication, heir to all the attraction and pitfalls of the enticing but difficult enterprise. My research on men's and women's conversations uncovered patterns similar to those described for children's groups.

For women, as for girls, intimacy is the fabric of relationships, and talk is the thread **9** from which it is woven. Little girls create and maintain friendships by exchanging secrets; similarly, women regard conversation as the cornerstone of friendship. So a woman expects her husband to be a new and improved version of a best friend. What is important is not the individual subjects that are discussed but the sense of closeness, of a life shared, that emerges when people tell their thoughts, feelings, and impressions.

Bonds between boys can be as intense as girls', but they are based less on talk- **10** ing, more on doing things together. Since they don't assume talk is the cement that binds a relationship, men don't know what kind of talk women want, and they don't miss it when it isn't there.

Boys' groups are larger, more inclusive, and more hierarchical, so boys must **11** struggle to avoid the subordinate position in the group. This may play a role in women's complaints that men don't listen to them. Some men really don't like to listen, because being the listener makes them feel one down, like a child listening to adults or an employee to a boss.

But often when women tell men, "You aren't listening," and the men protest, **12** "I am," the men are right. The impression of not listening results from misalignment in the mechanics of conversation. The misalignment begins as soon as a man and a woman take physical positions. This became clear when I studied videotapes made by psychologist Paul Dorval of children and adults talking to their same-sex best friends. I found that at every age, the girls and women faced each other directly, their eyes anchored on each other's faces. At every age, the boys and men sat at angles to each other and looked elsewhere in the room, periodically glancing at each other. They were obviously attuned to each other, often mirroring each other's movements. But the tendency of men to face away can give women the impression they aren't listening even when they are. A young woman in college was frustrated: Whenever she told her boyfriend she wanted to talk to him, he would lie down on the floor, close his eyes and put his arm over his face. This signaled to her, "He's taking a nap." But he insisted he was listening extra hard. Normally, he looks around the room, so he is easily distracted. Lying down and covering his eyes helped him concentrate on what she was saying.

Analogous to the physical alignment that women and men take in conversation **13** is their topical alignment. The girls in my study tended to talk at length about one topic, but the boys tended to jump from topic to topic. The second-grade girls exchanged stories about people they knew. The second-grade boys teased, told jokes, noticed things in the room, and talked about finding games to play. The sixth-grade girls talked about problems with a mutual friend. The sixth-grade boys talked about fifty-five different topics, none of which extended over more than a few turns.

Listening to Body Language

Switching topics is another habit that gives women the impression men aren't lis- **14** tening, especially if they switch to a topic about themselves. But the evidence of the tenth-grade boys in my study indicates otherwise. The tenth-grade boys sprawled across their chairs with bodies parallel and eyes straight ahead, rarely looking at each other. They looked as if they were riding in a car, staring out the windshield. But they were talking about their feelings. One boy was upset because a girl had told him he had a drinking problem, and the other was feeling alienated from all his friends.

Now, when a girl told a friend about a problem, the friend responded by ask- **15** ing probing questions and expressing agreement and understanding. But the boys dismissed each other's problems. Todd assured Richard that his drinking was "no big problem" because "sometimes you're funny when you're off your butt." And when Todd said he felt left out, Richard responded, "Why should you? You know more people than me."

Women perceive such responses as belittling and unsupportive. But the boys **16** seemed satisfied with them. Whereas women reassure each other by implying, "You shouldn't feel bad because I've had similar experiences," men do so by implying, "You shouldn't feel bad because your problems aren't so bad."

There are even simpler reasons for women's impression that men don't listen. **17** Linguist Lynette Hirschman found that women make more listener-noise, such as "mhm," "uhuh," and "yeah," to show "I'm with you." Men, she found, more often give silent attention. Women who expect a stream of listener noise interpret silent attention as no attention at all.

Women's conversational habits are as frustrating to men as men's are to women. Men who expect silent attention interpret a stream of listener noise as overreaction or impatience. Also, when women talk to each other in a close, comfortable setting, they often overlap, finish each other's sentences, and anticipate what the other is about to say. This practice, which I call "participatory listenership," is often perceived by men as interruption, intrusion, and lack of attention. **18**

A parallel difference caused a man to complain about his wife, "She just wants to talk about her own point of view. If I show her another view, she gets mad at me." When most women talk to each other, they assume a conversationalist's job is to express agreement and support. But many men see their conversational duty as pointing out the other side of an argument. This is heard as disloyalty by women, and refusal to offer the requisite support. It is not that women don't want to see other points of view, but that they prefer them phrased as suggestions and inquiries rather than as direct challenges. **19**

In his book *Fighting for Life*, Walter Ong points out that men use "agonistic" or warlike, oppositional formats to do almost anything; thus discussion becomes debate and conversation becomes a competitive sport. In contrast, women see conversation as a ritual means of establishing rapport. If Jane tells a problem and June says she has a similar one, they walk away feeling closer to each other. But this attempt at establishing rapport can backfire when used with men. Men take too literally women's ritual "troubles talk," just as women mistake men's ritual challenges for real attack. **20**

The Sounds of Silence

These differences begin to clarify why women and men have such different expectations about communication in marriage. For women, talk creates intimacy. Marriage is an orgy of closeness: you can tell your feelings and thoughts, and still be loved. Their greatest fear is being pushed away. But men live in a hierarchical world, where talk maintains independence and status. They are on guard to protect themselves from being put down and pushed around. **21**

This explains the paradox of the talkative man who said of his silent wife, "She's the talker." In the public setting of a guest lecture, he felt challenged to show his intelligence and display his understanding of the lecture. But at home, where he has nothing to prove and no one to defend against, he is free to remain silent. For his wife, being home means she is free from the worry that something she says might offend someone, or spark disagreement, or appear to be showing off; at home she is free to talk. **22**

The communication problems that endanger marriage can't be fixed by mechanical engineering. They require a new conceptual framework about the role of talk in human relationships. Many of the psychological explanations that have become second nature may not be helpful, because they tend to blame either women (for not being assertive enough) or men (for not being in touch with their feelings). A sociolinguistic approach by which male–female conversation is seen as cross-cultural communication allows us to understand the problem and forge solutions without blaming either party. **23**

Once the problem is understood, improvement comes naturally, as it did to the young woman and her boyfriend who seemed to go to sleep when she wanted to talk. Previously, she had accused him of not listening, and he had refused to change **24** his behavior, since that would be admitting fault. But then she learned about and explained to him the differences in women's and men's habitual ways of aligning themselves in conversation. The next time she told him she wanted to talk, he began, as usual, by lying down and covering his eyes. When the familiar negative reaction bubbled up, she reassured herself that he really was listening. But then he sat up and looked at her. Thrilled, she asked why. He said, "You like me to look at you when we talk, so I'll try to do it." Once he saw their differences as cross-cultural rather than right and wrong, he independently altered his behavior.

Women who feel abandoned and deprived when their husbands won't listen to   **25** or report daily news may be happy to discover their husbands trying to adapt once they understand the place of small talk in women's relationships. But if their husbands don't adapt, the women may still be comforted that for men, this is not a failure of intimacy. Accepting the difference, the wives may look to their friends or family for that kind of talk. And husbands who can't provide it shouldn't feel their wives have made unreasonable demands. Some couples will still decide to divorce, but at least their decisions will be based on realistic expectations.

In these times of resurgent ethnic conflicts, the world desperately needs cross-   **26** cultural understanding. Like charity, successful cross-cultural communication should begin at home.

■ **Reading Comprehension Questions**

1. The word *concurred* in "women frequently complain that their husbands don't talk to them. This man quickly concurred . . . and said, 'She's the talker in our family'" (paragraph 1) means
   a. delayed
   b. left
   c. agreed
   d. questioned

2. The word *hierarchical* in "Boys' groups are . . . more hierarchical, so boys must struggle to avoid the subordinate position in the group" (paragraph 11) means
   a. intimately connected
   b. organized by status
   c. tolerant
   d. useful

3. Which of the following would be a good alternative title for this selection?
   a. Men's Silence at Home
   b. Divorce Today
   c. Men's and Women's Expectations of Marriage
   d. Communicating Across the Gender Divide

4. Which sentence best expresses the main idea of the selection?
   a. Women and men are both frustrated by the bad habits of the opposite sex.
   b. The divorce rate would diminish if men and women understood each other's modes of communication.
   c. For men, discussion is debate, and conversation is a competitive sport.

      d. In one study, girls tended to talk at length about a single topic, and the boys tended to jump from topic to topic.

5. *True or false?* The majority of divorced men cite lack of communication as the reason for their divorce.

6. When grade ten boys talked about their feelings, they
      a. lay on the floor with their eyes closed
      b. looked straight ahead as if they were riding in a car
      c. frequently interrupted and finished each other's sentences
      d. made "listener-noise" such as "mhm" and "uhuh"

7. In paragraph 22, the author implies that, in general, women
      a. do not really talk much at home
      b. are not really intelligent enough to understand their husbands' comments
      c. offend people more than men do
      d. fear disapproval if they display too much knowledge in public

8. *True or false?* The author suggests that intimacy between male friends may be based more on activity than on conversation.

9. The author implies that
      a. men often listen more than their wives or girlfriends realize
      b. the differences between men's and women's communication styles are established during the teen years
      c. married men communicate differently from single men
      d. men and women are incapable of adapting to each other's conversational needs

10. The author implies that
      a. boys do their most honest communication while riding in cars
      b. differences in the socialization of boys and girls directly influence adult communication
      c. girls tend to have one "best friend" while boys typically have many very close friends
      d. in order to save their marriages, women should adopt the male communication style

■ Discussion Questions

About Content

1. Why did the man in the first paragraph look "puzzled and hurt" when people laughed at him?

2. What are the "tangible inequities" noted in paragraph 4 and why are these not the subjects of many women's complaints?

3. What "crossed signal" or "misalignment" occurred when the college woman in paragraph 12 tried to talk to her boyfriend?

4. What solution does Tannen offer for the problems of male–female communication, and what example does she use to illustrate that solution? How well do you think her solution would work?

About Structure

5. In comparing and contrasting males and females, which method of organization does Tannen use: one side at a time or point by point? Why might she have chosen this method?

6. Generally, the author provides brief examples as she contrasts male and female communication. But in two cases she offers extended examples about specific couples. Why do you think she does this, and why does she return to those examples later in the essay?

7. How would you outline paragraph 13? What is the main point? What secondary points support it?

About Style and Tone

8. What is unusual about the wordings of the headings within the essay? Why might the author have chosen such ways to phrase her concepts, relative to the essay's content?

9. In which paragraphs does Tannen use first-person pronoun point of view? In which does she write from the third-person viewpoint? Why might she have chosen to use these points of view where she did?

Writing Assignments

Assignment 1

What is an area besides communication in which you notice significant differences between male and female behaviour? Write an essay in which you compare and contrast your observations in that area. Below are examples of activities you might consider writing about:

> How males and females shop for groceries
> How males and females clean their apartments
> How males and females pursue a potential girlfriend or boyfriend

Prewriting for this assignment will help you determine if you have enough to say about a given topic. For instance, freewriting may reveal that grocery shopping can be considered under three appropriate headings or criteria for comparison or contrast. Three supporting paragraphs could cover the following:

> How often males and females shop for groceries
> (Once a week? Every day? When the cupboard is bare?)

> What kinds of foods males and females tend to choose
> (Lots of fruits and vegetables? Microwave meals-in-a-box? A long list of foods or only a few things such as bread, milk, and coffee?)

> Once in the supermarket, how do males and females go about shopping? (By carefully following a list? By going slowly up and down all the aisles? By looking for bargains? By rushing through just a few sections?)

Support your points by describing the behaviour of people you know or have observed. Include your thoughts about possible causes of the differences you notice, and be prepared to arrive at a conclusion or two, based on your findings.

Assignment 2

Tannen discusses the different body language used by men and women while communicating. Prepare for an essay on body language by spending some time observing your fellow students. For instance, you might notice how they do the following:

> Pass through doors
> Chat with friends
> Enter and leave a car
> Find a seat in a classroom
> Study at a library
> Congregate in hallways or cafeterias
> Behave in classroom discussions

Take careful notes as you observe. Then, drawing on your observations, write an essay, using the third-person point of view, comparing and contrasting the body language of college men and women. Divide your observations into three categories for which you have sufficient support, such as classroom behaviour, behaviour with people of one's own gender, and behaviour with those of the opposite sex.

Assignment 3

What is the "cement that binds a relationship" (as Tannen calls it in paragraph 10) between you and the person you consider your closest friend? This could be a same-sex friend, an opposite-sex friend, a spouse, or another family member. Write an essay in which you explore and analyze the ties that bind the two of you together. Are they common interests, shared conversations, a shared history, similarities in personality, or problems overcome together? Following are a sample thesis statement and topic sentences for this assignment.

> *Thesis:* Several important ties keep my friendship with my best friend, Lindsay, very strong.
>
> *Topic sentences:*
> a. Our friendship began in kindergarten, and we shared many happy childhood experiences.
> b. In addition, Lindsay and I have rich memories of having supported each other through many difficult times.
> c. Last of all, Lindsay and I share several strong interests.

Narration · Description · Examples · Process · Cause and Effect · Comparison and Con
Definition · Division and Classification · Argumentation · Narration · Description · Exam
Process · Cause and Effect · Comparison and Contrast · Definition · Division and Classific
Argumentation · Narration · Description · Examples · Process · Cause and Effect · Compariso
Contrast · Definition · Division and Classification · Argumentation · Narration · Descriptio

Reading Comprehension Chart

Write an X through the numbers of any questions you missed while answering the comprehension questions for each selection in Part 5, "Readings for Writing." Then write in your comprehension score. The chart will make clear any skill question you get wrong repeatedly, so that you can pay special attention to that skill in the future.

Selection	Vocabulary in Context	Subject or Title	Thesis or Main Idea	Key Details	Inferences	Comprehension Score
Banas	1 2	3	4	5 6 7	8 9 10	%
Bodett	1 2	3	4	5 6 7	8 9 10	%
Clark	1 2	3	4	5 6 7	8 9 10	%
Davis	1 2	3	4	5 6 7	8 9 10	%
Dunayer	1 2	3	4	5 6 7	8 9 10	%
Durning	1 2	3	4	5 6 7	8 9 10	%
Engkent	1 2	3	4	5 6 7	8 9 10	%
Gregory	1 2	3	4	5 6 7	8 9 10	%

Selection	Vocabulary in Context	Subject or Title	Thesis or Main Idea	Key Details	Inferences	Comprehension Score
Hoffert	1 2	3	4	5 6 7	8 9 10	%
Keeshig-Tobias	1 2	3	4	5 6 7	8 9 10	%
Lamanna and Reidmann	1 2	3	4	5 6 7	8 9 10	%
Laurence	1 2	3	4	5 6 7	8 9 10	%
Marshall	1 2	3	4	5 6 7	8 9 10	%
McMurtry	1 2	3	4	5 6 7	8 9 10	%
Mustafa	1 2	3	4	5 6 7	8 9 10	%
O'Keeney	1 2	3	4	5 6 7	8 9 10	%
Sherry	1 2	3	4	5 6 7	8 9 10	%
Suzuki	1 2	3	4	5 6 7	8 9 10	%
Tannen	1 2	3	4	5 6 7	8 9 10	%
Taylor	1 2	3	4	5 6 7	8 9 10	%
Tija	1 2	3	4	5 6 7	8 9 10	%

Index

a, an, 458
Abbreviations, 429
Abstract. *See* Summary
accept, except, 458
Action verbs, 358
Active voice, 104, 397
Added-detail fragments, 367
Addition signals, 77
Adequate details, 61
Adjectives, 409–412
Adverbs, 411–412
advice, advise, 458
affect, effect, 459
all ready, already, 454
among, between, 459
Analogy, 238
Announcements, 54
Antecedent, 399, 401
Apostrophe
    contractions, 431
    ownership/possession, 432
    plurals, 434
    points to remember, 432
    possessive pronouns, 434
    words ending in *-s*, 435
Argumentation essays, 267–282
    common ground, 269
    differing viewpoints, 269–270
    first draft, 276
    prewriting, 275–280
    rebut differing viewpoints, 270
    revising, 276–277
    rewriting, 278
    student essays, 271–273
    tactful/courteous language, 268
Articles, 466
Artificial language, 106
Assignment, nature/length, 153
Audience, 154

Background information, 84
Banas, Casey, "Why Are Student Turned Off?," 557
beside, besides, 459
between, among, 459
BIBCAT, 319
Bluebook of Canadian Business, 324
Bodett, Tom, "Wait Divisions," 519
Body (supporting paragraphs), 15–17
Body sentences, 8
Book stacks, 322
Book, overview, 3, 22–23
brake, break, 454

Canadian Periodical Index (CPI), 324
Capital letters
    books/newspapers, etc., 423
    commercial products, 423
    companies/organizations, etc., 423
    days of week/months/holidays, 423
    family relationships, 424
    first word of sentence/direct
        quotation, 422
    geographical locations, 425

    historical periods/events, 425
    I, 422
    languages, 425
    opening/closing letter, 426
    persons, 422
    places, 422
    race/nationality, 425
    school sources, 425
    titles of persons, 425
    unnecessary use, 426–427
Cause and effect essays, 211–222
    logic check, 219
    prewriting, 215–216, 219–221
    revising, 216–217
    rewriting, 219–221
    student essays, 212–213
Change-of-direction signals, 77
"Choose Your Battles" (Clark), 607
Chronological order, 74
Citations, 340–344, 354
Clark, Andrew, "Choose Your Battles," 607
Classification. *See* Division and classification essays
Clause, 373n
Cliché, 463
Clustering, 32–33
"Coffee" (Durning), 579
Coherence, 72–73, 134–137
Colon, 450
Comma, 441–449
    complete thoughts, 445
    direct quotations, 446
    everyday material, 447
    interruptions, 444–445
    introductory material, 443–444
    items in series, 442–443
    uses, 442
Comma splice, 373
Comparing, 409–411
Comparison and contrast essays, 223–240
    methods of development, 224–226
    one-side-at-a-time structure, 225
    point-by-point structure, 226
    prewriting, 230–232, 234, 237
    rewriting, 232, 236
    student essays, 226–228
Complex sentence, 109
Compound sentence, 108
Compound subject, 391
Concise words, 105
Concluding paragraph, 17, 87–89
Conclusion signals, 77
Consistent point of view, 99
Consistent pronoun point of view, 100–101
Continuous tenses, 395
Contraction, 431
Contrast. *See* Comparison and contrast essays
Coordination, 108
Count nouns, 466
course, coarse, 454
CPI, 324

Dangling modifiers, 416–419
Dash, 451

Davis, Glenda, "How To Do Well On a Job Interview," 524
Dead-end statement, 55
Deductive structure, 9
Definition essays, 241–253
    prewriting, 245–251
    revising, 248–249
    rewriting, 250–252
    student essays, 242–244
Demonstrative pronoun, 407
Dependent clause, 373n
Dependent statement, 362
Dependent thought, 109
Dependent-word fragments, 361–364
Describing, 199
Descriptive essays, 172–184
    detail listing, 180
    dominant impression, 179
    organizing principle, 180
    prewriting, 177–180, 182
    rewriting, 180–183
    sensory details, 180
    student essays, 173–175
Detail listing, 180
Details, 58–62, 180
Diagramming, 32
Dialog, 325
Direct quotation, 439, 446
Directory searches, 330
Division and classification essays, 254–266
    first draft, 260
    list making, 260
    outline, 260
    prewriting, 259–264
    revising, 261
    rewriting, 262, 264–265
    student essays, 255–257
Documentation of sources, 340–344, 354
Domain names, 326
Dominant impression, 179
Draft. *See* First draft
Dunayer, Joan, "Here's To Your Health," 574
Durning, Alan, "Coffee," 579

EBSCOhost, 325
Editing, 20, 43–45, 113–114
Editing tests, 476–488
effect, affect, 459
Electric Library Canada, 324
Electronic books, 322
Electronic research databases, 324
Ellipses, 338
Emphatic order, 75
Engkent, Garry, "Why My Mother Can't Speak English," 530
English as second language. *See* ESL pointers
ERIC, 325
ESL pointers, 466–475
    adjectives, 473–474
    articles, 466–469
    count/non-count nouns, 466–467
    idiomatic verb structures, 471–472
    present/past participles, 474
    progressive tense, 470

pronoun subjects/linking verbs, 469
proper nouns, 468
repeated subjects, 469
subjects/verbs, 469–473
time/place, 474–475
transitive verbs, 470–471
Essay
diagram, 17–18
one-three-one, 17
overview, 6
structure, 13–17
traditional, 5–6, 13–17
Essay development, 151–152
argumentation, 267–282
cause and effect, 211–222
comparison and contrast, 223–240
definition, 241–253
description, 172–184
division and classification, 254–266
examples, 185–197
narration, 159–171
process, 198–210
Essay exams, 285–293
anticipate exam questions, 286–287
direction words, 289–290
learning skills during semester, 285–286
organization/clarity, 291
outline the exam answer, 290–291
preparation, 286–289
prepare/memorize outline answers,
287–288
study skills, 286–288
write timed responses to questions, 288
Essay outline diagram, 39
Evaluation report, 308. *See also* Review/
evaluation report
Examples essays, 185–197
prewriting, 189–191, 193–195
revising, 191–192
rewriting, 193–194
student essays, 186–188
except, accept, 458
Exposition, 151
Expository essay narrative, 164

False third-person, 155
fewer, less, 459
Final personal review, 158
Final thought, 87–88
First draft, 19, 40–41
argumentation essay, 276
division and classification essay, 260
summary, 304–305
First-person approach, 154–155
First Search, 325
"Five Parenting Styles" (Lamanna/ Reidmann),
544
Focused freewriting, 28–29
Foreign students. *See* ESL pointers
former, latter, 459
Fragments. *See* Sentence fragments
Freewriting, 27–29
ftp, 327
Fused sentences, 373
Future perfect progressive tense, 395
Future perfect tense, 395
Future progressive tense, 395
Future tense, 394

General statements, 84

Gerund, 397
good, well, 412
Google, 328
Gopher, 327
Grammar, 357–453. *See also* Punctuation
marks
Grammar checker, 20
Gregory, Dick, "Shame," 495

"He Was a Boxer When I Was Small"
(Keeshig-Tobias), 538
hear, here, 455
Helping verbs, 395–396
"Here's To Your Health" (Dunayer), 574
Hoffert, Paul, "A Work Community," 603
hole, whole, 455
Homonyms, 454–458
"How To Do Well On a Job Interview"
(Davis), 524
"How to Make it in College, Now That
You're Here" (O'Keeney), 583
Hypertext tranfer protocol (http), 326, 327
Hyphen, 452

Illustration signals, 77
Immigrant students. *See* ESL pointers
"In Praise of the F Word" (Sherry), 591
Incident, 85
Indefinite pronoun, 392, 400
Independent clause, 373n
Indirect quotations, 438–439
Infinitive, 396
Inflated words, 107
Informative analysis, 199
InfoTrac, 325
-ing fragments, 364–365
Internet, 326–332
business/technological journals, 330
directory searchs, 330
domain names, 326
evaluation of material, 327–328
Internet-wide searches, 329
keywords, 330–331
mailing lists, 331
metasearcher, 328
newsgroups, 331
plagiarism, 339
protocols, 326–327
reference books, 332
search engines, 328–329
time requirement, 327
URL, 326
writing a research paper, 335–336
Introductory paragraph, 15, 83–87
Irregular verbs, 385–387
its, it's, 455

Keeshig-Tobias, Lenore, "He Was a Boxer
When I Was Small," 538
Keywords, 330–331
knew, new, 455
know, no, 455
Know your subject, 154

Lamanna, Mary Ann, "Five Parenting
Styles," 544
latter, former, 459
Laurence, Margaret, "Where the World
Began," 550
learn, teach, 460
less, fewer, 459

Library, 319–325
catalogue, 319–322
electronic books, 322
electronic research databases, 324
online search services, 325
periodicals, 322–324
stacks, 322
writing a research paper, 334
Library catalogue, 319–322
Linking sentences, 80
Linking verbs, 358
List making, 30–32, 260
Logic check, 219
loose, lose, 460

Mailing list, 331
Main point, 164
Manuscript form, 420–421
Mapping, 32
Marshall, Jeannie, "Sometimes the Words
Don't Come," 562
McMurtry, John "Smash Thy Neighbor," 501
Medline, 325
Metasearcher, 328
Misplaced modifiers, 413–415
Missing-subject fragments, 369
Modem, 326
Modifiers
dangling, 416–419
misplaced, 413–415
"Monster, The" (Taylor), 566
Mustafa, Naheed, "My Body Is My Own
Business," 508
"My Body Is My Own Business" (Mustafa), 508

Narrative essays, 159–171
discover your point, 164
focusing on writing goals, 166
ordering, 164
peer review, 166
point of view, 164
prewriting, 163–165, 167, 168
revising, 168, 169
student essays, 160–161
supporting evidence, 164
Natural language, 106
new, knew, 455
Newsgroups, 327, 331
no, know, 455
Non-count nouns, 466–467
Nonstandard forms of regular verbs, 388
Note taking, 338
Noun, 466
Numbers, 428–429

O'Keeney, Brian, "How to Make it in
College, Now That You're Here," 583
Object pronoun, 406
"Of Lemons and Lemonade," (Tija), 513
One-side-at-a-time structure, 225
One-three-one essay, 17
Online plagiarism, 339
Online search services, 325
Openers, 110
Organization, methods of, 74–76
Outline, 11–12, 34–39, 260
Overstatement, 54
Overview of book, 3, 22–23

"Pain of Animals, The" (Suzuki), 596
Paragraph length, 12
Paragraph-level transitions, 80

Paragraphs
  concluding, 17, 87–89
  introductory, 15, 83–87
  length, 12
  supporting, 15–17
Parallelism, 98
Parentheses, 451–452
Participle, 397
passed, past, 455
Passive voice, 104, 397
Past participle, 383
Past perfect progressive tense, 395
Past perfect tense, 395
Past progressive tense, 395
Past tense, 394
Past tense endings, 384
peace, piece, 456
Peer review, 156–157, 166
Perfect tenses, 394–395
Periodicals, 322–324
Personal review, 158
Plagiarism, 339
plain, plane, 456
Plural subject, 389
Point and support, 7, 13
Point-by-point structure, 226
Point of view, 99, 164
Possessive pronouns, 406–407, 434
Précis. *See* Summary
Prediction, 88
Preposition, 359, 406
Prepositional phrase, 358
Prescribing, 199
Present participle, 383
Present perfect progressive tense, 395
Present perfect tense, 394
Present progressive tense, 395
Present tense, 394
Present tense endings, 384
Pretentious words, 106–107
Prewriting, 26–33
  argumentation essays, 275–280
  cause and effect essays, 215–216, 219–221
  clustering, 32–33
  comparison and contrast essays, 230–232, 234, 237
  definition essays, 245–251
  descriptive essays, 177–180, 182
  division and classification essays, 262, 264–265
  examples essays, 189–191, 193–195
  freewriting, 27–29
  list making, 30–32
  narrative essays, 163–165, 167, 168
  process essays, 204–205
  questioning, 29–30
  word processing, 19
principal, principle, 456
Process essays, 198–210
  prewriting, 204–205
  rewriting, 205–206
  student essays, 199–200
  what is required, 199
Progressive (continuous) tenses, 395
Pronoun agreement, 399–401
Pronoun reference, 401–402
Pronouns
  demonstrative, 407
  indefinite, 392, 400
  object, 406

possessive, 406–407
subject, 404–405
transitions, as, 81–82
Proofreading, 20, 114
Proper nouns, 468
Proquest, 325
Punctuation marks. *See also* Grammar
  apostrophe, 431–435
  colon, 450
  comma, 442–449
  dash, 451
  hyphen, 452
  parentheses, 451–452
  quotation marks, 436–441
  semicolon, 450–451
Purpose, 154

Qualifier, 466
Questioning, 29–30
Questions, 86, 88
quiet, quite, 460
Quotation, 86
Quotation marks
  direct quotations, 439
  exact words of speaker, 436–437
  indirect quotations, 438–439
  quotation within quotation, 441
  titles of short works, 439–440
  uses, 440–441
Quotation within a quotation, 441

Readers' Guide, 323, 324
Reading comprehension chart, 620–621
Readings, 491–619
Recommendation, 89
Redundancy, 54
Regular verbs, 383, 388
Reidmann, Agnes, "Five Parenting Styles," 544
Repeated subjects, 469
Repeated words, 81
Reports, 308. *See also* Review/evaluation report
Research paper, 334–354. *See also* Internet, Library
  citations, 340–344, 354
  direct quotation, 338
  documentation of sources, 340–344, 354
  format, 340
  gather information, 337
  limit the topic, 336
  model paper, 345–354
  notetaking, 338
  outline, 337–338
  plagiarism, 339
  purpose, 336–337
  select topic which can be researched, 334–336
  time requirement, 337
Review/evaluation report, 308–318
  discover/state criteria, 310
  focus, 310
  model report, 314–317
  points to remember, 314
  summary, 309
  write the evaluation, 313–314
Revising, 41–43
  argumentation essays, 276–277
  cause and effect essays, 216–217
  definition essays, 248–249
  descriptive essays, 177–180, 182

division and classification essays, 261
examples essays, 191–192
narrative essays, 168, 169
strategies, 97
word processing, 20
right, write, 456
Run-ons, 373–382
  comma/joining word, 375–376
  comma splices, 373
  fused sentences, 373
  period/capital letter, 374–375
  semicolon, 378
  semicolon-transitional word, 379
  subordination, 380
  summary (review of chapter), 380
  words to be careful with, 374

Second complete thought, 108
Second-person approach, 155
Semicolon, 450–451
Sensory details, 180
Sentence fragments, 361–372
  added-detail fragments, 367
  dependent-word fragments, 361–364
  -ing fragments, 364–365
  missing-subject fragments, 369
  summary (review of chapter), 370
  to fragments, 364–365
Sentence-level transitions, 77–79
Sentence openings, 110
Sentence skills, 137–139, 357–453
Series, 111
"Sex, Lies, and Conversation" (Tannen), 612
"Shame" (Gregory), 495
Sherry, Mary, "In Praise of the F Word," 591
Simple tenses, 394
Singular subject, 389
Slang, 462
"Smash Thy Neighbor" (McMurtry), 501
"Sometimes the Words Don't Come" (Marshall), 562
Space signals, 77
Special openers, 110
Specific details, 58–61
Spell checker, 20
Starting up, 25
Stilted language, 106
Stories, 85
Strong comma, 378. *See also* Semicolon
Study skills, 286–288
Subject
  compound, 391
  finding, 357, 358
  plural, 389
  singular, 389
Subject pronoun, 404–405
Subject-verb agreement, 389–393
  compound subjects, 391
  general rule, 389
  indefinite pronouns, 392
  verb before subject, 390
  words between subject/verb, 389
Subordination, 380
Subtopic, 9
Summary, 294–307
  first draft, 304–305
  list main points, 301–304
  listing/editing/drafting, 297–298
  present tense, 304
  preview/review the article, 300–301

previewing/reviewing source material, 295–297
Summary (final thought), 87–88
Support, 131–134
Supporting evidence, 9, 57–62, 164
Supporting paragraphs, 15–17
Suzuki, David, "The Pain of Animals," 596
Synonyms, 82

Taking notes, 338
Tannen, Deborah, "Sex, Lies, and Conversation," 612
Taylor, Deems, "The Monster," 566
teach, learn, 460
Telnet, 327
than, then, 456
their, there, they're, 457
Thesis statement, 13, 52–57
Third-person approach, 156
Three-dimensional support, 12
threw, through, 457
Tija, Sherwin, "Of Lemons and Lemonade," 513
Time order, 74–75
Time signals, 77
Title, 89–90
Titles of books/movies, etc., 423, 439–440
to, too, two, 457
to fragments, 364–365
Topic, choosing, 25
Topic sentence, 8
Transitional sentences, 80
Transitions, 76–83
    functions, 76

pronouns, 81–82
repeated words, 81
sentence-level, 80
synonyms, 82
Transitive verbs, 470–471
two, to, too, 457

Uniform resource locator (URL), 326
Unity, 129–131
Unnatural-sounding sentences, 106
URL, 326
Usenet groups, 327, 331

Vague support, 59
Verb tenses, 99, 383–384, 394–395
Verbal fragments, 364–365
Verbals, 396–397
Verbs
    action, 358
    active/passive voice, 398
    agreement with subject, 389–393
    finding, 357–359
    helping, 395–396
    irregular, 385–387
    nonstandard form, 388
    regular, 383, 388
    tenses, 383–384, 394–395
Viewpoint, 154–156, 164

"Wait Divisions" (Bodett), 519
wear, where, 457
weather, whether, 457
Web browser, 326
well, good, 412

"Where the World Began" (Laurence), 550
whole, hole, 455
whose, who's, 458
"Why Are Student Turned Off?" (Banas), 557
"Why My Mother Can't Speak English" (Engkent), 530
Word choice, 462–465
Word processing, 18–21
Wordiness, 105
"Work Community, A" (Hoffert), 603
Works cited, 340–344, 354
write, right, 456
Writing
    discovery, as, 4–5
    skill, as, 4
Writing process, 24–50
    beginning to write, 25
    clustering, 32–33
    editing, 43–45
    first draft, 40–41
    freewriting, 27–29
    list making, 30–32
    outline, 34–39
    overview, 27
    prewriting, 26–33
    questioning, 29–30
    revising, 41–43
    steps in process, 27

you, 155
your, you're, 458

CORRECTION SYMBOLS

Here is a list of symbols your instructor may use when marking essays. The numbers in parentheses refer to the pages that explain the skill involved.

Agr   Correct the mistake in agreement of subject and verb (389–393) or pronoun and the word the pronoun refers to (399–403).

Apos   Correct the apostrophe mistake (431–435).

Bal   Balance the parts of the sentence so they have the same (parallel) form (98–99).

Cap   Correct the mistake in capital letters (422–427).

Coh   Revise to improve coherence (72–83; 134–137).

Comma   Add a comma (442–449).

CS   Correct the comma splice (373–382).

DM   Correct the dangling modifier (416–419).

Det   Support or develop the topic more fully by adding details (57–62; 131–134).

Frag   Attach the fragment to a sentence or make it a sentence (361–372).

lc   Use a lower case (small) letter rather than a capital (426).

MM   Correct the misplaced modifier (413–415).

¶   Indent for a new paragraph.

No ¶   Do not indent for a new paragraph.

Pro   Correct the pronoun mistake (404–408).

Quot   Correct the mistake in quotation marks (436–441).

R-O   Correct the run-on (373–382).

Sp   Correct the spelling error.

Trans   Supply or improve a transition (76–83; 91–94).

Und   Underline.

Verb   Correct the verb or verb form (357–360; 383–388; 394–398).

Wordy   Omit needless words (105–106).

WW   Replace the marked word with a more accurate one.

?   Write clearly the illegible word.

/   Eliminate the word, letter, or punctuation mark so slashed.

∧   Add the omitted word or words.

;/:/-/—/   Add the semicolon (450) or colon (450) or hyphen (452) or dash (451).

✓   You have something fine or good here: an expression, a detail, an idea.